The Complete Works of
WASHINGTON
IRVING

Richard Dilworth Rust
General Editor

MISCELLANEOUS
WRITINGS
1803-1859

Volume II

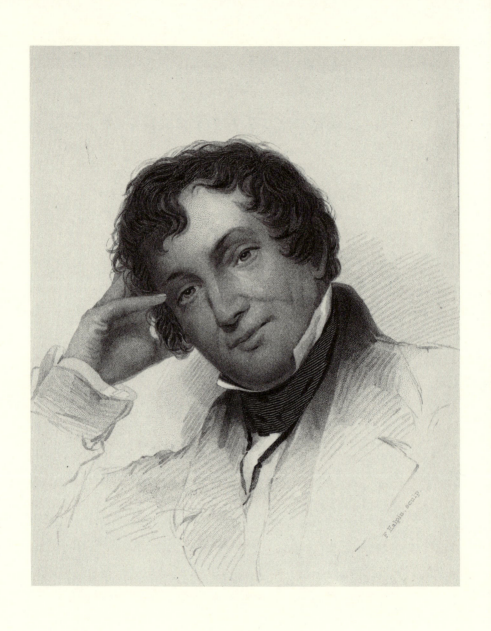

Washington Irving
1851

WASHINGTON IRVING

MISCELLANEOUS WRITINGS
1803-1859

Volume II

Edited by
Wayne R. Kime

Twayne Publishers
Boston
1981

Published by Twayne Publishers

A Divison of G. K. Hall & Co.

Copyright © 1981 by

G. K. Hall & Co.

The Complete Works of Washington Irving

Volume XXIX

CENTER FOR EDITIONS OF
AMERICAN AUTHORS
AN APPROVED TEXT
MODERN LANGUAGE
ASSOCIATION OF AMERICA
®

Library of Congress Cataloging in Publication Data

Irving, Washington, 1783–1859.
Miscellaneous writings, 1803–1859.

(The Complete works of Washington Irving; v. 29)
Includes index.
I. Kime, Wayne R.
PS2063.A2K55   818′.209   80–19108
ISBN 0–8057–8520–5

Manufactured in the United States of America

For my mother, Betty Kime Wendt

ILLUSTRATIONS

FRONTISPIECE

Washington Irving, 1851
An engraving by F. Halpin from
a sketch by Charles Martin

INTERIOR ILLUSTRATIONS

Washington Irving, 1858
An engraving by John Sartain from
a sketch by the same artist
(page 179)

Washington Irving
A photograph from an unfinished painting
by Charles Loring Elliott
(page 329)

CONTENTS

Prose Writings, 1829–1855

*Narratives of Spanish History Left Unpublished
at Irving's Death*

*Other Prose Writings Left Unpublished
at Irving's Death*

EDITORIAL APPENDIX

PROSE WRITINGS
1829-1855

[ADVERTISEMENT OF AN ABRIDGMENT OF
THE LIFE AND VOYAGES OF CHRISTOPHER COLUMBUS]

ADVERTISEMENT.—Having been informed, that some person in the United States had undertaken to fabricate a less voluminous work out of my History of the Life and Voyages of Columbus, I have thought proper immediately to execute my original intention of making an Abridgement of the History, to adapt it for general circulation. In this, I trust, I have given a satisfactory abstract of every thing of essential importance in the larger work, and have preserved those parts nearly entire, which have been considered the most striking and characteristic. It is probable, also, that the narrative has gained a spirit in many parts, by the omission of details which caused prolixity, but which could not be omitted in what professed to be a complete and circumstantial history of the subject.

I have felt the more hurt at this attempt to supersede my work with the public, from having always considered it a peculiar offering to my countrymen, whose good opinion, however the contrary may have been insinuated, has never ceased to be the leading object of my ambition, and the dearest wish of my heart: and I must confess that, in assiduously laboring at this history of the first discovery of our country, I have been chiefly animated by the hope, that the interest of the subject would cause the work to remain among my countrymen, and with it, a remembrance of the author, when all the frail productions of his fancy might have perished and been forgotten.

WASHINGTON IRVING.

SEVILLE, December, 1828.

[May, 1830]

[REVIEW OF A CHRONICLE OF
THE CONQUEST OF GRANADA]

There are a few places scattered about this "working-day world" which seem to be elevated above its dull prosaic level, and to be clothed with the magic lights and tints of poetry. They possess a charmed name, the very mention of which, as if by fairy power, conjures up splendid scenes and pageants of the past; summons from "death's dateless night" the shadows of the great and good, the brave and beautiful, and fills the mind with visions of departed glory. Such is pre-eminently the case with Granada, one of the most classical names in the history of latter ages. The very nature of the country and the climate contributes to bewitch the fancy. The Moors, we are told, while in possession of the land, had wrought it up to a wonderful degree of prosperity. The hills were clothed with orchards and vineyards, the valleys embroidered with gardens, and the plains covered with waving grain. Here were seen in profusion the orange, the citron, the fig, the pomegranate, and the silk-producing mulberry. The vine clambered from tree to tree, the grapes hung in rich clusters about the peasant's cottage, and the groves were rejoiced by the perpetual song of the nightingale. In a word, so beautiful was the earth, so pure the air, and so serene the sky of this delicious region, that the Moors imagined the paradise of their prophet to be situate in that part of the heaven which overhung their kingdom of Granada.

But what has most contributed to impart to Granada a great and permanent interest, is the ten years' war of which it was the scene, and which closed the splendid drama of Moslem domination in Spain. For nearly eight centuries had the Spaniards been recovering, piece by piece, and by dint of the sword, that territory which had been wrested from them by their Arab invaders in little more than as many months. The kingdom of Granada was the last strong hold of Moorish power, and the favourite abode of Moorish luxury. The final struggle for it was maintained with desperate valour; and the compact nature of the country, hemmed in by the ocean and by lofty mountains, and the continual recurrence of the names of the same monarchs and commanders throughout the war, give to it a peculiar distinctness, and an almost epic unity.

But though this memorable war had often been made the subject of romantic fiction, and though the very name possessed a spell upon the imagination, yet it had never been fully and distinctly treated. The world at large had been content to receive a strangely perverted idea of it, through Florian's romance of "Gonsalvo of Cordova;" or through the legend, equally fabulous, entitled "The Civil Wars of Granada," by Ginez Perez de la Hita, the pretended work of an Arabian contemporary, but in reality a Spanish fabrication.* It had been woven over with love tales and scenes of sentimental gallantry, totally opposite to its real character; for it was, in truth, one of the sternest of those iron contests which have been sanctified by the title of "holy wars." In fact, the genuine nature of the war placed it far above the need of any amatory embellishments. It possessed sufficient interest in the striking contrast presented by the combatants, of Oriental and European creeds, costumes, and manners; and in the hardy and hare-brained enterprises, the ro-mantic adventures, the picturesque forays through mountain regions, the daring assaults and surprisals of cliff-built castles and cragged fortresses, which succeeded each other with a variety and brilliancy beyond the scope of mere invention.

The time of the contest also contributed to heighten the interest. It was not long after the invention of gunpowder, when fire-arms and artillery mingled the flash, smoke, and thunder of modern warfare with the steely splendour of ancient chivalry, and gave an awful magnificence and terrible sublimity to battle; and when the old Moorish towers and castles, that for ages had frowned defiance to the battering-rams and catapults of classic tactics, were toppled down by the lombards of the Spanish engineers. It was one of those cases in which history rises su-perior to fiction. The author seems to have been satisfied of this fact, by the manner in which he has constructed the present work. The idea of it, we are told, was suggested to him, while in Spain, occupied upon his History of the Life and Voyages of Columbus. The application of the great navigator to the Spanish sovereigns, for patronage to his project of discovery, was made during their crusade against the Moors of Granada, and continued throughout the residue of that war. Columbus followed the court in several of its campaigns, mingled occasionally in the contest, and was actually present at the grand catastrophe of the enterprise, the surrender of the metropolis. The researches of Mr. Irving, in tracing the movements of his hero, led him to the various chronicles of the reign of Ferdinand and Isabella. He became deeply interested in the details of the war, and was induced, while collecting materials for the biography he had in hand, to make preparation also for the present history. He subsequently made a tour in Andalusia, visited the ruins of the Moorish towns, fortresses, and castles, and the wild mountain

---

* The following censure on the work of La Hita is passed by old Padre Eche-varría, in his "Paseos por Granada," or "Walks through Granada." "Esta es una historia toda fabulosa, cuyo autor se ignora, por mas que corra con el nombre de alguno, llena de cuentos y quimeras, en la que apenas si hallaràn seis verdades, y estas desfiguradas." Such is the true character of a work which has hitherto served as a fountain of historic fact concerning the conquest of Granada.

passes and defiles which had been the scenes of the most remarkable events of the war; and passed some time in the ancient palace of the Alhambra, the once favourite abode of the Moorish monarchs in Granada. It was then, while his mind was still excited by the romantic scenery around him, and by the chivalrous and poetical associations which throw a moral interest over every feature of Spanish landscape, that he completed these volumes.

His great object appears to have been, to produce a complete and authentic body of facts relative to the war in question, but arranged in such a manner as to be attractive to the reader for mere amusement. He has, therefore, diligently sought for his materials among the ancient chronicles, both printed and in manuscript, which were written at the time by eye-witnesses, and, in some instances, by persons who had actually mingled in the scenes recorded. These chronicles were often diffuse and tedious, and occasionally discoloured by the bigotry, superstition, and fierce intolerance of the age; but their pages were illumined, at times, with scenes of high emprize, of romantic generosity, and heroic valour, which flashed upon the reader with additional splendour, from the surrounding darkness. It has been the study of the author, to bring forth these scenes in their strongest light; to arrange them in clear and lucid order; to give them somewhat of a graphic effect, by connecting them with the manners and customs of the age in which they occurred, and with the splendid scenery amidst which they took place; and thus, while he preserved the truth and chronological order of events, to impart a more impressive and entertaining character to his narrative, than regular histories are accustomed to possess. By these means his chronicle, at times, wears almost the air of romance; yet the story is authenticated by frequent reference to existing documents, proving that he has substantial foundation for his most extraordinary incidents.

There is, however, another circumstance, by which Mr. Irving has more seriously impaired the *ex-facie* credibility of his narrative. He has professed to derive his materials from the manuscripts of an ancient Spanish monk, Fray Antonio Agapida, whose historical productions are represented as existing in disjointed fragments, in the archives of the Escurial and other conventual libraries. He often quotes the very words of the venerable friar; particularly when he bursts forth in exaggerated praises of the selfish policy or bigot zeal of Ferdinand; or chaunts, "with pious exultation, the united triumphs of the cross and the sword." This friar is manifestly a mere fiction—a stalking-horse, from behind which the author launches his satire at the intolerance of that persecuting age, and at the errors, the inconsistencies, and the self-delusions of the singular medley of warriors, saints, politicians, and adventurers engaged in that holy war. Fray Antonio, however, may be considered as an incarnation of the blind bigotry and zealot extravagance of the "good old orthodox Spanish chroniclers;" and, in fact, his exaggerated sallies of loyalty and religion are taken, almost word for word, from the works of some one or other of the monkish historians. Still, though this fictitious personage has enabled the author to indulge his satirical vein at once more freely and more modestly, and has diffused over his page something of the quaintness of the cloister, and the tint of the country and the period, the use of such machinery has thrown a doubt upon the absolute verity of his history; and it will take some time, before the general mass of readers become convinced that the pretended manuscript of Fray Antonio Agapida is, in truth, a faithful digest of actual documents.

The chronicle opens with the arrival of a Spanish cavalier at Granada, with a demand of arrears of tribute, on the part of Ferdinand and Isabella, from Muley Aben Hassan, the Moorish king. This measure is well understood to have been a crafty device of Ferdinand. The tribute had become obsolete, and he knew it would be indignantly refused; but he had set his heart on driving the Moors out of their last Spanish dominions, and he now sought a cause of quarrel.

> "Muley Aben Hassan received the cavalier in state, seated on a magnificent divan, and surrounded by the officers of his court, in the hall of ambassadors, one of the most sumptuous apartments of the Alhambra. When De Vera had delivered his message, a haughty and bitter smile curled the lip of the fierce monarch. 'Tell your sovereigns,' said he, 'that the kings of Granada who used to pay tribute in money to the Castilian crown, are dead. Our mint at present coins nothing but blades of scimitars and heads of lances.'"
> —vol. i. p. 10.

The fiery old Moslem had here given a very tolerable pretext for immediate war; yet King Ferdinand forbore to strike the blow. He was just then engaged in a contest with Portugal, the cause of which Mr. Irving leaves unnoticed, as irrelevant to his subject. It is, however, a curious morsel of history, involving the singular and romantic fortunes of the Fair Juana of Castile, by many, considered the rightful heir to the crown. It is illustrative, also, of the manners of the age of which this chronicle peculiarly treats, and of the character and policy of the Spanish sovereign who figures throughout its pages; a brief notice of it, therefore, may not be unacceptable.

Henry IV. of Castile, one of the most imbecile of kings and credulous of husbands, had lived for five years in sterile wedlock with his queen, a gay and buxom princess of Portugal, when, at length, she rejoiced him by the birth of the Infanta Juana. The horn of the king was, of course, exalted on this happy occasion, but the whisper was diligently circulated about the court, that he was indebted for the tardy honours of paternity to the good offices of Don Beltran de Cuevas, Count of Ledesma, a youthful and gallant cavalier, who had enjoyed the peculiar favour and intimacy of the queen. The story soon took wind, and became a theme of popular clamour. Henry, however, with the good easy faith, or passive acquiescence of an imbecile mind, continued to love and honour his queen, and to lavish favours on her paramour, whom he advanced in rank, making him his prime minister, and giving him the title of Duke of Albuquerque. Such blind credulity is not permitted, in this troublesome world, to kings more than to common men. The public were furious; civil commotions took place; Henry was transiently deposed, and was only reinstated in his royal dignity, on signing a treaty, by which he divorced his wife, disowned her child, and promised to send them both to Portugal. His connubial faith ultimately revived, in defiance of every trial, and on his death-bed he recognized the Infanta Juana as his daughter and legitimate successor. The public, however, who will not allow even kings to be infallible judges in cases of the kind, persisted in asserting the illegitimacy of the Infanta; and gave her the name of *La Beltranaja*, in allusion to her supposed father, Don Beltran.[*] No judicial investigation took place, but the question was decided as a point of faith, or a notorious fact; and the youthful princess, though of great beauty and merit, was set aside, and the crown adjudged to her father's sister, the renowned Isabella.

It should be observed, however, that the charge of illegitimacy is maintained principally by Spanish writers; the Portuguese historians reject it as a calumny. Even the classic Mariana expresses an idea that it might have been an invention or exaggeration, founded on the weakness of Henry IV. and the amorous temperament of his queen,[†] and artfully devised to favour the views of the crafty Ferdinand, who laid claim to the crown as the rightful inheritance of his spouse, Isabella.

Young, beautiful, and unfortunate, the discarded princess was not long in want of a champion in that heroic age. Her mother's brother, the brave Alonzo V. of Portugal, surnamed *el Lidiador*, or the Combatant, from his exploits against the Moors of Africa, stepped forward as her vindicator, and marched into Spain at the head of a gallant army, to place her on the throne. He asked her hand in marriage, and it was yielded. The espousals were publicly solemnised at Placentia, but were not consummated, the consanguinity of the parties obliging them to wait for a dispensation from the Pope.

All the southern provinces of Castile, with a part of Gallicia, declared in favour of Juana, and town after town yielded to the arms or

[*] Pulgar, Chron. de los Reyes Catolicos, c. 1, note A.
[†] Mariana, lib. xxii., c. 20.

the persuasion of Alonzo, as he advanced. The majority of the kingdom, however, rallied round the standard of Ferdinand and Isabella. The latter assembled their warrior nobles at Valladolid, and amidst the chivalrous throng that appeared glittering in arms, was Don Beltran, Duke of Albuquerque, the surmised father of Juana. His predicament was singular and delicate. If, in truth, the father of Juana, natural affection called upon him to support her interests: if she were not his child, then she had an unquestionable right to the crown, and it was his duty, as a true cavalier, to support her claim. It is even said that he had pledged himself to Alonzo, to stand forth in loyal adherence to the virgin queen; but when he saw the array of mailed warriors and powerful nobles that thronged round Ferdinand and Isabella, he trembled for his great estates, and tacitly mingled with the crowd.* The gallant inroad of Alonzo into Spain was attended with many vicissitudes; he could not maintain his footing against the superior force of Ferdinand, and being defeated in a decisive battle, between Zamora and Toro, was obliged to retire from Castile. He conducted his beautiful and yet virgin bride into Portugal, where she was received as queen with great acclamations. There leaving her in security, he repaired to France, to seek assistance from Louis XI. During this absence, Pope Sixtus IV. granted the dispensation for his marriage. It was cautiously worded, and secretly given, that it might escape the knowledge of Ferdinand, until carried into effect. It authorized the king of Portugal to marry any relative not allied to him in the first degree of consanguinity, but avoided naming the bride.†

The negociation of Alonzo at the court of France was protracted during many weary months, and was finally defeated by the superior address of Ferdinand. He returned to Portugal, to forget his vexations in the arms of his blooming bride; but even here he was again disappointed by the crafty intrigues of his rival. The pliant pontiff had been prevailed upon to issue a patent bull, overruling his previous dispensation, as having been obtained without naming both of the persons to be united in marriage, and as having proved the cause of wars and bloodshed.‡ The royal pair were thus obliged to meet in the relations of uncle and niece, instead of husband and wife. Peace was finally negociated by the intervention of friends, on the condition that Donna Juana should either take the veil and become a nun, or should be wedded to Don Juan, the infant son and heir of Ferdinand and Isabella, as soon as he should arrive at a marriageable age. This singular condition,

---

* Pulgar, part ii., cap. xxii.

† Zurita, Annales.

‡ Zurita.

which would place her on the throne from which she had been excluded, has been adduced as a proof of her legitimate right.

Alonzo V. was furious, and rejected the treaty; but Donna Juana shrunk from being any longer the cause of war and bloodshed, and determined to devote herself to celibacy and religion. All the entreaties of the king were of no avail: she took the irrevocable vows, and, exchanging her royal robes for the humble habit of a Franciscan nun, entered the convent of Santa Clara, with all the customary solemnities; not having yet completed her nineteenth year, and having been four years a virgin wife. All authors concur in giving her a most amiable and exemplary character; and Garibay says "she was named, for her virtues, *La Excellenta*, and left a noble example to the world. Her retirement," he adds, "occasioned great affliction to King Alonzo, and grief to many others, who beheld so exquisite a lady reduced to such great humility."*

The king, in a transport of tender melancholy, took a sudden resolution, characteristic of that age, when love and chivalry and religion were strangely intermingled. Leaving his capital on a feigned pretence, he repaired to a distant city, and there, laying aside his royal state, set forth on a pilgrimage to Jerusalem, attended merely by a chaplain and two grooms. He had determined to renounce the pomp, and glories, and vanities of the world; and, after humbling himself at the holy sepulchre, to devote himself to a religious life. He sent back one of his attendants with letters, in which he took a tender leave of Donna Juana, and directed his son to assume the crown. His letters threw the court into great affliction; his son was placed on the throne, but several of the ancient courtiers set out in pursuit of the pilgrim king. They overtook him far on his journey, and prevailed on him to return and resume his sceptre, which was dutifully resigned to him by his son. Still restless and melancholy, Alonzo afterwards undertook a crusade for the recovery of the holy sepulchre, and proceeded to Italy with a fleet and army; but was discouraged from the enterprise by the coldness of Pope Pius II. He then returned to Portugal; and his love melancholy reviving in the vicinity of Donna Juana, he determined, out of a kind of romantic sympathy, to imitate her example, and to take the habit of St. Francis. His sadness and depression, however, increased to such a degree as to overwhelm his forces, and he died, in 1481, at Cintra, in the chamber in which he was born.†

We cannot close the brief record of this romantic story without noticing the subsequent fortunes of Donna Juana. She resided in the monastery of Santa Anna, with the seclusion of a nun, but the state of a princess. The fame of her beauty and her worth drew suitors to the

* Garibay, Compend. Hist., lib. xxxv., cap. 19.
† Faria y Sousa, Hist. Portugal, p. iii. cap. xiii.

cloisters; and her hand was solicited by the youthful king of Navarre, Don Francisco Phebus, surnamed the Handsome. His courtship, however, was cut short by his sudden death, in 1483, which was surmised to have been caused by poison.* For six-and-twenty years did the royal nun continue shut up in holy seclusion from the world. The desire of youth and the pride of beauty had long passed away, when suddenly, in 1505, Ferdinand himself, her ancient enemy, the cause of all her sorrows and disappointments, appeared as a suitor for her hand. His own illustrious queen, the renowned Isabella, was dead, and had bequeathed her hereditary crown of Castile to their daughter, for whose husband, Philip I., he had a jealous aversion. It was supposed that the crafty and ambitious monarch intended, after marrying Juana, to revive her claim to that throne, from which his own hostility had excluded her. His conduct in this instance is another circumstance strongly in favour of the lawful right of Juana to the crown of Castile. The vanity of the world, however, was dead in the tranquil bosom of the princess, and the grandeur of a throne had no longer attraction in her eyes. She rejected the suit of the most politic and perfidious of monarchs; and, continuing faithful to her vows, passed the remainder of her days in the convent of Santa Anna, where she died in all the odour of holiness, and of immaculate and thrice-proved virginity, which had passed unscorched even through the fiery ordeal of matrimony.

To return to Mr. Irving's narrative.—Ferdinand having successfully terminated the war with Portugal, and seated himself and Isabella firmly on the throne of Castile, turned his attention to his contemplated project —the conquest of Granada. His plan of operations was characteristic of his cautious and crafty nature. He determined to proceed step by step, taking town after town, and fortress after fortress, before he attempted the Moorish capital. "I will pick out the seeds of this pomegranate one by one," said the wary monarch, in allusion to Granada,—the Spanish name both for the kingdom and the fruit. The intention of the Catholic sovereign did not escape the eagle eye of old Muley Aben Hassan. Being, however, possessed of great treasures, and having placed his territories in a warlike posture, and drawn auxiliary troops from his allies, the princes of Barbary, he felt confident in his means of resistance. His subjects were fierce of spirit, and stout of heart—inured to the exercises of war, and patient of fatigue, hunger, thirst, and nakedness. Above all, they were dexterous horsemen, whether heavily armed and fully appointed, or lightly mounted, *a la geneta*, with merely lance and target. Adroit in all kinds of stratagems, impetuous in attack, quick to disperse, prompt to rally and to return like a whirlwind to the charge, they were considered the best of troops for daring inroads, sudden scourings, and

* Abarca, Reyes de Aragon, Rey 30, cap. 2.

all kinds of partisan warfare. In fact, they have bequeathed their wild and predatory spirit to Spain; and her bandaleros, her contrabandistas, and her guerrillas, her marauders of the mountain, and scamperers of the plain, may all be traced back to the belligerent era of the Moors.

The truce which had existed between the Catholic sovereign and the king of Granada contained a singular clause, characteristic of the wary and dangerous situation of the two neighbouring nations, with respect to each other. It permitted either party to make sudden inroads and assaults upon towns and fortresses, provided they were done furtively and by stratagem, without display of banner or sound of trumpet, or regular encampment, and that they did not last above three days. This gave rise to frequent enterprises of a hardy and adventurous character, in which castles and strong-holds were taken by surprise, and carried sword in hand. Monuments of these border scourings, and the jealous watchfulness awakened by them, may still be seen by the traveller in every part of Spain, but particularly in Andalusia. The mountains which formed the barriers of the Christian and Moslem territories are still crested with ruined watch towers, where the helmed and turbaned sentinels kept a look-out on the Vega of Granada, or the plains of the Guadalquivir. Every rugged pass has its dismantled fortress, and every town and village, and even hamlet, of mountain or valley, its strong tower of defence. Even on the beautiful little stream of the Guadayra, which now winds peacefully among flowery banks and groves of myrtles and oranges, to throw itself into the Guadalquivir, the Moorish mills, which have studded its borders for centuries, have each its battlemented tower, where the miller and his family could take refuge until the foray which swept the plains, and made hasty sack and plunder in its career, had passed away. Such was the situation of Moor and Spaniard in those days, when the sword and spear hung ready on the wall of every cottage, and the humblest toils of husbandry were performed with the weapon close at hand.

The outbreaking of the war of Granada is in keeping with this picture. The fierce old king, Muley Aben Hassan, had determined to anticipate his adversary, and strike the first blow. The fortress of Zahara was the object of his attack; and the description of it may serve for that of many of those old warrior towns which remain from the time of the Moors, built, like eagle nests, among the wild mountains of Andalusia.

> "This important post was on the frontier, between Ronda and Medina Sidonia, and was built on the crest of a rocky mountain, with a strong castle perched above it, upon a cliff so high that it was said to be above the flight of birds or drift of clouds. The streets, and many of the houses, were mere excavations, wrought out of the living rock. The town had but one gate, opening to the

west, and defended by towers and bulwarks. The only ascent to this cragged fortress was by roads cut in the rock, and so rugged as in many places to resemble broken stairs. Such was the situation of the mountain fortress of Zahara, which seemed to set all attack at defiance, insomuch that it had become so proverbial throughout Spain, that a woman of forbidding and inaccessible virtue was called a Zahareña. But the strongest fortress and sternest virtue have their weak points, and require unremitting vigilance to guard them: let warrior and dame take warning from the fate of Zahara."

Muley Aben Hassan made a midnight attack upon this fortress during a howling wintry storm, which had driven the very sentinels from their posts. He scaled the walls, and gained possession of both town and castle before the garrison were roused to arms. Such of the inhabitants as made resistance were cut down, the rest were taken prisoners, and driven, men, women, and children, like a herd of cattle to Granada.

The capture of Zahara was as an electric shock to the chivalry of Spain. Among those roused to action was Don Rodrigo Ponce de Leon, Marquis of Cadiz, who is worthy of particular notice as being the real hero of the war. Florian has assigned this honour, in his historical romance, to Gonsalvo of Cordova, surnamed the Great Captain, who, in fact, performed but an inferior part in these campaigns. It was in the subsequent war of Italy that he acquired his high renown. Rodrigo Ponce de Leon is a complete exemplification of the Spanish cavalier of the olden time. Temperate, chaste, vigilant, and valorous; kind to his vassals, frank toward his equals, faithful and loving to his friends, terrible yet magnanimous to his enemies; contemporary historians extol him as the mirror of chivalry, and compare him to the immortal Cid. His ample possessions extended over the most fertile parts of Andalusia, including many towns and fortresses. A host of retainers, ready to follow him to danger or to death, fed in his castle hall, which waved with banners taken from the Moors. His armouries glittered with helms and cuirasses, and weapons of all kinds, ready burnished for use, and his stables were filled with hardy steeds, trained to a mountain scamper. This ready preparation arose not merely from his residence on the Moorish border: he had a formidable foe near at hand, in Juan de Guzman, Duke of Medina Sidonia, one of the most wealthy of Spanish nobles. We shall notice one or two particulars of his earlier life, which our author has omitted, as not within the scope of his chronicle, but which would have given additional interest to some of its scenes. An hereditary feud subsisted between these two noblemen; and as Ferdinand and Isabella had not yet succeeded in their plan of reducing the independent and dangerous power of the nobles of Spain, the whole province of Andalusia was convulsed by their strife. They waged war against each other like sovereign princes, regarding neither the authority of the crown nor the welfare of the country. Every fortress and castle became a strong hold of their partisans, and a kind of club law prevailed over the land, like the *faust recht* once exercised by the robber counts of Germany. The sufferings of the province awakened the solicitude of Isabella, and brought her to Seville, where, seated on a throne in a great hall of the Alcazar or Moorish palace, she held an open audience to receive petitions and complaints. The nobles of the province hastened to do her homage. The Marquis of Cadiz alone did not appear. The Duke of Medina Sidonia accused him of having been treasonably in the interest of Portugal, in the late war of the succession; of exercising tyrannical sway over certain royal domains; of harassing the subjects of the crown with his predatory bands, and keeping himself aloof in warlike defiance, in his fortified city of Xeres. The continued absence of the marquis countenanced these charges, and they were reiterated by the relations and dependents of the duke, who thronged and controlled the ancient city of Seville. The indignation of the queen was roused, and she determined to reduce the supposed rebel by force of arms. Tidings of these events were conveyed to Ponce de Leon, and roused him to vindicate his honour with frankness and decision. He instantly set off from Xeres, attended by a single servant. Spurring across the country, and traversing the hostile city, he entered the palace by a private portal, and penetrating to the apartment of the queen, presented himself suddenly before her.

> " 'Behold me here, most potent sovereign!' exclaimed he, 'to answer any charge in person. I come not to accuse others, but to vindicate myself; not to deal in words, but in deeds. It is said that I hold Xeres and Alcala fortified and garrisoned, in defiance of your authority: send and take possession of them, for they are yours. Do you require my patrimonial hereditaments? From this chamber I will direct their surrender; and here I deliver up my very person into your power. As to the other charges, let investigation be made; and if I stand not clear and loyal, impose on me whatever pain or penalty you may think proper to inflict.' "*

Isabella saw in the intrepid frankness of the marquis strong proof of innocence, and declared, that had she thought him guilty, his gallant confidence would have insured her clemency. She took possession of the fortresses surrendered, but caused the Duke to give up equally his military posts, and to free Seville from these distracting contests, ordered either chief to dwell on his estate. Such was the feud betwixt these rival

* Pulgar, c. lxx., &c.

nobles at the time when the old Moorish king captured and sacked Zahara.

The news of this event stirred up the warrior spirit of Ponce de Leon to retaliation. He sent out his scouts, and soon learnt that the town of Alhama was assailable. "This was a large, wealthy, and populous place, which, from its strong position on a rocky height, within a few leagues of the Moorish capital, had acquired the appellation of the 'Key of Granada.'" The marquis held conference with the most important commanders of Andalusia, excepting the Duke of Medina Sidonia, his deadly foe, and concerted a secret march through the mountain passes to Alhama, which he surprised and carried. We forbear to follow the author in his detail of this wild and perilous enterprise, the success of which struck deep consternation in the Moors of Granada. The exclamation of "Ay de mi, Alhama!—Wo is me, Alhama!" was in every mouth. It has become the burthen of a mournful Spanish ballad, supposed of Moorish origin, which has been translated by Lord Byron.

The Marquis of Cadiz and his gallant companions, now in possession of Alhama, were but a handful of men, in the heart of an enemy's country, and were surrounded by a powerful army, led by the fierce King of Granada. They despatched messengers to Seville and Cordova, describing their perilous situation, and imploring aid. Nothing could equal the anguish of the Marchioness of Cadiz on hearing of the danger of her lord. She looked round in her deep distress for some powerful noble, competent to raise the force requisite for his deliverance. No one was so competent as the Duke of Medina Sidonia. To many, however, he would have seemed the last person to whom to apply; but she judged of him by her own high and generous mind, and did not hesitate. The event showed how well noble spirits understand each other.

> "He immediately despatched a courteous letter to the marchioness, assuring her, that, in consideration of the request of so honourable and estimable a lady, and to rescue from peril so valiant a cavalier as her husband, whose loss would be great, not only to Spain, but to all Christendom, he would forego the recollection of all past grievances, and hasten to his relief. The duke wrote at the same time to the alcaydes of his towns and fortresses, ordering them to join him forthwith at Seville, with all the force they could spare from their garrisons. He called on all the chivalry of Andalusia to make a common cause in the rescue of those Christian cavaliers; and he offered large pay to all volunteers who would resort to him with horses, armour, and provisions. Thus all who could be incited by honour, religion, patriotism, or thirst of gain, were induced to hasten to his standard; and he took the field with an army of five thousand horse and fifty thousand foot."

Ferdinand was in church at Medina del Campo when he heard of the achievement and the peril of his gallant cavaliers, and set out instantly to aid in person in their rescue. He wrote to the Duke of Medina Sidonia to pause for him on the frontier; but it was a case of life and death: the duke left a message to that effect for his sovereign, and pressed on his unceasing march. He arrived just in time, when the garrison, reduced to extremity by incessant skirmishes and assaults, and the want of water, and resembling skeletons rather than living men, were on the point of falling into the hands of the enemy. Muley Aben Hassan, who commanded the siege in person, tore his beard when his scouts brought him word of their arrival.

> "They had seen from the heights the long columns and flaunting banners of the Christian army approaching through the mountains. To linger would be to place himself between two bodies of the enemy. Breaking up his camp, therefore, in all haste, he gave up the siege of Alhama, and hastened back to Granada; and the last clash of his cymbals scarce died upon the ear from the distant hills, before the standard of the Duke of Medina Sidonia was seen emerging in another direction from the defiles of the mountains.... It was a noble and gracious sight to behold the meeting of those two ancient foes, the Duke of Medina Sidonia and the Marquis of Cadiz. When the marquis beheld his magnanimous deliverer approaching, he melted into tears: all past animosities only gave the greater poignancy to present feelings of gratitude and admiration; they clasped each other in their arms; and, from that time forward, were true and cordial friends."

Having duly illustrated these instances of chivalrous hardihood and noble magnanimity, the author shifts his scene from the Christian camp to the Moslem hall, and gives us a peep into the interior of the Alhambra, and the domestic policy of the Moorish monarchs. The old King of Granada was perplexed, not merely with foreign wars, but with family feuds, and seems to have evinced a kind of tiger character in both. He had several wives, two of whom were considered as sultanas, or queens. One, named Ayxa, was of Moorish origin, and surnamed *La Horra*, or *The Chaste*, from the purity of her manners. Fatima, the other, had been originally a Christian captive, and was called, from her beauty, *Zoroya*, or *The Light of Dawn*. The former had given birth to his eldest son, Abdalla, or Boabdil, commonly called *El Chico*, or *the Younger*; and the latter had brought him two sons. Zoroya abused the influence that her youth and beauty gave her over the hoary monarch, inducing him to repudiate the virtuous Ayxa, and exciting his suspicions against Boabdil to such a degree, that he determined upon his death. It was the object of Zoroya, by these flagitious means, to secure the succession for one of her own children.

> "The sultana Ayxa was secretly apprized of the cruel design of the old monarch. She was a woman of talents and courage, and, by means of her female attendants, concerted a plan for the escape of her son. A faithful servant was instructed to wait below the Alhambra, in the dead of the night, on the banks of the river Darro, with a fleet Arabian courser. The sultana, when the castle was in a state of deep repose, tied together the shawls and scarfs of herself and her female attendants, and lowered the youthful prince from the tower of Comares. He made his way in safety down the steep rocky hill to the banks of the Darro, and, throwing himself on the Arabian courser, was thus spirited off to the city of Guadix. Here he lay for some time concealed, until, gaining adherents, he fortified himself in the place, and set his tyrant father at defiance. Such was the commencement of those internal feuds which hastened the downfall of Granada. The Moors became separated into two hostile factions, headed by the father and the son, and several bloody encounters took place between them; yet they never failed to act with all their separate force against the Christians, as a common enemy."

It is proper, in this place, to remark, that the present chronicle gives an entirely different character to Boabdil from that by which he is usually described. It says nothing of his alleged massacre of the Abencerrages, nor of the romantic story of his jealous persecution and condemnation of his queen, and her vindication in combat by Christian knights. The massacre, in fact, if it really did take place, was the deed of his tiger-hearted father; the story of the queen is not to be found in any contemporary chronicle, either Spanish or Arabian, and is considered by Mr. Irving as a mere fabrication. Boabdil appears to have been sometimes rash, at other times irresolute, but never cruel.

As a specimen of the predatory war that prevailed about the borders, we would fain make some extracts from a foray of the old Moorish king into the lands of the Duke of Medina Sidonia, who had foiled him before Alhama; but this our limits forbid. It ends triumphantly for Muley Hassan; and Boabdil el Chico, in consequence, found it requisite for his popularity to strike some signal blow that might eclipse the brilliant exploits of the rival king, his father. He was in the flower of his age, and renowned at joust and tourney, but as yet unproved in the field of battle. He was encouraged to make a daring inroad into the Christian territories by the father of his favourite sultana, Ali Atar,

alcayde of Loxa, a veteran warrior, ninety years of age, whose name
was the terror of the borders.

"Boabdil assembled a brilliant army of nine thousand foot and
seven hundred horse, comprising the most illustrious and valiant of
the Moorish chivalry. His mother, the Sultana Ayxa La Horra,
armed him for the field, and gave him her benediction as she girded
his cimeter to his side. His favourite wife, Morayma, wept, as she
thought of the evils that might befal him. 'Why dost thou weep,
daughter of Ali Atar?' said the high-minded Ayxa; 'these tears become not the daughter of a warrior, nor the wife of a king. Believe
me, there lurks more danger for a monarch within the strong walls
of a palace, than within the frail curtains of a tent. It is by perils
in the field, that thy husband must purchase security on his throne.'
But Morayma still hung upon his neck, with tears and sad forebodings; and when he departed from the Alhambra, she betook
herself to her mirador, which looks out over the vega, whence she
watched the army as it passed in shining order along the road that
leads to Loxa; and every burst of warlike melody that came swelling on the breeze was answered by a gush of sorrow. . . . .
"At Loxa, the royal army was reinforced by old Ali Atar, with
the chosen horsemen of his garrison, and many of the bravest warriors of the border towns. The people of Loxa shouted with exultation, when they beheld Ali Atar armed at all points, and once more
mounted on his Barbary steed, which had often borne him over
the borders. The veteran warrior, with nearly a century of years
upon his head, had all the fire and animation of a youth at the
prospect of a foray, and careered from rank to rank with the
velocity of an Arab of the desert. The populace watched the army
as it paraded over the bridge, and wound into the passes of the
mountains; and still their eyes were fixed upon the pennon of Ali
Atar, as if it bore with it an assurance of victory."

The enemy has scarcely had a day's ravage in the Christian land,
when the alarm-fires give notice that the Moor is over the border. Our
limits do not permit us to give this picture of the sudden rising of a
frontier in those times of Moorish inroad. We pass on to the scene of
action, when the hardy Count de Cabra came up with the foe, having
pressed fearlessly forward at the head of a handful of household troops
and retainers.

"The Moorish king descried the Spanish forces at a distance,
although a slight fog prevented his seeing them distinctly, and
ascertaining their numbers. His old father-in-law, Ali Atar, was by

his side, who, being a veteran marauder, was well acquainted with all the standards and armorial bearings of the frontiers. When the king beheld the ancient and long-disused banner of Cabra emerging from the mist, he turned to Ali Atar, and demanded whose ensign it was. The old borderer was for once at a loss, for the banner had not been displayed in battle in his time. 'Sire,' replied he, after a pause, 'I have been considering that standard, but do not know it. It appears to be a dog, which is a device borne by the towns of Baeza and Ubeda. If it be so, all Andalusia is in movement against you; for it is not probable that any single commander or community would venture to attack you. I would advise you, therefore, to retire.'

"The Count of Cabra, in winding down the hill towards the Moors, found himself on a much lower station than the enemy. He therefore ordered, in all haste, that his standard should be taken back, so as to gain the vantage ground. The Moors, mistaking this for a retreat, rushed impetuously towards the Christians. The latter, having gained the height proposed, charged down upon them at the same moment, with the battle cry of 'Santiago!' and, dealing the first blows, laid many of the Moorish cavaliers in the dust.

"The Moors, thus checked in their tumultuous assault, were thrown into confusion, and began to give way,—the Christians following hard upon them. Boabdil el Chico endeavoured to rally them. 'Hold! hold! for shame!' cried he: 'let us not fly, at least until we know our enemy!' The Moorish chivalry were stung by this reproof, and turned to make front, with the valour of men who feel that they are fighting under their monarch's eye. At this moment, Lorenzo de Porres, alcayde of Luque, arrived with fifty horse and one hundred foot, sounding an Italian trumpet from among a copse of oak-trees, which concealed his force. The quick ear of old Ali Atar caught the note. 'That is an Italian trumpet,' said he to the king: 'the whole world seems in arms against your majesty!' The trumpet of Lorenzo de Porres was answered by that of the Count de Cabra in another direction; and it seemed to the Moors as if they were between two armies. Don Lorenzo, sallying from among the oaks, now charged upon the enemy. The latter did not wait to ascertain the force of this new foe. The confusion, the variety of alarms, the attacks from opposite quarters, the obscurity of the fog, all conspired to deceive them as to the number of their adversaries. Broken and dismayed, they retreated fighting; and nothing but the presence and remonstrances of the king prevented their retreat from becoming a headlong flight."

The skirmishing retreat lasted for about three leagues; but on the

banks of the Mingonzalez the rout became complete. The result is related by a fugitive from the field.

"The sentinels looked out from the watch-towers of Loxa, along
the valley of the Xenil, which passes through the mountains. They
looked, to behold the king returning in triumph, at the head of
his shining host, laden with the spoil of the unbeliever. They looked,
to behold the standard of their warlike idol, the fierce Ali Atar,
borne by the chivalry of Loxa, ever foremost in the wars of the
border.

"In the evening of the 21st of April, they descried a single
horseman, urging his faltering steed along the banks of the river.
As he drew near, they perceived, by the flash of arms, that he
was a warrior; and, on nearer approach, by the richness of his
armour, and the caparison of his steed, they knew him to be a
warrior of rank.

"He reached Loxa faint and aghast; his Arabian courser covered
with foam, and dust, and blood, panting and staggering with
fatigue, and gashed with wounds. Having brought his master in
safety, he sank down and died, before the gate of the city. The
soldiers at the gate gathered round the cavalier, as he stood, mute
and melancholy, by his expiring steed. They knew him to be the
gallant Cidi Caleb, nephew of the chief alfaqui of the albaycen
of Granada. When the people of Loxa beheld this noble cavalier
thus alone, haggard and dejected, their hearts were filled with
fearful forebodings.

"'Cavalier,' said they, 'how fares it with the king and army?'
He cast his hand mournfully towards the land of the Christians.
'There they lie!' exclaimed he: 'the heavens have fallen upon them!
all are lost—all dead!'

"Upon this, there was a great cry of consternation among the
people, and loud wailings of women; for the flower of the youth
of Loxa were with the army. An old Moorish soldier, scarred in
many a border battle, stood leaning on his lance by the gateway.
'Where is Ali Atar?' demanded he eagerly. 'If he still live, the army
cannot be lost.'

"'I saw his turban cleft by the Christian sword,' replied Cidi
Caleb. 'His body is floating in the Xenil.'

"When the soldier heard these words, he smote his breast, and
threw dust upon his head; for he was an old follower of Ali Atar."

The unfortunate Boabdil was conducted a captive to Vaena, a frontier
town among the mountains; and the ruined towers of the old time-worn
castle are still pointed out to the traveller in which he was held in

honourable durance by the hardy Count de Cabra. Ferdinand at length liberated him, on stipulation of an ample tribute, and vassalage, with military service, to the Castilian crown. It was his policy to divide the Moors, by fomenting a civil war between the two rival kings; and his foresight was justified by the result. The factions of the father and the son broke forth again with redoubled fury, and Moor was armed against Moor, instead of uniting against the common foe.

Muley Aben Hassan became infirm through vexation as well as age, and blindness was added to his other calamities. He had, however, a brother, named Abdalla, but generally called El Zagal, or the Valiant, younger, of course, than himself, yet well stricken in years, who was alike distinguished for cool judgment and fiery courage, and for most of the other qualities which form an able general. This chief, whose martial deeds run through the present history, became the ruler of his brother's realm, and was soon after raised by acclamation to the throne, even before the ancient king's decease, which shortly followed, and not without suspicion of foul play. The civil war, which had commenced between father and son, was kept up between uncle and nephew. The latter, though vacillating and irresolute, was capable of being suddenly aroused to prompt and vigorous measures. The voice of the multitude, changeful as the wind, fluctuated between El Chico and El Zagal, according as either was successful; and, in depicting the frequent, and almost ludicrous, vicissitudes of their power and popularity, the author has indulged a quiet vein of satire, on the capricious mutability of public favour.

The varied and striking scenes of daring foray and mountain maraud, of military pomp and courtly magnificence, which occur throughout the work, make selection difficult. The following extract shows the splendour of a Spanish camp, and the varied chivalry assembled from different Christian powers.

> "Great and glorious was the style with which the catholic sovereigns opened another year's campaign of this eventful war. It was like commencing another act of a stately and heroic drama, where the curtain rises to the inspiring sound of martial melody, and the whole stage glitters with the array of warriors and the pomp of arms. The ancient city of Cordova was the place appointed by the sovereigns for the assemblage of the troops; and, early in the spring of 1486, the fair valley of the Guadalquivir resounded with the shrill blast of trumpet, and the impatient neighing of the war horse. In this splendid era of Spanish chivalry, there was a rivalship among the nobles, who most should distinguish himself by the splendour of his appearance, and the number and equipments of his feudal followers. . . . Sometimes they passed through

the streets of Cordova at night, in cavalcade, with great numbers of lighted torches, the rays of which, falling upon polished armour, and nodding plumes, and silken scarfs, and trappings of golden embroidery, filled all beholders with admiration. But it was not the chivalry of Spain alone, which thronged the streets of Cordova. The fame of this war had spread throughout Christendom: it was considered a kind of crusade; and catholic knights from all parts hastened to signalize themselves in so holy a cause. There were several valiant chevaliers from France, among whom the most distinguished was Gaston du Léon, seneschal of Toulouse. With him came a gallant train, well armed and mounted and decorated with rich surcoats and penaches of feathers. These cavaliers, it is said, eclipsed all others in the light festivities of the court. They were devoted to the fair; but not after the solemn and passionate manner of the Spanish lovers: they were gay, gallant, and joyous in their amours, and captivated by the vivacity of their attacks. They were at first held in light estimation by the grave and stately Spanish knights, until they made themselves to be respected by their wonderful prowess in the field.

"The most conspicuous of the volunteers, however, who appeared in Cordova on this occasion, was an English knight, of royal connexion. This was the Lord Scales, Earl of Rivers, related to the Queen of England, wife of Henry VII. He had distinguished himself, in the preceding year, at the battle of Bosworth Field, where Henry Tudor, then Earl of Richmond, overcame Richard III. That decisive battle having left the country at peace, the Earl of Rivers, retaining a passion for warlike scenes, repaired to the Castilian court, to keep his arms in exercise in a campaign against the Moors. He brought with him a hundred archers, all dexterous with the long bow and the cloth-yard arrow; also two hundred yeomen, armed cap-à-piè, who fought with pike and battleaxe— men robust of frame, and of prodigious strength. The worthy Padre Fray Antonio Agapida describes this stranger knight and his followers with his accustomed accuracy and minuteness. 'This cavalier,' he observes, 'was from the island of England, and brought with him a train of his vassals; men who had been hardened in certain civil wars which had raged in their country. They were a comely race of men, but too fair and fresh for warriors; not having the sunburnt, martial hue of our old Castilian soldiery. They were huge feeders, also, and deep carousers; and could not accommodate themselves to the sober diet of our troops, but must fain eat and drink after the manner of their own country. They were often noisy and unruly, also, in their wassail; and their quarter of the camp was prone to be a scene of loud revel and sudden brawl.

They were withal of great pride; yet it was not like our inflammable Spanish pride: they stood not much upon the *pundonor* and high punctilio, and rarely drew the stiletto in their disputes; but their pride was silent and contumelious. Though from a remote and somewhat barbarous island, they yet believed themselves the most perfect men upon earth; and magnified their chieftain, the Lord Scales, beyond the greatest of our grandees. With all this, it must be said of them that they were marvellous good men in the field, dexterous archers, and powerful with the battleaxe. In their great pride and self-will, they always sought to press in the advance, and take the post of danger, trying to outvie our Spanish chivalry. They did not rush forward fiercely, or make a brilliant onset, like the Moorish and Spanish troops, but they went into the fight deliberately, and persisted obstinately, and were slow to find out when they were beaten. Withal, they were much esteemed, yet little liked, by our soldiery, who considered them stanch companions in the field, yet coveted but little fellowship with them in the camp. Their commander, the Lord Scales, was an accomplished cavalier, of gracious and noble presence, and fair speech. It was a marvel to see so much courtesy in a knight brought up so far from our Castilian court. He was much honoured by the king and queen, and found great favour with the fair dames about the court; who, indeed, are rather prone to be pleased with foreign cavaliers. He went always in costly state, attended by pages and esquires, and accompanied by noble young cavaliers of his country, who had enrolled themselves under his banner, to learn the gentle exercise of arms. In all pageants and festivals, the eyes of the populace were attracted by the singular bearing and rich array of the English earl and his train, who prided themselves in always appearing in the garb and manner of their country; and were, indeed, something very magnificent, delectable, and strange to behold.' "

Ferdinand led this gallant army to besiege Loxa, a powerful city on the Moorish frontier, before which he had formerly been foiled. The assault was made in open day, by a detachment which had been thrown in the advance, and which was bravely and fiercely met and repelled by the Moors.

"At this critical juncture, King Ferdinand emerged from the mountains with the main body of the army, and advanced to an eminence commanding a full view of the field of action. By his side was the noble English cavalier, the Earl of Rivers. This was the first time he had witnessed a scene of Moorish warfare. He looked with eager interest at the chance-medley fight before him—the wild career of cavalry, the irregular and tumultuous rush of infantry, and Christian helm and Moorish turban intermingling in deadly struggle. His high blood mounted at the sight; and his very soul was stirred within him, by the confused war-cries, the clangour of drums and trumpets, and the reports of arquebuses, that came echoing up the mountains. Seeing the king was sending a reinforcement to the field, he entreated permission to mingle in the affray, and fight according to the fashion of his country. His request being granted, he alighted from his steed. He was merely armed *en blanco;* that is to say, with morion, back piece, and breastplate; his sword was girded by his side, and in his hand he wielded a powerful battleaxe. He was followed by a body of his yeomen, armed in like manner, and by a band of archers, with bows made of the tough English yew-tree. The earl turned to his troops, and addressed them briefly and bluntly, according to the manner of his country. 'Remember, my merry men all,' said he, 'the eyes of strangers are upon you; you are in a foreign land, fighting for the glory of God and the honour of merry old England!' A loud shout was the reply. The earl waved his battleaxe over his head. 'St. George for England!' cried he; and, to the inspiring sound of this old English war-cry, he and his followers rushed down to the battle, with manly and courageous hearts.

"The Moors were confounded by the fury of these assaults, and gradually fell back upon the bridge: the Christians followed up their advantage, and drove them over it tumultuously. The Moors retreated into the suburb, and Lord Rivers and his troops entered with them pell-mell, fighting in the streets and in the houses. King Ferdinand came up to the scene of action with his royal guard, and the infidels were all driven within the city walls. Thus were the suburbs gained by the hardihood of the English lord, without such an event having been premeditated."

Various striking events marked the progress of the war—ingenious and desperate manœuvres on the part of El Zagal, and persevering success in the well-judged policy of Ferdinand. A spell of ill fortune seemed to surround the old Moorish king ever since the suspicious death of his brother and predecessor, Muley Aben Hassan, which was surmised to have been effected through his connivance; and his popularity sunk with his versatile subjects. The Spaniards at length laid siege to the powerful city of Baza, the key to all the remaining possessions of El Zagal. The peril of the Moorish kingdom of Granada resounded now throughout the east. The Grand Turk, Bajazet II., and his deadly foe the Grand Soldan of Egypt, or of Babylon, as he is termed by the old chroniclers, suspended their bloody feuds to check this ruinous war. A singular embassy from the latter of these potentates now entered the Spanish camp.

"While the holy Christian army was beleaguering the infidel city of Baza, there rode into the camp, one day, two reverend friars of the order of Saint Francis. One was of portly person, and authoritative air. He bestrode a goodly steed, well conditioned, and well caparisoned; while his companion rode behind him upon a humble hack, poorly accoutred, and, as he rode, he scarcely raised his eyes from the ground, but maintained a meek and lowly air. The arrival of two friars in the camp was not a matter of much note; for, in these holy wars, the church militant continually mingled in the affray, and helmet and cowl were always seen together; but it was soon discovered that these worthy saints errant were from a far country, and on a mission of great import. They were, in truth, just arrived from the Holy Land, being two of the saintly men who kept vigil over the sepulchre of our blessed Lord at Jerusalem. He, of the tall and portly form, and commanding presence, was Fray Antonio Millan, prior of the Franciscan convent in the Holy City. He had a full and florid countenance, a sonorous voice, and was round, and swelling, and copious, in his periods, like one accustomed to harangue, and to be listened to with deference. His companion was small and spare in form, pale of visage, and soft, and silken, and almost whispering, in speech. 'He had a humble and lowly way,' says Agapida; 'evermore bowing the head, as became one of his calling. Yet. he was one of the most active, zealous, and effective brothers of the convent; and, when he raised his small black eye from the earth, there was a keen glance out of the corner, which showed that, though harmless as a dove, he was, nevertheless, as wise as a serpent.' These holy men had come, on a momentous embassy, from the Grand Soldan of Egypt, who, as head of the whole Moslem sect, considered himself bound to preserve the kingdom of Granada from the grasp of unbelievers. He despatched, therefore, these two holy friars, with letters to the Castilian sovereigns, insisting that they should desist from this war, and reinstate the Moors of Granada in the territory of which they had been dispossessed: otherwise, he threatened to put to death all the Christians beneath his sway, to demolish their convents and temples, and to destroy the holy sepulchre."

It may not be uninteresting to remark, that Christopher Columbus, in the course of his tedious solicitation to the Spanish court, was present at this siege; and it is surmised that, in conversations with these diplomatic monks, he was first inspired with that zeal for the recovery of the holy sepulchre which, throughout the remainder of his life, continued to animate his fervent and enthusiastic spirit, and beguile him into magnificent schemes and speculations. The ambassadors of the Soldan, meantime, could produce no change in the resolution of Ferdinand. Baza yielded after more than six months' arduous siege, and was followed by the surrender of most of the fortresses of the Alpuxarra mountains; and, at length, the fiery El Zagal, tamed by misfortunes, and abandoned by his subjects, surrendered his crown to the Christian sovereigns, for a stipulated revenue or productive domain.

Boabdil el Chico remained the sole and unrivalled sovereign of Granada, the vassal of the Christian sovereigns, whose assistance had supported him in his wars against his uncle. But he was now to prove the hollow-hearted friendship of the politic Ferdinand. Pretences were easily found where a quarrel was already predetermined, and he was presently required to surrender the city and crown of Granada. A ravage of the Vega enforced the demand, and the Spanish armies laid siege to the metropolis. Ferdinand had fulfilled his menace;—he had picked out the seeds of the pomegranate. Every town and fortress had successively fallen into his hand, and the city of Granada stood alone. He led his desolating armies over this paradise of a country, and left scarcely a living animal or a green blade on the face of the land,—and Granada, the queen of gardens, remained a desert. The history closes with the last scene of this eventful contest—the surrender of the Moorish capital.

> "Having surrendered the last symbol of power, the unfortunate Boabdil continued on towards the Alpuxarras, that he might not behold the entrance of the Christians into his capital. His devoted band of cavaliers followed him in gloomy silence; but heavy sighs burst from their bosoms, as shouts of joy and strains of triumphant music were borne on the breeze from the victorious army. Having rejoined his family, Boabdil set forward with a heavy heart for his allotted residence, in the valley of Porchena. At two leagues distance, the cavalcade, winding into the skirts of the Alpuxarras, ascended an eminence commanding the last view of Granada. As they arrived at this spot, the Moors paused involuntarily to take a farewell gaze at their beloved city, which a few steps more would shut from their sight for ever. Never had it appeared so lovely in their eyes. The sunshine, so bright in that transparent climate, lighted up each tower and minaret, and rested gloriously upon the crowning battlements of the Alhambra; while the vega spread its enamelled bosom of verdure below, glistening with the

silver windings of the Xenil. The Moorish cavaliers gazed with a silent agony of tenderness and grief upon that delicious abode, the scene of their loves and pleasures. While they yet looked, a light cloud of smoke burst forth from the citadel; and, presently, a peal of artillery, faintly heard, told that the city was taken possession of, and the throne of the Moslem kings was lost for ever. The heart of Boabdil, softened by misfortunes and overcharged with grief, could no longer contain itself. 'Allah achbar!—God is great!' said he; but the words of resignation died upon his lips, and he burst into a flood of tears. His mother, the intrepid sultana Ayxa la Horra, was indignant at his weakness. 'You do well,' said she, 'to weep like a woman for what you failed to defend like a man!' The vizier, Aben Comixa, endeavoured to console his royal master. 'Consider, sire,' said he, 'that the most signal misfortunes often render men as renowned as the most prosperous achievements, provided they sustain them with magnanimity.' The unhappy monarch, however, was not to be consoled. His tears continued to flow. 'Allah achbar!' exclaimed he, 'when did misfortunes ever equal mine!' From this circumstance, the hill, which is not far from Padul, took the name of Feg Allah Achbar; but the point of view commanding the last prospect of Granada is known among Spaniards by the name of *el ultimo suspiro del Moro,* or 'the last sigh of the Moor.' "

Here ends the Chronicle of the Conquest of Granada, for here the author lets fall the curtain. We shall, however, extend our view a little further. The rejoicings of the Spanish sovereigns were echoed at Rome, and throughout Christendom. The venerable chronicler, Pedro Abarca, assures us that King Henry VII. of England celebrated the conquest by a grand procession to St. Paul's, where the Chancellor pronounced an eloquent eulogy on King Ferdinand, declaring him not only a glorious captain and conqueror, but also entitled to a seat among the Apostles.[*]

The pious and politic monarch governed his new kingdom with more righteousness than mercy. The Moors were at first a little restive under the yoke; there were several tumults in the city; and a quantity of arms were discovered in a secret cave. Many of the offenders were tried, condemned, and put to death; some being quartered, others cut in pieces; and the whole mass of infidel inhabitants was well sifted, and purged of upwards of forty thousand delinquents. This system of wholesome purgation was zealously continued by Fray Francisco (afterwards Cardinal) Ximenes, who, seconded by Fernando de Talavera, Archbishop of Granada, and clothed in the terrific power of the In-

---

[*] Abarca, Anales de Aragon, p. 30.

quisition, undertook the conversion of the Moors. We forbear to detail the various modes—sometimes by blandishment, sometimes by rigour, sometimes exhorting, sometimes entreating, sometimes hanging, sometimes burning,—by which the hard hearts of the infidels were subdued, and above fifty thousand coaxed, teased, and terrified into baptism.

One act of Ximenes has been the subject of particular regret. The Moors had cultivated the sciences while they lay buried in Europe, and were renowned for the value of their literature. Ximenes, in his bigoted zeal to destroy the Koran, extended his devastation to the indiscriminate destruction of their works, and burnt five thousand manuscripts on various subjects, some of them very splendid copies, and others of great intrinsic worth, sparing a very few, which treated chiefly of medicine. Here we shall pause, and not pursue the subject to the further oppression and persecution, and final expulsion, of these unhappy people; the latter of which events is one of the most impolitic and atrocious recorded in the pages of history.

Centuries have elapsed since the time of this chivalrous and romantic struggle, yet the monuments of it still remain, and the principal facts still linger in the popular traditions and legendary ballads with which the country abounds. The likenesses of Ferdinand and Isabella are multiplied, in every mode, by painting and sculpture, in the churches, and convents, and palaces of Granada. Their ashes rest in sepulchral magnificence in the royal chapel of the cathedral, where their effigies in alabaster lie side by side before a splendid altar, decorated in relief with the story of their triumph. The anniversary of the surrender of the capital is still kept up by fêtes, and ceremonies, and public rejoicings. The standard of Ferdinand and Isabella is again unfurled and waved to the sound of trumpets. The populace are admitted to rove all day about the halls and courts of the Alhambra, and to dance on its terraces; the ancient alarm-bell resounds at morn, at noon, and at nightfall; great emulation prevails among the damsels to ring a peal,—it is a sign they will be married in the course of the opening year. But this commemoration is not confined to Granada alone. Every town and village of the mountains on the Vega has the anniversary of its deliverance from Moorish thraldom; when ancient armour, and Spanish and Moorish dresses, and unwieldy arquebuses, from the time of the conquest, are brought forth from their repositories—grotesque processions are made—and sham battles, celebrated by peasants, arrayed as Christians and Moors, in which the latter are sure to be signally defeated, and sometimes, in the ardour and illusion of the moment, soundly rib-roasted.

In traversing the mountains and vallies of the ancient kingdom, the traveller may trace with wonderful distinctness the scenes of the principal events of the war. The muleteer, as he lolls on his pack-saddle, smoking his cigar or chaunting his popular romance, pauses to point out some wild, rocky pass, famous for the bloody strife of infidel and Christian, or some Moorish fortress butting above the road, or some solitary watch-tower on the heights, connected with the old story of the conquest. Gibralfaro, the warlike hold of Hamet el Zegri, formidable even in its ruins, still frowns down from its rocky height upon the streets of Malaga. Loxa, Alhama, Zahara, Ronda, Guadix, Baza, have all their Moorish ruins,—rendered classic by song and story. The "Last sigh of the Moor" still lingers about the height of Padul: the traveller pauses on the arid and thirsty summit of the hill, commanding a view over the varied bosom of the Vega, to the distant towers of Granada. A humble cabin is erected by the way side, where he may obtain water to slake his thirst, and the very rock is pointed out from whence the unfortunate Boabdil took his last look, and breathed the last farewell, to his beloved Alhambra.

Every part of Granada itself retains some memorial of the taste and elegance, the valour and voluptuousness of the Moors, or some memento of the strife that sealed their downfall. The fountains which gush on every side are fed by the aqueducts once formed by Moslem hands; the Vega is still embroidered by the gardens they planted, where the remains of their ingenious irrigation spread the verdure and freshness of a northern climate, under the cloudless azure of a southern sky. But the pavilions that adorned these gardens; and where, if romances speak true, the Moslem heroes solaced themselves with the loves of their Zaras, their Zaidas, and their Zelindas, have long since disappeared. The orange, the citron, the fig, the vine, the pomegranate, the aloe, and the myrtle, shroud and overwhelm with oriental vegetation the crumbling ruins of towers and battlements. The Vivarrambla, once the scene of chivalric pomp and splendid tourney, is degraded to a market-place; the Gate of Elvira, from whence so many a shining array of warriors passed forth to forage the land of the Christians, still exists, but neglected and dismantled, and tottering to its fall. The Alhambra rises from amidst its groves, the tomb of its former glory. The fountains still play in its marble halls, and the nightingale sings among the roses of its gardens; but the halls are waste and solitary; the owl hoots from its battlements, the hawk builds in its warrior towers, and bats flit about its royal chambers. Still the fountain is pointed out where the gallant Abencerrages were put to death; the Mirador, where Morayma sat, and wept the departure of Boabdil, and watched for his return; and the broken gateway, from whence the unfortunate monarch issued forth to surrender his fortress and his kingdom; and which, at his request, was closed up, never to be entered by mortal footstep. At the time when the French abandoned this fortress, after its temporary occupation a few years since, the tower of the gateway was blown up;

the walls were rent and shattered by the explosion, and the folding doors hurled into the garden of the convent of Los Martiros. The portal, however, was closed up with stones, by persons who were ignorant of the tradition connected with it, and thus the last request of poor Boabdil continued unwittingly to be performed. In fact, the story of the gateway, though recorded in ancient chronicle, has faded from general recollection, and is only known to two or three ancient inhabitants of the Alhambra, who inherit it with other local traditions from their ancestors.

[February, 1831]

[REVIEW OF ALEXANDER SLIDELL'S
A YEAR IN SPAIN]

This is, altogether, one of the most amusing books of travels that we have read for a long time; and what is more, it relates to a country which though by no means distant, is comparatively but little known—a country, in fact, where the "far wandering" foot of the all pervading Englishman but seldom rambles. The stream of Cockney tourists; of burly citizens with their wondering wives; their half gawky, half dandy sons, and their novel-struck, poet-ridden daughters, with albums, port-folios and drawing books—that incessant and overwhelming stream which inundates all the rest of Europe, is turned off and completely repelled by the mountain barrier of the Pyrenees. The frightful stories of Spanish robbers and assassins, of Spanish blunderbusses and Spanish knives; of rugged roads, and comfortless inns, of bigotry, priestcraft, poverty, dirt, vermin, and all other kinds of dangers, evils and annoy-ances, with which the ear of the simple tourist is beguiled, deter the crowd of gentlemen and ladies who "travel at their ease" from venturing into that land of peril. Hence it is rare indeed that the well balanced, well laden and well filled travelling carriage of a sleek English family is seen rolling down the southern declivities of the Pyrenees, and those trophies of Cockney comfort, and Cockney civilization, the beefsteak and the tea kettle, which mark the progress of English travel, and have been introduced even in Greece and the Holy Land, are as yet unknown in the Ventas and Posadas of the Peninsula.

We are pleased, therefore, to meet with a work which gives us a familiar peep into that unhackneyed country, though we doubt whether some of the scenes and adventures recorded in the present work will not have the effect of still more increasing the before-mentioned disinclination of the comfort loving and cautious traveller.

The author has modestly withheld his name through diffidence, it would appear, of the success of this, his maiden production. Happening, however, to be accidentally informed on the subject, and feeling assured that the volumes before us cannot fail to give him an honourable rank in the rising literature of his country, we have no hesitation in betraying his incognito, and announcing him as Lieutenant Alexander Slidell, a young officer in the Navy of the United States.

It would appear that the Lieutenant, having a long leave of absence from his ship, undertook in 1826, a land cruise of observation and instruction on the continent of Europe; and, having traversed a part of France, entered Spain by the way of Perpignan, with the intention of passing a year in the Peninsula.

There were two things which we doubt not the worthy Lieutenant regarded as sore disadvantages for his undertaking, but which we consider as having most fortunately concurred to give his work the very entertaining character it possesses. The first was that, according to his own account, he had received but an imperfect education. The second, that he had but little money. The first threw him upon his own resources, and made him depend more upon his mother wit, and his every day observation and experience, in making his book, than upon the hackneyed information and associations derived from libraries. The second obliged him to adopt cheap modes of conveyance, and to live among the people rather than in the solitude of hotels. The consequence of both is a series of scenes and characters of Spanish life, taken from among the popular classes, and which remind us continually of what we have chuckled over in the pages of Don Quixote and Gil Blas. They are given with the microscopic minuteness, the persevering and conscientious fidelity of a Flemish painter, yet there is a graphic touch, and a lively colouring about them that prevents their ever becoming tedious. He has resorted but little to his imagination even for the embellishment of his facts, but has contented himself with setting down precisely every thing he saw, and felt and experienced. It is in fact the log book of his land cruize. Throughout it bears evidence of a youthful, kind and happy spirit, and of fresh, unhackneyed feelings; there is a certain vein of humour and bonhommie running through it, also, that gives it peculiar zest, and not the least amusing circumstances about it are the whimsical shifts and expedients to which the narrowness of the Lieutenant's purse now and then obliges him to resort in travelling, and which he records with delightful frankness and simplicity; the facility and good humour with which, from his rough nautical experience, he was enabled to put up with wind and weather and hard fare and hard lodging, that would have dismayed and discomfited a landsman; and the true sea-faring relish with which he enjoyed every snug berth or savoury meal; exulting over dishes that almost required the strong stomach of a midshipman or a Sancho Panza.

Of the verity of many parts of his narrative we happen ourselves to have personal proof, having about the same time visited various parts of Spain and known some of the characters, and heard of some of the most striking facts which he records. But enough of this prelude. We cannot do justice either to the author or the reader more completely than by letting the former speak for himself, and presenting a few of his graphical scenes, that will best permit of being extracted.

And first we give a most characteristic and amusing sketch of a French officer and his fair travelling companion, whom our author encountered in the Diligence after leaving Perpignan. The little touch about the officer's morning toilette is *impayable*.

"My attention, when the day had dawned, was first attracted to the portion of the diligence in which I rode. My former companion was beside me, and in front of us were a lady and gentleman. The latter was an officer, some thirty or forty years old, with a mixture of fearlessness and good-humor in his countenance. He wore the broad-breasted capote of blue, peculiar to the French infantry, and had the number of his regiment engraven upon each of his buttons. A leathern sword-belt hung from his left pocket flap, and on his head was a military bonnet of cloth, with a *fleur-de-lys* in front. His beard was of some days' standing, indicating the time he had been upon his journey; and his long moustaches hung about his mouth, neglected and crest-fallen. When the sun rose, however, he hastened to twist them up, until they stood fiercely from his face; then, having run his fingers through his hair, and replaced his bonnet on one side, his toilette might be said to be complete, and he turned with an air of confidence to look at the lady beside him.

"She was much younger than himself, and very beautiful. Her hair and eyes were as black as they could be; and her features, full of life and animation, were of a mellow brown, which, while it looked rich and inviting, had, besides, an air of durability. It was somewhat difficult to understand the relation subsisting between the officer and the lady. He had come to the diligence with her, made her accept of his cloak to keep off the cold air of the morning, and was assiduous in his attentions to her comfort. Their conversation soon showed, however, that their acquaintance was but of recent date; that the lady was going to Figueras, to join her husband, a sub-lieutenant in the garrison; that the officer had been on *congé* from his regiment at Barcelona, whither he was now return-

ing; and that they had travelled together accidentally from Narbonne. The difference between the French and most other nations,
and the secret of their enjoying themselves in almost any situation,
is, simply, that they endeavour to content themselves with the
present, and draw from it whatever amusement it may be capable
of affording. *Utiliser ses moments* is a maxim which they not only
utter frequently, but follow always. They make the most of such
society as chance may send them, are polite to persons whom they
never expect to see again, and thus often begin, where ruller spirits
end, by gaining the good will of all who come near them. In this
way our officer had turned his time to good account, and was
already on excellent terms with his fair companion. Nor was he
inattentive to us, but exceedingly courteous and polite; so that,
instead of frowning defiance upon each other, and putting ourselves at ease without regarding the comfort of the rest, we all
endeavoured to be agreeable, and even to prefer each the con-
venience of his fellow-travellers to his own."—vol. i. pp. 9–11.

The doughty French *sabreur* seems to have followed his own maxim,
Utiliser ses moments, with the fair lady, during the journey, but to have
been little prepared for the natural circumstance, the meeting with the
husband at the end of it.

"As soon as we drove up to the *posada*, a party of wild Catalans
rushed forth from the stable-yard to assist in carrying away our
team; and the conductor, who had long since abdicated his elevated
station, and descending along the iron steps placed at the side of
the diligence, had taken his stand upon the lowest one, supported
by a rope from above, now jumped to the ground and hastened
to release us from our captivity. Our captain alighted first, and
having refreshed himself by a well-bred stretch, was just holding
out his hand to assist his female friend, when he was suddenly
saved the trouble by a stout, fine-looking fellow, a sub-lieutenant
of chasseurs, who stepped in before him. This was a rough Pro-
vençal with a black beard, who had fought his way to his present
station without fear or favor. He was evidently the husband of the
lady; for she, declining the captain's courtesy, jumped into his arms
and embraced him. The husband seemed pleased enough to find
himself once more so near *sa petite*, and when he had called some
soldiers, who were standing by, to carry his wife's bandboxes, he
took her under his arm, and carried her away in a hurry to his
quarters, his spurs jingling at each step, and his sabre clattering
after him over the pavement. The captain twisted his moustaches,
and glared fiercely after the receding couple; but as the man was

only exercising an honest privilege, he said not a word, but bade
the conductor hand him down his sword, and when he had thrust
it through his belt, we all went into the posada."—vol. i. pp. 20, 21.

We cannot refrain from giving another casual picture of this Drawcansir
worthy at Barcelona; it is one of those characteristic scenes, those
interieurs as the French call them, that let one in at a single glance to
the whole economy of life of the individual.

> "Before separating, however, we had exchanged addresses with
> our companion the captain, and received an invitation to visit him
> at his quarters. We took an early occasion of redeeming our prom-
> ise, and at length found him out in a little room, overlooking one
> of the narrowest streets of Barcelona. As we entered, he was
> sitting thoughtfully on his bed, with a folded paper in his hand,
> one foot on the ground, the other swinging. A table, upon which
> were a few books, and a solitary chair, formed the only furniture
> of the apartment; while a schaiko, which hung from the wall by
> its nailed throat-lash, a sword, a pair of foils and masks, an ample
> cloak of blue, and a small portmanteau containing linen and uni-
> form, constituted the whole travelling equipage and moveable estate
> of this marching officer. We accommodated ourselves, without ad-
> mitting apologies, on the bed and the chair, and our host set about
> the task of entertaining us, which none can do better than a French-
> man. He had just got a letter from a widow lady, whose acquain-
> tance he had cultivated when last in Barcelona, and was musing
> upon the answer. Indeed, his amatory correspondence seemed very
> extensive; for he took one billet, which he had prepared, from the
> cuff of his capote, and a second from the fold of his bonnet, and
> read them to us. They were full of extravagant stuff, rather re-
> markable for warmth than delicacy; instead of a signature at the
> bottom, they had a heart transfixed with an arrow, and were folded
> in the shape of a cocked hat. As for the widow, he did not know
> where to find words sweet enough for her; and protested that he
> had half a mind to send her the remaining one of a pair of mous-
> taches, which he had taken from his lip after the campaign of
> Russia, and which he presently produced, of enormous length, from
> a volume of tactics."—vol. i. pp. 34, 35.

We forbear extracting from the work the various descriptions of the
country, which are given with considerable accuracy and with much
vivacity of colouring: we prefer dedicating the narrow limits afforded
us to the scenes of busy life and the personal anecdotes, which give
stirring interest to the work, and which, in fact, convey so much char-

acteristic and local information. We cannot refrain from inserting a picture of a Spanish Diligence; the starting of it from the court yard at Barcelona will remind many a traveller of a French Diligence getting under way, which may be compared to a mountain in labor, and is almost attended by an earthquake.

"By the time I had snugly adjusted myself in my corner of the cabriolet, and made all the knowing and comfortable arrangements of an experienced traveller, an absentee, for whom we had been waiting, arrived and took his seat beside me. This done, the door was closed with a slam, the iron steps were turned up with a grating sound, the guttural *'Arre!'* rattled out by the *mayoral* was repeated by the *zagal*, and our ponderous diligence heaved itself into motion, as it were, with a universal groan.

"In riding from Perpignan to Barcelona, the horses had been exchanged for mules very shortly after crossing the boundary. In Spain mules are generally preferred to horses both as beasts of burden and of draught, and are seen before the most elegant carriages. Horses are employed for the saddle, to make a display in cities; but to travel any distance, even in this way, the mule is preferred as an easier-gaited and hardier animal, capable of enduring the extremes of hunger and fatigue. Hence the mule commands a much higher price. The female, being of showy figure, with limbs beautifully formed and sinewy, is used for draught; while the *macho* or male, the most stubborn and stupid animal in the world, is laden upon the back, doomed to carry burdens, and to all kinds of ignominious labor. The team which now drew us through the silent streets of Barcelona consisted of seven mules; six of which drew in pairs, abreast of each other, while the seventh went alone at the head, and was honored with the name of capitana. Their harness was very different from any thing I had yet seen; for, while the two wheel mules were attached to the carriage in the ordinary way, all the rest had long rope traces, which, instead of leading to the pole, were attached to the carriage itself, and kept from dragging on the ground in descending hills by a leathern strap fastened to the end of the pole, through which they all passed. The leading mule only was guided by lines; the rest had their halters tied to the traces of capitana, and were thus obliged to follow all her motions, while the two hindmost had stout ropes fastened to their head-stalls for checking them on the descent. Nor was mere ornament disregarded in their equipment. Their bodies were smoothly shaven, to enable them better to endure the heat; but in this an eye was had to decoration by leaving the hair in partial stripes: the tail preserved enough of its garniture to furnish a neat fly

brush, and the hair on the haunches was clipped into a curious fret-
work, not a little resembling the embroidery of a hussar's pantaloons. They were besides plentifully adorned with plumes and
tassels of gaily-colored worsted, and had many bells about the head
to cheer them on the journey. As for our guides, they consisted of
a zagal and mayoral, or postilion and conductor. The zagal with
whom we set out from Barcelona was a fine-looking, athletic young
man, dressed in the Catalan costume, with a red cap of unusual
length reaching far down his back. The *mayoral*, who was much
older, was in similar attire; but rather more rolled up in jackets
and blankets, as became the cool air of the morning and his own
sedentary station on the front of the diligence."—pp. 54–57.

"The manner, too, in which these Catalans managed their mules
was quite peculiar. The zagal kept talking with one or the other
of them the whole time, calling them by their names, and apparently
endeavouring to reason them into good conduct, and make them
keep in a straight column, so that each might draw his share of the
burden, and not rub against his neighbour. I say he called them
by their names, for every mule in Spain has its distinctive appellation, and those that drew our diligence were not exceptions. Thus,
beside Capitana, we had Portugesa, Arragonesa, Coronela, and
a variety of other cognomens, which were constantly changing
during the journey to Valencia. Whenever a mule misbehaved,
turning from the road or failing to draw its share, the zagal would
call its name in an angry tone, lengthening out the last syllable,
and laying great emphasis on it. Whether the animals really knew
their names, or that each was sensible when it had offended, the
voice of the postilion would usually restore order. Sometimes when
the zagal called to Coronela, and Portugesa obeyed the summons by
mistake, he would cry, sharply, *Aquella otra!*— 'That other one!'—
and the conscience-stricken mule would quickly return to its duty.
When expostulation failed, blows were sure to follow: the zagal
would jump to the ground, run forward, and beat and belabor the
delinquent; sometimes jumping upon the mule immediately behind
it, and continuing the discipline for a half hour together. The
activity of these fellows is, indeed, wonderful. Of the twenty miles
which usually compose a stage, they run at least ten, and, during a
part of the remainder, stand upon one foot at the step of the
diligence. In general, the zagal ran up hill, flogging the mules
the whole way, and stopping occasionally at the road-side to pick
up a store of pebbles, which he stowed in his sash, or more frequently in his long red cap. At the summit he would take the
mule's tail in his hand, and jump to his seat before the descent
commenced. While descending, he would hold his cap in one hand,

and with the other throw a stone first at one mule, then at another, to keep them all in their proper stations, that the ropes might not hang on the ground and get entangled round their legs. These precautions would not always produce the desired effect; the traces would sometimes break or become entangled, the mules be brought into disorder, and a scene of confusion follow. This happened several times in one stage, when a vicious mule had been put among the team to be broken to harness. It was, indeed, an obstinate and perverse animal, and even more stupid than perverse. It would jump first to one side, then to the other, and kick the ribs of its neighbour without mercy. When, at length, it had succeeded in breaking its own traces and entangling its legs in those of its companions, it would stand as quiet as a lamb until the damage was repaired, and then renew the same scene of confusion. Nor did the more rational mules behave themselves much better. They would start to one side when the zagal cried out *Arre!* and when he whistled for them to stop, they would sometimes go the faster. If one had occasion to halt, the rest would not obey the hissing signal of the postilion, but drag the reluctant animal forward; and presently after, the mule which had been most unwilling to stop would be itself taken with a similar inclination, and receive similar treatment from its comrades; whereas the horses of a French diligence would all have halted sympathetically at the invitation of the driver. I hate a mule most thoroughly; for there is something abortive in every thing it does, even to its very bray. An ass, on the contrary, has something hearty and whole-souled about it. Jack begins his bray with a modest whistle, rising gradually to the top of his powers, like the progressive eloquence of a well-adjusted oration, and then as gradually declining to a natural conclusion; but the mule commences with a voice of thunder, and then, as if sorry for what he has done, he stops like a bully when throttled in the midst of a threat, or a clown who has begun a fine speech and has not courage to finish it."—pp. 64–67.

[We proceed to a scene of a different character, and one in which the minuteness and evident veracity of the detail produce an effect, that could never have been attained by the most romantic exaggeration. The author takes his seat about two in the morning in the cabriolet or front part of a Diligence from Tarragona, and gives many amusing particulars concerning his fellow-travellers, who, one after another, all surrender themselves to slumber. Thus powerfully invited by the example of those near him, the Lieutenant catches the drowsy infection, and having nestled snugly into his corner, soon loses entirely the realities of existence 'in that mysterious state which Providence has provided as a cure for every ill.' In short, he is indulged with a dream, which transports him into the midst of his own family circle beyond the Atlantic; but from this comfortable and sentimental nap he is soon aroused by the sudden stopping of the Diligence, and a loud clamour all about him.]

"There were voices without speaking in accents of violence, and whose idiom was not of my country. I now roused myself, rubbed my eyes, and directed them out of the windows.

"By the light of a lantern that blazed from the top of the diligence, I could discover that this part of the road was skirted by olive trees, and that the mules, having come in contact with some obstacle to their progress, had been thrown into confusion, and stood huddled together, as if afraid to move, gazing upon each other, with pricked ears and frightened aspect. A single glance to the right hand gave a clue to the mystery. Just beside the fore wheel of the diligence stood a man dressed in that wild garb of Valencia which I had seen for the first time in Amposta. His red cap, which flaunted far down his back, was in front drawn closely over his forehead, and his striped manta, instead of being rolled round him, hung unembarrassed from one shoulder. Whilst his left leg was thrown forward in preparation, a musket was levelled in his hands, along the barrel of which his eye glared fiercely upon the visage of the conductor. On the other side, the scene was somewhat different. Pepe, being awake when the interruption took place, was at once sensible of its nature. He had abandoned the reins, and jumped from his seat to the road side, intending to escape among the trees. Unhappy youth, that he should not have accomplished his purpose! He was met by the muzzle of a musket when he had scarce touched the ground, and a third ruffian appearing at the same moment from the treacherous concealment of the very trees towards which he was flying, he was effectually taken and brought round into the road, where he was made to stretch himself upon his face, as had already been done with the conductor.

"I could now distinctly hear one of these robbers—for such they were—inquire in Spanish of the mayoral as to the number of passengers; if any were armed; whether there was any money in the diligence; and then, as a conclusion to the interrogatory, demanding *La bolsa!* in a more angry tone. The poor fellow meekly obeyed. He raised himself high enough to draw a large leathern purse from an inner pocket, and stretching his hand upward to deliver it, said, *Toma usted caballero, pero no me quita usted la vida!* 'Take it, cavalier; but do not take away my life!' The robber, however, was pitiless. Bringing a stone from a large heap collected for the repair of the road, he fell to beating the mayoral upon the head with it. The unhappy man sent forth the most piteous cries for *miseri-cordia* and *piedad*. He might as well have asked pity of the stone that smote him, as of the wretch who wielded it. In his agony he invoked *Jesu Christo, Santiago Apostol y Martir, La Virgin del Pilar,* and all those sacred names held in awful reverence by the people, and most likely to arrest the rage of his assassin. All in vain: the murderer redoubled his blows, until growing furious in the task, he laid his musket beside him, and worked with both hands upon his victim. The cries for pity which blows had first excited, blows at length quelled. They had gradually increased with the suffering to the most terrible shrieks, then declined into low and inarticulate moans, until a deep-drawn and agonized gasp for breath and an occasional convulsion alone remained to show that the vital principle had not yet departed.

"It fared even worse with Pepe, though, instead of the cries for pity, which had availed the mayoral so little, he uttered nothing but low moans that died away in the dust beneath him. One might have thought that the extreme youth of the lad would have ensured him compassion: but no such thing. The robbers were doubtless of Amposta, and, being known to him, dreaded discovery. When both the victims had been rendered insensible, there was a short pause, and a consultation in a low tone between the ruffians; who then proceeded to execute their plans. The first went round to the left side of the diligence, and, having unhooked the iron shoe and placed it under the wheel, as an additional security against escape, opened the door of the interior, and mounted on the steps, I could hear him distinctly utter a terrible threat in Spanish, and demand an ounce of gold from each of the passengers. This was answered by an expostulation from the Valencian shopkeeper, who said that they had not so much money, but what they had would be given willingly. There was then a jingling of purses, some pieces dropping on the floor in the hurry and agitation of the moment. Having remained a short time at the door of the interior, he did not come to the cabriolet, but passed at once to the rotunda. Here he used greater caution, doubtless from having seen the evening before, at Amposta, that it contained no women, but six young students, who were all stout fellows. They were made to come down, one by one, from their strong hold, deliver their money and watches, and then lie flat upon their faces in the road.

"Meanwhile, the second robber, after consulting with his companion, returned to the spot where the zagal Pepe lay rolling from side to side. As he went towards him, he drew a knife from the folds of his sash, and having opened it, placed one of his naked legs on either side of his victim. Pushing aside the jacket of the youth, he bent forward and dealt him repeated blows in every part of the body. The young priest, my companion, shrunk back shuddering into his corner, and hid his face within his trembling fingers; but my own eyes seemed spell-bound, for I could not withdraw them from the cruel spectacle, and my ears were more sensible than ever. Though the windows at the front and sides were still closed, I could distinctly hear each stroke of the murderous knife, as it entered its victim. It was not a blunt sound as of a weapon that meets with positive resistance; but a hissing noise, as if the household implement, made to part the bread of peace, performed unwillingly its task of treachery. This moment was the unhappiest of my life; and it struck me at the time, that if any situation could be more worthy of pity than to die the dog's death of poor Pepe, it was to be compelled to witness his fate, without the power to aid him.

"Having completed the deed to his satisfaction, this cold-blooded murderer came to the door of the cabriolet, and endeavoured to open it. He shook it violently, calling to us to assist him; but it had chanced hitherto that we had always got out on the other side, and the young priest, who had never before been in a diligence, thought, from the circumstance, that there was but one door, and therefore answered the fellow that he must go to the other side. On the first arrival of these unwelcome visitors, I had taken a valuable watch which I wore from my waistcoat pocket, and slipped it into my boot; but when they fell to beating in the heads of our guides, I bethought me that the few dollars I carried in my purse might not satisfy them, and replaced it again in readiness to be delivered at the shortest notice. These precautions were, however, unnecessary. The third ruffian, who had continued to make the circuit of the diligence with his musket in his hand, paused a moment in the road ahead of us, and having placed his head to the ground as if to listen, presently came and spoke in an undertone to his companions. They stood for a moment over the mayoral, and struck his head with the butts of their muskets, whilst the fellow who had before used the knife returned to make a few farewell thrusts, and in another moment they had all disappeared from around us.

"In consequence of the darkness, which was only partially dispelled in front of the diligence by the lantern which had enabled me to see what occurred so immediately before me, we were not at once sensible of the departure of the robbers, but continued near half an hour after their disappearance in the same situation in which they left us. The short breathings and the chattering of teeth, lately so audible from within the interior, gradually subsided, and were succeeded by whispers of the females, and soon after by words pronounced in a louder tone; whilst our mangled guides, by groans and writhings, gave evidence of returning animation. My companion and I slowly let down the windows beside us, and, having looked round a while, opened the door and descended. The door of the interior stood open as it had been left, and those within sat each in his place in anxious conversation. In the rear of the coach was a black heap on the ground, which I presently recognised for the six students who had occupied the rotunda, and who, lying flat upon their faces, made the oddest figure one can conceive, rolled up in their black cloaks, with their cocked hats of the same solemn color·emerging at intervals from out the heap. As we came cautiously towards them, they whispered among each other, and then first one lifted his head to look at us, and then another, until finding that we were their fellow-travellers, they all rose at once like a cloud, notwithstanding a threat which the robbers had made to them at their departure, to wait by the road-side and shoot down the first who should offer to stir. It will readily occur to the reader that if resistance to this bold and bloody deed could have been made at all, it might have been by these six young men, who, being together and acquainted with each other, might have acted in concert, whereas the rest of the party were as completely separated as though they had been in distinct vehicles. But if it be considered that they had been awakened suddenly by armed ruffians, that they were destitute of weapons, and knew not the number of their assailants, it will appear more natural that they should have acted precisely as they did.

"Our first care, when thus left to ourselves, was to see if any thing could be done for our unfortunate guides. We found them rolling over in the dust and moaning inarticulately, excepting that the conductor would occasionally murmur forth some of those sainted names whose aid he had vainly invoked in the moment of tribulation. Having taken down the light from the top of the coach, we found them so much disfigured with bruises and with blood that recognition would have been impossible. The finery of poor Pepe, his silver buttons and his sash of silk were scarcely less disfigured than his features. There happened to be in our party a student of medicine, who now took the lead in the Samaritan office of binding, with pieces of linen and pocket handkerchiefs, the wounds of these unhappy men." [—pp. 88–96.]

[The wounded men were at length placed in a cart, and sent back slowly to Amposta, the mayoral showing some signs of returning sensibility, but the unfortunate Pepe evidently in his last agony. The Diligence proceeded on its route, and stopped to breakfast at Vinaroz. This picture of a mother's affliction mingling with her habitual household cares is] wonderfully touching, and reminds us of a similar conflict in the mind of the poor fisherman's wife in the Antiquary who had lost her son. An exquisite touch of nature worthy of the mighty Scottish master—and, in fact, only to be struck off by a master hand.

> "The kitchen of the posada at Vinaroz offered a scene of unusual confusion. The hostess was no other than the mother of Pepe, a very decent-looking Catalan woman, who, I understood, had been sent there the year before by the Diligence Company, which is concerned in all the inns at which their coaches stop throughout the line. She had already been told of the probable fate of her son, and was preparing to set off for Amposta in the deepest affliction; and yet her sorrow, though evidently real, was singularly combined with her habitual household cares. The unusual demand for breakfast by fourteen hungry passengers had created some little confusion, and the poor woman, instead of leaving these matters to take care of themselves, felt the force of habit, and was issuing a variety of orders to her assistant; nor was she unmindful of her appearance, but had already changed her frock and stockings, and thrown on her mantilla, preparatory to departure. It was indeed a singular and piteous sight to see the poor perplexed woman changing some fish that were frying, lest they should be burnt on one side, adjusting and repinning her mantilla, and sobbing and crying all the while. When the man came, however, to say that the mule was in readiness, everything was forgotten but the feelings of the mother, and she hurried off in deep and unsuppressed affliction."—pp. 101, 102.

We may as well add here the catastrophe of this tragical tale. From information received by the Lieutenant after his arrival in Madrid it appears that poor Pepe breathed his last about eight hours after the attack, and long before his widowed mother could arrive to close the eyes of her child. The mayoral lingered for about a week and then shared the fate of Pepe. The three robbers were detected and taken into custody. Two of them were townsmen and all three acquaintances of Pepe, whom they had doubtless murdered to prevent discovery.

We ourselves passed over the scene of the robbery between two and three years after the event. There were two crosses to mark the bloody spot. The mayoral and the zagal of our Diligence, the successors of those who had been murdered, pointed to the crosses with the *sang froid* with which Spaniards from long habitude contemplate mementos of the kind. The mayoral shewed the very place where his predecessor had been beaten to death. On our expressing horror at the detail he readily concurred, though he appeared more indignant at the manner in which the crime had been committed than at the crime itself. "It is the ugliest murder (el asesinato lo mas feo) that has been committed in this neighborhood for a long time past. Look you Sir, to shoot a man with a blunderbuss or to stab him with a knife is quite another kind of thing, but to beat his brains out with a stone is to treat him, not like a Christian, but like a dog!"—Not having the mayoral's experience in these matters we did not pretend to gainsay his criticism; it was evident that a frequent occurrence of such scenes had rendered him discriminating.

After his dismal affair with the robbers the Lieutenant pursues his journey to Madrid meeting with no adventure of importance, though with a variety of pleasant incidents and characteristic personages, all which he describes with happy minuteness. In traversing the naked plains of La Mancha he beholds the windmills mistaken of yore for giants by the Knight of the Sorrowful Countenance, and which still remain battling with the winds and domineering over the dreary waste as in the days of Don Quixote. He passed in sight of the village of Toboso, once graced by the presence of the gentle Dulcinea, but he looked in vain for the grove in which the Sorrowful Knight awaited the return of Sancho from his tender embassy. In fact the early scenes of the knight's adventures, which our imaginations had been used to grace with sylvan and rural beauties, are all laid in the central provinces of Spain, on naked cheerless plains, destitute of tree or even shrub, and it shews the magic power of genius that it can clothe such dreary landscapes with illusive charms to the eye of the traveller, and people them with the most amusing associations.

The author's account of his arrival and his first sallying forth into the streets of Madrid is full of lively and accurate picturing, nor can we refrain from extracting his description of his language master, Don Diego Redondo y Moreno, who may serve as the representative of a numerous class in Spain. Don Diego had been a clerk in the office of the Minister of State, under the constitution, but on the overthrow thereof had been displaced on suspicion of liberal principles and remained what is termed an impurificado.

> "The reader is not perhaps aware, that on the return of despotism in Spain, Juntas of Purification were established in all parts of the kingdom, before which all persons who had held offices under the abolished system were bound to appear and adduce evidence that they had not been remarkable for revolutionary zeal, nor over active in support of the Constitution, before they could be admitted to any new employment. Such as come out clean from this investigation, from being *impurificados* or unpurified, become *indefinidos* or indefinites, who are ready to be employed, and have a

nominal half-pay. These indefinidos have long formed a numerous class in Spain, and now more so than ever. They are patient waiters upon Providence, who, being on the constant look out for a god-send, never think of seeking any new means to earn a livelihood. They may be seen in any city in Spain, lounging in the coffee-houses, where they pick their teeth and read the gazette, but never spend any thing; or else at the public walk, where they may readily be known, if they be military officers of rank, by the bands of gold lace which bind the cuffs of their surtouts of blue or snuff color, and by their military batons, or still more readily by the huge cocked hats of oil-cloth with which they cover their sharp and starved features.

"Many impurificados of the present day have been prevented from offering themselves for purification by the scandal of their past conduct; but a far greater number are deterred by the rapacity and corruption of the purifying tribunals. Don Diego being both a peaceable and poor man, was probably among the last class. Indeed, I was afterwards assured that he was, and that he had been repeatedly solicited by various emissaries, one of whom came from the girl of the president of the Junta, and offered, for a stipulated sum, to pave the way to his thorough purification. Whether he looked on the nominal pay of an indefinido as dearly purchased by an immediate expenditure, or that he never had enough money at one time to gratify official or sub-official rapacity, he still continued impurificado, and gained his bread the best way he could, as a copyist and instructor of the Castilian. This he was well qualified to teach, for, though he had never read a dozen books besides the Quijote, and was as ignorant of the past as of the future history of his country, he had, nevertheless, pursued all the studies usual among his countrymen, wrote a good hand, was an excellent Latinist, and perfect master of his own language.

"The dress of Don Diego had evidently assimilated itself to his fallen fortunes. His hat hung in his hand greasy and napless; his boots, from having long been strangers to blacking, were red and foxy, while his pea-green frock, which, when the cold winds descended from the Guadarrama, served likewise as a surcoat, looked brushed to death and threadbare. He had, nevertheless, something of a supple and jaunty air with him, showed his worked ruffles and neckcloth to the best advantage, and flourished a little walking wand with no contemptible grace. So much for his artificial man, which was after the fashion of Europe; the natural man might have bespoke a native of Africa. Though called *redondo*, or round, in his own right, he was exceedingly spare and meagre; but he better deserved the cognomen of *moreno*, or black, though he had it in right of his wife, who was of a fair complexion, for his face was strongly indicative of Moorish blood. It showed features the reverse of prominent, and very swarthy; coal-black hair and whiskers, and blacker eyes, which expressed a singular combination of natural ardor and habitual sluggishness."—pp. 167–169.

[We know the original of this most accurate picture, for it was our lot to pursue the study of pure Castilian under his instructions. Poor Don Diego! Nature had certainly intended him for a higher sphere for he had a most gentlemanlike indolence and love of leisure, nor did ever *impurificado* await the dispensations of Providence with more inert resignation. As to his outward garb, it varied with his fortune: whenever an additional scholar or two made cash more plentiful, the pea-green threadbare gaberdine disappeared, he figured in somewhat of a fashionable suit, gallanted his wife to the Prado on Sundays, and even indulged in the occasional extravagance of a ticket to a bull-fight; but the least reverse of fortune sent] his finery to the pawn brokers, and again reduced him to the "sere and yellow leaf."

Under the guidance of Don Diego Redondo y Moreno the Lieutenant sallies forth in quest of lodgings, and is conducted to the house of one Don Valentin, another of those indefinite or unpurified worthies, who have been ruined in Spain by the frequent reverses in politics. An amusing and characteristic sketch is given of his history, and of his domestic establishment. As to his person, he was tall, gaunt and bony; with a thin, wrinkled, sallow face, set off by black and bristly hair, and illumined by but a single eye. The Lieutenant dislikes his looks; abominates his long, stiffbacked boots, notwithstanding they are decorated with tassels, nor is he to be reconciled to the coarseness of his square tailed coat, and scanty pantaloons, by a shirt and cravat elaborately embroidered. His dislike of the landlord extends to the house; he determines that he is not and will not be pleased with it, and is bowing his way out with all due courtesy, when, at the top of the narrow stair case, he is met full in the face by the daughter of mine host, Doña Florencia, just returning from mass.

"She might be nineteen or thereabout, a little above the middle size, and finely proportioned; with features regular enough, and hair and eyes not so black as is common in her country, a circumstance upon which, when I came to know her better, she used to pride herself; for, in Spain, auburn hair, and even red, is looked upon as a great beauty. She had on a mantilla of lace, pinned to her hair and falling gracefully about her shoulders, and a *basquiña* of black silk, trimmed with cords and tassels, and loaded at the bottom with lead, to make it fit closely, and show a shape which was

really a fine one. Though high in the neck, it did not descend so low
as to hide a well turned ankle, covered with a white stocking and
a small black shoe, bound over the instep by a riband of the same
color.

"As I said before, I was met full in the face by this damsel of
La Rioja, to whose cheek the ascent of three pairs of stairs had
given a color not common in Madrid, and to herself not habitual.
Her whole manner showed that satisfaction which people who feel
well and virtuously always experience on reaching the domestic
threshold. She was opening and shutting her fan with vivacity, and
stopped short in the midst of a little song, a great favorite in Andalusia, which begins,

> 'O no! no quiero casarme!
> Ques mejor, ques mejor ser soltera!'

> 'O no! I care not to marry!
> 'Tis better, 'tis better live single!'

"We came for a moment to a stand in front of each other, and
then I drew back to let her pass, partly from a sense of courtesy,
partly, perhaps, from a reluctance to depart. With the ready tact
which nowhere belongs to the sex so completely as in Spain, she
asked me in, and I at once accepted the invitation, without caring
to preserve my consistency."—pp. 190, 191.

In fine, the worthy Lieutenant, who throughout his work shews the
susceptibility of a sailor for female charms, beholds the whole establishment with different eyes now that it is graced by the presence of Doña
Florencia. He finds the lodgings the very thing of which he was in
search, and even more convenient than anything he had hoped to find.
He at once takes possession of them, and during the whole of his residence in Madrid appears to have flourished under the single though
guardian eye of Don Valentin and the gentler regards of Doña Florencia.
She is a perfect picture of a Spanish girl. Frank, amicable, disinterested,
uninstructed yet intelligent; with a surpassing fondness for fine stockings and spangled shoes.

But it would be wrong to put the reader off with this individual portrait of a Spanish female; when we have a general picture of a Madrid
beauty sketched off by our author with the practiced pencil of a landsman, and the thorough devotion of a sailor. It would appear by the
sudden burst of enthusiasm in the last sentence that the worthy Lieutenant had become enamoured of the goddess of his own creation.

"The *Madrileña* is rather under than above the middle size, with a faultless shape, seen to advantage through the elastic folds of her basquiña. Her foot is, however, her chief care; for, not content with its natural smallness and beauty, she binds it with narrow bandages of linen, so as to reduce it to smaller dimensions, and to give it a finer form. Though her complexion be pale, it is never defiled by rouge. Her teeth are pearly, lips red, eyes full, black, and glowing; her step is short and quick, yet graceful; and the restless play of her hands and arms, as she adjusts her mantilla or flutters her fan, is but a just index to the impatient ardor of her temperament. As she moves forward, she looks with an undisturbed yet pensive eye upon the men that surround her; but if you have the good fortune to be an acquaintance, her face kindles into smiles, she beams benignantly upon you, and returns your salute with an inviting shake of her fan in token of recognition. Then, if you have a soul, you lay it at once at her feet, are ready to become her slave for ever."—pp. 300, 301.

As our object is chiefly to exemplify our author's talent at sketching familiar pictures of life and manners, which we think quite peculiar and felicitous, we pass over without notice, his discussions of public places, public institutions and the other ordinary topics which abound in all books of travels, and on which he acquits himself very sensibly and creditably, but much in the usual style of tourists. We cannot, however, shew equal indifference to the following description of his setting off from Aranjuez; attended by a ragged, misbegotten boy named Jose, whom he had picked as a lacquey de place. It was an outset that might rival one of the picturesque sallies of Don Quixote and Sancho Panza.

"After being detained a day longer at Aranjuez than I had contemplated, for want of a conveyance, my little friend Jose at length procured me the means of reaching Toledo. Indeed, I was just thinking of the expediency of departing afoot, on the fourth morning of my absence from Madrid, when Jose knocked at my door, and told me that he had got a horse for me, and that he was to go along, to bring him back, on a borrico. I liked this arrangement well. So, paying my bill and packing up my sack, I sallied out into the courtyard, to commence my journey. I did not expect to be very splendidly mounted, but my astonishment and confusion were indeed great, on finding that I had to ride upon a miserable *rocin*, that had lost its hair by some disease, especially upon the tail, which was as long and as naked as the trunk of an elephant. The only flesh the animal had left seemed to have descended into the legs, and as for his hips, his backbone, and ribs, they were everywhere conspicuous, save where concealed by a huge pack-saddle, stuffed with straw and covered with canvas. What made the matter still worse, the master of the beast, an old man in a brown cloak, held his hand before me, as I was approaching to take a nearer view, and told me that if it was *igual* to me, he would take the two dollars beforehand. I explained to the old man how very possible it was that his horse would not live to complete the journey; to which he replied, with some indignation, that he would carry me to *las Indias*, much more to Toledo. As he continued to hold out his hand with a resolute air, I dropped the required sum into it, and grasping the pack-saddle for want of a mane, I vaulted at once into the seat. The back of the poor animal cracked and twisted under the burthen, and as he gave some indications of a disposition to lie down, I drew forcibly upon the halter. Thus roughly handled, his neck bent backward like a broken bow, and, making retrograde steps, he backed full upon Jose, who, well pleased with the idea of so long an excursion, was drawn up behind, upon a little mouse-coloured ass, with the game-bag, which contained all my travelling equipage, hung round his neck and hanging from his shoulder. Three or four sound blows from the cudgel of Jose, accompanied by a kick under the belly from the master of the beast, corrected this retrograde motion, which being changed for an advance, we sallied out of the inn and took our way through the market-place, to the admiration of all Aranjuez."—vol. ii. pp. 15–17.

We subjoin a truly Spanish repast made by the Lieutenant and his squire in a solitary Venta, on a dish of new laid eggs fried in oil.

"The eggs were soon emptied into an earthen dish, where they floated at large in a sea of oil; the dish was placed on a low table, which, for want of a bench—the only one in the house being occupied by the party of the muleteer—we drew close to the door, so as to take our seats upon the sill. Now that we had our meal before us, however, it was not so easy to eat it. The bread and the wine, indeed, gave us no trouble; but the eggs were as much beyond our reach, as fishes that you see in the water, but have no means of catching. In vain did we ask for a spoon or a fork. Our hostess only regretted that she could do nothing for us. Until a week before, she had two wooden spoons and one horn one, for the accommodation of cavaliers, who did not carry their own utensils; but some *quintas*, or conscripts, had passed by, on their way to the frontier of Portugal, and halted during the heat of the day at her house. Since then, she had seen nothing either of her horn spoon or of the two wooden ones, and she never meant to buy another. As our invention was sharpened by hunger, Jose and I bethought ourselves to cut the bread into slices, and to use two pieces as chop-sticks, after the manner of the Chinese. In this way, and by lending each other occasional assistance in catching a refractory egg, we were enabled to drive them, one by one, into a corner, and draw them out, until nothing remained but the oil." [—pp. 20, 21.]

The departure of the Lieutenant from Toledo was in quite a different style. He took his seat in a *coche de coleras*, an antique lumbering vehicle, such as may be seen in ancient Spanish pictures of the seventeenth century,· which was drawn by six mules. We give the description of his travelling companions in his own words, for the Lieutenant is always inspired when a female is to be described. In fact the most experienced writer for the annuals could not have touched off a female groupe more happily.

"I was not the sole occupant of the coche. It was brimming full of young girls, who were going a short distance from the city, partly for the sake of the ride, but chiefly to take leave of one of their number, who was to keep on to Madrid, whither she was going to serve a *Condesa*. I soon found, from their conversation, that two of them were daughters of the old man. The eldest, a close-built, fast-sailing little frigate, with an exquisitely pointed foot, a brilliant eye, and a pretty arch face—not at all the worse for two or three pock-marks—was the newly married wife of the zagal. The one who was now about to leave her home, for the first time, was a younger sister of the bride, and the rest were cousins and neighbours. They had all grown up together, and now, as they were whirled furiously down the hill-side that leads away from Toledo, were as merry as crickets, laughing, giggling, and shouting to such of their acquaintances as they passed. By and by, however, we got to the bottom of the valley, and began to toil up the opposite ascent. The excitation of the moment was over, and they remembered, that at the top of the hill they were to part with Beatriz. Their laughing ceased, the smiles passed from their countenances, a painful expression came instead, and, when the coach at length stopped, they were all in tears. Poor Beatriz! she cried and kissed them all; and when they got down from the coach, and left her all alone, she sobbed aloud, and was half ready to follow them.

"Margarita, the eldest sister, seeing poor Beatriz so much afflicted, begged her husband to let her go along and come back the next trip. Andres would not at first listen to the proposal, but fastened the door. When she began, however, to grow angry at the refusal, he took the trouble, like a thoughtful husband, to explain how in-

convenient it would be for her to go without any preparations; if
she had but spoken in the morning, or the night before, the thing
would have been easily settled. All these reasons availed nothing.
Margarita grew more and more vexed, until Andres was driven
from his resolution. He slowly opened the door, saying with a half-
displeased air, '*Entre usted!*' Contrary to all reasonable calculations,
she stirred not a step towards accepting the offer, and her embarrassment and vexation seemed only to grow greater, at thus losing
the cause of her displeasure. By this time, the old man, who had
thought it was all over when he had kissed the children, began
to grow impatient, and gave the word of command. Away went
the mules. Andres would not part in anger. He went to receive a
farewell kiss from his wife; but Margarita turned away pettishly,
striking her little foot on the ground and shaking her head, as
though she would have torn her mantilla. Without more ado, he
left her to her ill-humour, and overtaking the coach, caught the
left mule by the tail, and leaped to the wooden platform beside
his father.

"Meantime, Beatriz and I put our heads out of the window; she
from interest and affection, I from curiosity. The girls remained
where we left them, throwing up their handkerchiefs, and sending
after us a thousand kind words and well-wishes. Margarita alone
stood motionless in the same place, with her head turned away.
Gradually, however, she moved round to catch a sight of us; and
when she saw that her husband was not looking at her, seemed to
be sorry for what she had done, shook her fan at him fondly, and
cried out at the top of her voice, 'Until we meet, Andrew!'—'*Hasta
la vista, Andres!*' But it was too late, he would not hear, and beating
the mule nearest him with great energy, we were soon descending
the opposite hill. The last I saw of Margarita, she had hid her face
in her hands, and her companions were drawing round to offer
consolation." [—pp. 50–53.]

[We have given a tragical adventure with robbers during the Lieutenant's journey to Madrid. We now present, as a *pendant*, a comic
account of another robbery, which took place on his route to Cordova.]

"Leaving Madrilejos, we travelled on, through a solitary country,
until we came to the venta of Puerto Lapiche, the very house in
which Don Quixote watched over his armour and was dubbed
knight errant in the beginning of his adventurous career. The conductor had taken his seat beside me in the rotunda, and we were
yet talking over the exploits of that renowned hero, when our conversation was suddenly and unceremoniously interrupted by the

discharge of muskets, the loud shouting of eager, angry voices, and the clattering of many hoofs. Here, indeed, is an adventure, thought I.—O for Don Quixote to protect us!—In the next moment the diligence stopped, and on looking out at the window, the cause of this interruption became manifest.

"Our four wild partisans were seen flying at a fearful rate, closely pursued by eight still more desperate looking fellows, dressed in sheepskin jackets and breeches, with leathern leggings, and montera caps, or cotton handkerchiefs, on their heads. Each had four pistols at his saddle-bow, a steel sabre at his side, a long knife thrust through the belt of his cartouch-box, and a carabine, in this moment of preparation, held across his horse's neck in front of him. It was an animated scene this, such as I had frequently before seen on canvas, in Wouverman's spirited little pictures of robber broils and battle scenes, but which I had never before been so highly favored as to witness in reality.

"Whilst this was going on in the road behind us, we were made to get down by one of the party, who had been left to take care of us, and who now shouted in rapid succession the words '*Ajo! a tierra! boca abajo, ladrones!*' As this is the robber formula throughout Spain, its translation may not be unacceptable to the reader. Let him learn, then, that ajo means garlic, and the remainder of the salutation, 'To the ground! mouths in the dust, robbers!' Though this formula was uttered with great volubility, the present was doubtless the first attempt of the person from whom it proceeded; a youth scarce turned of twenty, and evidently a novice—a mere Gil Blas—at the business. We did not, however, obey him the less quickly, and took our seats as ordered, upon the ground, in front of the mules and horses, so that they could only advance by passing over us; for he was so much agitated, that his musket shook like the spout of a fire-engine, and we knew full well that in such situations a frightened is not less to be dreaded than a furious man. Our conductor, to whom this scene offered no novelty, and who was anxious to oblige our visitors, placed himself upon his hands and knees, like a frog when he is about to jump, and asked if that was the right way. He took care, however, to turn his unpleasant situation to account, putting a huge watch into the rut of the road, and covering it carefully with sand. Some of the party imitated this grasshopper attitude, and Fray Antonio availed himself of the occasion and the devotional posture to bring up the arrears of his Paters and Aves.

"We had not been long thus, before the captain of the band returned, leaving five of his party to take care of the guards, three of whom stood their ground and behaved well. Indeed, their chief

was no other than the celebrated Polinario, long the terror of La
Mancha, until he had been brought over to guard the diligence,
and had turned royalist volunteer. We could distinctly hear them
cursing and abusing the robbers, and daring them to come *tantos
por tantos*—man for man. As honor, however, was not the object
of these sturdy cavaliers, they contented themselves with keeping
the guard in check, whilst their comrades were playing their part
at the diligence. The first thing the captain did, when he rode
among us, was to call to the conductor for his hat; after which he
bade him mount upon the diligence, and throw down whatever
was there. He cautioned him at the same time to look around, and
see if any thing was coming—adding, with a terrible voice, as he
half lifted his carabine, 'And take care'—'*Y cuidado!*' The conductor
quietly obeyed, and the captain having told us to get up and not
be alarmed, as no harm was intended, called to us to put our
watches and money into the conductor's hat, which he held out
for the purpose, much in the ordinary way of making a collection,
except that instead of coming to us, he sat very much at his ease
upon his horse, and let us come to him. I threw my purse in, and
as it had nine or ten silver dollars, it made a very good appearance,
and fell with a heavy chink. Then, grasping the bunch of brass
keys and buttons which hung from my fob, I drew out the huge
watch which I had bought at Madrid, in contemplation of some
such event, and whose case might upon emergency have served
the purpose of a warming-pan. Having looked with a consequential
air at the time, which it marked within six hours, I placed it carefully in the hat of the conductor. The collection over, the captain
emptied purses, watches, and loose money all together into a large
leathern pocket which hung from his girdle, and then let the hat
drop under his horse's hoofs.

" '*Cuñado!*'—'Brother-in-law!' said the captain, to one of the
worthies, his companions, 'take a look into those trunks and boxes,
and see if there be any thing in them that will suit us.'—'*Las llaves,
señores!*'—'The keys, gentlemen!' 'And do you, zagal, cast me loose
those two horses on the lead; a fine fellow is that near horse with
the saddle.' The two persons thus summoned set about obeying
with a very different grace. Our cuñado dismounted at once, and
hitched his horse to the friar's trunk. He then took from the crupper
of his saddle a little bundle, which being unrolled expanded into
a prodigious long sack, with a yawning mouth in the middle. This
he threw over his arm, with the mouth uppermost, and with a
certain professional air. He was a queer, systematic little fellow
this, with a meek and Joseph cast of countenance, that in a market-
place would have inspired the most profound confidence. Having

called for the owner of the nearest trunk, the good friar made his appearance, and he accosted him with great composure. 'Open it yourself, padre; you know the lock better than I do.' The padre complied with becoming resignation, and the worthy trunk inspector proceeded to take out an odd collection of loose breeches that were secured with a single button, robes of white flannel, and handkerchiefs filled with snuff. He had got to the bottom without finding aught that could be useful to any but a friar of Mercy, and there were none such in the fraternity, when, as a last hope, he pulled from one corner something square that might have been a box of diamonds, but which proved to be only a breviary fastened with a clasp. The trunk of the Biscayan came next, and as it belonged to a sturdy trader from Bilboa, furnished much better picking. Last of all he came to mine; for I had delayed opening it, until he had called repeatedly for the key, in the hope that the arrival of succour might hurry the robbers away, or at least that this double sack would fill itself from the others, which was certainly very charitable. The countenance of our cuñado brightened up when he saw the contents of my well-filled trunk; and not unlike Sancho of old, when he stumbled upon the portmanteau of the disconsolate Cardenio in the neighbouring Sierra Morena, he went down upon one knee, and fell to his task most inquisitively. Though the sack was already filled out to a very bloated size, yet there remained room for nearly all my linen and summer clothing, which was doubtless preferred in consideration of the approaching heats. My gold watch and seal went in search of its silver companion; for Señor Cuñado slipped it slily into his side pocket, and, though there be no secrets among relations, I have my doubts whether to this day he has ever spoke of it to his brother-in-law.

"Meantime, our female companion had made acquaintance with the captain of the band, who for a robber was quite a conscientious and conversable person. He was a stout athletic man, about forty years old, with a weather-beaten face and long whiskers, which grew chiefly under his chin, in the modern fashion, and like the beard of a goat. It chanced that among the other contents of the trunk was a brass weight neatly done up and sealed, which our minister had procured from the Spanish Mint, and was sending with some despatches to the United States. This shone well, and had a golden look, so that our cuñado would have put it in his pocket, but I showed him that it was only brass; and when he had smelled and tasted it, and convinced himself that there was neither meat nor drink in it, he told me I might ask the captain, who graciously relinquished it to me. He also gave orders not to open the trunk of the lady, and then went on to apologize for the trouble

he was giving us, and had well-nigh convinced us that he was
doing a very praiseworthy act. He said that if the proprietors of
the diligence would procure his pardon, and employ him as escort,
he would serve them three months for nothing—'*Tres meses de
valde. Soy Felipe Cano, y, por mal nombre, el Cacaruco*'—said he—
'I am Philip Cano, nick-named the Cacaruco. No ratcatcher am
I; but a regular robber. I have no other profession or means of
bringing up a large family with any decency*.'

"In twenty minutes after the arrival of these unwelcome visiters,
they had finished levying their contribution, and drew together
to move off. The double sack of the inspector was thrown over the
back of one of the horses that had been taken from the diligence;
for in this part of the country the leaders of the teams were generally horses. The horse now loaded with such a singular burden
was a spirited animal, and seemed to understand that all was not
right; for he kicked away among the guns and sabres of the robbers,
until one of them, thus roughly handled, drew his sword to kill
him, and would have executed his purpose, had he not been re-
strained by Cacaruco. Before the robbers departed, the postilion
told Cacaruco that he had nothing in the world but the two horses,
and that if he lost them he was a ruined man: he begged him, at
least, to leave him the poorer of the two. After a short parley, the
request was granted, and then they moved off at a walk, talking and
gesticulating, without once looking back. We kept sight of them
for near half an hour, as they moved towards a ravine which lay
at the foot of a neighbouring mountain.

"We now commenced packing up the remnant of our wardrobes.
It was a sorrowful scene. Here a box emptied of some valuable
articles, and the shavings in which it had been packed driven in
every direction by the wind; there another, which had been broken
in by the but of a musket, that had passed with little ceremony
through the shade of an astral lamp; here shirts, and there waist-
coats—and there a solitary pair of red flannel drawers; everywhere,
however, sorrowful faces and plaintive lamentations. I tried to console myself, as I locked my trunk, with reflecting upon the trouble
I had found the day before in shutting it down—how I had tugged,
and grated my teeth, and jumped upon it; but this was poor consolation. My little portmanteau, yesterday so bloated and big, now
looked lean and flabby. I put my foot upon it, and it sunk slowly

"* A ratcatcher means one who does not follow the profession habitually, but
only makes it a subsidiary pursuit. Thus, a contrabandista who has been plundered
and dismounted by an aduanero, and who requites himself on some unhappy
traveller, and a carbonero, who leaves his charcoal heap to put himself in ambush
at the road-side, are both *rateros*."

under the pressure. I now looked round for the robbers. They were still seen in the distance, moving away at a walk, and followed by the horse, upon which was mounted that insatiate sack, which would have touched the ground on either side, had it not been crammed so full as to keep it from touching the horse's ribs. There was a singular association of ideas between the fatness of the bag and the leanness of my trunk; and as I still stood with one foot on my trunk and turning my thumbs about each other, I set up a faint whistle, as a baffled man is apt to do. By a singular coincidence I happened to hit upon that very waltz in the Freyschutz where the music seems to accompany the waltzers, and gradually dies away as they disappear from the stage; and that at a moment too when the robbers, having crossed a slight elevation, were descending into the hollow beyond. The apropos seemed excellent; so I continued to whistle, winding up as the heads of the robbers bobbed up and down, and just blew the last note as they sank below the horizon."
—pp. 65–74.

We have already exceeded our usual limits, yet we cannot forbear making one more extract which shews the worthy Lieutenant in a situation of more imminent jeopardy than any other of this his most eventful and adventurous land cruize. He had performed the journey from Cordova in one of those huge Galeras, or covered waggons, which as they slowly toil across the naked plains of Spain, resemble great ships traversing the ocean. Among the motley crew of this ark was a Spanish curate, a handsome galliard priest of about thirty years of age, with whom the Lieutenant, with his usual facility, became very sociable. When they landed together in "Fair Seville's famous city" the Lieutenant was for seeking an inn, but the provident priest, who had doubtless been accustomed to beat up that part of the country, recommended a *casa de pupilos,* or boarding house; where they would find "more comfort, more retirement and at the same time *more society.*" A barber of Seville, with the proverbial promptness of his craft, pointed them out a house of the kind kept by a widow lady, where they could not fail to be accommodated to their hearts' content.

They accordingly enter a house furnished in the delightful Andalusian style, with an interior court and babbling fountain; they ascend a stair case, enter a saloon, the windows of which open on balconies and are shaded by striped, red and white awnings, and, for the rest, we leave the Lieutenant to tell his own story.

"There were few ornaments here; unless, indeed, three young women—the two daughters and niece of the ancient hostess—who sat with their embroidery in the cool balcony, might be so esteemed.

One of them was at least five and twenty; the next might be eighteen
—a dark-haired, dark-eyed damsel, with a swarthy Moorish complexion and passionate temperament. The niece was a little girl from
Ecija, the native place of the whole family, who had come to Seville
to witness the splendors of the holy week. She was just beginning
to lose the careless animation, the simplicity, and the prattle of the
child in the suppressed demeanour, the softness, the voice and
figure of a woman. She looked as though she might have talked and
acted like a child a week or two ago in Ecija, but had been awakened to new and unknown feelings by the scenes of Seville. As for
the Morisca, she touched the guitar and sang, not only with passion
and feeling, but with no mean taste, for she went frequently to the
Italian opera. The other two waltzed like true Andaluzas, as I had
occasion to see that very evening.

"Such being the state of affairs, the curate and I decided that
we would go no farther, and accordingly accepted the rooms that
were offered us, and agreed to take our meals with the family. Nor
did we afterwards regret our precipitation, for the house was in
all things delightful. As for myself, it furnished me with a favorable
opportunity of seeing something of those Sevillanas, of whose
charms and graces, of whose sprightliness and courtesy, I had already heard such favorable mention. With these, and some other
specimens which I saw of the sex, as it is in Seville, I was indeed
delighted;—delighted with their looks, their words and actions, their
Andalusian Spanish, their seducing accent, and their augmentatives
and diminutives, from *grandissimo* to *poquito* and *chiqui-ti-ti-ti-to.*—
Every thing is very big or very little in the mouth of a Sevillana:
she is a superlative creature, and is ever in the superlative.

"There was one thing, however, in my situation in this *casa de
pupilos* which was new and singular, to say nothing of its incon-
venience, and which may furnish a curious study of Spanish customs. This was the position of my bedchamber. It had a grated
window looking on the street, and a door opening into the courtyard. Next it was a long room, running to the back of the building.
This also was a bedchamber, and the bedchamber of the old lady
and of the three niñas of Ecija, who slept on cots ranged along
the room. But it may not be amiss to tell how I came by this information. Now it chanced that the partition wall betwixt my room
and this next did not extend to the ceiling, nor, indeed, more than
two-thirds of the way up, the remainder being left open to admit
a free circulation of air, and keep the rooms cool; for Seville, in
summer, is little better than an oven. This being the case, I could
hear every thing that was going on next me. We used to commend
each other to God over the wall very regularly every night before

going to sleep, and presently I used to hear the old woman snore. The girls, however, would go on talking in a whisper, that they might not disturb their mother. In the morning again, we always woke at the same hour and with the customary salutations. Sometimes, too, I would be aroused in the dead of the night, and kept from sleeping for hours, just by the cracking of a cot, as one of my fair neighbors turned over; or may be on no greater provocation than the suppressed moan of a troubled dreamer, or the half-heard sigh of one just awoke from some blissful vision to a sense of disappointment." [—pp. 161–164.]

We can readily imagine the anxiety of the reader to know how our modern Telemachus extricated himself from the delicious perils of this Island of Calypso, and we confess that we feel a mischievous pleasure in balking his curiosity. If he wishes information on the subject let him consult the book itself. In a word, we here take leave altogether of the Lieutenant, consigning him to the tender mercies of the fair Sevillanas, and the guardianship of his friend the curate; albeit that we vehemently suspect the latter of being very little of a Mentor.

In casting our eyes back over the extracts we have made, we find they are almost entirely confined to the personal adventures, and travelling sketches of the author, and if these pages should meet his eye, he may complain that we have not done justice to his graver matter, to the statistical and historical lore which he has accumulated in various parts of his work. We, therefore, before concluding would assure the reader, that he will find throughout these volumes abundance of judicious remark and valuable information, and in the latter part of the second volume an ample dissertation on the general state of Spain. All this, however, is such matter as may be found in the pages of almost any sensible tourist; we have therefore preferred confining ourselves to those features of the work as are peculiar to the author, and calculated as we think to give him a distinct and a popular reputation; and we think we cannot do him better service than to advise him, should he make another essay in authorship, to trouble himself very little with an attempt to be erudite, but to give us as amply and minutely as possible his own adventures, observations and experience, and never to fear being egotistical, for when he is most so, he is most entertaining, and, in fact, most instructive. We conclude in hearty good will towards the Lieutenant, hoping that he may continue his cruizes by land and water, that he may have as many adventures as Sindbad, as happy an exit out of them, that he may survive to record them all in a book, and that we may have the gratification of reading it.

[1832]

[DEDICATORY LETTER IN *POEMS, BY WILLIAM CULLEN BRYANT, AN AMERICAN*]

TO

S A M U E L   R O G E R S, E s q.

MY DEAR SIR,

During an intimacy of some years' standing, I have uniformly remarked a liberal interest on your part in the rising character and fortunes of my country, and a kind disposition to promote the success of American talent, whether engaged in literature or the arts. I am induced, therefore, as a tribute of gratitude, as well as a general testimonial of respect and friendship, to lay before you the present volume, in which, for the first time, are collected together the fugitive productions of one of our living poets, whose writings are deservedly popular throughout the United States.

Many of these poems have appeared at various times in periodical publications; and some of them, I am aware, have met your eye, and received the stamp of your approbation. They could scarcely fail to do so, characterised as they are by a purity of moral, an elevation and refinement of thought, and a terseness and elegance of diction, congenial to the bent of your own genius and to your cultivated taste. They appear to me to belong to the best school of English poetry, and to be entitled to rank among the highest of their class.

The British public has already expressed its delight at the graphic descriptions of American scenery and wild woodland characters, contained in the works of our national novelist, Cooper. The same keen eye and fresh feeling for nature, the same indigenous style of thinking and local peculiarity of imagery, which give such novelty and interest to the pages of that gifted writer, will be found to characterise this volume, condensed into a narrower compass and sublimated into poetry.

The descriptive writings of Mr. Bryant are essentially American. They transport us into the depths of the solemn primeval forest—to the shores of the lonely lake—the banks of the wild nameless stream, or the brow of the rocky upland rising like a promontory from amidst a wide ocean of foliage; while they shed around us the glories of a climate fierce in its extremes, but splendid in all its vicissitudes. His close observation of the phenomena of nature, and the graphic felicity of his details, prevent his descriptions from ever becoming general and common-place; while he has the gift of shedding over them a pensive grace that blends them all into harmony, and of clothing them with moral associations that make them speak to the heart. Neither, I am convinced, will it be the least of his merits in your eyes, that his writings are imbued with the independent spirit, and the buoyant aspirations incident to a youthful, a free, and a rising country.

It is not my intention, however, to enter into any critical comments on these poems, but merely to introduce them, through your sanction, to the British public. They must then depend for success on their own merits; though I cannot help flattering myself that they will be received as pure gems, which, though produced in a foreign clime, are worthy of being carefully preserved in the common treasury of the language.

I am, my dear Sir,
Ever most faithfully yours,
WASHINGTON IRVING.

London, March 1832.

[ADDRESS AT THE IRVING DINNER, MAY 30, 1832]

Mr. Irving rose greatly agitated by the warm cheering with which he was hailed. He observed that he believed most of his hearers were sensible of his being wholly unused to public speaking: but he should be wanting in the feelings of human nature, if he were not roused and excited by the present scene. He proceeded in, as nearly as can be recollected, the following words. "I find myself, after a long absence of seventeen years, surrounded by the friends of my youth, by those whom in my early days I was accustomed to look up to with veneration, by others, whom though personally new to me, I recognize as the sons of the patriarchs of my native city. The manner in which I have been received by them has rendered this the proudest, the happiest moment of my life. And what has rendered it more poignant, is that I had been led at times to doubt my standing in the affections of my countrymen. Rumours and suggestions had reached me that absence had impaired their kind feelings; that they considered me alienated in heart from my country. Gentlemen, I was too proud to vindicate myself from such a charge—nor should I have alluded to it at this time, if the warm and affectionate reception I have met with on all sides since my landing, and the overpowering testimonial of regard here offered me, had not proved that my misgivings were groundless.

Never, certainly, did a man return to his native place after so long an absence under happier auspices: on every side I see changes, it is

true, but they are the changes of rapid improvement and growing prosperity. Even the countenances of my old associates and townsmen have
appeared to me but lightly affected by the lapse of years, though perhaps it was the glow of ancient friendship and heartfelt welcome, beaming from them, that prevented me from seeing the ravages of time.

As to my native city, from the time I approached the coast I had
indications of its growing greatness. We had scarce descried the land,
when a thousand sails of all sizes and descriptions gleaming along the
horizon and all standing to or from one point, shewed that we were in
the neighborhood of a vast commercial emporium. As I sailed up our
beautiful bay, with a heart swelling with old recollections and delightful associations, I was astonished to see its once wild features brighten-
ing with populous villages and noble piles, and a seeming city extending
itself over heights which I had left covered with groves and forests. But
how shall I describe my emotions when our city rose to sight, seated in
the midst of its watery domain; and stretching away to a vast extent;
when I beheld a glorious sunshine lighting up spires and domes, some
familiar to memory, others new and unknown, and beaming upon a
forest of masts of every nation, extending as far as the eye could reach?
I have gazed with admiration on many a fair city and stately harbour,
but my admiration was cold and ineffectual, for I was a stranger and
had no property in the soil. Here, however, my heart throbbed with
pride and joy as I admired—I had a birthright in the brilliant scene
before me—

'This was my own—my native land!'

It has been asked, 'Can I be content to live in this country?' Whoever asks that question must have but an inadequate idea of its blessings
and delights. What sacrifice of enjoyment have I to reconcile myself to?
I come from gloomier climes to one of brilliant sunshine and inspiring
purity. I come from countries lowering with doubt and danger, where the
rich man trembles and the poor man groans; where all repine at the
present and dread the future. I come from these to a country where all
is life and animation; where I hear on every side the sound of exultation; where every one speaks of the past with triumph, the present with
delight, the future with glowing and confident anticipation. Is not this
a community in which one may rejoice to live? Is not this a city by
which one may be proud to be received as the son? Is not this a land in
which one may be happy to fix his destiny, and ambitious, if possible,
to found a name?

I am asked how long I mean to remain here.——As long as I live!"

Mr. Irving concluded by proffering as a toast: "Our City—May God
continue to prosper it."

[October, 1832]

[REVIEW OF HENRY WHEATON'S
HISTORY OF THE NORTHMEN]

We are misers in knowledge as in wealth. Open inexhaustible mines to us on every hand, yet we return to grope in the exhausted stream of past opulence, and sift its sands for ore; place us in an age when history pours in upon us like an inundation, and the events of a century are crowded into a lustre; yet we tenaciously hold on to the scanty records of foregone times, and often neglect the all-important present to discuss the possibility of the almost forgotten past.

It is worthy of remark, that this passion for the antiquated and the obsolete appears to be felt with increasing force in this country. It may be asked, what sympathies can the native of a land, where every thing is in its youth and freshness, have with the antiquities of the ancient hemisphere? What inducement can he have to turn from the animated scene around him, and the brilliant perspective that breaks upon his imagination, to wander among the mouldering monuments of the olden world, and to call up its shadowy lines of kings and warriors from the dim twilight of tradition?—

> "Why seeks he, with unwearied toil,
>   Through death's dark walls to urge his way,
> Reclaim his long asserted spoil,
>   And lead oblivion into day?"

We answer, that he is captivated by the powerful charm of contrast. Accustomed to a land where every thing is bursting into life, and history itself but in its dawning, antiquity has, in fact, for him the effect of novelty; and the fading, but mellow, glories of the past, which linger in the horizon of the Old World, relieve the eye, after being dazzled with the rising rays which sparkle up the firmament of the New.

It is a mistake, too, that the political faith of a republican requires him, on all occasions, to declaim with bigot heat against the stately and traditional ceremonials; the storied pomps and pageants of other forms of government; or even prevents him from, at times, viewing them with interest, as matters worthy of curious investigation. Independently of the themes they present for historical and philosophical inquiry, he may regard them with a picturesque and poetical eye, as he regards the Gothic edifices rich with the elaborate ornaments of a gorgeous and intricate style of architecture, without wishing to exchange therefor the

stern but proud simplicity of his own habitation; or, as he admires the
romantic keeps and castles of chivalrous and feudal times, without desiring to revive the dangerous customs and warlike days in which they
originated. To him the whole pageantry of emperors and kings, and
nobles, and titled knights, is, as it were, a species of poetical machinery,
addressing itself to his imagination, but no more affecting his faith than
does the machinery of the heathen mythology affect the orthodoxy of
the scholar, who delights in the strains of Homer and Virgil, and wanders
with enthusiasm among the crumbling temples and sculptured deities of
Greece and Rome; or do the fairy mythology of the East, and the de-
monology of the North, impair the Christian faith of the poet or the
novelist who interweaves them in his fictions.

We have been betrayed into these remarks, in considering the work
before us, where we find one of our countrymen, and a thorough republican, investigating with minute attention some of the most antiquated
and dubious tracts of European history, and treating of some of its exhausted and almost forgotten dynasties; yet evincing throughout the
enthusiasm of an antiquarian, the liberality of a scholar, and the enlightened toleration of a citizen of the world.

The author of the work before us, Mr. Henry Wheaton, has for some
years filled the situation of Chargé d'Affaires at the court of Denmark.
Since he has resided at Copenhagen, he has been led into a course of
literary and historic research, which has ended in the production of the
present history of those Gothic and Teutonic people, who, inhabiting
the northern regions of Europe, have so often and so successfully made
inroads into other countries, more genial in climate and abundant in
wealth. A considerable part of his book consists of what may be called
conjectural or critical history, relating to remote and obscure periods
of time, previous to the introduction of Christianity, historiography, and
the use of Roman letters among those northern nations. At the outset,
therefore, it assumes something of an austere and antiquarian air, which
may daunt and discourage that class of readers who are accustomed to
find history carefully laid out in easy rambling walks through agreeable
landscapes, where just enough of the original roughness is left to produce the picturesque and romantic. Those, however, who have the
courage to penetrate the dark and shadowy boundary of our author's
work, grimly beset with hyperborean horrors, will find it resembling
one of those enchanted forests described in northern poetry,—embosom-
ing regions of wonder and delight, for such as have the hardihood to
achieve the adventure. For our own part, we have been struck with the
variety of adventurous incidents crowded into these pages, and with the
abundance of that poetical material which is chiefly found in early history; while many of the rude traditions of the Normans, the Saxons, and
the Danes have come to us with the captivating charms of early asso-

ciation, recalling the marvellous tales and legends that have delighted us in childhood.

The first seven chapters may be regarded as preliminary to the narrative, or, more strictly, historical part of the book. They trace the scanty knowledge possessed by Greek and Roman antiquity of the Scandinavian north; the earliest migrations from that quarter to the west, and south, and east of Europe; the discovery of Iceland by the Norwegians; with the singular circumstances which rendered that barren and volcanic isle, where ice and fire contend for mastery, the last asylum of Pagan faith and Scandinavian literature. In this wild region they lingered until the Latin alphabet superseded the Runic character, when the traditionary poetry and oral history of the north were consigned to written records, and rescued from that indiscriminate destruction which overwhelmed them on the Scandinavian continent.

The government of Iceland is described by our author as being more properly a patriarchal aristocracy than a republic; and he observes that the Icelanders, in consequence of their adherence to their ancient religion, cherished and cultivated the language and literature of their ancestors, and brought them to a degree of beauty and perfection which they never reached in the christianized countries of the north, where the introduction of the learned languages produced feeble and awkward, though classical imitation, instead of graceful and national originality.

When, at the end of the tenth century, Christianity was at length introduced into the island, the national literature, though existing only in oral tradition, was full blown, and had attained too strong and deep a root in the affections of the people to be eradicated, and had given a charm and value to the language with which it was identified. The Latin letters, therefore, which accompanied the introduction of the Romish religion, were merely adapted to designate the sounds heretofore expressed by Runic characters, and thus contributed to preserve in Iceland the ancient language of the north, when exiled from its parent countries of Scandinavia. To this fidelity to its ancient tongue, the rude and inhospitable shores of Iceland owe that charm which gives them an inexhaustible interest in the eyes of the antiquary, and endears them to the imagination of the poet. "The popular superstitions," observes our author, "with which the mythology and poetry of the north are interwoven, continued still to linger in the sequestered glens of this remote island."

The language in itself appears to have been worthy of this preservation, since we are told that "it bears in its internal structure a strong resemblance to the Latin and Greek, and even to the ancient Persian and Sanscrit, and rivals in copiousness, flexibility and energy, every modern tongue."

Before the introduction of letters, all Scandinavian knowledge was perpetuated in oral tradition by their Skalds, who, like the rhapsodists of ancient Greece, and the bards of the Celtic tribes, were at once poets and historians. We boast of the encouragement of letters and literary men in these days of refinement; but where are they more honored and rewarded than they were among these barbarians of the north? The Skalds, we are told, were the companions and chroniclers of kings, who entertained them in their trains, enriched them with rewards, and sometimes entered the lists with them in trials of skill in their art. They in a manner bound country to country, and people to people, by a delightful link of union, travelling about as wandering minstrels, from land to land, and often performing the office of ambassadors between hostile tribes. While thus applying the gifts of genius to their divine and legitimate ends, by calming the passions of men, and harmonizing their feelings into kindly sympathy, they were looked up to with mingled reverence and affection, and a sacred character was attached to their calling. Nay, in such estimation were they held, that they occasionally married the daughters of princes, and one of them was actually raised to a throne in the fourth century of the Christian era.

It is true the Skalds were not always treated with equal deference, but were sometimes doomed to experience the usual caprice that attends upon royal patronage. We are told that Canute the Great retained several at his court, who were munificently rewarded for their encomiastic lays. One of them having composed a short poem in praise of his sovereign, hastened to recite it to him, but found him just rising from table, and surrounded by suitors.

> "The impatient poet craved an audience of the king for his lay, assuring him it was 'very short.' The wrath of Canute was kindled, and he answered the Skald with a stern look,—'Are you not ashamed to do what none but yourself has dared,—to write a short poem upon me?—unless by the hour of dinner tomorrow you produce a *drapa* above thirty strophes long on the same subject, your life shall pay the penalty.' The inventive genius of the poet did not desert him: he produced the required poem, which was of the kind called *Tog-drapa*, and the king liberally rewarded him with fifty marks of silver.
>
> "Thus we perceive how the flowers of poetry sprung up and bloomed amidst eternal ice and snows. The arts of peace were successfully cultivated by the free and independent Icelanders. Their Arctic isle was not warmed by a Grecian sun, but their hearts glowed with the fire of freedom. The natural divisions of the country by icebergs and lava streams insulated the people from each other, and the inhabitants of each valley and each hamlet formed, as it were, an independent community. These were again reunited in the

general national assembly of the Al-thing, which might not be unaptly likened to the Amphyctionic council or Olympic games, where all the tribes of the nation convened to offer the common rites of their religion, to decide their mutual differences, and to listen to the lays of the Skald, which commemorated the exploits of their ancestors. Their pastoral life was diversified by the occupation of fishing. Like the Greeks, too, the sea was their element, but even their shortest voyages bore them much farther from their native shores than the boasted expedition of the Argonauts. Their familiarity with the perils of the ocean, and with the diversified manners and customs of foreign lands, stamped their national character with bold and original features, which distinguished them from every other people.

"The power of oral tradition, in thus transmitting, through a succession of ages, poetical or prose compositions of considerable length, may appear almost incredible to civilized nations accustomed to the art of writing. But it is well known, that even after the Homeric poems had been reduced to writing, the rhapsodists who had been accustomed to recite them could readily repeat any passage desired. And we have, in our own times, among the Servians, Calmucks, and other barbarous and semi-barbarous nations, examples of heroic and popular poems of great length thus preserved and handed down to posterity. This is more especially the case where there is a perpetual order of men, whose exclusive employment is to learn and repeat, whose faculty of the memory is thus improved and carried to the highest pitch of perfection, and who are relied upon as historiographers to preserve the national annals. The interesting scene presented this day in every Icelandic family, in the long nights of winter, is a living proof of the existence of this ancient custom. No sooner does the day close, than the whole patriarchal family, domestics and all, are seated on their couches in the principal apartment, from the ceiling of which the reading and working lamp is suspended; and one of the family, selected for that purpose, takes his seat near the lamp, and begins to read some favorite Saga, or it may be the works of Klopstock and Milton (for these have been translated into Icelandic,) whilst all the rest attentively listen, and are at the same time engaged in their respective occupations. From the scarcity of printed books in this poor and sequestered country, in some families the Sagas are recited by those who have committed them to memory, and there are still instances of itinerant orators of this sort, who gain a livelihood during the winter by going about, from house to house, repeating the stories they have thus learnt by heart."

The most prominent feature of Icelandic verse according to our author, is its alliteration. In this respect it resembles the poetry of all rude periods of society. That of the eastern nations, the Hebrews and the Persians, is full of this ornament; and it is found even among the classic poets of Greece and Rome. These observations of Mr. Wheaton are supported by those of Dr. Henderson,* who states that the fundamental rule in Icelandic poetry required that there should be three words in every couplet having the same initial letter, two of which should be in the former hemistich, and one in the latter. The following translation from Milton is furnished as a specimen.

> "Vid that Villu diup
> Vard annum slæga,
> Bölverk Bidleikat
> Barmi vitis á."

"Into this wild abyss the wary Fiend
Stood on the brink of Hell and looked;"—

As a specimen of the tales related by the Skalds, we may cite that of Sigurd and the beauteous Brynhilda, a royal virgin, who is described as living in a lonely castle, encircled by magic flames.

In the Teutonic lay, Brynhilda is a mere mortal virgin; but in the Icelandic poem she becomes a Valkyria, one of those demi-divinities, servants of Odin or Woden in the Gothic mythology, who were appointed to watch over the fate of battle, and were, as their name betokens, selectors of the slain. They were clothed in armor, and mounted on fleet horses, with drawn swords, and mingled in the shock of battle, choosing the warrior-victims, and conducting them to Valhalla, the hall of Odin, where they joined the banquet of departed heroes, in carousals of mead and beer.

The first interview of the hero and heroine is wildly romantic. Sigurd, journeying toward Franconia, sees a flaming light upon a lofty mountain: he approaches it, and beholds a warrior in full armor asleep upon the ground. On removing the helmet of the slumberer, he discovers the supposed knight to be an Amazon. Her armor clings to her body, so that he is obliged to separate it with his sword. She then arises from her death-like sleep, and apprises him that he has broken the spell by which she lay entranced. She had been thrown into this lethargic state by Odin, in punishment for having disobeyed his orders. In a combat between two knights, she had caused the death of him who should have had the victory.

This romantic tale has been agreeably versified by William Spencer,

---

* Henderson's Iceland. Edinb. 1819. Appendix III.

an elegant and accomplished genius, who has just furnished the world with sufficient proofs of his talents to cause regret that they did not fall to the lot of a more industrious man. We subjoin the fragments of his poem cited by our author.

"O strange is the bower where Brynhilda reclines,
Around it the watch-fire high bickering shines!
Her couch is of iron, her pillow a shield,
And the maiden's chaste eyes are in deep slumber sealed;
Thy charm, dreadful Odin, around her is spread,
From thy wand the dread slumber was poured on her head.
O whilom in battle so bold and so free,
Like a *Vikingr* victorious she roved o'er the sea.
The love-lighting eyes, which are fettered by sleep,
Have seen the sea-fight raging fierce o'er the deep;
And mid the dread wounds of the dying and slain,
The tide of destruction poured wide o'er the plain.

"Who is it that spurs his dark steed at the fire?
Who is it, whose wishes thus boldly aspire
To the chamber of shields, where the beautiful maid
By the spell of the mighty All-Father is laid?
It is Sigurd the valiant, the slayer of kings,
With the spoils of the Dragon, his gold and his rings."

BRYNHILDA.

*   *   *   *   *   *

"Like a Virgin of the Shield I roved o'er the sea,
My arm was victorious, my valor was free.
By prowess, by Runic enchantment and song,
I raised up the weak, and I beat down the strong;
I held the young prince mid the hurly of war,
My arm waved around him the charmed scimitar;
I saved him in battle, I crowned him in hall,
Though Odin and Fate had foredoomed him to fall:
Hence Odin's dread curses were poured on my head;
He doomed the undaunted Brynhilda to wed.
But I vowed the high vow which gods dare not gainsay,
That the boldest in warfare should bear me away:
And full well I knew that thou, Sigurd, alone
Of mortals the boldest in battle hast shone;
I knew that none other the furnace could stem,
(So wrought was the spell, and so fierce was the flame,)

Save Sigurd the glorious, the slayer of kings,
With the spoils of the Dragon, his gold and his rings."

The story in the original runs through several cantos, comprising varied specimens of those antique Gothic compositions, which, to use the words of our author,

"are not only full of singularly wild and beautiful poetry, and lively pictures of the manners and customs of the heroic age of the ancient north, its patriarchal simplicity, its deadly feuds, and its fanciful superstition, peopling the earth, air, and waters with deities, giants, genii, nymphs, and dwarfs; but there are many exquisite touches of the deepest pathos, to which the human heart beats in unison in every age and in every land."

Many of these hyperborean poems, he remarks, have an oriental character and coloring in their subjects and imagery, their mythology and their style, bearing internal evidence of their having been composed in remote antiquity, and in regions less removed from the cradle of the human race than the Scandinavian north. "The oldest of this fragmentary poetry," as he finely observes, "may be compared to the gigantic remains, the wrecks of a more ancient world, or to the ruins of Egypt and Hindostan, speaking a more perfect civilization, the glories of which have long since departed."

Our author gives us many curious glances at the popular superstitions of the north, and those poetic and mythic fictions which pervaded the great Scandinavian family of nations. The charmed armor of the warrior; the dragon who keeps a sleepless watch over buried treasure; the spirits or genii that haunt the rocky tops of mountains, or the depths of quiet lakes; and the elves or vagrant demons which wander through forests, or by lonely hills; these are found in all the popular superstitions of the north. Ditmarus Blefkenius tells us that the Icelanders believed in domestic spirits, which woke them at night to go and fish; and that all expeditions to which they were thus summoned were eminently fortunate. The water-sprites, originating in Icelandic poetry, may be traced throughout the north of Europe. The Swedes delight to tell of the Ström-kerl, or boy of the stream, who haunts the glassy brooks that steal gently through green meadows, and sits on the silver waves at moonlight, playing his harp to the elves who dance on the flowery margin. Scarcely a rivulet in Germany also but has its Wasser-nixe, or water-witches, all evidently members of the great northern family.

Before we leave this enchanted ground, we must make a few observations on the Runic characters, which were regarded with so much awe in days of yore, as locking up darker mysteries and more potent spells than the once redoubtable hieroglyphics of the Egyptians. The Runic alphabet, according to our author, consists properly of sixteen letters. Northern tradition attributes them to Odin, who, perhaps, brought them into Scandinavia, but they have no resemblance to any of the alphabets of central Asia. Inscriptions in these characters are still to be seen on rocks and stone monuments in Sweden, and other countries of the north, containing Scandinavian verses in praise of their ancient heroes. They were also engraven on arms, trinkets, amulets, and utensils, and sometimes on the bark of trees, and on wooden tablets, for the purpose of memorials or of epistolary correspondence. In one of the Eddaic poems, Odin is represented as boasting the magic power of the Runic rhymes, to heal diseases and counteract poison; to spell-bind the arms of an enemy; to lull the tempest; to stop the career of witches through the air; to raise the dead, and extort from them the secrets of the world of spirits. The reader who may desire to see the letters of this all-potent alphabet, will find them in Mallet's Northern Antiquities.

In his sixth chapter, Mr. Wheaton gives an account of the religion of Odin, and his migration, with a colony of Scythian Goths, from the banks of the Tanais, in Asia, to the peninsula of Scandinavia, to escape the Roman legions. Without emulating his minute and interesting detail, we will merely and briefly state some of the leading particulars, and refer the curious reader to the pages of his book.

The expedition of this mythological hero is stated to have taken place about seventy years before the Christian era, when Pompey the Great, then consul of Rome, finished the war with Tigranes and Mithridates, and carried his victorious arms throughout the most important parts of Asia. We quote a description of the wonderful vessel Skidbladner, the ship of the gods, in which he made the voyage.

> " 'Skidbladner,' said one of the genii, when interrogated by Gangler, 'is one of the best ships, and most curiously constructed. It was built by certain dwarfs, who made a present of it to Freyr. It is so vast that there is room to hold all the deities, with their armor. As soon as the sails are spread, it directs its course, with a favorable breeze, wherever they desire to navigate; and when they wish to land, such is its marvellous construction, that it can be taken to pieces, rolled up, and put in the pocket.' 'That is an excellent ship, indeed,' replied Gangler, 'and must have required much science and magic art to construct.' "—p. 118.

With this very convenient, portable, and pocketable ship, and a crew of Goths of the race of Sviar, called by Tacitus Suiones, the intrepid Odin departed from Scythia, to escape the domination of the Romans, who were spreading themselves over the world. He took with him also his twelve pontiffs, who were at once priests of religion and judges of the law. Whenever sea or river intervened, he launched his good ship Skidbladner, embarked with his band, and sailed merrily over; then landing, and pocketing the transport, he again put himself at the head of his crew, and marched steadily forward. To add to the facilities of these primitive emigrants, Odin was himself a seer and a magician. He could look into futurity; could strike his enemies with deafness, blindness, and sudden panic; could blunt the edge of their weapons, and render his own warriors invisible. He could transform himself into bird, beast, fish, or serpent, and fly to the most distant regions, while his body remained in a trance. He could, with a single word, extinguish fire, control the winds, and bring the dead to life. He carried about with him an embalmed and charmed head, which would reply to his questions, and give him information of what was passing in the remotest lands. He had, moreover, two most gifted and confidential ravens, who had the gift of speech, and would fly, on his behests, to the uttermost parts of the earth. We have only to believe in the supernatural powers of such a leader, provided with such a ship, and such an oracular head, attended by two such marvellously-gifted birds, and backed by a throng of staunch and stalwart Gothic followers, and we shall not wonder that he found but little difficulty in making his way to the peninsula of Scandinavia, and in expelling the aboriginal inhabitants, who seem to have been but a diminutive and stunted race; although there are not wanting fabulous narrators, who would fain persuade us there were giants among them. They were gradually subdued and reduced to servitude, or driven to the mountains, and subsequently to the desert wilds and fastnesses of Norrland, Lapland, and Finland, where they continued to adhere to that form of polytheism called Fetishism, or the adoration of birds and beasts, stocks and stones, and all the animate and inanimate works of creation.

As to Odin, he introduced into his new dominions the religion he had brought with him from the banks of the Tanais; but, like the early heroes of most barbarous nations, he was destined to become himself an object of adoration; for though to all appearance he died, and was consumed on a funeral pile, it was said that he was translated to the blissful abode of Godheim, there to enjoy eternal life. In process of time it was declared, that, though a mere prophet on earth, he had been an incarnation of the Supreme Deity, and had returned to the sacred hall of Valhalla, the paradise of the brave, where, surrounded by his late companions in arms, he watched over the deeds and destinies of the children of men.

The primitive people who had been conquered by Odin and his followers, seem to have been as diminutive in spirit as in form, and withal a rancorous race of little vermin, whose expulsion from their native land awakens but faint sympathy; yet candor compels us to add, that their conquerors are not much more entitled to our esteem, although their hardy deeds command our admiration. The author gives a slight sketch of the personal peculiarities which discriminated both, extracted from an Eddaic poem, and which is worthy of notice, as accounting, as far as the authority is respected, for some of the diversities in feature and complexion of the Scandinavian races.

> "The slave caste, descended from the Aboriginal Finns, were distinguished from their conquerors by black hair and complexion. . . . The caste of freemen and freeholders, lords of the soil which they cultivated, and descended from the Gothic conquerors, had reddish hair, fair complexion, and all the traits which peculiarly mark that famous race . . . —while the caste of the illustrious Jarls and the Herser, earls and barons, were distinguished by still fairer hair and skin, and by noble employments and manners: from these descended the kingly race, skilled in Runic science, in manly exercises, and the military art."

The manners, customs, and superstitions of these northern people, which afterwards, with various modifications, pervaded and stamped an indelible character on so great a part of Europe, deserve to be more particularly mentioned; and we give a brief view of them, chiefly taken from the work of our author, and partly from other sources. The religion of the early Scandinavians taught the existence of a Supreme Being, called Thor, who ruled over the elements, purified the air with refreshing showers, dispensed health and sickness, wielded the thunder and lightning, and with his celestial weapon, the rainbow, launched unerring arrows at the evil demons. He was worshipped in a primitive but striking manner, amidst the solemn majesty of nature, on the tops of mountains, in the depths of primeval forests, or in those groves which rose like natural temples on islands surrounded by the dark waters of lonely and silent lakes. They had, likewise, their minor deities, or genii, whom we have already mentioned, who were supposed to inhabit the sun, the moon, and stars,—the regions of the air, the trees, the rocks, the brooks and mountains of the earth, and to superintend the phenomena of their respective elements. They believed, also, in a future state of torment for the guilty, and of voluptuous and sensual enjoyment for the virtuous.

This primitive religion gave place to more complicated beliefs. Odin, elevated, as we have shown, into a divinity, was worshipped as the Supreme Deity, and with him was associated his wife Freya; from these are derived our Odensday,—Wodensday or Wednesday,—and our Freytag, or Friday. Thor, from whom comes Thursday, was now more limited in his sway, though he still bent the rainbow, launched the thunderbolt, and controlled the seasons. These three were the principal deities, and held assemblies of those of inferior rank and power. The mythology had also its devil, called Loke, a most potent and malignant spirit, and supposed to be the cause of all evil.

By degrees the religious rites of the northern people became more artificial and ostentatious; they were performed in temples, with something of Asiatic pomp. Festivals were introduced of symbolical and mystic import, at the summer and the winter solstice, and at various other periods; in which were typified, not merely the decline and renovation of nature and the changes of the seasons, but the epochs in the moral history of man. As the ceremonials of religion became more dark and mysterious, they assumed a cruel and sanguinary character; prisoners taken in battle were sacrificed by the victors, subjects by their kings, and sometimes even children by their parents. Superstition gradually spread its illusions over all the phenomena of nature, and gave each some occult meaning; oracles, lots, auguries, and divination gained implicit faith; and soothsayers read the decrees of fate in the flight of birds, the sound of thunder, and the entrails of the victim. Every man was supposed to have his attendant spirit, his destiny, which it was out of his power to avert, and his appointed hour to die;—Odin, however, could control or alter the destiny of a mortal, and defer the fatal hour. It was believed, also, that a man's life might be prolonged if another would devote himself to death in his stead.

The belief in magic was the natural attendant upon these superstitions. Charms and spells were practised, and the Runic rhymes, known but to the gifted few, acquired their reputation among the ignorant multitude, for an all-potent and terrific influence over the secrets of nature and the actions and destinies of man.

As war was the principal and the only noble occupation of these people, their moral code was suitably brief and stern. After profound devotion to the gods, valor in war was inculcated as the supreme virtue, cowardice as the deadly sin. Those who fell gloriously in war were at once transported to Valhalla, the airy hall of Odin, there to partake of the eternal felicities of the brave. Fighting and feasting, which had constituted their fierce joys on earth, were lavished upon them in this supernal abode. Every day they had combats in the listed field,—the rush of steeds, the flash of swords, the shining of lances, and all the maddening tumult and din of battle;—helmets and bucklers were riven,—horses and riders overthrown, and ghastly wounds exchanged; but at the setting of the sun all was over; victors and vanquished met unscathed in glorious companionship around the festive board of Odin in Valhalla's hall, where they partook of the ample banquet, and quaffed full horns of beer and fragrant mead. For the just who did not die in fight, a more peaceful but less glorious elysium was provided;—a resplendent golden palace, surrounded by verdant meads and shady groves and fields of spontaneous fertility.

The early training of their youth was suited to the creed of this warlike people. In the tender days of childhood they were gradually hardened by athletic exercises, and nurtured through boyhood in difficult and daring feats. At the age of fifteen they were produced before some public assemblage, and presented with a sword, a buckler, and a lance: from that time forth they mingled among men, and were expected to support themselves by hunting or warfare. But though thus early initiated in the rough and dangerous concerns of men, they were prohibited all indulgence with the softer sex until matured in years and vigor.

Their weapons of offence were bow and arrow, battle-axe and sword, and the latter was often engraved with some mystic characters, and bore a formidable and vaunting name.

The helmets of the common soldiery were of leather, and their bucklers leather and wood; but warriors of rank had helmets and shields of iron and brass, sometimes richly gilt and decorated; and they wore coats of mail, and occasionally plated armor.

A young chieftain of generous birth received higher endowments than the common class. Beside the hardy exercise of the chase and the other exercises connected with the use of arms, he was initiated betimes into the sacred science of the Runic writing, and instructed in the ancient lay, especially if destined for sovereignty, as every king was the pontiff of his people. When a prince had attained the age of eighteen, his father usually gave him a small fleet and a band of warriors, and sent him on some marauding voyage, from which it was disgraceful to return with empty hands.

Such was the moral and physical training of the Northmen, which prepared them for that wide and wild career of enterprise and conquest which has left its traces along all the coasts of Europe, and thrown communities and colonies, in the most distant regions, to remain themes of wonder and speculation in after ages. Actuated by the same roving and predatory spirit which had brought their Scythian ancestors from the banks of the Tanais, and rendered daring navigators by their experience along the stormy coasts of the north, they soon extended their warlike roamings over the ocean, and became complete maritime marauders, with whom piracy at sea was equivalent to chivalry on shore, and a freebooting cruise to a heroic enterprise.

For a time, the barks in which they braved the dangers of the sea, and infested the coasts of England and France, were mere canoes, formed from the trunks of trees, and so light as readily to be carried on men's shoulders, or dragged along the land. With these they suddenly swarmed upon a devoted coast, sailing up the rivers, shifting from stream to stream, and often making their way back to the sea by some different river from that they had ascended. Their chiefs obtained the appellation of sea-kings, because, to the astonished inhabitants of the invaded coasts, they seemed to emerge suddenly from the ocean, and when they had finished their ravages, to retire again into its bosom as to their native home; and they were rightly named, in the opinion of the author of a northern Saga, seeing that their lives were passed upon the waves, and "they never sought shelter under a roof, or drained their drinking horn at a cottage fire."

Though plunder seemed to be the main object of this wild ocean chivalry, they had still that passion for martial renown, which grows up with the exercise of arms, however rude and lawless, and which in them was stimulated by the songs of the skalds.

We are told that they were "sometimes seized with a sort of phrenzy, a *furor Martis*, produced by their excited imaginations dwelling upon the images of war and glory, and perhaps increased by those potations of stimulating liquors in which the people of the north, like other uncivilized tribes, indulged to great excess. When this madness was upon them, they committed the wildest extravagances, attacked indiscriminately friends and foes, and even waged war against the rocks and trees. At other times they defied each other to mortal combat in some lonely and desert isle."

Among the most renowned of these early sea-kings was Ragnar Lodbrok, famous for his invasion of Northumbria, in England, and no less famous in ancient Sagas for his strange and cruel death. According to those poetic legends, he was a king of Denmark, who ruled his realms in peace, without being troubled with any dreams of conquest. His sons, however, were roving the seas with their warlike followers, and after a time tidings of their heroic exploits reached his court. The jealousy of Ragnar was excited, and he determined on an expedition that should rival their achievements. He accordingly ordered "the Arrow," the signal of war, to be sent through his dominions, summoning his "champions" to arms. He had ordered two ships of immense size to be built, and in them he embarked with his followers. His faithful and discreet queen, Aslauga, warned him of the perils to which he was exposing himself, but in vain. He set sail for the north of England, which had formerly been invaded by his predecessors. The expedition was driven back to port by a tempest. The queen repeated her warnings and entreaties, but finding them unavailing, she gave him a magical garment that had the virtue to render the wearer invulnerable.

> "Ragnar again put to sea, and was at last shipwrecked on the English coast. In this emergency his courage did not desert him, but he pushed forward with his small band to ravage and plunder. Ella collected his forces to repel the invader. Ragnar, clothed with the enchanted garment he had received from his beloved Aslauga, and armed with the spear with which he had slain the guardian serpent of Thora, four times pierced the Saxon ranks, dealing death

on every side, whilst his own body was invulnerable to the blows of his enemies. His friends and champions fell one by one around him, and he was at last taken prisoner alive. Being asked, who he was he preserved an indignant silence. Then king Ella said:—'If this man will not speak, he shall endure so much the heavier punishment for his obduracy and contempt.' So he ordered him to be thrown into the dungeon full of serpents, where he should remain till he told his name. Ragnar, being thrown into the dungeon, sat there a long time before the serpents attacked him; which being noticed by the spectators, they said he must be a brave man indeed whom neither arms nor vipers could hurt. Ella, hearing this, ordered his enchanted vest to be stripped off, and, soon afterwards, the serpents clung to him on all sides. Then Ragnar said, 'how the young cubs would roar if they knew what the old boar suffers,' and expired with a laugh of defiance."—pp. 152, 153.

The death-song of Ragnar Lodbrok will be found in an appendix to Henderson's Iceland, both in the original and in a translation. The version, however, which is in prose, conveys but faintly the poetic spirit of the original. It consists of twenty-nine stanzas, most of them of nine lines, and contains, like the death-song of a warrior among the American Indians, a boastful narrative of his expeditions and exploits. Each stanza bears the same burden:

> "Hiuggom ver med hiarvi."
> "We hewed them with our swords."

Lodbrok exults that his achievements entitle him to admission among the gods; predicts that his children shall avenge his death; and glories that no sigh shall disgrace his exit. In the last stanza he hails the arrival of celestial virgins sent to invite him to the Hall of Odin, where he shall join the assembly of heroes, sit upon a lofty throne, and quaff the mellow beverage of barley. The last strophe of his death-song is thus rendered by Mr. Wheaton:

> "Cease my strain! I hear Them call
> Who bid me hence to Odin's hall!
> High seated in their blest abodes.
> I soon shall quaff the drink of Gods.
> The hours of Life have glided by,—
> I fall! but laughing will I die!
> The hours of Life have glided by,—
> I fall! but laughing will I die! !"

The sons of Ragnar, if the Sagas may be believed, were not slow in revenging the death of their parent. They were absent from home on warlike expeditions at the time, and did not hear of the catastrophe until after their return to Denmark. Their first tidings of it were from the messengers of Ella, sent to propitiate their hostility. When the messengers entered the royal hall, they found the sons of Ragnar variously employed. Sigurdr Snakeseye was playing at chess with his brother Huitserk the Brave; while Björn Ironside was polishing the handle of his spear in the middle pavement of the hall. The messengers approached to where Ivar, the other brother, was sitting, and saluting him with due reverence, told him they were sent by King Ella to announce the death of his royal father.

"As they began to unfold their tale, Sigurdr and Huitserk dropped their game, carefully weighing what was said. Björn stood in the midst of the hall, leaning on his spear: but Ivar diligently inquired by what means, and by what kind of death, his father had perished: which the messengers related, from his first arrival in England, till his death. When, in the course of their narrative, they came to the words of the dying king, 'how the young whelps would roar if they knew their father's fate,' Björn grasped the handle of his spear so fast, that the prints of his fingers remained; and when the tale was done, dashed the spear in pieces. Huitserk pressed the chess-board so hard with his hands, that they bled.

"Ivar changed color continually, now red, now black, now pale, whilst he struggled to suppress his kindling wrath.

"Huitserk the Brave, who first broke silence, proposed to begin their revenge by the death of the messengers; which Ivar forbad, commanding them to go in peace, wherever they would, and if they wanted any thing they should be supplied.

"Their mission being fulfilled, the delegates, passing through the hall, went down to their ships; and the wind being favorable, returned safely to their king. Ella, hearing from them how his message had been received by the princes, said that he foresaw that of all the brothers, Ivar or none was to be feared."—pp. 188, 189.

The princes summoned their followers, launched their fleets and attacked King Ella in the spring of 867.

"The battle took place at York, and the Anglo-Saxons were entirely routed. The sons of Ragnar inflicted a cruel and savage retaliation on Ella for his barbarous treatment of their father.

"After this battle, Northumbria appears no more as a Saxon kingdom, and Ivar was made king over that part of England which his ancestors had possessed, or into which they had made repeated incursions."—pp. 189, 190.

Encouraged by the success that attended their enterprises in the northern seas, the Northmen now urged their adventurous prows into more distant regions, besetting the southern coasts of France with their fleets of light and diminutive barks. Charlemagne is said to have witnessed the inroad of one of their fleets from the windows of his palace, in the harbor of Narbonne; upon which he lamented the fate of his successors, who would have to contend with such audacious invaders. They entered the Loire, sacked the city of Nantz, and carried their victorious arms up to Tours. They ascended the Garonne, pillaged Bordeaux, and extended their incursion even to Toulouse. They also entered the Seine in 845, ravaging its banks, and pushing their enterprise to the very gates of Paris, compelled the monarch Charles to take refuge in the monastery of St. Denis, where he was fain to receive the piratical chieftain, Regnier, and to pay him a tribute of 7000 pounds of silver, on condition of his evacuating his capital and kingdom. Regnier, besides immense booty, carried back to Denmark, as trophies of his triumph, a beam from the abbey of St. Germain, and a nail from the gate of Paris; but his followers spread over their native country a contagious disease which they had contracted in France.

Spain was, in like manner, subject to their invasions. They ascended the Guadalquivir, attacked the great city of Seville, and demolished its fortifications, after severe battles with the Moors, who were then sovereigns of that country, and who regarded these unknown invaders from the sea as magicians, on account of their wonderful daring, and still more wonderful success. As the author well observes, "the contrast between these two races of fanatic barbarians, the one issuing forth from the frozen regions of the north, the other from the burning sands of Asia and Africa, forms one of the most striking pictures presented by history."

The Straits of Gibraltar being passed by these rovers of the north, the Mediterranean became another region for their exploits. Hastings, one of their boldest chieftains, and father of that Hastings who afterwards battled with King Alfred for the sovereignty of England, accompanied by Björn Ironside and Sydroc, two sons of Ragnar Lodbrok, undertook an expedition against Rome, the capital of the world, tempted by accounts of its opulence and splendor, but not precisely acquainted with its site. They penetrated the Mediterranean with a fleet of one hundred barks, and entered the port of Luna in Tuscany, an ancient city, whose high walls and towers, and stately edifices, made them mistake it for imperial Rome.

"The inhabitants were celebrating the festival of Christmas in the cathedral, when the news was spread among them of the arrival of a fleet of unknown strangers. The church was instantly deserted, and the citizens ran to shut the gates, and prepared to defend their town. Hastings sent a herald to inform the count and bishop of Luna that he and his band were Northmen, conquerors of the Franks, who designed no harm to the inhabitants of Italy, but merely sought to repair their shattered barks. In order to inspire more confidence, Hastings pretended to be weary of the wandering life he had so long led, and desired to find repose in the bosom of the Christian church. The bishop and the count furnished the fleet with the needful succor; Hastings was baptised; but still his Norman followers were not admitted within the city walls. Their chief was then obliged to resort to another stratagem: he feigned to be dangerously ill; his camp resounded with the lamentations of his followers; he declared his intention of leaving the rich booty he had acquired to the church, provided they would grant him sepulture in holy ground. The wild howl of the Normans soon announced the death of their chieftain. The inhabitants followed the funeral procession to the church, but at the moment they were about to deposit his apparently lifeless body, Hastings started up from his coffin, and seizing his sword, struck down the officiating bishop. His followers instantly obeyed this signal of treachery: they drew from under their garments their concealed weapons, massacred the clergy and others who assisted at the ceremony, and spread havoc and consternation throughout the town. Having thus become master of Luna, the Norman chieftain discovered his error, and found that he was still far from Rome, which was not likely to fall so easy a prey. After having transported on board his barks the wealth of the city, as well as the most beautiful women, and the young men capable of bearing arms or of rowing, he put to sea, intending to return to the north.

"The Italian traditions as to the destruction of this city resemble more nearly the romance of Romeo and Juliet, than the history of the Scandinavian adventurer. According to these accounts, the prince of Luna was inflamed with the beauty of a certain young empress, then travelling in company with the emperor her husband. Their passion was mutual, and the two lovers had recourse to the following stratagem, in order to accomplish their union. The empress feigned to be grievously sick: she was believed to be dead; her funeral obsequies were duly celebrated; but she escaped from the sepulchre, and secretly rejoined her lover. The emperor had no sooner heard of their crime, than he marched to attack the residence of the ravisher, and avenged himself by the entire destruction of the once flourishing city of Luna. The only point of resemblance between these two stories consists in the romantic incident of the destruction of the city by means of a feigned death, a legend which spread abroad over Italy and France."

The last and greatest of the sea-kings, or pirate heroes of the north, was Rollo, surnamed Ferus Fortis, the Lusty Boar or Hardy Beast, from whom William the Conqueror comes in lineal, though not legitimate, descent. Our limits do not permit us to detail the early history of this warrior, as selected by our author from among the fables of the Norman chronicles, and the more simple, and, he thinks, more veritable narratives in the Icelandic Sagas. We shall merely state that Rollo arrived with a band of Northmen, all fugitive adventurers, like himself, upon the coast of France; ascended the Seine to Rouen, subjugated the fertile province then called Neustria; named it Normandy from the Northmen, his followers, and crowned himself first Duke.

> "Under his firm and vigorous rule, the blessings of order and peace were restored to a country which had so long and so cruelly suffered from the incursions of the northern adventurers. He tolerated the Christians in their worship, and they flocked in crowds to live under the dominion of a Pagan and barbarian, in preference to their own native and Christian prince (Charles the Simple) who was unwilling or incapable to protect them."

Rollo established in his duchy of Normandy a feudal aristocracy, or rather it grew out of the circumstances of the country. His followers elected him duke, and he made them counts and barons and knights. The clergy also pressed themselves into his great council or parliament. The laws were reduced to a system by men of acute intellect, and this system of feudal law was subsequently transplanted by William the Conqueror into England, as a means of consolidating his power and establishing his monarchy.

> "Rollo is said also to have established the Court of Exchequer as the supreme tribunal of justice; and the perfect security afforded by the admirable system of police established in England by King Alfred is likewise attributed to the legislation of the first Duke of Normandy."—p. 257.

Trial by battle, or judicial combat, was a favorite appeal to God by the warlike nations of Scandinavia, as by most of the barbarous tribes who established themselves on the ruin of the Roman empire. It had fallen into disuse in France, but was revived by Rollo in Normandy, although the clergy were solicitous to substitute the ordeal of fire and water, which brought controversies within their control. The fierce Norman warriors disdained this clerical mode of decision, and strenuously insisted on the appeal to the sword. They afterwards, at the conquest, introduced the trial by combat into England, where it became a part of the common law.*

A spirit of chivalry and love of daring adventure, a romantic gallantry towards the sex, and a zealous devotion were blended in the character of the Norman knights. These high and generous feelings they brought with them into England, and bore with them in their crusades into the Holy Land. Poetry also continued to be cherished and cultivated among them, and the Norman troubadour succeeded to the Scandinavian skald. The Dukes of Normandy and Anglo-Norman kings were practisers as well as patrons of this delightful art; and Henry I., surnamed Beauclerc, and Richard Cœur de Lion, were distinguished among the poetical composers of their day.

> "The Norman minstrels," to quote the words of our author, "appropriated the fictions they found already accredited among the people for whom they versified. The British King Arthur, his fabled knights of the Round Table, and the enchanter Merlin, with his wonderful prophecies; the Frankish monarch Charlemagne and his paladins; and the rich inventions of Oriental fancy borrowed from the Arabs and the Moors."—p. 262.

---

* A statue or effigy of Rollo, over a sarcophagus, is still to be seen in the cathedral at Rouen, with a Latin inscription, stating that he was converted to Christianity in 913, and died in 917, and that his bones were removed to this spot from their place of original sepulture, in A.D. 1063. The ancient epitaph, in rhyming monkish Latin, has been lost, except the following lines:

> Dux Normanorum
> Cunctorum,
> Norma Bonorum.
> Rollo, Ferus fortis,
> Quem gens Normanica mortis
> Invocat articulo,
> Clauditur hoc tumulo.

> *Imitation.*

> Rollo, that hardy Boar
> Renowned of yore,
> Of all the Normans Duke;
> Whose name with dying breath
> In article of death,
> All Norman knights invoke;
> That mirror of the bold,
> This tomb doth hold.

We have thus cursorily accompanied our author in his details of the origin and character, the laws and superstitions, and primitive religion, and also of the roving expeditions and conquests of the Northmen; and we give him credit for the judgment and candor and careful research, with which he has gleaned and collated his interesting facts, from the rubbish of fables and fictions with which they were bewildered and obscured.

Another leading feature in his work, is the conversion of the Northmen, and the countries from which they came, to the Christian faith. An attempt to condense or analyze this part of his work would lead us too far, and do injustice to the minuteness and accuracy of his details. We must, for like reasons, refer the reader to the work itself for the residue of its contents. We shall merely remark, that he goes over the same ground with the English historians, Hume, Turner, Lingard, and Palgrave, gleaning from the original authorities whatever may have been omitted by them. He has also occasionally corrected some errors into which they have fallen, through want of more complete access or more critical attention to the Icelandic sagas and the Danish and Swedish historians, who narrated the successful invasion of England by the Danes, under Canute, and its final conquest by William of Normandy.

We shall take leave of our author with some extracts from the triumphant invasion of William, premising a few words concerning his origin and early history. Robert Duke of Normandy, called Robert the Magnificent by his flatterers, but more commonly known as Robert the Devil, from his wild and savage nature, had an amour with Arlette, the daughter of a tanner, or currier, of Falaise, in Normandy. The damsel gave birth to a male child, who was called William. While the boy was yet in childhood, Robert the Devil resolved to expiate his sins by a pilgrimage to the Holy Land; and compelled his counts and barons to swear fealty to his son. "Par ma foi," said Robert, "je ne vous laisserai point sans seigneur. J'ai un petit bâtard qui grandira s'il plâit à Dieu. Choisissez-le dès à présent, et je le saiserai devant vous de ce duché comme mon successeur." The Norman lords placed their hands between the hands of the child, and swore fidelity to him according to feudal usage. Robert the Devil set out on his pious pilgrimage, and died at Nice. The right of the boy William was contested by Guy, Count of Burgundy, and other claimants, but he made it good with his sword, and then confirmed it by espousing Matilda, daughter of the Count of Flanders.

On the death of Edward the Confessor, King of England, Harold, from his fleetness surnamed Harefoot, one of the bravest nobles of the realm, assumed the crown, to the exclusion of Edgar Atheling, the lawful heir. It was said that Edward had named Harold to succeed him. William Duke of Normandy laid claim to the English throne. We have not room in this review to investigate his title, which was little more than bare pretension. He alleged that Edward the Confessor had promised to bequeath to him the crown; but his chief reliance was upon his sword. Harold, while yet a subject, had fallen by accident within the power of William, who had obtained from him, by cajolery and extortion, an oath, sworn on certain sacred reliques, not to impede him in his plans to gain the English crown.

William prepared an expedition in Normandy, and published a war ban, inviting adventurers of all countries to join him in the invasion of England, and partake the pillage. He procured a consecrated banner from the Pope under the promise of a portion of the spoil, and embarked a force of nearly sixty thousand men on board four hundred vessels and above a thousand boats.

> "The ship which bore William preceded the rest of the fleet, with the consecrated banner of the Pope displayed at the mast-head, its many-colored sails embellished with the lions of Normandy, and its prow adorned with the figure of an infant archer bending his bow and ready to let fly his arrow."

William landed his force at Pevensey, near Hastings, on the coast of Sussex, on the 28th of September, 1066; and we shall state from the Norman chronicles some few particulars of this interesting event, not included in the volume under review. The archers disembarked first,— they had short vestments and cropped hair; then the horsemen, armed with coats of mail, caps of iron, straight two-edged swords, and long powerful lances; then the pioneers and artificers, who disembarked, piece by piece, the materials for three wooden towers, all ready to be put together. The Duke was the last to land, for, says the chronicle, "there was no opposing enemy." King Harold was in Northumbria, repelling an army of Norwegian invaders.

As William leaped on shore, he stumbled and fell upon his face. Exclamations of foreboding were heard among his followers; but he grasped the earth with his hands, and raising them filled with it towards the heavens, "Thus," cried he, "do I seize upon this land, and by the splendor of God, as far as it extends, it shall be mine." His ready wit thus converted a sinister accident into a favorable omen. Having pitched his camp and reared his wooden towers near to the town of Hastings, he sent forth his troops to forage and lay waste the country; nor were even the churches and cemeteries held sacred to which the English had fled for refuge.

Harold was at York; reposing after a victory over the Norwegians, in which he had been wounded, when he heard of this new invasion. Undervaluing the foe, he set forth instantly with such force as he could muster, though a few days' delay would have brought great reinforcements. On his way he met a Norman monk, sent to him by William, with three alternatives: 1. To abdicate in his favor. 2. To refer their claims to the decision of the Pope. 3. To determine them by single combat. Harold refused all three, and quickened his march; but finding, as he drew nearer, that the Norman army was thrice the number of his own, he intrenched his host seven miles from their camp, upon a range of hills, behind a rampart of palisadoes and osier hurdles.

The impending night of the battle was passed by the Normans in warlike preparations, or in confessing their sins and receiving the sacrament, and the camp resounded with the prayers and chantings of priests and friars. As to the Saxon warriors, they sat round their camp-fires, carousing horns of beer and wine, and singing old national war-songs.

At an early hour in the morning of the 14th of October, Odo, Bishop of Bayeux, and bastard brother of the Duke, being the son of his mother Arlette, by a burgher of Falaise, celebrated mass, and gave his benediction to the Norman army. He then put a hauberk under his cassock, mounted a powerful white charger, and led forth a brigade of cavalry; for he was as ready with the spear as with the crosier, and for his fighting and other turbulent propensities, well merited his surname of Odo the Unruly.

The army was formed into three columns:—one composed of mercenaries from the countries of Boulogne and Ponthieu; the second of auxiliaries from Brittany and elsewhere; the third of Norman troops, led by William in person. Each column was preceded by archers in light quilted coats instead of armor, some with long bows, and others with cross-bows of steel. Their mode of fighting was to discharge a flight of arrows, and then retreat behind the heavy armed troops. The Duke was mounted on a Spanish steed, around his neck were suspended some of the reliques on which Harold had made oath, and the consecrated standard was borne at his side.

William harangued his soldiers, reminding them of the exploits of their ancestors, the massacre of the Northmen in England, and, in particular, the murder of their brethren the Danes. But he added another and a stronger excitement to their valor;—"Fight manfully, and put all to the sword; and if we conquer, we shall all be rich. What I gain, you gain; what I conquer, you conquer; if I gain the land, it is yours." We shall give, in our author's own words, the further particulars of this decisive battle, which placed a Norman sovereign on the English throne.

> "The spot which Harold had selected for this ever-memorable contest was a high ground, then called Senlac, nine miles from Hastings, opening to the south, and covered in the rear by an extensive wood. He posted his troops on the declivity of the hill in one

compact mass, covered with their shields, and wielding their enormous battle-axes. In the centre the royal standard, or gonfanon, was fixed in the ground, with the figure of an armed warrior, worked in thread of gold, and ornamented with precious stones. Here stood Harold, and his brothers Gurth and Leofwin, and around them the rest of the Saxon army, every man on foot.

"As the Normans approached the Saxon intrenchments, the monks and priests who accompanied their army retired to a neighboring hill to pray, and observe the issue of the battle. A Norman warrior, named Taillefer, spurred his horse in front of the line, and, tossing up in the air his sword, which he caught again in his hand, sang the national song of Charlemagne and Roland;—the Normans joined in the chorus, and shouted, 'Dieu aide! Dieu aide!' They were answered by the Saxons, with the adverse cry of 'Christ's rood! the holy rood!'

"The Norman archers let fly a shower of arrows into the Saxon ranks. Their infantry and cavalry advanced to the gates of the redoubts, which they vainly endeavored to force. The Saxons thundered upon their armor, and broke their lances with the heavy battle-axe, and the Normans retreated to the division commanded by William. The Duke then caused his archers again to advance, and to direct their arrows obliquely in the air, so that they might fall beyond and over the enemy's rampart. The Saxons were severely galled by the Norman missiles, and Harold himself was wounded in the eye. The attack of the infantry and men-at-arms again commenced with the cries of 'Nôtre-Dame! Dieu aide! Dieu aide!' But the Normans were repulsed, and pursued by the Saxons to a deep ravine, where their horses plunged and threw the riders. The *mêlée* was here dreadful, and a sudden panic seized the invaders, who fled from the field, exclaiming that their duke was slain. William rushed before the fugitives, with his helmet in hand, menacing and even striking them with his lance, and shouting with a loud voice:— 'I am still alive, and with the help of God I still shall conquer!' The men-at-arms once more returned to attack the redoubts, but they were again repelled by the impregnable phalanx of the Saxons. The Duke now resorted to the stratagem of ordering a thousand horse to advance, and then suddenly retreat, in the hope of drawing the enemy from his intrenchments. The Saxons fell into the snare, and rushed out with their battle-axes slung about their necks, to pursue the flying foe. The Normans were joined by another body of their own army, and both turned upon the Saxons, who were assailed on every side with swords and lances, whilst their hands were employed in wielding their enormous battle-axes. The invaders now rushed through the broken ranks of their opponents into the intrenchments, pulled down the royal standard, and erected in its place the papal banner. Harold was slain, with his brothers Gurth and Leofwin. The sun declined in the western horizon, and with his retiring beams sunk the glory of the Saxon name.

"The rest of the companions of Harold fled from the fatal field, where the Normans passed the night, exulting over their hard-earned victory. The next morning, William ranged his troops under arms, and every man who passed the sea was called by name, according to the muster-roll drawn up before their embarkation at St. Valery. Many were deaf to that call. The invading army consisted originally of nearly sixty thousand men, and of these one-fourth lay dead on the field. To the fortunate survivors was allotted the spoil of the vanquished Saxons, as the first fruits of their victory; and the bodies of the slain, after being stripped, were hastily buried by their trembling friends. According to one narrative, the body of Harold was begged by his mother as a boon from William, to whom she offered as a ransom its weight in gold. But the stern and pitless conqueror ordered the corpse of the Saxon king to be buried on the beach, adding, with a sneer, 'He guarded the coast while he lived, let him continue to guard it now he is dead.' Another account represents that two monks of the monastery of Waltham, which had been founded by the son of Godwin, humbly approached the Norman, and offered him ten marks of gold for permission to bury their king and benefactor. They were unable to distinguish his body among the heaps of slain, and sent for Harold's mistress, Editha, surnamed 'the Fair' and 'the Swan's Neck,' to assist them in the search. The features of the Saxon monarch were recognized by her whom he had loved, and his body was interred at Waltham, with regal honors, in the presence of several Norman earls and knights."

We have reached the conclusion of Mr. Wheaton's interesting volume, yet we are tempted to add a few words more from other sources. We would observe that there are not wanting historians who dispute the whole story of Harold having fallen on the field of battle. "Years afterwards," we are told by one of the most curiously learned of English scholars, "when the Norman yoke pressed heavily upon the English, and the battle of Hastings had become a tale of sorrow, which old men narrated by the light of the embers, until warned to silence by the sullen tolling of the curfew," there was an ancient anchorite, maimed, and scarred, and blind of an eye, who led a life of penitence and seclusion in a cell near the Abbey of St. John at Chester. This holy man was once visited by Henry I., who held a long and secret discourse with him, and on his death-bed he declared to the attendant monks that he was Harold.[*] According to this account, he had been secretly conveyed from the field of battle to a castle, and thence to this sanctuary; and the finding and burying of his corpse by the tender Editha, is supposed to have been a pious fraud. The monks of Waltham, however, stood up stoutly for the authenticity of their royal reliques. They showed a tomb, enclosing a mouldering skeleton, the bones of which still bore the marks of wounds received in battle, while the sepulchre bore the effigies of the monarch, and this brief but pathetic epitaph:—*"Hic jacet Harold infelix."*

For a long time after the eventful battle of the conquest, it is said that traces of blood might be seen upon the field, and, in particular, upon the hills to the south-west of Hastings, whenever a light rain moistened the soil. It is probable they were discolorations of the soil, where heaps of the slain had been buried. We have ourselves seen broad and dark patches on the hill side of Waterloo, where thousands of the dead lay mouldering in one common grave, and where, for several years after the battle, the rank green corn refused to ripen, though all the other part of the hill was covered with a golden harvest.

William the Conqueror, in fulfilment of a vow, caused a monastic pile to be erected on the field, which, in commemoration of the event, was called the "Abbey of Battle." The architects complained that there were no springs of water on the site. "Work on! work on!" replied he, jovially; "if God but grant me life, there shall flow more good wine among the holy friars of this convent, than there does clear water in the best monastery of Christendom."

The abbey was richly endowed, and invested with archiepiscopal jurisdiction. In its archives was deposited a roll, bearing the names of the followers of William, among whom he had shared the conquered land. The grand altar was placed on the very spot where the banner of the hapless Harold had been unfurled, and here prayers were perpetually to be offered up for the repose of all who had fallen in the contest. "All this pomp and solemnity," adds Mr. Palgrave, "has passed away like a dream! The perpetual prayer has ceased forever; the roll of battle is rent; the escutcheons of the Norman lineages are trodden in the dust. A dark and reedy pool marks where the abbey once reared its stately towers, and nothing but the foundations of the choir remain for the gaze of the idle visiter, and the instruction of the moping antiquary."[†]

---

[*] Palgrave, Hist. Eng., Cap. XV.
[†] Palgrave, Hist. Eng., Cap. XV.

[March 1, 1834]

MATHEWS *NOT* AT HOME

Those who know Charles Mathews personally know that his very
troubles and tribulations are comic, and derive a whimsical effect from
his extreme nervous irritability. A letter from an American gentleman
in England to his friend in this city, dated about the first of December
last, gives the following anecdote in point.

"Mathews, who is on a provincial tour with his budget, was cast
away a few days since and nearly lost, not at sea, but in the Arabian
desert of Salisbury plain. He had been on a visit to the retired tragedian
Charles Young, and was crossing the plain in a curricle with the son
of that gentleman, when something got wrong in the traces and they
had to descend to adjust them. The spirited horses ran off with the
vehicle. Mathews was too lame to travel on foot, and his staff or
crutch, together with his upper covering, were in the curricle. As the
plain is a sort of trackless desert, his companion pointed out a spot at
some distance which he knew as a landmark, and where he promised
to come for him; and in the mean time set out after the carriage. Mathews
hobbled and crawled to the appointed spot, where he passed several
hours, making signals of distress whenever a distant horseman hove
in sight, but all in vain: and he now began to worry himself with the
dread of having to pass the night in that chilly desert. As he is the
most fidgetting and fretful of men, although the most comic of comedians,
it is said that he played off some of the most extraordinary tantrums on
the occasion; and cut some capers that would not have disgraced the
Knight of the Woful Countenance, when he played mad in the Sierra
Morena, to the dismay of the sage Sancho Panza. Fortunately Young
found the curricle at the distance of some miles, overturned near an
encampment of Gipsies, who had taken possession of it, together with the
trunks of Mathews, in one of which was the treasure of his dramatic
tour, about three hundred pounds in cash. The Gipsies, however, acted
out of character in giving up every article with scrupulous honesty.
Mathews was rescued by his friend before nightfall in a state of despair
and almost frenzy, and conveyed to a comfortable supper and beds; and,
when he resumed his performances, appended a very amusing narrative
of his adventure as a post-script to his budget."

[March 21, 1835]

NEWTON THE PAINTER

Letters from England give an interesting account of our talented but unfortunate countryman Gilbert Stuart Newton. His mental malady still continues, yet accompanied with circumstances that are calculated to soften the affliction of his friends. His hours and habits are perfectly regular, his deportment subdued and quiet. He is like one in a pleasant dream, and his amusements and occupations are all of an elegant nature. He has the range of a large garden for his recreation, where he walks early in the morning; and the rest of the day is devoted to reading, music, and painting. He has made more than twenty sketches of original subjects, all of them good and some of them equal to his very best things. They are from Shakespeare, Sterne, Goldsmith and the Bible; and some from fancies of his own. For instance, a child dressed like a soldier, marching through a garden and saluting the flowers, as if they were officers. This, he says, he remembers doing himself, when a child.

Leslie, his old friend and companion in art, visits him frequently, and they have long conversations together, in which Newton often acquits himself as well as ever he did. What he says is not always the repetition of former thoughts, but he occasionally reasons well, when a new subject is presented to him. It is said that Dr. Sutherland does not consider his case as altogether hopeless. In the mean-time it is consoling to think, that the malady which thus separates him from the world, is not likely to deprive it entirely of the gifts and graces of his genius, and that while the exercise of his elegant pencil beguiles the loneliness of his seclusion, it may still link him, in a delightful manner, with his friends and with the lovers of the fine arts.

[October 17, 1835]

AN UNWRITTEN DRAMA OF LORD BYRON

The reading world has, I apprehend, by this time become possessed of nearly every scrap of poetry and romance ever written by Lord Byron. It may be pleased, however, to know something of a dramatic poem which he did not write, but which he projected—and this is the story:—

The hero, whom we will call Alfonso, is a Spanish nobleman, just entering upon the career of life. His passions, from early and unrestrained indulgence, have become impetuous and ungovernable, and he follows their impulses with a wild and heedless disregard of consequences.

Soon after his entrance into the world, he finds himself followed, occasionally, in public places, by a person masked and muffled up so as to conceal both countenance and figure. He at first pays but little attention to the circumstance, considering the stranger some idle or impertinent lounger about society. By degrees, however, the frequent intrusion of this silent and observant follower becomes extremely irksome. The mystery, too, which ènvelopes him, heightens the annoyance. Alfonso is unable to identify him with any of his acquaintance,—his name, his country, his place of abode; all are unknown,—and it is impossible even to conjecture his motives for this singular espionage. It is carried, by degrees, to such lengths, that he becomes, as it were, Alfonso's shadow—his second self. Not only the most private actions of the latter pass under the scrutiny of this officious monitor, but his most secret thoughts seem known to him. Speak of him, he stands by his side; think of him, he feels his presence, though invisible, oppress and weigh upon his spirits, like a troubled atmosphere. Waking or sleeping, Alfonso has him in thought or in view. He crosses his path at every turn; like the demon in Faust, he intrudes in his solitude. He follows him in the crowded street, or the brilliant saloon; thwarting his schemes, and marring all his intrigues of love or of ambition. In the giddy mazes of the dance, in which Alfonso is addressing his fair partner with the honeyed words of seduction, he sees the stranger pass like a shadow before him; a voice, like the voice of his own soul, whispers in his ear; the words of seduction die from his lips; he no longer hears the music of the dance.

The hero of the drama becomes abstracted and gloomy. Youth, health, wealth, power—all that promised to give a zest to life, have lost their charm. The sweetest cup of pleasure becomes poison to him. Existence is a burthen. To add to his despair, he doubts the fidelity of the fair but frail object of his affection; and suspects the unknown to have supplanted him in her thoughts.

Alfonso now thirsts only for vengeance, but the mysterious stranger eludes his pursuit, and his emissaries in vain endeavour to discover his retreat. At length he succeeds in tracing him to the house of his mistress, and attacks him with the fury of frantic jealousy, taxes him with his wrongs, and demands *satisfaction*. They fight; his rival scarcely defends himself; at the first thrust he receives the sword of Alfonso in his bosom; and in falling, exclaims, "Are you satisfied!"

The mask and mantle of the unknown drop off, and Alfonso discovers his own image—the spectre of himself—he dies with horror!

The spectre is an allegorical being, the personification of conscience, or of the passions.

Such was the general plan of a poem which Lord Byron had in mind, several years since; and which he communicated, in conversation, to Captain Medwin, from whom I received it nearly in the foregoing words. The idea was taken from a Spanish play, called the *Embozado*, or the *Encapotado*,° and was furnished to Byron by Shelley, as his Lordship did not understand Spanish. The foregoing plan is evidently somewhat vague and immature, and would doubtless have undergone many modifications in the progress of being brought out. Lord Byron intended to treat it in the genuine spirit of Goethe, as displayed in his wild and extraordinary drama of Faust, and expected to make it very effective. It certainly afforded ample scope for the mystic, the misanthropic, the metaphysical, and the romantic, in which he so much delighted; and would have given him an opportunity of interweaving much of his own peculiar feelings and experience.

How far the plan he had in view agreed with the Spanish original, I have not been able to ascertain. The latter was said to be by Calderon; but it is not to be found in any edition of his works that I have seen. My curiosity being awakened on the subject, I made diligent inquiry, while in Spain, for the play in question, but it was not to be met with in any of the public libraries, or private collections; nor could the book-sellers give me any information about it. Some of the most learned and indefatigable collectors of Spanish literature informed me that a play of the kind, called the *Embozado of Cordova*, was somewhere in existence, but they had never seen it. The foregoing sketch of the plot may hereafter suggest a rich theme to a poet or dramatist of the Byron school.

[1835]

THE HAUNTED SHIP.

A TRUE STORY—AS FAR AS IT GOES

The world abounds with ghost-stories, but it is exceedingly difficult to get them at first hand; that is to say, from persons who have actually seen the ghosts: this may be the reason why they have fallen into some discredit with the dubious. I once, however, heard a story of the kind from one who came within an ace of being an eye-witness, and who

° I. E. A person muffled and disguised.

believed in it most honestly. He was a worthy captain of the sea; a native either of Nantucket or Martha's Vineyard, I forget which; at any rate, of a place noted for its breed of hardy mariners. I met with him in the ancient city of Seville, having anchored with his brig in the Guadalquivir, in the course of a wandering voyage. Our conversation one day turned upon the wonders and adventures of the sea; when he informed me that, among his multifarious cruisings, he had once made a voyage on board of a haunted ship. It was a vessel that had been met with drifting, half dismantled, and with flagging sails, about the sea near the Gulf of Florida, between the mainland and the Bahama banks. Those who boarded her found her without a living soul on board; the hatch-ways were broken open; the cargo had been rifled; the decks fore and aft were covered with blood; the shrouds and rigging were smeared with the same, as if some wretched beings had been massacred as they clung to them: it was evident that the ship had been plundered by pirates, and, to all appearance, the crew had been murdered and thrown overboard.

The ship was taken possession of by the finders, and brought to Boston, in New England; but the sailors who navigated her to port declared they would not make such another voyage for all the wealth of Peru. They had been harassed the whole way by the ghosts of the murdered crew; who at night would come up out of the companion-way and the fore-castle, run up the shrouds, station themselves on the yards, and at the mast-heads, and appear to perform all the usual duties of the ship.

As no harm had resulted from this ghostly seamanship, the story was treated lightly, and the vessel was fitted out for another voyage; but when ready for sea, no sailors could be got to embark in her. She lay for some time in Boston harbour, regarded by the superstitious seamen as a fated ship; and there she might have rotted, had not the worthy captain who related to me the story, undertaken to command her. He succeeded in getting some hardy tars, who stood less in awe of ghosts, to accompany him, and his brother-in-law sailed with him as chief mate.

When they had got fairly to sea, the hobgoblin crew began to play their pranks. At night there would be the deuce to pay in the hold: such racketing and rummaging, as if the whole cargo was overhauled; bales tumbled about, and boxes broken open; and sometimes it seemed as if all the ballast was shifted from side to side. All this was heard with dismay by the sailors; and even the captain's brother-in-law, who appears to have been a very sagacious man, was exceedingly troubled at it. As to the captain himself, he honestly confessed to me that he never saw nor heard any thing; but then he slept soundly, and, when once asleep, was hard to be awakened.

Notwithstanding all these ghostly vagaries, the ship arrived safe at the destined end of her voyage, which was one of the South American rivers under the line. The captain proposed to go in his boat to a town some distance up the river, leaving his ship in charge of his brother-in-law. The latter said he would anchor her opposite to an island in the river, where he could go on shore at night, and yet be at hand to keep guard upon her; but that nothing should tempt him to sleep on board. The crew all swore the same. The captain could not reasonably object to such an arrangement: so the ship was anchored opposite to the island, and the captain departed on his expedition.

For a time all went well; the brother-in-law and his sagacious comrades regularly abandoned the ship at night-fall, and slept on shore; the ghosts then took command, and the ship remained as quietly at anchor as though she had been manned by living bodies instead of hobgoblin sprites. One night, however, the captain's brother-in-law was awakened by a tremendous storm. He hastened to the shore. The sea was lashed up in foaming and roaring surges; the rain came down in torrents—the lightning flashed—the thunder bellowed. It was one of those sudden tempests only known at the tropics. The captain's brother-in-law cast a rueful look at the poor tossing and labouring ship. He saw numbers of uncouth beings busy about her, who were only to be descried by the flashes of lightning or by pale fires that glided about the rigging; he heard occasionally the piping of a boatswain's whistle, or the bellowing of a hoarse voice through a speaking-trumpet. The ghosts were evidently striving to save the ship; but a tropical storm is sometimes an over-match for ghost, or goblin, or even the ———— himself. In a word, the ship parted her cables, drove before the wind, stranded on the rocks, and there she laid her bones.

When the captain returned from his expedition up the river, he found his late gallant vessel a mere hulk, and received this wonderful account of her fate from his sagacious brother-in-law. Whether the wreck continued to be haunted or not, he could not inform me; and I forgot to ask whether the owners recovered anything from the underwriters, who rarely insure against accidents from ghosts.

Such is one of the nearest chances I have ever had of getting to the fountain-head of a ghost-story. I have often since regretted that the captain should have been so sound a sleeper, and that I did not see his brother-in-law.

[January 7, 1837]

[LETTER TO THE EDITOR OF THE
NEW YORK *AMERICAN*]

To the Editor of the New York American:

Sir,—I perceive a prolonged and angry discussion in the papers, with which my name has been strangely mingled. The manner in which I have become implicated, is this: in a trifling sketch of a French Creole village, inserted in one of the latest Annuals, I observed, incidentally, that the Virginians retain peculiarities characteristic of the times of Queen Elizabeth and Sir Walter Raleigh. By this remark, I have drawn upon me some very ungracious language from a writer of North Carolina, who charges me with a gross violation of the truth of history; and implies that I have committed an intentional wrong on his native State. Conscious of no intention to controvert any point of history; free from all disposition to do wrong or to give offence either to communities or individuals; and accustomed to observe, and to experience, the most courteous conduct in all dealings with my literary contemporaries; I was at a loss to what to attribute so indecorous an attack. I have since, however, understood that the feelings of the writer in question had previously become sore and irritable, in the course of a contest in the papers between himself and some Virginian writers, as to the claims of their respective States to certain historical associations with the names of Queen Elizabeth and Sir Walter Raleigh; and that my innocently intended paragraph, aforesaid, being quoted by one of his opponents, had drawn upon me his undiscriminating ire.

I have too great commiseration for any person laboring under a state of mental irritability to seek to exasperate his malady; and feel nothing but regret that any casual remark of mine should have fallen upon this sore spot in the mind of your correspondent.

As, however, the writer's misconception has been reiterated in the newspapers; and as some readers may imagine that I really stand convicted of a deliberate outrage upon historical truth, and hostility to the claims of North Carolina, I beg leave simply to put on record, that I have neither part nor interest in the claims of either of the belligerent parties. The opinion expressed in my unlucky paragraph, had no sinister view with respect to North Carolina. It merely expressed a general notion as to the manners of the Virginians, and an idea that they had taken their original stamp from colonists who had lived in England in the time of Queen Elizabeth and Sir Walter Raleigh, and had brought with them the habitudes and manners characteristic of that period.

If I am wrong in this idea, I plead ignorance, rather than submit to the imputation of wilfully misstating facts; but I believe that the most accurate researches will establish the correctness of the casual remark which has brought upon me so much ire. As to the people of North Carolina, they have always partaken of that general feeling which I have toward the people of the south, which is any thing but one of coldness or disrespect.

If, after this explanation, any disputatious writer should think fit to persist in resenting an imaginary offence, I shall leave him to the singular caprice of fighting shadows, and will only pray for his speedy restoration to a happier state of mind and greater courtesy of language.

Very respectfully, yours,
WASHINGTON IRVING.

Greenburgh, Jan. 4th, 1837.

[January 28, 1837]

[LETTER TO THE EDITOR OF *THE PLAINDEALER*]

TO THE EDITOR OF THE PLAINDEALER.

Sir: Living at present in the country and out of the way of the current literature of the day, it was not until this morning that I saw your paper of the 14th of January, or knew any thing of your animadversions on my conduct and character therein contained. Though I have generally abstained from noticing any attack upon myself in the public papers, the present is one which I cannot suffer to pass in silence.

In the first place, you have censured me strongly for having altered a paragraph in the London edition of Mr. Bryant's poems; and the remarks and comparisons in which you have indulged on the occasion would seem to imply, that I have a literary hostility to Mr. Bryant, and a disposition to detract from the measure of his well merited reputation.

The relation in which you stand to that gentleman, as his particular friend and literary associate, gives these animadversions the greater weight, and calls for a real statement of the case.

When I was last in London (I think in 1832), I received a copy of the American edition of Mr. Bryant's poems from some friend (I now forget from whom), who expressed a wish that it might be republished in England. I had not, at that time, the pleasure of a personal acquaintance with Mr. Bryant, but I felt the same admiration for his poems that you have expressed, and was desirous that writings, so honourable to American literature, should be known to the British public, and take their merited rank in the literature of the language. I exerted myself, therefore, to get them republished, by some London bookseller; but met with unexpected difficulties; poetry being declared quite unsaleable since the death of Lord Byron.

At length a bookseller was induced to undertake an edition, by my engaging, gratuitously, to edit the work, and to write something that might call public attention to it. I accordingly prefixed to the volume a dedicatory letter, addressed to Mr. Samuel Rogers, in which, while I expressed my own opinion of the poems, I took occasion to allude to the still more valuable approbation which I had heard expressed by that distinguished author; thus bringing the work before the British public with the high sanction of one of the most refined critics of the day. While the work was going through the press an objection was started to the passage in the poem of "Marion's Men:"

> And the British foeman trembles
> When Marion's name is heard.

It was considered as peculiarly calculated to shock the feelings of British readers on the most sensitive point; seeming to call in question the courage of the nation. It was urged that common decorum required the softening of such a passage in an edition exclusively intended for the British public; and I was asked what would be the feelings of American readers if such an imputation on the courage of their countrymen were inserted in a work presented for their approbation. These objections were urged in a spirit of friendship to Mr. Bryant, and with a view to his success, for it was suggested that this passage might be felt as a taunt or bravado, and might awaken a prejudice against the work, before its merits could be appreciated.

I doubt whether these objections would have occurred to me had they not been thus set forth; but, when thus urged, I yielded to them, and softened the passage in question, by omitting the adjective *British*, and substituting one of a more general signification. If this evinced "timidity of spirit," it was a timidity felt entirely on behalf of Mr. Bryant. I was not to be harmed by the insertion of the paragraph as it originally stood. I freely confess, however, that I have at all times almost as strong a repugnance to tell a painful or humiliating truth, *unnecessarily*, as I have to tell an untruth, under any circumstances. To speak the truth on all occasions is the indispensable attribute of man; to refrain from uttering disagreeable truths, *unnecessarily*, belongs, I think, to the character of a gentleman; neither, sir, do I think it incompatible with fair dealing, however little it may square with your notions of plaindealing.

The foregoing statement will shew how I stand with regard to Mr. Bryant. I trust his fame has suffered nothing by my republication of his works in London; at any rate, he has expressed his thanks to me by letter, since my return to this country; I was therefore, I confess, but little prepared to receive a stab from his bosom friend.

Another part of your animadversions is of a much graver nature, for it implies a charge of hypocrisy and double dealing which I indignantly repel as incompatible with my nature. You intimate that "in publishing a book of my own, I prepare one preface for my countrymen full of amor patriæ and professions of home feeling, and another for the London market in which such professions are studiously omitted." Your inference is that these professions are hollow, and intended to gain favour with my countrymen, and that they are omitted in the London edition through fear of offending English readers. Were I indeed chargeable with such baseness, I should well merit the contempt you invoke upon my head. As I give you credit, sir, for probity, I was at a loss to think on what you could ground such an imputation, until it occurred to me that some circumstances attending the publication of my "Tour on the Prairies," might have given rise to a misconception in your mind.

It may seem strange to those intimately acquainted with my character, that I should think it necessary to defend myself from a charge of *duplicity*; but as many of your readers may know me as little as you appear to do, I must again be excused in a detail of facts.

When my "Tour on the Prairies" was ready for the press, I sent a manuscript copy to England for publication, and at the same time, put a copy in the press at New York. As this was my first appearance before the American public since my return, I was induced, while the work was printing, to modify the introduction so as to express my sense of the unexpected warmth with which I had been welcomed to my native place, and my general feelings on finding myself once more at home, and among my friends. These feelings, sir, were genuine, and were not expressed with half the warmth with which they were entertained. Circumstances alluded to in that introduction had made the reception I met with from my countrymen, doubly dear and touching to me, and had filled my heart with affectionate gratitude for their unlooked for kindness. In fact, misconstructions of my conduct and misconceptions of my character, somewhat similar to those I am at present endeavouring to rebut, had appeared in the public press, and, as I erroneously supposed, had prejudiced the mind of my countrymen against me. The professions therefore to which you have alluded, were uttered, not to obviate such prejudices, or to win my way to the good will of my countrymen, but to express my feelings after their good will · had been unequivocally manifested. While I thought they doubted me, I remained silent; when I found they believed in me, I spoke. I have never been in the habit of beguiling them by fulsome professions of patriotism, those cheap passports to public favour; and I think I might for once have been indulged in briefly touching a chord, on which others have harped to so much advantage.

Now, sir, even granting I had "studiously omitted" all those professions in the introduction intended for the London market, instead of giving utterance to them after that article had been sent off, where, I would ask, would have been the impropriety of the act? What had the British public to do with those home greetings and those assurances of gratitude and affection which related exclusively to my countrymen, and grew out of my actual position with regard to them? There was nothing in them at which the British reader could possibly take offence; the omitting of them, therefore, could not have argued "timidity," but would have been merely a matter of good taste; for they would have been as much out of place repeated to English readers, as would have been my greetings and salutations to my family circle, if repeated out of the window for the benefit of the passers by in the street.

I have no intention, sir, of imputing to you any malevolent feeling in the unlooked for attack you have made upon me: I can see no motive you have for such hostility. I rather think you have acted from honest feelings, hastily excited by a misapprehension of facts; and that you have been a little too eager to give an instance of that "plaindealing" which you have recently adopted as your war cry. Plaindealing, sir, is a great merit, when accompanied by magnanimity, and exercised with a just and generous spirit; but if pushed too far, and made the excuse for indulging every impulse of passion or prejudice, it may render a man, especially in your situation, a very offensive, if not a very mischievous member of the community. Such I sincerely hope and trust may not be your case; but this hint, given in a spirit of caution, not of accusation, may not be of disservice to you.

In the present instance I have only to ask that you will give this article an insertion in your paper, being intended not so much for yourself, as for those of your readers who may have been prejudiced against me by your animadversions. Your editorial position of course gives you an opportunity of commenting upon it according to the current of your feelings; and, whatever may be your comments, it is not probable that they will draw any further reply from me. Recrimination is a miserable kind of redress in which I never indulge, and I have no relish for the warfare of the pen.

Very respectfully, your obedient servant,
WASHINGTON IRVING.

[February 17, 1837]

[LETTER TO WILLIAM CULLEN BRYANT]

To Mr. William Cullen Bryant, Esq.

Sir,—It was not until this moment that I saw your letter in the Plain-dealer of Saturday last. I cannot express to you how much it has shocked and grieved me. Not having read any of the comments of the editor of the Plaindealer on the letter which I addressed to him, and being in the country, out of the way of hearing the comments of others, I was totally ignorant of the construction put upon the passages of that letter, which you have cited.—Whatever construction these passages may be susceptible of, I do assure you, Sir, I never supposed, nor had the remotest intention to insinuate, that you had the least participation in the attack recently made upon my character by the editor of the above mentioned paper, or that you entertained feelings which could in any degree be gratified by such an attack. Had I thought you chargeable with such hostility, I should have made the charge directly and explicitly, and not by innuendo.

The little opportunity I have had, Sir, of judging of your private character, has only tended to confirm the opinion I had formed of you from your poetic writings, which breathe a spirit too pure, amiable and elevated, to permit me, for a moment, to think you capable of any thing ungenerous or unjust.

As to the alteration of a word in the London edition of your poems, which others have sought to nurture into a root of bitterness between us, I have already stated my motives for it, and the embarrassment in which I was placed. I regret extremely that it should not have met with your approbation, and sincerely apologize to you for the liberty I was persuaded to take: a liberty, I freely acknowledge, the least excusable with writings like yours, in which it is difficult to alter a word without marring a beauty.

Believe me, Sir, with perfect respect and esteem, very truly yours,

WASHINGTON IRVING.

Thursday morning, Feb. 16th.

[TOAST AT THE BOOKSELLERS' DINNER, MARCH 30, 1837]

Mr. Washington Irving being called upon for a toast observed, that he meant to propose the health of an individual whom he was sure all present would delight to honor—of Samuel Rogers, the Poet. Mr. Irving observed that, in a long intimacy with Mr. Rogers, he had ever found him an enlightened and liberal friend of America and Americans. Possessing great influence in the world of literature and the fine arts in Great Britain from his acknowledged soundness of judgement and refinement of taste, he had often exerted it in the kindest and most gracious manner in fostering, encouraging, and bringing into notice the talents of youthful American artists. He had also manifested, on all occasions, the warmest sympathy in the success of American writers, and the promptest disposition to acknowledge and point out their merits. "I am led to these remarks," added Mr. Irving, "by a letter received yesterday from Mr. Rogers acknowledging the receipt of a volume of Halleck's poems which I had sent to him; and expressing his opinion of their merits." Mr. Irving here read the following extract from the letter:

" 'With Mr. Halleck's poems I was already acquainted—particularly with the two first in the volume, and I cannot say how much I admired them always. They are better than any thing we can do just now on our side of the Atlantic, and I hope he will not be idle, but continue long to delight us. When he comes here again he must not content himself with looking on the outside of my house, as I am told he did once—but knock and ring and ask for me as for an old acquaintance.—I should say indeed if I am here to be found, for if he or you, my dear friend, delay your coming much longer, I shall have no hope of seeing either of you on this side of the grave.' " (Mr. Rogers is now in his seventy fifth year, and has recently been much out of health.)

Mr. Irving concluded by giving as a toast: "Samuel Rogers—the friend of American genius."

The company all rose and drank the health standing, with the greatest enthusiasm.

[March, 1839]

[LETTER OF "GEOFFREY CRAYON" TO THE
EDITOR OF THE *KNICKERBOCKER MAGAZINE*]

TO THE EDITOR OF THE KNICKERBOCKER.

Sir: I have observed that as a man advances in life, he is subject to a kind of plethora of the mind, doubtless occasioned by the vast accumulation of wisdom and experience upon the brain. Hence he is apt to become narrative and admonitory, that is to say, fond of telling long stories, and of doling out advice, to the small profit and great annoyance of his friends. As I have a great horror of becoming the oracle, or, more technically speaking, the "bore," of the domestic circle, and would much rather bestow my wisdom and tediousness upon the world at large, I have always sought to ease off this surcharge of the intellect by means of my pen, and hence have inflicted divers gossipping volumes upon the patience of the public. I am tired, however, of writing volumes; they do not afford exactly the relief I require; there is too much preparation, arrangement, and parade, in this set form of coming before the public. I am growing too indolent and unambitious for any thing that requires labor or display. I have thought, therefore, of securing to myself a snug corner in some periodical work, where I might, as it were, loll at my ease in my elbow chair, and chat sociably with the public, as with an old friend, on any chance subject that might pop into my brain.

In looking around, for this purpose, upon the various excellent periodicals with which our country abounds, my eye was struck by the title of your work—"THE KNICKERBOCKER." My heart leaped at the sight.

DIEDRICH KNICKERBOCKER, Sir, was one of my earliest and most valued friends, and the recollection of him is associated with some of the pleasantest scenes of my youthful days. To explain this, and to show how I came into possession of sundry of his posthumous works, which I have from time to time given to the world, permit me to relate a few particulars of our early intercourse. I give them with the more confidence, as I know the interest you take in that departed worthy whose name and effigy are stamped upon your title-page, and as they will be found important to the better understanding and relishing divers communications I may have to make to you.

My first acquaintance with that great and good man, for such I may venture to call him, now that the lapse of some thirty years has shrouded his name with venerable antiquity, and the popular voice has elevated him to the rank of the classic historians of yore, my first acquaintance with him was formed on the banks of the Hudson, not far from the wizard region of Sleepy Hollow. He had come there in the course of his researches among the Dutch neighborhoods for materials for his immortal history. For this purpose, he was ransacking the archives of one of the most ancient and historical mansions in the country. It was a lowly edifice, built in the time of the Dutch dynasty, and stood on a green bank, overshadowed by trees, from which it peeped forth upon the Great Tappan Zee, so famous among early Dutch navigators. A bright pure spring welled up at the foot of the green bank; a wild brook came babbling down a neighboring ravine, and threw itself into a little woody cove, in front of the mansion. It was indeed as quiet and sheltered a nook as the heart of man could require, in which to take refuge from the cares and troubles of the world; and as such, it had been chosen in old times, by Wolfert Acker, one of the privy councillors of the renowned Peter Stuyvesant.

This worthy but ill-starred man had led a weary and worried life, throughout the stormy reign of the chivalric Peter, being one of those unlucky wights with whom the world is ever at variance, and who are kept in a continual fume and fret, by the wickedness of mankind. At the time of the subjugation of the province by the English, he retired hither in high dudgeon; with the bitter determination to bury himself from the world, and live here in peace and quietness for the remainder of his days. In token of this fixed resolution, he inscribed over his door the favorite Dutch motto, "Lust in Rust," (pleasure in repose.) The mansion was thence called "Wolfert's Rust"—Wolfert's Rest; but in process of time, the name was vitiated into Wolfert's Roost, probably from its quaint cock-loft look, or from its having a weather-cock perched on every gable. This name it continued to bear, long after the unlucky Wolfert was driven forth once more upon a wrangling world, by the tongue of a termagant wife; for it passed into a proverb through the neighborhood, and has been handed down by tradition, that the cock of the Roost was the most henpecked bird in the country.

This primitive and historical mansion has since passed through many changes and trials, which it may be my lot hereafter to notice. At the time of the sojourn of Diedrich Knickerbocker, it was in possession of the gallant family of the Van Tassels, who have figured so conspicuously in his writings. What appears to have given it peculiar value, in his eyes, was the rich treasury of historical facts here secretly hoarded up, like buried gold; for it is said that Wolfert Acker, when he retreated from New Amsterdam, carried off with him many of the records and journals of the province, pertaining to the Dutch dynasty; swearing that they should never fall into the hands of the English. These, like the lost books of Livy, had baffled the research of former historians; but these did I find the indefatigable Diedrich diligently deciphering. He was already a sage in years and experience, I but an idle stripling; yet he did not despise my youth and ignorance, but took me kindly by the hand, and led me gently into those paths of local and traditional lore which he was so fond of exploring. I sat with him in his little chamber at the Roost, and watched the antiquarian patience and perseverance with which he deciphered those venerable Dutch documents, worse than Herculanean manuscripts. I sat with him by the spring, at the foot of the green bank, and listened to his heroic tales about the worthies of the olden time, the paladins of New Amsterdam. I accompanied him in his legendary researches about Tarrytown and Sing-Sing, and explored with him the spell-bound recesses of Sleepy Hollow. I was present at many of his conferences with the good old Dutch burghers and their wives, from whom he derived many of those marvellous facts not laid down in books or records, and which give such superior value and authenticity to his history, over all others that have been written concerning the New Netherlands.

But let me check my proneness to dilate upon this favorite theme; I may recur to it hereafter. Suffice it to say, the intimacy thus formed, continued for a considerable time; and in company with the worthy Diedrich, I visited many of the places celebrated by his pen. The currents of our lives at length diverged. He remained at home to complete his mighty work, while a vagrant fancy led me to wander about the world. Many, many years elapsed, before I returned to the parent soil. In the interim, the venerable historian of the New Netherlands had been gathered to his fathers, but his name had risen to renown. His native city, that city in which he so much delighted, had decreed all manner of costly honors to his memory. I found his effigy imprinted upon new-year cakes, and devoured with eager relish by holiday urchins; a great oyster-house bore the name of "Knickerbocker Hall;" and I narrowly escaped the pleasure of being run over by a Knickerbocker omnibus!

Proud of having associated with a man who had achieved such greatness, I now recalled our early intimacy with tenfold pleasure, and sought to revisit the scenes we had trodden together. The most important of these was the mansion of the Van Tassels, the Roost of the unfortunate Wolfert. Time, which changes all things, is but slow in its operations upon a Dutchman's dwelling. I found the venerable and quaint little edifice much as I had seen it during the sojourn of Diedrich. There stood his elbow-chair in the corner of the room he had occupied; the old-fashioned Dutch writing desk at which he had pored over the chronicles of the Manhattoes; there was the old wooden chest, with the archives left by Wolfert Acker, many of which, however, had been fired off as wadding from the long duck gun of the Van Tassels. The scene around the mansion was still the same; the green bank; the spring beside which I had listened to the legendary narratives of the historian; the wild brook babbling down to the woody cove, and the overshadowing locust trees, half shutting out the prospect of the Great Tappan Zee.

As I looked round upon the scene, my heart yearned at the recollection of my departed friend, and I wistfully eyed the mansion which he had inhabited, and which was fast mouldering to decay. The thought struck me to arrest the desolating hand of Time; to rescue the historic pile from utter ruin, and to make it the closing scene of my wanderings; a quiet home, where I might enjoy "lust in rust" for the remainder of my days. It is true, the fate of the unlucky Wolfert passed across my mind; but I consoled myself with the reflection that I was a bachelor, and that I had no termagant wife to dispute the sovereignty of the Roost with me.

I have become possessor of the Roost! I have repaired and renovated it with religious care, in the genuine Dutch style, and have adorned and illustrated it with sundry reliques of the glorious days of the New Netherlands. A venerable weather-cock, of portly Dutch dimensions, which once battled with the wind on the top of the Stadt-House of New Amsterdam, in the time of Peter Stuyvesant, now erects its crest on the gable end of my edifice; a gilded horse, in full gallop, once the weather-cock of the great Vander Heyden Palace of Albany, now glitters in the sunshine, and veers with every breeze, on the peaked turret over my portal: my sanctum sanctorum is the chamber once honored by the illustrious Diedrich, and it is from his elbow-chair, and his identical old Dutch writing desk, that I pen this rambling epistle.

Here then, have I set up my rest, surrounded by the recollections of early days, and the mementos of the historian of the Manhattoes, with that glorious river before me, which flows with such majesty through his works, and which has ever been to me a river of delight.

I thank God I was born on the banks of the Hudson! I think it an invaluable advantage to be born and brought up in the neighborhood of some grand and noble object in nature; a river, a lake, or a mountain. We make a friendship with it, we in a manner ally ourselves to it for life. It remains an object of our pride and affections, a rallying point, to call us home again after all our wanderings. "The things which we have learned in our childhood," says an old writer, "grow up with our souls, and unite themselves to it." So it is with the scenes among which we have passed our early days; they influence the whole course of our thoughts and feelings; and I fancy I can trace much of what is good and pleasant in my own heterogeneous compound, to my early companionship with this glorious river. In the warmth of my youthful enthusiasm, I used to clothe it with moral attributes, and almost to give it a soul. I admired its frank, bold, honest character; its noble sincerity and perfect truth. Here was no specious, smiling surface, covering the dangerous sand-bar or perfidious rock; but a stream deep as it was broad, and bearing with honorable faith the bark that trusted to its waves. I gloried in its simple, quiet, majestic, epic flow; ever straight forward. Once indeed, it turns aside for a moment, forced from its course by opposing mountains, but it struggles bravely through them, and immediately resumes its straightforward march. Behold, thought I, an emblem of a good man's course through life; ever simple, open, and direct; or if, overpowered by adverse circumstances, he deviate into error, it is but momentary; he soon recovers his onward and honorable career, and continues it to the end of his pilgrimage.

Excuse this rhapsody, into which I have been betrayed by a revival of early feelings. The Hudson is, in a manner, my first and last love; and after all my wanderings, and seeming infidelities, I return to it with a heart-felt preference over all the other rivers in the world. I seem to catch new life, as I bathe in its ample billows, and inhale the pure breezes of its hills. It is true, the romance of youth is past, that once spread illusions over every scene. I can no longer picture an Arcadia in every green valley; nor a fairy land among the distant mountains; nor a peerless beauty in every villa gleaming among the trees; but though the illusions of youth have faded from the landscape, the recollections of departed years and departed pleasures shed over it the mellow charm of evening sunshine.

Permit me then, Mr. Editor, through the medium of your work, to hold occasional discourse from my retreat, with the busy world I have abandoned. I have much to say about what I have seen, heard, felt, and thought, through the course of a varied and rambling life, and some lucubrations, that have long been encumbering my port-folio; together with divers reminiscences of the venerable historian of the New Netherlands, that may not be unacceptable to those who have taken an interest in his writings, and are desirous of any thing that may cast a light back upon our early history. Let your readers rest assured of one thing, that, though retired from the world, I am not disgusted with it; and that if, in my communings with it, I do not prove very wise, I trust I shall at least prove very good natured.

Which is all at present, from
Yours, etc.,
GEOFFREY CRAYON.

[May, 1839]

SLEEPY HOLLOW

Having pitched my tent, probably for the remainder of my days, in the neighborhood of Sleepy Hollow, I am tempted to give some few

particulars concerning that spell-bound region; especially as it has risen
to historic importance, under the pen of my revered friend and master,
the sage historian of the New Netherlands. Beside, I find the very existence of the place has been held in question by many; who, judging
from its odd name, and from the odd stories current among the vulgar
concerning it, have rashly deemed the whole to be a fanciful creation,
like the Lubber Land of mariners. I must confess there is some apparent
cause for doubt, in consequence of the coloring given by the worthy
Diedrich, to his descriptions of the Hollow; who, in this instance, has
departed a little from his usually sober if not severe style; beguiled,
very probably, by his predilection for the haunts of his youth, and by
a certain lurking taint of romance, whenever any thing connected with
the Dutch was to be described. I shall endeavor to make up for this
amiable error, on the part of my venerable and venerated friend, by presenting the reader with a more precise and statistical account of the
Hollow; though I am not sure that I shall not be prone to lapse, in the
end, into the very error I am speaking of, so potent is the witchery of
the theme.

I believe it was the very peculiarity of its name, and the idea of something mystic and dreamy connected with it, that first led me, in my
boyish ramblings, into Sleepy Hollow. The character of the valley seemed
to answer to the name; the slumber of past ages apparently reigned over
it; it had not awakened to the stir of improvement, which had put all the
rest of the world in a bustle. Here reigned good old long-forgotten fashions; the men were in homespun garbs, evidently the product of their
own farms, and the manufacture of their own wives; the women were in
primitive short gowns and petticoats, with the venerable sun-bonnets of
Holland origin. The lower part of the valley was cut up into small farms,
each consisting of a little meadow and corn-field; an orchard of sprawl-
ing, gnarled apple trees, and a garden, where the rose, the marigold, and
the hollyhock were permitted to skirt the domains of the capacious cabbage, the aspiring pea, and the portly pumpkin. Each had its prolific
little mansion, teeming with children; with an old hat nailed against
the wall for the house-keeping wren; a motherly hen, under a coop on
the grass-plot, clucking to keep around her a brood of vagrant chickens;
a cool stone well, with the moss-covered bucket suspended to the long
balancing pole, according to the antediluvian idea of hydraulics; and
its spinning-wheel humming within doors, the patriarchal music of home
manufacture.

The Hollow at that time was inhabited by families which had existed
there from the earliest times, and which, by frequent intermarriage, had
become so interwoven, as to make a kind of natural commonwealth. As
the families had grown larger, the farms had grown smaller, every new
generation requiring a new subdivision, and few thinking of swarming

from the native hive. In this way, that happy golden mean had been produced, so much extolled by the poets, in which there was no gold, and very little silver. One thing which doubtless contributed to keep up this amiable mean, was a general repugnance to sordid labor. The sage inhabitants of Sleepy Hollow had read in their Bible, which was the only book they studied, that labor was originally inflicted upon man as a punishment of sin; they regarded it, therefore, with pious abhorrence, and never humiliated themselves to it, but in cases of extremity. There seemed, in fact, to be a league and covenant against it, throughout the Hollow, as against a common enemy. Was any one compelled, by dire necessity, to repair his house, mend his fences, build a barn, or get in a harvest, he considered it a great evil, that entitled him to call in the assistance of his friends. He accordingly proclaimed a "bee," or rustic gathering; whereupon all his neighbors hurried to his aid, like faithful allies; attacked the task with the desperate energy of lazy men, eager to overcome a job; and when it was accomplished, fell to eating and drinking, fiddling and dancing, for very joy that so great an amount of labor had been vanquished, with so little sweating of the brow.

Yet let it not be supposed that this worthy community was without its periods of arduous activity. Let but a flock of wild pigeons fly across the valley, and all Sleepy Hollow was wide awake in an instant. The pigeon season had arrived! Every gun and net was forthwith in requisition. The flail was thrown down on the barn floor; the spade rusted in the garden; the plough stood idle in the furrow; every one was to the hill side, and stubble-field, at day break, to shoot or entrap the pigeons, in their periodical migrations.

So, likewise, let but the word be given that the shad were ascending the Hudson, and the worthies of the Hollow were to be seen launched in boats upon the river; setting great stakes, and stretching their nets, like gigantic spider-webs, half across the stream, to the great annoyance of navigators. Such are the wise provisions of Nature, by which she equalizes rural affairs. A laggard at the plough is often extremely industrious with the fowling-piece and fishing net; and whenever a man is an indifferent farmer, he is apt to be a first-rate sportsman. For catching shad and wild pigeons, there were none throughout the country to compare with the lads of Sleepy Hollow.

As I have observed, it was the dreamy nature of the name, that first beguiled me, in the holiday rovings of boyhood, into this sequestered region. I shunned, however, the populous parts of the Hollow, and sought its retired haunts, far in the foldings of the hills, where the Pocantico "winds its wizard stream," sometimes silently and darkly, through solemn woodlands; sometimes sparkling between grassy borders, in fresh green meadows; sometimes stealing along the feet of rugged heights, under the balancing sprays of beech and chestnut trees. A thousand crystal springs, with which this neighborhood abounds, sent down from the hill-sides their whimpering rills, as if to pay tribute to the Pocantico. In this stream I first essayed my unskilful hand at angling. I loved to loiter along it, with rod in hand, watching my float as it whirled amid the eddies, or drifted into dark holes, under twisted roots and sunken logs, where the largest fish are apt to lurk. I delighted to follow it into the brown recesses of the woods; to throw by my fishing gear, and sit upon rocks beneath towering oaks and clambering grape-vines; bathe my feet in the cool current, and listen to the summer breeze playing among the tree-tops. My boyish fancy clothed all nature around me with ideal charms, and peopled it with the fairy beings I had read of in poetry and fable. Here it was I gave full scope to my incipient habit of day-dreaming, and to a certain propensity to weave up and tint sober realities with my own whims and imaginings, which has sometimes made life a little too much like an Arabian tale to me, and this "working day world" rather like a region of romance.

The great gathering place of Sleepy Hollow, in those days, was the church. It stood outside of the Hollow, near the great highway; on a green bank, shaded by trees, with the Pocantico sweeping round it, and emptying itself into a spacious mill-pond. At that time, the Sleepy Hollow church was the only place of worship for a wide neighborhood. It was a venerable edifice, partly of stone and partly of brick, the latter having been brought from Holland, in the early days of the province, before the arts in the New Netherlands could aspire to such a fabrication. On a stone above the porch, were inscribed the names of the founders, Frederick Filipsen, a mighty patroon of the olden time, who reigned over a wide extent of this neighborhood, and held his seat of power at Yonkers; and his wife, Katrina Van Courtlandt, of the no less potent line of the Van Courtlandts of Croton, who lorded it over a great part of the Highlands.

The capacious pulpit, with its wide-spreading sounding board, were likewise early importations from Holland; as also the communion-table, of massive form and curious fabric. The same might be said of a weather-cock, perched on top of the belfry, and which was considered orthodox in all windy matters, until a small pragmatical rival was set up, on the other end of the church, above the chancel. This latter bore, and still bears, the initials of Frederick Filipsen, and assumed great airs in consequence. The usual contradiction ensued that always exists among church weather-cocks, which can never be brought to agree as to the point from which the wind blows, having doubtless acquired, from their position, the Christian propensity to schism and controversy.

Behind the church, and sloping up a gentle acclivity, was its capacious burying-ground, in which slept the earliest fathers of this rural neighborhood. Here were tombstones of the rudest sculpture; on which were inscribed, in Dutch, the names and virtues of many of the first settlers, with their portraitures curiously carved in similitude of cherubs. Long rows of grave-stones, side by side, of similar names, but various dates, showed that generation after generation of the same families had followed each other, and been garnered together in this last gathering place of kindred.

Let me speak of this quiet grave-yard with all due reverence, for I owe it amends for the heedlessness of my boyish days. I blush to acknowledge the thoughtless frolic with which, in company with other whipsters, I have sported within its sacred bounds, during the intervals of worship; chasing butterflies, plucking wild flowers, or vieing with each other who could leap over the tallest tomb-stones; until checked by the stern voice of the sexton.

The congregation was, in those days, of a really rural character. City fashions were as yet unknown, or unregarded, by the country people of the neighborhood. Steam-boats had not as yet confounded town with country. A weekly market-boat from Tarrytown, the "Farmers' Daughter," navigated by the worthy Gabriel Requa, was the only communication between all these parts and the metropolis. A rustic belle in those days considered a visit to the city in much the same light as one of our modern fashionable ladies regards a visit to Europe; an event that may possibly take place once in the course of a life-time, but to be hoped for, rather than expected. Hence the array of the congregation was chiefly after the primitive fashions existing in Sleepy Hollow; or if, by chance, there was a departure from the Dutch sun-bonnet, or the apparition of a bright gown of flowered calico, it caused quite a sensation throughout the church. As the dominie generally preached by the hour, a bucket of water was providently placed on a bench near the door, in summer, with a tin cup beside it, for the solace of those who might be athirst, either from the heat of the weather, or the drouth of the sermon.

Around the pulpit, and behind the communion-table, sat the elders of the church, reverend, gray-headed, leathern-visaged men, whom I regarded with awe, as so many apostles. They were stern in their sanctity, kept a vigilant eye upon my giggling companions and myself, and shook a rebuking finger at any boyish device to relieve the tediousness of compulsory devotion. Vain, however, were all their efforts at vigilance. Scarcely had the preacher held forth for half an hour, on one of his interminable sermons, than it seemed as if the drowsy influence of Sleepy Hollow breathed into the place: one by one the congregation sank into slumber; the sanctified elders leaned back in their pews, spreading their handkerchiefs over their faces, as if to keep off the flies; while the locusts in the neighboring trees would spin out their sultry summer notes, as if in imitation of the sleep-provoking tones of the dominie.

I have thus endeavored to give an idea of Sleepy Hollow and its church, as I recollect them to have been in the days of my boyhood. It was in my stripling days, when a few years had passed over my head, that I revisited them, in company with the venerable Diedrich. I shall never forget the antiquarian reverence with which that sage and excellent man contemplated the church. It seemed as if all his pious enthusiasm for the ancient Dutch dynasty swelled within his bosom at the sight. The tears stood in his eyes, as he regarded the pulpit and the communion-table; even the very bricks that had come from the mother country, seemed to touch a filial chord within his bosom. He almost bowed in deference to the stone above the porch, containing the names of Frederick Filipsen and Katrina Van Courtlandt, regarding it as the linking together of those patronymic names, once so famous along the banks of the Hudson; or rather as a key-stone, binding that mighty Dutch family connexion of yore, one foot of which rested on Yonkers, and the other on the Croton. Nor did he forbear to notice with admiration, the windy contest which had been carried on, since time immemorial, and with real Dutch perseverance, between the two weather-cocks; though I could easily perceive he coincided with the one which had come from Holland.

Together we paced the ample church-yard. With deep veneration would he turn down the weeds and branches that obscured the modest brown grave-stones, half sunk in earth, on which were recorded, in Dutch, the names of the patriarchs of ancient days, the Ackers, the Van Tassels, and the Van Warts. As we sat on one of the tomb-stones, he recounted to me the exploits of many of these worthies; and my heart smote me, when I heard of their great doings in days of yore, to think how heedlessly I had once sported over their graves.

From the church, the venerable Diedrich proceeded in his researches up the Hollow. The genius of the place seemed to hail its future historian. All nature was alive with gratulation. The quail whistled a greeting from the corn-field; the robin carolled a song of praise from the orchard; the loquacious cat-bird flew from bush to bush, with restless wing, proclaiming his approach in every variety of note, and anon would whisk about, and perk inquisitively into his face, as if to get a knowledge of his physiognomy; the wood-pecker, also, tapped a tattoo on the hollow apple-tree, and then peered knowingly round the trunk, to see how the great Diedrich relished his salutation; while the ground-squirrel scampered along the fence, and occasionally whisked his tail over his head, by way of a huzza!

The worthy Diedrich pursued his researches in the valley with characteristic devotion; entering familiarly into the various cottages, and gossipping with the simple folk, in the style of their own simplicity. I confess my heart yearned with admiration, to see so great a man, in his eager quest after knowledge, humbly demeaning himself to curry favor with the humblest; sitting patiently on a three-legged stool, patting the children, and taking a purring grimalkin on his lap, while he conciliated the good will of the old Dutch housewife, and drew from her long ghost stories, spun out to the humming accompaniment of her wheel.

His greatest treasure of historic lore, however, was discovered in an old goblin-looking mill, situated among rocks and water-falls, with clanking wheels, and rushing streams, and all kinds of uncouth noises. A horse-shoe, nailed to the door to keep off witches and evil spirits, showed that this mill was subject to awful visitations. As we approached it, an old negro thrust his head, all dabbled with flour, out of a hole above the water-wheel, and grinned, and rolled his eyes, and looked like the very hobgoblin of the place. The illustrious Diedrich fixed upon him, at once, as the very one to give him that invaluable kind of information, never to be acquired from books. He beckoned him from his nest, sat with him by the hour on a broken mill-stone, by the side of the waterfall, heedless of the noise of the water, and the clatter of the mill; and I verily believe it was to his conference with this African sage, and the precious revelations of the good dame of the spinning wheel, that we are indebted for the surprising though true history of Ichabod Crane and the headless horseman, which has since astounded and edified the world.

But I have said enough of the good old times of my youthful days; let me speak of the Hollow as I found it, after an absence of many years, when it was kindly given me once more to revisit the haunts of my boyhood. It was a genial day, as I approached that fated region. The warm sunshine was tempered by a slight haze, so as to give a dreamy effect to the landscape. Not a breath of air shook the foliage. The broad Tappan Sea was without a ripple, and the sloops, with drooping sails, slept on its glassy bosom. Columns of smoke, from burning brush-wood, rose lazily from the folds of the hills, on the opposite side of the river, and slowly expanded in mid air. The distant lowing of a cow, or the noontide crowing of a cock, coming faintly to the ear, seemed to illustrate, rather than disturb, the drowsy quiet of the scene.

I entered the Hollow with a beating heart. Contrary to my apprehensions, I found it but little changed. The march of intellect, which had made such rapid strides along every river and highway, had not yet, apparently, turned down into this favored valley. Perhaps the wizard spell of ancient days still reigned over the place, binding up the faculties of the inhabitants in happy contentment with things as they had been handed down to them from yore. There were the same little farms and farm-houses, with their old hats for the house-keeping wren; their stone wells, moss-covered buckets, and long balancing poles.

There were the same little rills, whimpering down to pay their tributes to the Pocantico; while that wizard stream still kept on its course, as of old, through solemn woodlands and fresh green meadows: nor were there wanting joyous holiday boys, to loiter along its banks, as I had done; throw their pin-hooks in the stream, or launch their mimic barks. I watched them with a kind of melancholy pleasure, wondering whether they were under the same spell of the fancy, that once rendered this valley a fairy land to me. Alas! alas! to me every thing now stood revealed in its simple reality. The echoes no longer answered with wizard tongues; the dream of youth was at an end; the spell of Sleepy Hollow was broken!

I sought the ancient church, on the following Sunday. There it stood, on its green bank, among the trees; the Pocantico swept by it in a deep dark stream, where I had so often angled; there expanded the mill-pond, as of old, with the cows under the willows on its margin, knee-deep in water, chewing the cud, and lashing the flies from their sides with their tails. The hand of improvement, however, had been busy with the venerable pile. The pulpit, fabricated in Holland, had been superseded by one of modern construction, and the front of the semi-Gothic edifice was decorated by a semi-Grecian portico. Fortunately, the two weather-cocks remained undisturbed on their perches, at each end of the church, and still kept up a diametrical opposition to each other, on all points of windy doctrine.

On entering the church, the changes of time continued to be apparent. The elders round the pulpit were men whom I had left in the game-some frolic of their youth, but who had succeeded to the sanctity of station of which they once had stood so much in awe. What most struck my eye, was the change in the female part of the congregation. Instead of the primitive garbs of homespun manufacture, and antique Dutch fashion, I beheld French sleeves, French capes, and French collars, and a fearful fluttering of French ribbands.

When the service was ended, I sought the church-yard in which I had sported in my unthinking days of boyhood. Several of the modest brown stones, on which were recorded, in Dutch, the names and virtues of the patriarchs, had disappeared, and had been succeeded by others of white marble, with urns, and wreaths, and scraps of English tomb-stone poetry, marking the intrusion of taste, and literature, and the English language, in this once unsophisticated Dutch neighborhood.

As I was stumbling about among these silent yet eloquent memorials of the dead, I came upon names familiar to me; of those who had paid the debt of nature during the long interval of my absence. Some I remembered, my companions in boyhood, who had sported with me on the very sod under which they were now mouldering; others who in those days had been the flower of the yeomanry, figuring in Sunday finery on the church green; others, the white-haired elders of the sanctuary, once arrayed in awful sanctity around the pulpit, and ever ready to rebuke the ill-timed mirth of the wanton stripling, who, now a man, sobered by years, and schooled by vicissitudes, looked down pensively upon their graves. "Our fathers," thought I, "where are they!—and the prophets, can they live for ever!"

I was disturbed in my meditations, by the noise of a troop of idle urchins, who came gambolling about the place where I had so often gambolled. They were checked, as I and my playmates had often been, by the voice of the sexton, a man staid in years and demeanor. I looked wistfully in his face; had I met him any where else, I should probably have passed him by without remark; but here I was alive to the traces of former times, and detected in the demure features of this guardian of the sanctuary, the lurking lineaments of one of the very playmates I have alluded to. We renewed our acquaintance. He sat down beside me, on one of the tomb-stones over which we had leaped in our juvenile sports, and we talked together about our boyish days, and held edifying discourse on the instability of all sublunary things, as instanced in the scene around us. He was rich in historic lore, as to the events of the last thirty years, and the circumference of thirty miles, and from him I learned the appalling revolution that was taking place throughout the neighborhood. All this I clearly perceived he attributed to the boasted march of intellect, or rather to the all-pervading influence of steam. He bewailed the times when the only communication with town was by the weekly market-boat, the "Farmers' Daughter," which, under the pilotage of the worthy Gabriel Requa, braved the perils of the Tappan Sea. Alas! Gabriel and the "Farmers' Daughter" slept in peace. Two steam-boats now splashed and paddled up daily to the little rural port of Tarrytown. The spirit of speculation and improvement had seized even upon that once quiet and unambitious little dorp. The whole neighborhood was laid out into town lots. Instead of the little tavern below the hill, where the farmers used to loiter on market days, and indulge in cider and gingerbread, an ambitious hotel, with cupola and verandahs, now crested the summit, among churches built in the Grecian and Gothic styles, showing the great increase of piety and polite taste in the neighborhood. As to Dutch dresses and sun-bonnets, they were no longer tolerated, or even thought of; not a farmer's daughter but now went to town for the fashions; nay, a city milliner had recently set up in the village, who threatened to reform the heads of the whole neighborhood.

I had heard enough! I thanked my old playmate for his intelligence, and departed from the Sleepy Hollow church, with the sad conviction that I had beheld the last lingerings of the good old Dutch times, in this once favored region. If any thing were wanting to confirm this impression, it would be the intelligence which has just reached me, that a bank is about to be established in the aspiring little port just mentioned. The fate of the neighborhood is, therefore, sealed. I see no hope of averting it. The golden mean is at an end. The country is suddenly to be deluged with wealth. The late simple farmers are to become bank directors, and drink claret and champagne; and their wives and daughters to figure in French hats and feathers; for French wines and French fashions commonly keep pace with paper money. How can I hope that even Sleepy Hollow can escape the general inundation? In a little while, I fear the slumber of ages will be at end; the strum of the piano will succeed to the hum of the spinning wheel; the trill of the Italian opera to the nasal quaver of Ichabod Crane; and the antiquarian visitor to the Hollow, in the petulance of his disappointment, may pronounce all that I have recorded of that once favored region, a fable.

GEOFFREY CRAYON.

[May, 1839]

[LETTER OF "HIRAM CRACKENTHORPE" TO THE EDITOR OF THE *KNICKERBOCKER MAGAZINE*]

TO THE EDITOR OF THE KNICKERBOCKER.

SIR: In your last number, I read with great interest an article entitled "The First Locomotive." It throws light upon an incident which has long been a theme of marvel in the Far West. You must know that I was one among the first band of trappers that crossed the Rocky Mountains. We had encamped one night on a ridge of the Black Hills, and were wrapped up in our blankets, in the midst of our first sleep, when we were roused by the man who stood sentinel, who cried out, "Wild fire, by ——!" We started on our feet, and beheld a streak of fire coming across the prairies, for all the world like lightning, or a shooting star. We had hardly time to guess what it might be, when it came up, whizzing, and clanking, and making a tremendous racket, and we saw something huge and black, with wheels and traps of all kinds; and an odd-looking being on top of it, busy as they say the devil is in a gale of wind. In fact, some of our people thought it was the old gentleman himself, taking an airing in one of his infernal carriages; others thought it was the opening of one of the seals in the Revelations. Some of the stoutest fellows fell on their knees, and began to pray; a Kentuckian plucked up courage enough to hail the infernal coachman as he passed, and ask whither he was driving; but the speed with which he whirled by, and the rattling of his machine, prevented our catching more than the last words: "Slam bang to etarnal smash!" In five minutes more, he was across the prairies, beyond the Black Hills, and we saw him shooting, like a jack-a-lantern, over the Rocky Mountains.

The next day we tracked his course. He had cut through a great drove of buffalo, some hundred or two of which lay cut up as though the butchers had been there; we heard of him afterward, driving through a village of Black Feet, and smashing the lodge of the chief, with all his family. Beyond the Rocky Mountains, we could hear nothing more of him; so that we concluded he had ended his brimstone career, by driving into one of the craters that still smoke among the peaks.

This circumstance, Sir, as I said, has caused much speculation in the Far West; but many set it down as a "trapper's story," which is about equivalent to a traveller's tale; neither would the author of "Astoria" and "Bonneville's Adventures" admit it into his works, though heaven knows he has not been over squeamish in such matters. The article in your last number, above alluded to, has now cleared up the matter, and henceforth I shall tell the story without fear of being hooted at. I make no doubt, Sir, this supposed infernal apparition was nothing more nor less than Jabez Doolittle, with his Locomotive, on his way to Astoria.

> "Who knows, who knows what wastes
> He is now careering o'er?"

as the song goes; perhaps scouring California; perhaps whizzing away to the North Pole. One thing is certain, and satisfactory; he is the first person that ever crossed the Rocky Mountains on wheels; his transit shows that those mountains are traversable with carriages, and that it is perfectly easy to have a rail-road to the Pacific. If such road should ever be constructed, I hope, in honor of the great projector who led the way, it may be called the "Doolittle Rail-road;" unless that name should have been given as characteristic, to some of the many railroads already in progress.

Your humble servant,
HIRAM CRACKENTHORPE, of St. Louis.

[August, 1839]

NATIONAL NOMENCLATURE

TO THE EDITOR OF THE KNICKERBOCKER.

SIR: I am somewhat of the same way of thinking, in regard to names, with that profound philosopher, Mr. Shandy, the elder, who maintained that some inspired high thoughts and heroic aims, while others entailed irretrievable meanness and vulgarity; insomuch that a man might sink under the insignificance of his name, and be absolutely "Nicodemused into nothing." I have ever, therefore, thought it a great hardship for a man to be obliged to struggle through life with some ridiculous or ignoble *"Christian* name," as it is too often falsely called, inflicted on him in infancy, when he could not choose for himself; and would give him free liberty to change it for one more to his taste, when he had arrived at years of discretion.

I have the same notion with respect to local names. Some at once prepossess us in favor of a place: others repel us, by unlucky associations of the mind; and I have known scenes worthy of being the very haunt of poetry and romance, yet doomed to irretrievable vulgarity, by some ill-chosen name, which not even the magic numbers of a HALLECK or a BRYANT could elevate into poetical acceptation.

This is an evil unfortunately too prevalent throughout our country. Nature has stamped the land with features of sublimity and beauty; but some of our noblest mountains and loveliest streams are in danger of remaining for ever unhonored and unsung, from bearing appellations totally abhorrent to the Muse. In the first place, our country is deluged with names taken from places in the old world, and applied to places having no possible affinity or resemblance to their namesakes. This betokens a forlorn poverty of invention, and a second-hand spirit, content to cover its nakedness with borrowed or cast-off clothes of Europe.

Then we have a shallow affectation of scholarship: the whole catalogue of ancient worthies is shaken out from the back of Lempriere's Classical Dictionary, and a wide region of wild country sprinkled over with the names of the heroes, poets, and sages of antiquity, jumbled into the most whimsical juxtaposition. Then we have our political god-fathers; topographical engineers, perhaps, or persons employed by government to survey and lay out townships. These, forsooth, glorify the patrons that give them bread; so we have the names of the great official men of the day scattered over the land, as if they were the real "salt of the earth," with which it was to be seasoned. Well for us is it, when these official great men happen to have names of fair acceptation; but wo unto us, should a Tubbs or a Potts be in power: we are sure, in a little while, to find Tubbsvilles and Pottsylvanias springing up in every direction.

Under these melancholy dispensations of taste and loyalty, there-fore, Mr. Editor, it is with a feeling of dawning hope, that I have lately perceived the attention of persons of intelligence beginning to be awakened on this subject. I trust if the matter should once be taken up, it will not be readily abandoned. We are yet young enough, as a country, to remedy and reform much of what has been done, and to release many of our rising towns and cities, and our noble streams, from names calculated to vulgarize the land.

I have, on a former occasion, suggested the expediency of searching out the original Indian names of places, and wherever they are striking and euphonious, and those by which they have been superseded are glaringly objectionable, to restore them. They would have the merit of originality, and of belonging to the country; and they would remain as reliques of the native lords of the soil, when every other vestige had disappeared. Many of these names may easily be regained, by reference to old title-deeds, and to the archives of states and counties. In my own case, by examining the records of the county clerk's office, I have discovered the Indian names of various places and objects in the neighborhood, and have found them infinitely superior to the trite, poverty-stricken names which had been given by the settlers. A beautiful pastoral stream, for instance, which winds for many a mile through one of the loveliest little valleys in the state, has long been known by the common-place name of the "Saw-mill River." In the old Indian grants, it is designated as the Neperan. Another, a perfectly wizard stream, which winds through the wildest recesses of Sleepy Hollow, bears the hum-drum name of Mill Creek: in the Indian grants, it sustains the euphonious title of the Pocantico.

Similar researches have released Long-Island from many of those paltry and vulgar names which fringed its beautiful shores; their Cow Bays, and Cow Necks, and Oyster Ponds, and Musquito Coves, which spread a spell of vulgarity over the whole island, and kept persons of taste and fancy at a distance.

It would be an object worthy the attention of the historical societies, which are springing up in various parts of the Union, to have maps executed of their respective states or neighborhoods, in which all the Indian local names should, as far as possible, be restored. In fact, it appears to me that the nomenclature of the country is almost of sufficient importance for the foundation of a distinct society; or rather, a corres-ponding association of persons of taste and judgment, of all parts of the Union. Such an association, if properly constituted and composed, comprising especially all the literary talent of the country, though it might not have legislative power in its enactments, yet would have the all-pervading power of the press; and the changes in nomenclature which it might dictate, being at once adopted by elegant writers in prose and

poetry, and interwoven with the literature of the country, would ultimately pass into popular currency.

Should such a reforming association arise, I beg to recommend to its
attention all those mongrel names that have the adjective *New* prefixed
to them, and pray they may be one and all kicked out of the country.
I am for none of these second-hand appellations, that stamp us a second-
hand people, and that are to perpetuate us a new country to the end of
time. Odds my life! Mr. Editor, I hope and trust we are to live to be
an old nation, as well as our neighbors, and have no idea that our cities,
when they shall have attained to venerable antiquity, shall still be
dubbed *New*-York, and *New*-London, and *new* this and *new* that, like
the Pont Neuf, (the New Bridge,) at Paris, which is the oldest bridge
in that capital, or like the Vicar of Wakefield's horse, which continued
to be called "the colt," until he died of old age.

Speaking of New-York, reminds me of some observations which I
met with some time since, in one of the public papers, about the name
of our state and city. The writer proposes to substitute for the present
names, those of the STATE OF ONTARIO, and the CITY OF MANHATTAN.
I concur in his suggestion most heartily. Though born and brought up
in the city of New-York, and though I love every stick and stone about
it, yet I do not, nor ever did, relish its name. I like neither its sound nor
its significance. As to its *significance*, the very adjective *new* gives to
our great commercial metropolis a second-hand character, as if referring
to some older, more dignified, and important place, of which it was a
mere copy; though in fact, if I am rightly informed, the whole name
commemorates a grant by Charles II. to his brother, the Duke of York,
made in the spirit of royal munificence, of a tract of country which did
not belong to him. As to the *sound*, what can you make of it, either in
poetry or prose? New-York! Why, Sir, if it were to share the fate of
Troy itself; to suffer ten years' siege, and be sacked and plundered; no
modern Homer would ever be able to elevate the name to epic dignity.

Now, Sir, ONTARIO would be a name worthy of the Empire State. It
bears with it the majesty of that internal sea which washes our north-
western shore. Or, if any objection should be made, from its not being
completely embraced within our boundaries, there is the MOHEGAN, one
of the Indian names for that glorious river, the Hudson, which would
furnish an excellent state appellation. So also New-York might be called
Manhatta, as it is named in some of the early records, and Manhattan
used as the adjective. Manhattan, however, stands well as a substantive,
and "Manhattanese," which I observe Mr. COOPER has adopted in some
of his writings, would be a very good appellation for a citizen of the
commercial metropolis.

A word or two more, Mr. Editor, and I have done. We want a NATIONAL
NAME. We want it poetically, and we want it politically. With the poet-

ical necessity of the case I shall not trouble myself. I leave it to our poets
to tell how they manage to steer that collocation of words "The United
States of North America," down the swelling tide of song, and to float
the whole raft out upon the sea of heroic poesy. I am now speaking of
the mere purposes of common life. How is a citizen of this republic to
designate himself? As an American? There are two Americas, each sub-
divided into various empires, rapidly rising in importance. As a citizen
of the United States? It is a clumsy, lumbering title, yet still it is not
distinctive; for we have now the United States of Central America; and
heaven knows how many "United States" may spring up under the
Proteus changes of Spanish America.

This may appear matter of small concernment; but any one that has
travelled in foreign countries, must be conscious of the embarrassment
and circumlocution sometimes occasioned by the want of a perfectly
distinct and explicit national appellation. In France, when I have announced myself as an American, I have been supposed to belong to one
of the French colonies: in Spain, to be from Mexico, or Peru, or some
other Spanish American country. Repeatedly have I found myself involved in a long geographical and political definition of my national
identity.

Now, Sir, meaning no disrespect to any of our co-heirs of this great
quarter of the world, I am for none of this coparceny in a name, that is
to mingle us up with the riff-raff colonies and off-sets of every nation of
Europe. The title of American may serve to tell the quarter of the world
to which I belong, the same as a Frenchman or an Englishman may call
himself a European; but I want my own peculiar national name, to rally
under. I want an appellation that shall tell at once, and in a way not to
be mistaken, that I belong to this very portion of America, geographical
and political, to which it is my pride and happiness to belong; that I am
of the Anglo-Saxon race which founded this Anglo-Saxon empire in the
wilderness; and that I have no part or parcel with any other race or
empire, Spanish, French, or Portuguese, in either of the Americas. Such
an appellation, Sir, would have magic in it. It would bind every part
of the confederacy together, as with a key-stone; it would be a passport
to the citizen of our republic, throughout the world.

We have it in our power to furnish ourselves with such a national
appellation, from one of the grand and eternal features of our country;
from that noble chain of mountains which formed its back-bone, and
ran through the "old confederacy," when it first declared our national
independence. I allude to the Appalachian or Alleghany mountains. We
might do this without any very inconvenient change in our present titles.
We might still use the phrase, "The United States," substituting Appala-
chia, or Alleghania, (I should prefer the latter,) in place of America.
The title of Appalachian, or Alleghanian, would still announce us as

Americans, but would specify us as citizens of the Great Republic. Even our old national cypher of U. S. A. might remain unaltered, designating the United States of Alleghania.

These are crude ideas, Mr. Editor, hastily thrown out, to elicit the ideas of others, and to call attention to a subject of more national importance than may at first be supposed.

Very respectfully yours,
GEOFFREY CRAYON.

[August, 1839]

DESULTORY THOUGHTS ON CRITICISM

"Let a man write never so well, there are now-a-days a sort of persons they call critics, that, egad, have no more wit in them than so many hobby-horses; but they'll laugh at you, Sir, and find fault, and censure things, that, egad, I'm sure they are not able to do themselves; a sort of envious persons, that emulate the glories of persons of parts, and think to build their fame by calumniation of persons that, egad, to my knowledge, of all persons in the world, are in nature the persons that do as much despise all that, as—a—In fine, I'll say no more of 'em!"

REHEARSAL.

All the world knows the story of the tempest-tossed voyager, who, coming upon a strange coast, and seeing a man hanging in chains, hailed it with joy, as the sign of a civilized country. In like manner we may hail, as a proof of the rapid advancement of civilization and refinement in this country, the increasing number of delinquent authors daily gibbetted for the edification of the public.

In this respect, as in every other, we are "going ahead" with accelerated velocity, and promising to outstrip the superannuated countries of Europe. It is really astonishing to see the number of tribunals incessantly springing up for the trial of literary offences. Independent of the high courts of Oyer and Terminer, the great quarterly reviews, we have innumerable minor tribunals, monthly and weekly, down to the Pie-poudre courts in the daily papers; in so much that no culprit stands so little chance of escaping castigation, as an unlucky author, guilty of an unsuccessful attempt to please the public.

Seriously speaking, however, it is questionable whether our national literature is sufficiently advanced, to bear this excess of criticism; and whether it would not thrive better, if allowed to spring up, for some time longer, in the freshness and vigor of native vegetation. When the worthy Judge Coulter, of Virginia, opened court for the first time in one of the upper counties, he was for enforcing all the rules and regulations that had grown into use in the old, long-settled counties. "This is all very well," said a shrewd old farmer; "but let me tell you, Judge Coulter, you set your coulter too deep for a new soil."

For my part, I doubt whether either writer or reader is benefitted by what is commonly called criticism. The former is rendered cautious and distrustful; he fears to give way to those kindling emotions, and brave sallies of thought, which bear him up to excellence; the latter is made fastidious and cynical; or rather, he surrenders his own independent taste and judgment, and learns to like and dislike at second hand.

Let us, for a moment, consider the nature of this thing called criticism, which exerts such a sway over the literary world. The pronoun *we*, used by critics, has a most imposing and delusive sound. The reader pictures to himself a conclave of learned men, deliberating gravely and scrupulously on the merits of the book in question; examining it page by page, comparing and balancing their opinions, and when they have united in a conscientious verdict, publishing it for the benefit of the world: whereas the criticism is generally the crude and hasty production of an individual, scribbling to while away an idle hour, to oblige a book-seller, or to defray current expenses. How often is it the passing notion of the hour, affected by accidental circumstances; by indisposition, by peevishness, by vapors or indigestion; by personal prejudice, or party feeling. Sometimes a work is sacrificed, because the reviewer wishes a satirical article; sometimes because he wants a humorous one; and sometimes because the author reviewed has become offensively celebrated, and offers high game to the literary marksman.

How often would the critic himself, if a conscientious man, reverse his opinion, had he time to revise it in a more sunny moment; but the press is waiting, the printer's devil is at his elbow; the article is wanted to make the requisite variety for the number of the review, or the author has pressing occasion for the sum he is to receive for the article; so it is sent off, all blotted and blurred; with a shrug of the shoulders, and the consolatory ejaculation: "Pshaw! curse it! it's nothing but a review!"

The critic, too, who dictates thus oracularly to the world, is perhaps some dingy, ill-favored, ill-mannered varlet, who, were he to speak by word of mouth, would be disregarded, if not scoffed at; but such is the magic of types; such the mystic operation of anonymous writing; such the potential effect of the pronoun *we*, that his crude decisions, fulminated through the press, become circulated far and wide, control the opinions of the world, and give or destroy reputation.

Many readers have grown timorous in their judgments, since the all-pervading currency of criticism. They fear to express a revised, frank opinion about any new work, and to relish it honestly and heartily, lest it should be condemned in the next review, and they stand convicted of bad taste. Hence they hedge their opinions, like a gambler his bets, and leave an opening to retract, and retreat, and qualify, and neutralize every unguarded expression of delight, until their very praise declines into a faintness that is damning.

Were every one, on the contrary, to judge for himself, and speak his mind frankly and fearlessly, we should have more true criticism in the world than at present. Whenever a person is pleased with a work, he may be assured that it has good qualities. An author who pleases a variety of readers, must possess substantial powers of pleasing; or, in other words, intrinsic merits; for otherwise we acknowledge an effect, and deny the cause. The reader, therefore, should not suffer himself to be readily shaken from the conviction of his own feelings, by the sweeping censures of pseudo critics. The author he has admired, may be chargeable with a thousand faults; but it is nevertheless beauties and excellencies that have excited his admiration; and he should recollect that taste and judgment are as much evinced in the perception of beauties among defects, as in a detection of defects among beauties. For my part, I honor the blessed and blessing spirit, that is quick to discover and extol all that is pleasing and meritorious. Give me the honest bee, that extracts honey from the humblest weed, but save me from the ingenuity of the spider, which traces its venom, even in the midst of a flower-garden.

If the mere fact of being chargeable with faults and imperfections is to condemn an author, who is to escape? The greatest writers of antiquity have, in this way, been obnoxious to criticism. Aristotle himself has been accused of ignorance; Aristophanes of impiety and buffoonery; Virgil of plagiarism, and a want of invention; Horace of obscurity; Cicero has been said to want vigor and connexion, and Demosthenes to be deficient in nature, and in purity of language. Yet these have all survived the censures of the critic, and flourished on to a glorious immortality. Every now and then, the world is startled by some new doctrines in matters of taste, some levelling attacks on established creeds; some sweeping denunciations of whole generations, or schools of writers, as they are called, who had seemed to be embalmed and canonized in public opinion. Such has been the case, for instance, with Pope, and Dryden, and Addison; who for a time have almost been shaken from their pedestals, and treated as false idols.

It is singular, also, to see the fickleness of the world with respect to its favorites. Enthusiasm exhausts itself, and prepares the way for dislike. The public is always for positive sentiments, and new sensations.

When wearied of admiring, it delights to censure; thus coining a double set of enjoyments out of the same subject. Scott and Byron are scarce cold in their graves, and already we find criticism beginning to call in question those powers which held the world in magic thraldom. Even in our own country, one of its greatest geniuses has had some rough passages with the censors of the press; and instantly criticism begins to unsay all that it has repeatedly said in his praise; and the public are almost led to believe that the pen which has so often delighted them, is absolutely destitute of the power to delight!

If, then, such reverses in opinion as to matters of taste can be so readily brought about, when may an author feel himself secure? Where is the anchoring-ground of popularity, when he may thus be driven from his moorings, and foundered even in harbor? The reader, too, when is he to consider himself safe in admiring, when he sees long-established altars overthrown, and his household deities dashed to the ground?

There is one consolatory reflection. Every abuse carries with it its own remedy or palliation. Thus the excess of crude and hasty criticism, which has of late prevailed throughout the literary world, and threatened to overrun our country, begins to produce its own antidote. Where there is a multiplicity of contradictory paths, a man must make his choice; in so doing, he has to exercise his judgment, and that is one great step to mental independence. He begins to doubt all, where all differ, and but one can be in the right. He is driven to trust to his own discernment, and his natural feelings; and here he is most likely to be safe. The author, too, finding that what is condemned at one tribunal, is applauded at another, though perplexed for a time, gives way at length to the spontaneous impulse of his genius, and the dictates of his taste, and writes in the way most natural to himself. It is thus that criticism, which by its severity may have held the little world of writers in check, may, by its very excess, disarm itself of its terrors, and the hardihood of talent become restored.

G. C.

[September, 1839]

COMMUNIPAW

TO THE EDITOR OF THE KNICKERBOCKER.

Sir: I observe, with pleasure, that you are performing, from time to time, a pious duty, imposed upon you, I may say, by the name you

have adopted as your titular standard, in following in the footsteps
of the venerable KNICKERBOCKER, and gleaning every fact concerning
the early times of the Manhattoes, which may have escaped his hand.
I trust, therefore, a few particulars, legendary and statistical, concerning a place which figures conspicuously in the early pages of
his history, will not be unacceptable: I allude, Sir, to the ancient and
renowned village of Communipaw, which, according to the veracious
Diedrich, and to equally veracious tradition, was the first spot where
our ever-to-be-lamented Dutch progenitors planted their standard, and
cast the seeds of empire, and from whence subsequently sailed the
memorable expedition, under Oloffe the Dreamer, which landed on
the opposite island of Manahatta, and founded the present city of
New York, the city of dreams and speculations.

Communipaw, therefore, may truly be called the parent of New
York; yet it is an astonishing fact, that, though immediately opposite
to the great city it has produced, and its red roofs and tin weathercocks
are actually to be descried, peering above the surrounding apple
orchards, it should be almost as rarely visited, and as little known
by the inhabitants of the metropolis, as if it had been locked up among
the Rocky Mountains. Sir, I think there is something unnatural in
this, especially in these times of ramble and research, when our citizens
are antiquity-hunting in every part of the world. Curiosity, like charity,
should begin at home; and I would enjoin it on our worthy burghers,
especially those of the real Knickerbocker breed, before they send
their sons abroad, to wonder and grow wise among the remains of
Greece and Rome, to let them make a tour of ancient Pavonia, from
Weehawk even to the Kills, and meditate with filial reverence on the
moss grown mansions of Communipaw.

Sir, I look upon this much neglected village as one of the most
remarkable places in the country. The intelligent traveller, as he looks
down upon it from the Bergen Heights, modestly nestled among its
cabbage gardens, while the great flaunting city it has begotten, is
stretching far and wide on the opposite side of the bay—the intelligent
traveller, I say, will be filled with astonishment—not, Sir, at the village
of Communipaw, which in truth is a very small village, but at the
almost incredible fact, that so small a village should have produced
so great a city. It looks to him, in truth, like some squat little dame,
with a tall grenadier of a son strutting by her side; or some motherly
little hen, that has unwittingly hatched out a long legged turkey.

But this is not all for which Communipaw is remarkable—Sir, it is
interesting on another account. It is, to the ancient province of the New
Netherlands, and the classic era of the Dutch dynasty, what Herculaneum and Pompeii are to ancient Rome and the glorious days of
the empire. Here every thing remains in statu quo, as it was in the

days of Oloffe the Dreamer, Walter the Doubter and the other worthies of the Golden Age: the same broad brimmed hats and broad bottomed breeches; the same knee buckles and shoe buckles; the same close quilled caps and linsey woolsey short gowns and petticoats; the same implements and utensils, and forms and fashions; in a word Communipaw, at the present day, is a picture of what New Amsterdam was before the conquest. The "intelligent traveller" aforesaid, as he treads its streets, is struck with the primitive character of every thing around him. Instead of Grecian temples for dwelling houses, with a great column of pine boards in the way of every window, he beholds high, peaked roofs, gable ends to the street with weather cocks at top, and windows of all sorts and sizes; large ones for the grown up members of the family and little ones for the little folk. Instead of cold marble porches; with close locked doors and brass knockers, he sees the doors hospitably open; the worthy burgher smoking his pipe on the old fashioned stoop in front, with his "vrouw" knitting beside him; and the cat and her kittens at their feet, sleeping in the sunshine.

Astonished at the obsolete and old world air of every thing around him, the intelligent traveller demands how all this has come to pass. Herculaneum and Pompeii remain, it is true, in statu quo; unaffected by the varying fashions of centuries; but they were buried by a volcano, and preserved in ashes. What charmed spell has kept this wonderful little place unchanged, though in sight of the most changeful city in the universe?—Has it, too, been buried under its cabbage gardens, and only dug out in modern days for the wonder and edification of the world? The reply involves a point of history, worthy of notice and record and reflecting immortal honor on Communipaw.

At the time when New Amsterdam was invaded and conquered by British foes, as has been related in the history of the venerable Diedrich, a great dispersion took place among the Dutch inhabitants. Many, like the illustrious Peter Stuyvesant, buried themselves in rural retreats in the Bowery; others, like Wolfert Acker, took refuge in various remote parts of the Hudson; but there was one staunch, unconquerable band that determined to keep together and preserve themselves, like seed corn, for the future fructification and perpetuity of the Knickerbocker race. These were headed by one Garret Van Horne, a gigantic Dutchman, the Pelayo of the New Netherlands. Under his guidance they retreated across the bay and buried themselves among the marshes of ancient Pavonia, as did the followers of Pelayo among the mountains of Asturias, when Spain was overrun by its Arabian invaders.

The gallant Van Horne set up his standard at Communipaw, and invited all those to rally under it who were true Dutchmen at heart, and determined to resist all foreign intermixture or encroachment. A strict non-intercourse was observed with the captured city; not a boat ever crossed to it from Communipaw, and the English language was rigorously tabooed throughout the village and its dependencies. Every man was sworn to wear his hat, cut his coat, build his house and harness his horses exactly as his father had done before him; and to permit nothing but the Dutch language to be spoken in his household.

As a citadel of the place and a strong hold for the preservation of every thing Dutch, the gallant Van Horne erected a lordly mansion, with a chimney perched at every corner, which thence derived the aristocratical name of "The House of the Four Chimnies." Hither he transferred many of the precious reliques of New Amsterdam; the great round crowned hat that once covered the capacious head of Walter the Doubter, and the identical shoe with which Peter the Headstrong kicked his pusillanimous counsellors down stairs. St. Nicholas, it is said, took this loyal house under his especial protection; and a Dutch soothsayer predicted, that as long as it should stand, Communipaw would be safe from the intrusion either of Briton or Yankee.

In this house would the gallant Van Horne and his compeers hold frequent councils of war as to the possibility of re-conquering the province from the British; and here would they sit for hours, nay days, together, smoking their pipes, and keeping watch upon the growing city of New York, groaning in spirit whenever they saw a new house erected, or ship launched, and persuading themselves that Admiral Van Tromp would one day or other arrive, to sweep out the invaders with the broom which he carried at his mast-head.

Years rolled by, but Van Tromp never arrived. The British strengthened themselves in the land; and the captured city flourished under their domination. Still the worthies of Communipaw would not despair; something or other they were sure would turn up to restore the power of the Hogen Mogens, the Lords States General; so they kept smoking and smoking, and watching and watching, and turning the same few thoughts over and over in a perpetual circle, which is commonly called deliberating. In the mean time, being hemmed up within a narrow compass, between the broad bay and the Bergen Hills, they grew poorer and poorer, until they had scarce the wherewithal to maintain their pipes in fuel during their endless deliberations.

And now must I relate a circumstance which will call for a little exertion of faith on the part of the reader; but I can only say that, if he doubts it, he had better not utter his doubts in Communipaw, as it is among the religious beliefs of the place. It is, in fact, nothing more or less than a miracle worked by the blessed St. Nicholas for the relief and sustenance of this loyal community.

It so happened, in this time of extremity, that, in the course of cleaning the House of the Four Chimnies, by an ignorant wench, who knew nothing of the historic value of the reliques it contained, the old hat of Walter the Doubter and the executive shoe of Peter the Headstrong were thrown out of doors as rubbish. But mark the consequence. The blessed St. Nicholas kept watch over these precious reliques and wrought out of them a wonderful providence.

The hat of Walter the Doubter, falling on a stercoraceous heap of manure in the rear of the house, began forthwith to vegetate. Its broad brims spread forth grandly and exfoliated, and its round crown swelled, and crimped and consolidated, until the whole became a prodigious cabbage, rivalling in magnitude the capacious head of the Doubter. In a word it was the origin of that renowned species of cabbage, known by all Dutch epicures, by the name of the Governor's Head, and which is, to this day, the glory of Communipaw.

On the other hand, the shoe of Peter Stuyvesant, being thrown into the river in front of the house, gradually hardened and concreted and became covered with barnacles, and at length, turned into a gigantic oyster; being the progenitor of that illustrious species known throughout the gastronomical world by the name of the Governor's Foot.

These miracles were the salvation of Communipaw. The sages of the place immediately saw in them the hand of St. Nicholas, and understood their mystic signification. They set to work with all diligence, to cultivate and multiply these great blessings; and so abundantly did the gubernatorial hat and shoe fructify and increase, that in a little time great patches of cabbages were to be seen extending from the village of Communipaw, quite to the Bergen Hills; while the whole bottom of the bay in front became a vast bed of oysters. Ever since that time this excellent community has been divided into two great classes, those who cultivate the land and those who cultivate the water. The former have devoted themselves to the nurture and edification of cabbages, rearing them in all their varieties; while the latter have formed parks and plantations under water, to which juvenile oysters are transplanted from foreign parts, to finish their education.

As these great sources of profit multiplied upon their hands, the worthy inhabitants of Communipaw began to long for a market at which to dispose of their superabundance. This gradually produced once more an intercourse with New York: but it was always carried on by the old people and the negroes; never would they permit the young folks of either sex to visit the city, lest they should get tainted with foreign manners, and bring home foreign fashions. Even to this day, if you see an old burgher in the market with hat and garb of antique Dutch fashion, you may be sure he is one of the old unconquered race of the "bitter blood" who maintain their strong hold at Communipaw.

In modern days the hereditary bitterness against the English has lost much of its asperity, or rather has become merged in a new source of jealousy and apprehension: I allude to the incessant and wide spreading irruptions from New England. Word has been continually brought back to Communipaw by those of the community who return from their trading voyages in cabbages and oysters, of the alarming power which the Yankees are gaining in the ancient city of New Amsterdam; elbowing the genuine Knickerbockers out of all civic posts of honor and profit; bargaining them out of their hereditary home-steads; pulling down the venerable houses with crow step gables which have stood since the time of the Dutch rule, and erecting in stead granite stores and marble banks; in a word, evincing a deadly determination to obliterate every vestige of the good old Dutch times.

In consequence of the jealousy thus awakened, the worthy traders from Communipaw confine their dealings as much as possible to the genuine Dutch families. If they furnish the Yankees at all, it is with inferior articles. Never can the latter procure a real "Governor's Head" or "Governor's Foot," though they have offered extravagant prices for the same, to grace their table on the annual festival of the New England Society.

But, what has carried this hostility to the Yankees to the highest pitch was an attempt made by that all pervading race to get possession of Communipaw itself. Yes, Sir—during the late mania for land specu-lation, a daring company of Yankee projectors landed before the village; stopped the honest burghers on the public highway; endeavored to bargain them out of their hereditary acres; displayed lithographic maps in which their cabbage gardens were laid out into town lots; their oyster parks into docks and quays, and even the House of the Four Chimnies metamorphosed into a bank, which was to enrich the whole neighborhood with paper money.

Fortunately, the gallant Van Hornes came to the rescue, just as some of the worthy burghers were on the point of capitulating. The Yankees were put to the rout with signal confusion; and have never since dared to shew their faces in the place; the good people continue to cultivate their cabbages and rear their oysters; they know nothing of banks nor joint stock companies, but treasure up their money in stocking feet at the bottom of the family chest, or bury it in iron pots as did their fathers and grandfathers before them.

As to the House of the Four Chimnies, it still remains in the great and tall family of the Van Hornes. Here are to be seen ancient Dutch corner cupboards, chests of drawers and massive clothes presses, quaintly carved and carefully waxed and polished; together with divers thick, black letter volumes, with brass clasps, printed of yore in Leyden and Amsterdam and handed down from generation to generation in the family, but never read. They are preserved in the archives, among sundry old parchment deeds, in Dutch and English, bearing the seals of the early governors of the province.

In this house the primitive Dutch holydays of Paas and Pinxter are faithfully kept up; and New Year celebrated with cookies and cherry bounce; nor is the festival of the blessed St. Nicholas forgotten, when all the children are sure to hang up their stockings and to have them filled according to their deserts, though, it is said, the good saint is occasionally perplexed in his nocturnal visits, which chimney to descend.

Of late this portentous mansion has begun to give signs of dilapidation and decay. Some have attributed this to the visits made by the young people to the city; and their bringing thence various modern fashions; and to their neglect of the Dutch language, which is gradually becoming confined to the older persons in the community. The house, too, was greatly shaken by high winds during the prevalence of the speculation mania, especially at the time of the landing of the Yankees. Seeing how mysteriously the fate of Communipaw is identified with this venerable mansion, we cannot wonder that the older and wiser heads of the community should be filled with dismay, whenever a brick is toppled down from one of the chimneys, or a weather cock is blown off from a gable end.

The present lord of this historic pile, I am happy to say, is calculated to maintain it in all its integrity. He is of patriarchal age, and is worthy of the days of the patriarchs. He has done his utmost to increase and multiply the true race in the land. His wife has not been inferior to him in zeal, and they are surrounded by a goodly progeny of children, and grandchildren, and great grandchildren, who promise to perpetuate the name of Van Horne, until time shall be no more. So be it!—Long may the horn of the Van Hornes continue to be exalted in the land! Tall as they are, may their shadows never be less! May the House of the Four Chimneys remain for ages the citadel of Communipaw, and the smoke of its chimneys continue to ascend, a sweet smelling incense in the nose of Saint Nicholas!

                              With great respect, Mr. Editor,
                                        Your obt. servt.,
                              HERMANUS VANDER DONK.

P. S. Just as I had concluded the foregoing epistle I received a piece of intelligence which fills me with concern. Would you think it, Mr. Editor? —In spite of every precaution of the worthy burghers of Communipaw, the Yankees have succeeded in gaining a foothold in the place! Finding every other mode ineffectual, one of them, a smooth tongued varlet, set to work clandestinely, to "spark it" with a Dutch heiress who owns a great cabbage garden in her own right. He has made himself master of the lady and the land; and the first notice the inhabitants had of the event was a lithographed map of the cabbage garden laid out in town lots and advertised for sale. Never did the defenders of Communipaw dream of having their flank turned in this nefarious manner! On the night of the wedding the main weather-cock of the House of the Four Chimnies was carried away in a whirlwind!—The greatest consternation reigns throughout the village!

[October, 1839]

CONSPIRACY OF THE COCKED HATS

TO THE EDITOR OF THE KNICKERBOCKER

Sir: I have read, with great satisfaction, the valuable paper of your correspondent, Mr. HERMANUS VANDERDONK, (who, I take it, is a descendant of the learned Adrian Vanderdonk, one of the early historians of the Nieuw-Nederlands,) giving sundry particulars, legendary and statistical, touching the venerable village of Communipaw, and its fate-bound citadel, the House of the Four Chimnies. It goes to prove, what I have repeatedly maintained, that we live in the midst of history, and mystery, and romance; and that there is no spot in the world more rich in themes for the writer of historic novels, heroic melo-dramas, and rough-shod epics, than this same business-looking city of the Manhattoes and its environs. He who would find these elements, however, must not seek them among the modern improvements and modern people of this monied metropolis, but must dig for them, as for Kidd the pirate's treasures, in out-of-the-way places, and among the ruins of the past.

Poetry and romance received a fatal blow at the overthrow of the ancient Dutch dynasty, and have ever since been gradually withering under the growing domination of the Yankees. They abandoned our hearths, when the old Dutch tiles were superseded by marble chimney-pieces; when brass andirons made way for polished grates, and the crackling and blazing fire of nut-wood gave place to the smoke and stench of Liverpool coal; and on the downfall of the last gable-end house, their requiem was tolled from the tower of the Dutch church in Nassau-street, by the old bell that came from Holland. But poetry and romance still live unseen among us, or seen only by the enlightened few, who are able to contemplate this city and its environs through the medium of tradition, and clothed with the associations of foregone ages.

Would you seek these elements in the country, Mr. Editor, avoid all turnpikes, rail-roads, and steam-boats, those abominable inventions, by which the usurping Yankees are strengthening themselves in the land, and subduing every thing to utility and common-place. Avoid all towns and cities of white clap-board palaces, and Grecian temples, studded with "Academies," "Seminaries," and "Institutes," which glisten along our bays and rivers; these are the strong holds of Yankee usurpation: but if haply you light upon some rough, rambling road, winding between stone fences, gray with moss, and overgrown with elder, poke-berry, mullen, and sweet-briar, with here and there a low red-roofed, white-washed farm house, cowering among apple and cherry trees; an old stone church, with elms, willows, and button-woods as old-looking as itself, and tomb-stones almost buried in their own graves; and, perad-venture, a small log school-house, at a cross-road, where the English is still taught with a thickness of the tongue, instead of a twang of the nose; should you, I say, light upon such a neighborhood, Mr. Editor, you may thank your stars that you have found one of the lingering haunts of poetry and romance.

Your correspondent, Sir, has touched upon that sublime and affecting feature in the history of Communipaw, the retreat of the patriotic band of Nederlanders, led by Van Horne, whom he justly terms the Pelayo of the New-Netherlands. He has given you a picture of the manner in which they ensconced themselves in the House of the Four Chimnies, and awaited with heroic patience and perseverance the day that should see the flag of the Hogen Mogens once more floating on the fort of New-Amsterdam.

Your correspondent, Sir, has but given you a glimpse over the threshold; I will now let you into the heart of the mystery of this most mysterious and eventful village. Yes, Sir, I will now

> —"unclasp a secret book;
> And to your quick conceiving discontents,
> I'll read you matter deep and dangerous,
> As full of peril and adventurous spirit,
> As to o'er walk a current, roaring loud,
> On the unsteadfast footing of a spear."

Sir, it is one of the most beautiful and interesting facts connected with the history of Communipaw, that the early feeling of resistance to foreign rule, alluded to by your correspondent, is still kept up. Yes, Sir, a settled, secret, and determined conspiracy has been going on for generations among this indomitable people, the descendants of the refugees from New-Amsterdam; the object of which is, to redeem their ancient seat of empire, and to drive the losel Yankees out of the land.

Communipaw, it is true, has the glory of originating this conspiracy;

and it was hatched and reared in the House of the Four Chimnies; but
it has spread far and wide over ancient Pavonia, surmounted the heights
of Bergen, Hoboken, and Weehawk, crept up along the banks of the
Passaic and the Hackensack, until it pervades the whole chivalry of the
country, from Tappan Slote, in the North, to Piscataway, in the South,
including the pugnacious village of Rahway, more heroically denominated
Spank-town.

Throughout all these regions, a great "in-and-in confederacy" prevails;
that is to say, a confederacy among the Dutch families, by dint of diligent and exclusive intermarriage, to keep the race pure, and to multiply.
If ever, Mr. Editor, in the course of your travels between Spank-town
and Tappan Slote, you should see a cosey, low-eaved farm house, teeming with sturdy, broad-built little urchins, you may set it down as one of
the breeding places of this grand secret confederacy, stocked with the
embryo deliverers of New-Amsterdam.

Another step in the progress of this patriotic conspiracy is the establishment, in various places within the ancient boundaries of the Nieuw-
Nederlands, of secret, or rather mysterious associations, composed of
the genuine sons of the Nederlanders, with the ostensible object of keeping up the memory of old times and customs, but with the real object of
promoting the views of this dark and mighty plot, and extending its
ramifications throughout the land.

Sir, I am descended from a long line of genuine Nederlanders, who,
though they remained in the city of New-Amsterdam after the conquest,
and throughout the usurpation, have never in their hearts been able to
tolerate the yoke imposed upon them. My worthy father, who was one
of the last of the cocked hats, had a little knot of cronies, of his own
stamp, who used to meet in our wainscotted parlor, round a nut-wood
fire, talk over old times, when the city was ruled by its native burgo-
masters, and groan over the monopoly of all places of power and profit
by the Yankees. I well recollect the effect upon this worthy little conclave, when the Yankees first instituted their New-England Society, held
their "national festival," toasted their "father land," and sang their foreign
songs of triumph within the very precincts of our ancient metropolis.
Sir, from that day, my father held the smell of codfish and potatoes, and
the sight of pumpkin pie, in utter abomination; and whenever the annual
dinner of the New-England Society came round, it was a sore anniversary
for his children. He got up in an ill humor, grumbled and growled
throughout the day, and not one of us went to bed that night, without
having had his jacket well trounced, to the tune of the "The Pilgrim
Fathers."

You may judge, then, Mr. Editor, of the exaltation of all true patriots
of this stamp, when the Society of Saint Nicholas was set up among us,
and intrepidly established, cheek by jole, alongside of the society of the

invaders. Never shall I forget the effect upon my father and his little knot of brother groaners, when tidings were brought them that the ancient banner of the Manhattoes was actually floating from the window of the City Hotel. Sir, they nearly jumped out of their silver-buckled shoes for joy. They took down their cocked hats from the pegs on which they had hanged them, as the Israelites of yore hung their harps upon the willows, in token of bondage, clapped them resolutely once more upon their heads, and cocked them in the face of every Yankee they met on the way to the banqueting-room.

The institution of this society was hailed with transport throughout the whole extent of the New-Netherlands; being considered a secret foothold gained in New-Amsterdam, and a flattering presage of future triumph. Whenever that society holds its annual feast, a sympathetic hilarity prevails throughout the land; ancient Pavonia sends over its contributions of cabbages and oysters; the House of the Four Chimnies is splendidly illuminated, and the traditional song of Saint Nicholas, the mystic bond of union and conspiracy, is chaunted with closed doors, in every genuine Dutch family.

I have thus, I trust, Mr. Editor, opened your eyes to some of the grand moral, poetical and political phenomena with which you are surrounded. You will now be able to read the "signs of the times." You will now understand what is meant by those "Knickerbocker Halls," and "Knickerbocker Hotels," and "Knickerbocker Lunches," that are daily springing up in our city, and what all these "Knickerbocker Omnibuses" are driving at. You will see in them so many clouds before a storm; so many mysterious but sublime intimations of the gathering vengeance of a great though oppressed people. Above all, you will now contemplate our bay and its portentous borders, with proper feelings of awe and admiration. Talk of the Bay of Naples, and its volcanic mountain! Why, Sir, little Communipaw, sleeping among its cabbage gardens, "quiet as gunpowder," yet with this tremendous conspiracy brewing in its bosom, is an object ten times as sublime (in a moral point of view, mark me,) as Vesuvius in repose, though charged with lava and brimstone, and ready for an eruption.

Let me advert to a circumstance connected with this theme, which cannot but be appreciated by every heart of sensibility. You must have remarked, Mr. Editor, on summer evenings, and on Sunday afternoons, certain grave, primitive-looking personages, walking the Battery, in close confabulation, with their canes behind their backs, and ever and anon turning a wistful gaze toward the Jersey shore. These, Sir, are the sons of Saint Nicholas, the genuine Nederlanders; who regard Communipaw with pious reverence, not merely as the progenitor, but the destined regenerator, of this great metropolis. Yes, Sir; they are looking with longing eyes to the green marshes of ancient Pavonia, as did the poor conquered Spaniards of yore toward the stern mountains of Asturias, wondering whether the day of deliverance is at hand. Many is the time, when, in my boyhood, I have walked with my father and his confidential compeers on the Battery, and listened to their calculations and conjectures, and observed the points of their sharp cocked hats evermore turned toward Pavonia. Nay, Sir, I am convinced that at this moment, if I were to take down the cocked hat of my lamented father from the peg on which it has hung for years, and were to carry it to the Battery, its centre point, true as the needle to the pole, would turn to Communipaw.

Mr. Editor, the great historic drama of New-Amsterdam is but half acted. The reigns of Walter the Doubter, William the Testy, and Peter the Headstrong, with the rise, progress, and decline of the Dutch dynasty, are but so many parts of the main action, the triumphant catastrophe of which is yet to come. Yes, Sir! the deliverance of the New-Nederlands from Yankee domination will eclipse the far-famed redemption of Spain from the Moors, and the oft-sung conquest of Granada will fade before the chivalrous triumph of New-Amsterdam. Would that Peter Stuyvesant could rise from his grave to witness that day!

Your humble servant,
ROLOFF VAN RIPPER.

[January, 1840]

[LETTER ON INTERNATIONAL COPYRIGHT TO THE EDITOR OF THE *KNICKERBOCKER MAGAZINE*]

TO THE EDITOR OF THE KNICKERBOCKER.

Sir: Having seen it stated, more than once, in the public papers, that I declined subscribing my name to the petition, presented to Congress during a former session, for an act of international copy-right, I beg leave, through your pages, to say, in explanation, that I declined, not from any hostility or indifference to the object of the petition, in favor of which my sentiments have always been openly expressed, but merely because I did not relish the phraseology of the petition, and because I expected to see the measure pressed from another quarter. I wrote about the same time, however, to members of Congress in support of the application.

As no other petition has been sent to me for signature, and as silence on my part may be misconstrued, I now, as far as my name may be thought of any value, enrol it among those who pray most earnestly to Congress for this act of international equity. I consider it due, not merely to foreign authors, to whose lucubrations we are so deeply indebted for constant instruction and delight, but to our own native authors, who are implicated in the effects of the wrong done by our present laws.

For myself, my literary career, as an author, is drawing to a close, and cannot be much affected by any disposition of this question; but we have a young literature springing up, and daily unfolding itself with wonderful energy and luxuriance, which, as it promises to shed a grace and lustre upon the nation, deserves all its fostering care. How much this growing literature may be retarded by the present state of our copy-right law, I had recently an instance, in the cavalier treatment of a work of merit, written by an American, who had not yet established a commanding name in the literary market. I undertook, as a friend, to dispose of it for him, but found it impossible to get an offer from any of our principal publishers. They even declined to publish it at the author's cost, alleging that it was not worth their while to trouble themselves about native works, of doubtful success, while they could pick and choose among the successful works daily poured out by the British press, *for which they had nothing to pay for copy-right*. This simple fact spoke volumes to me, as I trust it will do to all who peruse these lines. I do not mean to enter into the discussion of a subject that has already been treated so voluminously. I will barely observe, that I have seen few arguments advanced against the proposed act, that ought to weigh with intelligent and high-minded men; while I have noticed some that have been urged, so sordid and selfish in their nature, and so narrow in the scope of their policy, as almost to be insulting to those to whom they are addressed.

I trust that, whenever this question comes before Congress, it will at once receive an action prompt and decided; and will be carried by an overwhelming, if not unanimous, vote, worthy of an enlightened, a just, and a generous nation.

Your ob. Servt.,
WASHINGTON IRVING.

[February, 1840]

[ANECDOTE OF ADMIRAL HARVEY]

Old Admiral Sir ——— Harvey told me of his serving on the American station when he was a midshipman, in 1776. He was cast away in the Liverpool, in the month of February, on Rockaway beach. The boats were swamped in getting the crew to shore. The people of the neighborhood came down to the beach in waggons, took them up home, changed and dried their clothes and gave them supper. They remained quartered in this neighborhood for weeks, part of the time in tents, part of the time in farmhouses. Nothing could exceed the kindness of the people, particularly of the Quaker family of the Hicks's and another family, who received them always hospitably in their houses. They made great havoc among the bacon and beans, and passed their time pleasantly among the Quaker girls, who always, however, demeaned themselves with strict propriety; the old Quakers tolerated their youthful frolicks. When they came to pay off scores they expected to have a thundering bill. The good people would take nothing but the King's allowance. "You are people in distress," said they. "We will not take any thing out of your pockets."

He has never forgotten their kindness; it is true he has only been able to express his gratitude in words, but if he had ever met an American in distress he should have felt bound to befriend him. Whenever he has met an American or Quaker he has felt proud to acknowledge the obligation.

[March, 1840]

THE "EMPIRE OF THE WEST"

We would call the attention of our readers to a copious and able article in the January number of the *North American Review*, treating of "Discovery beyond the Rocky Mountains." It is a paper that should be read and meditated upon by every American. It gives a clear and compendious narrative of the progressive steps of discovery and occupation by which we acquired an indefeasible right to the Oregon territory, and places in a startling light the actual state of our affairs in that most important and interesting region.

The reader will here find that our claim to a country "equal in extent to the old United States, and stretching for nine or ten degrees of latitude along the great (Pacific) Ocean" has become almost nullified through the supineness of our own statesmen and the wily and grasping policy of foreign traders. He will here find how Astoria, our original seat of empire, has been turned into a British fortified post and trading-house; how a foreign flag has been hoisted at the mouth of the Columbia, and how a mere trading company has seated itself at that great western portal of our empire, and actually locked it against our own citizens.

What are the petty questions which occupy Congress, and distract it with clamorous contention, in comparison with the adjustment of this great territorial right, which involves empire? What is the North-East Boundary question, which concerns a mere strip of forest land, to this, on which depends our whole territory west of the Rocky Mountains, and our great high-way to the Pacific? A little more delay on our part, and wily Commerce will have woven its web over the whole country, and it will cost thousands of lives, and millions of treasure, to break the meshes. We cannot help quoting some observations of the reviewer to the above purport:

"We have continual cause to lament the undue prominence in the public mind, which trivial and secondary questions, the petty issues of petty party controversy, are allowed to usurp, to the postponement or neglect of matters infinitely more important in reality. The topics of popular discussion in newspapers and in conversation, as well as in the more formal and serious public debates, and the action of the government, make the fact to be continually obvious. Thus, in Congress, for minutes occupied in things of true consequence, hours, nay days are consumed on trivialities, which will speedily be forgotten, and pass away for ever, as transitory and as insignificant in themselves as the motes, which play in the sunlight of a summer's noon. It has been so under every administration, of whatever party or opinion, the United States have seen. Hence it was, that the intrigues of the British companies among the Indians of the United States, and their general intrusion into our territory in the region of the Upper Mississippi and Upper Missouri, though repeatedly the subject of complaint and remonstrance on the part of observant men, as in this case of Captain Lewis, did not engage due attention from the government, until those intrigues and that intrusion resulted in the conclusion to have been anticipated from them, a general Indian war, which ravaged and desolated the whole region of the United States on the Ohio, the Lakes, and the Upper Mississippi. Transferred to another part of the territory of the United States, the same British companies, we fear, are now preparing the same *dénouement* of a like tragedy, by the same means, which failed to arouse the active resistance of our government of old, until savage massacre and conflagration burst on our western settlements; but the operations of which, it is to be hoped, the government of the United States, warned by that example, will arrest by measures of suitable energy."

It is singular how penetrable and easy the passage is across the Rocky Mountains. It seems as if Nature had provided a high-way for the caravans of commerce to pass from the Atlantic to the Pacific regions of our immense empire. "The gradual rise of the country, in the vast slope from the Mississippi to the foot of the mountains," says Major Pitcher, in his report, "makes a considerable elevation, without perceptible increase, and then gaps or depressions let you through almost on a level." Wagons and carriages may cross the mountains without difficulty, and with little delay in the day's journey. In fact, Captain Bonneville passed over to the western side of the mountains with wagons, several years since, and so easy and gradual was the ascent, that he was only made aware of the great elevation to which he had attained, by the wood-work of his wheels coming loose, through the rarity of the atmosphere.

By the way, we should like to hear more of Lake Bonneville, that remarkable body of salt water on the western side of the mountains, mentioned in the narrative of the Captain's expeditions. It strikes us as one of the most singular phenomenons in that vast region of curiosities and wonders.

We are glad to see that the reviewer pays a passing tribute of praise to Mr. Nathaniel J. Wyeth. We have ever admired the spirited attempt of that enterprizing individual, "to rear once more the American flag in the lost domains of Astoria, and to regain for his country the opulent trade of the Columbia." We regret that his intrepid and persevering efforts could not have been aided and enforced by government, so as to enable him to maintain the foothold which he had effected in the country. He appears to have had an energy and a decision of character, and a scope of thought, that fitted him to follow out the great plans of Mr. Astor; all he wanted was the purse.

[April, 1840]

[ANECDOTE OF THE FRENCH REVOLUTION]

Before the French Revolution the Abbés were privileged persons in the fashionable world; a kind of general gossips in politics, literature, and court scandal. At the tables of the principal noblemen there would always be a vacant place left for any Abbé who might drop in, and the first that arrived took it. About dinner time the Abbés might be seen, neatly dressed, picking their way from one dry stone to another along the dirty streets of Paris, ringing or rapping at the great port-cochéres of the lordly hotels, and inquiring of the porters, "Is there a place at table?" If answered in the negative, away they would tittup in hopes of better luck at the next place of call.

An Abbé of this sponging order was seated one day in the bloody time of the Revolution, at the table of a nobleman, where there was a large company. In the midst of the repast, a cart drove by, carrying a number of persons to the guillotine. All the company ran to the windows, to see if they had any friends among the victims. The Abbé, being a short man, tried by standing on tip-toe to peep over the shoulders of those before him, but in vain; so he ran down to the port-cochére. As the cart went by one of the prisoners who knew the Abbé, bowed to him. The Abbé returned the salutation. "What!" cried some of the mob, "you are his friend!—You are of the same way of thinking!—Here citizens is another traytor!—Away with him!" The poor Abbé was hoisted into the cart in spite of his protestations, and hurried off to the guillotine.

In the mean time the noble company up stairs having satisfied their curiosity, resumed their seats at table. One chair however remained vacant, and after a while the question began to be asked—"Where is Monsieur the Abbé?—What has become of the Abbé—?" Alas! by that time the poor Abbé was headless!

[June, 1840]

[THE TAKING OF THE VEIL, AND THE CHARMING LETORIÉRES]

TO THE EDITOR OF THE KNICKERBOCKER.

Sir: I have already given you a few anecdotes of characters and events drawn from the French memoirs of the last century, and am inclined to while away an idle hour in giving you a few more. You may use your discretion, either in throwing them aside, or handing them to your readers. Respectfully yours,

GEOFFREY CRAYON.

———

One of the most remarkable personages in Parisian society, during the last century, was Renée Charlotte Victoire de Froulay de Tessè, Marchioness de Créqui. She sprang from the highest and proudest of the old French nobility, and ever maintained the most exalted notions of the purity and antiquity of blood; looking upon all families that could not date back further than three or four hundred years, as mere upstarts. When a beautiful girl, fourteen years of age, she was presented to Louis XIV., at Versailles, and the ancient monarch kissed her hand with great gallantry; after an interval of about eighty five years, when nearly a hundred years old, the same testimonial of respect was paid her at the Tuileries by Bonaparte, then First Consul, who promised her the restitution of the confiscated forests formerly belonging to her family. She was one of the most celebrated women of her time, for intellectual grace and superiority; and had the courage to remain at Paris, and brave all the horrors of the revolution, which laid waste the aristocratical world around her.

The memoirs she has left behind, abound with curious anecdotes and vivid pictures of Parisian life, during the latter days of Louis XIV., the regency of the Duke of Orleans, and the residue of the last century; and are highly illustrative of the pride, splendor, and licentiousness of the French nobility, on the very eve of their tremendous downfall.

I shall draw forth a few scenes from her memoirs, taken almost at random, and which, though given as actual and well known circumstances, have quite the air of romance.

THE TAKING OF THE VEIL.

All the great world of Paris were invited to be present at a grand ceremonial, to take place in the church of the Abbey Royal of Panthemont. Henrietta de Lenoncour, a young girl, of a noble family, of great beauty, and heiress to immense estates, was to take the black veil. Invitations had been issued in grand form, by her aunt and guardian, the Countess Brigitte de Rupelmonde, canoness of Mauberge. The circumstance caused great talk and wonder, in the fashionable circles of Paris; every body was at a loss to imagine why a young girl, beautiful and rich, in the very spring-time of her charms, should renounce a world which she was so eminently qualified to embellish and enjoy.

A lady of high rank, who visited the beautiful novice at the grate of her convent-parlor, got a clue to the mystery. She found her in great agitation: for a time she evidently repressed her feelings; but they at length broke forth in passionate exclamations. "Heaven grant me grace," said she, "some day or other to pardon my cousin Gondrecourt the sorrows he has caused me."

"What do you mean?—what sorrows, my child?" inquired her visiter. "What has your cousin done to affect you?"

"He is married!" cried she, in accents of despair, but endeavoring to repress her sobs.

"Married! I have heard nothing of the kind, my dear. Are you perfectly sure of it?"

"Alas! nothing is more certain; my aunt De Rupelmonde informed me of it."

The lady retired, full of surprise and commiseration. She related the scene in a circle of the highest nobility, in the saloon of the Marshal Prince of Beauvau, where the unaccountable self-sacrifice of the beautiful novice was under discussion.

"Alas!" said she, "the poor girl is crossed in love; she is about to renounce the world in despair, at the marriage of her cousin De Gondrecourt."

"What!" cried a gentleman present, "the Viscount de Gondrecourt married! Never was there a greater falsehood. And her 'aunt told her so!' Oh! I understand the plot. The countess is passionately fond of Gondrecourt, and jealous of her beautiful niece: but her schemes are vain; the Viscount holds her in perfect detestation."

There was a mingled expression of ridicule, disgust, and indignation, at the thought of such a rivalry. The Countess Rupelmonde was old enough to be the grand-mother of the Viscount. She was a woman of violent passions, and imperious temper; robust in person, with a masculine voice, a dusky complexion, green eyes, and powerful eye-brows.

"It is impossible," cried one of the company, "that a woman of the countess' age and appearance can be guilty of such folly. No, no; you mistake the aim of this detestable woman. She is managing to get possession of the estate of her lovely niece."

This was admitted to be the most probable; and all concurred in believing the countess to be at the bottom of the intended sacrifice; for although a canoness, a dignitary of a religious order, she was pronounced little better than a devil incarnate.

The Princess de Beauvau, a woman of generous spirit and intrepid zeal, suddenly rose from the chair in which she had been reclining. "My prince," said she, addressing her husband, "if you approve of it, I will go immediately and have a conversation on this subject with the archbishop. There is not a moment to spare. It is now past midnight; the ceremony is to take place in the morning. A few hours, and the irrevocable vows will be pronounced."

The prince inclined his head in respectful assent. The princess set about her generous enterprise with a woman's promptness. Within a short time, her carriage was at the iron gate of the archepiscopal palace, and her servants rang for admission. Two Switzers, who had charge of the gate, were fast asleep in the porter's lodge, for it was half-past two in the morning. It was some time before they could be awakened, and longer before they could be made to come forth.

"The Princess de Beauvau is at the gate!"

Such a personage was not to be received in deshabille. Her dignity and the dignity of the archbishop demanded that the gate should be served in full costume. For half an hour, therefore, had the princess to wait, in feverish impatience, until the two dignitaries of the porter's lodge arrayed themselves; and three o'clock sounded from the tower of Notre Dame, before they came forth. They were in grand livery, of a buff color, with amaranth galloons, plaited with silver, and fringed sword-belts reaching to their knees, in which were suspended long rapiers. They had small three-cornered hats, surmounted with plumes; and each bore in his hand a halbert. Thus equipped, at all points, they planted themselves before the door of the carriage; struck the ends of their halberts on the ground with emphasis; and stood waiting with official importance, but profound respect, to know the pleasure of the princess.

She demanded to speak with the archbishop. A most reverential bow and shrug accompanied the reply, that "His Grandeur was not at home."

Not at home! Where was he to be found? Another bow and shrug: "His Grandeur either was, or ought to be, in retirement in the seminary of St. Magloire; unless he had gone to pass the Fête of St. Bruno with the reverend Carthusian Fathers of the Rue d'Enfer; or perhaps he might have gone to repose himself in his castle of Conflans-sur-Seine. Though on farther thought, it was not unlikely he might have gone to sleep at St. Cyr, where the Bishop of Chartres never failed to invite him for the anniversary soirée of Madame de Maintenon."

The princess was in despair at this multiplicity of cross roads pointed out for the chase: the brief interval of time was rapidly elapsing; day already began to dawn; she saw there was no hope of finding the archbishop before the moment of his entrance into the church for the morning's ceremony; so she returned home quite distressed.

At seven o'clock in the morning, the princess was in the parlor of the monastery of De Panthemont, and sent in an urgent request for a moment's conversation with the Lady Abbess. The reply brought was, that the Abbess could not come to the parlor, being obliged to attend in the choir, at the canonical hours. The princess entreated permission to enter the convent, to reveal to the Lady Abbess in two words, something of the greatest importance. The Abbess sent word in reply, that the thing was impossible, until she had obtained permission from the Archbishop of Paris. The princess retired once more to her carriage, and now, as a forlorn hope, took her station at the door of the church, to watch for the arrival of the prelate.

After a while, the splendid company invited to this great ceremony began to arrive. The beauty, rank, and wealth of the novice had excited great attention; and, as every body was expected to be present on the occasion, every body pressed to secure a place. The street reverberated with the continual roll of gilded carriages and chariots; coaches of princes and dukes, designated by imperials of crimson velvet, and magnificent equipages of six horses, decked out with nodding plumes and sumptuous harnessing. At length the equipages ceased to arrive; empty vehicles filled the street; and, with a noisy and parti-colored crowd of lacqueys in rich liverys, obstructed all the entrances to De Panthemont.

Eleven o'clock had struck; the last auditor had entered the church; the deep tones of the organ began to swell through the sacred pile, yet still the archbishop came not! The heart of the princess beat quicker and quicker with vague apprehension; when a valet, dressed in cloth of silver, trimmed with crimson velvet, approached her carriage precipitately. "Madame," said he, "the archbishop is in the church; he entered by the portal of the cloister; he is already in the sanctuary; the ceremony is about to commence!"

What was to be done! To speak with the archbishop was now impossible, and yet, on the revelation she was to make to him, depended the fate of the lovely novice. The princess drew forth her tablets of enamelled gold, wrote a few lines therein with a pencil, and ordered her lacquey to make way for her through the crowd, and conduct her with all speed to the sacristy.

The description given of the church and the assemblage on this occasion, presents an idea of the aristocratical state of the times, and of the high interest awakened by the affecting sacrifice about to take place. The church was hung with superb tapestry, above which extended a band of white damask, fringed with gold, and covered with armorial escutcheons. A large pennon, emblazoned with the arms and alliances of the high-born damsel, was suspended, according to custom, in place of the lamp of the sanctuary. The lustres, girandoles, and candelabras of the king had been furnished in profusion, to decorate the sacred edifice, and the pavements were all covered with rich carpets.

The sanctuary presented a reverend and august assemblage of bishops, canons, and monks of various orders, Benedictines, Bernardines, Raccollets, Capuchins, and others, all in their appropriate robes and dresses. In the midst presided the Archbishop of Paris, Christopher de Beaumont; surrounded by his four arch priests and his vicars-general. He was seated with his back against the altar. When his eyes were cast down, his countenance, pale and severe, is represented as having been somewhat sepulchral and death-like; but the moment he raised his large dark, sparkling eyes, the whole became animated; beaming with ardor, and expressive of energy, penetration, and firmness.

The audience that crowded the church, was no less illustrious. Excepting the royal family, all that was elevated in rank and title, was there: never had a ceremonial of the kind attracted an equal concourse of the high aristocracy of Paris.

At length the grated gates of the choir creaked on their hinges, and Madame de Richelieu, the high and noble Abbess of De Panthemont, advanced to resign the novice into the hands of her aunt, the Countess Canoness de Rupelmonde. Every eye was turned with intense curiosity to gain a sight of the beautiful victim. She was sumptuously dressed, but her paleness and languor accorded but little with her brilliant attire. The Canoness de Rupelmonde conducted her niece to her praying desk, where, as soon as the poor girl knelt down, she sank as if exhausted. Just then a sort of murmur was heard at the lower end of the church, where the servants in livery were gathered. A young man was borne forth, struggling in convulsions. He was in the uniform of an officer of the guards of King Stanislaus, Duke of Lorraine. A whisper circulated that it was the young Viscount de Gondrecourt, and that he was a lover of the novice. Almost all the young nobles present hurried forth to proffer him sympathy and assistance.

The Archbishop of Paris remained all this time seated before the altar; his eyes cast down, his pallid countenance giving no signs of interest or participation in the scene around him. It was noticed that in one of his hands, which was covered with a violet glove, he grasped firmly a pair of tablets, of enamelled gold.

The Canoness de Rupelmonde conducted her niece to the prelate, to make her profession of self-devotion, and to utter the irrevocable vow. As the lovely novice knelt at his feet, the archbishop fixed on her his dark beaming eyes, with a kind but earnest expression. "Sister!" said he, in the softest and most benevolent tone of voice, "What is your age?"

"Nineteen years, Monseigneur;" eagerly interposed the Countess de Rupelmonde.

"*You* will reply to me by and by, Madame," said the archbishop, drily. He then repeated his question to the novice, who replied in a faltering voice, "Seventeen years."

"In what diocese did you take the white veil?"

"In the diocese of Toul."

"How!" exclaimed the archbishop vehemently. "In the diocese of Toul? The chair of Toul is vacant! The Bishop of Toul died fifteen months since; and those who officiate in the chapter are not authorized to receive novices. Your noviciate, Mademoiselle, is null and void, and we cannot receive your profession!"

The archbishop rose from his chair, resumed his mitre, and took the crozier from the hands of an attendant.

"My dear brethren," said he, addressing the assembly. "there is no necessity for our examining and interrogating Mademoiselle de Lenoncour on the sincerity of her religious vocation. There is a canonical impediment to her professing for the present; and, as to the future, we reserve to ourselves the consideration of the matter: interdicting to all other ecclesiastical persons the power of accepting her vows, under penalty of interdiction, of suspension, and of nullification; all which is in virtue of our metropolitan rights, contained in the terms of the bull *cum proximis: 'Adjutorium nostrum in nomine Domini!'* " pursued he chanting in a grave and solemn voice, and turning toward the altar to give the benediction of the holy sacrament.

The noble auditory had that habitude of reserve, that empire, or rather tyranny, over all outward manifestations of internal emotions, which belongs to high aristocratical breeding. The declaration of the archbishop, therefore, was received as one of the most natural and ordinary things in the world, and all knelt down and received the pontifical benediction with perfect decorum. As soon, however, as they were released from the self-restraint imposed by etiquette, they amply indemnified themselves; and nothing was talked of for a month, in the fashionable saloons of Paris, but the loves of the handsome Viscount and the charming Henrietta; the wickedness of the canoness; the active benevolence and admirable address of the Princess de Beauvau; and the great wisdom of the archbishop; who was particularly extolled for his delicacy in defeating this manœuvre without any scandal to the aristocracy, or public stigma on the name of De Rupelmonde, and without any departure from pastoral gentleness, by adroitly seizing upon an informality, and turning it to beneficial account, with as much authority as charitable circumspection.

As to the Canoness de Rupelmonde, she was defeated at all points in her wicked plans against her beautiful niece. In consequence of the caveat of the archbishop, her superior ecclesiastic, the Abbess de Panthemont, formally forbade Mademoiselle de Lenoncour to resume the white veil and the dress of a noviciate, and instead of a novice's cell, established her in a beautiful apartment as a boarder. The next morning the Canoness de Rupelmonde called at the convent to take away her niece; but, to her confusion, the Abbess produced a lettre-de-cachet, which she had just received, and which forbade Mademoiselle to leave the convent with any other person save the Prince de Beauvau.

Under the auspices and the vigilant attention of the prince, the whole affair was wound up in the most technical and circumstantial manner. The Countess de Rupelmonde, by a decree of the Grand Council, was divested of the guardianship of her niece. All the arrears of revenues, accumulated during Mademoiselle de Lenoncour's minority, were rigorously collected, the accounts scrutinized and adjusted, and her noble fortune placed safely and entirely in her hands.

In a little while the noble personages who had been invited to the ceremony of taking the veil, received another invitation, on the part of the Countess dowager de Gondrecourt, and the Marshal Prince de Beauvau, to attend the marriage of Adrien de Gondrecourt, Viscount of Jean-sur-Moselle, and Henrietta de Lenoncour, "Countess de Hevouwal," etc., which duly took place in the chapel of the archepiscopal palace at Paris.

So much for the beautiful Henrietta de Lenoncour. We will now draw forth a companion picture of a handsome young cavalier, who figured in the gay world of Paris about the same time, and concerning whom the ancient Marchioness writes with the lingering feeling of youthful romance.

THE CHARMING LETORIÉRES.

"A good face is a letter of recommendation," says an old proverb; and it was never more verified than in the case of the Chevalier Letoriéres. He was a young gentleman of good family, but who, according to the Spanish phraze, had nothing but his cloak and sword, (Capa y espada) that is to say, his gentle blood and gallant bearing, to help him forward in the world. Through the interest of an uncle, who was an abbé, he received a gratuitous education at a fashionable college, but finding the terms of study too long, and the vacations too short, for his gay and indolent temper, he left college without saying a word, and launched himself upon Paris, with a light heart and still lighter pocket. Here he led a life to his humour; it is true, he had to make scanty meals, and to lodge in a garret; but what of that?—He was his own master; free from all task or restraint. When cold or hungry, he sallied forth, like others of the chamelion order, and banqueted on pure air and warm sunshine in the public walks and gardens; drove off the thoughts of a dinner, by amusing himself with the gay and grotesque throngs of the metropolis; and, if one of the poorest, was one of the merriest gentlemen upon town. Wherever he went, his good looks and frank, graceful demeanour, had an instant and magical effect in securing favor. There was but one word to express his fascinating powers; he was "charming."

Instances are given of the effect of his winning qualities upon minds of coarse, ordinary mould. He had once taken shelter from a heavy shower under a gateway. A hackney coachman, who was passing by, pulled up and asked him if he wished a cast in his carriage. Letoriéres declined, with a melancholy and dubious shake of the head. The coachman regarded him wistfully, repeated his solicitations, and wished to know what place he was going to. "To the Palace of Justice, to walk in the galleries; but I will wait here until the rain is over."

"And why so?" inquired the coachman, pertinaciously.

"Because, I've no money;—do let me be quiet."

The coachman jumped down, and, opening the door of his carriage, "It shall never be said," cried he, "that I left so charming a young gentleman to weary himself and catch cold, merely for the sake of twenty four sous."

Arrived at the Palace of Justice, he stopped before the saloon of a famous restaurateur, opened the door of the carriage, and, taking off his hat very respectfully, begged the youth to accept of a Louis d'or. "You will meet with some young gentlemen within" said he, "with whom you may wish to take a hand at cards. The number of my coach is 144. You can find me out, and repay me whenever you please."

The worthy Jehu was, some years afterward, made coachman to the Princess Sophia of France, through the recommendation of the handsome youth he had so generously obliged.

Another instance in point is given with respect to his taylor, to whom he owed four hundred livres. The taylor had repeatedly dunned him, but was always put off with the best grace in the world. The wife of the taylor urged her husband to assume a harsher tone.—He replied that he could not find it in his heart to speak roughly to so charming a young gentleman.

"I've no patience with such want of spirit!" cried the wife; "you have not the courage to shew your teeth: but I'm going out to get change for this note of a hundred crowns; before I come home I'll seek this 'charming' youth myself, and see whether he has the power to charm me. I'll warrant he won't be able to put *me* off with fine looks and fine speeches."

With these and many more vaunts, the good dame sallied forth. When she returned home, however, she wore quite a different aspect. "Well," said her husband, "how much have you received from the 'charming' young man?"

"Let me alone," replied the wife: "I found him playing on the guitar, and he looked so handsome, and was so amiable and genteel, that I had not the heart to trouble him."

"And the change for the hundred crown note?" said the taylor.

The wife hesitated a moment: "Faith," cried she, "you'll have to add the amount to your next bill against him.—The poor young gentleman had such a melancholy air, that—I know not how it was,—but—I left the hundred crowns on his mantle-piece in spite of him!"

The captivating looks and manners of Letoriéres made his way, with equal facility, in the great world. His high connexions entitled him to presentation at court, but some questions arose about the sufficiency of his proofs of nobility; whereupon the king, who had seen him walking in the gardens of Versailles, and been charmed with his appearance, put an end to all demurs of etiquette, by making him a Viscount.

The same kind of fascination is said to have attended him throughout his career. He succeeded in various difficult family suits on questions of honors and privileges; he had merely to appear in court, to dispose the judges in his favor. He at length became so popular, that, on one occasion, when he appeared at the theatre, on recovering from a wound received in a duel, the audience applauded him on his entrance. Nothing, it is said, could have been in more perfect good taste and high breeding than his conduct on this occasion. When he heard the applause, he rose in his box, stepped forward and surveyed both sides of the house, as if he could not believe that it was himself they were treating like a favorite actor, or a prince of the blood.

His success with the fair sex may easily be presumed; but he had too much honor and sensibility to render his intercourse with them a series of cold gallantries and heartless triumphs. In the course of his attendance upon court, where he held a post of honor about the king, he fell deeply in love with the beautiful Princess Julia, of Savoy Carignan. She was young, tender, and simple hearted and returned his love with equal fervor. Her family took the alarm at this attachment, and procured an order that she should inhabit the Abbey of Montmartre, where she was treated with all befitting delicacy and distinction, but not permitted to go beyond the convent walls. The lovers found means to correspond. One of their letters was intercepted, and it is even hinted that a plan of elopement was discovered. A duel was the consequence, with one of the fiery relatives of the princess. Letoriéres received two sword wounds in his right side. His wounds were serious, yet, after two or three days' confinement, he could not resist his impatience to see the princess. He succeeded in scaling the walls of the abbey, and obtaining an interview in an arcade, leading to the cloister of the cemetery. The interview of the lovers was long and tender. They exchanged vows of eternal fidelity; and flattered themselves with hopes of future happiness, which they were never to realize. After repeated farewells the princess reentered the convent, never again to behold the charming Letoriéres. On the following morning his corpse was found stiff and cold on the pavement of the cloister!

It would seem that the wounds of the unfortunate youth had been reopened by his efforts to get over the wall; that he had refrained from calling assistance lest he should expose the princess, and that he had bled to death, without any one to aid him; or to close his dying eyes.

Of these romances of real life, drawn from what profess to be authentic memoirs, and characteristic of aristocratical French life during the early part of the last century, I shall for the present, Mr. Editor, take my leave. Yours, etc.,

G. C.

[July, 1840]

LETTER FROM GRANADA

TO THE EDITOR OF THE KNICKERBOCKER.

Sir: The following letter was scribbled to a friend during my sojourn in the Alhambra, in 1829. As it presents scenes and impressions noted down at the time, I venture to offer it for the consideration of your readers. Should it prove acceptable, I may from time to time give other letters, written in the course of my various ramblings, and which have been kindly restored to me by my friends.

Yours,   G. C.

Granada, 1829.

MY DEAR ————:

Religious festivals furnish, in all Catholic countries, occasions of popular pageant and recreation; but in none more so than in Spain, where the great end of religion seems to be, to create holidays and ceremonials. For two days past, Granada has been in a gay turmoil with the great annual fête of Corpus Christi. This most eventful and romantic city, as you well know, has ever been the rallying point of a mountainous region, studded with small towns and villages. Hither, during the time that Granada was the splendid capital of a Moorish kingdom, the Moslem youth repaired from all points, to participate in chivalrous festivities; and hither the Spanish populace, at the present day, throng from all parts of the surrounding country, to attend the festivals of the church.

As the populace like to enjoy things from the very commencement, the stir of Corpus Christi began in Granada on the preceding evening. Before dark, the gates of the city were thronged with the picturesque peasantry from the mountain villages, and the brown laborers from the Vega, or vast fertile plain. As the evening advanced, the Vivarambla thickened and swarmed with a motley multitude. This is the great square in the centre of the city, famous for tilts and tourneys, during the times of Moorish domination, and incessantly mentioned in all the old Moorish ballads of love and chivalry. For several days the hammer had resounded throughout this square. A gallery of wood had been erected all round it, forming a covered way for the grand procession of Corpus Christi. On this eve of the ceremonial, this gallery was a fashionable promenade. It was brilliantly illuminated, bands of music were stationed in balconies on the four sides of the square, and all the fashion and beauty of Granada, and all its population that could boast a little finery of apparel, together with the *majos* and *majas*, the beaux and belles of the villages, in their gay Andalusian costumes, thronged this covered walk, anxious to see and to be seen. As to the sturdy peasantry of the Vega, and such of the mountaineers as did not pretend to display, but were content with hearty enjoyment, they swarmed in the centre of the square; some in groups, listening to the guitar and the traditional ballad; some dancing their favorite boléro; some seated on the ground making a merry though frugal supper; and some stretched out for their night's repose.

The gay crowd of the gallery dispersed gradually toward midnight; but the centre of the square resembled the bivouac of an army; for hundreds of the peasantry, men, women, and children, passed the night there, sleeping soundly on the bare earth, under the open canopy of heaven. A summer's night requires no shelter in this genial climate; and with a great part of the hardy peasantry of Spain, a bed is a superfluity which many of them never enjoy, and which they affect to despise. The common Spaniard spreads out his manta, or mule-cloth, or wraps himself in his cloak, and lies on the ground, with his saddle for a pillow.

The next morning I revisited the square at sun-rise. It was still strewed with groups of sleepers: some were reposing from the dance and revel of the evening; others had left their villages after work, on the preceding day, and having trudged on foot the greater part of the night, were taking a sound sleep to freshen them for the festivities of the day. Numbers from the mountains, and the remote villages of the plain, who had set out in the night, continued to arrive, with their wives and children. All were in high spirits; greeting each other, and exchanging jokes and pleasantries. The gay tumult thickened as the day advanced. Now came pouring in at the city gates, and parading through the streets, the deputations from the various villages, destined to swell the grand procession. These village deputations were headed by their priests, bearing their respective crosses and banners, and images of the blessed Virgin and of patron saints; all which were matters of great rivalship and jealousy among the peasantry. It was like the chivalrous gatherings of ancient days, when each town and village sent its chiefs, and warriors, and standards, to defend the capital, or grace its festivities.

At length all these various detachments congregated into one grand pageant, which slowly paraded round the Vivarambla, and through the principal streets, where every window and balcony was hung with tapestry. In this procession were all the religious orders, the civil and military authorities, and the chief people of the parishes and villages: every church and convent had contributed its banners, its images, its reliques, and poured forth its wealth, for the occasion. In the centre of the procession walked the archbishop, under a damask canopy, and surrounded by inferior dignitaries and their dependants. The whole moved to the swell and cadence of numerous bands of music, and, passing through the midst of a countless yet silent multitude, proceeded onward to the cathedral.

I could not but be struck with the changes of times and customs, as I saw this monkish pageant passing through the Vivarambla, the ancient seat of modern pomp and chivalry. The contrast was indeed forced upon the mind by the decorations of the square. The whole front of the wooden gallery erected for the procession, extending several hundred feet, was faced with canvass, on which some humble though patriotic artist had painted, by contract, a series of the principal scenes and exploits of the conquest, as recorded in chronicle and romance. It is thus the romantic legends of Granada mingle themselves with every thing, and are kept fresh in the public mind.

Another great festival at Granada, answering in its popular character to our Fourth of July, is *El Dia de la Toma*; "The day of the Capture:" that is to say, the anniversary of the capture of the city by Ferdinand and Isabella. On this day all Granada is abandoned to revelry. The alarm-bell on the Torre de la Campana, or watch-tower of the Alhambra, keeps up a clangor from morn till night; and happy is the damsel that can ring that bell: it is a charm to secure a husband in the course of the year.

The sound, which can be heard over the whole Vega, and to the top of the mountains, summons the peasantry to the festivities. Throughout the day the Alhambra is thrown open to the public. The halls and courts of the Moorish monarchs resound with the guitar and castanet, and gay groups, in the fanciful dresses of Andalusia, perform those popular dances which they have inherited from the Moors.

In the mean time a grand procession moves through the city. The banner of Ferdinand and Isabella, that precious relique of the conquest, is brought forth from its depository, and borne by the Alferez Mayor, or grand standard-bearer, through the principal streets. The portable camp-altar, which was carried about with them in all their campaigns, is transported into the chapel royal, and placed before their sepulchre, where their effigies lie in monumental marble. The procession fills the chapel. High mass is performed in memory of the conquest; and at a certain part of the ceremony, the Alferez Mayor puts on his hat, and waves the standard above the tomb of the conquerors.

A more whimsical memorial of the conquest is exhibited, on the same evening at the theatre, where a popular drama is performed, entitled AVE MARIA. This turns on the oft-sung achievement of Hernando del Pulgar, surnamed *El de las Hazañas*, "He of the Exploits," the favorite hero of the populace of Granada.

During the time that Ferdinand and Isabella beseiged the city, the young Moorish and Spanish knights vied with each other in extravagant bravados. On one occasion Hernando del Pulgar, at the head of a handful of youthful followers, made a dash into Granada at the dead of the night, nailed the inscription of AVE MARIA, with his dagger, to the gate of the principal mosque, as a token of having consecrated it to the Virgin, and effected his retreat in safety.

While the Moorish cavaliers admired this daring exploit, they felt bound to revenge it. On the following day, therefore, Tarfe, one of the stoutest of the infidel warriors, paraded in front of the Christian army, dragging the sacred inscription of AVE MARIA at his horse's tail. The cause of the Virgin was eagerly vindicated by Garcilaso de la Vega, who slew the Moor in single combat, and elevated the inscription of AVE MARIA, in devotion and triumph, at the end of his lance.

The drama founded on this exploit is prodigiously popular with the common people. Although it has been acted time out of mind, and the people have seen it repeatedly, it never fails to draw crowds, and so completely to engross the feelings of the audience, as to have almost the effect on them of reality. When their favorite Pulgar strides about with many a mouthy speech, in the very midst of the Moorish capital, he is cheered with enthusiastic bravos; and when he nails the tablet of AVE MARIA to the door of the mosque, the theatre absolutely shakes with shouts and thunders of applause. On the other hand, the actors who play the part of the Moors, have to bear the brunt of the temporary indignation of their auditors; and when the infidel Tarfe plucks down the tablet to tie it to his horse's tail, many of the people absolutely rise in fury, and are ready to jump upon the stage to revenge this insult to the Virgin.

Beside this annual festival at the capital, almost every village of the Vega and the mountains has its own anniversary, wherein its own deliverance from the Moorish yoke is celebrated with uncouth ceremony and rustic pomp.

On these occasions, a kind of resurrection takes place of ancient Spanish dresses and armor; great two-handed swords, ponderous arquebusses, with match-locks, and other weapons and accoutrements, once the equipments of the village chivalry, and treasured up from generation to generation, since the time of the conquest. In these hereditary and historical garbs, some of the most sturdy of the villagers array themselves as champions of the faith, while its ancient opponents are represented by another band of villagers, dressed up as Moorish warriors. A tent is pitched in the public square of the village, within which is an altar, and an image of the Virgin. The Spanish warriors approach to perform their devotions at this shrine, but are opposed by the infidel Moslems, who surround the tent. A mock-fight succeeds, in the course of which the combatants sometimes forget that they are merely playing a part, and exchange dry blows of grievous weight: the fictitious Moors, especially, are apt to bear away pretty evident marks of the pious zeal of their antagonists. The contest, however, invariably terminates in favor of the good cause. The Moors are defeated and taken prisoners. The image of the Virgin, rescued from thraldom, is elevated in triumph; and a grand procession succeeds, in which the Spanish conquerors figure with great vain-glory and applause, and their captives are led in chains, to the infinite delight and edification of the populace. These annual festivals are the delight of the villagers; who expend considerable sums in their celebration. In some villages they are occasionally obliged to suspend them for want of funds; but when times grow better, or they have been enabled to save money for the purpose, they are revived with all their grotesque pomp and extravagance.

To recur to the exploit of Hernando del Pulgar. However extravagant and fabulous it may seem, it is authenticated by certain traditional usages, and shows the vain-glorious daring that prevailed between the youthful warriors of both nations, in that romantic war. The mosque thus consecrated to the Virgin, was made the cathedral of the city after the conquest; and there is a painting of the Virgin beside the royal chapel, which was put there by Hernando del Pulgar. The lineal representative of the hare-brained cavalier has the right, to this day, to enter the church, on certain occasions, on horseback, to sit within the choir, and to put on his hat at the elevation of the host, though these privileges have often been obstinately contested by the clergy.

The present lineal representative of Hernando del Pulgar is the Marquis de Salar, whom I have met occasionally in society. He is a young man of agreeable appearance and manners, and his bright black eyes would give indication of his inheriting the fire of his ancestor. When the paintings were put up in the Vivarambla, illustrating the scenes of the conquest, an old gray-headed family servant of the Pulgars was so delighted with those which related to the family hero, that he absolutely shed tears, and hurrying home to the Marquis, urged him to hasten and behold the family trophies. The sudden zeal of the old man provoked the mirth of his young master; upon which, turning to the brother of the Marquis, with that freedom allowed to family servants in Spain, "Come, Señor," cried he, "you are more grave and considerate than your brother; come and see your ancestor in all his glory!"

———

Within two or three years after the above letter was written, the Marquis de Salar was married to the beautiful daughter of the Count ————, mentioned by the author in his anecdotes of the Alhambra. The match was very agreeable to all parties, and the nuptials were celebrated with great festivity.

[October, 1841]

AMERICAN RESEARCHES IN ITALY

LIFE OF TASSO: RECOVERY OF A LOST PORTRAIT OF DANTE.

TO THE EDITOR OF THE KNICKERBOCKER.

Sir: Permit me through the pages of your Magazine to call the attention of the public to the learned and elegant researches in Europe of one of our countrymen, Mr. R. H. WILDE, of Georgia, formerly a member of the House of Representatives. After leaving Congress, Mr. Wilde a few years since spent about eighteen months in travelling through different parts of Europe, until he became stationary for a time in Tuscany. Here he occupied himself with researches concerning the private life of Tasso, whose mysterious and romantic love for the Princess Leonora, his madness and imprisonment, had recently become the theme of a literary controversy, not yet ended; curious in itself, and rendered still more curious by some alledged manuscripts of the poet's, brought forward by Count Alberti. Mr. Wilde entered into the investigation with the enthusiasm of a poet, and the patience and accuracy of a case-hunter; and has produced a work, now in the press, in which the "vexed questions" concerning Tasso are most ably discussed, and lights thrown upon them by his letters, and by various of his sonnets, which last are rendered into English with rare felicity. While Mr. Wilde was occupied upon this work, he became acquainted with Signor Carlo Liverati, an artist of considerable merit, and especially well versed in the antiquities of Florence. This gentleman mentioned incidentally one day, in the course of conversation, that there once and probably still existed in the *Bargello*, anciently both the prison and palace of the republic, an authentic portrait of DANTE. It was believed to be in fresco, on a wall which afterward, by some strange neglect or inadvertency, had been covered with white-wash. Signor Liverati mentioned the circumstance merely to deplore the loss of so precious a portrait, and to regret the almost utter hopelessness of its recovery.

As Mr. Wilde had not as yet imbibed that enthusiastic admiration for Dante which possesses all Italians, by whom the poet is almost worshipped, this conversation made but a slight impression on him at the time. Subsequently, however, his researches concerning Tasso being ended, he began to amuse his leisure hours with attempts to translate some specimens of Italian lyric poetry, and to compose very short biographical sketches of the authors. In these specimens, which as yet exist only in manuscript, he has shown the same critical knowledge of the Italian language, and admirable command of the English, that characterize his translations of Tasso. He had not advanced far in these exercises, when the obscure and contradictory accounts of many incidents in the life of Dante caused him much embarrassment, and sorely piqued his curiosity. About the same time he received, through the courtesy of Don Neri dei Principi Corsini, what he had long most fervently desired, a permission from the Grand Duke to pursue his investigations in the secret archives of Florence, with power to obtain copies therefrom. This was a rich and almost unwrought mine of literary research; for to Italians themselves, as well as to foreigners, their archives for the most part have been long inaccessible. For two years Mr. Wilde devoted himself with indefatigable ardor, to explore the records of the republic during the time of Dante. These being written in barbarous Latin and semi-Gothic characters, on parchment more or less discolored and mutilated, with ink sometimes faded, were rendered still more illegible by the arbitrary abbreviations of the notaries. They require in fact an especial study; few even of the officers employed in the "*Archivio delle Riformagione*" can read them currently and correctly.

Mr. Wilde however persevered in his laborious task with a patience severely tried, but invincible. Being without an index, each file, each book, required to be examined page by page, to ascertain whether any particular of the immortal poet's political life had escaped the untiring industry of his countrymen. This toil was not wholly fruitless, and several interesting facts obscurely known, and others utterly unknown by the Italians themselves, are drawn forth by Mr. Wilde from the oblivion of these archives.

While thus engaged, the circumstance of the lost portrait of Dante was again brought to Mr. Wilde's mind, but now excited intense interest. In perusing the notes of the late learned Canonico Moreri on Filelfo's life of Dante, he found it stated that a portrait of the poet by Giotto was formerly to be seen in the Bargello. He learned also that Signor Scotti, who has charge of the original drawings of the old masters in the imperial and royal gallery, had made several years previously an ineffectual attempt to set on foot a project for the recovery of the lost treasure. Here was a new vein of inquiry, which Mr. Wilde followed up with his usual energy and sagacity. He soon satisfied himself, by reference to Vasari, and to the still more ancient and decisive authority of Filippo Villani, who lived shortly after the poet, that Giotto, the friend and contemporary of Dante, did undoubtedly paint his likeness in the place indicated. Giotto died in 1336, but as Dante was banished, and was even sentenced to be burned, in 1302, it was obvious the work must have been executed before that time; since the portrait of one outlawed and capitally convicted as an enemy to the commonwealth would never have been ordered or tolerated in the chapel of the royal palace. It was clear then, that the portrait must have been painted between 1290 and 1302.

Mr. Wilde now revolved in his own mind the possibility that this precious relic might remain undestroyed under its coat of white-wash, and might yet be restored to the world. For a moment he felt an impulse to undertake the enterprise; but feared that, in a foreigner from a new world, any part of which is unrepresented at the Tuscan court, it might appear like an intrusion. He soon however found a zealous coadjutor. This was one Giovanni Aubrey Bezzi, a Piedmontese exile, who had long been a resident in England, and was familiar with its language and literature. He was now on a visit to Florence, which liberal and hospitable city is always open to men of merit who for political reasons have been excluded from other parts of Italy. Signor Bezzi partook deeply of the enthusiasm of his countrymen for the memory of Dante, and sympathized with Mr. Wilde in his eagerness to retrieve if possible the lost portrait. They had several consultations as to the means to be adopted to effect their purpose, without incurring the charge of undue officiousness. To lessen any objections that might occur they resolved to ask for nothing but permission to search for the fresco painting at their own expense; and should any remains of it be found, then to propose to the nobility and gentry of Florence an association for the purpose of completing the undertaking, and effectually recovering the lost portrait.

For the same reason the formal memorial addressed to the Grand Duke was drawn up in the name of Florentines; among whom were the celebrated Bartolini, now President of the School of Sculpture in the Imperial and Royal Academy, Signor Paolo Ferroni, of the noble family of that name, who has exhibited considerable talent for painting, and Signor Gasparini, also an artist. This petition was urged and supported with indefatigable zeal by Signor Bezzi; and being warmly countenanced by Count Nerli and other functionaries, met with more prompt success than had been anticipated. Signor Marini, a skilful artist, who had succeeded in similar operations, was now employed to remove the whitewash by a process of his own, by which any fresco painting that might exist beneath would be protected from injury. He set to work patiently and cautiously. In a short time he met with evidence of the existence of the fresco. From under the coat of white-wash the head of an angel gradually made its appearance, and was pronounced to be by the pencil of Giotto.

The enterprise was now prosecuted with increased ardor. Several months were expended on the task, and three sides of the chapel-wall were uncovered; they were all painted in fresco by Giotto, with the history of the Magdalen, exhibiting her conversion, her penance, and her beatification. The figures, however, were all those of saints and angels: no historical portraits had yet been discovered, and doubts began to be entertained whether there were any. Still the recovery of an indisputable work of Giotto's was considered an ample reward for any toil; and the Ministers of the Grand Duke, acting under his directions, assumed on his behalf the past charges and future management of the enterprise.

At length, on the uncovering of the fourth wall, the undertaking was crowned with complete success. A number of historical figures were brought to light, and among them the undoubted likeness of Dante. He was represented in full length, in the garb of the time, with a book under his arm, designed most probably to represent the "*Vita Nuova*," for the "Comedia" was not yet composed, and to all appearance from thirty to thirty-five years of age. The face was in profile, and in excellent preservation, excepting that at some former period a nail had unfortunately been driven into the eye. The outline of the eyelid was perfect, so that the injury could easily be remedied. The countenance was extremely handsome, yet bore a strong resemblance to the portraits of the poet taken later in life.

It is not easy to appreciate the delight of Mr. Wilde and his coadjutors at this triumphant result of their researches; nor the sensation produced, not merely in Florence but throughout Italy, by this discovery of a veritable portrait of Dante, in the prime of his days. It was some such sensation as would be produced in England by the sudden discovery of a perfectly well authenticated likeness of Shakspeare; with a difference in intensity proportioned to the superior sensitiveness of the Italians.

The recovery of this portrait of the "divine poet" has occasioned fresh inquiry into the origin of the masks said to have been made from a cast of his face taken after death. One of these masks, in the possession of the Marquess of Torrigiani, has been pronounced as certainly the *original*. Several artists of high talent have concurred in this opinion; among these may be named Jesi, the first engraver in Florence; Seymour Kirkup, Esq., a painter and antiquary; and our own countryman Powers, whose genius, by the way, is very highly appreciated by the Italians.

We may expect from the accomplished pen of Carlo Torrigiani, son of the Marquess, and who is advantageously known in this country, from having travelled here, an account of this curious and valuable relic, which has been upward of a century in the possession of his family.

Should Mr. Wilde finish his biographical work concerning Dante, which promises to be a proud achievement in American literature, he intends, I understand, to apply for permission to have both likenesses copied, and should circumstances warrant the expense, to have them engraved by eminent artists. We shall then have the features of Dante while in the prime of life as well as the moment of his death.

G. C.

[1850]

[MEMOIR OF THOMAS CAMPBELL]

MESSRS. HARPER AND BROTHERS.

Gentlemen:—I feel much obliged to you for the perusal you have afforded me of the biography of Campbell, but fear I have nothing of importance to add to the copious details which it furnishes. My acquaintance with Campbell commenced in, I think, 1810, through his brother Archibald, a most amiable, modest, and intelligent man, but more of a mathematician than a poet. He resided at that time in New York, and had received from his brother a manuscript copy of "O'Connor's Child; or, the Flower of Love Lies Bleeding," for which he was desirous of finding a purchaser among the American publishers. I negotiated the matter for him with a publishing house in Philadelphia, which offered a certain sum for the poem, provided I would write a biographical sketch of the author to be prefixed to a volume containing all his poetical works. To secure a good price for the poet, I wrote the sketch, being furnished with facts by his brother; it was done, however, in great haste, when I was "not in the vein," and, of course, was very slight and imperfect. It served, however, to put me at once on a friendly footing with Campbell, so that, when I met him for the first time a few years subsequently in England, he received me as an old friend. He was living at that time in his rural retreat at Sydenham. His modest mansion was fitted up in a simple style, but with a tact and taste characteristic of the occupants.

Campbell's appearance was more in unison with his writings than is generally the case with authors. He was about thirty seven years of age; of the middle size, lightly and genteelly made; evidently of a delicate, sensitive organization, with a fine intellectual countenance and a beaming poetic eye.

He had now been about twelve years married. Mrs. Campbell still retained much of that personal beauty for which he praises her in his letters written in the early days of matrimony; and her mental qualities seemed equally to justify his eulogies: a rare circumstance, as none are more prone to dupe themselves in affairs of the heart than men of lively imaginations. She was, in fact, a more suitable wife for a poet than poet's wives are apt to be; and for once a son of song had married a reality and not a poetical fiction.

I had considered the early productions of Campbell as brilliant indications of a genius yet to be developed, and trusted that, during the long interval which had elapsed, he had been preparing something to fulfill the public expectation; I was greatly disappointed, therefore, to find that, as yet, he had contemplated no great and sustained effort. My disappointment in this respect was shared by others, who took the same interest in his fame, and entertained the same idea of his capacity. "There he is, cooped up in Sydenham," said a great Edinburgh critic* to me, "simmering his brains to serve up a little dish of poetry, instead of pouring out a whole caldron."

Scott, too, who took a cordial delight in Campbell's poetry, expressed himself to the same effect. "What a pity is it," said he to me, "that Campbell does not give full sweep to his genius. He has wings that would bear him up to the skies, and he does now and then spread them grandly, but folds them up again and resumes his perch, as if afraid to launch away. The fact is, he is a bugbear to himself. The brightness of his early success is a detriment to all his future efforts. *He is afraid of the shadow that his own fame casts before him.*"

Little was Scott aware at the time that he, in truth, was a "bugbear" to Campbell. This I infer from an observation of Mrs. Campbell's in reply to an expression of regret on my part that her husband did not attempt something on a grand scale. "It is unfortunate for Campbell," said she, "that he lives in the same age with Scott and Byron." I asked why. "Oh," said she, "they write so much and so rapidly. Now Campbell writes slowly, and it takes him some time to get under way; and just as he has fairly begun, out comes one of their poems, that sets the world agog and quite daunts him, so that he throws by his pen in despair."

I pointed out the essential differences in their kinds of poetry, and the qualities which insured perpetuity to that of her husband. "You can't persuade Campbell of that," said she. "He is apt to undervalue his own works, and to consider his own little lights put out whenever they come blazing out with their great torches."

I repeated the conversation to Scott some time afterward, and it drew forth a characteristic comment.

"Pooh!" said he, good humoredly, "how can Campbell mistake the matter so much. Poetry goes by quality, not by bulk. My poems are mere cairngorms, wrought up, perhaps, with a cunning hand, and may pass well in the market as long as cairngorms are the fashion; but they are mere Scotch pebbles after all; now Tom Campbell's are real diamonds, and diamonds of the first water."

I have not time at present to furnish personal anecdotes of my intercourse with Campbell, neither does it afford any of a striking nature. Though extending over a number of years, it was never very intimate. His residence in the country, and my own long intervals of absence on the Continent, rendered our meetings few and far between. To tell the truth, I was not much drawn to Campbell, having taken up a wrong notion concerning him from seeing him at times when his mind was ill at ease, and preyed upon by secret griefs. I thought him disposed to be

* Jeffrey.

querulous and captious, and had heard his apparent discontent attributed to jealous repining at the success of his poetical contemporaries. In a word, I knew little of him but what might be learned in the casual intercourse of general society; whereas it required the close communion of confidential friendship to sound the depths of his character and know the treasures of excellence hidden beneath its surface. Besides, he was dogged for years by certain malignant scribblers, who took a pleasure in misrepresenting all his actions, and holding him up in an absurd and disparaging point of view. In what this hostility originated I do not know, but it must have given much annoyance to his sensitive mind, and may have affected his popularity. I know not to what else to attribute a circumstance to which I was a witness during my last visit to England. It was at an annual dinner of the Literary Fund, at which Prince Albert presided, and where was collected much of the prominent talent of the kingdom. In the course of the evening Campbell rose to make a speech. I had not seen him for years, and his appearance showed the effect of age and ill health; it was evident, also, that his mind was obfuscated by the wine he had been drinking. He was confused and tedious in his remarks; still, there was nothing but what one would have thought would be received with indulgence, if not deference, from a veteran of his fame and standing; a living classic. On the contrary, to my surprise, I soon observed signs of impatience in the company; the poet was repeatedly interrupted by coughs and discordant sounds, and as often endeavored to proceed; the noise at length became intolerable, and he was absolutely clamored down, sinking into his chair overwhelmed and disconcerted. I could not have thought such treatment possible to such a person at such a meeting.

Hallam, author of the "Literary History of the Middle Ages," who sat by me on this occasion, marked the mortification of the poet, and it excited his generous sympathy. Being shortly afterward on the floor to reply to a toast, he took occasion to advert to the recent remarks of Campbell, and in so doing called up in review all his eminent achievements in the world of letters, and drew such a picture of his claims upon popular gratitude and popular admiration as to convict the assembly of the glaring impropriety they had been guilty of—to soothe the wounded sensibility of the poet, and send him home to, I trust, a quiet pillow.

I mention these things to illustrate the merit of the piece of biography which you are about to lay before the American world. It is a great act of justice to the memory of a distinguished man, whose character has not been sufficiently known. It gives an insight into his domestic as well as his literary life, and lays open the springs of all his actions and the causes of all his contrariety of conduct. We now see the real difficulties he had to contend with in the earlier part of his literary career; the worldly cares which pulled his spirit to the earth whenever it would wing its way to the skies; the domestic afflictions, tugging at his heart-strings even in his hours of genial intercourse, and converting his very smiles into spasms; the anxious days and sleepless nights preying upon his delicate organization, producing that morbid sensitiveness and nervous irritability which at times overlaid the real sweetness and amenity of his nature, and obscured the unbounded generosity of his heart.

The biography does more: it reveals the affectionate considerateness of his conduct in all the domestic relations of life. The generosity with which he shared his narrow means with all the members of his family, and tasked his precarious resources to add to their relief; his deep-felt tenderness as a husband and a father, the source of exquisite home-happiness for a time, but ultimately of unmitigated wretchedness; his constant and devoted friendships, which in early life were almost romantic passions, and which remained unwithered by age; his sympathies with the distressed of every nation, class, and condition; his love of children, that infallible sign of a gentle and amiable nature; his sensibility to beauty of every kind; his cordial feeling toward his literary contemporaries, so opposite to the narrow and despicable jealousy imputed to him; above all, the crowning romance of his life, his enthusiasm in the cause of suffering Poland, a devotion carried to the height of his poetic temperament, and, in fact, exhausting all that poetic vein which, properly applied, might have produced epics: these and many more traits set forth in his biography bring forth his character in its true light; dispel those clouds which malice and detraction may at times have cast over it; and leave it in the full effulgence of its poetic glory.

This is all, gentlemen, that the hurried nature of personal occupations leaves me leisure to say on this subject. If these brief remarks will be of any service in recommending the biography to the attention of the American public, you are welcome to make such use of them as you may think proper; and I shall feel satisfaction in putting on record my own recantation of the erroneous opinion I once entertained, and may have occasionally expressed, of the private character of an illustrious poet, whose moral worth is now shown to have been fully equal to his exalted genius.

Your obedient servant,
WASHINGTON IRVING.

[November 22, 1851]

CORRECTION OF A MISSTATEMENT RESPECTING *ASTORIA*

To the Editors of the Literary World:

GENTLEMEN—A quotation from Mr. Schoolcraft's work in your last number has drawn from me the following note to that gentleman, which I will thank you to insert in your next.

Yours very truly,
WASHINGTON IRVING.

Nov. 10, 1851.

TO HENRY R. SCHOOLCRAFT, ESQ.

SUNNYSIDE, *Nov.* 10, 1851.

DEAR SIR—In your "Personal Memoirs," recently published, you give a conversation with the late Albert Gallatin, Esq., in the course of which he made to you the following statement:

"Several years ago John Jacob Astor put into my hands the journal of his traders on the Columbia, desiring me to use it. I put it into the hands of Malte Brun, at Paris, who employed the geographical facts in his work, but paid but little respect to Mr. Astor, whom he regarded merely as a merchant seeking his own profit, and not a discoverer. He had not even sent a man to observe the facts in the natural history. Astor did not like it. He was restive several years, and then gave Washington Irving $5,000 to take up the MSS. This is the History of 'Astoria.'"

Now, sir, I beg leave to inform you that this is *not* the History of "Astoria." Mr. Gallatin was misinformed as to the part he has assigned me in it. The work was undertaken by me through a real relish of the subject. In the course of visits in early life to Canada I had seen much of the magnates of the North West Company and of the hardy trappers and fur traders in their employ, and had been excited by their stories of adventurous expeditions into the "Indian country." I was sure, therefore, that a narrative, treating of them and their doings, could not fail to be full of stirring interest, and to lay open regions and races of our country, as yet but little known. I never asked, nor received of Mr. Astor a farthing on account of the work. He paid my nephew, who was then absent practising law in Illinois, for coming on, examining and collating manuscript journals, accounts and other documents, and preparing what lawyers would call a brief, for me. Mr. Fitzgreene Halleck, who was with Mr. Astor at the time, determined what the compensation of my nephew ought to be. When the brief was finished, I paid my nephew an additional consideration on my own account, and out of my own purse. It was the compensation paid by Mr. Astor to my nephew which Mr. Gallatin may have heard of, and supposed it was paid to myself; but even in that case the amount, as reported to him, was greatly exaggerated.

Mr. Astor signified a wish to have the work brought out in a superior style, supposing that it was to be done at his expense. I replied that it must be produced in the style of my other works, and at my expense and risk; and that whatever profit I was to derive from it must be from its sale and my bargain with the publishers. This is the true History of "Astoria," as far as I was concerned in it.

During my long intimacy with Mr. Astor, commencing when I was a young man, and ending only with his death, I never came under a pecuniary obligation to him of any kind. At a time of public pressure and imprudent investments, when, having invested a part of my very moderate means in wild lands, I was straitened and obliged to seek accommodations from monied institutions, he repeatedly urged me to accept loans from him, but I always declined. He was too proverbially rich a man for me to permit the shadow of a pecuniary favor to rest on our intercourse.

The only monied transaction between us was my purchase of a share in a town he was founding at Green Bay; for this I paid cash, though he wished the amount to stand on mortgage. The land fell in value, and some years afterwards, when I was in Spain, Mr. Astor, of his own free will, took back the share from my agent and repaid the original purchase money. This, I repeat, was the only monied transaction that ever took place between us; and by this I lost four or five years' interest of my investment.

My intimacy with Mr. Astor was perfectly independent and disinterested. It was sought originally on his part, and grew up, on mine, out of the friendship he spontaneously manifested for me, and the confidence he seemed to repose in me. It was drawn closer when, in the prosecution of my literary task, I became acquainted, from his papers and his confidential conversations, with the scope and power of his mind, and the grandeur of his enterprizes. His noble project of the ASTOR LIBRARY, conceived about the same time, and which I was solicitous he should carry into execution during his lifetime, was a still stronger link of intimacy between us.

He was altogether one of the most remarkable men I have ever known: of penetrating sagacity, massive intellect, and possessing elements of greatness of which the busy world around him was little aware: who, like Malte Brun, regarded him "merely as a merchant seeking his own profit."

Very respectfully,
Your friend and servant,
WASHINGTON IRVING.

[1851]

THE CATSKILL MOUNTAINS

The Catskill, Katskill, or Cat River Mountains derived their name, in the time of the Dutch domination, from the Catamounts by which they were infested; and which, with the bear, the wolf and the deer, are still to be found in some of their most difficult recesses. The interior of these mountains is in the highest degree wild and romantic; here are rocky precipices mantled with primeval forests; deep gorges walled in by beetling cliffs, with torrents tumbling as it were from the sky; and savage glens rarely trodden excepting by the hunter. With all this internal rudeness, the aspect of these mountains toward the Hudson at times is eminently bland and beautiful, sloping down into a country softened by cultivation and bearing much of the rich character of Italian scenery about the skirts of the Apennines.

The Catskills form an advanced post, or lateral spur of the great Alleganian or Appalachian system of mountains which sweeps through the interior of our continent, from Southwest to Northeast, from Alabama to the extremity of Maine, for nearly fourteen hundred miles, belting the whole of our original confederacy and rivalling our great system of lakes in extent and grandeur. Its vast ramifications comprise a number of parallel sierras and lateral groups; such as the Cumberland Mountains, the Blue Ridge, the Alleganies, the Delaware and Lehigh, the Highlands of the Hudson, the Green Mountains of Vermont and the White Mountains of New Hampshire. In many of these vast ranges or sierras, Nature still reigns in indomitable wildness: their rocky ridges, their rugged clefts and defiles teem with magnificent vegetation. Here are locked up mighty forests that have never been invaded by the axe; deep umbrageous valleys where the virgin soil has never been outraged by the plough; bright streams flowing in untasked idleness, unburthened by commerce, unchecked by the milldam. It is in fact the great poetical region of our Country; resisting, like the tribes which once inhabited it, the taming hand of cultivation; and maintaining a hallowed ground for fancy and the muses.

It is a magnificent and all pervading feature of our Country, that might have given it a name and a poetical one, had not the all controlling powers of commonplace determined otherwise.

The Catskill Mountains, as I have observed, maintain all the internal wildness of the wilderness of mountains with which they are connected. Their detached position, overlooking a wide lowland region with the majestic Hudson rolling through it, has given them a distinct character; and rendered them at all times a rallying point for romance and fable. Much of the fanciful associations with which they have been clothed may be owing to the beautiful atmospherical effects to which they are subject; which in my mind constitute one of the great charms of Hudson River scenery. To me at least they have ever been the fairy region of the Hudson. I speak however from early impressions; made in the happy days of boyhood; when all the world had a tinge of fairy land. I shall never forget my first view of these mountains. It was in the course of a voyage up the Hudson in the good old times before steam boats and rail roads had driven all poetry and romance out of travel. A voyage up the Hudson in those days, was equal to a voyage to Europe at present, and cost almost as much time: but we enjoyed the river in those days, we relished it as we did our wine, sip by sip, not gulping all down at a draught without tasting it. My whole voyage up the Hudson was full of wonder and romance. I was a lively boy, somewhat imaginative, of easy faith, and prone to relish every thing which partook of the marvellous. Among the passengers on board of the sloop was a veteran Indian trader, on his way to the lakes to traffic with the natives. He had discovered my propensity and amused himself throughout the voyage by telling me Indian legends and grotesque stories about every noted place on the river, such as Spuyten Devil Creek, The Tappan Sea, The Devil's Dans Kammer and other hobgoblin places. The Catskill Mountains especially called forth a host of fanciful traditions. We were all day slowly tiding along in sight of them, so that he had full time to weave his whimsical narratives. In these mountains he told me, according to Indian belief, was kept the great treasury of storm and sunshine, for the region of the Hudson. An old squaw spirit had charge of it, who dwelt on the highest peak of the mountain, where she kept day and night shut up in her wigwam, letting out only one at a time. She made new moons every month and hung them up in the sky, cutting up the old ones into stars. The great Manitou, or Master Spirit, employed her to manufacture clouds; sometimes she wove them out of cobwebs, gossamers and morning dew, and sent them off flake after flake, to float in the air and give light summer showers. Sometimes she would brew up black thunder storms and send down drenching rains; to swell the streams and sweep every thing away. He had many stories, also, about mischievous spirits who infested the mountains in the shape of animals and played all kinds of pranks upon Indian hunters, decoying them into quagmires and morasses, or to the brinks of torrents and precipices.* All these were doled out to me as I lay on the deck throughout a long summer's day, gazing upon these mountains, the ever changing shapes and hues of which seemed to realize the magical influences in question. Sometimes they seemed to approach; at others to recede; during the

---

* Some of these Indian superstitions about the Catskill Mountains have already been spoken of in a postscript to Rip Van Winkle, in the revised edition of the Sketch Book.

heat of the day they almost melted into a sultry haze; as the day declined they deepened in tone; their summits were brightened by the last rays of the sun, and later in the evening their whole outline was printed in deep purple against an amber sky. As I beheld them thus shifting continually before my eye, and listened to the marvellous legends of the trader, a host of fanciful notions concerning them was conjured into my brain, which have haunted it ever since.

As to the Indian superstitions concerning the treasury of storms and sunshine, and the cloud weaving spirits, they may have been suggested by the Atmospherical Phenomena of those mountains; the clouds which gather round their summits and the thousand aerial effects which indicate changes of weather over a great extent of country. They are epitomes of our variable climate and are stamped with all its vicissitudes. And here let me say a word in favor of those vicissitudes, which are too often made the subject of exclusive repining. If they annoy us occasionally by changes from hot to cold, from wet to dry, they give us one of the most beautiful climates in the world. They give us the brilliant sunshine of the south of Europe with the fresh verdure of the north. They float our summer sky with clouds of gorgeous tints or fleecy whiteness, instead of leaving it like molten brass; they send down cooling showers to refresh the panting earth and keep it green. Our seasons are all poetical; the phenomena of our heavens are full of sublimity and beauty. Even winter with us has none of its proverbial gloom. It may have its howling winds, and thrilling frosts and whirling snow storms; but it has its long intervals of cloudless sunshine, when the snow clad earth gives redoubled splendor to a day; when at night the stars beam with intense lustre, or the moon floods the whole landscape with her limpid radiance. Our spring too with its sudden transition; bursting at once into leaf and blossom, redundant with vegetation and vociferous with life! The splendors of our summer; its morning voluptuousness and its evening glory; its airy palaces of sun gilt clouds piled up in a deep azure sky; and its purifying gusts of almost tropical grandeur, when the forked lightning and the bellowing thunder volley from the battlements of heaven and shake the sultry atmosphere; and the sublime melancholy of our autumn, magnificent in its decay; withering down the pomp and pride of a woodland country, yet reflecting back from its yellow forests the golden serenity of the sky. Surely we may say that in our climate "the heavens declare the glory of the Lord, and the firmament sheweth forth his handy work: day unto day uttereth speech; and night unto night sheweth forth knowledge."

A word more concerning the Catskills. It is not the Indians only to whom they have been a kind of wonder land. In the early times of the Dutch dynasty we find them themes of golden speculation among even the sages of New Amsterdam. During the administration of Wilhelmus

Kieft there was a meeting between the Director of the New Netherlands and the chiefs of the Mohawk nation to conclude a treaty of peace. On this occasion the Director was accompanied by Mynheer Adrian Van der Donk, Doctor of Laws and subsequently historian of the colony. The Indian chiefs as usual painted and decorated themselves for the ceremony. One of them in so doing made use of a pigment, the weight and shining appearance of which attracted the notice of Kieft and his learned companion, who suspected it to be ore. They procured a lump of it, and took it back with them to New Amsterdam. Here it was submitted to the inspection of Johannes de la Montagne, an eminent Huguenot doctor of medicine, one of the Councillors of the New Netherlands. The supposed ore was forthwith put in a crucible and assayed, and to the great exultation of the junto yielded two pieces of gold, worth about three guilders. This golden discovery was kept a profound secret. As soon as the treaty of peace was adjusted with the Mohawks, William Kieft despatched a trusty officer with a few men under guidance of an Indian, who undertook to conduct them to the place whence the ore had been procured. We have no account of this gold hunting expedition, nor of its whereabouts, excepting that it was somewhere in the Catskill Mountains. The exploring party brought back a bucketful of ore. Like the former specimen it was submitted to the crucible of De la Montagne, and was equally productive of gold. All this we have on the authority of Doctor Van der Donk, who was an eye witness of the process and its result, and records the whole in his Description of the New Netherlands.

William Kieft now dispatched a confidential agent, one Arent Corsen, to convey a sackful of the precious ore to Holland. Corsen embarked at New Haven in a British vessel bound to England, whence he was to cross to Holland. The ship set sail about Christmas, but never reached her port. All on board perished.

In 1647, when the redoubtable Petrus Stuyvesant took command of the New Netherlands, William Kieft embarked on his return to Holland, provided with further specimens of the Catskill Mountain ore; from which he doubtless indulged golden anticipations. A similar fate attended him with that which had befallen his agent. The ship in which he had embarked was cast away, and he and his treasure were swallowed in the waves.

Here closes the golden legend of the Catskills; but another one of similar import succeeds. In 1649, about two years after the shipwreck of Wilhelmus Kieft, there was again rumor of precious metals in the mountains. Mynheer Brant Arent Van Slechtenhorst, agent of the Patroon of Rensselaerswyck, had purchased on behalf of the patroon a tract of the Catskill lands, and leased it out in farms. A Dutch lass in the household of one of the farmers found one day a glittering substance, which on being examined was pronounced silver ore. Brant Van Slechtenhorst forthwith sent his son from Rensselaerswyck to explore the mountains in quest of the supposed mines. The young man put up at the farmer's house, which had recently been erected on the margin of a mountain stream. Scarcely was he housed when a furious storm burst forth in the mountains. The thunders rolled, the lightnings flashed, the rain came down in cataracts; the stream was suddenly swollen to a furious torrent thirty feet deep; the farm house and all its contents were swept away, and it was only by dint of excellent swimming that young Slechtenhorst saved his own life and the lives of his horses. Shortly after this a feud broke out between Peter Stuyvesant and the Patroon of Rensselaerswyck on account of the right and title to the Catskill Mountains, in the course of which the elder Slechtenhorst was taken captive by the potentate of the New Netherlands and thrown in prison at New Amsterdam.

We have met with no record of any further attempt to get at the treasures of the Catskills; adventurers may have been discouraged by the ill luck which appeared to attend all who meddled with them; as if they were under the guardianship of the same spirits or goblins who once haunted the mountains and ruled over the weather.

That gold and silver ore was actually procured from these mountains in days of yore we have historical evidence to prove, and the recorded word of Adrian Van der Donk, a man of weight who was an eye witness. If gold and silver were once to be found there, they must be there at present. It remains to be seen, in these gold hunting days, whether the quest will be revived, and some daring adventurer fired with a true Californian spirit will penetrate the mysteries of these mountains and open a golden region on the borders of the Hudson.

[REMARKS AT THE COOPER MEMORIAL MEETING, FEBRUARY 24, 1852]

I was sorry to find it reported that I intended to deliver an address this evening. I have no talent for public speaking; if I had I would be most happy to do justice to the genius of one whose writings entitle him to the love, respect, and admiration of every American. I appear before you, on this occasion, as Chairman of the Committee of Arrangements, to present to you the Hon. DANIEL WEBSTER, who will preside at this meeting.

[1855]

CONVERSATIONS WITH TALMA
FROM ROUGH NOTES IN A COMMON-PLACE BOOK.

PARIS, *April* 25th, 1821.—Made a call with a friend this morning to be introduced to Talma, the great French tragedian. He has a suite of apartments in a hotel in the Rue des Petites Augustines but is about to build a town residence. He has also a country retreat a few miles from Paris of which he is extremely fond, and is continually altering and improving it. He had just arrived from the country and his apartment was rather in confusion; the furniture out of place and books lying about. In a conspicuous part of the saloon was a coloured engraving of John Kemble, for whom he expresses great admiration and regard.

Talma is about five feet seven or eight inches, English, in height and somewhat robust. There is no very tragic or poetic expression in his countenance; his eyes are of a bluish grey, with at times a peculiar cast; his face is rather fleshy yet flexible, and he has a short thick neck. His manners are open, animated and natural. He speaks English well and is prompt, unreserved and copious in conversation.

He received me in a very cordial manner, and asked if this was my first visit to Paris. I told him I had been here once before; about fourteen years since.

"Ah! that was in the time of the Emperor!" cried he with a sudden gleam of the eye.

"Yes—just after his coronation as King of Italy."

"Ah, those were the heroic days of Paris. Every day some new victory! The real chivalry of France rallied round the Emperor—the youth and talent and bravery of the nation. Now you see the courts of the Tuileries crowded by priests and an old worn out nobility, brought back by foreign bayonets."

He consoled himself by observing that the national character had improved under its reverses. Its checks and humiliations had made the nation more thoughtful. "Look at the young men from the colleges," said he, "how serious they are in their demeanor. They walk together in the public promenades, conversing always on political subjects, but discussing politics philosophically and scientifically. In fact the nation is becoming as grave as the English."

He thinks too that there is likely to be a great change in the French drama. "The public," said he, "feel greater interest in scenes that come home to common life, and in the fortunes of every day people, than in the distresses of the heroic personages of classic antiquity. Hence they never come to the Théâtre Français, excepting to see a few great actors, while they crowd to the minor theatres to witness representations of scenes in ordinary life. The revolution," added he, "has caused such vivid and affecting scenes to pass before their eyes that they can no longer be charmed by fine periods and declamation. They require character, incident, passion, life."

He seems to apprehend another revolution, and that it will be a bloody one. "The nation," said he, "that is to say, the younger part of it, the *children of the revolution,* have such a hatred of the priests and the noblesse that they would fly upon them like wolves upon sheep."

On coming away, he accompanied us to the door. In passing through the antechamber I pointed to children's swords and soldier caps lying on a table. "Ah!" cried he with animation, "the amusements of the children nowadays are all military. They will have nothing to play with but swords, guns, drums and trumpets."

Such are the few brief notes of my first interview with Talma. Some time afterwards I dined in company with him at Beauvillier's Restaurant. He was in fine spirits: gay and earnest by turns, and always perfectly natural and unreserved.

He spoke with pleasure of his residence in England. He liked the English. They were a noble people; but he thought the French more amiable and agreeable to live among. "The intelligent and cultivated English," he said, "are disposed to do generous actions, but the common people are not so liberal as the same class among the French: they have bitter national prejudices. If a French prisoner escaped in England the common people would be against him." In France it was otherwise. "When the fight was going on round Paris," said he, "and Austrian and other prisoners were brought in wounded and conducted along the Boulevards, the Parisian populace shewed great compassion for them and gave them money, bread and wine."

Of the liberality of the cultivated class of English he gave an anecdote. Two French prisoners had escaped from confinement and made their way to a sea port, intending to get over on a boat to France. All their money however was exhausted, and they had not wherewithal to hire a boat. Seeing a banker's name on a door they went in, stated their case frankly and asked for pecuniary assistance, promising to repay it faithfully. The banker at once gave them one hundred pounds. They offered a bill on receipt; but he declined it. "If you be not men of honor," said he, "such paper would be of no value, and if you are men of honor there is no need of it." This circumstance was related to Talma by one of the parties thus obliged.

In the course of conversation we talked of the theatre. Talma had been a close observer of the British stage and was alive to many of its merits. He spoke of his efforts to introduce into French acting the familiar style occasionally used by the best English tragedians, and of the difficulties he encountered in the stately declamation and constantly recurring rhymes of French tragedy. Still he found, he said, every familiar touch of nature immediately appreciated and applauded by the French audiences. Of Shakespeare he expressed the most exalted opinion, and said he should like to attempt some of his principal characters in English, could he be sure of being able to render the text without a foreign accent. He had represented his character of Hamlet, translated into French, in the Théâtre Français, with great success, but he felt how much more powerful it would be if given as Shakespeare had written it. He spoke with admiration of the individuality of Shakespeare's characters; and the varied play of his language, giving such a scope for familiar touches of pathos and tenderness and natural outbreaks of emotion and passion. All this, he observed, required quite a different style of acting from the well balanced verse, flowing periods and recurring rhymes of the French drama; and it would doubtless require much study and practice to catch the spirit of it. "And after all," added he laughing, "I should probably fail. Each stage has its own peculiarities which belong to the nation, and cannot be thoroughly caught, nor perhaps thoroughly appreciated by strangers."

––––––––

[To the foregoing scanty notes were appended some desultory observations made at the time and suggested by my conversations with Talma. They were intended to form the basis of some speculations on the French literature of the day, which were never carried out. They are now given very much in the rough style in which they were jotted down; with some omissions and abbreviations, but no heightenings nor additions.]

––––––––

The success of a translation of Hamlet in the Théâtre Français appears to me an era in the French drama. It is true the play has been sadly mutilated and stripped of some of its most characteristic beauties in the attempt to reduce it to the naked stateliness of the pseudo-classic drama, but it retains enough of the wild magnificence of Shakespeare's imagination to give it an individual character on the French stage. Though the ghost of Hamlet's father does not actually tread the boards, yet it is supposed to hover about his son, unseen by other eyes, and the admirable acting of Talma conveys to the audience a more awful and mysterious idea of this portentous visitation than could be produced by any visible spectre. I have seen a lady carried fainting from the boxes, overcome by its effect upon her imagination. In this translation and modification of the original play Hamlet's mother stabs herself before the audience; a catastrophe hitherto unknown on the grand theatre, and repugnant to the French idea of classic rule.

The popularity of this play is astonishing. On the evenings of its representation the doors of the theatre are besieged at an early hour. Long before the curtain rises the house is crowded to overflowing; and throughout the performance the audience passes from intervals of breathless attention to bursts of ungovernable applause.

The success of this tragedy may be considered one of the triumphs of what is denominated the romantic school; and another has been furnished by the overwhelming reception of Marie Stuart, a modification of the German tragedy of Schiller. The critics of the old school are sadly alarmed at these foreign innovations, and tremble for the ancient decorum and pompous proprieties of their stage. It is true both Hamlet and Marie Stuart have been put in the strait waistcoat of Aristotle, yet they are terribly afraid they will do mischief and set others madding. They exclaim against the apostacy of their countrymen in bowing to foreign idols—and against the degeneracy of their taste; after being accustomed from infancy to the touching beauties and harmonious numbers of Athalie, Polyeucte and Merope, in relishing these English and German monstrosities, and that through the medium of translation. —All in vain. The nightly receipts at the doors outweigh, with managers, all the invectives of the critics, and Hamlet and Marie Stuart maintain triumphant possession of the boards.

Talma assures me that it begins to be quite the fashion in France to admire Shakespeare, and those who cannot read him in English enjoy him diluted in French translations.

It may at first create a smile of incredulity that foreigners should pretend to feel and appreciate the merits of an author, so recondite at times, as to require commentaries and explanations even to his own countrymen; yet it is precisely writers like Shakespeare, so full of thought, of character and passion, that are most likely to be relished even when but partially understood. Authors whose popularity arises from beauty of diction and harmony of numbers are ruined by translation; a beautiful turn of expression, a happy combination of words and phrases, and all the graces of perfect euphony, are limited to the language in which they are written. Style cannot be translated. The most that can be done is to furnish a parallel and render grace for grace. Who can form an idea of the exquisite beauties of Racine when translated into a foreign tongue? But Shakespeare triumphs over translation. His scenes are so exuberant in original and striking thoughts, and masterly strokes of nature, that he can afford to be stripped of all the magic of his style. His volumes are like the magician's cave in Aladdin, so full of jewels and precious things, that he who does but penetrate for a moment, may bring away enough to enrich himself.

The relish for Shakespeare however, which according to Talma is daily encreasing in France, is, I apprehend, but one indication of a general revolution which is taking place in the national taste. The French character, as Talma well observes, has materially changed during the last thirty years. The present generation (the "children of the revolution," as Talma terms them) who are just growing into the full exercise of talent, are a different people from the French of the old regime. They have grown up in rougher times and among more adventurous and romantic habitudes. They are less delicate in tact, but stronger in their feelings, and require more stimulating aliment. The Frenchman of the camp, who has bivouacked on the Danube and the Wolga; who has brought back into peaceful life the habits of the soldier; who wears fierce moustaches, swaggers in his gait and smokes tobacco, is of course a different being in his literary tastes from the Frenchman of former times, who was refined but finical in dress and manners; wore powder and delighted in perfumes and polished versification.

The whole nation, in fact, has been accustomed for years to the glitter of arms and the parade of soldiery: to tales of battles, sieges and victories. The feverish drama of the revolution and the rise and fall of Napoleon have passed before their eyes like a tale of Arabian enchantment. Though these realities have passed away; the remembrances of them remain, with a craving for the strong emotions which they excited.

This may account in some measure for that taste for the romantic which is growing upon the French nation: a taste vehemently but vainly reprobated by their critics. You see evidence of it in every thing; in their paintings; in the engravings which fill their printshops; in their songs, their spectacles and their works of fiction. For several years it has been making its advances without exciting the jealousy of the critics, its advances being apparently confined to the lower regions of literature and the arts. The circulating libraries have been filled with translations of English and German romances and tales of ghosts and robbers, and the theatres of the boulevards occupied by representations of melodrames. Still the higher regions of literature remained unaffected, and the national theatre retained its classic stateliness and severity. The critics consoled themselves with the idea that the romances were only read by women and children, and the melodrames admired by the ignorant and vulgar. But the children have grown up to be men and women; and the tinge given to their imaginations in early life is now to have an effect on the forthcoming literature of the country. As yet they depend for their romantic aliment upon the literature of other nations, especially the English and Germans, and it is astonishing with what promptness the Scottish novels, notwithstanding their dialects, are translated into French, and how universally and eagerly they are sought after.

In poetry Lord Byron is the vogue; his verses are translated into a kind of stilted prose and devoured with extacy, they are *si sombre*! His likeness is in every print shop. The Parisians envelop him with melancholy and mystery and believe him to be the hero of his own poems; or some thing of the vampyre order. A French poem has lately appeared in imitation of him;* the author of which has caught in a great degree his glowing style and deep and troubled emotions. The great success of this production ensures an inundation of the same kind of poetry from inferior hands. In a little while we shall see the petty poets of France, like those of England, affecting to be moody and melancholy; each wrapping himself in a little mantle of mystery and misanthropy, vaguely accusing himself of heinous crimes and affecting to despise the world.

That this taste for the romantic will have its way, and give a decided tone to French literature, I am strongly inclined to believe. The human mind delights in variety and abhors monotony even in excellence. Nations, like individuals, grow sated with artificial refinements, and their pampered palates require a change of diet, even though it be for the worse. I should not be surprised, therefore, to see the French breaking away from rigid rule; from polished verse, easy narrative, the classic drama, and all the ancient delights of elegant literature, and rioting in direful romances, melodramatic plays, turgid prose and glowing, rough written poetry.

PARIS, 1821.

[1855]

[MEMOIR OF WASHINGTON ALLSTON]

I first became acquainted with Washington Allston early in the Spring of 1805. He had just arrived from France; I from Sicily and Naples. I was then not quite twenty two years of age; he a little older. There was something, to me, inexpressibly engaging in the appearance and manners of Allston. I do not think I have ever been more completely captivated on a first acquaintance. He was of a light and graceful form; with large blue eyes, and black silken hair, waving and curling round a pale expressive countenance. Every thing about him bespoke the man of intellect and refinement. His conversation was copious, animated and highly graphic; warmed by a general sensibility and benevolence, and enlivened at times by a chaste and gentle humor.

A young man's intimacy took place immediately between us, and we

* The Missennienes.

were much together during my brief sojourn at Rome. He was taking a general view of the place before settling himself down to his professional studies. We visited together some of the finest collections of paintings, and he taught me how to visit them to the most advantage; guiding me always to the masterpieces, and passing by the others without notice. "Never attempt to enjoy every picture in a great collection," he would say, "unless you have a year to bestow upon it. You may as well attempt to enjoy every dish in a Lord Mayor's feast. Both mind and palate get confounded by a great variety and rapid succession, even of delicacies. The mind can only take in a certain number of images and impressions distinctly; by multiplying the number you weaken each and render the whole confused and vague. Study the choice pieces in each collection; look upon none else, and you will afterwards find them hanging up in your memory."

He was exquisitely sensible to the graceful and the beautiful and took great delight in paintings which excelled in colour; yet he was strongly moved and roused by objects of grandeur: I well recollect the admiration with which he contemplated the sublime statue of Moses by Michael Angelo, and his mute awe and reverence on entering the stupendous pile of St. Peter's. Indeed the sentiment of veneration so characteristic of the elevated and poetic mind was continually manifested by him. His eyes would dilate; his pale countenance would flush; he would breathe quick and almost gasp in expressing his feelings when excited by any object of grandeur and sublimity.

We had delightful rambles together about Rome and its environs; one of which came near changing my whole course in life. We had been visiting a stately villa, with its gallery of paintings; its marble halls; its terraced gardens set out with statues and fountains, and were returning to Rome about sunset. The blandness of the air, the serenity of the sky, the transparent purity of the atmosphere and that nameless charm which hangs about an Italian landscape, had derived additional effect from being enjoyed in company with Allston, and pointed out by him with the enthusiasm of an artist. As I listened to him and gazed upon the landscape, I drew in my mind a contrast between our different pursuits and prospects. He was to reside among these delightful scenes; surrounded by masterpieces of art; by classic and historic monuments; by men of congenial minds and tastes, engaged like him in the constant study of the sublime and beautiful. I was to return home to the dry study of the law; for which I had no relish, and, as I feared, but little talent.

Suddenly the thought presented itself, "Why might I not remain here and turn painter?" I had taken lessons in drawing before leaving America, and had been thought to have some aptness, as I certainly had a strong inclination for it. I mentioned the idea to Allston and he caught at it with eagerness. Nothing could be more feasible. We would take an apartment together. He would give me all the instruction and assistance in his power, and was sure I would succeed.

For two or three days the idea took full possession of my mind; but I believe it owed its main force to the lovely evening ramble in which I first conceived it and to the romantic friendship I had formed with Allston. Whenever it recurred to mind it was always connected with beautiful Italian scenery, palaces, and statues, and fountains and terraced gardens, and Allston as the companion of my studio. I promised myself a world of enjoyment in his society, and in the society of several artists with whom he had made me acquainted, and pictured forth a scheme of life all tinted with the rainbow hues of youthful promise.

My lot in life, however, was differently cast. Doubts and fears gradually clouded over my prospect; the rainbow tints faded away; I began to apprehend a sterile reality. So I gave up the transient but delightful project of remaining in Rome with Allston and turning painter.

My next meeting with Allston was in America after he had finished his studies in Italy; but, as we resided in different cities, we saw each other only occasionally. Our intimacy was closer some years afterwards when we were both in England. I then saw a great deal of him during my visits to London, where he and Leslie resided together. Allston was dejected in spirits from the loss of his wife, but I thought a dash of melancholy had increased the amiable and winning graces of his character. I used to pass long evenings with him and Leslie; indeed Allston, if any one would keep him company, would sit up until cock crowing, and it was hard to break away from the charms of his conversation. He was an admirable story teller; for a ghost story none could surpass him. He acted the story as well as told it.

I have seen some anecdotes of him in the public papers, which represent him in a state of indigence and almost despair; until rescued by the sale of one of his paintings. This is an exaggeration. I subjoin an extract or two from his letters to me, relating to his most important pictures. The first, dated May 9th 1817, was addressed to me at Liverpool, where he supposed I was about to embark for the United States.

"Your sudden resolution of embarking for America has quite thrown me, to use a sea phrase, all a-back. I have so many things to tell you of—to consult you about, &c., and am such a sad correspondent, that before I can bring my pen to do its office 'tis a hundred to one but the occasions for which your advice would be wished will have passed and gone. One of these subjects (and the most important) is the large picture I talked of soon beginning, the Prophet Daniel interpreting the *handwriting on the wall* before Belshazzar. I have made a highly finished sketch of it, and I wished much to have your remarks on it. But as your sudden departure will deprive me of this advantage, I must beg, should any hints on the subject occur to you during your voyage, that you will favor me with them, at the same time you let me know that you are again safe in our good country.

"I think the composition the best I ever made. It contains a multitude of figures and (if I may be allowed to say it) they are without confusion. Don't you think it a fine subject? I know not any that so happily unites the magnificent and the awful. A mighty sovereign surrounded by his whole court, intoxicated with his own state in the midst of his revellings, palsied in a moment under the spell of a preternatural hand suddenly tracing his doom on the wall before him: his powerless limbs, like a wounded spider's, shrunk up to his body, while his heart, *compressed to a point*, is only kept from vanishing by the terrific suspense that animates it during the interpretation of his mysterious sentence. His less guilty but scarcely less agitated Queen, the panic-struck courtiers and concubines, the splendid and deserted banquet table, the half arrogant, half astounded magicians, the holy vessels of the Temple (shining as it were in triumph through the gloom) and the calm solemn contrast of the prophet, standing like an animated pillar in the midst, breathing forth the oracular destruction of the empire!—The picture will be twelve feet high by seventeen feet long.—Should I succeed in it to my wishes, I know not what may be its fate. But I leave the future to Providence.—Perhaps I may send it to America."

The next letter from Allston which remains in my possession is dated London, 13 March 1818. In the interim he had visited Paris in company with Leslie and Newton; the following extract gives the result of the excitement caused by a study of the masterpieces in the Louvre.

"Since my return from Paris I have painted two pictures, in order to have something in the present exhibition at the British gallery; the subjects the Angel Uriel in the Sun, and Elijah in the Wilderness. Uriel was immediately purchased, (at the price I asked, 150 guineas) by the Marques of Stafford, and the directors of the British Institution moreover presented me a *donation* of a hundred and fifty pounds, 'as a mark of their *approbation* of the talent evinced,' &c. The manner in which this was done was highly complimentary; and I can only say that it was full as gratifying as it was unexpected. As both these pictures together cost me but ten weeks, I do not regret having deducted that time from the Belshazzar, to whom I have since returned with redoubled vigour. I am sorry I did not exhibit Jacob's Dream. If I had dreamt of this success I certainly would have sent it there."

Leslie in a letter to me speaks of the picture of Uriel seated on the sun. "The figure is colossal, the attitude and air very noble and the form heroic without being over charged. In the colour he has been equally successful, and with a very rich and glowing tone he has avoided *positive* colours, which would have made him too material. There is neither red, blue nor yellow on the picture, and yet it possesses a harmony equal to the best pictures of Paul Veronese."

The picture made what is called a "decided hit" and produced a great sensation; being pronounced worthy of the old masters. Attention was immediately called to the artist. The Earl of Egremont, a great connoisseur and patron of the arts, sought him in his studio; eager for any production of his pencil. He found one admirable picture there of which he became the glad possessor. The following is an extract from Allston's letter to me on the subject.

"Leslie tells me he has informed you of the sale of Jacob's Dream. I do not remember if you have seen it. The manner in which Lord Egremont bought it was particularly gratifying—to say nothing of the price, which is no trifle to me at present. But Leslie having told you all about it I will not repeat it. Indeed by the account he gives me of his letter to you he seems to have puffed me off in grand style. Well—you know I don't *bribe* him to do it. And, 'if they will buckle praise upon my back' —why, I can't help it!—Leslie has just finished a very beautiful little picture of Anne Page inviting Master Slender into the house. Anne is exquisite; soft and feminine, yet arch and playful. She is all she should be. Slender also is very happy; he is a good parody on Milton's 'linked sweetness long drawn out.' Falstaff and Shallow are seen through a window in the back ground. The whole scene is very picturesque, and beautifully painted. 'Tis his best picture. You must not think this praise the 'return in kind.' I give it because I really admire the picture, and I have not the smallest doubt, that he will do great things, when he is once freed from the necessity of painting portraits."*

Lord Egremont was equally well pleased with the artist as with his works and invited him to his noble seat at Petworth, where it was his delight to dispense his hospitalities to men of genius. The road to fame and fortune was now open to Allston; he had but to remain in England and follow up the signal impression he had made.

Unfortunately, previous to this recent success he had been disheartened by domestic affliction, and by the uncertainty of his pecuniary prospects, and had made arrangements to return to America. I arrived in London a few days before his departure, full of literary schemes, and delighted with the idea of our pursuing our several arts in fellowship. It was a sad blow to me to have this day dream again dispelled. I urged him to remain and complete his grand painting of Belshazzar's Feast; the study of which gave promise of the highest kind of excellence. Some of the best patrons of the art were equally urgent. He was not to be persuaded, and I saw him depart with still deeper and more painful regret than I

---

* This picture was formerly in the possession of Philip Hone, Esq., and is probably still in New York.

had parted with him in our youthful days at Rome. I think our separation was a loss to both of us—to me a grievous one. The companionship of such a man was invaluable. For his own part, had he remained in England for a few years longer, surrounded by every thing to encourage and stimulate him, I have no doubt he would have been at the head of his art. He appeared to me to possess more than any contemporary the spirit of the old masters; and his merits were becoming widely appreciated. After his departure he was unanimously elected a member of the Royal Academy.

The next time I saw him was twelve years afterwards, on my return to America; when I visited him at his studio at Cambridge in Massachusetts and found him, in the gray evening of life; apparently much retired from the world, and his grand picture of Belshazzar's Feast yet unfinished.

To the last he appeared to retain all those elevated, refined and gentle qualities which first endeared him to me.

Such are a few particulars of my intimacy with Allston; a man whose memory I hold in reverence and affection, as one of the purest, noblest and most intellectual beings that ever honored me with his friendship.

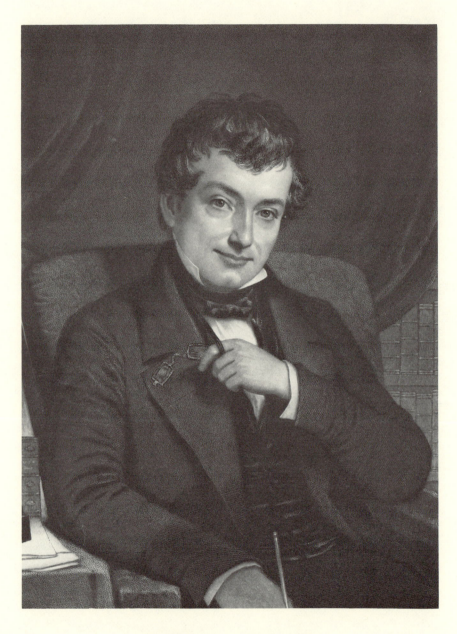

Washington Irving, 1858

An engraving by John Sartain from a sketch by the same artist.

NARRATIVES OF SPANISH HISTORY
LEFT UNPUBLISHED AT
IRVING'S DEATH

[1827–1847]

[THE CHRONICLE OF PELAYO]

[CHAPTER I

Obscurity of the ancient chronicles—The loves of Doña Lucia and the Duke of Favila—Birth of Pelayo, and what happened thereupon; his early fortunes, and his tutelage under the veteran Count Grafeses.]

It is the common lamentation of Spanish historians that, in the obscure and melancholy space of time which succeeded the perdition of their country, its history is a mere wilderness of dubious facts, wild exaggerations and evident fables. Many learned men in cells and cloisters have passed their lives in the weary and fruitless task of attempting to correct incongruous events and reconcile absolute contradictions. The worthy Jesuit Pedro Abarca confesses that, for more than forty years, during which he had been employed in theological controversies, he had never found any questions so obscure and inexplicable as those rising out of this portion of Spanish history; and that the only fruit of an indefatigable, prolix, and even prodigious study of the subject, was a melancholy and mortifying indecision.*

Let us console ourselves, therefore, in our attempts to thread this mazy labyrinth with the reflection that, if we occasionally err and become bewildered, we do but share the errors and perplexities of our graver and more laborious predecessors; and that, if we occasionally stray into the flowery bye-ways of fanciful tradition, we are as likely to arrive at the truth as those who travel by more dry and dusty, but not more authenticated paths.

We premise these suggestions before proceeding to cull, from the midst of the fables and extravagancies of ancient chronicles, a few particulars of the story of Pelayo, the deliverer of Spain; whose name, like that of William Wallace the hero of Scotland, will ever be linked with the glory of his country; but linked, like his, by a band in which fact and fiction are indissolubly mingled.

In the ensuing pages it is our intention to give little more than an abstract of an old chronicle teeming with extravagancies, yet containing facts of admitted credibility, and presenting pictures of Spanish life, partly sylvan, partly chivalrous, which have all the quaint merit of the curious delineations in old tapestry.

---

* Abarca, *Anales de Aragon.* Ante regno, § 2.

The origin of Pelayo is wrapped in great obscurity, though all writers concur in making him of royal Gothic lineage. The chronicle in question makes Pelayo the offspring of a love affair in the court of Ezica, one of the last of the Gothic kings, who held his seat of government at Toledo. Among the noble damsels brought up in the royal household was the beautiful Lucia, niece and maid of honor to the queen. A mutual passion subsisted between her and Favila, the youthful Duke of Cantabria, one of the most accomplished cavaliers of the kingdom. The duke, however, had a powerful rival in the Prince Witiza, son to the king, and afterwards known for the profligacy of his reign by the name of Witiza the Wicked. The prince, to rid himself of a favored rival, procured the banishment of Favila to his estates in Cantabria; not, however, before he had been happy in his loves in stolen interviews with the fair Lucia. The cautious chronicler, however, lets us know that a kind of espousal took place by the lovers plighting their faith with solemn vows before an image of the Virgin, and as the image gave no sign of dissent by way of forbidding the bans, the worthy chronicler seems to consider them as good as man and wife.

After the departure of the duke, the prince renewed his suit with stronger hope of success but met with a repulse which converted his love into implacable and vengeful hate.

The beautiful Lucia continued in attendance on the queen, but soon became sensible of the consequences of her secret and informal nuptials so tacitly sanctioned by the Virgin. In the process of time, with great secrecy, she gave birth to a male child, whom she named Pelayo. For fifteen days the infant was concealed in her apartment, and she trusted all was safe, when, to her great terror, she learnt that her secret had been betrayed to Prince Witiza and that search was to be made for the evidence of her weakness.

The dread of public scorn and menace' of a cruel death overcame even the feelings of a mother. Through means of a trusty female of her chamber she procured a little ark, so constructed as to be impervious to water. She then arrayed her infant in costly garments, wrapping it in a mantle of rich brocade, and, when about to part with it, kissed it many times and laid it in her lap and wept over it. At length the child was borne away by the Dueña of her ,chamber and a faithful handmaid. It was dark midnight when they conveyed it to the borders of the Tagus, where it washes the rocky foundations of Toledo. Covering it from the dew and night air, they committed the ark to the eddying current, which soon swept it from the shore. As it glided down the rapid stream, says the ancient chronicle, they could mark its course even in the darkness of the night; for it was surrounded by a halo of celestial light.* They knew not how to account for this prodigy, says the same authentic writer, until they remembered that the mother had blessed the child with the sign of the cross and had baptised it with her own hand. Others, however, explain this marvel differently, for in this child, say they, was centered the miraculous light which was afterwards to shine forth with comfort and deliverance in the darkest hour of Spain.

The chronicle quoted by Fray Antonio Agapida goes on to state what befel the fair Lucia after the departure of the child. Her apartments were searched at early dawn, but no proof appeared to substantiate the charges made against her. The Prince Witiza persisted in accusing her publicly of having brought disgrace upon her line by her frailty. A cavalier of the court, suborned by him, supported the accusation by an oath and offered to maintain the truth of it by his sword. A month was granted by the king for the afflicted lady to find a champion, and a day appointed for the lists; if none appeared, or if her champion were overcome, she was to be considered guilty and put to death. The day arrived, the accusing knight was on the ground in complete armor; proclamation was made, but no one stepped forward to defend the lady. At length a trumpet sounded; an unknown knight with visor closed, entered the lists. The combat was long and doubtful, for it would appear as if the Holy Virgin was not perfectly satisfied with the nature of the espousals which had taken place before her image. At length the accusing knight was overcome and slain, to the great joy of the court and all the spectators, and the beautiful Lucia was pronounced as immaculate as the Virgin her protectress.

The unknown champion of course proved to be the Duke of Cantabria. He obtained a pardon of the king for returning from banishment without the royal permission; what is more, he obtained permission formally to espouse the lady whose honor he had so gallantly established. Their nuptials were solemnized in due form and with great magnificence, after which he took his blooming bride to his castle in Cantabria to be out of reach of the persecutions of the Prince Witiza.

Having made this brief abstract of what occupies many a wordy page in the ancient chronicle, we return to look after the fortunes of the infant Pelayo when launched upon the waves in the darkness of the night.

The ark containing this future hope of Spain, continues the old chronicle, floated down the current of the golden Tagus, where that renowned river winds through the sylvan solitudes of Estremadura. All night, and throughout the succeeding day and the following night, it made its tranquil way; the stream ceased its wonted turbulence

---

* El Moro Rasis, *La Destruycion de España*. Rojas, *Hist. Toledo*, p. 2, L. 4, c. 1.

and dimpled round it; the swallow circled round it with lively chirp and sportive wing, the breezes whispered musically among the reeds, which bowed their tall heads as it passed; such was the bland influence of the protection of the Virgin.

Now so it happened that at this time there lived in a remote part of Estremadura an ancient cavalier, a hale and hearty bachelor, named the Count Grafeses. He had been a warrior in his youth, but now, in a green and vigorous old age, had retired from camp and court to a domain on the banks of the Tagus, inherited from his Gothic ancestors. His great delight was in the chase, which he followed successfully in the vast forests of Estremadura. Every morning heard the woods resounding with the melody of hound and horn; and the heads of stags, of wolves and wild boars, vied in his castle hall with the helms and bucklers and lances, and the trophies of his youthful and martial days.

The jovial count was up at early dawn pursuing a boar in the thick forest bordering the Tagus when he beheld the little ark floating down the stream. He ordered one of his huntsmen to strip and enter the river and bring the ark to land. On opening it, he was surprized to behold within an infant wrapped in costly robes, but pale and wan and apparently almost exhausted. Beside it was a purse of gold, and on its bosom a cross of rubies and a parchment scroll, on which was written, "Let this infant be honorably entertained; he is of illustrious lineage; his name is Pelayo."

The good count shrewdly surmised the cause of this perilous exposure of a helpless infant. He had a heart kind and indulgent toward the weaker sex, as the heart of a genial old bachelor is prone to be; and while he looked with infinite benevolence upon the beauteous child, felt a glow of compassion for the unknown mother. Commanding his huntsman to be silent as to what he had witnessed, he took the infant in his arms and returned with it to his castle.

Now so it happened that the wife of his steward had, about a week before, been delivered of a child which lived but a very few days, leaving the mother in great affliction. The count gave her the infant, and the money found with it, and told her the story of the ark, with a strong injunction of secrecy; entreating her to take charge of the child and rear it as her own. The good woman doubted the story, and strongly suspected her master of having fallen into an error in his old age; she received the infant, however, as a gift from heaven sent to console her in her affliction; and pressed it with tears to her bosom; for she thought of the child she had lost.

Pelayo, therefore, was reared on the banks of the Tagus as the offspring of the steward and his wife and the adopted son of the count. That veteran cavalier bore in mind, however, that his youthful charge

was of illustrious lineage, and took a delight in accomplishing him
in all things befitting a perfect hidalgo. He placed him astride of a
horse almost as soon as he could walk; a lance and cross bow were
his earliest playthings, and he was taught to hunt the small game of
the forest until strong enough to accompany the count in his more
rugged sports. Thus he was inured to all kinds of hardy exercises and
rendered heedless of danger and fatigue. Nor was the discipline of his
mind neglected. Under the instructions of a neighboring friar he
learned to read in a manner that surpassed the erudition of his foster-
father, for he could con more correctly all the orizons of the Virgin,
and listened to mass and attended all the ceremonies of the church
with a devotion truly exemplary. Some ancient chroniclers have gone
so far as to say that he even excelled in clerkly craft; but this is most
likely fond exaggeration.

Time glided by. King Ezica was gathered to his fathers and his son
Witiza reigned in his stead. All the chivalry of the kingdom was summoned to Toledo to give splendor to his coronation. The good old
count prepared, among the rest, to appear at a court from which he
had long been absent. His ancient serving-men were arrayed in the
antiquated garbs in which they had figured in his days of youthful
gallantry, and his household troops in the battered armor which had
seen hard service in the field, but which had long rusted in the armory.
He determined to take with him his adopted son Pelayo, now seven
years of age. A surcoat was made for him from the mantle of rich
brocade in which he had been found wrapped in the ark. A palfrey
was also caparisoned for him in warlike style. It was a rare sight, says
the old chronicler, to see the antiquated chivalry of the good Count
Grafeses parading across the bridge of the Tagus, or figuring in the
streets of Toledo, in contrast to the silken and shining retinues of the
more modern courtiers; but the veteran was hailed with joy by many
of the ancient nobles, his early companions in arms. The populace
too, when they beheld the youthful Pelayo ambling by his side on his
gentle palfrey, were struck with the chivalrous demeanor of the boy
and the perfect manner in which he managed his steed.

[CHAPTER II

What happened to Pelayo at the Court of Witiza.]

Among the nobles, continues the old chronicle, who appeared in Toledo
to do homage to the new king, was Favila, Duke of Cantabria. He had
left his wife in their castle among the mountains, for the fair Lucia was
still in the meridian of her beauty, and he feared lest the sight of her

might revive the passion of Witiza. They had no other fruit of their union but a little daughter of great beauty called Lucinda, and they still mourned in secret the loss of their first born. The duke was related to Count Grafeses; and when he first beheld Pelayo his heart throbbed, he knew not why, and he followed him with his eyes in all his youthful sports. The more he beheld him the more his heart yearned toward him, and he entreated the count to grant him the youth for a time as a page; to be reared by him in all the offices of chivalry, as was the custom in the houses of warlike nobles in those days.

The count willingly complied with his request, knowing the great prowess of the Duke of Cantabria who was accounted a mirror of knightly virtue. "For my own part," said he, "I am at present but little capable of instructing the boy; for many years have passed since I gave up the exercise of arms, and little am I worth at present excepting to blow the horn and follow the hound."

When the ceremonies of the coronation were over, therefore, the Duke of Cantabria departed for his castle accompanied by the young Pelayo and the count, for the good old cavalier could not yet tear himself from his adopted child.

As they drew near the castle, the Duchess came forth with a grand retinue; for they were as petty sovereigns in their domains. The duke presented Pelayo to her as her page and the youth knelt to kiss her hand, but she raised him and kissed him on the forehead; and as she regarded him the tears stood in her eyes.

"God bless thee gentle page," said she, "and preserve thee to the days of manhood; for thou hast in thee, the promise of an accomplished cavalier. Joyful must be the heart of the mother who can boast of such a son!"

On that day, when the dinner was served with becoming state, Pelayo took his place among the other pages in attendance, who were all children of nobles; but the Duchess called him to her as her peculiar page. He was arrayed in his surcoat of brocade, made from the mantle in which he had been folded in the ark, and round his neck hung the cross of rubies.

As the Duchess beheld these things she turned pale and trembled. "What is the name of thy son?" said she to Count Grafeses. "His name," replied the count, "is Pelayo." "Tell me of a truth," demanded she still more earnestly, "is this indeed thy son?"—The count was not prepared for so direct a question. "Of a truth," said he, "he is but the son of my adoption; yet is he of noble lineage." The Duchess again addressed him with tenfold solemnity. "On thy honor as a knight do not trifle with me. Who are the parents of this child?" The count, moved by her agitation, briefly told the story of the ark. When the Duchess heard it—she gave a great sigh and fell as one dead. On reviving she embraced

Pelayo with mingled tears and kisses and proclaimed him as her long lost son.

[CHAPTER III

How Pelayo lived among the mountains of Cantabria. His adventure with the needy hidalgo of Gascony and the rich merchant of Bordeaux—Discourse of the holy hermit.]

The authentic Agapida passes over many pages of the ancient chronicle narrating the early life of Pelayo, presenting nothing of striking importance. His father, the Duke of Cantabria, was dead, and he was carefully reared by his widowed mother at a castle in the Pyrenees, out of the reach of the dangers and corruptions of the court. Here that hardy and chivalrous education was continued which had been commenced by his veteran foster-father on the banks of the Tagus. The rugged mountains around abounded with the bear, the wild boar and the wolf; and in hunting these he prepared himself for the conflicts of the field.

The old chronicler records an instance of his early prowess in the course of one of his hunting expeditions on the immediate borders of France. The mountain passes and the adjacent lands were much infested and vexed by marauders from Gascony. The Gascons, says the worthy Agapida, were a people ready to lay their hands upon every thing they met. They used smooth words when necessary but force when they dared. Though poor they were proud; there was not one who did not plume himself upon being a hijo de algo, or son of somebody. Whenever Pelayo, therefore, hunted on the borders infested by these people he was attended by a page conducting his horse, with his buckler and lance; to be at hand in case of need.

At the head of a band of fourteen of these self-styled hidalgos of Gascony was a broken down cavalier by the name of Arnaud. He and four of his comrades were well armed and mounted, the rest were mere scamper grounds on foot armed with darts and javelins. This band was the terror of the border: here to day, gone tomorrow; sometimes in one pass of the mountains; sometimes in another; sometimes they made descents into Spain, harassing the roads and marauding the country, and were over the mountains again and into France before a force could be sent against them.

It so happened that while Pelayo with a number of his huntsmen was on the border, this Gascon cavalier and his crew were on the maraud. They had heard of a rich merchant of Bordeaux who was to pass through the mountains on his way to one of the ports of Biscay with which several of his vessels traded, and that he would carry with him much money for the purchase of merchandize. They determined to ease him of his money bags; for, being hidalgos who lived by the sword, they considered all peaceful men of trade as lawful spoil, sent by heaven for the supply of men of valour and gentle blood.

As they waylaid a lonely defile they beheld the merchant approaching. He was a fair and portly man, whose looks bespoke the good cheer of his native city. He was mounted on a stately and well fed steed; beside him on palfreys paced his wife, a comely dame, and his daughter, a damsel of marriageable age, and fair to look upon. A young man, his nephew, who acted as his clerk, rode with them and a single domestic followed.

When the travellers had advanced within the defile the bandeleros rushed from behind a rock and set upon them. The nephew fought valiantly and was slain; the servant fled; the merchant, though little used to the exercise of arms and of unwieldy bulk, made courageous defence, having his wife and daughter and his money bags at hazard. He was wounded in two places and overpowered.

The freebooters were disappointed at not finding the booty they expected; and, putting their swords to the breast of the merchant, demanded where was the money with which he was to traffic in Biscay. The trembling merchant informed them that a trusty servant was following him at no great distance with a stout hackney laden with bags of money. Overjoyed at this intelligence they bound their captives to trees and awaited the arrival of the treasure.

In the mean time Pelayo was on a hill near a narrow pass awaiting a wild boar which his huntsmen were to rouse. While thus posted, the merchant's servant who had escaped came running in breathless terror, but fell on his knees before Pelayo and craved his life in the most piteous terms, supposing him another of the robbers. It was some time before he could be persuaded of his mistake and made to tell the story of the robbery. When Pelayo heard the tale he perceived that the robbers in question must be the Gascon hidalgos upon the scamper. Taking his armor from the page he put on his helmet, slung his buckler round his neck, took lance in hand and, mounting his horse, compelled the trembling servant to guide him to the scene of the robbery. At the same time he despatched his page to summon as many of his huntsmen as possible to his assistance.

When the robbers saw Pelayo advancing through the forest, the sun sparkling upon his rich armor; and saw that he was attended but by a single page, they considered him a new prize, and Arnaud and two of his companions mounting their horses advanced to meet him. Pelayo put himself in a narrow pass between two rocks where he could only be attacked in front, and, bracing his buckler and lowering his lance, awaited their coming.

"Who and what are ye," cried he, "and what seek ye on this land?"

"We are huntsmen," replied Arnaud, "in quest of game; and lo it runs into our toils."

"By my faith," said Pelayo, "thou wilt find the game easier roused than taken; have at thee for a villain."

So saying he put spurs to his horse and charged upon him. Arnaud was totally unprepared for so sudden an assault; having scarce anticipated a defence. He hastily couched his lance, but it merely glanced on the shield of Pelayo, who sent his own through the middle of his breast, and threw him out of his saddle to the earth. One of the other robbers made at Pelayo and wounded him slightly in the side, but received a blow over the head, which cleft his scull cap and sank into his brain. His companion, seeing him fall, galloped off through the forest.

By this time three or four of the robbers on foot had come up, and assailed Pelayo. He received two of their darts on his buckler, a javelin razed his cuirass, and his horse received two wounds. Pelayo then rushed upon them and struck one dead; the others, seeing several huntsmen advancing, took to flight: two were overtaken and made prisoners; the rest escaped by clambering among rocks and precipices.

The good merchant of Bordeaux and his family beheld this scene with trembling and amazement. They almost looked upon Pelayo as something more than mortal, for they had never witnessed such feats of arms. Still they considered him as a leader of some rival band of robbers, and when he came up and had the bonds loosened by which they were fastened to the trees, they fell at his feet and implored for mercy. It was with difficulty he could pacify their fears; the females were soonest reassured, especially the daughter, for the young maid was struck with the gentle demeanour and noble countenance of Pelayo, and said to herself, "Surely nothing wicked can dwell in so heavenly a form."

Pelayo now ordered that the wounds of the merchant should be dressed; and his own examined. When his cuirass was taken off his wound was found to be but slight; but his men were so exasperated at seeing his blood, that they would have put the two captive Gascons to death, had he not forbad them. He now sounded his hunting horn, which echoed from rock to rock, and was answered by shouts and horns, from various parts of the mountains. The merchant's heart misgave him, he again thought he was among robbers; nor were his fears allayed when he beheld in a little while more than forty men assembling together from various parts of the forest; clad in hunting dresses, with boar spears, darts and hunting swords, and each leading a hound by a long cord. All this was a new and a wild world to the astonished

merchant, nor was his uneasiness abated when he beheld his servant
arrive leading the hackney laden with money. "Certainly," said he to
himself, "this will be too tempting a spoil for these wild men of the
mountains."

The huntsmen brought with them a boar which they had killed, and
being hungry from the chace they lighted a fire at the foot of a tree,
and each cutting off such portion of the boar as he liked best roasted
it at the fire, and ate it with bread taken from his wallet. The merchant,
his wife, and daughter, looked at all this and wondered, for they had
never beheld so savage a repast. Pelayo then enquired of them if they
did not desire to eat; they were too much in awe of him to decline,
though they felt a loathing at the idea of this hunter's fare. Linen
cloths were, therefore, spread under the shade of a great oak, to skreen
them from the sun; and when they had seated themselves round it,
they were served, to their astonishment, not with the flesh of the boar,
but with dainty viands, such as the merchant had scarcely hoped to
find, out of the walls of his native city of Bordeaux.

While they were eating, the young damsel, the daughter of the
merchant, could not keep her eyes from Pelayo. Gratitude for his
protection, admiration of his valour, had filled her heart; and when she
regarded his noble countenance, now that he had laid aside his helmet,
she thought she beheld something divine. The heart of the tender
Donzella, says the old historian, was kind and yielding; and had Pelayo
thought fit to ask the greatest boon that love and beauty could bestow,
doubtless meaning, her own fair hand—she would not have had the
cruelty to say him nay. Pelayo, however, had no such thoughts. The
love of woman had never yet entered in his heart; and though he
regarded the damsel as the fairest maiden he had ever beheld, her
beauty caused no perturbation in his breast.

When the repast was over, Pelayo offered to conduct the merchant
and his family through the passes of the mountains, which were yet
dangerous from the scattered band of Gascons. The bodies of the slain
marauders were buried, and the corpse of the nephew of the merchant
was laid upon one of the horses captured in the battle. They then formed
their cavalcade and pursued their way slowly up one of the steep and
winding defiles of the Pyrenees.

Towards sunset they arrived at the dwelling of a holy hermit. It was
hewn out of the solid rock, a cross was over the door, and before it was
a spreading oak, with a sweet spring of water at its foot. Here the body
of the merchant's nephew was buried, close by the wall of this sacred
retreat, and the hermit performed a mass for the repose of his soul.
Pelayo then obtained leave from the holy father that the merchant's wife
and daughter should pass the night within his cell; and the hermit made
beds of moss for them and gave them his benediction; but the damsel

found little rest, so much were her thoughts occupied by the youthful cavalier who had delivered her from death or dishonour.

When all were buried in repose, the hermit came to Pelayo who was sleeping by the spring under the tree, and he awoke him and said, "Arise my son, and listen to my words." Pelayo arose and seated him on a rock, and the holy man stood before him, and the beams of the moon fell on his silver hair and beard. And he said, "This is no time to be sleeping; for know that thou art chosen for a great work. Behold the ruin of Spain is at hand, destruction shall come over it like a cloud, and there shall be no safeguard. For it is the will of heaven that evil shall for a time have sway, and whoever withstands it shall be destroyed. But thou, tarry not to see these things; for thou canst not relieve them. Depart on a pilgrimage, and visit the sepulchre of our blessed Lord in Palestine, and purify thyself by prayer, and enrol thyself in the order of chivalry, and prepare for the work of the redemption of thy country. When thou shalt return, thou wilt find thyself a stranger in the land. Thy residence will be in wild dens and caves of the earth which thy young foot has never trodden. Thou wilt find thy countrymen harbouring with the beasts of the forest and the eagles of the mountains. The land which thou leavest smiling with cornfields, and covered with vines and olives, thou wilt find overrun with weeds and thorns and brambles; and wolves will roam where there have been peaceful flocks and herds. But thou wilt weed out the tares, and destroy the wolves, and raise again the head of thy suffering country."

Much further discourse had Pelayo with this holy man, who revealed to him many of the fearful events that were to happen, and counselled him the way in which he was to act.

When the morning sun shone upon the mountains, the party assembled round the door of the hermitage and made a repast by the fountain under the tree. Then having received the benediction of the hermit, they departed and travelled through the forests and defiles of the mountain, in the freshness of the day; and when the merchant beheld his wife and daughter thus secure by his side, and the hackney laden with his treasure following close behind him, his heart was light in his bosom, and he carolled as he went. But Pelayo rode in silence, for his mind was deeply moved by the revelations and the counsel of the hermit; and the daughter of the merchant ever and anon regarded him with eyes of tenderness and admiration, and deep sighs spoke the agitation of her bosom.

At length they came to where the forests and the rocks terminated, and a secure road lay before them; and here Pelayo paused to take his leave, appointing a number of his followers to attend and guard them to the nearest town.

When they came to part, the merchant and his wife were loud in their thanks and benedictions; but for some time the daughter spake never a word. At length she raised her eyes, which were filled with tears, and looked wistfully at Pelayo, and her bosom throbbed, and after a struggle between strong affection and virgin modesty her heart relieved itself by words.

"Señor," said she, "I know that I am humble and unworthy of the notice of so noble a cavalier, but suffer me to place this ring on a finger of your right hand, with which you have so bravely rescued us from death; and when you regard it you shall consider it as a memorial of your own valour, and not of one who is too humble to be remembered by you." With these words she drew a ring from off her finger and put it upon the finger of Pelayo; and having done this she blushed and trembled at her own boldness, and stood as one abashed, with her eyes cast down upon the earth.

Pelayo was moved at her words, and at the touch of her fair hand, and at her beauty as she stood thus troubled and in tears before him; but as yet he knew nothing of woman, and his heart was free from the snares of love. "Amiga" (friend), said he, "I accept thy present and will wear it in remembrance of thy goodness." The damsel was cheered by these words, for she hoped she had awakened some tenderness in his bosom; but it was no such thing, says the ancient chronicler; for his heart was ignorant of love, and was devoted to higher and more sacred matters. Yet certain it is that he always guarded well that ring.

They parted, and Pelayo and his huntsmen remained for some time on a cliff on the verge of the forest, watching that no evil befel them about the skirts of the mountain: and the damsel often turned her head to look at him, until she could no longer see him for the distance and the tears that dimmed her eyes.

And, for that he had accepted her ring, she considered herself wedded to him in her heart, and never married; nor could be brought to look with eyes of affection upon any other man; but for the true love which she bore Pelayo she lived and died a virgin.

And she composed a book, continues the old chronicler, which treated of love and chivalry and the temptations of this mortal life; and one part discoursed of celestial things; and it was called the "Contemplations of Love;" because at the time she wrote it she thought of Pelayo, and of his having received her jewel and called her by the gentle name of Amiga. And often thinking of him, and of her never having beheld him more, in tender sadness she would take the book which she had written, and would read it for him, and while she repeated the words of love which it contained, she would fancy them uttered by Pelayo and that he stood before her.*

* El Moro Rasis, *Destruycion de España*, Part 2, c. 101.

[CHAPTER IV

Pilgrimage of Pelayo, and what befell him on his return to Spain.]

Pelayo, according to the old chronicle before quoted, returned to his home deeply impressed with the revelations made to him by the saintly hermit, and prepared to set forth upon the pilgrimage to the holy sepulchre. Some historians have alleged that he was quickened to this pious expedition by fears of violence from the wicked King Witiza; but at this time Witiza was in his grave and Don Roderick swayed the Gothic sceptre; the sage Agapida is therefore inclined to attribute the pilgrimage to the mysterious revelation already mentioned.

Having arranged the concerns of his household, chosen the best suit of armor from his armory and the best horse from his stable, and supplied himself with jewels and store of gold for his expenses, he took leave of his mother and his sister Lucinda as if departing upon a distant journey in Spain, and, attended only by his page, set out upon his holy wayfaring. Descending from the rugged Pyrenees he journeyed through the fair plains of France to Marseilles, where laying by his armour and leaving his horses in safe keeping, he put on a pilgrim's garb, with staff and scrip and cockleshell, and embarked on board of a galley bound for Sicily. From Messina he voyaged in a small bark to Rhodes; thence in a galliot with a number of other pilgrims to the Holy Land. Having passed a year of pious devotion at the Holy Sepulchre; and visited all the places rendered sacred by the footsteps of our Lord, and of his mother the ever blessed Virgin, and having received the order of knighthood, he turned his steps toward his native land.

The discreet Agapida here pauses and forbears to follow the ancient chronicler further in his narration, for an interval of obscurity now occurs in the fortunes of Pelayo. Some who have endeavored to ascertain and connect the links of his romantic and eventful story have represented him as returning from his pilgrimage in time to share in the last struggle of his country and as signalizing himself in the fatal battle on the banks of the Guadalete. Others declare that, by the time he arrived in Spain, the perdition of the country was complete; that infidel chieftains bore sway in the palaces of his ancestors; that his paternal castle was a ruin; his mother in her grave, and his sister Lucinda carried away into captivity.

Stepping lightly over this disputed ground, the cautious Agapida resumes the course of the story where Pelayo discovers the residence of his sister in the city of Gijon, on the Atlantic coast at the foot of the Asturian Mountains. It was a formidable fortress chosen by Taric as a military post to control the sea-bord and hold in check the Christian patriots who had taken refuge in the neighboring mountains. The commander of this redoubtable fortress was a renegade chief, who has been variously named by historians; and who held the sister of Pelayo a captive; though others affirm that she had submitted to become his wife, to avoid a more degrading fate. According to the old chronicle already cited, Pelayo succeeded by artifice in extricating her from his hands and bearing her away to the mountains. They were hotly pursued, but Pelayo struck up a steep and rugged defile where scarcely two persons could pass abreast, and partly by his knowledge of the defiles, partly by hurling down great masses of rock to check his pursuers, effected the escape of his sister and himself to a secure part of the mountains. Here they found themselves in a small green meadow, blocked up by a perpendicular precipice, whence fell a stream of water with great noise, into a natural basin or pool, the source of the river Deva. Here was the hermitage of one of those holy men who had accompanied the Archbishop Urbano in his flight from Toledo and had established a sanctuary among these mountains. He received the illustrious fugitives with joy, especially when he knew their rank and story, and conducted them to his retreat. A kind of ladder led up to an aperture in the face of the rock about two pike lengths from the ground. Within was a lofty cavern capable of containing many people, with an inner cavern of still greater magnitude. The outer cavern served as a chapel, having an altar, a crucifix and an image of the blessed Mary.

This wild retreat had never been molested; not a Moslem turban had been seen within the little valley. The cavern was well known to the Gothic inhabitants of the mountains and the adjacent valleys. They called it the cave of Santa Maria; but it is more commonly known to fame by the name of Covadonga. It had many times been a secure place of refuge to suffering Christians, being unknown to their foes, and capable of being made a natural citadel. The entrance was so far from the ground that, when the ladder was removed, a handful of men could defend it from all assault. The small meadow in front afforded pasturage and space for gardens; and the stream that fell from the rock was from a never failing spring. The valley was high in the mountains; so high that the crow seldom winged its flight across it, and the passes leading to it were so steep and dangerous that single men might set whole armies at defiance.

Such was one of the wild fastnesses of the Asturias which formed the forlorn hope of unhappy Spain. The anchorite too was one of those religious men permitted by the conquerors, from their apparently peaceful and inoffensive lives, to inhabit lonely chapels and hermitages, but whose cells formed places of secret resort and council for the patriots of Spain, and who kept up an intercourse and understanding among the scattered remnants of the nation. The holy man knew all the Christians of the Asturias, whether living in the almost inaccessible caves and dens of the cliffs, or in the narrow valleys imbedded among the mountains. He represented these to Pelayo as brave and hardy and ready for any desperate enterprize that might promise deliverance, but they were disheartened by the continued subjection of their country, and on the point, many of them, of descending into the plains, and submitting, like the rest of their countrymen, to the yoke of the conquerors.

When Pelayo considered all these things he was persuaded the time was come for effecting the great purpose of his soul. "Father," said he, "I will no longer play the fugitive nor endure the disgrace of my country and my line. Here in this wilderness will I rear once more the royal standard of the Goths, and attempt, with the blessing of God, to shake off the yoke of the invader."

The hermit hailed his words with transport; as prognostics of the deliverance of Spain. Taking staff in hand, he repaired to the nearest valley inhabited by Christian fugitives. "Hasten in every direction," said he, "and proclaim far and wide among the mountains, that Pelayo, a descendant of the Gothic kings, has unfurled his banner at Covadonga as a rallying point for his countrymen."

The glad tidings ran like wildfire throughout all the regions of the Asturias. Old and young started up at the sound and seized whatever weapons were at hand. From mountain cleft and secret glen issued forth stark and stalwart warriors, grim with hardship and armed with old Gothic weapons that had rusted in caves since the battle of the Guadalete. Others turned their rustic implements into spears and battle axes, and hastened to join the standard of Pelayo. Every day beheld numbers of patriot warriors arriving in the narrow valley or rather glen of Covadonga, clad in all the various garbs of ancient Spain, for here were fugitives from every province, who had preferred liberty among the sterile rocks of the mountains, to ease and slavery in the plains. In a little while Pelayo found himself at the head of a formidable force, hardened by toil and suffering, fired with old Spanish pride, and rendered desperate by despair. With these he maintained a warlike sway among the mountains. Did any infidel troops attempt to penetrate to their strong hold, the signal fires blazed from height to height, the steep passes and defiles bristled with armed men, and rocks were hurled upon the heads of the intruders.

By degrees the forces of Pelayo encreased so much in number, and in courage of heart, that he sallied forth occasionally from the mountains; swept the sea coast; assailed the Moors in their towns and villages; put many of them to the sword, and returned laden with spoil to the mountains.

His name now became the terror of the infidels and the hope and consolation of the Christians. The heart of old Gothic Spain was once more lifted up and hailed his standard as the harbinger of happier days.

Her scattered sons felt again as a people, and the spirit of empire arose once more among them. Gathering together from all parts of the Asturias in the valley of Cangas, they resolved to elect their champion their sovereign. Placing the feet of Pelayo upon a shield, several of the starkest warriors raised him aloft, according to ancient Gothic ceremonial, and presented him as king. The multitude rent the air with their transports, and the mountain cliffs which so long had echoed nothing but lamentations, now resounded with shouts of joy.* Thus terminated the interregnum of Christian Spain, which had lasted since the overthrow of King Roderick and his host on the banks of the Guadalete, and the new king continued with augmented zeal his victorious expeditions against the infidels.

CHAPTER V

The battle of Covadonga.

Tidings soon spread throughout Spain that the Christians of the Asturias were in arms and had proclaimed a king among the mountains. The veteran chief, Taric el Tuerto, was alarmed for the safety of the sea-bord, and dreaded lest this insurrection should extend into the plains. He despatched, therefore, in all haste a powerful force from Cordova, under the command of Ibrahim Alcamar, one of his most experienced captains, with orders to penetrate the mountains and crush this dangerous rebellion. The perfidious Bishop Oppas, who had promoted the perdition of Spain, was sent with this host; in the hope that through his artful eloquence Pelayo might be induced to lay down his arms and his newly assumed sceptre.

The army made rapid marches and in a few days arrived among the narrow valleys of the Asturias. The Christians had received notice of their approach and fled to their fastnesses. The Moors found the valleys silent and deserted; there were traces of men, but not a man was to be seen. They passed through the most wild and dreary defiles among impending rocks, here and there varied by small green strips of mountain meadow, and directed their march for the lofty valley or rather glen of Covadonga, whither they learnt from their scouts that Pelayo had retired.

The newly elected king, when he heard of the approach of this mighty force, sent his sister, and all the women and children to a distant and secret part of the mountains. He then chose a thousand of his best armed and most powerful men and placed them within the cave. The lighter

* Morales, *Cronicon de España*, L. 13, c. 2.

armed and less vigorous he ordered to climb to the summit of the impending rocks and conceal themselves among the thickets with which they were crowned. This done he entered the cavern and caused the ladder leading to it to be drawn up.

In a little while the bray of distant trumpets and the din of atabals resounded up the glen, and soon the whole gorge of the mountain glistened with armed men; squadron after squadron of swarthy Arabs spurred into the valley; which was soon whitened by their tents. The veteran Ibrahim Alcamar, trusting that he had struck dismay into the Christians by this powerful display, sent the crafty Bishop Oppas to parley with Pelayo, and persuade him to surrender.

The bishop advanced on his steed until within a short distance of the cave, and Pelayo appeared at its entrance with lance in hand. The silver tongued prelate urged him to submit to the Moslem power, assuring him that he would be rewarded with great honours and estates. He represented the mildness of the conquerors to all who submitted to their sway, and the hopelessness of resistance. "Remember," said he, "how mighty was the power of the Goths who vanquished both the Romans and Barbarians, yet how completely was it broken down and annihilated by these people.—If the whole nation in arms could not stand before them, what canst thou do with thy wretched cavern and thy handful of mountaineers? Be counselled then, Pelayo; give up this desperate attempt; accept the liberal terms offered thee: abandon these sterile mountains and return to the plains to live in wealth and honour under the magnanimous rule of Taric."

Pelayo listened to the hoary traitor with mingled impatience and disdain. "Perdition has come upon Spain," replied he, "through the degeneracy of her sons, the sins of her rulers, like the wicked King Witiza thy brother, and the treachery of base men like thee. But when punishment is at an end, mercy and forgiveness succeed. The Goths have reached the lowest extreme of misery, it is for me to aid their fortune in the turn, and soon I trust will it arise to its former grandeur. As to thee, Don Oppas, thou shalt stand abhorred among men; false to thy country; traitorous to thy king; a renegado Christian and an apostate priest."

So saying he turned his back upon the bishop and retired into his cave.

Oppas returned pale with shame and malice to Alcamar. "These people," said he, "are stiff-necked in their rebellion; their punishment should be according to their obstinacy, and should serve as a terror to evil-doers; not one of them should be permitted to survive."

Upon this Alcamar ordered a grand assault upon the cavern; and the slingers and cross-bow men advanced in great force, and with a din of atabals and trumpets that threatened to rend the very rocks. They discharged showers of stones and arrows at the mouth of the cavern, but their missiles rebounded from the face of the rock, and many of them fell upon their own heads. This is recorded as a miracle by pious chroniclers of yore, who affirm that the stones and arrows absolutely turned in the air and killed those who had discharged them.

When Alcamar and Oppas saw that the attack was ineffectual, they brought up fresh forces and made preparations to scale the mouth of the cavern. At this moment, says the old chronicle, a banner was put in the hand of Pelayo, bearing a white cross on a blood-red field, and inscribed on it, in Chaldean characters, was the name of Jesus. And a voice spake unto him and said, "Arouse thy strength; go forth in the name of Jesus Christ, and thou shalt conquer." Who gave the banner and uttered the words has never been known; the whole, therefore, stands recorded as a miracle.

Then Pelayo elevated the banner. "Behold," said he, "a sign from heaven,—a sacred cross sent to lead us on to victory."

Upon this the people gave a great shout of joy; and when the Saracens heard that shout within the entrails of the mountain their hearts quaked, for it was like the roar of the volcano giving token of eruption.

Before they could recover from their astonishment, the Christians issued in a torrent from the cave, all fired with rage and holy confidence. By their impetuous assault they bore back the first rank of their adversaries and forced it upon those behind, and as there was no space in that narrow valley to display a front of war, or for many to fight at a time, the numbers of the foe but caused their confusion. The horse trampled on the foot, and the late formidable host became a mere struggling and distracted multitude. In the front was carnage and confusion, in the rear terror and fright; wherever the sacred standard was borne, the infidels appeared to fall before it as if smitten by some invisible hand rather than by the Christian band.

Early in the fight Pelayo encountered Ibrahim Alcamar. They fought hand to hand on the border of the pool from which springs the river Deva, and the Saracen was slain upon the margin of that pool, and his blood mingled with its waters.

When the Bishop Oppas beheld this he would have fled, but the valley was closed up by the mass of combatants, and Pelayo overtook him and defied him to the fight. But the bishop, though armed, was as craven as he was false, and yielding up his weapons implored for mercy. So Pelayo spared his life, but sent him bound to the cavern.

The whole Moorish host now took to headlong flight. Some attempted to clamber to the summit of the mountains, but they were assailed by the troops stationed there by Pelayo; who showered down darts and arrows and great masses of rock, making fearful havoc.

The great body of the army fled by the road leading along the ledge or shelf overhanging the deep ravine of the Deva; but as they crowded in one dense multitude upon the projecting precipice, the whole mass suddenly gave way, and horse and horseman, tree and rock were precipitated in one tremendous ruin into the raging river. Thus perished a great part of the flying army. The venerable Bishop Sebastiano, who records this event with becoming awe as another miracle wrought in favour of the Christians, assures us that, in his time, many years afterwards, when, during the winter season the Deva would swell, and rage and tear away its banks, spears, and scimitars and corselets, and the mingled bones of men and steeds would be uncovered, being the wrecks and reliques of the Moslem host, thus marvellously destroyed.*

Note. To satisfy all doubts with respect to the miraculous banner of Pelayo, that precious relique is still preserved in the sacred chamber of the church of Oviedo, richly ornamented with gold and precious stones. It was removed to that place, by order of Alonzo the Third, from the church of Santa Cruz near Cangas, which was erected by Favila, the son and successor of Pelayo, in memory of this victory.

CHAPTER VI

Pelayo becomes King of Leon—His death.

When Pelayo beheld his enemies thus scattered and destroyed, he saw that heaven was on his side and proceeded to follow up his victory. Rearing the sacred banner he descended through the valleys of the Asturias, his army augmenting, like a mountain torrent, as it rolled along; for the Christians saw in the victory of Covadonga a miraculous interposition of providence in behalf of ruined Spain, and hastened from all parts to join the standard of the deliverer.

Emboldened by numbers, and by the enthusiasm of his troops, Pelayo directed his march towards the fortress of Gijon. The renegado Magued, however, did not await his coming. His heart failed him on hearing of the defeat and death of Alcamar, the destruction of the Moslem army, and the augmenting force of the Christians, and abandoning his post, he marched towards Leon with the greatest part of his troops. Pelayo received intelligence of his movements, and advancing rapidly through the mountains encountered him in the valley of Ollalas. A bloody battle ensued on the banks of the river which flows through that valley. The sacred banner was again victorious; Magued was slain by the hand of

---

* Judicio Domini actum est, ut ipsius montis pars se a fundamentis evolvens, sexaginta tria millia caldeorum stupenter in fulmina projecit, atque eos omnes opressit. Ubi usque nunc ipse fluvius dum tempore hyemali alveum suum implet, ripasque dissoluit, signa armorum, et ossa eorum evidentissime ostendit.—*Sebastianus Salmanticensis Episc.*

Pelayo, and so great was the slaughter of his host, that for two days the river ran red with the blood of the Saracens.

From hence Pelayo proceeded rapidly to Gijon which he easily carried by assault. The capture of this important fortress gave him the command of the sea-board, and of the skirts of the mountains. While reposing himself after his victories, the Bishop Oppas was brought in chains before him, and the Christian troops called loudly for the death of that traitor and apostate. But Pelayo recollected that he had been a sacred dignitary of the church, and regarded him as a scourge in the hand of heaven for the punishment of Spain. He would not, therefore, suffer violent hands to be laid upon him, but contented himself with placing him where he could no longer work mischief. He accordingly ordered him to be confined in one of the towers of Gijon, with nothing but bread and water for his subsistence. There he remained a prey to the workings of his conscience, which filled his prison with horrid spectres of those who had perished through his crimes. He heard wailings and execrations in the sea breeze that howled round the tower, and in the roaring of the waves that beat against its foundations, and in a little time he was found dead in his dungeon, hideously distorted, as if he had died in agony and terror.*

The sacred banner that had been elevated at Covadonga never sank nor receded, but continued to be the beacon of deliverance to Spain. Pelayo went on from conquest to conquest encreasing and confirming his royal power. Having captured the city of Leon he made it the capital of his kingdom, and took there the title of the King of Leon. He moreover adopted the device of the city for his arms; a blood-red lion rampant, in a silver field; this long continued to be the arms of Spain, until in after times the lion was quartered with the castle, the device of Burgos, capital of Old Castile.

We forbear to follow this patriot prince through the rest of his glorious career. Suffice it to say that he reigned long and prosperously; extending on all sides the triumphs of his arms; establishing on solid foundations the reviving empire of Christian Spain; and that after a life of constant warfare, he died in peace in the city of Cangas; and lies buried with his queen, Gaudiosa, in the church of Santa Eulalia near to that city.

Here ends the Legend of Pelayo.

* *La Destruycion de España*, Part 3.

[1827]

[THE SUCCESSORS OF PELAYO.   FAVILA]

The good King Pelayo having reared once more the standard of Spain and of the church, and established his little kingdom in the mountains of the Asturias, died, as has been noted, in the Year of Grace 737, and his son Favila succeeded to the throne.

This was a youth of great parts and promise, hardy, vigorous and daring, fitted to extend by dint of sword, the rude mountain kingdom left him by his father. He is accused, however, of levity and rashness. Of neglecting the stern cares of his government, to indulge in his own amusements, and of exposing to the rude dangers of the mountain chase and inglorious contests with the wild beasts of the forest, that life which ought to have been devoted to the defense of his country and the noble contests of the faith. Favila, however, was young; age might have matured his judgement and directed his courage rightly. He reigned but two short years and in those there is nothing recorded derogatory to his memory, but the youthful rashness that led to his untimely end.

One of the first cares of his reign was to erect the hermitage or chapel of Santa Cruz, already mentioned, in honour of the sainted warriors who had fallen in the battles of his father. In this pious act he was assisted by his young and beautiful wife Froyliuba. The hermitage stood on a mound in the green valley of Cangas. It was scarce completed when the Moors made an inroad and laid waste the valleys. Favila was instantly in the field with his cavaliers; pursued and overtook the Moors, vanquished them, regained the booty they were bearing away and returned flushed with victory to his youthful bride, who was in his camp, in the valley of Cangas, hard by the chapel of Santa Cruz. In the buoyancy of youthful spirits, Favila now determined to sally forth to the chase among the mountains without taking off his armour. He was clad in his shirt of mail, with his buckler on his arm and his sword in his belt. His wife Froyliuba was seized with a sudden foreboding of some impending evil. She entreated the king to lay aside his armour, to forego the chase for that day and to repose himself after the battle. Finding he persisted in his intention, she redoubled her entreaties; taking hold of the skirt of his surcoat and imploring him with tears in her eyes, and the most endearing accents, to dismount from his horse, and remain that day in his tent.

The youthful monarch made light of her forebodings; and was not to be persuaded from his purpose. He took a hawk on his fist, and with gay air bade farewell to the queen. She embraced and kissed him at parting with strong emotion, and as she watched him as he rode off thoughtlessly with his hunting train for the mountains, her heart was filled with dismal apprehensions.

The king ascended a mountain, which rises from the valley of Cangas, and is called Sobremonte, near to the town of Helgueras. In a narrow glen of the mountain, the huntsmen and dogs dislodged a huge bear from a thicket, which retreating to a rock, turned to make battle. The king, rashly confiding in his own prowess, forbade any one to interfere and took the combat to himself. Throwing the hawk from his fist and dismounting, he drew his sword, braced his shield, and pursued the bear among the rocks. Closing with the animal he gave him a thrust in the flank, but the bear sprang upon him, seized him with a terrible embrace, tore him with his teeth, and left him bleeding and strangled on the earth before any one could come to his assistance. Thus, say the ancient chronicles, did Don Favila throw away a life that should have been devoted to his kingdom and his faith: for kings, on whose lives depends the welfare of their realms, have no right to risk them, even in war, without the utmost necessity.

A cross still marks the spot where the unfortunate king fell a victim to his youthful temerity. His death was greatly deplored, particularly by his wife and his sister Hermasinda, who erected a holy monastery to his memory, with a church dedicated to St. Peter, prince of the apostles. It is situated in Cangas Donis on the banks of the Sella about half a league from the hermitage of Santa Cruz. It is one of the most beautiful specimens of Gothic architecture of that time, and though many ages have passed since it was erected, the workmanship is as fresh as if it had just been left by the hand of the artist.* In this church repose the ashes of King Favila, his queen, and his loving sister, with her spouse Alonzo the Catholic; but no other are interred within the walls.

In a little chapel of St. Michael, outside of the church, are gathered the remains of many cavaliers and hidalgos of that time and territory. The story of the death of Favila is sculptured with great art in various parts of the church, and in truth it is the subject of that device which is seen in various parts of Spain, where an armed cavalier is seen contending with a bear, who is rending the buckler from his arm. The frequency of the device shews either how universally the death of Favila was deplored by all good Christians, or how important the lesson of his death was considered to the early Spanish princes, who were much given to the rude and perilous amusement of the chase.

* Sandoval, *El Rey Alonzo el Catholico.*

[1827–1847]

CHRONICLE OF THE OMMIADES

[CHAPTER I

Of the youthful fortunes of Abderahman.]

"Blessed be God!" exclaims an Arabian historian: "In his hands alone is the destiny of princes. He overthrows the mighty and humbles the haughty to the dust; and he raises up the persecuted and afflicted from the very depths of despair."

The illustrious house of Omeya, one of the two lines descended from Mahomet, had swayed the sceptre at Damascus for nearly a century, when a rebellion broke out headed by Abu al Abbas Safah, who aspired to the throne of the Caliphs, as being descended from Abbas the uncle of the Prophet. The rebellion was successful. Meruan, the last caliph of the house of Omeya, was defeated and slain. A general proscription of the Ommiades took place. Many of them fell in battle: many were treacherously slain in places where they had taken refuge; above seventy of the most noble and distinguished were murdered at a banquet to which they had been invited, and their dead bodies, covered with cloths, were made to serve as tables for the horrible festivity. Others were driven forth forlorn and desolate wanderers in various parts of the earth, pursued with relentless hatred; for it was the determination of the usurper that not one of the proscribed family should escape. Abu al Abbas took possession of their stately palaces and delicious gardens, and founded the powerful dynasty of the Abbassides, which, for several centuries, maintained dominion in the East.

"Blessed be God!" again exclaims the Arabian historian: "It was written in his eternal decrees that, notwithstanding the fury of the Abbassides, the noble stock of Omeya should not be destroyed. One fruitful branch remained to flourish with glory and greatness in another land."

When the sanguinary proscription of the Ommiades took place, two young princes of that line, brothers, by the names of Solyman and Abderahman, were spared for a time. Their personal graces, noble demeanour and winning affability, had made them many friends, while their extreme youth rendered them objects of but little dread to the usurper. Their safety, however, was but transient. In a little while the suspicions of Abu al Abbas were aroused. The unfortunate Solyman fell beneath the scymetar of the executioner. His brother Abderahman was warned of his danger in time. Several of his friends hastened to him, bringing him jewels, a disguise and a fleet horse. "The emissaries of the caliph," said they, "are in search of thee; thy brother lies weltering in his blood—fly to the desert, there is no safety for thee in the habitations of man!"

Abderahman took the jewels, clad himself in the disguise and mounting the steed fled for his life. As he passed a lonely fugitive by the palaces of his ancestors in which his family had long held sway, their very walls seemed disposed to betray him, as they echoed the swift clattering of his steed.

Abandoning his native country Syria, where he was liable at each moment to be recognized and taken, he took refuge among the Bedouin Arabs; a half savage race of shepherds. His youth, his inborn majesty and grace, and the sweetness and affability that shone forth in his azure eyes, won the hearts of these wandering men. He was but twenty years of age, and had been reared in the soft luxury of a palace, but he was tall and vigorous and in a little while hardened himself so completely to the rustic life of the fields that it seemed as though he had passed all his days in the rude simplicity of a shepherd's cabin.

His enemies, however, were upon his traces and gave him but little rest. By day he scoured the plains, with the Bedouins, hearing in every blast the sound of pursuit, and fancying in every distant cloud of dust a troop of the caliph's horsemen. His night was passed in broken sleep and frequent watchings, and at the earliest dawn he was the first to put the bridle to his steed.

Wearied by these perpetual alarms, he bade farewell to his friendly Bedouins, and leaving Egypt behind, sought a safer refuge in Western Africa. The province of Barca was at that time governed by Aben Habib, who had risen to rank and fortune under the fostering favor of the Ommiades. "Surely," thought the unhappy prince, "I will receive kindness and protection from this man; he will rejoice to shew his gratitude for the benefits showered upon him by my kindred."

Abderahman was young and as yet knew little of mankind. None are so hostile to the victim of power as those whom he has befriended. They fear being suspected of gratitude by his persecutors and involved in his misfortunes.

The unfortunate Abderahman had halted for a few days to repose himself among a horde of Bedouins, who had received him with their characteristic hospitality. They would gather round him in the evenings to listen to his conversation, regarding with wonder this gently spoken stranger from the more refined country of Egypt. The old men marvelled to find so much knowledge and wisdom in such early youth, and the young men, won by his frank and manly carriage, entreated him to remain among them.

In the mean time the Wali Aben Habib, like all the governors of distant posts, had received orders from the caliph to be on the watch for the fugitive prince. Hearing that a young man, answering the description, had entered the province alone, from the frontiers of Egypt, on a steed worn down by travel, he sent forth horsemen in his pursuit, with orders to bring him to him dead or alive. The emissaries of the wali traced him to his resting place and coming upon the encampment in the dead of the night demanded of the Arabs whether a young man, a stranger from Syria, did not sojourn among their tribe. The Bedouins knew by the description that the stranger must be their guest, and feared some evil was intended him. "Such a youth," said they, "has indeed sojourned among us, but he has gone with some of our young men to a distant valley to hunt the lion." The emissaries enquired the way to the place and hastened on to surprize their expected prey.

The Bedouins repaired to Abderahman, who was still sleeping. "If thou hast aught to fear from man in power," said they, "arise and fly; for the horsemen of the wali are in quest of thee. We have sent them off for a time on a wrong errand, but they will soon return."

"Alas! whither shall I fly!" cried the unhappy prince. "My enemies hunt me like the ostrich of the desert. They follow me like the wind and allow me neither safety nor repose."

Six of the bravest youths of the tribe stepped forward. "We have steeds," said they, "that can outstrip the wind, and hands that can hurl the javelin. We will accompany thee in thy flight, and will fight by thy side while life lasts and we have weapons to wield."

Abderahman embraced them with tears of gratitude. They mounted their steeds and made for the most lonely parts of the desert. By the faint light of the stars they passed through dreary wastes and over hills of sand. The lion roared and the hyæna howled unheeded, for they fled from man, more cruel and relentless when in pursuit of blood than the savage beasts of the desert.

At sun rise they paused to refresh themselves beside a scanty well surrounded by a few palm trees. One of the young Arabs climbed a tree and looked in every direction, but not a horseman was to be seen.

"We have outstripped pursuit," said the Bedouins, "whither shall we conduct thee; where is thy home and the land of thy people?"

"Home have I none!" replied Abderahman, mournfully, "nor family, nor kindred! My native land is to me a land of destruction; and my people seek my life!"

The hearts of the youthful Bedouins were touched with compassion at these words, and they marvelled that one so young and gentle should have suffered such great sorrow and persecution.

Abderahman sat by the well and mused for a time. At length, breaking silence, "In the midst of Mauritania," said he, "dwells the tribe of Zeneta. My mother was of that tribe; and perhaps when her son presents himself a persecuted wanderer at their door, they will not turn him from the threshold."

"The Zenetes," replied the Bedouins, "are among the bravest and most hospitable of the people of Africa; never did the unfortunate seek refuge among them in vain, nor was the stranger repulsed from their door." So they mounted their steeds with renewed spirits and journeyed with all speed to Tahart, the capital of the Zenetes.

When Abderahman entered the place followed by his six rustic Arabs, all wayworn and travel stained, his noble and majestic demeanour shone through the simple garb of a Bedouin. A crowd gathered round him as he alighted from his weary steed. Confiding in the well known character of the tribe, he no longer attempted concealment.

"You behold before you," said he, "one of the proscribed house of Omeya. I am that Abderahman upon whose head a price has been set, and who has been driven from land to land. I come to you as my kindred. My mother was of your tribe, and she told me, with her dying breath, that, in all time of need I would find a home and friends among the Zenetes."

The words of Abderahman went straight to the hearts of his hearers. They pitied his youth and his great misfortunes, while they were charmed by his frankness and by the manly graces of his person. The tribe was of a bold and generous spirit and not to be awed by the frown of power. "Evil be upon us and upon our children," said they, "if we deceive the trust thou hast placed in us."

One of the noblest xeques then took Abderahman to his house and treated him as his own child; and the principal people of the tribe strove who most should cherish him and do him honour; endeavoring to obliterate by their kindness the recollection of his past misfortunes.

Abderahman had resided some time among the hospitable Zenetes when one day two strangers of venerable appearance, attended by a small retinue, arrived at Tahart. They gave themselves out as merchants, and from the simple style in which they travelled, excited no attention. In a little while they sought out Abderahman, and, taking him apart: "Hearken," said they, "Abderhman, of the royal line of Omeya; we are ambassadors, sent on the part of the principal Moslems of Spain to offer thee, not merely an asylum, for that thou hast already, among these brave Zenetes, but an empire! Spain is a prey to distracting factions, and can no longer exist as a dependance upon a throne too remote to watch over its welfare. It needs to be independent of Asia and Africa and to be under the government of a good prince, who shall reside within it and devote himself entirely to its prosperity, a prince with sufficient title to silence all rival claims, and bring the warring parties into unity and peace; and at the same time with sufficient ability and virtue to ensure the welfare of his dominions. For this purpose the eyes of all the honorable leaders in Spain have been turned to thee, as a descendant of the royal line of Omeya, and an offset from the same stock as our holy prophet. They have heard of thy virtues, and of thy admirable constancy under misfortunes, and invite thee to accept the sovereignty of one of the noblest countries in the world. Thou wilt have some difficulties to encounter from hostile men, but thou wilt have on thy side the bravest captains that have signalized themselves in the conquest of the unbelievers."

The ambassadors ceased, and Abderahman remained for a time lost in wonder and admiration. "God is great!" exclaimed he at length, "there is but one God who is god, and Mahomet is his prophet! Illustrious ambassadors, you have put new life into my soul, for you have shewn me something to live for. In the few years that I have lived, troubles and sorrows have been heaped upon my head and I have become inured to hardships and alarms. Since it is the wish of the valiant Moslems of Spain, I am willing to become their leader, and defender, and devote myself to their cause, be it happy or disastrous."

The ambassadors now cautioned him to be silent as to their errand, and to depart secretly for Spain. "The sea bord of Africa," said they, "swarms with your enemies, and a powerful faction in Spain would intercept your landing did they know your name and rank, and the object of your coming."

But Abderahman replied, "I have been cherished in adversity by these brave Zenetes; I have been protected and honored by them when a price was set upon my head and to harbour me was great peril. How can I keep my good fortune from my benefactors and desert their hospitable roofs in silence? He is unworthy friendship who withholds confidence from his friend."

Charmed with the generosity of his feelings, the ambassadors made no opposition to his wishes. The Zenetes proved themselves worthy of his confidences. They hailed with joy the great change in his fortunes. The warriors and the young men pressed forward to follow and aid them with horse and weapon, "for the honours of a noble house and family," said they, "can be maintained only by lances and horsemen." In a few days he set forth with the ambassadors, at the head of nearly a thousand horsemen, skilled in war, and exercised in the desart, and a large body of infantry, armed with lances. The venerable xeque with whom he had resided, blessed him, and shed tears over him at parting, as though he had been his own child, and when the youth passed over the threshold, the house was filled with lamentations.

CHAPTER II

[Landing of Abderahman in Spain—Condition of the Country.]

Abderahman ben Omeya arrived in safety on the coast of Andalusia and landed at Almunecar, or Malaga, with his little band of warlike Zenetes. Spain was at that time in great confusion. Upwards of forty years had elapsed since the Conquest. The civil wars in Syria and Egypt and occasional revolts in Africa had caused frequent overflowings of different tribes into Spain, which was a place of common refuge. Hither too came the fragments of defeated armies, desperate in fortune, with weapons in their hands. These settled themselves in various parts of the peninsula which thus became divided between the Arabs of Yemen, the Egyptians, the Syrians and the Alabdaries. The distractions of its eastern and African provinces prevented the main government at Damascus from exercising any control over its distant and recently acquired territory in Spain which soon became broken up into factions and a scene of all kinds of abuses. Every sheik and wali considered the town or province committed to his charge an absolute property; and practised the most arbitrary extortions. These excesses at length became insupportable, and at a convocation of the principal leaders it was determined, as a means of ending these dissensions, to unite all the Moslem provinces of the peninsula under one Emir or General Governor. Yusuf el Fehri, an ancient man, of honorable lineage being of the tribe of Koreish, and a descendant of Ocba the conqueror of Africa, was chosen for this station. He began his reign with policy and endeavored to conciliate all parties. At the head of the Egyptian faction was a veteran warrior named Samael to whom Yusuf gave the government of Toledo, and to his son that of Saragossa. At the head of the Alabdaries was Amer ben Amru, Emir of the Seas; his office being suppressed, Yusuf gave him in place thereof the government of the noble city of Seville. Thus he proceeded distributing honors and commands and flattered himself that he secured the loyalty and good will of every one whom he benefited.

"Who shall pretend," says the Arabian sage, "to content the human heart by benefits; when even the bounties of Allah are ineffectual?" In seeking to befriend all parties Yusuf created for himself inveterate enemies. Amer ben Amru, powerful from his wealth and connexions and proud of his descent from Mosab the standard bearer of the prophet in the battle of Beder, was indignant that Samael and his son, with whom he was at deadly feud, should be appointed to such important commands. He demanded one of those posts for himself and was refused. An insurrection and a civil war was the consequence; and the country was laid waste with fire and sword. The inhabitants of the villages fled to the cities for refuge; flourishing towns disappeared from the face of the earth, or were reduced to heaps of rubbish.

In these dismal times, say the Arabian chroniclers, the very heavens gave omens of the distress and desolation of the earth. At Cordova two pale and livid suns were seen shedding a baleful light. In the north appeared a flaming scythe and the heavens were red as blood. These were regarded as presages of direful calamities and bloody wars.

At the time of the landing of Abderahman in Spain Yusuf had captured Saragossa, in which was Amer ben Amru, with his son and secretary, and loading them in chains and putting them on camels, he set out on his return to Cordova. He had halted one day in a valley called Wadaramla and was reposing with his family in his tent while his people and the prisoners made a repast in the open air. The heart of the old emir was lifted up for he thought there was no one to dispute with him the domination of Spain. In the midst of his exultation some horsemen were seen spurring up the valley, bearing the standard of the Wali Samael.

That officer arrived covered with dust and exhausted with fatigue. He brought tidings of the arrival of Abderahman and that the whole seabord was flocking to his standard. Messenger after messenger arrived confirming the fearful tidings, and adding that this descendant of the Omeyas had been secretly invited to Spain by Amru and his party.

Yusuf waited not to ascertain the truth of this accusation. In a transport of fury he ordered that Amru, his son, and secretary should be cut to pieces. His orders were instantly executed; "and this cruelty," adds the Arabian chronicler, "lost him the favor of Allah; for from that time success deserted his standard."

[CHAPTER III

Triumphs of Abderahman—The palm-tree which he planted, and the verses he composed thereupon—Insurrections—His enemies subdued— Undisputed sovereign of the Moslems of Spain—Begins the famous mosque in Cordova—His death.]

Abderahman had indeed been hailed with joy on his landing. The old people hoped to find tranquility under the sway of one supreme chieftain, descended from their Ancient Caliphs: the young men were rejoiced to have a youthful warrior to lead them on to victories; and the populace, charmed with his fresh and manly beauty, his majestic yet gracious and affable demeanor, shouted, "Long live Abderahman, Miramamolin of Spain!"

In a few days the youthful sovereign saw himself at the head of more than twenty thousand men from the neighborhood of Elvira, Almeria, Malaga, Xeres, and Sidonia. Fair Seville threw open its gates at his approach, and celebrated his arrival with public rejoycings. He continued his march into the country, vanquished one of the sons of Yusuf before the gates of Cordova, and obliged him to take refuge within its walls, where he held him in close siege. Hearing, however, of the approach of Yusuf, the father, with a powerful army, he divided his forces, and leaving ten thousand men to press the siege, he hastened with the other ten to meet the coming foe.

Yusuf had indeed mustered a formidable force, from the east and south of Spain, and accompanied by his veteran general Samael, came with confident boasting to drive this intruder from the land. His confidence encreased on beholding the small army of Abderahman. Turning to Samael, he repeated, with scornful sneer, a verse from an Arabian poetess which says:

"How hard is our lot; we come, a thirsty multitude, and lo! but this cup of water to share among us."

There was indeed a fearful odds. On the one side were two veteran generals, grown grey in victory, with a mighty host of warriors seasoned in the wars of Spain. On the other side was a mere youth, scarce attained to manhood, with a hasty levy of half disciplined troops; but the youth was a prince flushed with hope and aspiring after fame and empire; and surrounded by a devoted band of warriors from Africa, whose example infused zeal into the little army.

The encounter took place at daybreak. The impetuous valour of the Zenetes carried every thing before it. The cavalry of Yusuf was broken, and driven back upon the infantry, and before noon the whole host was put to headlong flight. Yusuf and Samael were borne along in the torrent of the fugitives, raging and storming, and making ineffectual efforts to rally them. They were separated widely in the confusion of the flight, one taking refuge in the Algarves, the other in the kingdom of Murcia. They afterwards rallied, and reunited their forces and made another desperate stand near to Almunecar. The battle was obstinate and bloody, but they were again defeated, and driven, with a handful of followers, to take refuge in the rugged mountains adjacent to Elvira.

The spirit of the veteran Samael gave way before these fearful reverses. "In vain, Oh Yusuf," said he, "do we contend with the prosperous star of this youthful conqueror: the will of Allah be done; let us submit to our fate, and sue for favorable terms, while we have yet the means of capitulation."

It was a hard trial for the proud spirit of Yusuf, that had once aspired to uncontrolled sway, but he was compelled to capitulate. Abderahman was as generous as brave. He granted the two grey headed generals the most honorable conditions; and even took the veteran Samael into favor, employing him, as a mark of confidence, to visit the eastern provinces of Spain, and restore them to tranquility. Yusuf, having delivered up Elvira and Granada, and complied with other articles of his capitulation, was permitted to retire to Murcia and rejoin his son Muhamad. A general amnesty to all chiefs and soldiers who should yield up their strong holds, and lay down their arms, completed the triumph of Abderahman, and brought all hearts into obedience. Thus terminated this severe struggle for the domination of Spain; and thus the illustrious family of Omeya, after having been cast down and almost exterminated in the East, took new root, and sprang forth prosperously in the West.

Wherever Abderahman appeared, he was received with rapturous acclamations. As he rode through the cities, the populace rent the air with shouts of joy; the stately palaces were crowded with spectators, eager to gain a sight of his graceful form, and beaming countenance; and when they beheld the mingled majesty and benignity of their new monarch, and the sweetness and gentleness of his whole conduct, they extolled him as something more than mortal; as a beneficent genius, sent for the happiness of Spain.

In the interval of peace which now succeeded Abderahman occupied himself in promoting the useful and elegant arts, and in introducing into Spain the refinements of the East. Considering the building and ornamenting of cities among the noblest employments of the tranquil hours of princes, he bestowed great pains upon beautifying the city of Cordova and its environs. He reconstructed banks and dykes, to keep the Guadalquivir from overflowing its borders, and on the terraces thus formed, he planted delightful gardens. In the midst of these, he erected a lofty tower, commanding a view of the vast and fruitful valley, enlivened by the windings of the river. In this tower would he pass hours of meditation, gazing on the soft and varied landscape, and inhaling the bland and balmy airs of that delightful region. At such times, his thoughts would recur to the past, and the misfortunes of his youth; the massacre of his family would rise to view, mingled with tender recollections of his native country, from which he was exiled. In these melancholy musings, he would sit with his eyes fixed upon a palm tree which he had planted in the midst of his garden. It is said to have been the first ever planted in Spain; and to have been the parent stock of all the palm trees which grace the southern provinces of the peninsula. The heart of Abderahman yearned towards this tree; it was the offspring of his native country, and like him, an exile. In one of his moods of tenderness he composed verses upon it, which have since become famous throughout the world. The following is a rude but literal translation:

"Beauteous Palm! thou also wert hither brought a stranger; but thy roots have found a kindly soil, thy head is lifted to the skies, and the sweet airs of Algarve fondle and kiss thy branches.

"Thou hast not known like me the storms of adverse fortune. Bitter tears wouldst thou shed, couldst thou feel my woes. Repeated griefs have overwhelmed me. With early tears, I bedewed the palms on the banks of the Euphrates; but neither tree nor river heeded my sorrows, when driven by cruel fate, and the ferocious Abu al Abbas, from the scenes of my childhood and the sweet objects of my affection.

"To thee no remembrance remains of my beloved country; I, unhappy! can never recall it without tears!"

The generosity of Abderahman to his vanquished foes, was destined to be abused. The veteran Yusuf, in visiting certain of the cities which he had surrendered, found himself surrounded by zealous partizans, ready to peril life in his service. The love of command revived in his bosom, and he repented the facility with which he suffered himself to be persuaded to submission. Flushed with new hopes of success, he caused arms to be secretly collected and deposited in various villages most zealous in their professions of devotion, and raising a considerable body of troops, seized upon the castle of Almodovar.

The rash rebellion was short lived. At the first appearance of an army, sent by Abderahman, and commanded by Abdelmelec, governor of Seville, the villages which had so recently professed loyalty to Yusuf, hastened to declare their attachment to the monarch, and to give up the concealed arms. Almodovar was soon retaken, and Yusuf, driven to the environs of Lorca, was surrounded by the cavalry of Abdelmelec. The veteran endeavored to cut a passage through the enemy, but after fighting with desperate fury, and with a force of arm incredible in one of his age, he fell beneath blows from weapons of all kinds, so that after the battle, his body could scarcely be recognized, so numerous were the wounds. His head was cut off and sent to Cordova, where it was placed in an iron cage, over the gate of the city.

The old lion was dead, but his whelps survived. Yusuf had left three sons, who inherited his warlike spirit, and were eager to revenge his death. Collecting a number of the scattered adherents of their house, they surprized and seized upon Toledo, during the absence of Temam, its wali or commander. In this old warrior city, built upon a rock, and almost surrounded by the Tagus, they set up a kind of robber hold, scouring the surrounding country, levying tribute, seizing upon houses, compelling the peasantry to join their standard. Every day cavalgadas of horses and mules laden with spoil, with flocks of sheep, and droves of cattle, came pouring over the bridges on either side of the city, and thronging in at the gates, the plunder of the surrounding country. Those of the inhabitants who were still loyal to Abderahman, dared not lift up their voices, for men of the sword bore sway. At length one day,

when the sons of Yusuf, with their choicest troops, were out on a
maraud, the watchmen on the towers gave the alarm. A troop of scattered horsemen were spurring towards the gates. The banners of the
sons of Yusuf were descried. Two of them spurred into the city, followed by a handful of warriors, covered with confusion and dismay.
They had been encountered and defeated by the Wali Temam, and
one of the brothers had been slain.

The gates were secured in all haste, and the walls were scarcely
manned, when Temam appeared before them with his troops, and
summoned the city to surrender. A great internal commotion ensued
between the loyalists and the insurgents; the latter, however, had
weapons in their hands and prevailed, and for several days, trusting
to the strength of their rock built fortress, they set the wali at defiance.
At length some of the loyal inhabitants of Toledo, who knew all its
secret and subterraneous passages, some of which if chroniclers may
be believed have existed since the days of Hercules, if not of Tubal
Cain, introduced Temam and a chosen band of his warriors, into the
very center of the city, where they suddenly appeared as if by magic.
A panic seized upon the insurgents. Some sought safety in submission,
some in concealment, some in flight. Casim, one of the sons of Yusuf,
escaped in disguise; the youngest, Muhamad, was taken, and was sent
captive to the king accompanied by the head of his brother who had
been slain in battle.

When Abderahman beheld the youth laden with chains, he remembered his own sufferings in his early days, and had compassion on him;
but, to prevent him from doing further mischief he imprisoned him in
a tower of the wall of Cordova.

In the mean time Casim, who had escaped, managed to raise another
band of war. Spain, in all ages a *guerilla* country, prone to partizan
warfare, and petty maraud, was at that time infested by bands of
licentious troops, who had sprung up in the civil wars; their only object
pillage, their only dependence the sword, and ready to flock to any
new and desperate standard, that promised the greatest licence. With
a ruffian force thus levied, Casim scoured the country, took Sidonia
by storm, and surprized Seville while in a state of unsuspecting security.

Abderahman put himself at the head of his faithful Zenetes, and took
the field in person. By the rapidity of his movements the insurgents were
defeated, Sidonia and Seville speedily retaken, and Casim was made
prisoner. The generosity of Abderahman was again exhibited towards
this unfortunate son of Yusuf. He spared his life, and sent him to be
confined in a tower at Toledo.

The veteran Samael had taken no part in these insurrections, but had
attended faithfully to the affairs intrusted to him by Abderahman. The
death of his old friend and colleague Yusuf, however, and the subsequent

disasters of his family, filled him with despondency. Fearing the inconstancy of fortune, and the dangers incident to public employ, he entreated the king to be permitted to retire to his house in Seguenza and indulge a privacy and repose suited to his advanced age. His prayer was granted. The veteran laid by his arms, battered in a thousand conflicts, hung his sword and lance against the wall, and, surrounded by a few friends gave himself up, apparently, to the sweets of quiet and unambitious leisure.

Who can count, however, upon the tranquil content of a heart nurtured amid the storms of war and ambition? Under the ashes of this outward humility were glowing the coals of faction. In his seemingly philosophical retirement Samael was concerting with his friends new treason against Abderahman. His plot was discovered; his house was suddenly surrounded by troops and he was conveyed to a tower at Toledo, where in the course of a few months, he died in captivity.

The magnanimity of Abderahman was again put to the proof, by a new insurrection at Toledo. Hixem ben Adra, a relative of Yusuf, seized upon the Alcazar, or citadel, slew several of the loyal adherents of the king, liberated Casim from his tower, and summoning all the banditti of the country, soon mustered a force of ten thousand men. Abderahman was quickly before the walls of Toledo, with the troops of Cordova, and his devoted Zenetes. The rebels were brought to terms, and surrendered the city, on promise of general pardon, which was extended even to Hixem and Casim. When the chieftains saw Hixem and his principal confederates in the power of Abderahman, they advised him to put them all to death. "A promise given to traitors and rebels," said they, "is not binding, when it is to the interest of the state that it should be broken."

"No!" replied Abderahman, "if the safety of my throne were at stake, I would not break my word." So saying, he confirmed the amnesty and granted Hixem ben Adra a worthless life, to be employed in further treason.

Scarcely had Abderahman returned from this expedition, when a powerful army, sent by the caliph, landed from Africa on the coast of the Algarves. The commander, Aly ben Mogueth, Emir of Cairvan, elevated a rich banner which he had received from the hands of the caliph. Wherever he went he ordered the Caliph of the East to be proclaimed by sound of trumpet, denouncing Abderahman as a usurper, the vagrant member of a family proscribed and execrated in all the mosques of the east.

One of the first to join his standard was Hixem ben Adra, so recently pardoned by Abderahman. He seized upon the citadel of Toledo, and repairing to the camp of Aly, offered to deliver the city into his hands.

Abderahman, as bold in war as he was gentle in peace, took the field with his wonted promptness; overthrew his enemies with great slaughter, drove some to the sea coast to regain their ships, and others to the mountains. The body of Aly was found on the field of battle. Abderahman caused the head to be struck off and conveyed to Cairvan, where it was affixed at night to a column in the public square with this inscription: "Thus Abderahman, the descendant of the Omeyas, punishes the rash and arrogant."

Hixem ben Adra escaped from the field of battle, and excited further troubles, but was eventually captured by Abdelmelec, who ordered his head to be struck off on the spot, lest he should again be spared through the wonted clemency of Abderahman.

Notwithstanding these signal triumphs, the reign of Abderahman was disturbed by further insurrections, and by another descent from Africa, but he was victorious over them all; striking the roots of his power deeper and deeper into the land. Under his sway the government of Spain became more regular and consolidated, and acquired an independence of the empire of the east. The caliph continued to be considered as first pontiff and chief of the religion, but he ceased to have any temporal power over Spain.

Having again an interval of peace, Abderahman devoted himself to the education of his children. Suleiman, the eldest, he appointed wali or governor of Toledo; Abdallah, the second, was entrusted with the command of Merida; but the third son, Hixem, was the delight of his heart, the son of Howara, his favorite sultana, whom he loved throughout life with the utmost tenderness. With this youth, who was full of promise, he relaxed from the fatigues of government, joining in his youthful sports amidst the delightful gardens of Cordova, and teaching him the gentle art of falconry, of which the king was so fond that he received the name of the Falcon of Coraixi.

While Abderahman was thus indulging in the gentle propensities of his nature, mischief was secretly at work. Muhamad, the youngest son of Yusuf, had been for many years a prisoner in the tower of Cordova. Being passive and resigned, his keepers relaxed their vigilance and brought him forth from his dungeon. He went groping about, however, in broad daylight as if still in the darkness of his tower. His guards watched him narrowly, lest this should be a deception, but were at length convinced that the long absence of light had rendered him blind. They now permitted him to descend frequently to the lower chambers of the tower, and to sleep there occasionally, during the heats of summer. They even allowed him to grope his way to the cistern in quest of water for his ablutions.

A year passed in this way without any thing to excite suspicion. During all this time, however, the blindness of Muhamad was entirely a deception, and he was concerting a plan of escape through the means of some friends of his father, who found means to visit him occasionally. One sultry evening in midsummer, the guards had gone to bathe in the Guadalquivir leaving Muhamad alone in the lower chambers of the tower. No sooner were they out of sight and hearing than he hastened to the window of the stair case leading down to the cistern, lowered himself as far as his arms would reach, and dropped without injury to the ground. Plunging into the Guadalquivir he swam across to a thick grove on the opposite side, where his friends were waiting to receive him. Here, mounting a horse which they had provided for an event of the kind, he fled across the country, by solitary roads, and made good his escape to the mountains of Jaen.

The guardians of the tower dreaded for some time to make known his flight to Abderahman. When at length it was told to him he exclaimed, "All is the work of eternal wisdom; it is intended to teach us that we cannot benefit the wicked without injuring the good. The flight of that blind man will cause much trouble and bloodshed."

His predictions were verified. Muhamad reared the standard of rebellion in the mountains; the seditious and discontented of all kinds hastened to join it, together with soldiers of fortune, or rather wandering banditti, and he had soon six thousand men well armed, hardy in habits, and desperate in character. His brother Casim, also, reappeared about the same time, in the mountains of Ronda, at the head of a daring band, that laid all the neighboring valleys under contribution.

Abderahman summoned all his alcaydes from their various military posts, to assist in driving the rebels from their mountain fastnesses into the plains. It was a dangerous, and protracted toil, for the mountains were frightfully wild and rugged. He entered them with a powerful host, driving the rebels from height to height and valley to valley, and harassing them by a galling fire from thousands of cross bows. At length, a decisive battle took place near the river Guadalemar. The rebels were signally defeated; four thousand fell in action, many were drowned in the river, and Muhamad, with a few horsemen, escaped to the mountains of the Algarves.

Here he was hunted by the alcaydes from one desolate retreat to another; his few followers grew tired of sharing the disastrous fortunes of a fated man: one by one deserted him, and he himself deserted the remainder, fearing they might give him up, to purchase their own pardon.

Lonely and disguised he plunged into the depths of the forests, or lurked in dens and caverns, like a famished wolf, often casting back his thoughts with regret to the time of his captivity in the gloomy tower of Cordova. Hunger at length drove him to Alarcon, at the risk of being discovered. Famine and misery, however, had so wasted and changed him, that he was not recognized. He remained nearly a year

in Alarcon, unnoticed and unknown, yet constantly tormenting himself
with the dread of discovery, and with groundless fears of the vengeance
of Abderahman. Death at length put an end to his wretchedness.

A milder fate attended his brother Casim. Being defeated in the
mountains of Murcia, he was conducted in chains to Cordova. On
coming into the presence of Abderahman, his once fierce and haughty
spirit, broken by distress, gave way; he threw himself on the earth,
kissed the dust beneath the feet of the king, and implored his clemency.
The benignant heart of Abderahman was filled with melancholy rather
than exultation, at beholding this wreck of the once haughty family
of Yusuf a suppliant at his feet, and suing for mere existence. He thought
upon the mutability of fortune and felt how insecure are all her favors.
He raised the unhappy Casim from the earth, ordered his irons to be
taken off, and, not content with mere forgiveness, treated him with
honor, and gave him possessions in Seville where he might live in
state conformable to the ancient dignity of his family. Won by this
great and persevering magnanimity, Casim ever after remained one
of the most devoted of his subjects.

All the enemies of Abderahman were at length subdued; he reigned
undisputed sovereign of the Moslems of Spain; and so benign was his
government that every one blessed the revival of the illustrious line of
Omeya. He was at all times accessible to the humblest of his subjects;
the poor man ever found in him a friend, and the oppressed a protector.
He improved the administration of justice; established schools for public
instruction; encouraged poets and men of letters and cultivated the
sciences. He built mosques in every city that he visited; inculcated
religion by example as well as by precept; and celebrated all the festivals
prescribed by the Koran, with the utmost magnificence.

As a monument of gratitude to God for the prosperity with which he
had been favored, he undertook to erect a mosque in his favorite city
of Cordova, that should rival in splendor the great mosque of Damascus,
and excel the one recently erected in Bagdad by the Abbassides, the
supplanters of his family.

It is said that he himself furnished the plan for this famous edifice,
and even worked on it, with his own hands, one hour in each day, to
testify his zeal and humility in the service of God, and to animate his
workmen. He did not live to see it completed, but it was finished according to his plans by his son Hixem. When finished, it surpassed the
most splendid mosques of the east. It was six hundred feet in length
and two hundred and fifty in breadth. Within were twenty eight
aisles, crossed by nineteen, supported by a thousand and ninety three
columns of marble. There were nineteen portals covered with plates
of bronze, of rare workmanship. The principal portal was covered with
plates of gold. On the summit of the grand cupola, were three gilt

balls, surmounted by a golden pomegranate. At night, the mosque was illuminated with four thousand seven hundred lamps, and great sums were expended in amber and aloes, which were burnt as perfumes. The mosque remains to this day, shorn of its ancient splendor yet still one of the grandest Moslem monuments in Spain.

Finding himself advancing in years, Abderahman assembled in his capital of Cordova the principal governors and commanders of his kingdom, and in presence of them all, with great solemnity, nominated his son Hixem as the successor to the throne. All present made an oath of fealty to Abderahman during his life and to Hixem after his death. The prince was younger than his brothers Suleiman and Abdallah; but he was the son of Howara, the tenderly beloved sultana of Abderahman, and her influence, it is said, gained him this preference.

Within a few months afterwards Abderahman fell grievously sick at Merida. Finding his end approaching, he summoned Hixem to his bedside. "My son," said he, "the angel of death is hovering over me; treasure up, therefore, in thy heart this dying counsel, which I give through the great love I bear thee. Remember that all empire is from God, who gives and takes it away according to his pleasure. Since God through his divine goodness, has given us regal power and authority, let us do his holy will, which is nothing else than to do good to all men, and especially to those committed to our protection. Render equal justice, my son, to the rich and the poor, and never suffer injustice to be done within thy dominion, for it is the road to perdition. Be merciful and benignant to those dependent upon thee. Confide the government of the cities and provinces to men of worth and experience; punish without compassion those ministers who oppress thy people with exorbitant exactions. Pay thy troops punctually; teach them to feel a certainty in thy promises; command them with gentleness but firmness, and make them in truth the defenders of the state, not its destroyers. Cultivate unceasingly the affections of thy people, for in their good will consists the security of the state, in their distrust its peril, in their hatred its certain ruin. Protect the husbandmen who cultivate the earth, and yield us necessary sustenance; never permit their fields and groves and gardens to be disturbed. In a word, act in such wise that thy people may bless thee and may enjoy, under the shadow of thy wings, a secure and tranquil life. In this consists good government; if thou dost practise it, thou wilt be happy among thy people, and renowned throughout the world."

Having given this excellent counsel, the good King Abderahman blessed his son Hixem, and shortly after, died; being but in the sixtieth year of his age. He was interred with great pomp; but the highest honors that distinguished his funeral were the tears of real sorrow shed upon his grave. He left behind him a name for valour, justice, and magnanimity,

and forever famous as being the founder of the glorious line of the
Ommiades in Spain.

HIXEM

[CHAPTER IV

*Rebellion of the brothers of Hixem—A Holy war proclaimed—
Completion of the great mosque—Death of Hixem.*]

787

"In the hand of God," says the Arabian chronicler, "is power and
dominion; he giveth and taketh away; he layeth one in the dust and
setteth up another in his stead." Scarcely had the funeral train of the
good King Abderahman passed by, and scarce were the tears dried
from the eyes of the mourners when his son Hixem made his progress
through the streets of Merida with a splendid train of chivalry, amid
the acclamations of the multitude hailing him as Miramamolin or
King of Spain.

He was thirty years of age, of a majestic presence, surnamed Aladil,
or the just, for the equity of his dealings, and al Rahdi, or the benign,
for the gentleness of his spirit. The very commencement of his beneficent reign, however, was disturbed by tempests. His two elder brothers
Suleiman and Abdallah, indignant at the preference shewn him by
their deceased father, rose in rebellion. Various sanguinary battles
took place. "It was grievous," says the Arabian chronicler, "to see
brethren of the same faith contending with tenfold greater wrath and
cruelty than if they had been contending with the enemies of the
prophet."

Hixem, however, though gentle in peace, proved himself formidable
in war. The insurgents were defeated with great loss. Suleiman took
refuge in the mountains, and Abdallah shut himself up in the iron
bound city of Toledo. The latter was invested by the army of Hixem
for upwards of two months and reduced to famishing extremity. Seeing
there was no hope of succor from his brother Suleiman, nor any possibility of holding out for a much longer period; Abdallah sent forth
his vizier to the commander of the army, craving safe passage for
messengers to the king charged with propositions for a surrender. A
passport was granted, but it was Abdallah himself who sallied forth in
disguise, accompanied by his vizier. The deception was undiscovered,
and two cavaliers of the besieging army were ordered to accompany
the supposed messengers to the king at Cordova. On coming in sight

of the royal Alcazar or palace Abdallah sent his vizier in advance to announce his approach. When Hixem heard that his brother was coming in this suppliant manner, his heart yearned toward him, and hastening forth he threw himself upon his neck and took him once more into his affection. Toledo was given up to the king; he did not reinstate Abdallah in power but he gave him a royal residence situated in the neighborhood of that city, in the rich and delightful vega watered by the Tagus.

Hixem would fain have drawn to him his brother Suleiman by assurances of equal favor, but the latter haughtily spurned his proffers. He displayed his standard in the mountains of Murcia, the ancient region of Tadmir, summoning the turbulent and disaffected to join him in a war against the king. Hixem was grieved at the necessity of once more taking up arms against a brother. He prepared to take the field with a powerful army, but sent the vanguard a day in advance under the command of his youthful son Alhakem. It was the first time the prince had ever been in command; in the vanguard was the flower of the Moorish chivalry. The enemy was overtaken in the fields of Lorca. Full of youthful fire and eager to distinguish himself, the prince, without waiting for the arrival of his father with the main army, made a headlong charge upon the foe, though greatly superior in number. The rash courage of the prince was successful; after a severe conflict in which the field was covered with the dead bodies of kindred enemies, the insurgents were routed and took refuge in the mountains.

When Hixem arrived at the field of battle he found the soldiers of Alhakem burying the dead. The youthful conqueror, flushed with triumph, laid the banners of Suleiman at the feet of his father. Hixem embraced him with tenderness and passed encomiums on the valor of himself and his cavaliers. When he was alone with him, however, he addressed to him a few words suggested by the experience of maturer years. "A daring spirit, my son," said he, "is excellent in war, but it should be governed by prudence and reflexion. Never aim at a brilliant, but hazardous blow when a little delay would ensure a complete victory. Seek the service of the cause, more than personal distinction. An eagerness to enjoy a triumph without competition, often causes the loss of a battle and brings disgrace upon him who with selfish rashness has risqued it. Courage, my son, is the glory of the youthful soldier, but caution is the staunch merit of the accomplished veteran."

Suleiman was absent from his army when it was thus suddenly attacked and routed. He was returning to it when he met with scattered fugitives. "Fly!" cried they. "All is lost, and the enemy is in pursuit." "Hard is my fortune!" said he in tones of bitter despondency. Then without adding another word he turned his bridle and rode towards Valencia. He was followed by several cavaliers; but every day thinned their number, as he was harassed by the warriors of the king, and took no certain course, wandering like a man in despair. Arrived in the neighborhood of Denia he shut himself up in a strong fortress, whence he wrote to Hixem entreating forgiveness and oblivion of the past and like clemency with that shewn to his brother Abdallah.

Hixem readily forgave his repentant brother but on condition that he should establish himself in some city of Africa; and to facilitate his departure the king bought of him his possessions in Spain for sixty thousand mitcales of gold. Suleiman took up his residence in the city of Tangier and gave his brother no further molestation.

Other rebellions occurred in the east of Spain but were speedily subdued, and Hixem found himself seated firmly on the throne established by his father.

"During these lamentable wars and dissensions among true believers," says the Arabian chronicler, "the Christians had regained possession of many cities in the north of Spain and the southern provinces of France. To regain these, Hixem ordered that an algihed or holy war should be proclaimed, on the same day and the same hour, from the khatib or pulpit of every mosque throughout his dominions. By this every musulman was called upon to aid with his person, if young, or with arms, horses and contributions, if too old to take the field; and ineffable blessings were promised to such as should display zeal in the righteous cause.

The call was not in vain. An army of thirty thousand men commanded by Abdelwahid, the Hagib of the King, marched towards the Asturias, ravaging the country about Astonga and a part of Galicia, making immense booty and carrying off many captives with great droves of cattle. A young Christian prince named Alphonso, however, hastily assembled a body of troops; intercepted the Moslems in the defiles of the mountains, rescued the prisoners, retook the booty and obliged Abdelwahid to retreat with loss and humiliation."

The youthful prince here spoken of by the Arabian chronicler was Alphonso the Chaste, to whom his father Bermudo the Deacon had resigned the sceptre of the Asturias, as being more fitted by his warlike qualities to defend it.

Another army of greater force, led by Abdallah ben Abdelmelic, passed the Pyrenees and made a descent upon the plains of France; took Narbonne, sacked it with fire and sword, and laid waste the environs. The affrighted inhabitants abandoned their dwellings and fled into the interior of the country, or hid themselves in dens and caves.

The victorious army of Islam pursued its destructive course to the neighborhood of Carcassone. There it was met by a powerful force composed of the counts of the frontier with their vassals. A sanguinary battle took place between Carcassone and Narbonne in which Abdallah was victorious. "The sword of Islam," says the Arabian historian, "made such slaughter among the unbelievers, that God alone who created them knows the number of the slain." Abdallah reconducted his army into Spain laden with gold and silver and precious stuffs, the spoil of these Gallic cities. Great were the rejoicings in Cordova when the army poured into its gates, all glittering with the riches gained in this holy war. Hixem rendered thanks to Allah for the protection shewn to his arms; and in pious gratitude devoted all his share of the spoil to the completion of the great mosque of Cordova which had been commenced by his father.

Hixem had proved himself formidable in war, but his delight was in the gentle arts of peace. He devoted much of his time to rural occupations; planting groves and orchards, and embellishing the environs of Cordova with gardens. He fostered literature also and entertained distinguished poets at his court; he even wrote verses himself, which were praised for their elegance. He had the felicity, so rare with monarchs, to be truly beloved by his people, for he exercised over them a gentle and paternal sway. The poor blessed him for his bounteous charity; his captive subjects were never suffered to languish in foreign chains; and the widow and the fatherless found in him a protector.

Hixem was one day recreating himself in his delightful garden near Cordova, attending to his favorite plants and flowers, when an astrologer whom he entertained at his court approached with gloomy aspect. "Señor," said he, "time is short; work rather for eternity."

"Why do you address to me that sentence?" demanded the king. "I entreat you Señor," replied the astrologer, "to ask me no further. What I said was uttered in an unguarded moment." Hixem insisted upon knowing his secret meaning, assuring him that nothing he might say should cause displeasure. "Then," said the astrologer, "prepare Oh Hixem for thy latter end, for it is written in the decrees of heaven that within two years thou shalt die!"

The king heard these words without a change of countenance and ordered a rich garment to be given to the astrologer. He pursued his amusements in the garden until his accustomed hour; heard music and singing; played at chess as he was wont, repeating many times the exclamation, "My trust is in God; in him will I hope."

Still the astrologer's words had sunk deep in his heart. Awakened to the uncertainty of life, he assembled the principal commanders and governors of his kingdom in the seventh year of his reign and solemnly named his son Alhakem, then twenty two years of age, his wali alhadi, or future successor, obliging them all to take the prince by the hand and swear to him fealty and obedience.

The prediction of the astrologer was verified. He fell ill in the following year, and after giving to his son the golden advice which he had received from his own father, and which he had so faithfully and prosperously followed, he died in the thirty eighth year of his age and the eighth year of his reign. He was interred with great magnificence; his son Alhakem made his funeral oration, and the tears and blessings of his subjects proved how beneficent had been his reign.

[ALHAKEM

CHAPTER V

Character of Alhakem—His uncles Suleiman and Abdallah take the field against him—Siege of Toledo—Capture of Narbonne—Suleiman slain in battle—Flight of Abdallah—Alhakem returns in triumph to Cordova.]

AH AD
180 796

"To Allah," says the Arabian chronicler, "is it given to look beyond the outward form and read the heart of man." Cordova resounded with acclamations when Alhakem, the son of Hixem, ascended the throne of Moslem Spain. He was in the flower of youth, comely in form and feature and graceful in every action. As he passed in glorious cavalcade through the principal streets, proclaimed at every corner, the populace hailed him as a worthy successor of Hixem and Abderahman and invoked blessings on his head. Alhakem had, indeed, received every advantage of education and example: he was learned beyond his age, and of a quick and subtle genius; but vain and presumptuous; he was also quick to anger; and what was mere passion in his youth, hardened into cruelty as he advanced in years.

At the outset of his reign his uncles Suleiman and Abdallah renewed their pretensions to the sovereignty of Spain, in the rights of primogeniture. Suleiman brought over from Africa a great host, composed of the loose rabble of the African towns and the wild sons of the desert; inflamed with the idea of plundering the rich cities of Spain and occupying its fertile valleys. On landing, he proclaimed himself King of Spain, as oldest son of the former Miramamolin, Abderahman ben Omeya.

Abdallah, who was residing on the estate granted him by Hixem near to Toledo, got possession of that city with its powerful Alcazar, and made a strong party among the commanders of several neighboring fortresses. About the same time Alhakem heard of hostilities breaking out on the frontiers of France; the Franks having retaken Narbonne and Giron and made an invasion of the rich provinces along the Mediterranean.

The youthful king, full of the fire and confidence natural to his years, was not to be daunted by this varied front of war. He marched at once to the siege of Toledo, and despatched some of his best troops and ablest commander to repel the invading Franks. He soon learnt, however, that the invasion was more dangerous than he had apprehended; the alcaydes of his frontier towns being in secret league with the Franks, who were overrunning the whole eastern part of his dominions. Leaving an experienced general, therefore, by the name of Amru, to maintain the siege of Toledo, he set off with the flower of his chivalry; swept through Arragon and Catalonia, driving the Franks before him, and retaking Huesca, Girona, and Barcelona. Thence he continued his victorious career into the provinces of Afranc or France; rearing again the banner of the prophet in those regions which had been overrun by true believers, in the holy war levied by his father.

On taking the city of Narbonne he put every man to the sword and carried the women and children into captivity. He then recrossed the Pyrenees; and pursued his homeward march, making a great parade of the spoils and captives taken in the land of the unbelievers; so that he was regarded with admiration and greeted by the surname of Almudafar, or, the fortunate conqueror.

During his absence his uncles Suleiman and Abdallah had augmented their forces by adventurers and desperadoes from all quarters; they had kindled the flames of revolt in Murcia and Valencia, and erected their standard in the vicinity of Toledo, where, confident in their numbers, and in the success which had attended their arms in various encounters with the generals of the king, they now awaited his coming in full anticipation of a victory.

The conflict took place in the neighborhood of Toledo; where their rabble army was soon routed with great slaughter by the veteran troops of Alhakem. Suleiman and Abdallah took refuge in Murcia where they collected the scattered ruins of their army, and being reenforced by the insurgents of those parts, were soon enabled to take the field in greater numbers than before.

Alhakem hastened to encounter them. He was met by the light African cavalry of Suleiman, with whom he had several sharp skirmishings. A general battle succeeded of a deadly and unnatural kind. It was the house of Omeya divided against itself; kindred fighting with kindred. Suleiman and Abdallah displayed the characteristic valor of their race; they were making their last stand for empire. The battle raged throughout the day; and as the sun went down upon that bloody field it was yet uncertain who would be the victors.

Alhakem now made a charge with the choicest of his troops upon the centre of the enemy and threw them into confusion. Suleiman rallied his flying forces, and seemed, for a time, to stay the course of victory with his single scymetar. His brother Abdallah came to his assistance; when Alhakem, at the head of his Zenetes, pressed forward to engage hand to hand with his uncles.

At this critical moment; when the blood of the Omeyas was about to be shed by each other's sword, an arrow from an unknown hand pierced the throat of Suleiman. He fell from his horse and was trampled to death under the feet of his own cavalry. His brother Abdallah saw him fall, and, despairing of success, suffered himself to be borne off in the throng of his flying army.

The forces of Alhakem remained under arms all night, expecting, from the superior number of the enemy, a renewal of the battle in the morning. During that gloomy night the wounded lay mingled with the dead, uttering their groans in vain, for no one came to their relief. Those who were unhurt lay stretched upon the ground with their weapons in their hands, seeking in feverish sleep to recover from the past, and to gather fresh strength for the morning conflict. At the first gleam of dawn the trumpet startled them awake. No trumpet was heard from the camp of the enemy. The sun rose upon a dismal field strewed with the dead and the dying, but not a hostile spear was to be seen. In the darkness of the night the enemy had retreated to the mountains.

Among the dead was found the body of the unfortunate Suleiman; transfixed with an arrow, and trampled in the dust. It was borne in triumph to the presence of Alhakem by some of his devoted followers. "Such," cried they, "be the fate of all the enemies of our Lord the King. Praised be the name of Allah who alone giveth victory."

The heart of Alhakem was not yet hardened. In the pale features of his uncle he beheld a resemblance to his father, and overcome by sudden tenderness and sorrow, wept over the body. He caused it to be interred with honour befitting the remains of a prince of the illustrious line of Omeya; and remained with his whole army to perform the obsequies with impressive pomp.

He would not permit any pursuit after his uncle Abdallah, who retreated through the mountains towards Denia followed by numbers of his African troops, and ultimately found refuge in Valencia where he was much beloved. Thence he sent messages to his nephew offering to give up all pretensions to the crown and to submit to his commands on receiving assurance of amnesty.

The message reached Alhakem in a favorable moment; when his anger was appeased by victory, and his heart softened at the grave of his unfortunate uncle Suleiman. He gave Abdallah the amnesty required, with permission to reside wherever he should choose, only claiming his two sons as hostages. Abdallah immediately went to Tangiers in Africa, sending his sons as stipulated to Alhakem. The king received them with great affection and gave his sister Alkinza in marriage to the eldest, whose name was Esfah. He allowed Abdallah a monthly sum for his support and a further sum to be paid at the end of every year; and permitted that he should reside at a favorite country retreat near Valencia.

He pardoned all the leaders who had joined the standard of his uncles and took many of their African troops into his service. Thus, having terminated these civil wars with so much success and moderation, he returned in triumph to Cordova where he was received with enthusiasm by the inhabitants. Happy would it have been for him, and glorious for his name, had he always tempered his triumphs with equal clemency.

[C H A P T E R   V I

Jusuf ben Amru in command of Toledo—His insolent rule—Vows bloody vengeance against the inhabitants—A dark scene of murder.]

805

At the time that Alhakem pursued his uncles into the lands of Murcia, the city of Toledo surrendered itself to his general, Amru. That commander left his son Jusuf in command of the place, and departed with his warriors to join the king. Jusuf ben Amru was the last person to be entrusted with the command of a place like Toledo. It was a city of great importance, from its central situation, its natural strength, its numerous population and immense wealth. It was full too of warlike Christians, ever ready to fly to arms, and who submitted with great impatience to the Moslem yoke. It was a post to be intrusted to an experienced and wary veteran, whose wisdom had outlived his passions, and who would know how to be strict without severity, and lenient without connivance. Jusuf ben Amru, on the contrary, was young, hot headed and arrogant. He treated Toledo as a conquered place, and ruled with such cruelty and insolence, that an exasperated multitude surrounded and stoned his house and wounded several of his guards. Jusuf trembled for his life. Fortunately the principal inhabitants, hearing the tumult, came to his assistance and calmed their enraged townsmen.

No sooner was the danger over than the arrogance of Jusuf revived, and he vowed bloody vengeance on the people. The same nobles who had protected him now took him prisoner, and confined him in a fortress to prevent his further endangering the public safety. They at the same time wrote to the king, complaining of the rash passions of the young man left to govern them.

The king shewed these letters to Amru. "Your son," said he, "is too young and impetuous for so critical a command; he must come and serve on the frontiers."

Amru, though grey in years, was equally vindictive, but more politic than his son; he determined to take cruel revenge for what he considered an insult offered to his family; and for that purpose obtained again the command of Toledo. He commenced harassing the people by measures apparently taken for their good. He levied incessant exactions for repairing the walls, strengthening the towers, and enlarging the Alcazar or citadel. These exactions bore heavy upon the people of Toledo, but they were far from satisfying his thirst for vengeance. The Alcazar, in which he resided, stood on the brow of a rocky hill overlooking the waters of the Tagus. He erected a strong tower adjacent to it, with a deep vault or pit beneath.

Soon after these events Alhakem sent a body of five thousand cavalry to the eastern provinces, under charge of his son Abderahman, a youth of only fifteen years of age. As these troops passed near Toledo the prince pitched his tents on the banks of the Tagus. Amru went forth to render him respect, and invited him to pass the night in the Alcazar. The prince accepted and entered the city with a chosen guard of cavalry, and Amru invited all the principal inhabitants to a banquet to be given that night in the Alcazar. He then told the prince that Toledo was full of factions and dangerous men, and that it was necessary many heads should fall to prevent rebellion, and that now was an opportunity to effect it—without risk. The prince cautioned him against a measure that should render him abhorrent to the people; but does not appear to have made strong opposition.

At night the Alcazar was lighted up with great splendor, and there was the sound of music and festivity. As the guests arrived those destined to destruction were introduced through the portal of the tower; the moment they entered their heads were struck off, and their blood made to flow into the pit. In this way four hundred of the noblest cavaliers of Toledo fell beneath the sword of the executioner. In the mean while the banquet went on, the torches blazed, and the sound of music and minstrelsy echoed through the shining halls of the Alcazar, and no one knew of the dark scene of murder that was going on within its vaults. On the following day the heads of the slaughtered cavaliers were exhibited on the walls of the Alcazar, and it was given out as a punishment, by command of the king, for the insurrection against the son of Amru. The people were overcome with fear and horror but dared not utter a murmur. The vengeance of Allah, however, was soon manifested, for both Amru and his son perished shortly after the perpetration of this cruelty.

[CHAPTER VII

Esfah and the dismissed vizier—Rage of Alhakem against Esfah and how it was softened.]

When Alhakem gave his sister in marriage to his cousin Esfah, he at the same time made that prince wali or governor of the city of Merida. He gave him also one of his principal favorites as vizier, who, however, soon made himself so disagreeable to Esfah that he dismissed him from his office. The degraded vizier immediately repaired to the king at Cordova, full of bitter complaints of the treatment he had experienced, mingled with calumnies against Esfah, calculated to alarm the jealous and suspicious nature of Alhakem. The king was incensed at the dismissal of his favorite, and alarmed at the fancied abuse of the powers confided to Esfah. In one of his moments of passion, he sent the vizier back to Merida with peremptory orders to Esfah to deliver up to him the government of the city and province. The prince treated the vizier with contempt, and sent for answer to Alhakem that he was surprized that his tried loyalty and affection should have no weight against the slanders of a dismissed vizier; and that he wondered at his turning off a grandson of Abderahman as though he had been a common servant. This reply threw Alhakem into one of his transports of rage, and he sent the captain of his cavalry to arrest Esfah.

The latter shut the gates of the city and refused admission to the cavalry, but offered no other resistance. Upon this Alhakem departed himself, resolving to enter the city by force and inflict a sanguinary punishment. Esfah feared to draw upon the inhabitants the wrath of the king and prepared to sally, with a few cavaliers, by one gate of the city, as Alhakem should enter by another. The loyal citizens opposed this resolution, offering to defend him to the last drop of blood.

The beautiful Alkinza, the wife of Esfah and sister of Alhakem, put an end to the contest by a woman's spirit and self devotion. Attended only by two servants of her household she sallied forth on horseback, traversed the camp of the besiegers, and suddenly appearing before her brother threw herself at his feet as the mediator for her husband. The heart of Alhakem was taken by surprize; he raised his sister from the earth and folded her tenderly to his bosom. The accents of her voice softened his anger, her explanations removed his doubts, he forgave all that had passed, and entered Merida with her by his side, amidst the shouts and blessings of the people. He was reconciled to his cousin

Esfah; restored him to his command, and in place of the scene of
terror and suffering he had intended to enact in Merida, he remained
for some time in the city partaking in public festivities and rejoicings.

[CHAPTER VIII

Conspiracy against Alhakem—Its terrific suppression.]

During the absence of Alhakem at Merida, treason was busy in his
capital of Cordova. The public were disappointed in him. Instead of
the benignity which they had promised themselves from his youth,
he governed with severity, and his sternness encreased with his years.
Many were scandalized also at a treaty which he had recently made
with a Christian king of Galicia, considering it a disgrace to form
alliance with a chief of the unbelievers; but the most moving cause is
said to have been the massacre at Toledo, which they ascribed to the
cruel policy of Alhakem, and in which many of the nobles of Cordova
had lost friends and relatives. Taking the advantage of the absence of
the king, therefore, a conspiracy was formed against his crown and
life. The chief conspirator was Yahye, a xeque or chief of the council,
and many of the nobles of the city were concerned. They fixed upon
the Prince Casim, cousin to the king and brother to Esfah, as successor
to the crown. He was grandson of Abderahman ben Omeya equally
with the present king and of an elder line. They supposed he must
feel an envious hostility to Alhakem in secret, and a present animosity
on account of the transactions at Merida and the deposition of his
brother. They began to talk with him vaguely and by obscure hints,
until, being gradually encouraged by him, they opened their whole
plot, to take away the life of the king and place one of the grandsons
of Abderahman upon the throne. Casim saw himself in their power and
affected to accede to their plans; but immediately sent a private
message to Alhakem entreating him to return immediately to Cordova,
for the safety of the empire. On his arrival Casim informed him of the
conspiracy as far as the plan had been revealed to him. Alhakem re-
strained his fury at the intelligence and ordered Casim to continue
to treat with the conspirators, until he should discover the whole
extent of the danger and devise effectual means to prevent it. In a few
days Casim presented the names of three hundred cavaliers, who
were sworn to slay Alhakem, as he entered the mosque at the hour of
evening prayers. Only two days remained before the time appointed
for the attempt. Alhakem did not close his eyes until his vengeance
was completed. That night mysterious and terrific scenes occurred in
the principal dwellings of the city. By the third watch of the night

Alhakem gazed with horrid satisfaction on the heads of the three hundred cavaliers, piled in the court of his palace. By day light they were suspended on hooks about the public place, and over each was written: "A traitor and enemy of his king."

The people were struck with horror at this fearful spectacle; the greater part were ignorant of the cause and feared to make any inquiry.

After this event Alhakem for eight years of his reign was no more troubled by rebellions or seditions. He had various battles with Christians both of the mountains of Spain, and the frontiers of France, in which his arms as usual were crowned with success. His youthful son Abderahman accompanied him in these wars, and at times had almost exclusive command. He not only relieved his father from the toils of war, but took upon himself the affairs of state, and at length was solemnly named by his father the future successor to the crown; all the dignitaries of the kingdom, as usual, taking the oath of fidelity; the foremost of whom were Esfah and Casim; the cousins of the king.

An interval of peace now prevailed throughout the kingdom. Alhakem, leaving the cares of government to his son, buried himself in the retirement of his Alcazar, or in the voluptuous bowers of his gardens, and gave himself up to mere sensual pleasures. He was surrounded by every thing that could minister delight to the senses, and attended by crowds of beautiful slaves of both sexes, skilled in music and dancing.

The various seditions which had taken place during his reign, had made him restless and suspicious. His Alcazar was surrounded with guards who kept watch night and day. There were three thousand Musarabs of Andalusia, and two thousand slaves, that watched without, and many armed eunuchs within the palace. The numerous and sanguinary executions he had made, likewise, had encreased a natural hardness of heart and given him a thirst for blood, and scarce a day passed that he did not issue sentences of death for every kind of crime. The public lost all admiration for his valour in his cruelty, and they felt indignant at the want of confidence in their loyalty evinced by such crowds of guards about his palace, for his father and grandfather had considered themselves sufficiently guarded by the affections of their people.

The cruelty of Alhakem and the discontents of his subjects at length produced a fearful convulsion. He had imposed a tribute upon certain merchandize, for the support of his guards. Several persons at first refused to pay it and had a contest with the collectors. Ten of the delinquents were seized in the midst of tumult and confusion. Enraged at this opposition to his decrees, Alhakem ordered that the unfortunate men should be impaled. The execution took place in a public square on a day of festival in the moon Ramazan. A great crowd from the

southern suburb of Cordova was present, and stifled indignation scowled
in every visage. In the press and confusion an inhabitant of the suburb
was struck and wounded by a soldier. His companions and neighbors
immediately attacked the soldier with stones. He galloped, wounded and
bloody, to the city guard; pursued by the multitude. The guard issued
forth to protect their comrade but were likewise assaulted and driven
to the very gates of the royal Alcazar. The cries of the soldiers and the
shouts of the multitude reached the king in the depths of his retirement. In one of his transports of ungovernable fury he seized his arms,
nor could the entreaties of his son and of various of his chieftains
mitigate his rage, or rather his frenzy. Sallying forth at the head of
his cavalry he charged furiously upon the multitude, cutting them
down and trampling them under foot. They fled in headlong terror to
their suburb; such as could get to their houses shut themselves up.
Some of the lowest of the populace made a faint resistance; the slaughter
was dreadful; the public sewers ran with blood. Three hundred were
taken prisoners, whom the king ordered to be impaled in a row along
the banks of the river from the bridge to the last of the mills. He then
gave up the suburb to be pillaged by his troops for three days successively, with this one exception, that no harm should be done to the
females. The whole arrabal or suburb was then razed to the ground,
and the king enjoined on his successors that it should never be rebuilt.
At the end of three days he ordered the bodies of those impaled to be
taken from the stakes, and granted assurance of life to the miserable
survivors of the suburb, on condition that they should leave Cordova
forever.

The unhappy exiles took a mournful farewell of their beloved country;
some wandered about in the villages and hamlets in the neighborhood
of Toledo, or took refuge in that city. More than fifteen thousand
passed into Africa, and thence into Egypt, where, arriving at Alexandria,
and being opposed by the inhabitants, in their despair they attacked
the city, entered it by force of arms, made a terrible massacre and
remained masters of the place. After some time the governor of Egypt,
by orders of the Caliph Almamon, ransomed the city from them by a
large sum of gold and a permission to choose some island of the
Grecian Sea for a residence.

They chose that of Crete, which was at that time nearly unin-
habited. Here they founded an independent government, placing at
its head their leader Omar ben Zoaïb Abu Hafas. Their numbers were
soon encreased by people from Irack and Egypt. They became rovers
of the seas, and having twenty ships they scoured the Grecian Sea
and plundered its islands so as to become wealthy with spoil. Seeing
themselves in possession of such great riches they desired to return
and enjoy them in their native country. Upon this, their commander

burnt the fleet; and when they railed at him for the act, lamenting their banishment from the sweet country of their youth, he rebuked them with severity. "How much better and more pleasant," said he, "is this island which flows with milk and honey than your arid deserts. Here among beautiful captives you will soon forget your ancient loves; and enjoying all the pleasures of life, will behold a new generation growing up to be the pride and comfort of your age."

With these words the exiles were comforted; and making up their minds to pass their lives upon the island they founded on its eastern part the famous city of Candy. Such was the fate of the exiles of Cordova.

The blind and ungovernable fury of Alhakem on this occasion lost Cordova more than twenty thousand of its most vigorous and useful inhabitants. Not content with having demolished the southern suburb, he left to his successors a solemn prohibition to restore it, but to suffer it to remain an open field. From this circumstance he was ever afterwards named Alrabdi, or he of the suburb, and Abu el Aasi, or the cruel, for the hardness and ferocity of his heart.

[CHAPTER IX

Of the war on the frontiers and on the sea—Death of King Alhakem.]

[A portion of the text of this chapter is lost.]
by their means to dispel the horrors seated in his soul. If they did not appear immediately his impatience became furious. One night at a late hour he called up Jacinto, a servant who was accustomed to anoint his beard. The servant was slow in coming, and when he appeared with a flask of musk Alhakem seized it in a rage and wounded him with it in the head. The trembling Jacinto humbly ventured to expostulate. "Fear not—," said Alhakem wildly, "that we shall lack ointment, even though we shed it with profusion, for that it might not fail us have I ordered so many heads to be struck off." Sometimes he would assemble all his commanders and soldiery, and distribute arms and horses among them as if for some warlike expedition, and then suddenly dismiss them and send them to their homes. At other times he would call his cadis and viziers from their beds at midnight as if for urgent consultation, and then make his slaves dance and sing before them, as if they were only summoned for recreation.*

In this way he passed four wretched years, full of gloom, and repen-

---

* His melancholy sometimes took a poetic vein and vented itself in verses of a plaintive nature; some of which still exist. (See Conde, 1, 257.)

tance, and occasionally disordered by temporary frenzy. At length his melancholy and the fever which preyed upon him overpowered his frame and he died in horror and despair, after a troubled reign of about twenty six years. "Glory," concludes the Arabian chronicler, "be to him whose kingdom is eternal and without change."*

* Loado sea aquel cuyo imperio es eterno y sin contrariedades.—Conde, C. 37.

[1827–1847]

CHRONICLE OF FERNAN GONZALEZ,

COUNT OF CASTILE

[INTRODUCTION]

At the time of the general wreck of Spain by the sudden tempest of Arab invasion, many of the inhabitants took refuge in the mountains of the Asturias; burying themselves in narrow valleys difficult of access, wherever a constant stream of water afforded a green bosom of pasture land and scanty fields for cultivation. For mutual protection they gathered together in small villages called castros or castrellos, with watch towers and fortresses on impending cliffs, in which they might shelter and defend themselves in case of sudden inroad. Thus arose the kingdom of the Asturias, subject to Pelayo and the kings his successors, who gradually extended their dominions, built towns and cities and after a time fixed their seat of government at the city of Leon.

An important part of the region over which they bore sway was ancient Cantabria, extending from the Bay of Biscay to the Duero and called Castile from the number of castles with which it was studded. They divided it into seignories, over which they placed civil and military governors called counts; a title said to be derived from the Latin *comes*, a companion; the person enjoying it being admitted to the familiar companionship of the king, entering into his councils in time of peace and accompanying him to the field in time of war. The title of Count was therefore more dignified than that of Duke in the time of the Gothic kings.

The power of these counts encreased to such a degree that four of them formed a league to declare themselves independent of the Crown of Leon. Ordoño II., who was then king, received notice of it, and got them into his power by force as some assert, but as others maintain, by perfidious artifice. At any rate they were brought to court, convicted of treason and publicly beheaded. The Castilians flew to arms to revenge their deaths. Ordoño took the field with a powerful army, but his own death defeated all his plans.

The Castilians now threw off allegiance to the kingdom of Leon and elected two judges to rule over them; one in a civil, the other in a military capacity. The first who filled those stations were Nuño Rasura and Lain Calvo; two powerful nobles, the former descended from Diego

Porcello, a count of Lara; the latter, ancestor of the renowned Cid Campeador.

Nuño Rasura, the civil and political judge, was succeeded by his son Gonzalo Nuño; who married Doña Ximena, a daughter of one of the counts of Castile put to death by Ordoño II. From this marriage came Fernan Gonzalez, the subject of the following chronicle.

[CHAPTER I

Installation of Fernan Gonzalez as Count of Castile—His first campaign against the Moors—Victory of San Quirce—How the count disposed of the spoils.]

The renowned Fernan Gonzalez, the most complete hero of his time, was born about the year 887. Historians trace his descent to Nuño Belchidez, nephew of the Emperor Charlemagne, and Doña Sula Bella, granddaughter to the Prince Don Sancho, rightful sovereign of Spain, but superceded by Roderick, the last of the Gothic kings.

Fernan Gonzalez was hardily educated among the mountains in a strong place called Maron, in the house of Martin Gonzalez, a gallant and veteran cavalier. From his earliest years he was enured to all kinds of toils and perils: taught to hunt, to hawk, to ride the great horse, to manage sword, lance and buckler; in a word he was accomplished in all the noble exercises befitting a cavalier.

His father Gonzalo Nuño died in 903 and his elder brother Rodrigo in 904, without issue; and such was the admiration already entertained of Fernan Gonzalez by the hardy mountaineers and old Castilian warriors, that, though scarce seventeen years of age, he was unanimously elected to rule over them. His title is said to have been Count, Duke, and Consul, under the seignory of Alonzo the Great, King of Leon. A cortes or assemblage of the nobility and chivalry of Castile and of the mountains met together at the recently built city of Burgos to do honor to his installation. Sebastian, the renowned Bishop of Oca, officiated.

In those stern days of Spain the situation of a sovereign was not that of silken ease and idle ceremonial. When he put the rich crown upon his head, he encircled it likewise with shining steel. With the sceptre were united the lance and shield, emblems of perpetual war against the enemies of the faith. The cortes took this occasion to pass the following laws for the government of the realm.

1. Above all things the people should observe the law of God, the canons and statutes of the holy fathers; the liberty and privileges of the church and the respect due to its ministers. 2. No person should prosecute another, out of Castile, at any tribunal of justice or of arms,

under pain of being considered a stranger. 3. All Jews and Moors who refused to acknowledge the Christian faith, should depart from Castile within two months. 4. That the cavaliers of noble blood should treat their tenants and vassals with love and gentleness. 5. That he who slew another or committed any other grave offense should make equal measure of atonement. 6. That no one should take the property of another; but, if oppressed by poverty, should come to the count, who ought to be as a father to all. 7. That all should unite and be of one heart and aid one another in defence of their faith and of their country.

Such were the ordinances of the ancient cortes of Burgos; brief and simple and easy to be understood: not as at the present day, multifarious and perplexed, to the confusion and ruin of clients and the enrichment of lawyers.

Scarce was the installation ended, and while Burgos was yet abandoned to festivity, the young count, with the impatient ardor of youth, caused the trumpets to sound through the streets a call to arms. A captain of the Moorish king of Toledo was ravaging the territory of Castile at the head of seven thousand troops, and against him the youthful count determined to make his first campaign. In the spur of the moment but one hundred horsemen and fifteen hundred footsoldiers could be collected; but with this slender force the count prepared to take the field. Ruy Velazquez, a valiant cavalier, remonstrated against such rashness, but in vain. "I owe," said the count, "a death to the grave; the debt can never be paid so honorably as in the service of God and my country. Let every one, therefore, address himself heart and hand to this enterprize; for, if I come face to face with this Moor I will most assuredly give him battle." So saying, he knelt before Bishop Sebastian of Salamanca and craved his benediction. The reverend prelate invoked on his head the blessing and protection of heaven, for his heart yearned toward him; but when he saw the youthful warrior about to depart, he kindled as it were, with a holy martial fire, and ordering his steed to be saddled he sallied forth with him to the wars.*

The little army soon came upon traces of the enemy in fields laid waste and the smoking ruins of villages and hamlets. The count sent out scouts to clamber every height and explore every defile. From the summit of a hill they beheld the Moors encamped in a valley which was covered with the flocks and herds swept from the neighboring country. The camp of the marauders was formidable as to numbers; with various standards floating in the breeze; for in this foray were engaged the Moorish chiefs of Saragossa, Denia and Seville, together with many valiant Moslems who had crossed the straits from Africa to share in what they considered a holy enterprise. The scouts observed, however,

* Sandoval, *ut supra*, p. 298.

that the most negligent security reigned throughout the camp; some reposing, others feasting and revelling; all evidently considering themselves safe from any attack.

Upon hearing this the count led his men secretly and silently to the assault and came upon the Moors in the midst of their revelry, before they had time to buckle on their armour. The infidels, however, made a brave though confused resistance; the camp was strewn with their dead; many were taken prisoners and the rest began to falter. The count killed their captain general with his own hand, in single fight, as he was bravely rallying his troops. Upon seeing him fall the Moors threw down their weapons and fled.

Immense booty was found in the Moorish camp; partly the rich arms and equipments of the infidel warriors, partly the plunder of the country. An ordinary victor would have merely shared the spoils with his soldiery, but the count was as pious as he was brave, and moreover had by his side the venerable Bishop of Salamanca as counsellor. Contenting himself, therefore, with distributing one third among his soldiery, he shared the rest with God, devoting a large part to the church and to the relief of souls in purgatory; a pious custom which he ever after observed. He moreover founded a church on the field of battle, dedicated to St. Quirce, on whose festival (the 16th July) this victory was obtained. To this church was subsequently added a monastery, where a worthy fraternity of monks were maintained in the odour of sanctity, to perpetuate the memory of this victory. All this was doubtless owing to the providential presence of the good bishop on this occasion; and this is one instance of the great benefit derived from those priests and monks and other purveyors of the church, who hovered about the Christian camps throughout all these wars with the infidels.

[CHAPTER II

Of the sally from Burgos, and surprise of the Castle of Lara—Capitulation of the town—Visit to Alonzo the Great, King of Leon.]

Count Fernan Gonzalez did not remain idle after the victory of San Quirce. There was at this time an old castle, strong but much battered in the wars, which protected a small town, the remains of the once flourishing city of Lara. It was the ancient domain of his family, but was at present in possession of the Moors. In sooth it had repeatedly been taken and retaken; for, in those iron days, no castle nor fortress remained long under the same masters. One year it was in the hands of the Christians, the next of the Moors. Some of these castles with their dependent towns were sacked, burnt and demolished; others remained silent and deserted, their original owners fearing to reside in them; and their ruined towers were only tenanted by bats and owls and screaming birds of prey. Lara had lain for a time in ruins after being captured by the Moors, but had been rebuilt by them with diminished grandeur, and they held a strong garrison in the castle, whence they sallied forth occasionally to ravage the lands of the Christians. The Moorish chieftain of Lara, as has been observed, was among the associated marauders who had been routed in the battle of San Quirce; and the Count Fernan Gonzalez thought this a favorable time to strike for the recovery of his family domain, now that the infidel possessor was weakened by defeat and could receive no succour.

Appointing Rodrigo Velazquez and the Count Don Vela Alvarez to act as governors of Castile during his absence, the count sallied forth from Burgos with a brilliant train of chivalry. Among the distinguished cavaliers who attended him were Martin Gonzalez, Don Gonzalo Gustios, Don Velasco, and Don Lope de Biscaya, which last brought a goodly band of stout Biscayans. The alfarez or standard bearer was Orbita Velazquez, who had distinguished himself in the battle of San Quirce. He bore as a standard a great cross of silver, which shone gloriously in front of the host, and is preserved, even to the present day, in the church of St. Pedro de Arlanza. One hundred and fifty noble cavaliers well armed and mounted, with many esquires and pages of the lance, and three thousand foot soldiers, all picked men, formed this small but stout hearted army.

The count led his troops with such caution that they arrived in the neighborhood of Lara without being discovered. It was the Vigil of St. John, the country was wrapped in evening shadows, and the count was enabled to approach near to the place to make his observations. He perceived that his force was too inconsiderable to invest the town and fortress. Beside, about two leagues distant, was the gaunt and rock built castle of Carazo, a presidio or strong hold of the Moors whence he might be attacked in the rear should he linger before the fortress. It was evident, therefore, that, whatever was to be effected must be done promptly and by sudden surprize. Revolving these things in his mind he put his troops in ambush in a deep ravine where they took their rest while he kept watch upon the castle; maturing his plans against the morrow. In this way he passed his midsummer's night, the Vigil of the blessed St. John.

The festival of St. John is observed as well by Mahometans as Christians. During the night bonfires blazed on the hilltops and the sound of music and festivity was heard from within the town. When the rising sun shone along the valley of the Arlanza the Moors in the castle, unsuspicious of any lurking danger, threw open the gates and issued forth to recreate themselves in the green fields and along the banks of the river. When they had proceeded to a considerable distance, and a hill shut them from view, the count with his eager followers issued silently but swiftly from their hiding place and made directly for the castle. On the way they met with another band of Moors who had likewise come forth for amusement. The count struck the leader to the earth with one blow of his lance; the rest were either slain or taken prisoners; so that not one escaped to give the alarm.

Those of the garrison who had remained in the castle, seeing a Christian force rushing up to the very walls, hastened to close the gates, but it was too late. The count and his cavaliers burst them open and put every one to the sword who made opposition. Leaving Don Belasco and a number of soldiers to guard the castle, the count hastened with the rest in pursuit of the Moors who were solemnizing the day on the banks of the Arlanza. Some were reclining on the grass; others were amusing themselves with music and the popular dance of the Zambra, while their arms lay scattered among the herbage.

At sight of the Christians they snatched up their weapons and made a desperate though vain resistance. Within two hours almost all were either slain or captured; a few escaped to the neighboring mountains of Carazo. The town, seeing the castle in the hands of the Christians and the garrison routed and destroyed, readily capitulated; and the inhabitants were permitted to retain unmolested possession of their houses, on agreeing to pay to the count the same tribute which had been exacted from them by the Moorish king. Don Belasco was left alcayde of the fortress, and the count returned covered with glory to his capital of Burgos.

The brilliant victories and hardy deeds of arms with which the youthful Count of Castile had commenced his reign excited the admiration of Alonzo the Great, King of Leon, and he sent missives urging him to appear at his royal court. The count accordingly set forth with a cavalcade of his most approved knights and many of his relatives, sumptuously armed and arrayed and mounted on steeds richly caparisoned. It was a pageant befitting a young and magnificent chief, in the freshness and pleasance of his years.

The king came out of the city to meet him attended by all the pomp and grandeur of his court. The count alighted and approached to kiss the king's hand; but Alonzo alighted also and embraced him with great affection, and the friendship of these illustrious princes continued without interruption throughout the life of the king.

[CHAPTER III

Expedition against the Fortress of Muñon—Desperate defence of the Moors—Enterprise against Castro Xeriz.]

Many are the doughty achievements recorded in ancient chronicles, of this most valorous cavalier; among others is his expedition with a chosen band against the castle of Muñon; a place of great importance, which stood at no great distance from Burgos. He sallied from his capital in an opposite direction, to delude the Moorish scouts; but making a sudden turn, came upon the fortress by surprize; broke down the gates and forced his way in at the head of his troops having nothing but a dagger in his hand, his lance and sword having been broken in the assault. The Moors fought desperately from court to tower; from tower to wall; and when they saw all resistance vain many threw themselves from the battlements into the ditch rather than be made captives. Leaving a strong garrison in the place the count returned to Burgos.

His next enterprize was against Castro Xeriz, a city with a strong castle, which had been a thorn in the side of Castile, the Moorish garrison often sweeping the road between Burgos and Leon; carrying off travellers, capturing cattle and plundering convoys of provisions and merchandize. The count advanced against this place in open day, ravaging the country and announcing his approach by clouds of smoke from the burning habitations of the Moors. Abdallah, the alcayde of the fortress, would have made peace, but the count refused all terms. "God," said he, "has appointed me to rescue his holy inheritance from the power of infidels; nothing is to be negotiated but by the edge of the sword."

Abdallah then made a sally with a chosen band of his cavaliers. They at first careered lightly with their Arabian steeds and launched their Moorish darts, but the Christians closed in the old Gothic style, fighting hand to hand. Abdallah fell by the sword of the count, and his followers fled with loosened reins back to the city. The Christians followed hard upon them strewing the ground with dead. At the gate of the city they were met by Almondir, the son of Abdallah, who disputed the gate way and the street inch by inch until the whole place ran with blood. The Moors driven from the streets took refuge in the castle; where Almondir inspirited them to a desperate defence until a stone struck him as he stood on the battlements and he fell to the earth, dead. Having no leader to direct them, the Moors surrendered. When the town was cleared of the dead and order restored, the count divided the spoils, allotting the houses among his followers and peopling the place with Christians. He gave the command of it to Layn Bermudez, with the title of Count. From him descended an illustrious line of cavaliers

termed de Castro, whose male line became extinct in Castile but continued to flourish in Portugal. The place is said to have been called
Castro Xeriz, in consequence of the blood shed in this conflict, xeriz,
in the Arabic language, signifying bloody.[*]

[CHAPTER IV

*How the Count of Castile and the King of Leon make a triumphant
foray into the Moorish country—Capture of Salamanca—Of the chal-
lenge brought by the herald, and of the count's defiance.*]

Count Fernan Gonzalez was restless, daring and impetuous; he seldom
suffered lance to rest on wall or steed in stable, and no Moorish
commander could sleep in quiet who held town or tower in his
neighborhood. King Alonzo the Great became emulous of sharing in
his achievements, and they made a campaign together against the
Moors. The count brought a splendid array of Castilian chivalry into
the field together with a host of Montaneses, hardy and vigorous troops
from the Asturias, excellent for marauding warfare. The King of Leon
brought his veteran bands, seasoned to battle. With their united forces
they ravaged the Moorish country, marking their way with havoc and
devastation; arrived before Salamanca they took that city by storm
after a brave defence; and gave it up to be sacked by the soldiery.
After which such of the Moors as chose to remain in it were suffered to
retain their possessions as vassals to the king. Having accomplished
this triumphant foray they returned, each one to his capital.

The Count of Castile did not repose long in his palace. One day a
Moorish herald magnificently dressed rode into the city of Burgos,
bringing Fernan Gonzalez a cartel of defiance. It was from a vaunting
Moor named Acefali, who had entered the territories of Castile with a
powerful force of horse and foot, giving out that he had come to
measure strength and prowess with the count in battle. Don Fernan
Gonzalez replied to the defiance with weapon in hand at the head of
his warriors. A pitched battle ensued, which lasted from early morn
until evening twilight. In the course of the fight the count was in
imminent peril, his horse being killed under him and himself surrounded, but he was rescued by his cavaliers. After great bloodshed
the Moors were routed and pursued beyond the borders. The spoil
gained in this battle was devoutly expended in repairing the churches
of Castile and the Montaneses.

[*] Sandoval, p. 301.

[CHAPTER V

A night assault upon the castle of Carazo—The Moorish maiden who betrayed the garrison.]

In those warlike times of Spain every one lived with sword in hand; there was scarcely a commanding cliff or hill top but had its castle. Moors and Christians regarded each other from rival towers and battlements perched on opposite heights, and were incessantly contending for the dominion of the valleys.

We have seen that Count Fernan Gonzalez had regained possession of the ancient town and fortress of Lara; the domain of his ancestors; but it will be recollected that within two leagues' distance stood the Moorish presidio of Carazo. It was perched like an eagle's nest on the summit of a mountain, and the cragged steepness of its position and its high and thick walls seemed to render it proof against all assault. The Moors who garrisoned it were fierce marauders, who used to sweep down like birds of prey from their lofty nest, pounce upon the flocks and dwellings of the Christians, make hasty ravage and bear away their spoils to the mountain top. There was no living with safety or tranquillity within the scope of their maraudings.

Intelligence of their misdeeds was brought to the count at Burgos. He determined to have that castle of Carazo whatever might be the cost; for this purpose he called a council of his chosen cavaliers. He did not conceal the peril of the enterprize, from the crag built situation of the castle; its great strength and the vigilance and valor of its garrison. Still the Castilian cavaliers offered themselves to carry the fortress or die.

The count sallied secretly from Burgos with a select force and repaired in the night time to Lara, that the Moors might have no intimation nor suspicion of his design. In the midst of the next night the castle gate was quietly opened and they issued forth as silently as possible; pursuing their course in the deep shadows of the valley until they came to the foot of the mountain of Carazo. Here they remained in ambush, and sent forth scouts. As the latter prowled about the day began to dawn and they heard a female voice singing above them on the side of the mountain. It was a Moorish damsel coming down, with a vessel upon her head. She descended to a fountain which gushed forth beneath a grove of willows, and as she sang she began to fill her vessel with water. The spies issued from their concealment, seized her and carried her to Count Fernan Gonzalez.

Overcome by terror or touched by conviction, the Moorish damsel threw herself on her knees before the count; declared her wish to turn Christian, and offered, in proof of her sincerity, to put him in a way of gaining possession of the castle. Being encouraged to proceed, she told

him that there was to be a marriage feast that day in the castle, and
of course a great deal of revelry which would put the garrison off of its
guard. She pointed out a situation where he might lie in ambush with
his troops in sight of the tower, and promised when a favorable moment
presented for an attack to give a signal with a light.

The count regarded her for a time with a fixed and earnest gaze but
saw no faltering nor change of countenance. The case required bold
measures combined with stratagem, so he confided in her and permitted
her to return to the castle. All day he lay in ambush with his troops;
each man his hand upon his weapon to guard against surprise. The
distant sound of revelry from the castle, with now and then the clash
of cymbals, the bray of trumpets and a strain of festive music, shewed
the revelry that reigned within. Night came on; hour after hour passed
away; lights gleamed from walls and windows; but none resembling the
appointed signal. It was almost midnight and the count began to fear
the Moorish damsel had deceived him, when to his great joy he saw the
signal light gleaming from one of the towers.

He now sallied forth with his men, and all, on foot, clambered up
the steep and rugged height. They had almost attained the foot of the
towers when they were descried by a sentinel who cried with a loud
voice, "The foe! the foe! to arms! to arms!" The count, followed by his
hardy cavaliers, rushed forward to the gate crying, "God and Saint
Millan!" The whole castle was instantly in an uproar. The Moors were
bewildered by the sudden surprize and the confusion of a night assault.
They fought bravely but irregularly. The Christians had but one plan
and one object. After a hard struggle and great bloodshed they forced
the gate and made themselves masters of the castle.

The count remained several days fortifying the place and garrisoning
it, that it might not fall again into the possession of the Moors. He
bestowed magnificent rewards on the Moorish damsel who had thus
betrayed her countrymen; she embraced the Christian faith, to which
she had just given such a signal proof of devotion, though it is not said
whether the count had sufficient confidence in her conversion and her
newly moulted piety to permit her to remain in the fortress she had
betrayed.

Having completed his arrangements the count departed on his return
and encountered on the road his mother Doña Nuña Fernandez, who,
exulting in his success, had set out to visit him at Carazo. The mother
and son had a joyful meeting and gave the name of Contreras to the
place of their encounter.

[CHAPTER VI

Death of Alonzo, King of Leon—The Moors determined to strike a fresh blow at the count, who summons all Castile to his standard— Of his hunt in the forest while waiting for the enemy, and of the hermit that he met with.]

Alonzo the Great was now growing old and infirm, and his queen and sons, taking advantage of his age and feebleness, endeavored by harsh treatment to compel him to relinquish the Crown. Count Fernan Gonzalez interceded between them, but in vain; and Alonzo was at length obliged to surrender his crown to his eldest son, Don Garcia. The aged monarch then set out upon a pilgrimage to the shrine of St. Iago; but, falling ill of his mortal malady, sent for the count to come to him to his death bed at Zamora. The count hastened thither with all zeal and loyalty. He succeeded in effecting a reconciliation between Alonzo and his son Don Garcia in his dying moments, and was with the monarch when he quietly breathed his last. The death of the king gave fresh courage to the Moors, and they thought this a favorable moment to strike a blow at the rising power of the count. Abderahman was at this time King of Cordova and Miramamolin, or sovereign, of the Moors in Spain. He had been enraged at the capture of the castle of Carazo, and the other victories of the count, and now that the latter had no longer the King of Leon to back him, it was thought he might, by a vigorous effort, be completely crushed. Abderahman accordingly assembled at Cordova a great army of Moorish warriors, both those of Spain and Africa; and sent them, under the command of Almanzor, to ravage the country of Count Fernan Gonzalez. This Almanzor was the most valiant Moorish general in Spain, and one on whom Abderahman depended as upon his right hand.

On hearing of the impending danger, Count Fernan Gonzalez summoned all men of Castile, capable of bearing arms, to repair to his standard at Muñon. His force when assembled was but small, but was composed of the bravest chivalry of Castile, any one knight of which he esteemed equal to ten Moors. One of the most eminent of his cavaliers was Don Gonzalo Gustios, of Lara, who brought seven valiant sons to the field; the same afterwards renowned in Spanish story as the Seven Princes of Lara. With Don Gonzalo came also his wife's brother Ruy or Rodrigo Velazquez, a cavalier of great prowess.

In the mean time tidings continued to arrive of the great force of the enemy, which was said to cover the country with its tents. The name of the Moorish general Almanzor likewise inspired great alarm. One of the count's cavaliers, therefore, Gonzalo Diaz, counselled him not to venture upon an open battle against such fearful odds; but rather to make a tula, or ravaging inroad into the country of the Moors, by way of compelling them to make a truce. The count, however, rejected his advice. "As to their numbers," said he, "one lion is worth ten sheep, and thirty wolves could kill thirty thousand lambs. As to that Moor Almanzor, be assured we shall vanquish him, and the greater his renown the greater will be the honor of the victory."

The count now marched his little army to Lara, where he paused to await the movements of the enemy. While his troops were lying there he mounted his horse one day and went forth with a few attendants to hunt in the forests which bordered the river Arlanza. In the course of the chase he roused a monstrous boar and pursued it among rocks and brakes until he became separated from his attendants. Still following the track of the boar he came to the foot of a rocky precipice, up which the animal mounted by a rugged and narrow path, where the horse could not follow. The count alighted, tied his horse to an oak and clambered up the path, assisting himself at times with his boar spear. The path led to a close thicket of cedars surrounding a small edifice partly built of stone and partly hewn out of the solid rock. The boar had taken refuge within, and had taken his stand behind what appeared to be a mass of stone. The count was about to launch his javelin when he beheld a cross of stone standing on what he now perceived was an altar, and he knew that he was in a holy place. Being as pious as he was brave, the good count now knelt before the altar and asked pardon of God for the sin he had been on the point of committing; and when he had finished this prayer he added another for victory over the foe.

While he was yet praying there entered a venerable monk, Fray Pelayo by name; who seeing him to be a Christian knight, gave him his benediction. He informed the count that he resided in this hermitage in company with two other monks, Arsenio and Silvano. The count marvelled much how they could live there in a country overrun by enemies, and which had for a long time, and but recently, been in the power of the infidels. The hermit replied that in the service of God they were ready to endure all hardships. It is true they suffered much from cold and hunger, being obliged to live chiefly on herbs and roots; but by secret paths and tracks they were in communication with other hermitages scattered throughout the country, so that they were enabled to aid and comfort each other. They could also secretly sustain in the faith the Christians who were held in subjection by the Moors; and afford them places of refuge and concealment in cases of extremity.

The count now opened his heart to the good hermit, revealing his name and rank, and the perils impending over him from the invasion of the infidel. As the day was far spent Fray Pelayo prevailed upon him to pass the night in the hermitage, setting before him barley bread and such simple fare as his cell afforded.

Early in the morning the count went forth and found the hermit seated beneath a tree on a rock whence he could look far and wide out of the forest and over the surrounding country. The hermit then accosted him as one whose holy and meditative life and mortifications of the flesh had given to look into the future almost with the eye of prophecy. "Of a truth, my son," said he, "there are many trials and hardships in store for thee, but be of good cheer; thou wilt conquer these Moors and wilt encrease thy power and possessions." He now revealed to the count certain signs and portents which would take place during battle. "When thou shalt see these," said he, "be assured that heaven is on thy side, and thy victory secure." The count listened with devout attention. "If these things do indeed come to pass," said he, "I will found a church and convent in this place to be dedicated to St. Peter, the patron saint of this hermitage; and when I die my body shall be interred here." Receiving then the benediction of the holy friar, he departed.

[CHAPTER VII

The battle of the Ford of Cascajares.]

When Count Fernan Gonzalez returned to his troops he found them in great alarm at his absence, fearing some evil had befallen him, but he cheered them with an account of his adventure and of the good fortune predicted by the hermit.

It was in the month of May on the day of the Holy Cross that the Christian and Moslem armies came in sight of each other. The Moors advanced with a great sound of trumpets, atabals and cymbals, and their mighty host extended over hill and valley. When they saw how small was the force of the Christians they put up derisive shouts, and rushed forward to surround them.

Don Fernan Gonzalez remained calm and unmoved upon a rising ground, for the hour was at hand when the sign of victory promised by the hermit, was to take place. Near by him was a youthful cavalier, Pedro Gonzalez by name; native of La Puente de Hitero, of fiery courage but vainglorious temper. He was cased in shining armour and mounted on a beautiful horse impatient of spirit as himself, and incessantly foaming and champing on the bitt and pawing the earth. As the Moors drew near, while there was yet a large space between them and the Christians, this fiery cavalier could no longer contain himself, but giving reins to his steed set off headlong to encounter the foe; when suddenly the earth opened, man and horse rushed downward into an abyss, and the earth closed as before.

A cry of horror ran through the Christian ranks and a panic was like to seize upon them, but Don Fernan Gonzalez rode in front of them exclaiming, "This is the promised sign of victory. Let us see how Castilians defend their lord, for my standard shall be borne into the thickest of the fight." So saying, he ordered Orbita Fernandez to advance his standard; and when his troops saw the silver cross glittering on high and borne toward the enemy, they shouted, "Castile! Castile!" and rushed forward to the fight. Immediately around the standard fought Don Gonzalo Gustios and his seven sons; and he was, say the old chroniclers, like a lion leading his whelps into the fight. Wherever they fought their way they might be traced by the bodies of bleeding and expiring infidels. Few particulars of this battle remain on record, but it is said the Moors were as if struck with sudden fear and weakness, and fled in confusion. Almanzor, himself, escaped by the speed of his horse, attended by a handful of his cavaliers.

In the camp of the Moors was found vast booty in gold and silver and other precious things: with sumptuous armour and weapons. When the spoil was divided and the troops were refreshed, Don Fernan Gonzalez went with his cavaliers in pious procession to the hermitage of San Pedro. Here he gave much silver and gold to the worthy Fray Pelayo, to be expended in masses for the souls of the Christian warriors who had fallen in battle, and in prayers for further victories over the infidels; after which he returned in triumph to his capital of Burgos.*

---

* It does not appear that Count Fernan Gonzalez kept his promise of founding a church and monastery on the site of the hermitage. The latter edifice remained to after ages. "It stands," says Sandoval, "on a precipice overhanging the river Arlanza, insomuch that it inspires dread to look below. It is extremely ancient; large enough to hold a hundred persons. Within the chapel is an opening like a chasm, leading down to a cavern larger than the church; formed in the solid rock, with a small window which overlooks the river. It was here the Christians used to conceal themselves."

As a corroboration of the adventure of the Count of Castile, Sandoval assures us that in his day the oak still existed to which Don Fernan Gonzalez tied his horse, when he alighted to scramble up the hill in pursuit of the boar. The worthy Fray Agapida, however, needed no corroboration of the kind, swallowing the whole story with the ready credence of a pious monk.

The action here recorded was known by the name of the battle of the Ford of Cascajares.

Sandoval gives a different account of the fate of the hermits. He says that Almanzor, in a rage at their prognostics, overthrew their chapel and without alighting from his horse ordered the three monks to be beheaded in his presence. "This martyrdom," he adds, "is represented in an ancient painting of the chapel which still exists."

[CHAPTER VIII

Of the message sent by the count to Sancho II. King of Navarre, and the reply—Their encounter in battle.]

The good Count of Castile was so inspirited by this signal victory over the Moors and their great general Almanzor; that he determined, now that he had a breathing spell from infidel warfare, to redress certain grievances sustained from one of his Christian neighbors. This was Don Sancho II., King of Navarre; surnamed Abarca, either from the abarcas or shepherd shoes which he had worn in early life when brought up in secrecy and indigence, during the overthrow of his country by the Moors; or from making his soldiers wear shoes of the kind in crossing the snowy Pyrenees. It was a name by which the populace delighted to call him.

This prince had recovered all Navarre from the infidels and even subjected to his crown all Biscay or Cantabria and some territory beyond the Pyrenees, on the confines of France. Not content with these acquisitions, he had made occasional inroads into Castile in consequence of a contest respecting the territories of Najarra and Rioxa, to which he laid claim. These incursions he repeated whenever he had peace or truce with the Moors.*

Count Fernan Gonzalez, having now time as has been observed, to attend to these matters, sent an ambassador to King Sancho charged with a courteous but resolute message. "I come, Señor," said the ambassador to the king, "by command of the Count Fernan Gonzalez of Castile, and this is what I am told to say. You have done him much wrong in times past by leaguing with the infidels and making inroads into his territories while he was absent or engaged in war. If you will amend your ways in this respect, and remedy the past, you will do him much pleasure; but, if you refuse, he sends you his defiance."

King Sancho Abarca was lost in astonishment and indignation at receiving such a message from a count of Castile. "Return to the count," said he, "and tell him I will amend nothing; that I marvel at his insolence and hold him for a madman for daring to defy me. Tell him he has listened to evil counsel, or a few trifling successes against the Moors have turned his brain; but it will be very different when I come to seek him, for there is not town or tower from which I will not drag him forth."†

The ambassador returned with this reply, nor did he spare the least of its scorn and bitterness. Upon this the count assembled his cavaliers

---

* Sandoval, *The Five Bishops*. Mariana, lib. 8, c. 5, p. 367. *Cron. Gen. de España*, part 3, c. 18, fol. 53.

† *Chron. Gen. de España, ut supra.*

and councillors and represented the case. He exhorted them to stand by him in seeking redress for this insult and injury to their country and their chieftain. "We are not equal in numbers to the enemy, but we are valiant men, united and true to each other, and one hundred good lances all in the hands of chosen cavaliers all of one heart and mind are worth three hundred, placed by chance in the hands of men who have no common tie." The cavaliers all assured him they would follow and obey him as loyal subjects of a worthy lord, and would prove their fealty in the day of battle.

A little army of staunch Castilians was soon assembled; the silver cross was again reared on high by the standard bearer Orbita Velazquez, and the count advanced resolutely a day's journey into the kingdom of Navarre, for his maxim was to strike quickly and sudden. King Sancho wondered at his daring but hastened to meet him with a greatly superior force. The armies came in sight of each other at a place called the Era de Gollanda.

The count now addressed his men. "The enemy," said he, "are more numerous than we; they are vigorous of body and light of foot and are dextrous in throwing darts. They will have the advantage if they attack us: but if we attack them and close manfully, we shall get the field of them before they have time to hurl their darts and wound us. For my part I shall make for the king. If I can but revenge the wrongs of Castile upon his person I care not how soon I die."

As the armies drew near each other the Castilians, true to the orders of their chieftain, put up the war cry, "Castile! Castile!" and rushing forward, broke through the squadrons of Navarre. "Then followed a fight so pitiless and deadly," says an old chronicler, "that the strokes of their weapons resounded through the whole country." The count sought King Sancho throughout the field; they met and recognized each other by their armorial bearings and devices. They fought with fury, until both fell from their horses as if dead. The Castilians cut their way through the mass of the enemy and surrounded their fallen chief. Some raised him from the earth while others kept off the foe. At first they thought him dead and were loud in their lamentations, but when the blood and dust were wiped from his face he revived and told them not to heed him, for his wounds were nothing; but to press on and gain the victory, for he had slain the King of Navarre.

At hearing this they gave a great shout and returned to the fight; but those of Navarre, seized with terror at the fall of their king, turned their backs and fled.

The count then caused the body of the king to be taken from among the slain and to be conducted back honorably attended, to Navarre. Thus fell Sancho Abarca, King of Navarre, and was succeeded by his son Don Garcia, surnamed the Trembler.

[CHAPTER IX

How the Count of Toulouse makes a campaign against Castile, and how he returns in his coffin.]

While the Count Fernan Gonzalez was yet ill of his wounds in his capital, and when his soldiers had scarce laid by their cuirasses and hung up their shields and lances, there was a fresh alarm of war. The Count of Toulouse and Poictiers, the close friend and ally of King Sancho Abarca, had come from France with a host to his assistance, but finding him defeated and slain, raised his standard to make a campaign, in his revenge, against the Castilians. The Navarrese all gathered round him, and now an army was on foot, more powerful than the one which had recently been defeated.

Count Fernan Gonzalez, wounded as he was, summoned his troops to march against this new enemy; but the war worn Castilians, vexed at being thus called again to arms before they had time to breathe, began to murmur. "This is the life of the very devil," said they, "to go about, day and night, without a moment's rest. This lord of ours is assuredly Satan himself, and we are lesser devils in his employ, always busy entrapping the souls of men. He has no pity for us so battered and worn, nor for himself so badly wounded. It is necessary that some one should talk with him and turn him from this madness."

Accordingly a hardy cavalier, Nuño Laynez, remonstrated with the count against further fighting until he should be cured of his wounds and his people should have time to repose; for mortal men could not support this kind of life. "Nor is this urged through cowardice," added he, "for your men are ready to fight for and defend you as they would their own souls."

"Well have you spoken, Nuño Laynez," replied the count, "yet for all this I am not minded to defer this fight. A day lost never returns. An opportunity foregone can never be recalled. The warrior who indulges in repose will never leave the memory of great deeds behind him. His name dies when his soul leaves his body. Let us, therefore, make the most of the days and hours allotted us and crowd them with such glorious deeds that the world shall praise us in all future time."

When Nuño Laynez repeated these generous words to the cavaliers, the blood glowed in their veins and they prepared themselves manfully for the field; nor did the count give them time to cool before he put himself at their head and marched to meet the enemy. He found them drawn up on the opposite side of a river which was swollen and troubled by recent rains. Without hesitation he advanced to ford it, but his troops were galled by flights of darts and arrows as they crossed; and received with lances on the water's edge; the bodies of many floated down the turbid stream, and many perished on the banks. They made good their crossing, however, and closed with the enemy. The fight was obstinate and the Castilians were hardly pressed; being so inferior in number. Don Fernan Gonzalez galloped along the front of the enemy. "Where is the Count of Toulouse?" cried he. "Let him come forth and face me, me, Fernan Gonzalez of Castile, who defy him to single combat!" The count answered promptly to the defiance. No one from either side presumed to interfere while the two counts encountered man to man and horse to horse like honorable and generous cavaliers. They rushed upon each other with the full speed of their horses; the lance of Don Fernan pierced through all the armour and accoutrements of the Count of Toulouse and bore him out of the saddle, and before he touched the earth his soul had already parted from his body. The men of Toulouse, seeing their chief fall dead, fled amain; but were pursued and three hundred of them taken.*

The field being won Count Fernan Gonzalez alighted and took off the armour of the Count of Toulouse, with his own hands, and wrapped him in a xemete or Moorish mantle of great value, which he had gained when he conquered Almanzor. He ordered a coffin to be made and covered with cloth of gold and studded with silver nails, and he put therein the body of the count, and delivered it to the captive cavaliers, whom he released, and furnished with money for their expenses, making them swear not to leave the body of the count until they had conducted it to Toulouse. So the count, who had come from France in such chivalrous state at the head of an array of shining warriors, returned in his coffin with a mourning train of vanquished cavaliers, while Count Fernan Gonzalez conducted his victorious troops in triumph back to Burgos.

This signal victory took place in the year of our Redemption 926, in the beginning of the reign of Alonzo the Monk on the throne of Leon and the Asturias.†

[CHAPTER X

How the count went to receive the hand of a princess, and was thrown into a dungeon—Of the stranger that visited him in his chains, and of the appeal that he made to the princess for his deliverance.]

Garcia II., who had succeeded to the throne of Navarre on the death of his father, was brave of soul though surnamed El Tembloso, or The Trembler. He was so called because he was observed to tremble on

---

* *Cron. Gen. de España, ut supra.*
† Mariana, lib. 8, c. 5, p. 367.

going into battle; but, as has been said of others, it was only the flesh that trembled, foreseeing the dangers into which the spirit would carry it. This king was deeply grieved at the death of his father, slain by Count Fernan Gonzalez, and would have taken vengeance by open warfare; but he was counselled by his mother the Queen Teresa to pursue a subtler course. At her instigation overtures were made to the count to settle all the feuds between Navarre and Castile by a firm alliance, and to this end it was proposed that the count should take to wife Doña Sancha, the sister of King Garcia, and daughter of King Sancho Abarca. The count accepted gladly the proffered alliance, for he had heard of the great merit and beauty of the princess and was pleased with so agreeable a mode of putting an end to all their contests. A conference was accordingly appointed between the count and King Garcia to take place at Ciruena, each to be attended only by five cavaliers.

The count was faithful to his compact and appeared at the appointed place with five of the bravest of his cavaliers; but the king arrived with five and thirty chosen men, all armed cap-a-pie. The count, suspecting treachery, retreated with his cavaliers into a neighboring hermitage, and barricading the door, defended himself throughout the day until nightfall. Seeing there was no alternative he at length capitulated and agreed to surrender himself a prisoner, and pay homage to the king on the latter assuring him under oath that his life should be secure. King Garcia the Trembler having in this wily manner gained possession of the count, threw him in irons and conducted him prisoner to Navarre; where he confined him in a strong castle called Castro Viejo. At his intercession, however, his five cavaliers were released and carried back to Castile the doleful tidings of his captivity.

Now it came to pass that a brave Norman count, who was performing a pilgrimage to St. Iago of Compostella, heard that the Count Fernan Gonzalez, whose renown had spread far and wide, lay in chains in Castro Viejo. Having a vehement desire to see the man of whom fame had spoken so loudly, he repaired to the castle and bribed his way to the prison of the count. When he entered and beheld so noble a cavalier in a solitary dungeon and in chains he was sore at heart. The count looked up with wonder as this stranger stood before him in pilgrim garb and with sorrowful aspect; but when he learnt his name, and rank, and the object of his visit, he gave him the right hand of friendship.

The pilgrim count left the castle more enamoured than ever of the character of Count Fernan Gonzalez. At a festival of the court he beheld the Princess Sancha, who had served as a lure to draw the good count into the power of his enemies, and he found her of surpassing beauty and of a gentle and loving demeanor; so he determined to seek an opportunity to speak with her in private, for surely, thought he, in such a bosom must dwell the soft pity of womanhood. Accordingly one day as the princess was walking in the garden with her ladies he presented himself before her in his pilgrim's garb; and prayed to speak with her apart, as if on some holy mission. And when they were alone, "How is this, Princess," said he, "that you are doing such great wrong to heaven, to yourself and to all Christendom?" The princess started and said, "What wrong have I done?" Then replied the pilgrim count, "Behold, for thy sake the noblest of cavaliers; the pride of Spain, the flower of chivalry, the hope of Christendom lies in a dungeon fettered with galling chains. What lady but would be too happy to be honored with the love of Count Fernan Gonzalez; and thou hast scorned it! How will it tell for thy fame in future times, that thou wast made a snare to capture an honorable knight; that the gentlest, the bravest, the most generous of cavaliers was inveigled by the love of thee to be thrown in a dungeon? How hast thou reversed the maxims of chivalry! Beauty has ever been the friend of valor; but thou hast been its foe! The fair hands of lovely dames have ever bestowed laurels and rewards on those gallant knights who sought and deserved their loves; thou hast bestowed chains and a dungeon. Behold, the Moors rejoice in his captivity while all Christians mourn. Thy name will be accursed throughout the land like that of Cava; but shouldst thou have the heroism to set him free, thou wilt be extolled above all Spanish ladies. Hadst thou but seen him as I have done; alone, abandoned, enchained, yet so noble, so courteous, so heroic in his chains that kings upon their thrones might envy the majesty of his demeanor. If thou couldst feel love for man thou shouldst do it for this knight, for I swear to thee on this cross which I bear that never was there king or emperor in the world so worthy of woman's love." When the pilgrim count had thus spoken, he left the princess to meditate upon his words.

[CHAPTER XI

Of the meditations of the princess, and their result. Her flight from the prison with the count, and perils of the escape—The nuptials.]

The Princess Sancha remained for some time in the garden revolving in her mind all that she had just heard, and tenderness for the Count Fernan Gonzalez began to awaken in her bosom; for nothing so touches the heart of woman as the idea of valour suffering for her sake. The more the princess meditated the more she became enamoured. She called to mind all she had heard of the illustrious actions of the count. She thought upon the pictures just drawn of him in prison; so noble, so majestic in his chains. She remembered the parting words of the pilgrim count, "Never was there king nor emperor so worthy of a woman's love." "Alas!" cried she, "was there ever a lady more unfortunate than I? All the love and devotion of this noble cavalier I might have had, and behold it has been made a mockery. Both he and myself have been wronged by the treachery of my brother."

At length the passion of the princess arose to such a height that she determined to deliver the count from the misery of which she had been made the instrument. So she found means one night to bribe the guards of his prison and made her way to his dungeon. When the count saw her he thought it a beautiful vision, or some angel sent from heaven to comfort him, for certainly her beauty surpassed the ordinary loveliness of woman.

"Noble cavalier," said the princess, "this is no time for idle words and ceremonies. Behold before you the Princess Doña Sancha. The word which my brother brake I am here to fulfil. You came to receive my hand, and, instead, you were thrown in chains. I come to yield you that hand and to deliver you from those chains. Behold, the door of your prison is open and I am ready to fly with you to the ends of the earth. Swear to me one word, and when you have sworn it I know your loyalty too well to doubt that you will hold your oath sacred. Swear that if I fly with you, you will treat me with the honour of a knight; that you will make me your wife and never leave me for any other woman."

The count sware all this on the faith of a Christian cavalier; and well did he feel disposed to keep his oath, for never before had he beheld such glorious beauty.

So the princess led the way, and her authority and her money had conquered the fidelity of the guards, so that they permitted the count to sally forth with her from the prison.

It was dark night, and they left the great road and climbed a mountain. The count was so fettered by his chains that he moved with difficulty, but the princess helped and sometimes almost carried him; for what will not delicate woman perform when her love and pity are fully aroused. Thus they toiled their way until the day dawned, when they hid themselves in the cliffs of the mountain among rocks and thickets. While thus concealed they beheld an archpriest of the castle mounted on a mule with a falcon on his fist, hawking about the lower part of the mountain. The count knew him to be a base and malignant man and watched his movements with great anxiety. He had two hounds beating about the bushes which at length got upon the traces of the count and princess and discovering them set up a violent barking. Alighting from his mule the archpriest clambered up to where the fugitives were concealed. He knew the count and saw that he had escaped. "Aha! traytor," cried he drawing his sword, "think not to escape from the power of the king." The count saw that resistance was in vain, for he was without weapon and in chains and the arch-priest was a powerful man, exceeding broad across the shoulders; he sought, therefore, to win him by fair words, promising that if he would aid him to escape he would give him a city in Castile for him and his heirs forever. But the archpriest was more violent than ever and held his sword at the breast of the count to force him back to the castle. Upon this the princess rushed forward and with tears in her eyes implored him not to deliver the count into the hands of his enemies. But the heart of the priest was inflamed by the beauty of the princess, and, thinking her at his mercy, "Gladly," said he, "will I assist the count to escape, but upon one condition." Then he whispered a proposal which brought a crimson glow of horror and indignation into the cheeks of the princess, and he would have laid his hand upon her; but he was suddenly lifted from the earth by the strong grasp of the count, who bore him to the edge of a precipice and flung him headlong down; and his neck was broken in the fall.

The count then took the mule of the archpriest, his hawk and his hounds, and after keeping in the secret parts of the mountain all day, he and the princess mounted the mule at night, and pursued their way, by the most rugged and unfrequented passes, toward Castile.

As the day dawned they found themselves in an open plain at the foot of the mountains, and beheld a body of horsemen riding toward them conducting a car, in which sat a knight in armour, bearing a standard. The princess now gave all up for lost. "These," said she, "are sent by my brother in pursuit of us; how can we escape, for this poor animal has no longer strength nor speed to bear us up the mountains." Upon this Count Fernan alighted, and drawing the sword of the arch-priest placed himself in a narrow pass. "Do you," said he to the princess, "turn back and hasten to the mountains, and dearly shall it cost him who attempts to follow you." "Not so!" replied the princess; "for the love of me hast thou been brought from thine own domain and betrayed into all these dangers, and I will abide to share them with thee." The count would have remonstrated, when to his astonish-ment, he saw as the car drew near that the knight seated in it was clad in his own armour with his own devices, and held his own banner in his hand. "Surely," said he crossing himself, "this is enchantment;" but on looking still nearer, he recognized among the horsemen Nuño Sandias and Nuño Laynez, two of his most faithful knights. Then his heart leaped for joy. "Fear nothing," cried he, to the princess; "behold my standard and behold my vassals. Those whom you feared as enemies shall kneel at your feet and kiss your hand in homage."

Now so it appears that the tidings of the captivity of the count had spread mourning and consternation throughout Castile, and the cavaliers assembled together to devise means for his deliverance. And certain of them had prepared this effigy of the count clad in his armour and bearing his banner and devices, and having done homage and sworn fealty to it as they would have done to the count himself, they had placed it in this car and set forth with it as a leader, making a vow, in the spirit of ancient chivalry, never to return to their homes until they should have delivered the count from his captivity.

When the cavaliers recognized the count they put up shouts of joy and kissed his hands and the hands of the princess in token of devoted loyalty. And they took off the fetters of the count and placed him in the car and the princess beside him, and returned joyfully to Castile.

Vain would be the attempt to describe the transports of the multitude as Count Fernan Gonzalez entered his noble capital of Burgos. The Princess Sancha, also, was hailed with blessings wherever she passed, as the deliverer of their lord and the saviour of Castile; and shortly afterwards her nuptials with the count were celebrated with feasting and rejoicing and tilts and tournaments which lasted for many days.

[CHAPTER XII

King Garcia confined in Burgos by the count—The princess intercedes for his release.]

The rejoicings for the marriage of Count Fernan Gonzalez with the beautiful Princess Sancha were scarcely finished, when King Garcia the Trembler came with a powerful army to revenge his various affronts. The count sallied forth to meet him, and a bloody and doubtful battle ensued. The Navarrese at length were routed, and the king was wounded and taken prisoner in single combat, by Count Fernan; who brought him to Burgos and put him in close confinement.

The Countess Doña Sancha was now almost as much afflicted at the captivity of her brother as she had been at that of the count, and interceded with her husband for his release. The count, however, retained too strong a recollection of the bad faith of King Garcia, and of his own treacherous and harsh imprisonment, to be easily moved; and the king was kept in duress for a considerable time. The countess then interested the principal cavaliers in her suit, reminding them of the services she had rendered them in aiding the escape of their lord. Through their united intercessions the count was induced to relent: so King Garcia the Trembler was released and treated with great honor, and sent back to his dominions with a retinue befitting his rank.

[CHAPTER XIII

Of the expedition against the ancient city of Sylo—The unwitting trespass of the count into a convent, and his compunction thereupon.]

Volumes would it take to follow the Count Fernan Gonzalez in his heroic achievements against the infidels; achievements which give to sober history almost the air of fable. I forbear to dwell at large upon one of his campaigns wherein he scoured the valley of Laguna; passed victoriously along the banks of the Douro, building towers and castles to keep the country in subjection; how he scaled the walls of the castle of Gormaz; being the first to mount, sword in hand; how by the valour of his arm he captured the city of Orma; how he took the town of Sandoval, the origin of the cavaliers of Sandoval who were anciently called Salvadores; how he made an inroad even to Madrid, then a strongly fortified village; and having taken and sacked it, returned in triumph to Burgos.

But it would be wronging the memory of this great and good cavalier to pass in silence over one of his exploits in which he gave a singular instance of his piety. This was in an expedition against the ancient city of Sylo. It was not a place of much value in itself, being situated in a cold and sterile country; but it had become a strong hold of the Moors, whence they carried on their warfare. This place the count carried by assault, entering it in full armour, on his steed; overturning and slaying all who opposed him. In the fury of his career he rode into a spacious edifice which he supposed to be a mosque, with the pious intention of slaying every infidel he might find within. On looking round, however, great was his astonishment at beholding images of saints; the blessed cross of our Saviour, and various other sacred objects which announced a church devoted to the veritable faith. Struck with remorse, he sprang from his horse, threw himself upon his knees, and, with many tears, implored pardon of God for the sin he had unknowingly committed. While he was yet on his knees, several monks of the order of St. Dominick approached, meagre in looks and squalid in attire, but hailing him with great joy as their deliverer. In sooth this was a convent of San Sebastian, the fraternity of which had remained captives among the Moors; supporting themselves poorly by making baskets; but permitted to continue in the exercise of their religion.

Still filled with pious compunction for the trespass he had made, the count ordered that the shoes be taken from his horse and nailed upon the door of the church; "for never," said he, "shall they tread any other ground after having trodden this holy place." From that day, we are told, it has been the custom to nail the shoes of horses on the portal of that convent, a custom which has extended to many other places.

The worthy Fray Prudencio de Sandoval records a marvellous memento of the expedition of the count against this city which remained, he says, until his day. Not far from the place, on the road which passes by Lara, is to be seen the print of his horse's hoof in a solid rock, which has received the impression as though it had been made in softened wax.* It is to be presumed that the horse's hoofs had been gifted with miraculous hardness in reward to the count for his pious oblation of the shoes.

[CHAPTER XIV

Of the Moorish host that came up from Cordova, and how the count repaired to the hermitage of San Pedro, and prayed for success against them, and received assurance of victory in a vision—Battle of Hazinas.]

The worthy Fray Antonio Agapida, from whose manuscripts this memoir is extracted, passes by many of the striking and heroic deeds of the count, which crowd the pages of ancient chroniclers, but the good friar ever is sure to dwell with delight upon any of those miraculous occurrences which took place in Spain in those days and which shewed the marked interposition of heaven in behalf of the Christian warriors in their battles with the infidels. Such was the renowned battle of Hazinas, "which," says Agapida, "for its miraculous events is worthy of eternal blazon."

Now so it was that the Moorish King of Cordova had summoned all the faithful, both of Spain and Africa, to assist him in recovering the lands wrested from him by the unbelievers and especially by Count Fernan Gonzalez in his late victories; and such countless legions of turbaned warriors were assembled that it was said they covered the plains of Andalusia, like swarms of locusts.

Hearing of their threatening approach the count gathered together his forces at Piedrafita, while the Moors encamped in Hazinas. When, however, he beheld the mighty host arrayed against him, his heart for once was troubled with evil forebodings; and calling to mind the cheering prognostications of the friar Pelayo on a like occasion, he resolved to repair again to that holy man for counsel. Leaving his camp, therefore, secretly, he set out accompanied by two cavaliers to seek the chapel which he had ordered to be built at the hermitage of San Pedro,

*Sandoval, p. 313.

on the mountain overhanging the river Arlanza, but when he arrived there he heard to his great grief that the worthy friar was dead.

Entering the chapel, however, he knelt down at the altar and prayed for success in the coming fight; humbly representing that he had never, like many of the kings and nobles of Spain, done homage to the infidels and acknowledged them for sovereigns. The count remained for a long time at prayer until sleep gradually stole over him; and as he lay slumbering before the altar the holy Fray Pelayo appeared before him in a vision, clad in garments as white as snow. "Why sleepest thou, Fernan Gonzalez?" said he; "arise and go forth, and know that thou shalt conquer those Moors. For, inasmuch as thou art a faithful vassal of the Most High, he has commanded the apostle St. Iago and myself, with many angels, to come to thy aid, and we will appear in the battle, clad in white armour, with each of us a red cross upon our pennon. Therefore arise, I say, and go hence with a valiant heart."

The count awoke, and while he was yet musing upon the vision he heard a voice saying, "Arise and get thee hence; why dost thou linger? Separate thy host into three divisions; enter the field of battle by the east, with the smallest division, and I will be with thee; and let the second division enter by the west, and that shall be aided by St. Iago, and let the third division enter by the north. Know that I am St. Millan who come to thee with this message."

The count departed joyfully from the chapel and returned to his army, and when he told his troops of this his second visit to the hermitage, and of the vision he had had, and how the holy friar San Pelayo had again assured him of victory, their hearts were lifted up, and they rejoiced to serve under a leader who had such excellent counsellors in war.

In the evening preceding the battle Don Fernan Gonzalez divided his forces as he had been ordered. The first division was composed of two hundred horsemen and six thousand infantry; hardy mountaineers, light of foot and of great valour. In the advance were Don Gonzalo Gustios of Salas and his seven sons and two nephews, and his brother Ruy Velazquez and a valiant cavalier named Gonzalo Diaz.

The second division was led by Don Lope de Biscaya, with the people of Burueba and Trevino and Old Castile and Castro and the Asturias. Two hundred horsemen and six thousand infantry.

The third division was led by the count himself, and with him went Ruy Cavia, and Nuño Cavia and the Velascos, whom the count that day dubbed knights, and twenty esquires of the count, whom he had likewise knighted. His division consisted of four hundred and fifty horse and fifteen hundred foot. And he told his men that if they should not conquer the Moors on the following day, they should draw off from the battle when he gave the word. Late at night when all the camp, excepting the centinels and guards, were buried in sleep, a light suddenly illumined the heavens and a great serpent was seen in the air, wounded and covered with blood and vomiting flames, and making a loud hissing, that awakened all the soldiers. They rushed out of their tents and ran hither and thither, running against each other in their affright. Count Fernan Gonzalez was awakened by their outcries; but before he came forth the serpent had disappeared. He rebuked the terrors of his people, representing to them that the Moors were great necromancers, and by their arts could raise devils to their aid; and that some Moorish astrologer had doubtless raised this spectrum to alarm them; but he bade them be of good heart, since they had St. Iago on their side, and might set Moor, astrologer and devil at defiance.

In the first day's fight Don Fernan fought hand to hand with a powerful Moor, who had desired to try his prowess with him. It was an obstinate contest, in which the Moor was slain, but the count so badly wounded that he fell to the earth, and had not his men surrounded and defended him he would have been slain or captured. The battle lasted all day long, and Gonzalo Gustios and his kindred warriors shewed prodigies of valor. Don Fernan, having had his wounds stanched, re-mounted his horse and galloped about, giving courage to his men; but he was covered with dust and blood and so hoarse that he could no longer be heard. The sun went down. The Moors kept on fighting, confiding in their great numbers. The count, seeing the night approaching, ordered the trumpets to be sounded, and collecting his troops made one general charge on the Moors and drove them from the field. He then drew off his men to their tents, where the weary troops found refreshment and repose, though they slept all night upon their arms.

On the second day the count rose before the dawn, and having attended mass like a good Christian, attended next to his horses, like a good cavalier; seeing with his own eyes that they were well fed and groomed and prepared for the field. The battle this day was obstinate as the day before, with great valour and loss on either side.

On the third day the count led forth his forces at an early hour, raising his silver standard of the cross and praying devoutly for aid. Then lowering their lances the Castilians shouted "St. Iago! St. Iago!" and rushed to the attack.

Don Gonzalo Gustios de Salas, the leader of one of the divisions, made a lane into the centre of the Moorish host, dealing death on either side. He was met by a Moorish cavalier of powerful frame. Covering themselves with their shields, they attacked each other with great fury; but the days of Gonzalo Gustios were numbered, and the Moor slew him, and with him fell a nephew of Count Fernan, and many of his principal cavaliers.

Count Fernan Gonzalez encountered the Moor who had just slain his friend. The infidel would have avoided him, having heard that never man escaped alive from a conflict with him; but the count gave him a furious thrust with his lance which stretched him dead upon the field.

The Moors, however, continued to press the count sorely, and their numbers threatened to overwhelm him. Then he put up a prayer for the aid promised in his vision, and of a sudden the apostle St. Iago appeared, with a great and shining company of angels in white bearing the device of a red cross and all rushing upon the Moors. The Moors were dismayed at the sight of this reinforcement to the enemy. The Christians on the other hand, recovered their forces, knowing the apostle St. Iago to be at hand. They charged the Moors with new vigor and put them to flight and pursued them for two days, killing and making captive. They then returned and gathered together the bodies of the Christians who had been slain, and buried them in the chapel of St. Pedro of Arlanza and in other hermitages. The bodies of the Moors were piled up and covered with earth, forming a mound which is still to be seen on the field of battle.

Some have ascribed to the signal worn in this battle by the celestial warriors the origin of the Cross of Calatrava.

[CHAPTER XV

The count imprisoned by the King of Leon—The countess concerts his escape—Leon and Castile united by the marriage of the Prince Ordoño with Urraca, the daughter of the count by his first wife.]

Not long after this most renowned and marvellous battle a Moorish captain named Aceyfa became a vassal of the Count Don Fernan. Under his protection and that of a rich and powerful Castilian cavalier named Diego Muñon he rebuilt Salamanca and Ledesma, and several places on the river Tormes which had been desolated and deserted in times past.

Ramiro the Second, who was at this time King of Leon, was alarmed at seeing a strong line of Moorish fortresses erected along the borders of his territories, and took the field with an army to drive the Moor Aceyfa from the land. The proud spirit of Count Fernan Gonzalez was aroused at this attack upon his Moorish vassal, which he considered an indignity offered to himself; so being seconded by Don Diego Muñon he marched forth with his chivalry to protect the Moor. In the present instance he had trusted to his own head and had neglected to seek advice of saint or hermit; so his army was defeated by King Ramiro, and himself and Don Diego Muñon taken prisoner. The latter was sent in chains to the castle of Gordon, but the count was carried to

Leon; where he was confined in a tower of the wall; which to this day is pointed out as his prison.*

All Castile was thrown into grief and consternation by this event, and lamentations were heard throughout the land, as though the count had been dead. The countess, however, did not waste time in tears, for she was a lady of most valiant spirit. She forthwith assembled five hundred cavaliers: chosen men of tried loyalty and devotion to the count. They met in the chapel of the palace and took an oath upon the holy evangelists to follow the countess through all difficulties and dangers and to obey implicitly all her commands for the rescue of their lord. With this band the countess departed secretly at nightfall and travelled rapidly until morning, when they left the roads and took to the mountains lest their march should be discovered. Arrived near to Leon, she halted her band in a thick woods on the mountain of Samosa, where she ordered them to remain in secrecy. Then clothing herself as a pilgrim with her staff and pannier, she sent word to King Ramiro that she was on a pilgrimage to St. Iago, and entreated that she might have permission to visit her husband in his prison. King Ramiro not merely granted her request, but sallied forth above a league from the city with a great retinue to do her honor. So the countess entered a second time the prison where the count lay in chains, and stood before him as his protecting angel. At sight of him in this miserable and dishonored state, however, the valor of spirit which had hitherto sustained her gave way, and tears flowed from her eyes. The count received her joyfully and reproached her with her tears; "for it becomes us," said he, "to submit to what is imposed upon us by God."

The countess now sent to entreat the king that while she remained with the count his chains should be taken off. The king again granted her request; and the count was freed from his irons and an excellent bed prepared in his prison.

The countess remained with him all night and concerted his escape. Before it was daylight she gave him her pilgrim's dress and staff, and the count went forth from the chamber disguised as his wife. The porter at the outer portal, thinking it to be the countess, would have waited for orders from the king; but the count, in a feigned voice, entreated not to be detained, lest he should not be able to perform his pilgrimage. The porter mistrusting no deceit opened the door. The count issued forth, repaired to a place pointed out by the countess, where the two cavaliers awaited him with a fleet horse. They all

---

* In the *Cronica General de España* this imprisonment is said to have been by King Sancho the Fat; but the cautious Agapida goes according to his favorite Sandoval in attributing it to King Ramiro, and in so doing he is supported by the *Chronicle* of Bleda, L. 3, c. 19.

sallied quietly forth from the city at the opening of the gates, until they found themselves clear of the walls, when they put spurs to their horses and made the best of their way to the mountain of Samosa. Here the count was received with shouts of joy by the cavaliers whom the countess had left there in concealment.

As the day advanced the keeper of the prison entered the apartment of Don Fernan but was astonished to find there the beautiful countess in place of her warrior husband. He conducted her before the king, accusing her of the fraud by which she had effected the escape of the count. King Ramiro was greatly incensed, and he demanded of the countess how she dared do such an act. "I dared," replied she, "because I saw my husband in misery and felt it my duty to relieve him, and I dared because I was the daughter of a king and the wife of a distinguished cavalier; as such I trust to your chivalry to treat me."

The king was charmed with her intrepidity. "Señora," said he, "you have acted well and like a noble lady, and it will redound to your laud and honor." So he commanded that she should be conducted to her husband in a manner befitting a lady of high and noble rank; and the count was overjoyed to receive her in safety, and they returned to their dominions and entered Burgos at the head of their train of cavaliers amidst the transports and acclamations of their people. And King Ramiro sought the amity of Count Fernan Gonzalez and proposed that they should unite their houses by some matrimonial alliance which should serve as a bond of mutual security. The count gladly listened to his proposals. He had a fair daughter named Urraca, by his first wife, who was now arrived at a marriageable age, so it was agreed that nuptials should be solemnized between her and the Prince Ordoño, son of King Ramiro; and all Leon and Castile rejoiced at this union which promised tranquility to the land.

[CHAPTER XVI

Moorish incursion into Castile—Battle of San Estevan—Of Pascual Vivas and the miracle that befell him—Death of Ordoño III.]

For several succeeding years of the career of this most redoubtable cavalier, the most edifying and praiseworthy traces which remain, says Fray Antonio Agapida, are to be found in the archives of various monasteries; consisting of memorials of pious gifts and endowments made by himself and his countess Doña Sancha.

In the process of time King Ramiro died and was succeeded by his son Ordoño III.; the same who had married Urraca, the daughter of Count Fernan. He was surnamed the Fierce, either from his savage temper or savage aspect. He had a stepbrother named Don Sancho; nephew, by the mother's side, of King Garcia of Navarre, surnamed the Trembler. This Don Sancho rose in arms against Ordoño at the very outset of his reign; seeking to deprive him of his crown. He applied for assistance to his uncle Garcia, and to Count Fernan Gonzalez, and it is said both favoured his pretensions. Nay, the count soon appeared in the field in company with King Garcia the Trembler in support of Prince Sancho. It may seem strange that he should take up arms against his own son-in-law; and so it certainly appeared to Ordoño III., for he was so incensed against the count that he repudiated his wife Urraca and sent her back to her father; telling him that since he would not acknowledge him as king he should not have him for son-in-law.

The kingdom now became a prey to civil wars; the restless part of the subjects of King Ordoño rose in rebellion, and every thing was in confusion. King Ordoño succeeded, however, in quelling the rebellion, and defended himself so ably against King Garcia and Count Fernan Gonzalez that they returned home without effecting their object.

About this time, say the records of Compostello, the sinful dissensions of the Christians brought on them a visible and awful scourge from heaven. A great flame, or, as it were, a cloud of fire passed throughout the land burning towns, destroying men and beasts and spreading horror and devastation even over the sea. It passed over Zamora, consuming a great part of the place; it scorched Castro Xeriz likewise, and Brebiesco and Pan Cervo, in its progress; and in Burgos one hundred houses were consumed.

"These," says the worthy Agapida, "were fiery tokens of the displeasure of heaven at the sinful conduct of the Christians in warring upon each other, instead of joining their arms like brethren in the righteous endeavor to extirpate the vile sect of Mahomet."

While the Christians were thus fighting among themselves, the Moors, taking advantage of their discord, came with a great army and made an incursion into Castile as far as Burgos. King Ordoño and Count Fernan Gonzalez, alarmed at the common danger, came to a reconciliation, and took arms together against the Moors: though it does not appear that the king received again his repudiated wife Urraca. These confederate princes gave the Moors a great battle near to San Estevan.

"This battle," says Fray Antonio Agapida, "is chiefly memorable for a miracle which occurred there;" and which is recorded by the good friar with an unction and perfect credence worthy of a monkish chronicler.

The Christians were encastelled at San Estevan de Gormaz which is near the banks of the Douro. The Moors had possession of the fortress of Gormaz, about a league further up the river on a lofty and rocky height.

The battle commenced at the dawn of day. Count Fernan Gonzalez, however, before taking the field repaired with his principal cavaliers to the church to attend the first morning's mass. Now at this time there was in the service of the count a brave cavalier named Pascual Vivas, who was as pious as he was brave, and would pray with as much fervor and obstinacy as he would fight. This cavalier made it a religious rule with himself, or rather had made a solemn vow, that, whenever he entered a church in the morning, he would on no account leave it until all the masses were finished.

On the present occasion the firmness of this brave but pious cavalier was put to a severe proof. When the first mass was finished the count and his cavaliers rose and sallied from the church in clanking armour, and soon after the sound of trumpet and quick tramp of steed told that they were off to the encounter. Pascual Vivas, however, remained kneeling all in armour, before the altar, waiting, according to custom, until all the masses should be finished. The masses that morning were numerous, and hour after hour passed away, yet still the cavalier remained kneeling all in armour, with weapon in hand, yet so zealous in his devotion that he never turned his head.

All this while the esquire of the cavalier was at the door of the church holding his war horse, and the esquire beheld with surprise the count and his warriors depart, while his lord remained in the chapel; and, from the height on which the chapel stood, he could see the Christian host encounter the Moors at the ford of the river; and could hear the distant sound of trumpets and din of battle; and at the sound the war horse pricked his ears, and snuffed the air and pawed the earth, and shewed all the eagerness of a noble steed to be among the armed men, but still Pascual Vivas came not out of the chapel. The esquire was wroth, and blushed for his lord, for he thought it was through cowardice and not piety that he remained in the chapel while his comrades were fighting in the field.

At length the masses were finished, and Pascual Vivas was about to sally forth when horsemen came riding up the hill with shouts of victory, for the battle was over and the Moors completely vanquished.

When Pascual Vivas heard this he was so troubled in mind that he dared not leave the chapel nor come into the presence of the count, for he said to himself, "Surely I shall be looked upon as a recreant knight who have hidden myself in the hour of danger." Shortly, however, came some of his fellow cavaliers summoning him to the presence of the count, and as he went, with a beating heart, they lauded him for the valor he had displayed and the great services he had rendered; saying that to the prowess of his arm they owed the victory. The good knight, imagining they were scoffing at him, felt still more cast down in spirit and entered the presence of the count covered with confusion. Here again he was received with praises and caresses at which he was greatly astonished but still thought it all done in mockery. When the truth came to be known, however, all present were filled with wonder, for it appeared as if this cavalier had been, at the same moment, in the chapel and in the field; for while he remained on his knees before the altar with his steed pawing the earth at the door, a warrior exactly resembling him, with the same arms, device and steed had appeared in the hottest of the fight; penetrating and overthrowing whole squadrons of Moors; that he had cut his way to the standard of the enemy, killed the standard bearer and carried off the banner in triumph. That his pourpoint and coat of mail were cut to pieces and his horse covered with wounds, yet still he fought on, and through his valor chiefly the victory was obtained.

What more moved astonishment was that for every wound received by the warrior and his steed in the field, there appeared marks on the pourpoint and coat of mail and upon the steed of Pascual Vivas; so that he had the semblance of having been in the severest press of the battle.

The matter was now readily explained by the worthy friars who followed the armies in those days, and who were skillful in expounding the miracles daily occurring in those holy wars. A miraculous intervention had been vouchsafed to Pascual Vivas. That his piety in remaining at his prayers might not put him to shame before sinful men, an angel bearing his form and semblance had taken his place in battle and fought while he prayed.

The matter being thus explained, all present were filled with pious admiration, and Pascual Vivas, if he ceased to be extolled as a warrior, came near being canonized as a saint.*

King Ordoño III. did not long survive this battle. Scarce had he arrived at Zamora on his way homeward, when he was seized with a mortal malady of which he died. He was succeeded by his brother Don Sancho; the same who had formerly endeavored to dispossess him of his throne.

---

* Exactly the same kind of miracle is recorded as happening in the same place to a cavalier of the name of Don Fernan Antolinez, in the service of the Count Garcia Fernandez. Fray Antonio Agapida has no doubt that the same miracle did actually happen to both cavaliers; "for in those days," says he, "there was such a demand for miracles that the same had frequently to be repeated:" witness the repeated appearance of Santiago in precisely the same manner, to save Christian armies from imminent danger of defeat, and achieve wonderful victories over the infidels: as we find recorded throughout the Spanish chronicles.

[CHAPTER XVII

King Sancho the Fat—Of the homage he exacted from Count Fernan Gonzalez, and of the strange bargain that he made with him for the purchase of his horse and falcon.]

King Sancho I., on ascending the throne, held a cortes at Leon, where all the great men of the kingdom and the princes who owed allegiance to him, were expected to attend and pay homage. As the court of Leon was excessively tenacious of its claim to sovereignty over Castile, the absence of Count Fernan Gonzalez was noticed with great displeasure by the king, who sent missives to him commanding his attendance. The count being proud of heart, and standing much upon the independence of Castile, was unwilling to kiss the hand of any one in token of vassalage. He was at length induced to stifle his repugnance and repair to the court, but he went in almost regal style and with a splendid retinue more like a sovereign making a progress through his dominions.

As he approached the city of Leon King Sancho came forth in great state to receive him and they met apparently as friends, but there was enmity against each other in their hearts.

The rich and gallant array with which Count Fernan made his entry in Leon was the theme of every tongue; but nothing attracted more notice than a falcon thoroughly trained which he carried on his hand; and an Arabian horse of wonderful beauty which he had gained in his wars with the Moors. King Sancho was seized with a vehement desire to possess this horse and falcon and offered to purchase them of the count. Don Fernan haughtily declined to enter into traffic; but offered them to the monarch as a gift. The king was equally punctilious in refusing to accept a favor; but as monarchs do not easily forego any thing on which they have set their hearts; it became evident to Count Fernan that it was necessary, for the sake of peace, to part with his horse and falcon. To save his dignity, however, he asked a price correspondent to his rank; for it was beneath a cavalier, he said, to sell his things cheap like a mean man. He demanded, therefore, one thousand marks of silver for the horse and falcon; to be paid on a stipulated day; if not paid on that day the price to be doubled on the next; and on each day's further delay, the price should in like manner be doubled. To these terms the king gladly consented, and the terms were specified in a written agreement which was duly signed and witnessed. The king thus gained the horse and falcon, but it will be hereinafter shewn that this indulgence of his fancy cost him dear.

This eager desire for an Arabian steed appears the more singular in Sancho the First, from his being so corpulent that he could not sit on horseback. Hence he is commonly known in history by the appellation of King Sancho the Fat. His unwieldy bulk may be one reason why he soon lost the favour of his warrior subjects; who looked upon him as a mere trencherman and bed presser, and not fitted to command men who lived in the saddle, and had rather fight than either eat or sleep.

King Sancho saw that he might soon have hard fighting to maintain his throne; and how could he figure as a warrior who could not mount on horseback? In his anxiety he repaired to his uncle Garcia, King of Navarre, surnamed the Trembler, who was an exceeding meagre man, and asked counsel of him what he should do to cure himself of this troublesome corpulency. Garcia the Trembler was totally at a loss for a recipe; his own leanness being a gift of nature: he advised him, however, to repair to Abderahman, the Miramamolin of Spain and King of Cordova; with whom he was happily at peace; and consult with him, and seek advice of the Arabian physicians resident at Cordova; the Moors being generally a spare and active people; and the Arabian physicians skillful above all others in the treatment of diseases.

King Sancho the Fat therefore sent amicable messages beforehand to the Moorish miramamolin, and followed them as fast as his corpulency would permit; and he was well received by the Moorish sovereign and remained for a long time at Cordova, diligently employed in decreasing his rotundity.

While the corpulent king was thus growing leaner discontent broke out among his subjects at home, and Count Fernan Gonzalez taking advantage of it stirred up an insurrection and placed upon the throne of Leon Ordoño the Fourth, surnamed the Bad, who was a kinsman of the late King Ordoño III.: and he moreover gave him his daughter for wife—his daughter Urraca, the repudiated wife of the late king.

If the good Count Fernan Gonzalez supposed he had fortified himself by this alliance, and that his daughter was now fixed for the second time, and more firmly than ever, on the throne of Leon, he was grievously deceived; for Sancho I. returned from Cordova at the head of a powerful host of Moors; and was no longer to be called the Fat, for he had so well succeeded under the regimen prescribed by the miramamolin and his Arabian physicians, that he could vault into the saddle with merely putting his hand upon the pommel.

Ordoño IV. was a man of puny heart; no sooner did he hear of the approach of King Sancho, and of his marvellous leanness and agility, than he was seized with terror, and abandoning his throne, and his twice repudiated spouse Urraca, he made for the mountains of Asturias; or as others assert, was overtaken by the Moors and killed with lances.

[CHAPTER XVIII

Further of the horse and falcon.]

King Sancho I. having reestablished himself on the throne and recovered the good will of his subjects by his leanness and horsemanship; sent a stern message to Count Fernan Gonzalez to come to his cortes or resign his Countship. The count was exceedingly indignant at this order and feared moreover that some indignity or injury would be offered him should he repair to Leon. He made the message known to his principal cavaliers and requested their advice. Most of them were of opinion that he should not go to the cortes. Don Fernan declared, however, that he would not act disloyally in omitting to do that, which the Counts of Castile had always performed; although he felt that he incurred the risk of death or imprisonment. Leaving his son Garcia Fernandez, therefore, in charge of his councillors, he departed for Leon with only seven cavaliers.

As he approached the gates of that city, no one came forth to greet him, as had always been the custom. This he considered an evil sign. Presenting himself before the king he would have kissed his hand, but the monarch withheld it. He charged the count with being vainglorious and disloyal: with having absented himself from the cortes and conspired against his throne; for all which he should make atonement; and should give hostages or pledges for his good faith before he left the court.

The count in reply accounted for his absenting himself from the cortes by the perfidious treatment he had formerly experienced at Leon. As to any grievances the king might have to complain of he stood ready to redress them; provided the king would make good his own written engagement, signed with his own hand and sealed with his own seal; to pay for the horse and falcon which he had purchased of the count on his former visit to Leon. Three years now had elapsed since the day appointed for the payment; and in the mean time the price had gone on daily doubling according to stipulation.

They parted mutually indignant; and after the count had retired to his quarters the king, piqued to maintain his royal word, summoned his major domo and ordered him to take a large amount of treasure and carry it to the Count of Castile in payment of his demand. So the major domo repaired to the count with a great sack of money to settle with him for the horse and hawk; but when he came to cast up the account, and double it each day that had intervened since the appointed day of payment, the major domo, though an expert man at figures, was totally confounded, and returning to the king assured him that all the money in the world would not suffice to pay the debt. King Sancho was totally at a loss how to keep his word and pay off a debt which was more than enough to ruin him. Grievously did he repent his first experience in traffic, and found that it is not safe even for a monarch to trade in horses.

In the mean time the count was suffered to return to Castile, but he did not let the matter rest here; for being sorely incensed at the indignities he had experienced, he sent missives to King Sancho urging his demand of payment for the horse and falcon; menacing otherwise to make seizures by way of indemnification. Receiving no satisfactory reply, he made a foray into the kingdom of Leon and brought off great spoil of sheep and cattle.

King Sancho now saw that the count was too bold and urgent a creditor to be trifled with. In his perplexity he assembled the estates of his kingdom and consulted them upon this momentous affair. His counsellors like himself were grievously perplexed between the sanctity of the royal word and the enormity of the debt. After much deliberation they suggested a compromise; the Count Fernan Gonzalez to relinquish the debt and in lieu thereof to be released from his vassalage.

The count agreed right gladly to this compromise, being thus relieved from all tribute and imposition and from the necessity of kissing the hand of any man in the world as his sovereign. Thus did King Sancho pay with the sovereignty of Castile for a horse and falcon; and thus were the Castilians relieved, by a skillful bargain in horse dealing, from all subjection to the kingdom of Leon.*

[CHAPTER XIX

The last campaign of Count Fernan—His death.]

The good Count Fernan Gonzalez was now well stricken in years. The fire of youth was extinct; the pride and ambition of manhood were over; instead of erecting palaces and lofty castles, he began now to turn his thoughts upon the grave and to build his last earthly habitation, the sepulchre.

Before erecting his own he had one built of rich and stately workmanship for his first wife, the object of his early love, and had her remains conveyed to it and interred with great solemnity. His own sepulchre, according to ancient promise, was prepared at the chapel and hermitage of San Pedro at Arlanza; where he had first communed with the holy Friar Pelayo. When it was completed he merely inscribed

* *Cronica* de Alonzo el Sabio, p. 3, c. 19.

upon it the word *Obijt*, leaving the rest to be supplied by others after his death.

When the Moors perceived that Count Fernan Gonzalez, once so redoubtable in arms, was old and infirm, and given to build tombs instead of castles, they thought it a favorable time to make an inroad into Castile. They passed the border, therefore, in great numbers, laying every thing waste and bearding the old lion in his very den.

The veteran had laid by sword and buckler, and had almost given up the world; but the sound of Moorish drum and trumpet called him back even from the threshold of the sepulchre. Buckling once more on his armour and bestriding his war steed, he summoned around him his Castilian cavaliers, seasoned like him in a thousand battles; and accompanied by his son Garcia Fernandez, who inherited all the valor of his father; issued forth to meet the foe; followed by the shouts and blessings of the populace, who joyed to see him once more in arms and glowing with his ancient fire.

The Moors were retiring from an extensive ravage laden with booty and driving before them an immense cavalgada; when they descried a squadron of cavaliers armed all in steel; emerging from a great cloud of dust, and bearing aloft the silver cross, the well known standard of Count Fernan Gonzalez. That veteran warrior came on as usual leading the way, sword in hand. The very sight of his standard had struck dismay into the enemy; they soon gave way before one of his vigorous charges; nor did he cease to pursue them until they took shelter within the very walls of Cordova. Here he wasted the surrounding country with fire and sword, and after thus braving the Moor in his very capital, returned triumphant to Burgos.

"Such," says Fray Antonio Agapida, "was the last campaign in this life of this most valorous cavalier;" and now, abandoning all further deeds of mortal enterprize in arms to his son Garcia Fernandez, he addressed all his thoughts, as he said, to prepare for his campaign in the skies. He still talked as a veteran warrior whose whole life had been passed in arms; but his talk was not of earthly warfare nor of earthly kingdom. He spoke only of the kingdom of heaven, and what he must do to make a successful inroad and gain an eternal inheritance in that blessed country.

He was equally indefatigable in preparing for his spiritual as for his mortal campaign. Instead, however, of mailed warriors tramping through his courts, and the shrill neigh of steed or clang of trumpet echoing among their walls; there were seen holy priests and barefoot monks passing to and fro, and the halls resounded with the sacred melody of litany and psalm. So pleased was heaven with the good works of this pious cavalier; and especially with rich donations to church and monasteries, which he made under the guidance of his spiritual counsellors;

that we are told it was given to him to foresee in vision the day and hour when he should pass from this weary life and enter the mansions of eternal rest.

Knowing that the time approached he prepared for his end like a good Christian. He wrote to the kings of Leon and Navarre in terms of great humility, craving their pardon for all past injuries and offences, and entreating them, for the good of Christendom, to live in peace and amity and make common cause for the defence of the faith.

Ten days before the time which heaven had appointed for his death he sent for the abbot of the chapel and convent of Arlanza, and bending his aged knees before him confessed all his sins. This done, as in former times he had shewn great state and ceremony in his worldly pageants, so now he arranged his last cavalgada to the grave. He prayed the abbot to return to his monastery and have his sepulchre prepared for his reception; and that the abbots of St. Sebastian and Silos and Quirce, with a train of holy friars, might come at the appointed day for his body; that thus, as he commended his soul to heaven through the hands of his confessor, he might, through the hands of these pious men, resign his body to the earth.

When the abbot had departed the count desired to be left alone; and clothing himself in a coarse friar's garb, he remained fervent in prayer for the forgiveness of all his sins. As he had been a valiant captain, all his life, against the enemies of the faith, so was he in death against the enemies of the soul. He died in the full command of all his faculties, making no groans nor contortions but rendering up his spirit with the calmness of a heroic cavalier.

We are told that when he died voices were heard from heaven in testimony to his sanctity; while the tears and lamentations of all Spain proved how much he was valued and beloved on earth. His remains were conveyed, according to his request, to the monastery of St. Pedro de Arlanza by a procession of holy friars with solemn chaunt and dirge. In the church of that convent they still repose, and two paintings are to be seen in the convent: one representing the count valiantly fighting with the Moors; the other conversing with St. Pelayo and St. Millan, as they appeared to him in vision before the battle of Hazinas.

The cross which he used as his standard is still treasured up in the sacristy of the convent. It is of massive silver, two ells in length, with our Saviour sculptured upon it, and above the head, in gothic letters, I.N.R.I. Below is Adam awaking from the grave, with the words of St. Paul, "Awake, thou who sleepest, and arise from the tomb; for Christ shall give thee life."

This holy cross still has the form at the lower end by which the standard bearer rested it in the pummel of his saddle.

"Inestimable," adds Fray Antonio Agapida, "are the reliques and remains of saints and sainted warriors." In after times, when Fernando the Third, surnamed the Saint, went to the conquest of Seville, he took with him a bone of this thrice blessed and utterly renowned cavalier, together with his sword and pennon, hoping through their efficacy to succeed in his enterprise. Nor was he disappointed; but what is marvellous to hear, but which we have on the authority of the good Bishop Sandoval, on the day on which King Fernando the Saint entered Seville in triumph, great blows were heard to resound within the sepulchre of the count at Arlanza, as if veritably his bones which remained behind exulted in the victory gained by those which had been carried to the wars. Thus were marvellously fulfilled the words of the holy psalm: "Exaltabant ossa humilitata."*

Here ends the chronicle of the most valorous and renowned Don Fernan Gonzalez, Count of Castile. Laus Deo.

* Sandoval, p. 334.

[1827–1847]

CHRONICLE OF FERNANDO THE SAINT

[CHAPTER I

The parentage of Fernando—Queen Berenguela—The Laras—Don Alvar conceals the death of King Henry—Mission of Queen Berenguela to Alfonso IX—She renounces the crown of Castile in favor of her son Fernando.]

Fernando III., surnamed the Saint, was the son of Alfonso III. King of Leon, and of Berenguela, a princess of Castile; but there were some particulars concerning his parentage which it is necessary clearly to state before entering upon his personal history.

Alfonso III. of Leon and Alfonso IX. King of Castile, were cousins, but there were dissensions between them. The King of Leon, to strengthen himself, married his cousin, the Princess Teresa, daughter of his uncle, the King of Portugal. By her he had two daughters. The marriage was annulled by Pope Celestine III. on account of their consanguinity, and, on their making resistance, they were excommunicated and the kingdom laid under an interdict. This produced an unwilling separation in 1195. Alfonso III. did not long remain single. Fresh dissensions having broken out between him and his cousin Alfonso IX. of Castile, they were amicably adjusted by his marrying the Princess Berenguela, daughter of that monarch. This second marriage, which took place about three years after the divorce, came likewise under the ban of the church and for the same reason, the near propinquity of the parties. Again the commands of the Pope were resisted, and again the refractory parties were excommunicated and the kingdom laid under an interdict.

The unfortunate King of Leon was the more unwilling to give up the present marriage, as the Queen Berenguela had made him the happy father of several children; one of whom he hoped might one day inherit the two crowns of Leon and Castile.

The intercession and entreaties of the bishops of Castile so far mollified the rigor of the Pope that a compromise was made; the legitimacy of the children by the present marriage was not to be affected by the divorce of the parents; and Fernando, the eldest, the subject of the present chronicle, was recognized as successor to his father to the throne of Leon. The divorced Queen Berenguela left Fernando in Leon and returned in 1204 to Castile to the court of her father Alfonso IX. Here she remained until the death of her father in 1214, who was succeeded by his son, Enrique or Henry I. The latter being only in his eleventh year, his sister the ex-Queen Berenguela was declared regent. She well merited the trust, for she was a woman of great prudence and wisdom, and a resolute and magnanimous spirit.

At this time the house of Lara had risen to great power. There were three brothers of that turbulent and haughty race, Don Alvar Nuñez, Don Fernan Nuñez and Don Gonzalo Nuñez. The Laras had caused great trouble in the kingdom during the minority of Prince Henry's father by arrogating to themselves the regency; and they now attempted in like manner to get the guardianship of the son; declaring it an office too important and difficult to be entrusted to a woman. Having a powerful and unprincipled party among the nobles and using great bribery among persons in whom Berenguela confided, they carried their point; and the virtuous Berenguela, to prevent civil commotions, resigned the regency into the hands of Don Alvar Nuñez de Lara, the head of that ambitious house. First, however, she made him kneel and swear that he would conduct himself toward the youthful King Enrique as a thorough friend and a loyal vassal, guarding his person and his kingdom from all harm; that he would respect the property of individuals, and undertake nothing of importance without the counsel and consent of Queen Berenguela. Furthermore that he would guard and respect the hereditary possessions of Queen Berenguela, left to her by her father; and would always serve her as his sovereign, the daughter of his deceased king. All this Don Alvar Nuñez solemnly swore upon the sacred evangelists and the Holy Cross.

No sooner, however, had he got the young king in his power than he shewed the ambition, rapacity and arrogance of his nature. He prevailed upon the young king to make him a count; he induced him to hold cortes without the presence of Queen Berenguela: issuing edicts in the king's name he banished refractory nobles, giving their offices and lands to his brothers; he levied exactions on rich and poor, and what is still more flagrant, he extended those exactions to the church. In vain did Queen Berenguela remonstrate; in vain did the Dean of Toledo thunder forth an excommunication; he scoffed at them both; for in the king's name he persuaded himself he had a tower of strength. He even sent a letter to Queen Berenguela in the name of the young king, demanding of her the castles, towns and ports which had been left to her by her father. The queen was deeply grieved at this letter, and sent a reply to the king that when she saw him, face to face, she would do with those possessions whatever he should command as her brother and sovereign.

On receiving this message the young king was shocked and distressed that such a demand should have been made in his name; but he was young and inexperienced, and could not openly contend with a man of Don Alvar's overbearing character. He wrote secretly to the queen, however, assuring her that the demand had been made without his knowledge; and saying how gladly he would come to her if he could, and be relieved from the thraldom of Don Alvar.

In this way the unfortunate prince was made an instrument in the hands of this haughty and arrogant nobleman, of inflicting all kinds of wrongs and injuries upon his subjects. Don Alvar constantly kept him with him; carrying him from place to place of his dominions, wherever his presence was necessary to effect some new measure of tyranny. He even endeavored to negociate a marriage between the young king and some neighboring princess, in order to retain an influence over him; but in this he was unsuccessful.

For three years had he maintained this iniquitous sway until one day in 1217, when the young king was with him at Palencia, and was playing with some youthful companions in the court yard of the episcopal palace, a tile, either falling from the roof of a tower, or sportively thrown by one of his companions, struck him in the head and inflicted a wound, of which he presently died.

This was a fatal blow to the power of Don Alvar. To secure himself from any sudden revulsion in the popular mind, he determined to conceal the death of the king as long as possible, and gave out that he had retired to the fortress of Tariego, whither he had the body conveyed, as if still living. He continued to issue dispatches from time to time in the name of the king and made various excuses for his non-appearance in public.

Queen Berenguela soon learnt the truth. According to the laws of Castile she was heiress to the crown, but she resolved to transfer it to her son, Fernando, who, being likewise acknowledged successor to the crown of Leon, would unite the two kingdoms under his rule. To effect her purpose she availed herself of the cunning of her enemy; kept secret her knowledge of the death of her brother and sent two of her confidential cavaliers, Don Lope Diaz de Haro, Señor of Biscay, and Don Gonsalvo Ruiz Giron, and Don Alonzo Tellez de Meneses to her late husband, Alfonso III. King of Leon, who, with her son Fernando, was then at Toro, entreating him to send the latter to her to protect her from the tyranny of Don Alvar. The prudent mother, however, forbore to let King Alfonso know of her brother's death, lest it might awaken in him ambitious thoughts about the Castilian crown.

This mission being sent, she departed with the cavaliers of her party for Palencia. The death of the King Enrique being noised about, she was honored as Queen of Castile, and Don Tello, the bishop, came forth in procession to receive her. The next day she proceeded to the castle of Duenas and, on its making some shew of resistance, took it by force.

The cavaliers who were with the queen endeavored to effect a reconciliation between her and Don Alvar, seeing that the latter had powerful

connexions, and through his partizans and retainers held possession of
the principal towns and fortresses; that haughty nobleman, however,
would listen to no proposals unless the Prince Fernando was given into
his guardianship, as had been the Prince Enrique.

In the mean time the request of Queen Berenguela had been granted
by her late husband, the King of Leon, and her son Fernando hastened
to meet her. The meeting took place at the castle of Otiella, and happy
was the anxious mother once more to embrace her son. At her command
the chevaliers in her train elevated him on the trunk of an elm tree for
a throne, and hailed him king with great acclamations.

They now proceeded to Valladolid, which at that time was a great and
wealthy town. Here the nobility and chivalry of Estramadura and other
parts hastened to pay homage to the queen. A stage was erected in the
market place, where the assembled states acknowledged her for queen
and swore fealty to her. She immediately, in presence of her nobles,
prelates and people, renounced the crown in favor of her son. The air
rang with the shouts of "Long live Fernando, King of Castile!" The bishops and clergy then conducted the king in state to the church. This
was on the 31st of August, 1217, and about three months from the death
of King Enrique.

Fernando was at this time about eighteen years of age; an accomplished cavalier; having been instructed in every thing befitting a prince
and a warrior.

[CHAPTER II

*King Alfonso of Leon ravages Castile—Captivity of Don Alvar—
Death of the Laras.*]

King Alfonso of Leon was exceedingly exasperated at the furtive manner
in which his son Fernando had left him, without informing him of King
Henry's death. He considered, and perhaps with reason, the transfer of
the crown of Castile by Berenguela to her son as a manoeuvre to evade
any rights or claims which he, King Alfonso, might have over her, notwithstanding their divorce; and he believed that both mother and son
had conspired to deceive and outwit him; and, what was especially
provoking, they had succeeded. It was natural for King Alfonso to have
become by this time exceedingly irritable and sensitive; he had been
repeatedly thwarted in his dearest concerns; excommunicated out of
two wives by the Pope, and now, as he conceived, cajoled out of a
kingdom.

In his wrath he flew to arms, a prompt and customary recourse of kings
in those days, when they had no will to consult but their own; and not-

withstanding the earnest expostulations and entreaties of holy men, he entered Castile with an army, ravaging the legitimate inheritance of his son, as if it had been the territory of an enemy. He was seconded in his outrages by Count Alvar Nuñez de Lara and his two bellicose brothers, who hoped still to retain power by rallying under his standard.

There were at this time full two thousand cavaliers with the youthful king, resolute men, well armed and well appointed, and they urged him to lead them against the King of Leon. Queen Berenguela, however, interposed and declared her son should never be guilty of the impiety of taking up arms against his father. By her advice King Fernando sent an embassy to his father, expostulating with him and telling him that he ought to be thankful to God that Castile was in the hands of a son disposed at all times to honor and defend him, instead of a stranger who might prove a dangerous foe.

King Alfonso, however, was not so to be appeased. By the ambassadors he sent proposals to Queen Berenguela that they reenter into wedlock, for which he would procure a dispensation from the Pope; they would then be jointly sovereigns of both Castile and Leon, and the Prince Fernando their son, should inherit both crowns. But the virtuous Berenguela recoiled from this proposal of a second nuptials. "God forbid," replied she, "that I should return to a sinful marriage; and as to the crown of Castile, it now belongs to my son, to whom I have given it with the sanction of God and the good men of this realm."

King Alfonso was more enraged than ever by this reply, and, being incited and aided by Count Alvar and his faction, he resumed his ravages; laying waste the country and burning the villages. He would have attacked Duenas, but found that place strongly garrisoned by Diego Lopez de Haro and Ruy Diaz de los Cameros; he next marched upon Burgos; but that place was equally well garrisoned by Lope Diaz de Haro and other stout Castilian cavaliers; so perceiving his son to be more firmly seated upon the throne than he had imagined; and that all his menaces and ravages were unavailing, he returned deeply chagrined to his kingdom.

King Fernando, in obedience to the dictates of his mother as well as of his own heart, abstained from any acts of retaliation on his father, but he turned his arms against Muñon and Lerma and Lara, and other places which either belonged to, or held out for Count Alvar, and having subdued them proceeded to Burgos, the capital of his kingdom, where he was received by the bishop and clergy with great solemnity; and whither the nobles and chivalry from all parts of Castile hastened to rally round his throne. The turbulent Count Alvar Nuñez de Lara and his brothers retaining other fortresses too strong to be easily taken, refused all allegiance, and made ravaging excursions, over the country. The prudent and provident Berenguela, therefore, while at Burgos, seeing that the troubles and contentions of the kingdom would cause great expense, and prevent much revenue, gathered together all her jewels of gold and silver and precious stones, and all her plate, and rich silks and other precious things, and caused them to be sold and gave the money to her son, to defray the cost of these civil wars.

King Fernando and his mother departed shortly afterward for Palencia; on their way they had to pass by Herrera, which at that time was the strong hold of Count Alvar. When the king came in sight Count Fernan Nuñez with his battalions was on the banks of the river, but drew within the walls. As the king had to pass close by with his retinue, he ordered his troops to be put in good order and gave it in charge to Alonzo Tellez and Suer Tellez and Alvar Ruyz to protect the flanks.

As the royal troops drew near, Count Alvar, leaving his people in the town, sallied forth with a few cavaliers to regard the army as it passed. Affecting great contempt for the youthful king and his cavaliers, he stood drawn up on a rising ground with his attendants, looking down upon the troops with scornful aspect, and rejecting all advice to retire into the town.

As the king and his immediate escort drew nigh their attention was drawn to this little body of proud warriors drawn up upon a bank and regarding them so loftily; and Alonzo Tellez and Suer Tellez, looking more closely, recognized Don Alvar and, putting spurs to their horses, dashed up the bank followed by several cavaliers. Don Alvar repented of his vain confidence too late; and seeing great numbers urging toward him, turned his reins and retreated toward the town. Still his stomach was too high for absolute flight, and the others, who spurred after him at full speed, overtook him. Throwing himself from his horse, he covered himself with his shield and prepared for defence. Alonzo Tellez, however, called to his men not to kill the count, but to take him prisoner. He was accordingly captured with several of his followers and borne off to the king and queen. The count had every thing to apprehend from their vengeance for his misdeeds. They used no personal harshness, however, but demanded from him that he should surrender all the castles and strong places held by the retainers and partizans of his brothers and himself; that he should furnish one hundred horsemen to aid in their recovery, and should remain a prisoner until those places were all in the possession of the crown.

Captivity broke the haughty spirit of Don Alvar. He agreed to those conditions, and, until they should be fulfilled, was consigned to the charge of Gonsalvo Ruiz Giron and confined in the castle of Valladolid. The places were delivered up in the course of a few months, and thus King Fernando became strongly possessed of his kingdom.

Stripped of power, state and possessions, Count Alvar and his brothers, after an ineffectual attempt to rouse the King of Leon to another campaign against his son, became savage and desperate, and made predatory excursions, pillaging the country; until Count Alvar fell mortally ill of hydropsy. Struck with remorse and melancholy, he repaired to Toro and entered the chivalrous order of Santiago; that he might gain the indulgences granted by the Pope to those who die in that order, and hoping, says an ancient chronicler, to oblige God, as it were, by that religious ceremony, to pardon his sins.* His illness endured seven months, and he was reduced to such poverty that at his death there was not money enough left by him to convey his body to Ucles; where he had requested to be buried, nor to pay for tapers for his funeral. When Queen Berenguela heard this she ordered that the funeral should be honorably performed at her own expense and sent a cloth of gold to cover the bier.†

The brother of Count Alvar, Don Fernan, abandoned his country in despair and went to Marocco, where he was well received by the miramamolin, and had lands and revenues assigned to him. He became a great favorite among the Moors, to whom he used to recount his deeds in the civil wars of Castile. At length he fell dangerously ill and caused himself to be taken to a suburb inhabited by Christians. There happened to be there at that time one Don Gonsalvo, a knight of the order of the Hospital of St. John de Acre, and who had been in the service of Pope Innocent III. Don Fernan finding his end approaching, entreated of the knight his religious habit, that he might die in it. His request was granted, and thus Count Fernan died in the habit of a knight hospitaliere of St. John de Acre, in Elbora, a suburb of Marocco. His body was afterwards brought to Spain and interred in a town on the banks of the Pisuerga, in which repose likewise the remains of his wife and children.

The Count Gonzalo Nuñez de Lara, the third of these brothers, also took refuge among the Moors. He was seized with violent disease in the city of Baeza, where he died. His body was conveyed to Campos a Zalmos which appertained to the Friars of the Temple, where the holy fraternity gave it the rites of sepulture with all due honor. Such was the end of these three brothers of the once proud and powerful house of Lara, whose disloyal deeds had harassed their country and brought ruin upon themselves.

* *Cronica Gotica,* por Don Alonzo Nuñez de Castro, p. 17.
† *Cronica General de España,* part 3, p. 370.

[CHAPTER III

Marriage of King Fernando—Campaign against the Moors—Aben Mohamed, King of Baeza, declares himself the vassal of King Fernando—They march to Jaen—Burning of the tower—Fernando commences the building of the cathedral at Toledo.]

King Fernando, aided by the sage counsels of his mother, reigned for some time in peace and quietness, administering his affairs with equity and justice. The good Queen Berenguela now began to cast about her eyes in search of a suitable alliance for her son and had many consultations with the Bishop Maurice of Burgos and other ghostly counsellors thereupon. They at length agreed upon the Princess Beatrix, daughter of the late Philip, Emperor of Germany, and the Bishop Maurice and Padre Fray Pedro de Arlanza were sent as envoys to the Emperor Frederick II., cousin of the princess, to negotiate the terms. An arrangement was happily effected and the princess set out for Spain. In passing through France she was courteously entertained at Paris by King Philip, who made her rich presents. On the borders of Castile, she was met at Victoria by the Queen Berenguela with a great train of prelates, monks and masters of the religious orders, and of abbesses and nuns; together with a glorious train of chivalry. In this state she was conducted to Burgos where the king and all his court came forth to receive her; and their nuptials were celebrated with great pomp and rejoicing.

King Fernando lived happily with his fair Queen Beatrix and his kingdom remained in peace; but by degrees he became impatient of quiet, and anxious to make war upon the Moors. Perhaps he felt called upon to make some signal assay in arms at present; having, the day before his nuptials, been armed a knight in the monastery of Las Huelgas; and in those iron days knighthood was not a matter of mere parade and ceremony but called for acts of valor and proofs of stern endurance.

The discreet Berenguela endeavored to dissuade her son from taking the field, considering him not of sufficient age. In all things else he was ever obedient to her counsels and even to her inclinations, but it was in vain that she endeavored to persuade him from making war upon the infidels. "God," would he say, "had put into his hands not merely a sceptre to govern, but a sword to avenge his country."

It was fortunate for the good cause moreover, add the Spanish chroniclers, that while the queen mother was endeavoring to throw a damper on the kindling fire of her son, a worthy prelate was at hand to stir it up into a blaze. This was the illustrious historian Rodrigo, Archbishop of Toledo, who now preached a crusade against the Moors, promising like indulgences with those granted to the warriors for the holy sepulchre. The consequence was a great assemblage of troops from all parts at Toledo.

King Fernando was prevented for a time from taking the field in person but sent in advance Don Lope Diaz de Haro and Gonsalvo Ruiz Giron and Alonzo Tellez de Meneses, with five hundred cavaliers well armed and mounted. The very sight of them effected a conquest over Aben Mohamed, the Moorish King of Baeza, insomuch that he sent an embassy to King Fernando, declaring himself his vassal.

When King Fernando afterwards took the field, he was joined by this Moorish ally at the Navas, or plains, of Tolosa; who was in company with him when the king marched to Jaen, to the foot of a tower, and set fire to it, whereupon those Moors who remained in the tower were burnt to death and those who leapt from the walls were received on the points of lances.

Notwithstanding the burnt offering of this tower, heaven did not smile upon the attempt of King Fernando to reduce the city of Jaen. He was obliged to abandon the siege, but consoled himself by laying waste the country. He was more successful elsewhere. He carried the strong town of Priego by assault, and gave the garrison their lives on condition of yielding up all their property and paying moreover eighty thousand maravedis of silver. For the payment of this sum they were obliged to give as hostages fifty five damsels of great beauty, and fifty cavaliers of rank, beside nine hundred of the common people. The king divided his hostages among his bravest cavaliers and the religious orders; but his vassal, the Moorish King of Baeza, obtained the charge of the Moorish damsels.

The king then attacked Loxa, and his men scaled the walls and burnt the gates, and made themselves masters of the place. He then led his army into the Vega of Granada, the inhabitants of which submitted to become his vassals and gave up all the Christian captives in that city, amounting to thirteen hundred.

Aben Mohamed, King of Baeza, then delivered to King Fernando the towers of Martos and Andujar, and the king gave them to Don Alvar Perez de Castro and placed with him Don Gonzalo Ybañez, Master of Calatrava, and Tello Alonzo Meneses, son of Don Alonzo Tellez, and other stout cavaliers, fitted to maintain frontier posts. These arrangements being made, and having ransacked every mountain and valley and taken many other places not herein specified; King Fernando returned in triumph to Toledo; where he was joyfully received by his mother Berenguela and his wife Beatrix.

Clerical historians do not fail to record with infinite satisfaction a signal instance of the devout and zealous spirit which King Fernando had derived from his constant communion with the reverend fathers of the church. As the king was one day walking with his ghostly adviser the archbishop in the principal church of Toledo, which was built in the Moresco fashion, having been a mosque of the infidels, it occurred, or more probably was suggested to him that, since God had aided him to encrease his kingdom and had given him such victories over the enemies of his holy faith; it became him to rebuild his holy temple, which was ancient and falling to decay, and to adorn it richly with the spoils taken from the Moors. The thought was promptly carried into effect. The king and the archbishop laid the first stone with great solemnity and in the fulness of time accomplished the mighty cathedral of Toledo, which remains the wonder and admiration of after ages.

[CHAPTER IV

Assassination of Aben Mohamed—His head carried as a present to Abullale, the Moorish King of Seville. Advance of the Christians into Andalusia—Abullale purchases a truce.]

The worthy Fray Antonio Agapida records various other victories and achievements of King Fernando in a subsequent campaign against the Moors of Andalusia; in the course of which his camp was abundantly supplied with grain by his vassal Aben Mohamed, the Moorish King of Baeza. The assistance rendered by that Moslem monarch to the Christian forces in their battles against those of his own race and his own faith, did not meet with the reward it merited; "doubtless," says Antonio Agapida, "because he halted half way in the right path and did not turn thorough renegado." It appears that his friendship for the Christians gave great disgust to his subjects, and some of them rose upon him, while he was sojourning in the city of Cordova, and sought to destroy him. Aben Mohamed fled by a gate leading to the gardens, to take shelter in the tower of Almodovar; but the assassins overtook him and slew him on a hill near the tower. They then cut off his head and carried it as a present to Abullale, the Moorish King of Seville, expecting to be munificently rewarded; but that monarch gave command that their heads should be struck off and their bodies thrown to the dogs, as traitors to their liege lords.*

King Fernando was grieved when he heard of the assassination of his vassal; and feared the death of Aben Mohamed might lead to a rising of the Moors. He sent notice to Andujar, to Don Alvar Perez de Castro and Alonzo Tellez de Meneses, to be on their guard; but the Moors, fearing punishment for some rebellious movements, abandoned the town and it fell into the hands of the king. The Moors of Martos did the like: the Alcazar of Baeza yielded also to the king, who placed in it Don Lope Diaz de Haro with five hundred men.

---

* *Cron. Gen. de España,* part 4, fol. 373.

Abullale, the Moorish sovereign of Seville, was alarmed at seeing the advances which the Christians were making in Andalusia; and attempted to wrest from their hands these newly acquired places. He marched upon Martos, which was not strongly walled. The Countess Doña Yrenia, wife to Don Alvar Perez de Castro, was in this place and her husband was absent. Don Tello Alonzo with a Spanish force hastened to her assistance. Finding the town closely invested, he formed his men into a troop and endeavored to cut his way through the enemy. A rude conflict ensued; the cavaliers fought their way forward, and Christian and Moor arrived pell mell at the gate of the town. Here the press was excessive. Fernan Gomez de Pudiello, a stout cavalier, who bore the pennon of Don Tello Alonzo, was slain; and the same fate would have befallen Don Tello himself, but that a company of esquires sallied from the town to his rescue.

King Abullale now encircled the town and got possession of the peña or rock which commands it, killing two hundred Christians who defended it.

Provisions began to fail the besieged; and they were reduced to slay their horses for food; and even to eat the hides. Don Gonsalvo Ybañez, Master of Calatrava, who was in Baeza, hearing of the extremity of the place came suddenly with seventy men and effected an entrance. The augmentation of the garrison only served to encrease the famine, without being sufficient in force to raise the siege. At length word was brought to Don Alvar Perez de Castro, who was with the king at Guadalaxara, of the imminent danger to which his wife was exposed. He instantly set off for her relief, accompanied by several cavaliers of note and a strong force. They succeeded in getting into Martos; recovered the peña or rock, and made such vigorous defence that Abullale abandoned the siege in despair. In the following year King Fernando led his host to take revenge upon this Moorish King of Seville; but the latter purchased a truce for one year, with three hundred maravedis of silver.*

[CHAPTER V

Aben Hud—Abullale purchases another year's truce. Fernando hears of the death of his father, the King of Leon, while pressing the siege of Jaen—He becomes sovereign of the two kingdoms of Leon and Castile.]

About this time a valiant sheik named Aben Abdallar Mohammed ben Hud, but commonly called Aben Hud, was effecting a great revolution in Moorish affairs. He was of the lineage of Aben Alfange, and bitterly opposed to the sect of Almohades, who for a long time had exercised

---

* *Cron. Gen. de España*, part 4, c. ii.

a tyrannical sway. Stirring up the Moors of Murcia to rise upon their oppressors; he put himself at their head; massacred all the Almohades that fell into his hands and made himself sheik or king of that region. He purified the mosques with water after the manner in which Christians purify their churches, as though they had been defiled by the Almohades. Aben Hud acquired a name among those of his religion for justice and good faith as well as valour; and after some opposition, gained sway over all Andalusia. This brought him in collision with King Fernando

☞   (Something is wanting here.)

laying waste fields of grain. The Moorish sovereign of Seville purchased another year's truce of him for three hundred thousand maravedis of silver: Aben Hud on the other hand collected a great force and marched to oppose him; but did not dare to give him battle. He went, therefore, upon Merida and fought with King Alfonso of Leon, father of King Fernando, where however he met with complete discomfiture.

On the following year King Fernando repeated his invasion of Andalusia and was pressing the siege of the city of Jaen, which he assailed by means of engines discharging stones; when a courier arrived in all speed from his mother informing him that his father Alfonso was dead and urging him to proceed instantly to Leon to enforce his pretensions to the crown. King Fernando accordingly raised the siege of Jaen, sending his engines to Martos, and repaired to Castile to consult with his mother; who was his counsellor on all occasions.

It appeared that in his last will King Alfonso had named his two daughters joint heirs to the crown. Some of the Leonese and Gallegos were disposed to place the Prince Alonzo, brother to King Fernando, on the throne; but he had listened to the commands of his mother and had resisted all suggestions of the kind; the larger part of the kingdom, including the most important cities, had declared for Fernando.

By the advice of his sagacious and intrepid mother therefore, and accompanied by her, King Fernando proceeded instantly into the kingdom of Leon with a powerful force. Wherever they went the cities threw open their gates to them. The princesses Doña Sancha and Doña Dulce with their mother Teresa would have assembled a force to oppose them; but the prelates were all in favor of King Fernando. On his approach to Leon the bishops and clergy and all the principal inhabitants came forth to receive him and conducted him to the cathedral, where he received their homage and was proclaimed king, with the *Te Deums* of the choir and the shouts of the people.

Doña Teresa, who with her daughters was in Galicia, finding the kingdom thus disposed of, sent to demand provision for herself and the two princesses; who in fact were step-sisters of King Fernando. Queen Berenguela, though she had some reason not to feel kindly disposed toward Doña Teresa, who she might think had been exercising a secret influence over her late husband, yet suppressed all such feelings, and undertook to repair in person to Galicia and negotiate this singular family question. She had an interview with Queen Teresa at Valencia de Merlio in Galicia and arranged a noble dower for her and an annual revenue to each of her daughters of thirty thousand maravedis of gold. The king then had a meeting with his sisters at Benevente, where they resigned all pretensions to the throne. All the fortified places which held for them were given up, and thus Fernando became undisputed sovereign of the two kingdoms of Castile and Leon.

[CHAPTER VI

Expedition of the Prince Alonzo against the Moors—Encamps on the banks of the Gaudalete—Aben Hud marches out from Xerez and gives battle—Prowess of Garcia Perez de Vargas—Flight and pursuit of the Moors—Miracle of the blessed Santiago.]

King Fernando III. having, through the sage counsel and judicious management of his mother the Queen Berenguela, made this amicable arrangement with his step-sisters, by which he gained possession of their inheritance, now found his territories to extend from the Bay of Biscay to the vicinity of the Guadalquivir, and from the borders of Portugal to those of Aragon and Valencia; and in addition to his titles of King of Castile and Leon, now called himself King of Spain, by seignorial right. Being at peace with all his Christian neighbors he now prepared to carry on with more zeal and vigor than ever his holy wars against the infidels. While making a progress, however, through his dominions, administering justice, he sent his brother, the Prince Alonzo, to make an expedition into the country of the Moors and to attack the newly risen power of Aben Hud.

As the Prince Alonzo was young and of little experience the king sent Don Alvar Perez de Castro, the Castilian, with him as his captain; he being stout of heart, strong of hand and skilled in war. The prince and his captain went from Salamanca to Toledo, where they recruited their force with a troop of cavalry. Thence they proceeded to Andujar, where they sent out corredores, or light foraging troops, who laid waste the country, plundering and destroying, and bringing off great booty. Thence they directed their ravaging course toward Cordova, assaulted and carried Palma and put all its inhabitants to the sword. Following the fertile valley of the Guadalquivir, they scoured the vicinity of Seville, and continued onward for Xerez, sweeping off cattle and sheep from the pastures of Andalusia; driving on long cavalgadas of horses and mules laden with spoil; until the earth shook with the tramping of their feet and their course was marked by clouds of dust and the smoke of burning villages.

In this desolating foray they were joined by two hundred horse and three hundred foot, Moorish allies, or rather vassals, being led by the son of Aben Mohamed, the King of Baeza.

Arrived within sight of Xerez they pitched their tents on the banks of the Guadalete; that fatal river, sadly renowned in the annals of Spain for the overthrow of Roderick and the perdition of his kingdom.

Here a good watch was set over the captured flocks and herds which covered the adjacent meadows; while the soldiers, fatigued with ravage, gave them up to repose on the banks of the river; or indulged in feasting and revelry; or gambled with each other for their booty.

In the meantime Aben Hud hearing of this inroad summoned all his chivalry of the sea-bord of Andalusia to meet him in Xerez. They hastened to obey his call; every leader spurred for Xerez with his band of vassals. Thither came also the King of the Gazules with seven hundred horsemen, Moors of Africa, light, vigorous and active; and the city was full of troops.

The camp of Don Alonzo had a formidable appearance at a distance, from the flocks and herds which surrounded it; the vast number of sumpter mules and the numerous captives; but when Aben Hud came to reconnoitre it he found that its aggregate force did not exceed three thousand five hundred men, a mere handful in comparison with his army, and those encumbered with cattle and booty. He anticipated therefore an easy victory. He now sallied forth from the city and took his position in the olive fields between the Christians and the city; while the African horsemen were stationed on each wing, with instructions to hem in the Christians on either side; for he was only apprehensive of their escaping. It is even said that he ordered great quantities of cords to be brought from the city and osier bands to be made by the soldiery; wherewith to bind the multitude of prisoners about to fall into their hands. His whole force he divided into seven battalions, each containing from fifteen hundred to two thousand cavalry. With these he prepared to give battle.

When the Christians thus saw an overwhelming force in front; cavalry hovering on either flank, and the deep waters of the Guadalete behind them they felt the perils of their situation.

In this emergency Alvar Perez de Castro shewed himself the able captain that he had been represented. Though apparently deferring to the prince in council, he virtually took the command, riding among the troops lightly armed, with truncheon in hand, encouraging every one by word and look and fearless demeanour. To give the most formidable appearance to their little host, he ordered that as many as possible of the footsoldiers should mount upon the mules and beasts of burden and form a troop to be kept in reserve. Before the battle he conferred the honor of knighthood on Garci Perez de Vargas, a cavalier destined to gain renown for hardy deeds of arms.

When the troops were all ready for the field, the prince exhorted them as good Christians, to confess their sins and obtain absolution. There was a goodly number of priests and friars with the army; as there generally was with all the plundering expeditions of this holy war, but there were not enough to confess all the army; those therefore who could not have a priest or monk for the purpose, confessed to each other.

Among the cavaliers were two noted for their valour; but who, though brothers-in-law, lived in mortal feud. One was Diego Perez, vassal to Alvar Perez and brother to him who had just been armed knight; the other was Pero Miguel, both natives of Toledo. Diego Perez was the one who had given cause of offence. He now approached his adversary and asked his pardon for that day only; that, in a time of such mortal peril, there might not be enmity and malice in their hearts. The priests added their exhortations to this request, but Pero Miguel sternly refused to pardon. When this was told to the prince and Don Alvar, they likewise entreated Don Miguel to pardon his brother-in-law. "I will," replied he, "if he will come to my arms and embrace me as a brother." But Diego Perez declined the fraternal embrace, for he saw danger in the eye of Pero Miguel and he knew his savage strength and savage nature, and suspected that he meant to strangle him. So Pero Miguel went into battle without pardoning his enemy who had implored forgiveness.

At this time, say the old chroniclers, the shouts and yells of the Moorish army, the sound of their cymbals, kettledrums and other instruments of warlike music were so great that heaven and earth seemed commingled and confounded. In regarding the storm of battle about to overwhelm him, Alvar Perez saw that the only chance was to form the whole army into one mass and by a headlong assault, to break the centre of the enemy. In this emergency he sent word to the prince, who was in the rear with the reserve, and had five hundred captives in charge, to strike off the heads of the captives and to join him with the whole reserve. This bloody order was obeyed. The prince came to the front, all formed together in one dense column and then with the war cry "Santiago! Santiago! Castile! Castile!" charged upon the centre of the enemy.

The Moors' line was broken by the shock. Squadron after squadron was thrown into confusion. Moors and Christians were intermingled until the field became one scene of desperate, chance medley fighting. Every Christian cavalier fought as if the salvation of the field depended upon his single arm. Garci Perez de Vargas, who had been knighted just before the battle, proved himself worthy of the honor. He had three horses killed under him and engaged in a desperate combat with the King of the Gazules whom at length he struck dead from his horse. This king had crossed from Africa on a devout expedition in the cause of the Prophet Mahomet. "Verily," says Antonio Agapida, "he had his reward."

Diego Perez was not behind his brother in prowess; and heaven favored him in that deadly fight notwithstanding that he had not been pardoned by his enemy. In the heat of the battle he had broken both sword and lance, whereupon tearing off a great knotted limb from an olive tree, he laid about him with such vigor and manhood that he who got one blow in the head from that war club never needed another. Don Alvar Perez who witnessed his feats was seized with delight. At each fresh blow that cracked a Moslem scull he would cry out, "Assi! Assi! Diego, Machucha, Machucha!"—"So! So! Diego, Smash them, Smash them!"—and from that day forward that stronghanded cavalier went by the name of Diego Machucha, or Diego the Smasher, and it remained the surname of several of his lineage.

At length the Moors gave way and fled for the gates of Xerez; being hotly pursued they stumbled over the bodies of the slain, and thus many were taken prisoners. At the gates the press was so great that they killed each other in striving to enter; and the Christian sword made slaughter under the walls.

The Christians gathered spoils of the field after this victory until they were fatigued with collecting them; and the precious articles found in the Moorish tents were beyond calculation. Their camp fires were supplied with the shafts of broken lances, and they found ample use for the cords and osier bands which the Moors had provided to bind their expected captives.

It was a theme of much marvel and solemn meditation that of all the distinguished cavaliers who entered into this battle not one was lost, excepting the same Pero Miguel who refused to pardon his adversary. What became of him no one could tell. The last that was seen of him he was in the midst of the enemy cutting down and overturning, for he was a valiant warrior and of prodigious strength. When the battle and pursuit were at an end and the troops were recalled by sound of trumpet he did not appear. His tent remained empty. The field of battle was searched, but he was nowhere to be found. Some supposed that, in his fierce eagerness to make havoc among the Moors, he had entered the gates of the city and there been slain; but his fate remained a mere matter of conjecture; and the whole was considered an awful warning that no Christian should go into battle without pardoning those who asked forgiveness.

"On this day," says the worthy Agapida, "it pleased heaven to work one if its miracles in favor of the Christian host, for the blessed Santiago appeared in the air on a white horse, with a white banner in one hand and a sword in the other, accompanied by a band of cavaliers in white. This miracle," he adds, "was beheld by many men of verity and worth," probably the monks and priests who accompanied the army; "as well as by numbers of Moors, who declared that the greatest slaughter was effected by those sainted warriors."

It may be as well to add that Fray Antonio Agapida is supported in this marvellous fact by Rodrigo, Archbishop of Toledo; one of the most learned and pious men of the age; who lived at the time and records it in his chronicle. It is a matter, therefore, placed beyond the doubts of the profane.

[CHAPTER VII

A bold attempt upon Cordova, the seat of Moorish power.]

About this time certain Christian cavaliers of the frontiers received information from Moorish captives that the noble city of Cordova was negligently guarded, so that the suburbs might easily be surprised. They immediately concerted a bold attempt and sent to Pedro and Alvar Perez, who were at Martos, entreating them to aid them with their vassals. Having collected a sufficient force and prepared scaling ladders, they approached the city on a dark night in January; amid showers of rain and howling blasts, which prevented their footsteps being heard. Arrived at the foot of the ramparts, they listened but could hear no sentinel. The guards had shrunk into the watch towers for shelter from the pelting storm, and the garrison was in profound sleep, for it was the mid-watch of the night.

Some, disheartened by the difficulties of the place, were for abandoning the attempt; but Domingo Muñoz, their adalid, or guide, encouraged them. Silently fastening together ladders of wood so as to be of sufficient length, they placed them against one of the towers. The first who mounted were Alvar Colodro and Benito de Banos, who were dressed as Moors and spoke the Arabic language. The tower which they scaled is to this day called the tower of Alvar Colodro. Entering it suddenly but silently they found four Moors asleep, whom they seized and threw over the battlements, and the Christians below immediately dispatched them. By this time a number more of Christians had mounted the ladder, and sallying forth sword in hand upon the wall they gained possession of several towers and of the gate of Martos. Throwing open the gate Pero Ruyz Tabur galloped in at the head of a squadron of horse, and by the dawn of day the whole suburb of Cordova, called the Axarquia, was in their possession; the inhabitants having hastily gathered such of their most valuable effects as they could carry with them, and taken refuge in the city.

The cavaliers now barricaded every street of the suburbs excepting the principal one, which was broad and straight; the Moors however, made frequent sallies upon them, or showered down darts and arrows and stones from the walls and towers of the city. The cavaliers soon found that they had got into warm quarters which it would cost them blood and toil to maintain. They sent off messengers therefore to Don Alvar Perez, then at Martos, and to King Fernando at Benevente, craving instant aid. The messenger to the king travelled day and night and found the king at table; when, kneeling down, he presented the letter with which he was charged.

No sooner had the king read the letter than he called for horse and weapon. All Benevente instantly resounded with the clang of arms and tramp of steed; couriers galloped off in every direction; rousing the towns and villages to arms; and ordering every one to join the king on the frontier. "Cordova! Cordova!" was the war cry. That proud city of the infidels; that seat of Moorish power! The king waited not to assemble a great force, but, within an hour after receiving the letter, was on the road with a hundred good cavaliers.

It was the depth of winter, the rivers were swollen with rain. The royal party were often obliged to halt on the bank of some raging stream until its waters should subside. The king was all anxiety and impatience. Cordova! Cordova! was the prize to be won, and the cavaliers might be driven out of the suburb before he could arrive to their assistance.

Arrived at Cordova he proceeded to the bridge of Alcolea where he pitched his tents and displayed the royal standard.

Before the arrival of the king Alvar Perez had hastened from the castle of Martos with a body of troops and thrown himself into the suburb. Many warriors both horse and foot had likewise hastened from the frontiers and from the various towns to which the king had sent his mandates. Some came to serve the king; others out of devotion to the holy faith; some to gain renown and not a few to aid in plundering the rich city of Cordova. There were many monks also who had come for the glory of God and the benefit of their convents.

When the Christians in the suburbs saw the royal standard flouting above the camp of the king they shouted for joy and in the exultation of the moment forgot all past dangers and hardships.

[CHAPTER VIII

A spy in the Christian camp—Death of Aben Hud—A vital blow to Moslem power—Surrender of Cordova to King Fernando.]

Aben Hud, the Moorish chief who had been defeated by Alvar Perez and Prince Alonzo before Xerez, was at this time in Ecija with a large force, and disposed to hasten to the aid of Cordova; but his recent defeat had made him cautious.

He had in his camp a Christian cavalier, Don Lorenzo Xuarez by name, who had been banished from Castile by King Fernando. This cavalier offered to go as a spy into the Christian camp accompanied by three Christian horsemen, and to bring accounts of its situation and strength. His offer was gladly accepted, and Aben Hud promised to do nothing with his forces until his return.

Don Lorenzo set out privately with his companions, and when he came to the end of the bridge he alighted and took one of the three with him, leaving the other two to guard the horses. He entered the camp without impediment and saw that it was small and of but little force; for, though recruits had repaired from all quarters, they had as yet arrived in but scanty numbers.

As Don Lorenzo approached the camp he saw a montero who stood sentinel. "Friend," said he, "do me the kindness to call to me some person who is about the king as I have something to tell him of great importance." The sentinel went in and brought out Don Otiella. Don Lorenzo took him aside and said, "Do you not know me? I am Don Lorenzo. I pray you tell the king that I entreat his permission to enter and communicate matters touching his safety."

Don Otiella went in and awoke the king, who was sleeping, and obtained permission for Don Lorenzo to enter. When the king beheld him he was wroth at his presuming to return from exile; but Don Lorenzo replied, "Señor, your majesty banished me to the land of the Moors to do me harm, but I believe it was intended by heaven for the welfare both of your majesty and myself." Then he apprised the king of the intention of Aben Hud to come with a great force against him; and of the doubts and fears he entertained lest the army of the king should be too powerful. Don Lorenzo, therefore, advised the king to draw off as many troops as could be spared from the suburbs of Cordova and to give his camp as formidable an aspect as possible; and that he would return and give Aben Hud such an account of the power of the royal camp as would deter him from the attack. "If," continued Don Lorenzo, "I fail in diverting him from his enterprise, I will come off with all my vassals and offer my self and all I can command, for the service of your majesty; and hope to be accepted for my good intentions.

As to what takes place in the Moorish camp, from hence in three days I will send your majesty letters by this my squire."

The king thanked Don Lorenzo for his good intentions and pardoned him, and took him as his vassal; and Don Lorenzo said, "I beseech your majesty to order that for three or four nights there be made great fires in various parts of the camp, so that in case Aben Hud should send scouts by night, there may be the appearance of a great host." The king promised it should be done, and Don Lorenzo took his leave. Rejoining his companions at the bridge, they mounted their horses and travelled all night and returned to Ecija.

When Don Lorenzo appeared in presence of Aben Hud he had the air of one fatigued and careworn. To the enquiries of the Moor he returned answers full of alarm, magnifying the power and condition of the royal forces. "Señor," added he, "if you would be assured of the truth of what I say send out your scouts, and they will behold the Christian tents whitening all the banks of the Guadalquivir and covering the country as the snow covers the mountains of Granada; or at night they will see fires on hill and dale illumining all the land."

This intelligence redoubled the doubts and apprehensions of Aben Hud. On the following day two Moorish horsemen arrived in all haste from Zaen, King of Valencia, informing him that King Jayme of Aragon was coming against that place with a powerful army, and offering him the supremacy of the place if he would hasten with all speed to its relief.

Aben Hud, thus perplexed between two objects, asked advice of his counsellors, among whom was the perfidious Don Lorenzo. They observed that the Christians, though they had possession of the suburbs of Cordova, could not for a long time master the place. He would have time, therefore, to relieve Valencia and then turn his arms and those of King Zaen against the host of King Fernando.

Aben Hud listened to their advice and marched immediately for Almeria, to take thence his ships to guard the port of Valencia. While at Almeria a Moor named Aben Arramin, and who was his especial favorite, invited him to a banquet. The unsuspecting Aben Hud threw off his cares for the time, and giving loose to conviviality in the house of his favorite drank freely of the wine cup that was insidiously pressed upon him until he became intoxicated. He was then suffocated by the traytor in a trough of water, and it was given out that he had died of apoplexy.

At the death of Aben Hud his host fell asunder, and every one hied him to his home, whereupon Don Lorenzo and the Christians who were with him hastened to King Fernando, by whom they were graciously received and admitted into his royal service.

The death of Aben Hud was a vital blow to Moslem power and spread confusion throughout Andalusia. When the people of Cordova heard of it, and of the dismemberment of his army, all courage withered from their hearts. Day after day the army of King Fernando was encreasing; the roads were covered with footsoldiers hastening to his standard; every hidalgo who could bestride a horse spurred to the banks of the Guadalquivir to be present at the downfall of Cordova. The noblest cavaliers of Castile were continually seen marching into the camp with banners flying and long trains of retainers.

The inhabitants held out as long as there was help or hope; but they were exhausted by frequent combats and long and encreasing famine, and now the death of Aben Hud cut off all chance of succour. With sad and broken spirits, therefore, they surrendered their noble city to King Fernando after a siege of six months and six days. The surrender took place on Sunday the twenty ninth day of July, on the feast of the glorious apostles St. Peter and St. Paul, in the year of the Incarnation one thousand two hundred and thirty six.

The inhabitants were permitted to march forth in personal safety but to take nothing with them. "Thus," exclaims the pious Agapida, "was the city of Cordova, the Queen of the Cities of Andalusia; which so long had been the seat of power and grandeur of the Moors, cleansed from all the impurities of Mahomet and restored to the dominion of the true faith."

King Fernando immediately ordered the cross to be elevated on the tower of the principal mosque, and beside it the royal standard; while the bishops, the clergy and all the people chaunted *Te Deum Laudamus* as a song of triumph for this great victory of the faith.* "The pious king," says Agapida, "having now gained full possession of the city began to repair, embellish and improve it. The Grand Mosque, which had been built with unparalleled splendor, in honor of the Arch-imposter Mahomet, and was the greatest and most magnificent in Spain, was now converted into a holy Catholic church. No pains were spared," continues he, "to cleanse it from every trace or taint of its former abominations." The bishops and other clergy walked round it in solemn procession sprinkling holy water in every nook and corner and performing all other rites and ceremonies necessary to purify and sanctify it. They erected an altar in it, also, in honor of the Virgin, and chaunted masses with great fervor and unction. In this way they consecrated it to the true faith and made it the cathedral of the city.

In this mosque were found the bells of the church of St. Iago in Gallicia, which the Alhagib Almazor in the year of our Redemption nine hundred and seventy five had brought off in triumph; and placed

* *Cron. Gen. de España*, part 4. Bleda, lib. 4, c. 10.

here, turned with their mouths upward to serve as lamps, and remain shining mementos of his victory. King Fernando ordered that these bells should be restored to the church of St. Iago, and Fray Antonio Agapida cites as an instance of even handed justice on the part of this excellent king, that as Christians had been obliged to bring those bells hither on their shoulders, so infidels were compelled in like manner to carry them back. "Great was the triumph," continues the worthy Agapida, "when these bells had their tongues restored to them and were once more enabled to fill the air with their holy clangour."

Having ordered all things for the security and welfare of the city, the king placed it under the government of Don Tello Alonzo de Meneses; he appointed Don Alvar Perez de Castro, also, General of the Frontier, having his strong hold in the castle of the Rock of Martos. The king then returned covered with glory to Toledo.

The fame of the recovery of the renowned city of Cordova, which for five hundred and twenty two years had been in the power of the infidels, soon spread throughout the kingdom, and people came crowding from every part to inhabit it. The gates which lately had been thronged with steel clad warriors were now besieged by peaceful wayfarers of all kinds; conducting trains of mules laden with their effects and all their household wealth; and so great was the throng that in a little while there were not houses sufficient to receive them.

King Fernando, having restored the bells to St. Iago, had others suspended in the tower of the mosque whence the muezzin had been accustomed to call the infidels to their worship. "When the pilgrims," says Fray Antonio Agapida, "who repaired to Cordova, heard the holy sound of these bells chiming from the tower of the cathedral, their hearts leaped for joy, and they invoked blessings on the head of the pious King Fernando."

[CHAPTER IX

Marriage of King Fernando to the Princess Juana—Famine at Cordova—Don Alvar Perez.]

When Queen Berenguela beheld King Fernando returning in triumph from the conquest of Cordova her heart was lifted up with transport, for there is nothing that more rejoices the heart of a mother than the true glory of her son. The queen, however, as has been abundantly shewn, was a woman of great sagacity and forecast. She considered that upwards of two years had elapsed since the death of the Queen Beatrix, and that her son was living in widowhood. It is true he was of quiet temperament and seemed sufficiently occupied by the cares of government and the wars for the faith; so that apparently he had no thought of further matrimony; but the shrewd mother considered likewise that he was in the prime and vigor of his days; renowned in arms, noble and commanding in person and gracious and captivating in manners, and surrounded by the temptations of a court. True he was a saint in spirit, but after all in flesh he was a man; and might be led away into those weaknesses very incident to, but highly unbecoming of the exalted state of princes. The good mother was anxious, therefore, that he should enter again into the secure and holy state of wedlock.

King Fernando was always a mirror of obedience to his mother, excepting when she endeavored to dissuade him from his wars with the Moors; he readily concurred with her views in the present instance, and left it to her judgment and discretion to make a choice for him. The choice fell upon the Princess Juana, daughter of the Count of Pothier and a descendant of Louis the Seventh of France. The marriage was negotiated by Queen Berenguela with the Count of Pothier; and the conditions being satisfactorily arranged the princess was conducted in due state to Burgos, where the nuptials were celebrated with great pomp and ceremony.

The king, as well as his subjects, was highly satisfied with the choice of the sage Berenguela, for the bride was young, beautiful and of stately form and conducted herself with admirable suavity and grace.

After the rejoicings were over King Fernando departed with his bride, and visited the principal cities and towns of Castile and Leon; receiving the homage of his subjects and administering justice according to the primitive forms of those days; when sovereigns attended personally to the petitions and complaints of their subjects, and went about hearing causes and redressing grievances.

In the course of his progress, while at Toledo, he received intelligence of a severe famine which prevailed at Cordova. The king thought readily to relieve the city by sending a large supply of money, and at the same time issuing orders to various parts to transport thither as much grain as possible. The calamity, however, went on encreasing. The conquest of Cordova had drawn thither great multitudes, expecting to thrive on the well known fertility and abundance of the country. But the Moors in the agitation of the time had almost ceased to cultivate their fields; the troops helped to consume the supplies on hand; there were few hands to labor and an infinity of mouths to eat; and the cry of famine went on daily growing more intense.

Upon this Don Alvar Perez, who had command of the frontier, set off to represent the case in person to the king; for one living word from the mouth is more effective than a thousand dead words from the pen. He found the king at Valladolid, deeply immersed in the religious exercises of holy week, and much did it grieve this saintly monarch, say his chroniclers, to be obliged even for a moment to quit the holy quiet of the church for the worldly bustle of the palace; to lay by the saint and enact the sovereign. Having heard the representations of Don Alvar Perez he forthwith gave him ample funds wherewith to maintain his castles, his soldiers and even the idlers who thronged about the frontier, and who would be useful subjects when the times should become settled. Satisfied also of the zeal and loyalty of Alvar Perez, which had been so strikingly displayed in the present instance, he appointed him adelantado of the whole frontier of Andalusia; an office equivalent to that at present called viceroy. Don Alvar hastened back to execute his mission and enter upon his new office. He took his station at Martos, in its rock built castle, which was the key of all that frontier; whence he could carry relief to any point of his command, and could make occasional incursions into the territories. The following chapter will shew the cares and anxieties which awaited him in his new command.

[CHAPTER X

Aben Alhamar, founder of the Alhambra—Fortifies Granada and makes it his capital—Attempts to surprise the Castle of Martos—Peril of the fortress—A woman's stratagem to save it—Diego Perez, the Smasher—Death of Count Alvar Perez de Castro.]

On the death of Aben Hud the Moorish power in Spain was broken up into factions, as has already been mentioned, but these factions were soon united under one head who threatened to be a formidable adversary to the Christians. This was Mohammed ben Alhamar, or Aben Alhamar, as he is commonly called in history. He was a native of Arjona, of noble descent, being of the Beni Nasar, or race of Nasar, and had been educated in a manner befitting his rank. Arrived at manly years, he had been appointed Alcayde of Arjona and Jaen and had distinguished himself by the justice and benignity of his rule. He was intrepid also, and ambitious; and during the late dissensions among the Moslems had extended his territories, making himself master of many strong places.

On the death of Aben Hud he made a military circuit through the Moorish territories and was everywhere hailed with acclamations, as the only one who could save the Moslem power in Spain from annihilation. At length he entered Granada amidst the enthusiastic shouts of the populace. Here he was proclaimed king and found himself at the head of the Moslems of Spain; being the first of his illustrious line that ever sat upon a throne. It needs nothing more to give lasting renown to Aben Alhamar than to say he was the founder of the Alhambra, that magnificent monument which to this day bears testimony to Moorish taste, and splendor. As yet, however, Aben Alhamar had not time to indulge in the arts of peace. He saw the storm of war that threatened his newly founded kingdom and prepared to buffet with it. The territories of Granada extended along the coast from Algeziras almost to Murcia, and inland as far as Jaen and Huescar. All the frontiers he hastened to put in a state of defence; while he strongly fortified the city of Granada, which he made his capital. By the Mahometan law every citizen is a soldier, and to take arms in defence of the country and the faith is a religious and imperative duty. Aben Alhamar, however, knew the unsteadiness of hastily levied militia and organized a standing force to garrison his forts and cities, the expense of which he defrayed from his own revenues. The Moslem warriors from all parts now rallied under his standard, and fifty thousand Moors, abandoning Valencia on the conquest of that country by the King of Aragon, hastened to put themselves under the dominion of Aben Alhamar.

Don Alvar Perez on returning to his post had intelligence of all these circumstances and perceived that he had not sufficient force to make head against such a formidable neighbor, and that in fact the whole frontier, so recently wrested from the Moors, was in danger of being reconquered. With his old maxim, therefore, "There is more life in one word from the mouth than in a thousand words from the pen," he determined to have another interview with King Fernando, and acquaint him with the imminent dangers impending over the frontier.

He accordingly took his departure with great secrecy; leaving his Countess and her women and donzellas in his castle of the Rock of Martos, guarded by his nephew Don Tello and forty chosen men.

The departure of Don Alvar Perez was not so secret however but that Aben Alhamar had notice of it by his spies, and he resolved to make an attempt to surprize the castle of Martos; which has been said, was the key to all this frontier.

Don Tello who had been left in command of the fortress was a young galliard, full of the fire, of youth, and he had several hardy and adventurous cavaliers with him, among whom was Diego Perez de Vargas, surnamed Machucha, or the Smasher; for his exploits at the battle of Xerez in smashing the heads of the Moors with the limb of an olive tree. These hot-blooded cavaliers, looking out like hawks from their mountain hold, were seized with an irresistible inclination to make a foray into the lands of their Moorish neighbors. On a bright morning they accordingly set forth, promising the donzellas of the castle to bring them jewels and rich silks, the spoils of Moorish women.

The cavaliers had not been long gone when the castle was alarmed by the sound of trumpets, and the watchman from the tower gave notice of a cloud of dust with Moorish banners and armour gleaming through it. It was in fact the Moorish king, Aben Alhamar, who pitched his tents before the castle.

Great was the consternation that reigned within the walls, for all the men were absent, excepting one or two necessary for the service of the castle. The dames and donzellas gave themselves up to despair, expecting to be carried away captive; perhaps to supply some Moorish harem. The Countess, however, was of an intrepid spirit and ready invention. Summoning her dueñas and damsels she made them arrange their hair and dress themselves like men; take weapons in hand and shew themselves between the battlements. The Moorish king was deceived and supposed the fort well garrisoned. He was deterred therefore from attempting to take it by storm. In the mean time she despatched a messenger by the postern gate with orders to speed swiftly in quest of Don Tello and tell him the peril of the fortress.

At hearing these tidings Don Tello and his companions turned their reins and spurred back for the castle, but on drawing nigh they saw from the hill, that it was invested by a numerous host who were battering the walls. It was an appalling sight, for it seemed hopeless to attempt to cut their way through such a force; yet their hearts were wrung with anguish at thinking of the Countess and her helpless donzellas exposed to such ferocious warfare.

Upon this Diego Perez de Vargas, surnamed Machucha, stepped forward and proposed to form a forlorn hope and attempt to force a passage to the castle. "If any of us succeed," said he, "we may save the Countess and the rock; if we fall we shall save our souls and act the parts of good cavaliers. This rock is the key of all the frontier, on which the king depends to get possession of the country. Shame would it be if Moors should capture it; above all if they should lead away our honored Countess and her ladies captive before our eyes while our lances remain unstained by blood and we unscarred with a wound. For my part I would rather die than see it. Life is but short; we should do in it our best. So in a word cavaliers, if you refuse to join me I will take my leave of you and do what I can with my single arm."

"Diego Perez," cried Don Tello, "You have spoken my very wishes; I will stand by you until the death, and let those who are good cavaliers and hidalgos follow our example."

The other cavaliers caught fire at these words; forming a solid squadron they put spurs to their horses and rushed down upon the Moors. The first who broke into the ranks of the enemy was Diego Perez, the Smasher, and he opened a way for the others. Their only object was to cut their way to the fortress, so they fought and pressed forward. The most of them got to the rock; some were cut off by the Moors and died like valiant knights, fighting to the last gasp.

When the Moorish king saw the daring of these cavaliers and that they had succeeded in reinforcing the garrison, he despaired of gaining the castle without much time, trouble and loss of blood. He persuaded himself, therefore, that it was not worth the price, and striking his tents, abandoned the siege. Thus the Rock of Martos was saved by the sagacity of the Countess and the prowess of Diego Perez de Vargas, otherwise called the Smasher.

In the mean time Don Alvar Perez de Castro had accomplished his mission to the king, whom he found at Hutiel. King Fernando received him with benignity, but seemed to think his zeal beyond his prudence; leaving so important a frontier so weakly guarded, sinking the viceroy in the courier, and coming so far to give by word of mouth what might easily have been communicated by letter. He felt the value, however, of his loyalty and devotion, but, furnishing him with ample funds, requested him to lose no time in getting back to his post. The count set out on his return, but it is probable the ardor and excitement of his spirit proved fatal to him, for he was seized with a violent fever when on the journey and died in the town of Orgaz.

[CHAPTER XI

Aben Hudiel, the Moorish King of Murcia, becomes the vassal of King Fernando—Aben Alhamar seeks to drive the Christians out of Andalusia—Fernando takes the field against him—Ravages of the king. His last meeting with the queen-mother.]

The death of Count Alvar Perez de Castro caused deep affliction to King Fernando; for he considered him the shield of the frontier. While he was at Cordova or at his Rock of Martos the king felt as assured of the safety of the border as though he had been there himself. As soon as he could be spared from Castile and Leon he hastened to Cordova to supply in person the loss the frontier had sustained in the person of his vigilant lieutenant. One of his first measures was to effect a truce of one year with the King of Granada; a measure which each adopted with great regret, compelled by his several policy: King Fernando to organize and secure his recent conquests; Aben Alhamar to regulate and fortify his newly founded kingdom. Each felt that he had a powerful enemy to encounter and a desperate struggle before him.

King Fernando remained at Cordova until the spring of the following year (1241) regulating the affairs of that noble city, assigning houses and castles to such of his cavaliers as had distinguished themselves in the conquest, and, as usual, making rich donations to towns and great tracts of land to the church and to different religious orders.* Leaving

* During this time there was an insurrection of a Moorish adventurer. See *Notas para la Vida*, p. 552.

his brother Alonzo with a sufficient force to keep an eye upon the King of Granada and hold him in check, King Fernando departed for Castile, making a circuit by Jaen and Baeza and Andujar and arriving in Toledo on the 4th of April. Here he received important propositions from Aben Hudiel, the Moorish King of Murcia. The death of Aben Hud had left that kingdom a scene of confusion. The alcaydes of the different cities and fortresses were at strife with each other, and many refused allegiance to Aben Hudiel. The latter too was in hostility with Aben Alhamar, the King of Granada, and he feared he would take advantage of his truce with King Fernando, and the distracted state of the kingdom of Murcia, to make an inroad. Thus desperately situated, Aben Hudiel had sent missives to King Fernando entreating his protection and offering to become his vassal.

The King of Castile gladly closed with this offer. He forthwith sent his son and heir the Prince Alfonso to receive the submission of the King of Murcia. As the prince was young and inexperienced in these affairs of state, he sent with him Don Pelayo de Correa, the Grand Master of Santiago; a cavalier of consummate wisdom and address, and also Rodrigo Gonzalez Giron. The prince was received in Murcia with regal honors; the terms were soon adjusted by which the Moorish king acknowledged vassalage to King Fernando and ceded to him one half of his revenues; in return for which the king graciously took him under his protection. The Alcaydes of Alicant, Elche, Oriola and several other places agreed to this covenant of vassalage, but it was indignantly spurned by the Wali of Lorca; he had been put in office by Aben Hud, and now that potentate was no more, he aspired to exercise an independent sway, and had placed alcaydes of his own party in Mula and Carthagena.

As the Prince Alfonso had come to solemnize the act of homage and vassalage proposed by the Moorish king, and not to extort submission from his subjects by force of arms, he contented himself with making a progress through the kingdom and receiving the homage of the acquiescent towns and cities, after which he rejoined his father in Castile.

It is conceived by the worthy Fray Antonio Agapida as well as by other monkish chroniclers, that this important acquisition of territory by the saintly Fernando was a boon from heaven in reward of an offering which he made to God of his daughter Berenguela; whom early in this year he dedicated as a nun in the convent of las Huelgas in Burgos; of which convent the king's sister Constanza was abbess.*

About this time it was that King Fernando gave an instance of his magnanimity and his chivalrous disposition. We have seen the deadly opposition he had experienced from the haughty house of Lara; and

* *Cronica del Rey Santo*, cap. 13.

the ruin which the three brothers brought upon themselves by their traitorous hostility. The anger of the king was appeased by their individual ruin; he did not desire to revenge himself upon their helpless families, nor to break down and annihilate a house lofty and honored in the traditions of Spain. One of the brothers, Don Fernan, had left a daughter, Doña Sancha Fernandez de Lara; there happened at this time to be in Spain a cousin german of the king, a prince of Portugal Don Fernando by name, who held the señoria of Serpa. Between this prince and Doña Sancha the king effected a marriage, whence has sprung one of the most illustrious branches of the ancient house of Lara.* The other daughters of Don Fernan, retained large possessions in Castile; and one of his sons will be found serving valiantly under the standard of the king.

In the mean time the truce with Aben Alhamar, the King of Granada, had greatly strengthened the hands of that monarch. He had received accessions of troops from various parts, had fortified his capital and his frontiers, and now fomented disturbances in the neighboring kingdom of Murcia; encouraging the refractory cities to persist in their refusal of vassalage; hoping to annex that kingdom to his own newly consolidated dominions.

The Wali of Lorca and his partizans the Alcaydes of Mula and Carthagena, thus instigated by the King of Granada, now encreased in turbulence and completely overawed the feeble handed Aben Hudiel. King Fernando thought this a good opportunity to give his son and heir his first essay in arms. He accordingly despatched the prince a second time to Murcia, accompanied as before by Don Pelayo de Correa, the Grand Master of Santiago; but he sent him now with a strong military force, to play the part of a conqueror. The conquest as may be supposed was easy; Mula, Lorca and Carthagena soon submitted; and the whole kingdom was reduced to vassalage; Fernando henceforth adding to his other titles King of Murcia. "Thus," says Fray Antonio Agapida, "was another precious jewel wrested from the kingdom of Antichrist and added to the crown of this saintly monarch."

But it was not in Murcia alone that King Fernando found himself called to contend with his new adversary, the King of Granada. That able and active monarch, strengthened as has been said during the late truce, had made bold forays in the frontiers recently conquered by King Fernando, and had even extended them to the neighborhood of Cordova. In all this he had been encouraged by some degree of negligence and inaction on the part of King Fernando's brother Alonzo, who had been left in charge of the frontier. The prince took the field against

* *Notas para la Vida del Santo Rey,* p. 554.

Aben Alhamar, and fought him manfully; but the Moorish force was too powerful to be withstood and the prince was defeated.

Tidings of this was sent to King Fernando, and of the great danger of the frontier; as Aben Alhamar, flushed with success, was aiming to drive the Christians out of Andalusia. King Fernando immediately set off for the frontier accompanied by the Queen Juana. He did not wait to levy a powerful force, but took with him a small number; knowing the loyalty of his subjects and their belligerent propensities, and that they would hasten to his standard the moment they knew he was in the field and exposed to danger. His force accordingly encreased as he advanced. At Andujar he met his brother Alonzo with the reliques of his lately defeated army; all brave and expert soldiers. He had now a commanding force, and leaving the queen with a sufficient guard at Andujar he set off with his brother Alonzo and Don Nuño Gonzalez de Lara, son of the Count Gonzalo, to scour the country about Arjona, Jaen and Alcandete. The Moors took refuge in their strong places, whence they saw with aching hearts the desolation of their country; olive plantations on fire; vineyards laid waste, groves and orchards cut down, and all the other modes of ravage practised in these unsparing wars.

The King of Granada did not venture to take the field; and King Fernando meeting no enemy to contend with; while ravaging the lands of Alcandete detached a part of his force under Don Rodrigo Fernandez de Castro, a son of the brave Alvar Perez lately deceased, and he associated with him Nuño Gonzalez, with orders to besiege Arjona. This was a place dear to Aben Alhamar, the King of Granada, being his native place where he had first tasted the sweets of power. Hence he was commonly called the King of Arjona.

The people of the place, though they had quailed before King Fernando, despised his officers and set them at defiance. The king himself, however, made his appearance on the following day with the remainder of his forces; whereupon Arjona capitulated.

While his troops were reposing from their fatigues, the king made some further ravages, and reduced several small towns to obedience. He then sent his brother Don Alonzo with sufficient forces to carry fire and sword into the Vega of Granada. In the mean time he returned to Andujar to the Queen Juana. He merely came, say the old chronicles, for the purpose of conducting her to Cordova; fulfilling always his duty as a cavalier, without neglecting that of a king.

The moment he had left her in her palace at Cordova he hastened back to join his brother in harassing the territories of Granada. He came in time; for Aben Alhamar, enraged at seeing the destruction of the vega, made such a vigorous sally that had Prince Alonzo been alone in command, he might have received a second lesson still more disastrous than the first. The presence of the king, however, put new spirits and valor into the troops; the Moors were driven back to the city and the Christians pursued them to the very gates. As the king had not sufficient forces with him to attempt the capture of this place, contenting himself with the mischief he had done, and with some more which he subsequently effected, he returned to Cordova to let his troops rest from their fatigues.

While the king was in this city a messenger arrived from his mother the Queen Berenguela informing him of her intention of coming to pay him a visit. A long time had elapsed since they had seen each other, and her extreme age rendered her anxious to embrace her son. The king, to prevent her from taking so long a journey, set off to meet her taking with him his Queen Juana. The meeting took place in Pezuelo near Burgos,* and was affecting on both sides, for never did son and mother love and honor each other more truly. In this interview the queen represented her age and encreasing weakness, and her incapacity to cope with the fatigues of public affairs; of which she had always shared the burden with the king. She therefore signified her wish to retire to her convent, to pass the remnant of her days in holy repose. King Fernando, who had ever found in his mother his ablest counsellor and best support, entreated her not to leave his side, in these arduous times, when the King of Granada on one side and the King of Seville on the other, threatened to put all his courage and resources to the trial. A long and earnest yet tender and affectionate conversation succeeded between them, which resulted in the queen mother's yielding to his solicitations. The illustrious son and mother remained together six weeks, enjoying each other's society, after which they separated, the king and queen for the frontier, and the queen mother for Toledo. They were never to behold each other again on earth, for the king never returned to Castile.

[CHAPTER XII

King Fernando's expedition to Andalusia—Siege of Jaen—Secret departure of Aben Alhamar for the Christian camp—He acknowledges himself the vassal of the king, who enters Jaen in triumph.]

It was in the middle of August 1245 that King Fernando set out on his grand expedition to Andalusia, whence he was never to return. All that autumn he pursued the same destructive course as in his preceding

---

* Some chronicles through mistake make it Pezuelo near Ciudad Real, in the mountains on the confines of Granada.

campaigns, laying waste the country with fire and sword in the vicinity of Jaen, and to Alcala la Real. The town too of Illora, built on a lofty rock and fancying itself secure, was captured and given a prey to flames; which was as a bale fire to the country. Thence he descended into the beautiful Vega of Granada, ravaging that earthly paradise. Aben Alhamar sallied forth from Granada with what forces he could collect, and a bloody battle ensued about twelve miles from Granada. A part of the troops of Aben Alhamar were hasty levies, inhabitants of the city and but little accustomed to combat; they lost courage, gave way and threw the better part of the troops in disorder; a retreat took place which ended in a headlong flight, in which there was great carnage.*

Content, for the present, with the ravage he had made and the victory he had gained, King Fernando now drew off his troops and repaired to his frontier hold of Martos where they might rest after their fatigues in security.

Here he was joined by Don Pelayo Perez Correa, the Grand Master of Santiago. This valiant cavalier, who was as sage and shrewd in council as he was adroit and daring in the field; had aided the youthful Prince Alfonso in completing the tranquilization of Murcia, and leaving him in the quiet administration of affairs in that kingdom had since been on a pious and political mission to the Court of Rome. He arrived most opportunely at Martos to aid the king with his counsels; for there was none in whose wisdom and loyalty the king had more confidence.

The grand master listened to all the plans of the king for the humiliation of the haughty King of Granada: he then gravely but most respectfully objected to the course the king was pursuing. He held the mere ravaging the country of little ultimate benefit. It harassed and irritated but did not destroy the enemy; while it fatigued and demoralized the army. To conquer the country they must not lay waste the field but take the towns. So long as the Moors retained their strong holds, so long they had dominion over the land. He advised therefore, as a signal blow to the power of the Moorish king, the capture of the city of Jaen. This was a city of immense strength, the bulwark of the kingdom; it was well supplied with provisions and the munitions of war; strongly garrisoned and commanded by Abu Omar, native of Cordova; a general of cavalry, and one of the bravest officers of Aben Alhamar. King Fernando had already besieged it in vain; but the reasoning of the grand master had either convinced his reason or touched his pride. He set himself down before the walls of Jaen, declaring he would never raise the siege until he was master of the place. For a long time the siege was carried on in the depth of winter, in defiance of rain and

---

* Conde, tome III. c. 5.

tempests. Aben Alhamar was in despair; he could not relieve the place; he could not again venture on a battle with the king after his late defeat. He saw that Jaen must fall; and feared it would be followed by the fall of Granada. He was a man of ardent spirit and quick and generous impulses. Taking a sudden resolution, he departed secretly for the Christian camp, and made his way to the presence of King Fernando. "Behold before you," said he, "the King of Granada. Resistance I find unavailing; I come trusting to your magnanimity and good faith to put myself under your protection and acknowledge myself your vassal." So saying he knelt and kissed the king's hand in token of homage.

King Fernando, say the old chroniclers, was not to be outdone in generosity. He raised his late enemy from the earth; embraced him as a friend, and left him in the sovereignty of his dominions; the good king however was as politic as he was generous. He received Aben Alhamar as a vassal: conditioned for the delivery of Jaen into his hands; for the yearly payment of one half of his revenues; for his attendance at the cortes as one of the nobles of the empire and his aiding Castile in war with a certain number of horsemen.

In compliance with these conditions Jaen was given up to the Christian king, who entered it in triumph, about the end of February.* His first care was to repair in grand procession bearing the holy cross to the principal mosque, which was purified and sanctified by the Bishop of Cordova and created into a cathedral and dedicated to the Most Holy Virgin Mary.

He remained some time in Jaen giving repose to his troops; regulating the affairs of this important place, disposing of houses and estates among his warriors who had most distinguished themselves, and amply rewarding the priests and monks who had aided him with their prayers.

As to Aben Alhamar, he returned to Granada relieved from apprehension of impending ruin to his kingdom, but deeply humiliated at having to come under the yoke of vassalage. He consoled himself by prosecuting the arts of peace; improving the condition of his people; building hospitals, founding institutions of learning, and beautifying his capital with those magnificent edifices which remain the admiration of posterity: for now it was that he commenced to build the Alhambra.

NOTE.—There is some dispute among historians as to the duration of the siege and the date of the surrender of Jaen. Some make the siege endure eight months; from August into the middle of April. The authentic Agapida adopts the opinion of the author of *Notas para la Vida del Santo Rey,* &c., who makes the siege begin on the 31st December and end about 26th February.

* *Notas para la Vida,* &c., p. 562.

[CHAPTER XIII

Axataf, King of Seville, exasperated at the submission of the King
of Granada—Rejects the propositions of King Fernando for a truce—
The latter is encouraged by a vision to undertake the conquest of the
city of Seville—Death of Queen Berenguela—A diplomatic marriage.]

King Fernando having reduced the fair kingdom of Granada to vassalage and fortified himself in Andalusia by the possession of the strong city of Jaen, bethought him now of returning to Castile. There was but one Moorish potentate in Spain whose hostilities he had to fear: this was Axataf, the King of Seville. He was the son of Aben Hud and succeeded to a portion of his territories. Warned by the signal defeat of his father at Xerez, he had forborne to take the field against the Christians, but had spared no pains and expense to put the city of Seville in the highest state of defense—strengthening its walls and towers; providing it with munitions of war of all kinds and exercising his people continually in the use of arms.

King Fernando was loth to leave this great frontier in its present unsettled state, with such a powerful enemy in the neighborhood who might take advantage of his absence to break into open hostility; still it was his policy to let the sword rest in the sheath until he had completely secured his new possessions. He sought, therefore, to make a truce with King Axataf, and, to enforce his propositions, it is said he appeared with his army before Seville in May 1246.* His propositions were rejected as it were at the very gate. It appears that the King of Seville was exasperated rather than dismayed by the submission of the King of Granada. He felt that on himself depended the last hope of Islamism in Spain; he trusted on aid from the coast of Barbary, with which his capital had ready communication by water; and he resolved to make a bold stand in the cause of his faith.

King Fernando retired indignant from before Seville, and repaired to Cordova with the pious determination to punish the obstinacy and humble the pride of this proud infidel by planting the standard of the cross on the walls of his capital. Seville once in his power, the rest of Andalusia would soon follow, and then his triumph over the Sect of Mahomet would be complete. Other reasons may have concurred to make him covet the conquest of Seville. It was a city of great splendor and wealth: situated in the midst of a fertile country, in a genial climate,

* *Notas para la Vida del Santo Rey,* p. 572.

under a benignant sky; and having by its river the Guadalquivir an open highway for commerce, it was the metropolis of all Morisma; a world of wealth and delight within itself.

These were sufficient reasons for aiming at the conquest of this famous city, but these were not sufficient to satisfy the holy friars who have written the history of this monarch; and who have found a reason more befitting his character of saint. Accordingly we are told by the worthy Fray Antonio Agapida, that at a time when the king was in deep affliction for the death of his mother, the Queen Berenguela, and was praying with great fervor, there appeared before him Saint Isidro, the great apostle of Spain, who had been Archbishop of Seville in old times before the perdition of Spain by the Moors. As the monarch gazed in reverend wonder at the vision the saint laid on him a solemn injunction to rescue from the empire of Mahomet his city of Seville, "que asi la llamo por suya en la patria, suya en la silla, y suya en la proteccion." "Such," says Agapida, "was the true reason why this pious king undertook the conquest of Seville;" and in this assertion he is supported by many Spanish chroniclers; and by the traditions of the church, the vision of San Isidro being read to this day among its services.[*]

The death of Queen Berenguela, to which we have just adverted, happened some months after the conquest of Jaen and submission of Granada. The grief of the king on hearing the tidings, we are told, was past description. For a time it quite overwhelmed him. "Nor is it much to be marvelled at," says an old chronicler; "for never did monarch lose a mother so noble and magnanimous in all her actions. She was indeed accomplished in all things; an example of every virtue; the mirror of Castile and Leon and all Spain; by whose counsel and wisdom the affairs of many kingdoms were governed. This noble queen," continues the chronicler, "was deplored in all the cities, towns and villages of Castile and Leon; by all people great and small but *especially by poor cavaliers*, to whom she was ever a benefactor."[†]

Another heavy loss to King Fernando about this time was that of the Archbishop of Toledo, Don Rodrigo, the great adviser of the king in all his expeditions and the prelate who first preached the grand crusade in Spain. He lived a life of piety, activity and zeal and died full of years, of honors and of riches; having received princely estates and vast revenues from the king in reward of his services in the cause.

These private afflictions for a time occupied the royal mind: the king was also a little disturbed by some rash proceedings of his son the

[*] Rodriguez, *Memorias del Santo Rey*, c. LVIII.
[†] *Cronica del Rey Don Fernando*, c. XIII.

hereditary Prince Alfonso, who, being left in the government of Murcia, took a notion of imitating his father in his conquests and made an inroad into the Moorish kingdom of Valencia, at that time in a state of confusion. This brought on a collision with King Jayme of Aragon, surnamed the Conqueror, who had laid his hand upon all Valencia as his by right of arms. There was thus danger of a rupture with Aragon, and of King Fernando having an enemy on his back, while busied in his wars in Andalusia. Fortunately King Jayme had a fair daughter, the Princess Violante, and the grave diplomatists of the two courts determined that, it were better the two children should marry, than the two fathers should fight. To this arrangement King Fernando and King Jayme gladly assented. They were both of the same faith; both proud of the name of Christian; both zealous in driving Mahometanism out of Spain, and in augmenting their empires with its spoils. The marriage was accordingly solemnized in Valladolid in the month of November in this same year: and now the saintly King Fernando turned his whole energies to this great and crowning achievement, the conquest of Seville; the emporium of Mahometanism in Spain.

Foreseeing as long as the mouth of the Guadalquivir was open, the city could receive reinforcements and supplies from Africa; the king held consultations with a wealthy man of Burgos, Ramon Bonifaz, or Boniface, by name, some say a native of France, one well experienced in maritime affairs and capable of fitting out and managing a fleet. This man he constituted his admiral and sent him to Biscay, to provide and arm a fleet of ships and galleys with which to attack Seville by water while the king should invest it by land.

[CHAPTER XIV

Investment of Seville—All Spain aroused to arms—Surrender of Alcala Del Rio—The fleet of Admiral Ramon Bonifaz advances up the Guadalquivir—Don Pelayo Correa Master of Santiago—His valorous deeds and the miracles wrought in his behalf.]

When it was bruited abroad that King Fernando the Saint intended to besiege the great city of Seville, all Spain was roused to arms. The masters of the various military and religious orders, the ricos hombres, the princes, cavaliers, hidalgos, and every one of Castile and Leon capable of bearing arms prepared to take the field. Many of the nobility of Catalonia and Portugal repaired to the standard of the king, as did other cavaliers of worth and prowess from lands far beyond the Pyrenees.

Prelates, priests and monks likewise thronged to the army; some to take care of the souls of those who hazarded their lives in this holy enterprize; others with a zealous determination to grasp buckler and lance, and battle with the arm of flesh against the enemies of God and the church.

At the opening of spring the assembled host issued forth in shining array from the gates of Cordova. After having gained possession of Carmona, and Lora, and Alcolea, and other neighboring places; some by voluntary surrender, others by force of arms; the king crossed the Guadalquivir, with great difficulty and peril, and made himself master of several of the most important posts in the neighborhood of Seville. Among these was Alcala del Rio, a place of great consequence, through which passed all the succours from the mountains to the city. This place was bravely defended by Axataf in person, the commander of Seville. He remained in Alcala with three hundred Moorish cavaliers, making frequent sallies upon the Christians, and effecting great slaughter. At length he beheld all the country around laid waste, the grain burnt or trampled down, the vineyards torn up, the cattle driven away and the villages consumed; so that nothing remained to give sustenance to the garrison or the inhabitants. Not daring to linger there any longer, he departed secretly in the night and retired to Seville, and the town surrendered to King Fernando.

While the king was putting Alcala del Rio in a state of defence, Admiral Ramon Bonifaz arrived at the mouth of the Guadalquivir with a fleet of thirteen large ships and several small vessels and galleys. While he was yet hovering about the land, he heard of the approach of a great force of ships from Tangier, Ceuta and Seville, and of an army to assail him from the shores. In this peril he sent in all speed for succour to the king. When it reached the sea coast the enemy had not yet appeared, wherefore thinking it a false alarm, the reinforcement returned to the camp. Scarcely, however, had it departed when the Africans came swarming over the sea and fell upon Ramon Bonifaz with a greatly superior force. The Admiral, in no ways dismayed, defended himself vigorously, sank several of the enemy, took a few prizes, and put the rest to flight, remaining master of the river. The king had heard of the peril of the fleet, and crossing the ford of the river had hastened to its aid, but when he came to the sea coast, he found it victorious, at which he was greatly rejoiced, and commanded that it should advance higher up the river.

It was on the twentieth of the month of August that King Fernando began formally the siege of Seville, having encamped his troops, small in number, but of stout hearts and valiant hands, near to the city on the banks of the river. From hence Don Pelayo Correa, the valiant Master of St. Iago, with two hundred and sixty horsemen, many of whom were warlike friars, attempted to cross the river at the ford below Aznal Farache. Upon this Aben Amaken, Moorish King of Niebla, sallied forth with a great host to defend the pass, and the cavaliers were exposed to imminent peril, until the king sent one hundred cavaliers to their aid, led on by Rodrigo Flores and Alonzo Tellez and Fernan Diañez.

Thus reinforced, the Master of St. Iago scoured the opposite side of the river, and with his little army of scarce four hundred horsemen, mingled monks and soldiers, spread dismay throughout the country. They attacked the town of Gelbes, and after a desperate combat, entered it sword in hand, slaying or capturing the Moors and making rich booty. They made repeated assaults upon the castle of Triana, and had bloody combats with its garrison, but could not take the place. This hardy band of cavaliers had pitched their tents and formed their little camp on the banks of the river, below the castle of Aznal Farache. This fortress was situated on an eminence above the river, and its massive ruins, remaining at the present day, attest its formidable strength.

When the Moors from their castle towers looked down upon this little camp of Christian cavaliers, and saw them sallying forth, and careering about the country and returning in the evenings with cavalgadas of sheep and cattle, and mules laden with spoil, and long trains of captives, they were exceedingly wroth. And they kept a watch upon them, and sallied forth every day to fight with them, and to intercept stragglers from their camp, and to carry off their horses. Then the cavaliers concerted together, and they lay in ambush one day in the road by which the Moors were accustomed to sally forth. And when the Moors had partly passed their ambush they rushed forth, and fell upon them, and killed and captured above three hundred, and pursued the remainder to the very gates of the castle. From that time the Moors were so disheartened that they made no further sallies.

Shortly after, the Master of St. Iago receiving secret intelligence that a Moorish sea captain had passed from Seville to Triana, on his way to succour the castle of Aznal Farache, placed himself, with a number of chosen cavaliers, in ambuscade at a pass by which the Moors were expected to come. After waiting a long time their scouts brought word that the Moors had taken another road and were nearly at the foot of the hill on which stood the castle. "Cavaliers," cried the master, "it is not too late; let us first use our spurs, and then our weapons, and if our steeds prove good, the day will yet be ours." So saying he put spurs to his horse, and the rest following his example, they soon came in sight of the Moors. The latter, seeing the Christians coming after them full speed, urged their horses up the hill, towards the castle; but the Christians overtook them and slew seven of those in the rear. In the skirmish Garci Perez struck the Moorish captain from his horse with a blow of his lance. The Christians rushed forward to take him prisoner. On seeing this the Moors turned back, threw themselves between their commander and his assailants and kept the latter in check, while he was conveyed into the castle. Several of them fell covered with wounds; the residue, seeing their chieftain safe, turned their reins and galloped for the castle, just entering in time to have the gates closed upon their pursuers.

Time and space permit not to recount the many other valorous deeds of Don Pelayo Correa, the good Master of St. Iago, and his band of cavaliers and monks. His little camp became a terror to the neighborhood and checked the sallies of the Moorish mountaineers from the Sierra Morena. In one of his enterprizes he gained a signal advantage over the foe, but the approach of night threatened to defraud him of his victory. Then the pious warrior lifted up his voice and supplicated the Virgin Mary in those celebrated words, "Santa Maria deten tu dia," ("Holy Mary detain thy day") for it was one of the days consecrated to the Virgin. The blessed Virgin listened to the prayer of her valiant votary; the day light continued in a supernatural manner, until the victory of the good Master of St. Iago was completed. In honour of this signal favour he afterwards erected a temple to the Virgin, by the name of Nuestra Señora de Tentudia.*

If any one should doubt this miracle, wrought in favour of this pious warrior and his soldiers of the cowl, it may be sufficient to relate another, which immediately succeeded and which shews how peculiarly he was under the favour of heaven. After the battle was over his followers were ready to faint with thirst, and could find no stream or fountain; and when the good master saw the distress of his soldiers, his heart was touched with compassion, and bethinking himself of the miracle performed by Moses, in an impulse of holy zeal and confidence, and in the name of the blessed Virgin, he struck a dry and barren rock with his lance, and instantly there gushed forth a fountain of water, at which all his Christian soldiery drank and were refreshed.† So much at present for the good Master of St. Iago, Don Pelayo Correa.

[CHAPTER XV

King Fernando changes his camp—Garci Perez and the seven Moors.]

King Fernando the Saint soon found his encampment on the banks of the Guadalquivir too much exposed to the sudden sallies and insults

---

* Zuniga, *Annales de Sevilla*, L. 1.

† Jacob Paranes, *Lib. de los Maestros de St. Iago. Corona Gotica,* T. 3, § xiii. Zuniga, *Annales de Sevilla.*

of the Moors. As the land was level they easily scoured the fields; carried off horses and stragglers from the camp, and kept it in continual alarm. He drew off therefore to a securer place, called Tablada, the same where at present is situated the hermitage of Neustra Señora de el Balme. Here he had a profound ditch digged all round the camp, to shut up the passes from the Moorish cavalry. He appointed patrols of horsemen also, completely armed, who continually made the rounds of the camp, in successive bands, at all hours of the day and night.[*] In a little while his army was encreased by the arrival of troops from all parts; nobles, cavaliers and rich men, with their retainers, nor were there wanting holy prelates, who assumed the warrior, and brought large squadrons of well armed vassals to the army. Merchants and artificers now daily arrived, and wandering minstrels, and people of all sorts, and the camp appeared like a warlike city; where rich and sumptuous merchandize was mingled with the splendour of arms; and the various colours of the tents and pavilions, and the fluttering standards and pennons, bearing the painted devices of the proudest houses of Spain, were gay and glorious to behold.

When the king had established the camp in Tablada he ordered that every day the foragers should sally forth in search of provisions and provender, guarded by strong bodies of troops. The various chiefs of the army took turns to command the guard who escorted the foragers. One day it was the turn of Garci Perez, the same cavalier who had killed the king of the Gazules. He was a hardy, iron warrior; seasoned, and scarred in warfare, and renowned among both Moors and Christians for his great prowess, his daring courage and his coolness in the midst of danger. Garci Perez had lingered in the camp until some time after the foragers had departed, who were already out of sight. He at length set out to join them accompanied by another cavalier. They had not proceeded far before they perceived seven Moorish genetes or light horsemen directly in their road. When the companion of Garci Perez beheld such a formidable array of foes he paused and said, "Señor Perez, let us return; the Moors are seven and we but two, and there is no law in the duello which obliges us to make front against such fearful odds."

To this Garci Perez replied, "Señor, forward, always forward; let us continue on our road, those Moors will never wait for us." The other cavalier, however, exclaimed against such rashness and turning the reins of his horse, returned as privately as possible to the camp and hastened to his tent.

All this happened within sight of the camp. The king was at the door of his royal tent, which stood on a rising ground and overlooked the

[*] *Corona Gotica*, T. 3, § viii.

place where this occurred. When the king saw one cavalier return and the other continue notwithstanding that there were seven Moors in the road; he ordered that some horsemen should ride forth to his aid.

Upon this Don Lorenzo Xuarez, who was with the king and had seen Garci Perez sally forth from the camp, said, "Your majesty may let that cavalier to himself—that is Garci Perez, and he has no need of aid against seven Moors. If the Moors know him they will not meddle with him, and if they do, your majesty will see what kind of a cavalier he is."

They continued to watch the cavalier, who rode on tranquilly, as if in no apprehension. When he drew nigh to the Moors, who were drawn up on each side of the road, he took his arms from his squire, and ordered him not to separate from him. As he was lacing his *morion*, an embroidered cap which he wore on his head fell to the ground without his perceiving it. Having laced the capellina he continued on his way, and his squire after him. When the Moors saw him near by, they knew by his arms that it was Garci Perez, and bethinking them of his great renown for terrible deeds in arms, they did not dare to attack him but went along the road even with him, he on one side, they on the other, making menaces.

Garci Perez went on his road with great serenity without making any movement. When the Moors saw that he heeded not their menaces, they turned round and went back to about the place where he had dropped his cap.

Having arrived at some distance from the Moors, he took off his arms to return them to the squire, and unlacing the capellina, found that the cap was wanting. He asked the squire for it but the latter knew nothing about it. Seeing that it had fallen he again demanded his arms of the squire and returned in search of it, telling his squire to keep close behind him and look out well for it. The squire remonstrated. "What Señor," said he, "will you return and place yourself in such great peril for a mere copia? Have you not already done enough for your honour, in passing so daringly by seven Moors, and have you not been singularly favoured by fortune in escaping unhurt—and do you seek again to tempt fortune for a cap?" "Say no more," replied Garci Perez. "That cap was worked for me by a fair lady; I hold it of great value. Besides dost thou not see that I have not a head to be without a cap?"—alluding to the baldness of his head, which had no hair in front. So saying he tranquilly returned towards the Moors. When Don Lorenzo Xuarez saw this he said to the king: "Behold! your majesty, how Garci Perez turns upon the Moors; since they will not make an attack he means to attack them. Now your majesty will see the noble valour of this cavalier if the Moors dare to await him." When the Moors beheld Garci Perez approaching they thought he meant to assault them; they drew off, not daring to encounter him. When Don Lorenzo saw this he exclaimed,

"Behold! your majesty, the truth of what I told you. These Moors dare not wait for him. I knew well the valour of Garci Perez and it appears the Moors are aware of it likewise."

In the mean time Garci Perez came to the place where the copia had fallen and beheld it upon the earth. Then he ordered his squire to dismount and pick it up, and putting it deliberately on his head he continued on his way to the foragers.

When he returned to the camp from guarding the herberos, Don Lorenzo asked him, in presence of the king, who was the cavalier who had set out with him from the camp, but had turned back on sight of the Moors; he replied that he did not know him, and was confused, for he perceived that the king had witnessed what had passed, and he was so modest withal that he was ever embarrassed when his deeds were praised in his presence.

Don Lorenzo repeatedly asked him who was the recreant cavalier, but he always replied that he did not know—although he knew full well; and saw him daily in the camp. But he was too generous to say any thing that should take away the fame of another, and he charged his squire that never, by word or look, he should betray the secret. So that, though enquiries were often made, the name of that cavalier was never discovered.

[CHAPTER XVI

Of the raft built by the Moors, and how it was boarded by Admiral Bonifaz—Destruction of the Moorish fleet—Succor from Africa.]

While the army of King Fernando the Saint harassed the city by land, and cut off its supplies, the bold Bonifaz with his fleet shut up the river, prevented all succour from Africa, and menaced to attack the bridge between Triana and Seville, by which the city derived its sustenance from the opposite country. The Moors saw their peril. If this pass were destroyed famine must be the consequence, and the multitude of their soldiers, on which at present they relied for safety, would then become the cause of their destruction.

So the Moors devised a machine, by which they hoped to sweep the river and involve the invading fleet in ruin. They made a raft so wide that it reached from one bank to the other. And they placed all around it, pots and vessels filled with resin, pitch, tar and other combustibles, forming what is called Greek fire; and upon it was a great number of armed men. And on each shore, from the castle of Triana on the one side, and from the city on the other, sallied forth legions of troops, to advance at the same time with the raft. And the raft was preceded by several vessels well armed, to attack the Christian ships, while the soldiers on the raft should hurl on board their pots of fire, and at length, setting all the combustibles in a blaze, should send the raft flaming into the midst of the hostile fleet and wrap it in one general conflagration.

When every thing was prepared the Moors set off, by land and water, confident of success. But they proceeded in a wild, irregular manner; shouting, and sounding drums and trumpets, and began to attack the Christian ships fiercely, but without concert, hurling their pots of fire from a distance, filling the air with smoke, but falling short of their enemy. The tumultuous uproar of their preparations had put all the Christians on their guard. The bold Bonifaz waited not to be assailed; he boarded the raft, attacked vigorously its defenders, put many of them to the sword and drove the rest into the water, and succeeded in extinguishing the Greek fire. He then encountered the ships of war, grappling them, and fighting hand to hand from ship to ship. The action was furious and bloody and lasted all the day. Many were cut down in fight, many fell into the water, and many in despair threw themselves in and were drowned.

The battle had raged no less fiercely upon the land. On the side of Seville the troops had issued from the camp of King Fernando, while on the opposite shore the brave Master of St. Iago, Don Pelayo Perez Correa, with his warriors and fighting friars, had made sharp work with the enemy. In this way a triple battle was carried on; there was the rush of squadrons, the clash of arms, and the din of drums and trumpets on either bank, while the river was covered with vessels, tearing each other to pieces as it were, their crews fighting in the midst of flames and smoke, the waves red with blood and filled with the bodies of the slain. At length the Christians were victorious; most of the enemies' vessels were taken or destroyed, and on either shore the Moors, broken and discomfited, fled, those on the one side for the gates of Seville, and those on the other, for the castle of Triana, pursued with great slaughter by the victors.

Notwithstanding the great destruction of their fleet, the Moors soon renewed their attempts upon the ships of Ramon Bonifaz, for they knew that the salvation of the city required the freedom of the river. Succour arrived from Africa, of ships, with troops and provisions; they rebuilt the fire ships which had been destroyed, and incessant combats, feints, and stratagems took place daily, both on land and water. The Admiral stood in great dread of the Greek fire used by the Moors. He caused large stakes of wood to be placed in the river to prevent the passage of the fire ships. This for some time was of avail; but the Moors, watching an opportunity when the centinels were asleep, came and threw cables round the stakes, and fastening the other ends to their vessels, made all sail and by the help of wind and oars, tore away the stakes and carried them off with shouts of triumph. The clamourous exultation of the Moors betrayed them. The Admiral Bonifaz was aroused. With a few of the lightest of his vessels he immediately pursued the enemy. He came upon them so suddenly, that they were too much bewildered either to fight or fly. Some threw themselves into the waves in affright, others attempted to make resistance and were cut down. The Admiral took four barks laden with arms and provisions, and with these returned in triumph to his fleet.*

[CHAPTER XVII

Of the stout prior, Ferran Ruyz, and how he rescued his cattle from the Moors—Further enterprises of the prior, and of the ambuscade into which he fell.]

It happened one day that a great part of the cavaliers of the army were absent, some making cavalgadas about the country, others guarding the foragers, and others gone to receive the Prince Alfonso, who was on his way to the camp from Murcia. At this time ten Moorish cavaliers, of the brave lineage of the Gazules, finding the Christian camp but thinly peopled, came prowling about, seeking where they might make a bold inroad. As they were on the lookout they came to that part of the camp where were the tents of the stout Friar Ferran Ruyz, Prior of the Hospital. The Stout Prior, and his fighting brethren, were as good at foraging as fighting. Around their quarters there were several sleek cows grazing, which they had carried off from the Moors. When the Gazules saw these they thought to make a good prize and to bear off the Prior's cattle as a trophy. Careering lightly round, therefore, between the cattle and the camp, they began to drive them towards the city. The alarm was given in the camp and six sturdy friars sallied forth on foot, with two cavaliers, in pursuit of the marauders. The Prior himself was roused by the noise; when he heard that the beeves of the church were in danger his ire was kindled, and buckling on his armour he mounted his steed and galloped furiously to the aid of his valiant friars, and the rescue of his cattle. The Moors attempted to urge on the lagging and full fed kine, but finding the enemy close upon them they were obliged to abandon their spoil among the olive trees and to retreat. The Prior then gave the cattle in charge to a squire to drive back to the camp. He would have returned himself, but his friars had con-

* *Corona Gotica*, L. 3, § 13. *Cronica General*, part 4. *Cronica de Santo Rey*, c. 55.

tinued on for some distance. The Stout Prior therefore gave spurs to his horse and galloped beyond them, to turn them back. Suddenly a great shout and cries arose before and behind him, and an ambuscade of Moors, both horse and foot, came rushing out of a ravine. The Stout Prior of St. Juan saw that there was no retreat; and he disdained to render himself a prisoner. Commending himself to his patron saint and bracing his shield, he charged bravely among the Moors and began to lay about him with a holy zeal of spirit and a vigorous arm of flesh. Every blow that he gave was in the name of St. Juan, and every blow laid an infidel in the dust. His friars, seeing the peril of their leader, came running to his aid, accompanied by a number of cavaliers. They rushed into the fight shouting, "St. Juan! St. Juan!" and began to deal such sturdy blows as savoured more of the camp than of the cloister. Great and fierce was this struggle between cowl and turban. The ground was strewn with bodies of the infidels; but the Christians were a mere handful among a multitude. A burly friar, commander of Sietefilla, was struck to the earth, and his shaven head cleft by a blow of a scymetar. Several squires and cavaliers, to the number of twenty, fell covered with wounds; yet still the Stout Prior and his brethren continued fighting with desperate fury, shouting incessantly, "St. Juan! St. Juan!" and dealing their blows with as good heart as they had ever dealt benedictions on their followers.

The noise of this skirmish, and the holy shouts of the fighting friars, resounded through the camp. The alarm was given, "The Prior of St. Juan is surrounded by the enemy! To the rescue! to the rescue!" The whole Christian host was in agitation, but none were so alert as those holy warriors of the church Don Garcia, Bishop of Cordova, and Don Sancho, Bishop of Coria. Hastily summoning their vassals, horse and foot, they bestrode their steeds, with cuirass over cassock, and lance instead of crosier, and set off at full gallop to the rescue of their brother saints.

When the Moors saw the warrior bishops and their retainers, scouring to the field, they gave over the contest and, leaving the Prior and his companions, they drew off towards the city. Their retreat was soon changed to a headlong flight, for the bishops, not content with rescuing the Prior, continued in pursuit of his assailants. The Moorish footsoldiers were soon overtaken and either slaughtered or made prisoners, nor did the horsemen make good their retreat into the city, until the powerful arm of the church had visited their rear with pious vengeance.* Nor did the chastisement of heaven end here. The Stout Prior of the Hospital being once aroused was full of ardour and enterprize. Concerting with the Prince Don Enrique and the Masters of Calatrava

* *Cronica General*, part 4, p. 338.

and Alcantara and the valiant Lorenzo Xuarez, they made a sudden assault by night on the suburb of Seville called Benaljofar, and broke their way into it with fire and sword. The Moors were roused from their sleep by the flames of their dwellings, and the shouts of the Christians. There was hard and bloody fighting. The Prior of the Hospital with his valiant friars were in the fiercest of the action, and their war cry of "St. Juan! St. Juan!" was heard in all parts of the suburb. Many houses were burnt; many sacked, many Moors slain or taken prisoners, and the Christian knights and warrior friars having gathered together a great cavalgada of the flocks and herds which were in the suburb, drove it off in triumph to the camp, by the light of the blazing dwellings.

A like inroad was made by the Prior and the same cavaliers, a few nights afterwards, into the suburb, called Macarena, which they laid waste in like manner, bearing off wealthy spoils. Such was the pious vengeance which the Moors brought upon themselves by meddling with the kine of the Stout Prior of the Hospital.

[CHAPTER XVIII

Bravado of the three cavaliers—Ambush at the bridge over the Guadayra—Desperate valor of Garci Perez—Grand attempt of Admiral Bonifaz on the bridge of boats—Seville dismembered from Triana.]

Of all the Christian cavaliers who distinguished themselves in this renowned Siege of Seville, there was none who surpassed in valour the bold Garci Perez de Vargas. This hardy knight was truly enamoured of danger, and like a gamester with his gold, he seemed to have no pleasure of his life except in putting it in constant jeopardy. One of the greatest friends of Garci Perez was Don Lorenzo Xuarez Gallinato, the same who had boasted of the valour of Garci Perez at the time that he exposed himself to be attacked by seven Moorish horsemen. They were not merely companions but rivals in arms; for in this siege it was the custom among the Christian knights to vie with each other in acts of daring enterprize.

One morning as Garci Perez, Don Lorenzo Xuarez and a third cavalier named Tello Alonzo were on horseback patrolling the skirts of the camp, a friendly contest rose between them as to who was the most adventurous in arms. To settle the question it was determined to put the proof to the Moors, by going alone and striking the points of their lances in the gate of the city.

No sooner was this mad bravado agreed upon than they turned the reins of their horses and made for Seville. The Moorish centinels from the towers of the gate saw three Christian knights advancing over the plain, and supposed them to be messengers or deserters from the army. When the cavaliers drew near each struck his lance against the gate, and wheeling round, put his spurs to his horse and retreated. The Moors, considering this a scornful defiance, were violently exasperated and sallied forth in great numbers to revenge the insult. They soon were hard on the traces of the Christian cavaliers. The first who turned to fight with them was Tello Alonzo, being of a fiery and impatient spirit. The second was Garci Perez; the third was Don Lorenzo, who waited until the Moors came up with them when he braced his shield, couched his lance and took the whole brunt of their charge. A desperate fight took place; for though the Moors were overwhelming in number the cavaliers were three of the most valiant warriors in Spain. The conflict was beheld from the camp. The alarm was given, the Christian cavaliers hastened to the rescue of their companions in arms; squadron after squadron pressed to the field, the Moors poured out reenforcements from the gate; in this way a general battle ensued which lasted a great part of the day until the Moors were vanquished and driven within their walls.

There was one of the gates of Seville, called the Gate of the Alcazar, which led out to a small bridge over the Guadayra. Out of this gate the Moors used to make frequent sallies, to fall suddenly upon the Christian camp, or to sweep off the flocks and herds about its outskirts, and then to scour back to the bridge, beyond which it was dangerous to pursue them.

The defence of this part of the camp was entrusted to those two valiant compeers in arms, Garci Perez de Vargas, and Don Lorenzo Xuarez; and they determined to take ample revenge upon the Moors for all the depredations they had committed. They chose therefore about two hundred hardy cavaliers, the flower of those seasoned warriors on the opposite side of the Guadalquivir, who formed the little army of the good Master of St. Iago. When they were all assembled together Don Lorenzo put them in ambush, in the way by which the Moors were accustomed to pass in their maraudings, and he instructed them in pursuing the Moors, to stop at the bridge, and by no means to pass beyond it, for between it and the city there was a great host of the enemy, and the bridge was so narrow that to retreat over it would be perilous in the extreme. This order was given to all, but was particularly intended for Garci Perez, to restrain his daring spirit which was ever apt to run into peril.

They had not been long in ambush when they heard the distant tramp of the enemy upon the bridge and found that the Moors were upon the forage. They kept close concealed and the Moors passed by them in

careless and irregular manner as men apprehending no danger. Scarce
had they gone by when the cavaliers rushed forth, charged into the
midst of them, and threw them all into confusion. Many were killed or
overthrown in the shock. The rest took to flight, and made at full speed
for the bridge. Most of the Christian soldiers, according to orders,
stopped at the bridge, but Don Lorenzo with a few of his cavaliers
followed the enemy half way across, making great havoc in that narrow
pass. Many of the Moors in their panic flung themselves from the bridge
and perished in the Guadayra. Others were cut down and trampled
under the hoofs of friends and foes. And Don Lorenzo in the heat of
the fight cried aloud incessantly, defying the Moors, and proclaiming
his name. "Turn hither! turn hither! 'Tis I, Lorenzo Xuarez!" But few
of the Moors cared to look him in the face.

Don Lorenzo now returned to his cavaliers, but on looking round,
Garci Perez was not to be seen. All were dismayed, fearing some evil
fortune had befallen him; when on casting their eyes beyond the bridge,
they saw him on the opposite side surrounded by Moors and fighting
with desperate valour.

"Garci Perez has deceived us," said Don Lorenzo, "and has passed
the bridge contrary to agreement. But to the rescue, comrades! Never
let it be said that so good a cavalier as Garci Perez was lost for want of
our assistance." So saying they all put spurs to their horses, rushed again
upon the bridge, and broke their way across cutting down and overturning the Moors and driving great numbers to fling themselves into
the river. When the Moors who had surrounded Garci Perez saw this
band of cavaliers rushing from the bridge, they turned to defend themselves. The contest was fierce, but broken; many of the Moors took
refuge in the river but the Christians followed and slew them among
the waves. They continued fighting for the remainder of the day, quite
up to the gate of the Alcazar, and if the chronicles of the times speak
with their usual veracity, full three thousand infidels bit the dust on
that occasion. When Don Lorenzo returned to the camp and was in
presence of the king and of numerous cavaliers, great encomiums were
passed upon his valour; but he modestly replied that Garci Perez had
that day made them good soldiers by force.

From that time forward the Moors attempted no further inroads
into the camp, so severe a lesson had they received from these brave
cavaliers.*

The city of Seville was connected with the suburb of Triana by a
strong bridge of boats, fastened together by massive chains of iron.
By this bridge a constant communication was kept up between Triana

---

* *Cronica General de España*, part 4. *Cronica del Rey Fernando el Santo*,
c. 60. *Corona Gotica*, T. 3, p. 126.

and the city, and mutual aid and support passed and repassed. While this bridge remained, it was impossible to complete the investment of the city, or to capture the castle of Triana.

The bold Admiral Bonifaz at length conceived a plan to break this bridge asunder, and thus to cut off all communication between the city and Triana. No sooner had this idea entered his mind than the bold Admiral landed and proceeded with great speed to the royal tent, to lay it before the king. Then a consultation was summoned by the king of ancient mariners and artificers of ships, and other persons learned in maritime affairs; and after Admiral Bonifaz had propounded his plan it was thought to be good, and all preparations were made to carry it into effect. And the Admiral took two of his largest and strongest ships, and fortified them at the prows with solid timber and with plates of iron. And he put within them a great number of chosen men, well armed and provided with every thing for attack and defence: and of one he took the command himself. It was the third day of May, the day of the most Holy Cross, that he chose for this grand and perilous attempt; and the pious King Fernando, to ensure success, ordered that a cross should be carried as a standard at the mast head of each ship.

On the third of May towards the hour of noon the two ships descended the Guadalquivir for some distance, to gain room to come up with greater violence. Here they waited the rising of the tide, and as soon as it was in full force, and a favorable wind had sprung up from the sea, they hoisted anchor, spread all sail, and put themselves in the midst of the current. The whole shores were lined on each side with Christian troops watching the event with great anxiety. The king and the Prince Alfonso with their warriors on the one side, had drawn close to the city to prevent the sallying forth of the Moors, while the good Master of St. Iago, Don Pelayo Perez Correa, kept watch upon the gates of Triana. The Moors crowded the tops of their towers, their wall and house tops, and prepared engines and weapons of all kinds to overwhelm the ships with destruction.

Twice the bold Admiral set all sail and started on his career, and twice the wind died away before he had proceeded half his course. Shouts of joy and derision rose from the walls and towers of Seville, while the warriors in the ships began to fear that their attempt would be unsuccessful. At length a fresh and strong wind arose that swelled every sail and sent the ships ploughing up the waves of the Guadalquivir. A dead silence prevailed among the hosts on either bank; even the Moors remained silent, in fixed and breathless suspence. When the ships arrived within reach of the walls of the city and the suburbs, a tremendous attack was commenced from every wall and tower; great engines discharged stones, and offensive weapons of all kinds, and

flaming pots of Greek fire. On the Tower of Gold were stationed catapults and vast cross-bows that were worked with cranks, and from
hence an iron shower was rained upon the ships. The Moors in Triana
were equally active; from every wall and turret, from house tops and
from the banks of the river an incessant assault was kept up with catapults, cross-bows, slings, darts, and every thing that could annoy.
Through all this tempest of war the ships kept on their course. The
first ship which arrived struck the bridge on the part towards Triana.
The shock resounded from shore to shore, the whole fabric trembled,
the ship recoiled and reeled, but the bridge was unbroken; and shouts
of joy rose from the Moors on each side of the river. Immediately after
came the ship of the Admiral. It struck the bridge just about the centre
with a tremendous crash. The iron chains which bound the boats
together snapped as if they had been flax. The boats were crushed and
shattered and flung wide asunder, and the ship of the Admiral proceeded in triumph through the open space. No sooner did the king and
the Prince Alfonso see the success of the Admiral, than they pressed
with their troops closely round the city and prevented the Moors from
sallying forth, while the ships, having accomplished their enterprize,
extricated themselves from their dangerous situation and returned in
triumph to their accustomed anchorage. This was the fatal blow that
dismembered Seville from Triana, and ensured the downfall of the city.

[CHAPTER XIX

Investment of Triana—Garci Perez and the Infanzon.]

On the day after the breaking of the bridge the king, the Prince Alfonso,
the Prince Enrique, the various masters of the orders and a great part
of the army, crossed the Guadalquivir, and commenced an attack on
Triana, while the bold Admiral Bonifaz approached with his ships and
assaulted the place from the water. But the Christian army was unpro-
vided with ladders or machines for the attack, and fought to great
disadvantage. The Moors, from the safe shelter of their walls and
towers, rained a shower of missiles of all kinds. As they were so high
above the Christians, their arrows, darts, and lances came with the
greater force. They were skilful with the cross-bow, and had engines
of such force that the darts which they discharged would sometimes
pass through a cavalier all armed, and bury themselves in the earth.*
The very women combatted from the walls and hurled down stones that
crushed the warriors beneath.

* *Cronica General*, part 4, p. 341.

While the army was closely investing Triana, and fierce encounters were daily taking place between Moor and Christian, there arrived at the camp of youthful Infanzon, or noble, of proud lineage. He brought with him a shining train of vassals, all newly armed and appointed, and his own armour, all fresh and lustrous, shewed none of the dints and bruises and abuses of the war. As this gay and gorgeous cavalier was patrolling the camp, with several cavaliers, he beheld Garci Perez pass by, in armour and accoutrements all worn and soiled by the hard service he had performed; and he saw a similar device to his own, of white waves, emblazoned on the scutcheon of this unknown warrior. Then the nobleman was highly ruffled and incensed, and he exclaimed, "How is this? who is this sorry cavalier that dares to bear these devices? By my faith he must either give them up or shew his reasons for usurping them." The other cavaliers exclaimed, "Be cautious how you speak. This is Garci Perez; a braver cavalier wears not sword in Spain. For all he goes thus modestly and quietly about, he is a very lion in the field, nor does he assume any thing that he cannot well maintain. Should he hear this which you have said, trust us he would not rest quiet until he had terrible satisfaction."

Now so it happened that certain mischief makers carried word to Garci Perez of what the nobleman had said, expecting to see him burst into fierce indignation, and defy the other to the field. But Garci Perez remained tranquil, and said not a word.

Within a day or two after, there was a sally from the castle of Triana, and a hot skirmish between the Moors and Christians. And Garci Perez and the Infanzon and a number of cavaliers pursued the Moors up to the barriers of the castle. Here the enemy rallied and made a fierce defence and killed several of the cavaliers. But Garci Perez put spurs to his horse and couching his lance charged among the thickest of the foes, and followed by a handful of his companions, drove the Moors to the very gates of Triana. The Moors, seeing how few were their pursuers, turned upon them, and dealt bravely with sword and lance and mace, while stones and darts and arrows were rained down from the towers above the gates. At length the Moors took refuge within the walls, leaving the field to the victorious cavaliers. Garci Perez drew off coolly and calmly, amidst a shower of missiles from the wall. He came out of the battle with his armour all battered and defaced: his helmet was bruised, the crest broken off and his buckler so dented and shattered that the device could scarcely be perceived. On returning to the barrier he found there the Infanzon, with his armour all uninjured and his armorial bearings as fresh as if just emblazoned, for the vaunting warrior had not ventured beyond the barrier. Then Garci Perez drew near to the Infanzon, and eyeing him from head to foot, "Señor cavalier," said he, "you may well dispute my right to wear this honorable device in my shield, since you see I take so little care of it that it is almost destroyed. You on the other hand are worthy of bearing it. You are the guardian angel of honour, since you guard it so carefully as to put it to no risk. I will only observe to you that the sword kept in the scabbard rusts, and the valour that is never put to the proof becomes sullied."*

At these words the Infanzon was deeply humiliated, for he saw that Garci Perez had heard of his empty speeches, and he felt how unworthily he had spoken of so valiant and magnanimous a cavalier. "Señor cavalier," said he, "pardon my ignorance and presumption. You alone are worthy of bearing these arms, for you derive not nobility from them, but ennoble them by your glorious deeds."

Then Garci Perez blushed at the praises he had thus drawn upon himself, and he regretted the harshness of his words towards the Infanzon, and he not merely pardoned him all that had passed, but gave him his hand in pledge of amity, and from that time they were close friends and companions in arms.†

[CHAPTER XX

Capitulation of Seville—Dispersion of the Moorish inhabitants—Triumphant entry of King Fernando.]

About this time there arrived in Seville a Moorish alfaqui named Orias, with a large company of warriors, who came to this war as if performing a pilgrimage, for it was considered a holy war no less by infidels than Christians. This Orias was of a politic and crafty nature, and he suggested to the commander of Seville a stratagem by which they might get Prince Alfonso in their power, and compel King Fernando to raise the siege by way of ransom. The counsel of Orias was adopted after a consultation with the principal cavaliers, and measures taken to carry it into execution. A Moor was sent, therefore, as if secretly and by stealth, to Prince Alfonso, and offered to put him in possession of the two towers of the wall, if he would come in person to receive them, which towers once in his possession, it would be easy to overpower the city.

Prince Alfonso listened to the envoy with seeming eagerness but suspected some deceit and thought it unwise to put his person in such jeopardy. Lest however there should be truth in his proposals, a party of chosen cavaliers were sent as if to take possession of the towers, and with them was Don Pero Nuñez de Guzman, disguised as the prince.

---

* *Cronica General*, part 4. *Corona Gotica*, T. 3, § 16.
† *Cronica General*, part 4. *Cronica del Rey Santo. Corona Gotica*, T. 3, § 16.

When they came to the place where the Moors had appointed to meet them, they beheld a party of infidels strongly armed; who advanced with sinister looks and attempted to surround Don Nuñez; but he being on his guard put spurs to his horse, and breaking through the midst of them escaped. His companions followed his example, all but one, who was struck from his horse and cut to pieces by the Moors.*

Just after this event there arrived a great reenforcement to the camp from the city of Cordova, bringing provisions and various munitions of war. Finding his army thus encreased the king had a consultation with Admiral Bonifaz and determined completely to cut off all communication between Seville and Triana, for the Moors still crossed the river occasionally by fording. When they were about to carry their plan into effect the crafty Alfaqui Orias crossed to Triana, accompanied by a number of Gazules. He was charged with instructions to the garrison and to concert some mode of reuniting their forces, or of effecting some blow upon the Christian camp: for unless they could effect a union and cooperation, it would be impossible to make much longer resistance.

Scarce had Orias passed, when the Christian sentinels gave notice. Upon this a detachment of the Christian army immediately crossed and took possession of the opposite shore, and Admiral Bonifaz stationed his fleet in the middle of the river. Thus the return of Orias was prevented, and all intercourse between the places, even by messenger, completely interrupted.

The city and Triana were now severally attacked and unable to render each other assistance. The Moors were daily diminishing in number; many slain in battle, many taken captive and many dying of hunger and disease. The Christian forces were daily augmenting, and were animated by continual success, whereas mutiny and sedition began to break out among the inhabitants of the city. The Moorish commander Axataf, therefore, seeing all further resistance vain, sent ambassadors to capitulate with King Fernando. It was a hard and humiliating struggle, to resign this fair city, the Queen of Andalusia, the seat of Moorish sway and splendour, and which had been under Moorish domination ever since the Conquest.

The valiant Axataf endeavoured to make various conditions; that King Fernando should raise the siege on receiving the tribute which had hitherto been paid to the miramamolin. This being peremptorily refused, he offered to give up a third of the city, and then a half, building at his own cost a wall to divide the Moorish part from the Christian. King Fernando, however, would listen to no such terms. He demanded the entire surrender of the place, with the exception of the persons and effects of the inhabitants, and permitting the commander to retain

* *Cronica General*, part 4, p. 424.

possession of St. Lucar, Aznal Farache and Niebla. The commander of Seville saw the sword suspended over his head, and had to submit; the capitulations of the surrender were signed, when Axataf made one last request, that he might be permitted to demolish the grand mosque and the principal tower (or Giralda) of the city.* He felt that these would remain perpetual monuments of his disgrace. The Prince Alfonso was present when this last demand was made, and his father looked at him significantly as if he desired the reply to come from his lips. The prince rose indignantly and exclaimed that if there should be a single tile missing from the temple or a single brick from the tower, it should be paid by so many lives that the streets of Seville should run with blood. The Moors were silenced by this reply; and prepared with heavy hearts to fulfill the capitulation. One month was allowed them for the purpose, the Alcazar or citadel of Seville being given up to the Christians as a security.

On the twenty-third day of November this important fortress was surrendered, after a siege of eighteen months. A deputation of the principal Moors came forth and presented King Fernando with the keys of the city; at the same time the aljamia, or council of the Jews, presented him with the key of Jewry, the quarter of the city which they inhabited. This key was notable for its curious workmanship. It was formed of all kinds of metals. The guards of it were wrought into letters, bearing the following signification,—"God will open—the king will enter." On the ring was inscribed in Hebrew,—"The King of kings will enter; all the world will behold him." This key is still preserved in the cathedral of Seville, in the place where repose the remains of the sainted King Fernando.†

During the month of grace the Moors sold such of their effects as they could not carry with them, and the king provided vessels for such as chose to depart for Africa. Upwards of one hundred thousand, it is said, were thus convoyed by Admiral Bonifaz, while upwards of two hundred thousand dispersed themselves throughout such of the territory of Andalusia as still remained in possession of the Moors.

When the month was expired, and the city was evacuated by its Moorish inhabitants, King Fernando the Saint entered in solemn triumph, in a grand religious and military procession. There were all the captains and cavaliers of the army, in shining armor, with the prelates,

---

* Mariana, L. 13, c. 7.

† In Castile, whenever the kings entered any place where there was a synagogue, the Jews assembled in council and paid to the Monteros, or bull-fighters, twelve maravedis each, to guard them, that they should receive no harm from the Christians; being held in such contempt and odium, that it was necessary they should be under the safeguard of the king, not to be injured or insulted.[1]

[1]Zuniga, Annales de Sevilla.

and masters of the religious and military orders, and the nobility of Castile, Leon, and Aragon, in their richest apparel. The streets resounded with the swelling notes of martial music and with the joyous acclamations of the multitude.

In the midst of the procession was the venerable effigy of the most Holy Mary, on a triumphal car of silver, wrought with admirable skill; and immediately after followed the pious king, with a drawn sword in his hand, and on his left was Prince Alfonso and the other princes.

The procession advanced to the principal mosque, which had been purified and consecrated as a Christian temple, where the triumphal car of the Holy Virgin was placed at the grand altar. Here the pious king knelt and returned thanks to heaven and the Virgin for this signal victory, and all present chanted *Te Deum Laudamus*.

[CHAPTER XXI

Death of King Fernando.]

When King Fernando had regulated every thing for the good government and prosperity of Seville, he sallied forth with his conquering army to subdue the surrounding country. He soon brought under subjection Xerez, Medina Sidonia, Alua, Bepel, and many other places near the seacoast; some surrendered voluntarily; others were taken by force; he maintained a strict peace with his vassal the King of Granada, but finding not sufficient scope for his arms in Spain, and being inflamed with a holy zeal in the cause of the faith, he determined to pass over into Africa and retaliate upon the Moslems their daring invasion of his country. For this purpose he ordered a powerful armada to be prepared in the ports of Cantabria, to be put under the command of the bold Admiral Bonifaz.

In the midst of his preparations, which spread consternation throughout Mauritania, the pious king fell dangerously ill at Seville of a dropsy. When he found his dying hour approaching, he made his death bed confession and requested the holy Sacrament to be administered to him. A train of bishops and other clergy, among whom was his son Philip, Archbishop of Seville, brought the Sacrament into his presence. The king rose from his bed, threw himself on his knees, with a rope round his neck and a crucifix in his hand, and poured forth his soul in penitence and prayer. Having received the Viatica and the holy Sacrament, he commanded all ornaments and insignia of royalty to be taken from his chamber. He assembled his children round his bedside, and blessed his son the Prince Alfonso as his firstborn and the heir of his throne, giving him excellent advice for the government of his kingdom, and charging him to protect the interests of his brethren. The pious king afterwards fell into an extacy or trance, in which he beheld angels watching round his bed to bear his soul to heaven. He awoke from this in a state of heavenly rapture, and asking for a candle, he took it in his hands and made his ultimate profession of the faith. He then requested the clergy present to repeat the litanies and to chaunt the *Te Deum Laudamus*. In chaunting the first verse of the hymn the king gently inclined his head with perfect serenity of countenance and rendered up his spirit. "The hymn," says the ancient chronicle, "which was begun on earth by men, was continued by the voices of angels, which were heard by all present." These doubtless were the angels which the king in his extacy had beheld around his couch, and which now accompanied him in his glorious ascent to heaven with songs of holy triumph. Nor was it in his chamber alone that these voices were heard, but in all the royal Alcazars of Seville the sweetest voices were heard in the air and seraphic music, as of angelic choirs, at the moment that the sainted king expired.* He died on the 30th of May, the vespers of the Holy Trinity, in the year of the Incarnation one thousand two hundred and forty-two, aged seventy-three years—having reigned thirty-five years over Castile and twenty over Leon.

Two days after his death, he was interred in his royal chapel in the Holy Church, in a sepulchre of alabaster which still remains. It is asserted by grave authors that at the time of putting his body in the sepulchre, the choir of angels again was heard chanting his eulogium, and filling the air with sweet melody in praise of his virtues.†

When Alhamar, the Moorish King of Granada, heard of his death, he caused great demonstrations of mourning to be made throughout his dominions. During his life he sent yearly a number of Moors with one hundred wax tapers, to assist at his exequies, which ceremony was observed by his successors, until the time of the conquest of Granada by Fernando the Catholic.‡

---

*Pablo de Espinosa, *Grandesas de Sevilla*, folio 146. *Cronica del Santo Rey*, c. 78. *Corona Gotica*, T. 3, p. 166.

† Argoti de Molina, *Nobleza de Andaluzia*, L. 1, c. 21. Tomas Bocio, *Signales de la Iglesia*, L. 20. Don Rodrigo Sanchez, Bishop of Palencia, part 3, c. 40.

‡ Pablo de Espinosa, folio 146.

Washington Irving

A photograph from an unfinished painting
by Charles Loring Elliott

OTHER PROSE WRITINGS
LEFT UNPUBLISHED AT
IRVING'S DEATH

[1822?]

[MY UNCLE]

My uncle was of an ancient family, and born to an easy fortune. He had been educated under the directions of a kind and indulgent mother, who was something of what is termed a blue stocking; and who was so attentive to the varied cultivation of his mind, that, by the time he had finished his education, he knew a little of every thing. His circumstances made it unnecessary that he should bind his mind to any pursuit, for a livelihood, and indeed his mother had always expressed a wish that he should lead the life of a gentleman and do nothing, as all his ancestors had done before him.

As it was his mind was never idle; he was what is termed a young man of universal acquirements. He was an amateur, a connoisseur and a dilettante. His taste however inclined more particularly to literature and the elegant arts. He was fond of paintings, and could paint a little himself; that is to say in a decent, gentlemanlike skimble skamble way, without much adherence to rule. It is true his paintings had never been admitted to any of the exhibitions; but then they had been abundantly praised by several artists of undoubted judgement, who dined with him very frequently.

My uncle was a gay fellow in his younger days, and considered himself a man that had seen the world, having figured at balls, masquerades and drawing rooms; his gaiety, however, was checked by some disappointment in love, the particulars of which it is needless to detail; they were rather of a gloomy nature. This seemed to effect quite a revolution in his character. His vanity expired; his spirits languished; there was a dash of softness, and even melancholy thrown into his nature; a tinge of what is commonly called sentiment. It remained with him through life, but it was so unaffected, and mingled so well with his other kind and generous and whimsical qualities, that it made him more agreeable than before.

He was recovering from the immediate effects of this blow, when new misfortunes overtook him. By the failure of a banking house he was stripped of his moderate though independent estate, and left almost a wreck upon the town. My uncle with all his knowledge of the world, did not know the art of being poor; that is to say, of having no money in his pocket, and yet keeping up appearances. Though he would economize rigidly on some small points, yet he was sure to be extravagant on others ten times as important. He was naturally compassionate and open handed; would give to a beggar what would straiten him the whole week afterwards, and never could reduce his gratuities to servants and waiters to the scale of his other expenses. Still he lived on without a murmur, gradually going down into poverty, while he lay on his sopha and read Horace, or strolled about his chamber and played the flute.

Just at this juncture my father arrived in town, and called on my uncle. He found him about twelve o'clock, just finishing his breakfast, in rather a melancholy mood. Travellers may talk of picturesque ruins; of temples crumbling into morsels of fine marbles and bits of rich frieze; but to my mind there is no ruin half so picturesque as that of a broken down gentleman; and such was my uncle. His room was full of petty, elegant knick-knacks; portfolios of drawings; musical instruments lying about among splendidly bound books of poetry. His very dress betrayed traces of former finery. Though he had adopted a stern frugality in all the recent additions to his wardrobe, yet his linen was still exquisitely fine; his old robe de chambre was of costly silk; he had a valuable cameo on his finger; and an old pair of sattin slippers peeped from under a sopha.

My father, who is a prompt, direct man, where the good of another is concerned, entered at once upon business, and enquired into my uncle's affairs. The latter gave them in three words, "he was ruined." My father talked something about future prospects, and tried to apply some of those commonplace maxims which are always at hand upon such occasions, but my uncle shook his head, and drew such a picture of his situation, his habits, and his peculiarities, that my father both laughed and cried; for there is nothing so touching as a careless, kind, broken spirit, jesting with its misfortunes.

"You shall go home with me, my dear Brother," said he at length, "and take up your quarters at the Hall; where you shall have your own way, be master of your time, do what you please, and wait until fortune turns her face towards you again."

My uncle was easily persuaded. His man John packed up his wardrobe and books, which filled several trunks, and in a few days he was fixed at the Hall.

All this part of his story I had from my father, for it happened many years since; while I was yet a boy. I recollect when my poor uncle came down to the country; it was quite a jubilee among us little folks; for he was a great friend to children, and used to join us in our sports. When he got out of the post chaise at the door, we scrambled about him, to welcome him. He caught us up in his arms, and embraced and kissed us. My little sister, who was a great favourite of his, threw her arms about his neck. "Do you love your poor Uncle?" said he, and as he said so the tears rushed into his eyes. I had never seen him so affected at meeting before; our meetings were always merry. I observed that he looked pale and thin; but I did not know of his circumstances, at the time; and if I had known them, I was too young to comprehend the sensitiveness of a proud yet delicate spirit; beaten down by misfortune.

My uncle's room was in one corner of the old Hall, on the second floor, looking out upon the garden; and commanding from between the trees, a peep at a rich distant country. He chose it because it was quiet and retired. It took him some days to arrange his trunks and books; and it was a matter of great curiosity for us to watch him as he opened his various repositories. Such gewgaws, and knick-knacks and trinkets as he had of every kind, which seemed to us of incredible value and rarity. Here he fitted up a little study, as it was termed, in which he used to pass part of his days reading, drawing, playing on the flute or violin, or as it is termed in literary labour.

It was a great treat for us to be admitted to his room, though he was apt to be a little nervous and uneasy, if we ranged too much about, and handled any of the various curiosities with which it was crowded. He used to give us little books to read; or teach us to draw, or tell us stories. He told us wonderful tales about the great city of London; and Gog and Magog; and London Bridge and the Monument. Sometimes he would stroll with us through the fields, and make us notice the birds and flowers; and would sit on the grass, and tell us tales of fairies that danced on the green; and sported in the flowers; and of Robin Goodfellow. He made us believe that the Hall was visited by fairies, who glided in at the casements on moonlight nights; and that they danced about the great kitchen hearth at midnight, when the servants were all gone to bed.

My mother would often rebuke him for filling our brains with such nonsense; and would very seriously assure us that there were no such beings as fairies and dwarfs and giants; but my uncle would give a faint laugh and exclaim, "Ah my dear Sister, let them believe in fairy land as long as possible. They'll find out, soon enough, what a sad matter of fact world they live in."

After he had been some time at the Hall, his literary inclinations seemed to encrease upon him. He passed more time in his room writing; was observed frequently to carry books thither, a volume at a time, until by degrees he had broken the sets of almost all the works in the family library. It is said that he occasionally wrote for the magazines, but of this I am not certain; I rather think his effusions were generally limited in their circulation to the family and the visitors at the Hall, by whom they were universally admired. My mother considered him one of the greatest writers of the day.

One of those chance windfalls which are continually happening in extensive family connexions made him once more independent. An old relative, whom neither he, nor any body else had ever cared for, died and left him his property. My uncle now divided his time between town and country. He set up a neat establishment in the west end; became a regular literary man upon town; lounged at all the bookshops; and was even an occasional visitor at Murray's drawing room. He gave literary dinners, which were much resorted to, particularly by the poorer and more hungry class of authors. He also became a great musical amateur and held weekly concerts at his own house, to the infinite disturbance of the neighbourhood. He was cried up as the very Pan of music; and uncouth looking personages, with strange foreign heads, and little odd hats upon them, might be seen popping in and out of his house at all times of day; humming opera airs; with fiddle cases under their arms, and flutes sticking out of their pockets.

Not long after the peace my uncle was recommended to visit the continent; his health having grown very precarious. He did so, and remained abroad for about a year, when he returned once more to the Hall, sadly altered and broken down. He lingered for a few months, and then gradually sunk into the grave.

[1828–1829]

[SIR DAVID WILKIE IN SPAIN]

The inconveniences of travelling in Spain, and the exaggerated ideas which strangers have of its roads, render it a country comparatively but little visited or known by the lovers of the fine arts. The English artists in particular, who throng to Italy, but seldom venture across the Pyrenees, and no English painter of renown has made a tour of the interior of Spain until the celebrated Wilkie, who passed the winter before last at Madrid and visited Seville last April. This intelligent artist is at the head of the English school; and is one of the very few painters of the present day who appear to have inherited the genius of the old masters. He is known throughout Europe by the engravings that have been multiplied of his works. He excels in representing scenes in familiar life, and in giving strong traits of peculiar and national characteristics. His works are remarkable for their truth to nature, and the wonderful exactness and beauty of the execution. They approach somewhat to the Flemish school, but are more free in style, nobler in their conceptions, and shew a politer taste and greater scope of thought.

This intelligent artist, who had already visited the best galleries in Italy, France and Germany, was astonished at the riches of art, both foreign and native, which were in a manner buried in Spain, and almost unknown out of its boundaries. The Royal Museum at Madrid was the theme of his most animated eulogiums. His opinion of the Spanish masters was continually encreasing during his residence in this country. Velasquez is well known and appreciated in England, but of Murillo, Mr. Wilkie observed, that much as he is admired abroad it is necessary to visit Spain and when in Spain to visit Seville, to know the variety and extent of his genius. He made a journey to this city expressly to examine the masterpieces of Murillo with which it abounds. The church of the Capuchin convent was repeatedly visited by this observing artist, who seemed to study with unwearied delight the glorious works treasured up there. It is but justice to bear testimony to the extreme urbanity of the good fathers of that convent, whose attention to amateurs visiting their chapel, has been the theme of praise of all the strangers who visit our city, and has been particularly mentioned by several English visitors. One thing that seemed to surprize Mr. Wilkie was to observe the many admirable paintings of the Spanish school, which had been executed before the time of Murillo, for there is an idea abroad that prior to his time the arts in Spain were but in an imperfect state. When he contemplated various noble productions, such as that of St. Thomas by Zurbaran—, the exclamation would involuntarily escape him—"And this too they had before Murillo!"

While in Madrid Mr. Wilkie composed three pictures on Spanish subjects. One was a scene in a Spanish Posada during the late wars. Another a Guerrilla going to battle, a third, the defence of Saragossa, in which he introduced a likeness of General Palafox. To these he intends to add a fourth, the subject of which will be the Guerrilla, returning wounded to his family. In these paintings he has shewn the result of his studies of the Spanish painters, as he has altered his former style of colouring and execution, and has introduced many effects of Murillo and Velasquez. The King of England, who is an admirable connoisseur of paintings, sent for Mr. Wilkie on his return, and purchased of him the works he had executed while in Spain. His majesty had a long conversation with him about the state of the arts in this country. He examined his paintings with great care and passed high encomiums on them. That of the posada appeared to please him best; though he was much struck by the likeness of Palafox. His majesty pointed out various parts of the paintings which reminded him of the style of Murillo and Velasquez, who are favorite masters with the King.

As Mr. Wilkie is the first great English artist who has visited this country it is gratifying to find that he has visited it with such a liberal spirit and discerning judgement, and is disposed to bear such ample testimony to the merits of the Spanish school. Since his return his observations on the Spanish masters; the exhibition of his paintings; and the sight of various sketches he has made, have caused a strong sensation in England and turned the attention of amateurs towards this country.

[1829–1832?]

THE VILLAGE CURATE

The Spanish peasants for the most part reside in villages and hamlets; their fields, vineyards and olive plantations are without inclosures, and often at a distance from their dwellings. They employ bold fellows to watch these grounds towards the time of harvest; who sleep in mere sheds or huts, of straw and rushes, or in cabins, built like cages among the branches of the trees. These men are generally armed with a musket and a knife; and patrol the fields at all hours. They are often mere vagabonds and desperadoes, too idle or vicious to follow an industrious course of life. Sometimes they are old soldiers, sometimes men who have been in prison, sometimes outcasts and fugitives from other parts of the country, who, like the storm, come no one knows from whence and go no one knows whither. They rarely want for courage, and it often borders on ferocity.

On an estate that lies in a lonely part of the country at some distance from Seville, there was a desperado of the kind employed to guard the olive orchards. No one knew his story; some said he had been condemned to the galleys for murder and had served out his term at Ceuta, others that he was a fugitive from justice for some unknown crime. No enquiry had been made into particulars when he was hired, for investigations of the kind are not often made in Spain, nor are they always safe. The guard was a dark looking, powerful man; a short Andalusian jacket and leathern hose set off his brawny figure; he wore two pistols stuck in a red woollen sash, his hat was drawn over his eyes, which scowled from under it with a ferocious expression, and he had a thick black bushy beard. He passed the greater part of his time in the fields, loitering about with his musket in his hand, looking more like a robber than a guardian. He spoke with no one, came seldom to the village, and remained there but a short time; no one sought his society; his looks caused universal distrust and every one stood in awe of him.

The steward of the estate where he kept watch had a daughter, about seventeen years of age, whose tender beauty had captivated the heart or rather excited the desires of this ruffian. He softened in his manners towards her, as much as his stern nature would allow, and took every occasion to plead his passion and to endeavour to seduce her. The young girl discouraged his advances, but she was timid and weak hearted, and was frightened by his violent character. She applied for counsel to her confessor the village curate, to whom she was accustomed to resort for advice on all occasions. The curate was straightforward and zealous in the discharge of his sacred office. He endeavoured to fortify this tender and timid lamb of his flock, thus menaced by the wolf. "Hold fast to thy integrity, my child," said he; "guard thy virtue above every thing, listen not to the voice of the tempter, nor regard his threats. Thy own weakness is all thou hast to fear; be true to thyself and thou mayst set the enemy at defiance."

The young girl promised to be guided by his advice, and departed strengthened in spirit. The guard however continued his solicitations, mingled with ferocious menaces; the poor girl resisted him steadfastly, being supported by the secret counsels of the curate, but she grew pale, and her wasted cheek told the struggles and anxieties the conflict cost her. At length she came one day to the curate, weeping and wringing her hands. The good man, as he saw her approach in this manner, supposed she had fallen a victim to the seducer. He spoke to her mildly, however, in the true Christian spirit. "I understand thee!" said he, "poor child, thou hast fallen!—but be comforted. Thy tears have washed away thy guilt; recollect the shepherd of our faith brings back the wandering lamb on his shoulders to the fold."—"No, my father," replied the damsel, blushing, "it is not that; thank God and thy good counsel, as yet I am free from sin—but it is for thee I am distressed. I have told him, as you advised me, that I would never speak with him again. He looked at me with a fearful brow that made me tremble. 'Well,' said he, 'I see how it is; thy scoundrel confessor is at the bottom of all this. Yes, I see it in thy eye, he is the cause that you treat me thus—enough—I quit you, and I quit this neighborhood forever; but before I go,' said he, striking his hand on his musket and shaking his head, 'this meddling priest shall feel my vengeance, and you shall have reason never to forget it.' With these words he left me. This is the cause of my distress. I know the terrible character of this man and the frightful things that are told of him. What is he not capable of doing, and what dreadful misfortunes may your kindness for me have brought upon your head?"

"Is this all?" said the worthy curate. "Then thank God it is no worse. Be not alarmed on my account. The threats of this man are only made to frighten thee. He will not attempt to injure me; or if he should," added the curate, with an intrepid air and sudden zeal, "I put my trust in God. Even should he take my life, to fall thus in the execution of my duty would give me a greater chance for heaven."

Notwithstanding that he had spoken in this stouthearted manner in the moment of excitement, the worthy curate, when left to himself, began to call to mind the dark and dangerous character of this man and the proneness of desperadoes of this kind in Spain to commit bloody acts of vengeance, from the natural violence of their passions and from the facility of escaping from justice. He bethought him too that in the discharge of his duties he was often to traverse lonely fields and the woods and olive orchards, where the ruffian might lurk unseen and waylay him without danger of being discovered. He fortified himself, however, with the thought that he was in the hand of God, and he continued to go about the neighborhood as usual, visiting his parishioners.

He was going one day towards sunset, along a hollow way of the forest, overhung with fir trees, with the setting sun shining up it, when he beheld at a distance the guard coming towards him with his musket on his shoulder. There was no avoiding him; and to turn and fly were useless. As the ruffian advanced he looked like a giant in the dusty sunshine. "It is all over with me," thought the poor curate. "My hour is come." He endeavoured to summon up Christian resignation, and the martyr spirit; but the flesh was weak and clinged to mortality, and in spite of all his hopes of heaven, life at that moment seemed sweet and desirable. He advanced notwithstanding, and when they had come near to each other both of them paused. The ruffian took his gun from his shoulder, held it athwart as if about to cock it, and stood looking for a moment at the curate. The latter looked at him in silence, with a mild countenance, and a serene and lofty brow, where peace and good will to man were contrasted with the dark scowl of the murderer. By degrees the musket of the ruffian sank to the earth; his eye sank also; he mused for a moment. Then suddenly rousing himself—"God be with thee, father," said he, and throwing his musket on his shoulder struck off into the forest and never again was seen in that neighbourhood.

[1833?]

THE LOG HOUSE HOTEL

We had ridden a few miles from St. Charles, through a hot sun, when about two o'clock we stopped before a new log house, called Green's Hotel, kept by a decent young couple; the husband was absent on a deer hunt; but we were received by a tall, long sided negro, in tow cloth jacket and trowsers, who came out, perspiration streaming and steaming from every pore. The horses were given in charge to him with directions that they should be well fed.

"Massa, dey shall be fed in style," was the reply. "We shall require to be fed also, Sambo." "Never fear, gentlemen, you'll have a good dinner as sure as eggs is chickens. Dis house is famous all along the road. They talk of it in Illinois and Boone's Lick—and recommend travellers to it." Then sticking his arms akimbo and wagging his head he called with a tone of absolute authority—"What de hell ye doing dere when you know dere's business in the house?" The person to whom this authoritative speech was made was behind the barn and out of sight. We looked to see the tardy recreant, when a little black imp about six years old, in ragged linen trowsers, came running forth.

In a few minutes there was a tremendous outcry from the poultry yard, cocks, hens, chickens scampering, fluttering and cackling in every direction, over and under fences, across the road, into the barn, out of the barn, into the potato patch, out of the potato patch, through the orchard, across the stableyard, chased by the long negro, the little negro, a strapping negress, two little white girls, with sticks, stones and all other missiles. One gallant rooster who had strutted away his hour in the farmyard was knocked down. In an instant the tall negro seized him, whirled him round by the neck until the headless body fell bouncing and bounding on the ground. "There," cried he, "you must be cooked for the strangers."

This done the chace was continued,—the tall negro armed with a long stick chasing a fowl which eluded every blow and ran under the log house. The little negro was sent in after it, like a terrier into a rat hole, while the big negro stood sentry without, to knock down the quarry should it attempt to escape. The little negro scrambled on all fours, or rather sprawled along the ground, but the fowl was too nimble for him.

"Make haste dere," cries Sambo, "or I'll come after you with a d——d big stick! Dere's a chicken dere as fat as mud."

The chicken is at length captured, slain and consigned to the cook: and our dinner was now secure.

While the repast was in preparation our friend Sambo set out a pitcher of water, a flask of whiskey and a basin of sugar; and came in repeatedly to prompt us to partake. "Gentlemen," he would cry, "there's cold water and capital whiskey and sugar all gratis, for travellers, no charge—nothing at all to pay." I observed that he never passed the whiskey flask without helping himself, and by degrees he grew more and more eloquent, and let us in to a part of his history.

He told us he was born in Virginny and came from thence to Kentucky, then to Tennessee, then here in Missouri; each change, he said, was for the best, but Missouri was his paradise. One lived so easy here, he said. There was no hard work as in tobacco plantations, things were raised so easy, pork, corn, vegetables, and all brought cash. He could make a little money here for himself and meant to buy himself free.

"And do you think you'll be better off?" said I.

Oh yes, he would have holyday when he pleased and go to musters and shooting matches.

"Yes," added I, "and play the fool and get married."

"Yes Massa—and leave off drinking and dress!"

What reform a poor varlet in a tow cloth trowsers was to make in dress I could not conceive, unless to return to the primitive simplicity of the fig leaf.

Sambo now bustled forth, but had not been long gone when he popped his black head into the room again.

"Ah gentlemen—I told you so—you'll have a dinner worth sitting down to. Fried chicken! brown and juicy. It does one good only to smell 'em. I told mistress she must give fried chicken for the honor of Virginny."

The dinner at length was served, and in effect was good and savory. In the midst of the repast however we were aroused by a loud uproar in the hen yard and heard our friend Sambo in violent quarrel with another negro, who had resisted his domineering spirit, which had been aggravated and inflamed by frequent visits to the whiskey bottle. The storm of words encreased—it threatened to break forth in blows, when our little Frenchman Antoine sprang forth, seized a plank in his hand, flourished it over the heads of the belligerents and produced an instant though growling cessation of hostilities.

Our repast was concluded without further interruption—our horses were harnessed and saddled, and having paid the very moderate bill of our hostess we sallied forth. Poor Sambo, completely crestfallen, stood by the waggon, looking like a culprit. As we mounted we put a piece of money into his hands. His countenance immediately brightened—he gave a glance at the coin; slipped it into his pocket with a toss of his head. "Ah," said he, "dat's what it is to have to do wid gentlemen."

[1827–1838]

[HISTORY OF THE CONQUEST OF MEXICO]

At the time when the kingdom of Mexico was about to be invaded by strangers and the downfall of the throne of its Indian monarchs was at hand, strange portents were seen in the heavens and the earth, but none which surpasses the following, attested by too many Spanish historians of gravity and veracity to be for a moment doubted.

There lived near the foot of the mountains which encircle the great plains of Mexico an Indian of the name of Itztupulcan. He was a simple and virtuous man, his drink was the water of the brook, and his food the maize of his fields and the fruit of his groves. He had toiled one day in his fields and during the noontide heat reposed himself under the shade of a palm tree by the side of a fountain. Scarcely had he fallen asleep when he was awakened by a rushing sound in the air and, looking up, beheld a huge eagle hovering over him. The enormous bird swooped down and seizing him in his talons, but without doing him injury, bore him aloft far above the tops of the trees, until his little hut, and grove and field of maize, diminished to a mere speck in the vast landscape. He continued sailing over forests, lakes and rocks, until he soared away into the bosom of the mountains. Here the eagle mounted to the face of a great precipice overhung with trees and alighted at the entrance of a spacious cavern. It lay open to the south, and looked over the vast valley of Mexico, the great lake shining in the midst and the city a mere dark island on the water. The eagle paused at the entrance of the cavern and waving his wings, exclaimed with a human voice, "Behold, O Almighty Sovereign! I have done what thou hast commanded me." Itztupulcan looked round but beheld no one to whom the words were addressed. The mouth of the cavern was hung with weeds and vines that almost shut out the light of the day. A voice resounded from within,— "Advance Itztupulcan, favored of Heaven, advance and behold the mystery of the sleeper." The knees of the Indian smote together and he obeyed trembling. As he advanced, a light beamed up from the interior of the cavern and he beheld its walls shining with veins of gold and sparkling with precious stones. A light vapour floated in the air filling the cave with a spicy and pleasant odour. On turning an angle of the rock, he beheld before him a man fast asleep, reclining on a bed of flowers and oderiferous herbs. He was clad in royal robes and in his hand he held, instead of a sceptre, a reed filled with aromatic *pebete* which flamed like a torch, and illumined the whole cavern, sweetening the air with its fragrance. But while the sleeper lay thus buried in balmy slumber, a huge and terrible serpent, whose scaly folds were coiled round the rocks, hung over him with fiery eyes and forked tongue, ready to dart upon his prey.

The voice resounded again. "Itztupulcan, favoured of Heaven, knowest thou the sleeper before thee?"

The Indian looked again and great drops of sweat stood upon his forehead. "Verily," said he, "if I were not deep in the midst of the mountains, I would say that this is the person of my Lord, the King Montezuma."

"Even so," replied the voice. "And thus he is sunk in luxury and forgetfulness, so deep is he steeped in sensuality, that he has lost all sense of feeling. Wouldst thou know the truth of this, take the reed which he holds burning in his hand and put it to his thigh, and thou wilt see that his very senses are benumbed."

The Indian hesitated to obey, for he was filled with the reverence which the Mexicans entertain for the persons of their kings, and he feared to approach the hideous serpent. But the voice exclaimed again, "Advance, fear not, but do as I bid thee, for I am greater than Montezuma and can shield thee from all harm; fear nothing but my displeasure."

Then Itztupulcan put forth his trembling hand, and took the flaming reed from the loose grasp of the sleeper, and applied it to his thigh, but the king moved not, nor did he show any sign of pain.

"Behold," said the voice, "even thus is it with Montezuma; he sees not, he hears not, he feels not the dangers that are around him. Hasten then to awaken him; tell him the time is come when he must atone for his pride and tyranny; that ruin is impending over him, and the downfall of his empire is at hand."

Scarcely had the voice uttered these words when the eagle again seized Itztupulcan in his talons and bearing him out of the cavern soared away with him over forests and cliffs, and deep dark valleys, until poising himself for a moment in the air he descended swiftly to the earth and left him by the fountain under the palm tree near his humble cabin.

Itztupulcan now hastened to the city of Mexico; he presented himself at the portal of Montezuma, who was in one of his palaces of pleasure built in the midst of the lake. It was guarded by the youthful nobles, sumptuously attired in gold and jewels and feathers of a thousand gorgeous dyes. Scarcely could he gain admittance to Montezuma, who was surrounded by his wives, and sunk in voluptuousness. When Itztupulcan recounted the wonderful sight he had witnessed in the mountain the king was filled with indignation, for he looked upon it as an idle tale, and he was wearied with the evil portents that were daily announced to him. He seized a javelin and would have struck the bearer of ill tidings, but a thrilling pain in his thigh arrested his hand, and looking to the place, he found the mark of the flaming torch which had been applied to his effigy, the sleeper on the mountain. Consternation now seized upon all present. The king in his terror ordered that Itztupulcan should be seized and sacrificed as an offering to appease the gods, but he had already fled from the palace. His cabin was searched but remained vacant, nor was it ever known what became of him, but it is supposed he was borne away by the same power that had made this revelation to him, and that he passed the remainder of his days in some peaceful retreat of the mountains far beyond the reach of the ills that soon overwhelmed his unhappy country.

[1850?]

ILLUSTRATION TO THE LEGEND OF PRINCE AHMED

It would appear that Eben Bonabben was mistaken in affirming that Solomon had been taught the language of birds by the Queen of Sheba; he knew it before he became acquainted with her; it having been miraculously bestowed upon him with all other kinds of knowledge. Indeed according to Arabian tradition it was through his knowledge of the language of birds that he first became informed of the existence of such a person as the Queen of Sheba and a Lapwing which served as a diplomatic agent between the parties, and thus the thing came to pass. Solomon, having finished the temple of Jerusalem, went on a pilgrimage to Mecca, whence he proceeded to Yemen, or Arabia the happy. On his journeys he used to be attended by his court, and by legions of genii and armies of birds. For the facility of travelling he had an immense carpet of green silk, of magic properties. On this was placed his throne, whereon he seated himself; his courtiers on his right hand and the genii on his left. On giving the word this carpet would be elevated in the air, with all that were thereon, and transported whithersoever he desired; the birds flying in a cloud over head, to keep off the ardent rays of the sun. To the birds were assigned their several functions; that of the Lapwing was to discover hidden springs in the deserts; at which she was wonderfully sagacious, alighting and striking with her bill where water was to be discovered; upon which the genii digged and laid open the fountain head, and drew water for Solomon and his host.

One day when Solomon had encamped in the desert, the Lapwing failed to appear when summoned to perform her accustomed task: whereupon Solomon vowed to punish her severely unless she could give a sufficient excuse for her absence.

After a time the delinquent bird appeared before him but advanced with an intrepid air. "Be not angry with thy servant, oh son of David," said the Lapwing, "for I have been gathering tidings for thee of a far country of which thou knowest nothing. As I was taking a wide circuit in the air I encountered a bird of my acquaintance who told me such wonders of Saba that I prevailed upon her to conduct me thither. There I beheld a country filled with riches and delights, and a magnificent city and a queen named Balkis, who sat on a throne of gold and silver, and precious stones, and was surrounded by all the splendor befitting a mighty sovereign: but she and her subjects had turned aside from the path of truth and worshipped the sun, instead of the true God."

Solomon regarded the Lapwing with a doubtful eye: "We shall see" said he, "whether thou hast spoken the truth or art a liar." He then wrote a letter to the following effect. "From the Servant of God, Solomon the son of David, unto Balkis, Queen of Saba. In the name of the most merciful God, I offer you peace and truth. Resist not, but come and yield yourselves up to me, and receive from me the knowledge of the true religion." This letter he perfumed with musk and sealed it with his signet, and gave it to the Lapwing. "If thou be a faithful and honest little bird," said he, "and hast spoken the truth, prove it by taking this letter to the Queen of Saba and bringing me a reply." The Lapwing took the letter and sped away for the kingdom of Saba. She beheld Queen Balkis surrounded by her nobles and her army; and circling in the air, dropped the letter in her bosom, after which she alighted on a neighboring tree to note what should follow.

When Balkis read the letter she was troubled in mind; for she had heard of the great power of Solomon and feared that he would enter her city by force and lay it waste. After consulting with her nobles, therefore, she determined to send an embassy to Solomon, bearing rich presents. Having heard this resolution the Lapwing again took flight and brought back the intelligence to Solomon. The latter prepared to receive the ambassadors in state befitting his riches and grandeur. He had a large square enclosed with gold and silver moulded in the form of bricks; and here he awaited the introduction of the ambassadors seated on his throne and surrounded by his court and army. The ambassadors arrived and displayed their presents: there were five hundred slaves of either sex, chosen for their beauty, all dressed in the same manner; bearing presents of gold and precious stones and rich stuffs, and musk, and amber and other things of value. But Solomon regarded these presents with contempt. "Will ye put me off with riches?" said he. "God has given me enough thereof to satisfy the heart of man. Return to the people of Saba. Tell them I call upon them to surrender themselves to me; and to acknowledge the religion of the true God; otherwise I will drive them out of their city and make them contemptible on the face of the earth."

This threat being reported to Balkis by her ambassadors determined her to repair to Solomon and pay him homage.

Arabian traditions add several miracles which took place during this visit: some of which are recorded by Mahomet himself in the twenty seventh chapter of the Koran; which miracles were effected by Solomon, or rather by the genii which he had at his command.

(The above is from Sale's Koran. De Herbelot, &c. &c.)

[1851]

[A VOYAGE UP THE HUDSON RIVER IN 1800]

My first voyage up the Hudson was made in early boyhood, in the good old times before steamboats and railroads had annihilated time and space, and driven all poetry and romance out of travel. A voyage to Albany then, was equal to a voyage to Europe at present, and took almost as much time. We enjoyed the beauties of the river in those days; the features of nature were not all jumbled together, nor the towns and villages huddled one into the other by railroad speed as they are now.

I was to make the voyage under the protection of a relative of mature age; one experienced in the river. His first care was to look out for a favorite sloop and captain, in which there was great choice.

The constant voyaging in the river craft by the best families of New York and Albany, made the merits of captains and sloops matters of notoriety and discussion in both cities. The captains were mediums of communication between separated friends and families. On the arrival of one of them at either place he had messages to deliver and commissions to execute which took him from house to house. Some of the ladies of the family had, peradventure, made a voyage on board of his sloop, and experienced from him that protecting care which is always remembered with gratitude by female passengers. In this way the captains of Albany sloops were personages of more note in the community than captains of European packets or steamships at the present day. A sloop was at length chosen; but she had yet to complete her freight and secure a sufficient number of passengers. Days were consumed in "drumming up" a cargo. This was a tormenting delay to me who was about to make my first voyage, and who, boy-like, had packed up my trunk on the first mention of the expedition. How often that trunk had to be unpacked and repacked before we sailed!

* * * At length the sloop actually got under way. As she worked slowly out of the dock into the stream, there was a great exchange of last words between friends on board and friends on shore, and much waving of handkerchiefs when the sloop was out of hearing.

Our captain was a worthy man, native of Albany, of one of the old Dutch stocks. His crew was composed of blacks, reared in the family and belonging to him; for negro slavery still existed in the State. All his communications with them were in Dutch. They were obedient to his orders; though they occasionally had much previous discussion of the wisdom of them, and were sometimes positive in maintaining an opposite opinion. This was especially the case with an old gray-headed negro, who had sailed with the captain's father when the captain was a mere boy, and who was very crabbed and conceited on points of seamanship. I observed that the captain generally let him have his own way.

* * * What a time of intense delight was that first sail through the Highlands. I sat on the deck as we slowly tided along at the foot of those stern mountains, and gazed with wonder and admiration at cliffs impending far above me, crowned with forests, with eagles sailing and screaming around them; or listened to the unseen stream dashing down precipices; or beheld rock, and tree, and cloud, and sky reflected in the glassy stream of the river. And then how solemn and thrilling the scene as we anchored at night at the foot of these mountains, clothed with overhanging forests; and every thing grew dark and mysterious; and I heard the plaintive note of the whip-poor-will from the mountain-side, or was startled now and then by the sudden leap and heavy splash of the sturgeon.

* * * But of all the scenery of the Hudson, the Kaatskill Mountains had the most witching effect on my boyish imagination. Never shall I forget the effect upon me of the first view of them predominating over a wide extent of country, part wild, woody, and rugged; part softened away into all the graces of cultivation. As we slowly floated along, I lay on the deck and watched them through a long summer's day; under-going a thousand mutations under the magical effects of atmosphere; sometimes seming to approach; at other times to recede; now almost melting into hazy distance, now burnished by the setting sun, until, in the evening, they printed themselves against the glowing sky in the deep purple of an Italian landscape.

In the foregoing pages I have given the reader my first voyaging amid Hudson scenery. It has been my lot, in the course of a somewhat wandering life, to behold some of the rivers of the old world, most renowned in history and song, yet none have been able to efface or dim the pictures of my native stream thus early stamped upon my memory. My heart would ever revert to them with a filial feeling, and a recurrence of the joyous associations of boyhood; and such recollections are, in fact, the true fountains of youth which keep the heart from growing old.

To me the Hudson is full of storied associations, connected as it is with some of the happiest portions of my life. Each striking feature brings to mind some early adventure or enjoyment; some favorite companion who shared it with me; some fair object, perchance, of youthful admiration, who, like a star, may have beamed her allotted time and passed away.

[1851?]

[A JOURNEY TO SACKETT'S HARBOR IN 1814]

While I was jogging thus pensively on, my horse scarce dragging a snail's pace, and seemingly, like his rider, sunk into a reverie, I was suddenly startled by a loud rustling on the right; a beautiful doe came bounding through the thickets, leaped lightly over a fallen pine, and alighted in the road just before me. The poor animal seemed transfixed with astonishment at beholding another tenant of these solitudes; it gazed at me for an instant with the most picturesque surprise, and then launching away to the left, I presently heard it plunge into the river.

I had now been for some time travelling through close woodland, my views bounded on every side by impassive forest, when I came to where the face of the country sinks for a considerable distance, and forms a vast terrace of ten miles in breadth, and then sinking again forms another broad terrace, or plain, until it reaches Lake Ontario. Nothing could exceed the grandeur of the effect when the view first burst upon my sight. I found myself upon the brow of a hill, down which the road suddenly made a winding descent. The trees on each side of the road, were like the side scenes of a theatre; while those which had hitherto bounded my view in front, seemed to have sunk from before me, and I looked forth upon a luxuriant and almost boundless expanse of country. The forest swept down from beneath my feet, and spread out into a vast ocean of foliage, tinted with all the brilliant dyes of autumn, and gilded by a setting sun. Here and there a column of smoke curling its light blue volumes into the air, rose as a beacon to direct the eye to some infant settlement, as to some haven in this sylvan sea. As my eye ranged over the mellow landscape, I could perceive where the country dipped again into its second terrace—the foliage beyond being more and more blended in the purple mist of sunset; until a glittering line of gold, trembling along the horizon, showed the distant waters of Ontario.

That evening I rested at a log-house in the midst of a forest. The next day I passed through a wilderness of pine trees, over causeways of rough logs, which preserved me from being almost buried in the mire of the light soil.

After toiling along this rough road, amidst the most lonely and savage scenery, I at length came to where the country suddenly opened— Sackett's Harbor lay before me; a town which had recently sprung up in the bosom of this wilderness; beyond it the lake spread its vast waters like an ocean, no opposing shore being visible; while a few miles from land rode a squadron of ships of war at anchor on the calm bosom of the lake, and looking as if they were balanced in the air.

EDITORIAL APPENDIX

Textual Commentary,
Discussions, and Lists by
Wayne R. Kime

LIST OF ABBREVIATIONS

The following symbols have been used in the editorial apparatus to designate the manuscript and previously published texts of Irving's *Miscellaneous Writings*:

[ADVERTISEMENT OF AN ABRIDGEMENT OF *THE LIFE AND VOYAGES OF CHRISTOPHER COLUMBUS*]

1A   New York *American*, April 4, 1829 (vol. X, No. 2852), p. 2 col. 4.

[REVIEW OF *A CHRONICLE OF THE CONQUEST OF GRANADA*]

C   *A Chronicle of the Conquest of Granada*. . . . 2 vols. London: John Murray, 1829.

1E   *Quarterly Review*, 43 (May 1830), 55–80.

1A   *A Chronicle of the Conquest of Granada*. . . . New York: G. P. Putnam, 1850. "Note to the Revised Edition," pp. xvi–xix.

2A   *Spanish Papers*, II, [378]–416.

[REVIEW OF ALEXANDER SLIDELL'S *A YEAR IN SPAIN*]

MSm   Author's manuscript, John Murray Ltd., London.

Y   *A Year in Spain. By a Young American*. 2 vols. London: John Murray, 1831.

1E   *Quarterly Review*, 44, no. 88 (February 1831), 319–42.

[DEDICATORY LETTER IN *POEMS, BY WILLIAM CULLEN BRYANT, AN AMERICAN*]

1E   *Poems by William Cullen Bryant, An American*. London: J. Andrews, 1832. Pp. [iii]–iv.

1A   *Irvingiana*, p. xiii.

2A   PMI, II, 475–77.

[ADDRESS AT THE IRVING DINNER, MAY 30, 1832]

MSv   Author's manuscript, University of Virginia.

1A   New York *Morning Courier*, June 2, 1832, p. 2 cols. 2–3.

2A   New York *American*, June 2, 1832, p. 2 cols. 2–3.

3A   New-York *Spectator*, 35 (June 5, 1832), p. 2 col. 4.

4A   Boston *Daily Advertiser and Patriot*, June 5, 1832, p. 1 col 4.

5A   *New-York Mirror*, 9, no. 49 (June 9, 1832), 386 col. 3–387 col. 1.

6A   PMI, II, 488–90.

[REVIEW OF HENRY WHEATON'S
HISTORY OF THE NORTHMEN]

H   Wheaton, Henry. *History of the Northmen, or Danes and Normans, from the Earliest Times to the Conquest of England by William of Normandy.* London: John Murray, 1831.

1A   *North American Review*, 35, no. 77 (October 1832), 342–71.
2A   *Spanish Papers*, II, [339]–77.

MATHEWS *NOT* AT HOME

MSv   Author's manuscript, University of Virginia.
1A   *New-York Mirror*, 11, no. 35 (March 1, 1834), 278 col. 3.

NEWTON THE PAINTER

MSn   Author's manuscript, Berg Collection, New York Public Library.
1A   *New-York Mirror*, 12, no. 38 (March 21, 1835), 303 col. 3.

AN UNWRITTEN DRAMA OF LORD BYRON

J   *"Unpublished note by Capt Medwin"* in *Journals*, III, pp. 710–12.

1A   *Knickerbocker Magazine*, 6 (August 1835), 142–44.
2A   *The Gift: A Christmas and New Year's Present for 1836.* Philadelphia: E. Carey & A. Hart, 1835. Pp. 166–71.

THE HAUNTED SHIP. A TRUE STORY—AS FAR AS IT GOES

1E   *Heath's Book of Beauty. 1836.* Edited by the Countess of Blessington. London: Longman, *et al.*, [1835]. Pp. [253]–57.

1A   *New-York Mirror*, 13, no. 28 (January 9, 1836), 218.
2A   *Friendship's Offering:—A Christmas, New Year and Birthday Present for MDCCCXLIX.* Boston: Phillips and Sampson, [1848]. Pp. 326–30.

[LETTER TO THE EDITOR OF THE NEW YORK *AMERICAN*]

1A   New York *American*, January 7, 1837, p. 2 col. 6.
2A   PMI, III, 100–01.

[LETTER TO THE EDITOR OF *THE PLAINDEALER*]

1A   *The Plaindealer*, 1, no. 9 (January 28, 1837), 131.
2A   PMI, III, 104–09.

[LETTER TO WILLIAM CULLEN BRYANT]

1A   New York *American*, February 17, 1837, p. 2 col. 6.
2A   *The Plaindealer*, 1, no. 12 (February 18, 1837), 186–87.

[TOAST AT THE BOOKSELLERS' DINNER, MARCH 30, 1837]

MSm   Author's manuscript, John S. H. Fogg Collection, Maine Historical Society.
1A   New York *American*, April 3, 1837, p. 2 cols. 3–4.
3A   PMI, III, 115–16.

[LETTER OF "GEOFFREY CRAYON" TO THE EDITOR OF
THE *KNICKERBOCKER MAGAZINE*]

1A	*Knickerbocker Magazine*, 13, no. 3 (March 1839), 206–10.
2A	*A Book of the Hudson.* New York: George Putnam [Printed by R. Craighead], 1849. P. [vii].
3A	*Homes of American Authors.* New York: George P. Putnam, 1853. Pp. 53–61.
4A	*Spanish Papers*, II, [417]–24.

SLEEPY HOLLOW

1A	*Knickerbocker Magazine*, 13, no. 5 (May 1839), 404–11.
2A	*Spanish Papers*, II, [425]–39.

[LETTER OF "HIRAM CRACKENTHORPE" TO THE EDITOR
OF THE *KNICKERBOCKER MAGAZINE*]

1A	*The Knickerbocker Sketch-Book. A Library of Select Litera-*
2A	*Knickerbocker Magazine*, 13, no. 5 (May 1839), 445–46.
	ture. Edited by Lewis Gaylord Clark. New York: Burgess and Stringer, 1845. Pp. [27]–29.

NATIONAL NOMENCLATURE

1A	*Knickerbocker Magazine*, 14, no. 2 (August 1839), 158–62.
2A	*Spanish Papers*, II, [440]–46.

DESULTORY THOUGHTS ON CRITICISM

1A	*Knickerbocker Magazine*, 14, no. 2 (August 1839), 175–78.
2A	*Spanish Papers*, II, [447]–52.

COMMUNIPAW

MSn	Author's manuscript, Berg Collection, New York Public Library.
MSnp	Author's manuscript as revised by Pierre M. Irving.
1A	*Knickerbocker Magazine*, 14, no. 3 (September 1839), 257–62.
4A	*Spanish Papers*, II [453]–62.

CONSPIRACY OF THE COCKED HATS

1A	*Knickerbocker Magazine*, 14, no. 4 (October 1839), 305–09.
2A	*Spanish Papers*, II, [463]–70.

[LETTER ON INTERNATIONAL COPYRIGHT TO THE EDITOR
OF THE *KNICKERBOCKER MAGAZINE*]

1A	*Knickerbocker Magazine*, 15, no. 1 (January 1840), 78–79.
2A	PMI, III, 149–51.

[ANECDOTE OF ADMIRAL HARVEY]

MSn	Author's manuscript, Manuscript Division, New York Public Library.
MSnc	Author's manuscript as revised by Lewis Gaylord Clark.
1A	*Knickerbocker Magazine*, 15, no. 2 (February 1840), 166–67.

THE "EMPIRE OF THE WEST"

MSv	Author's manuscript, University of Virginia.
MSvc	Author's manuscript, as revised by Lewis Gaylord Clark.
1A	*Knickerbocker Magazine*, 15, no. 3 (March 1840), 260–61.
N	*North American Review*, 50 (January 1840), 100–01, 113, 120, 124.

[ANECDOTE OF THE FRENCH REVOLUTION]

MSy	Author's manuscript, Yale University.
MSyc	Author's manuscript, as revised by Lewis Gaylord Clark.
1A	*Knickerbocker Magazine*, 15, no 4 (April 1840), 351.

[THE TAKING OF THE VEIL, AND THE CHARMING LETORIÉRES]

MSv	Author's manuscript, University of Virginia Library.
MSvc	Author's manuscript, as revised by Lewis Gaylord Clark.
1A	*Knickerbocker Magazine*, 15, no. 6 (June 1840), 513–21.

LETTER FROM GRANADA

1A	*Knickerbocker Magazine*, 16, no. 1 (July 1840), 57–61.
2A	*Spanish Papers*, II, [471]–79.

AMERICAN RESEARCHES IN ITALY

1A	*Knickerbocker Magazine*, 18, no. 4 (October 1841), 319–22.

[MEMOIR OF THOMAS CAMPBELL]

1A	Beattie, William. *The Life and Letters of Thomas Campbell*. 2 vols. New York: Harper & Brothers, 1850. I, xi–xvi.
2A	*Spanish Papers*, II, 135–42.

CORRECTION OF A MISSTATEMENT RESPECTING *ASTORIA*

MSt	Galley proof of the *Literary World* text, uncorrected, Sleepy Hollow Restorations, Tarrytown, New York.
MStc	Galley proof of the *Literary World* text, as corrected by the author.
1A	*Literary World*, 9, no. 251 (November 22, 1851), 408, cols. 1–3.

THE CATSKILL MOUNTAINS

MSt	Author's manuscript, Sleepy Hollow Restorations, Inc., Tarrytown, New York
2A	*The Home Book of the Picturesque*. New York: G. P. Putnam, 1852 [1851]. Pp. [71]–78.
5A	*Spanish Papers*, II [480]–87.

[REMARKS AT THE COOPER MEMORIAL MEETING, FEBRUARY 24, 1852]

1A	*Memorial of James Fenimore Cooper*. New York: G. P. Putnam, 1852. P. 23.

CONVERSATIONS WITH TALMA

MSy	Author's manuscript, "French Romance," Yale University.
MSh	Author's manuscript, "Conversations with Talma," Henry E. Huntington Library.
1A	*The Knickerbocker Gallery: A Testimonial to the Editor of the Knickerbocker Magazine from its Contributors.* New York: S. Hueston, 1855. Pp. [15]–22.
2A	*The Atlantic Souvenir for 1859....* New York: Derby and Jackson, 1859. Pp. [33]–40.
3A	*Spanish Papers,* II, [151]–60.

[MEMOIR OF WASHINGTON ALLSTON]

MSn	Author's manuscript, Manuscript Division, New York Public Library.
1A	Duyckinck, Evert A. and George L., eds. *Cyclopædia of American Literature* ... 2 vols. New York: Charles Scribner & Co., 1855. Volume II, pp. 14–16.
3A	*Spanish Papers,* II, [143]–50.

[THE CHRONICLE OF PELAYO]

MSy	Author's manuscript. "Pelayo and the Merchant's Daughter," Yale University.
MSv	Author's manuscript, University of Virginia.
1A	*Knickerbocker Magazine,* 15 (January 1840), 65–66.
4A	*Spanish Papers,* I, [209]–44.

[THE SUCCESSORS OF PELAYO. FAVILA]

MSv	Author's manuscript, University of Virginia.

CHRONICLE OF THE OMMIADES

MSb	Author's manuscript, pp. 21–40, Johns Hopkins University.
MSc	Author's manuscript, pp. 32–89 [bound], Columbia University.
MSca	Author's manuscript, pp. 62, 63, [unbound], Columbia University.
MSh	Author's manuscript, Hispanic Society of America.
MShc	Author's manuscript, Hispanic Society of America, as revised by Lewis Gaylord Clark.
MSn	Author's manuscript, Berg Collection, New York Public Library.
MSv	Author's manuscript, p. 31, University of Virginia.
1A	*Knickerbocker Magazine,* 15, no. 5 (May 1840), 427–40.
2A	*Spanish Papers,* I, [247]–73.

CHRONICLE OF FERNAN GONZALEZ, COUNT OF CASTILE

MSv	Author's manuscript, University of Virginia.
1A	*Spanish Papers,* I, [277]–350.

CHRONICLE OF FERNANDO THE SAINT

MSv	Author's manuscript, University of Virginia.
MSn	Author's manuscript, Berg Collection, New York Public Library.

MSva	Author's manuscript, pp. 185–86 [filed as "A Spanish Tale"], University of Virginia.
1A	*Spanish Papers*, I, [353]–451.

[MY UNCLE]

MSy	Author's manuscript, Beinecke Library, Yale University.

[SIR DAVID WILKIE IN SPAIN]

MSy	Author's manuscript, Beinecke Library, Yale University.

THE VILLAGE CURATE

MSw	Author's manuscript, Olin Library, Washington University.

THE LOG HOUSE HOTEL

MSw	Author's manuscript, Olin Library, Washington University.

[HISTORY OF THE CONQUEST OF MEXICO]

MSt	Facsimile of author's manuscript, in Joseph F. Taylor, "Washington Irving's Mexico: A Lost Fragment," *The Bookman*, 41 (1915), 667.
1A	Taylor, "Washington Irving's Mexico," pp. 668–69.

ILLUSTRATION TO THE LEGEND OF PRINCE AHMED

MSp	Author's manuscript, Princeton University Library.

[A VOYAGE UP THE HUDSON RIVER IN 1800]

1A	PMI, I, 40–43.

[A JOURNEY TO SACKETT'S HARBOR IN 1814]

1A	PMI, I, 317–18.

ARE	Author's Revised Edition of *The Works of Washington Irving*, 15 vols. (New York: George P. Putnam, 1848–1850)
Irvingiana	Evert A. Duyckinck, ed. *Irvingiana: A Memorial of Washington Irving* (New York: C. B. Richardson, 1860 [1859])
T	Twayne edition
Johnson	Samuel Johnson, *A Dictionary of the English Language*, 9th ed., 2 vols. (London: J. Johnson et al., 1806)
Walker	John Walker, *A Critical Pronouncing Dictionary* (London: G. G. J. and J. Robinson and T. Cadell, 1791)
Webster	Noah Webster, *A Compendious Dictionary of the English Language* (Hartford: Hudson and Goodwin, 1806)

The following further editorial symbols are employed throughout the editorial apparatus:

↑ ↓	Interlinear insertion
⟨ ⟩	Cancelled matter
[roman]	Editorial insertion

[*italics*]   Editorial comment
⟨? ?⟩
   or   Doubtful readings
[? ?]
undeciphered   Unrecovered word. When more than one word is unre-
                      covered, the fact is noted: e.g., "⟨*three undeciphered
                      words*⟩"

EXPLANATORY NOTES

The numbers before all notes indicate page and line or lines respectively. Chapter numbers, chapter or section titles, epigraphs, author's chapter or section summaries, texts, quotations, and footnotes are included in the line count. Only running heads and rules added by the printer to separate the running heads from the text are omitted from the count. The quotation from the text, to the left of the bracket, is the matter under discussion.

4.8 "death's dateless night"] Shakespeare, Sonnet XXX, line 6.

4.42 Florian's romance of "Gonsalvo of Cordova;"] Jean Pierre Claris de Florian (1755–1794) published his *Gonzalve de Cordoue, ou Grenade Reconquise* . . . at Paris in 1791. The work appeared in several editions thereafter and in 1801 was translated into Spanish.

5.1–2 "The Civil Wars of Granada," by Ginez Perez de la Hita] Pérez de Hita's influential *Historia de los Vandos de los Zegries y Abencerrajes Caualleros Mores de Granada, de las Civiles Guerras que Huvo en Ellas, y Batallas . . . entre Moros y Christianos . . .* first appeared in 1595 and was reprinted many times thereafter. A *Segunda Parte* was published in 1619.

5.40–43 "Esta . . . desfiguradas."] "This is a history totally fabulous, whose author is ignorant, however much he passes with the name of someone,—stuffed with tales and chimeras, in which scarcely six truths are to be found, and those distorted." The source of the quotation is Juan de Echeverría, *Paseos por Granada y sus Contornos . . .*, 2 vols. (Granada, 1814).

8.42 Pulgar, Chron. de los Reyes Catolicos] Fernando del Pulgar's *Chronica de los Muy Altos y Esclarecidos Reyes Chatolicos don Fernando y doña Isabel . . .*, 2 vols. (Valladolid, 1565) was reprinted in 1567 and 1780.

8.43 Mariana] Juan de Mariana's *Historia General de España* was first published in Latin and in partial form, with twenty books, in 1592, and augmented editions appeared at intervals. The first Spanish version was published in 1601 and the work was often reprinted thereafter.

9.41 Zurita, Annales] Jerónimo Zurita y Castro (1512–1580) *Anales de la Corona de Aragon . . .* first appeared in six volumes between 1562 and 1580. Further editions were published in 1610–1621 and 1668–1671.

10.42 Garibay, Compend. Hist.] Esteban Garibay y Zamalloa (1525–1599) first published *Los XL. Libros d'el Compendio Historial de las Chronicas y Vniuersal Historia . . . de España . . .* at Madrid in 1571. Subsequent editions were published in 1596 and 1628.

10.43 Faria y Sousa, Hist. Portugal] Manuel de Faria y (or e) Sousa (1590–1649) first published his *Historia del Reyno de Portugal . . .* at Madrid in 1628, under the title *Epitome de las Historias Portuguesas.* An English translation by John Stevens, *The History of Portugal . . .,* appeared in 1698.

11.43 Abarca, Reyes de Aragon] Pedro Abarca (1619–1693), *Los Reyes de Aragon en Anales Historicos, Distribvdos en Dos Partes . . . ,* 2 vols. (Madrid, 1682–1684).

15.15–16 a mournful Spanish ballad . . . translated by Lord Byron] Byron's "A Very Mournful Ballad on the Siege and Conquest of Alhama" has as its refrain "Wo is me, Alhama!"

27.39–41 Fray Francisco (afterwards Cardinal) Ximenes . . . Fernando de Talavera, Archbishop of Granada] Fray Ximenes (1436–1517) was made primate of Spain in 1495; in 1507 he was made a cardinal and inquisitor-general. Fernando or Hernando de Talavera (1428–1507) was confessor to Queen Isabella, and in 1492 he was named Archbishop of Granada.

29.43 when . . . this fortress] In August 1823 French forces had invaded Spain to help quell a revolution against the tyrannical King Ferdinand VII.

31.9–10 Lieutenant Alexander Slidell] Alexander Slidell Mackenzie (1803–1848), known until 1838 by the surname "Slidell," after the publication of *A Year in Spain* continued in the naval service but also pursued an active interest in authorship. His published works also include *Popular Essays on Naval Subjects* (1833), *The American in England* (2 vols., 1835), *Spain Revisited* (2 vols., 1836), a *Life of Commodore Oliver Hazard Perry* (2 vols., 1840), a *Life of Paul Jones* (2 vols., 1841), and *The Life of Stephen Decatur* (1846).

33.6 *Utiliser ses moments*] "Make use of one's moments."

34.4 Drawcansir] A blustering, vainglorious bully in Buckingham's *The Rehearsal* (1672).

42.4 the poor fisherman's wife in the Antiquary who had lost her son] Maggie Mucklebackit; see Walter Scott, *The Antiquary,* Chapters XXXI, XXXII.

43.17–18 Toboso . . . Dulcinea] A small town about sixty miles southeast of Toledo, Toboso was the home of Don Quixote's lady-love. See *Don Quixote,* Part II, Chapter 10.

43.32 under the constitution] The liberal Constitution of 1812. Upon his restoration to power in 1814, King Ferdinand VII promised to maintain the constitution but did not do so. In 1823, following the suppression of a rebellion against the king, the constitution was suspended.

45.17 "sere and yellow leaf."] Adapted from *Macbeth* V. iii. 23.

52.1 the celebrated Polinario] A highwayman, according to Henry D. Inglis "during eleven years, the dread of half of Spain," who ranged the northern part of the Sierra Morena and the southern parts of La Mancha. In his *Spain in 1830* (London, 1831), II, 10–13, Inglis gives an amusing account of Polinario's being reformed by the Archbishop of Gaen.

53.20–21 Sancho . . . the disconsolate Cardenio] See *Don Quixote*, Book III, Chapter 23.

57.11–13 our modern Telemachus . . . Island of Calypso] Telemachus was the son of Ulysses. See *The Odyssey*, Books XIV–XVI.

57.18 Mentor] A faithful friend of Ulysses, whose form Athene assumed when she accompanied Telemachus as guide and adviser in his search for his father.

60.25 'This . . . native land!'] Adapted from Walter Scott, *The Lay of the Last Minstrel*, Canto VI, stanza one.

62.20 Mr. Henry Wheaton] Wheaton (1785–1848), American jurist and diplomat, was U. S. chargé d'affaires to Denmark, 1827–1835, and Minister to Prussia, 1835–1846.

64.21 Canute the Great] A king of England, Denmark, and Norway, Canute (ca. 994–1035) was a son of Sweyn, King of Denmark.

65.2 the Amphyctionic council] A confederation for mutual protection of twelve Greek tribes, whose deputies met twice yearly, at Delphi and at Thermopylae.

65.20–21 Servians, Calmucks] That is, Serbians and Kalmucks; the latter are a confederacy of Mongol tribes in Sinkiang province, China.

65.35 Klopstock] Friedrich Gottlieb Klopstock (1724–1803), German poet, author of a religious epic in twenty cantos, the *Messias*, which first appeared in complete form in 1773.

66.6 Dr. Henderson] See Discussions of Adopted Readings 66.11–16.

66.30 Franconia] In medieval times an important duchy of Germany.

66.40 William Spencer] William Robert Spencer (1769–1834), poet and wit, published translations, adaptations, and in 1811 a volume of *Poems*. Byron thought his verses "pefectly aristocratic."

68.29 Ditmarus Blefkenius] Blefken was the author of an important early account of Iceland and Greenland and their peoples, *Islandia, sive Populorum & Mirabilium quæ in ea Insula Reperiuntur Accvratior Descriptio . . .* (Leiden, 1607).

69.16 Mallet's Northern Antiquities] The *Introduction a l'Histoire de Dannemarc* . . . of Paul Henri Mallet (1730–1807) was first translated into English, by Bishop Thomas Percy, as *Northern Antiquities: A Description of the Manners, Customs, Religion, and Laws of the Ancient Danes, and other Northern Nations* (London, 1770). Another edition in English appeared in 1809.

69.24–25 Pompey . . . Tigranes and Mithridates] In 66 B.C., Pompey was given command over all Roman territory in Asia. Pompey drove Mithridates IV Eupator, King of Pontus, and his son-in-law Tigranes I of Armenia, from the territories of Cappadocia and Syria which they had annexed. He drove Mithridates to the east end of the Black Sea, and he captured Tigranes.

74.19–20 Ragnar Lodbrok] Ragnar is supposed to have lived around 800 A.D. and is said to have been the son of King Sigurd of Sweden.

79.5 Rollo] Born about 860, Rollo was in his early career a Norwegian Viking or pirate.

81.14–15 the English historians, Hume, Turner, Lingard, and Palgrave] David Hume (1711–1776), Sharon Turner (1768–1847), John Lingard (1771–1851), and Francis Palgrave (1788–1861).

81.30–33 "Par . . . successeur."] "By my faith," said Robert, "I shall not leave you behind entirely without a lord. I have a little bastard who will be growing up if it pleases God. Choose him forthwith, and I shall invest him before you as my successor to this duchy."

86.40 Palgrave, Hist. Eng.] See Discussions of Adopted Readings 85.33–38.

87.3 Charles Mathews] Mathews (1776–1835), the English comedian, had visited the U. S. in 1822 and visited it again in 1834.

87.5–7 A letter from an American gentleman . . . the following anecdote] Irving's correspondent is unknown. However, for Mathews' own account of the incident see his letter to his wife, November 6, 1833, in *Memoirs of Charles Mathews, Comedian. By Mrs. Mathews* (London, 1839), IV, 214–19.

87.10–11 the retired tragedian Charles Young] Charles Mayne Young (1777–1856), English actor, had retired from the stage in 1832. At his farewell benefit at Covent Garden, Young had appeared as Hamlet; and, in his honor, Charles Mathews played as Polonius.

87.26–27 when he played mad in the Sierra Morena] See *Don Quixote*, Book III, Chapter 25.

88.4 Gilbert Stuart Newton] Newton (1797–1835) was born in Halifax, Nova Scotia, and contrary to Irving's suggestion he considered himself an Englishman. He was in the U. S. for ten months when at the height of his fame, in 1831 and 1832. Not long after his return to England he entered St. Luke's Hospital, London.

88.18 Leslie]   Charles Robert Leslie (1794–1859), the English painter.

88.22 Dr. Sutherland]   Alexander Robert Sutherland (d. 1861) was physician to St. Luke's Hospital for Lunatics from 1816 or before to 1842, when his son Alexander John Sutherland (1811–1867) succeeded him.

90.6–7 a Spanish play . . . furnished to Byron by Shelley]   In fact, the "play" was a scene from Calderon's *El Purgatorio de San Patricio* in which Ludovico Enio vainly attempts to kill a mantled figure ("un Hombre Embozado") who at last reveals himself to be Enio's second self.

90.25 the *Embozado of Cordova*]   Calderon wrote no such play. Irving was misled by Thomas Medwin, who quoted to him the title of the mysterious work as "the *Embozado* or *Encapotado*."

93.11–12 a writer of North Carolina]   Joseph Seawell Jones (*ca.* 1811–1855) was the author of *A Defense of the Revolutionary History of North Carolina from the Aspersions of Mr. Jefferson* (Boston and Raleigh, 1834). He also published *Memorials of North Carolina* (New York, 1838).

93.21 some Virginian writers]   George Tucker (1775–1861), political economist and author, was Professor of Moral Philosophy at the University of Virginia at the time he became involved in the newspaper controversy with Joseph Seawell Jones. Other Virginians whom Irving may have had in mind are unknown.

94.31 from some friend]   Gulian C. Verplanck (1786–1870); see PMI, II, 473.

99.15–16 a volume of Halleck's poems]   *Alnwick Castle, with Other Poems* (New York, 1836) was Fitz-Greene Halleck's most recent volume of verse; probably Irving sent a copy of it to Rogers.

99.19 the two first in the volume]   "Alnwick Castle" and "Marco Bozzaris."

101.12–13 Peter Stuyvesant]   Stuyvesant (1602–1682), the original of "Peter the Headstrong" in Irving's *A History of New York*, was the last Dutch governor of the New Netherlands.

102.4–5 Herculanean manuscripts]   The city of Herculaneum, at the foot of Mt. Vesuvius, was buried during an eruption of the volcano in 79 A.D. In 1709 the ancient city was rediscovered, and a century later (1806–1815) systematic explorations were conducted under the French. Among the remains were a number of carbonized manuscripts on sheets of papyrus; some of these had been deciphered by the time of Irving's writing.

107.26–28 Frederick Filipsen . . . his wife, Katrina Van Courtlandt]   Frederick Philipse (1626–1702), landed proprietor of New Netherland, came to America from Holland in 1647. In 1672 he began to

acquire a magnificent landed property which, following other acquisitions, was consolidated in 1693 in the Royal Patent of Philipsburgh
manor. Catherine Van Cortlandt, whom he married in 1692, was his
second wife.

108.18 Gabriel Requa] Requa (1760–1809), was one of a family of
Huguenot origin which had settled in Tarrytown, New York.

113.35–36 the opening of one of the seals in the Revelations] See
Revelations 6.1.

115.5 Mr. Shandy, the elder] Walter Shandy believed that "there was
a strange kind of magic bias, which good or bad names, as he called
them, irresistibly impressed upon our characters and conduct" (*The
Life and Opinions of Tristram Shandy, Gent.*, Vol. I [original edition],
Chapter XIX, in *The Works of Lawrence Sterne* [London, 1803], I,
59). The phrase "Nicodemused into nothing" (115.9) is from the same
source.

117.13 the Vicar of Wakefield's horse] In Chapter XII of Goldsmith's
The Vicar of Wakefield "the Colt, which was grown old," is traded
at a neighboring fair by the Vicar's son Moses, who after making a
further trade returns home with a gross of green spectacles.

119.11–18 "Let . . . 'em!" REHEARSAL.] George Villiers, Second Duke
of Buckingham, *The Rehearsal* (1672), Act I, Scene 2.

122.5 one of its greatest geniuses has had some rough passages] James
Fenimore Cooper, whose criticisms during the 1830's of abuses of
democracy in American society resulted in virulent attacks by Whig
editors against his books and his personal character.

123.11 expedition, under Oloffe the Dreamer] In the Author's Revised
Edition (1848), of *A History of New York*, see Book II, Chapters
5–7.

124.1 Walter the Doubter] The name given in *A History of New York*
to Wouter Van Twiller (1580?–1656?), Dutch governor of the New
Netherlands (1633–1637).

128.3 Paas and Pinxter] Easter and Whitsuntide (the week beginning
the seventh Sunday after Easter).

130.29 "unclasp a secret book . . . . spear."] *I Henry IV* I. iii. 188–93.

131.32 New-England Society] "The New-England Society in the City
and State of New York" adopted its constitution in 1805.

131.43 Society of Saint Nicholas] "The Saint Nicholas Society of the
City of New York" was organized February 28, 1835, and was incorporated April 17, 1841.

133.11 William the Testy] The name given in *A History of New York*
to William Kieft (1597–1647), governor of the New Netherlands
(1638–1647).

133.26–27 the petition . . . act of international copy-right] The first

American movement for international copyright was made in 1837, when Henry Clay presented a petition on the subject. The matter was referred to a Senate committee, including Clay, Daniel Webster, and James Buchanan, who reported in favor of the full protection of literary property. No further action was taken, however.

135.3 Sir ———— Harvey] Sir Eliab Harvey (1758–1830), English admiral, was in 1776 sent out to North America in the ship *Mermaid*, from which he was later transferred to the *Eagle*, then carrying the flag of Lord Howe. He returned to England in October 1778.

136.10–11 the North-East Boundary question] A treaty of 1783 defined the northeast boundary of the United States as extending from the source of the St. Croix River due north to the highlands or watershed between the Atlantic and St. Lawrence systems, thence along those highlands to the northwesternmost head of the Connecticut River. Disputes over this definition lasted until 1842, when the Webster-Ashburton Treaty resulted in adoption of the present boundary.

136.35 Captain Lewis] Meriwether Lewis (1774–1809), co-leader with William Clark of an official expedition from the United States to the Pacific Coast, 1803–1806.

137.9–10 Major Pitcher, in his report] In "Discovery Beyond the Rocky Mountains," the article in the *North American Review*, 50 (January 1840), the passage being quoted here is cited (p. 120) as from "a memoir addressed to the War Department by Major Joshua Pitcher," published in *Senate Documents*, 21st Congress, Second Session, I, No. 39.

137.24 Mr. Nathaniel J. Wyeth] Wyeth (1802–1856), trader and explorer, between 1832 and 1837 organized and led two attempts to exploit the Columbia River and lands adjoining it for fish, furs, timber, and agricultural resources. His schemes failed, chiefly owing to timorous and financially inadequate support. Some of Wyeth's activities are described by Irving in an appendix to *The Adventures of Captain Bonneville, U.S.A.*, from which the quotation on 137.25–27 was adapted in "Discovery Beyond the Rocky Mountains," p. 124. Irving's quotation departs somewhat from the *North American Review* text.

138.28 I have already given you a few anecdotes] In "The Knight of Malta," *Knickerbocker Magazine*, 15 (February 1840), 108–18; reprinted in *Wolfert's Roost* (1855).

139.14 The memoirs she has left behind] The seven-volume *Souvenirs de la Marquise de Créquy* (1714–1803) appeared at Paris in 1834–1835. Irving derives his material for "The Taking of the Veil" from *Souvenirs*, III, 108–33, and for "The Charming Letoriéres" from IV, 25–34.

144.3–4 the bull *cum proximis*: '*Adjutorium nostrum in nomine Domini.*']
   In his reference to a papal bull entitled "*Cum proximis*" Irving follows
   his source, the Marquise de Crequi; but no bull exists having that
   title. Probably the original intended reference was to a brief by Pope
   Gregory XIII, *Cum pro munere* (1580), which decreed that no changes
   were to be made to the "Corpus Juris Canonici," or Body of Canon
   Law, then in preparation. The *Corpus*, which served as exemplar for
   all subsequent editions, appeared at Rome in 1582.
      The Latin phrases, which translate "Our help [is] in the name of
   the Lord," are from the Ordinary of the Mass immediately preceding
   the "Confiteor."
152.23 Marquis de Salar]   Fernando Pérez del Pulgar, the sixth Marquis
   of Salar, married Carmen, the daughter of the Count de Luque; the
   latter two are described by Irving in *The Alhambra* (1832), II, 47–54.
153.9 R. H. WILDE]   Wilde (1789–1847), a lawyer, was a U. S. con-
   gressman from Georgia in 1815–1817 and 1828–1835. In addition to
   his published historical researches (see Explanatory Notes 153.20),
   Wilde wrote popular lyrics.
153.18 Count Alberti]   See Count Mariano Alberti's *Manoscritti inediti
   di Torquato Tasso, ed Altri Pregevoli Documenti, per Servire alla
   Biografia del Medesimo . . .*, ed. Romualdo Gentilucci (Lucca, 1837).
153.20 a work, now in the press]   Wilde, *Conjectures and Researches
   Concerning the Love, Madness, and Imprisonment of Torquato Tasso
   . . .*, 2 vols. (New York, 1842).
154.30–31 the notes of the late learned Canonico Moreri on Filelfo's life
   of Dante]   The references are to Francesco Filelfo (1398–1481?),
   Italian philologist and poet, and to Louis Moréri, D. D. (1643–1680),
   author of *Le Grand Dictionnaire Historique . . .* (Lyons, 1674), which
   work had passed through twenty editions by 1759, when the final one
   appeared. However, no reference to Filelfo appears in the articles on
   Dante in any of the several editions of the *Dictionnaire* consulted in
   the preparation of this edition.
154.38 Vasari]   Giorgio Vasari (1512–1574), Italian painter, architect,
   and author, whose *Le Vite de piv Eccelenti Architetti, Pittori, et
   Scvltori* (1550) was available in English translation as *Lives of the
   Most Emient Painters, Sculptors, and Architects.*
154.38–39 Filippo Villani]   Villani (1325?–1405) was the author of
   Liber de Origine Civitatis Florentiae et eiusdem Famosis Civibus and
   also of a commentary on the first canto of Dante's *Divine Comedy*.
   The latter work is rich with information laying bare the historical
   allegory in the poem.
155.9 Giovanni Aubrey Bezzi]   The results of Bezzi's activities include a
   translation into English of Giorgio Vasari's *Life of Giovanni Angelico*

de Fiesole (London, 1850) and an anthology, *Readings in Italian Prose Literature. With Biographical Sketches* (London, 1852).

156.36 Should Mr. Wilde finish his biographical work] "The Life and Times of Dante" was left incomplete at Wilde's death and has never been published. The manuscript is at the Library of Congress.

158.43 Jeffrey] Francis Jeffrey (1773–1850), co-founder of the *Edinburgh Review* in 1802 and until 1829 its editor.

159.28 Hallam, author of the "Literary History of the Middle Ages,"] Henry Hallam (1777–1859) was the author of, among other works, an *Introduction to the Literature of Europe, in the Fifteenth, Sixteenth, and Seventeenth Centuries,* 4 vols. (London, 1837–1839) and a *View of the State of Europe During the Middle Ages,* 2 vols. (London, 1818). He wrote no work having the title mentioned by Irving, which is probably a confusion of the above two titles.

160.20 the cause of suffering Poland] After the suppression of a Polish national uprising, followed by the partition of Poland; see Explanatory Notes I, 138.34–35

161.13 Albert Gallatin, Esq.] Gallatin (1761–1849), Swiss-born American statesman and financier, shared with Schoolcraft an enthusiastic interest in the culture of the American Indian.

161.17 Malte Brun] Conrad Malte-Brun (1775–1826) was the author of an encyclopedic study, *Précis de la Géographie Universelle . . . ,* which appeared in eight volumes between 1810 and 1829. As early as 1824 various English translations of the then unfinished work began to appear, under the title *Universal Geography; or, A Description of All the Parts of the World.*

166.3–4 Adrian Van der Donk] Van der Donck (1620–*ca.* 1655), colonist and lawyer, was the author of a work, more descriptive than historical since in preparing it he was denied access to official records, *Beshrivinge von Nieuw Nederlandt* (Amsterdam, 1655). An English translation by Jeremiah Johnson, entitled *Description of the New Netherlands,* is in *New-York Historical Society Collections,* second series, I (New York, 1841), [125]–242.

166.10 Johannes de la Montagne] Van der Donck's account of de la Montagne and his part in this incident is as follows: "We acted with it [the mineral received from the Indian] as we best could, under the direction of a certain Johannes de la Montagne, doctor in medicine, and counselor in New Netherland, a man of intelligence, who had some knowledge or science in these matters. To be brief; it was put into a crucible, and after it had been thought to be long enough in the fire, it was taken out, and two pieces of gold were found in it, which were both judged to be worth about three guilders. This proof was at first kept very still" (*Description,* p. 161).

166.41 Brant Arent Van Slechtenhorst . . . Rensselaerswyck] In 1646 Van Slechtenhorst was appointed director of the colony of Rensselaerswyck, succeeding Arendt van Curler. In 1653 he sent his son Gerrit to the Catskill Mountains in order to search for a hypothesized source of silver in that region.

168.4 with a friend] John Howard Payne.

168.12 John Kemble] John Philip Kemble (1755–1823), the English actor.

168.22 the Emperor] In May 1804 Napoleon I was proclaimed Emperor of the French, which title he held until his abdication ten years later.

171.7–8 Marie Stuart, a modification of the German tragedy of Schiller] Schiller's five-act tragedy in blank verse, *Maria Stuart: Ein Trauerspiel*, was first performed at Weimar in 1800. A French translation was produced at the Théâtre Français in March 1820, and a three-act imitation in French was published in August of the same year.

171.16 Athalie, Polyeucte, Merope] Tragedies composed, respectively, by Racine (1691), Corneille (1641 or 1642), and Voltaire (1736).

173.35 The Missennienes] Casimir Delavigne (1793–1843) was the author of *Les Messéniennes* (1818), elegaic verses inspired by the sufferings of Greece and the trials of France after Waterloo. For discussion of his indebtedness to the example of Byron, see Edmond Estéve, *Byron et le Romantisme Français . . . de 1812 a 1850* (Paris, 1907), p. 116 and Index.

174.18–19 statue of Moses by Michael Angelo] In the church of San Pietro in Vincoli, Rome.

175.21 he and Leslie resided together] For Charles Leslie's account of his relationship with Allston during this period see his *Autobiographical Recollections*, ed. Tom Taylor (Boston, 1860), pp. 21–31.

177.2 Paul Veronese] Popular name of Paolo Caglieri (1528–1588), painter of the Venetian school, celebrated as a colorist.

177.5 Earl of Egremont] George O'Brien Wyndham (1751–1837), Earl of Egremont, was renowned as a public benefactor and patron of the arts.

177.18 Anne Page inviting Master Slender into the house] See *The Merry Wives of Windsor* I. i. 276.

177.20–21 Milton's 'linked sweetness long drawn out.'] "L'Allegro," line 138.

177.42 Philip Hone] Hone (1780–1851), mayor of New York for one year, 1825–1826, was active in Whig politics and in civic and charitable undertakings.

180.29 Pelayo, the deliverer of Spain] Pelayo, or Pelagius, successor to Roderick the Goth (see Irving's "Legend of Don Roderick" in *The*

Crayon Miscellany), created the Kingdom of the Asturias, in lands formerly dominated by the Moslems, *ca.* 718–737 A.D.

180.30 William Wallace] Wallace (*ca.* 1274–1305), the Scottish patriot, carried on a devastating campaign of guerilla warfare in northern England for several years before being captured and condemned for treason.

180.38 Abarca, *Anales de Aragon*] See Explanatory Notes 11.43.

182.43 El Moro Rasis, *La Destruycion de España.* Rojas, *Hist. Toledo*] Ahmed Ibn Mohammed Ibn Moosa Al Razee (Latinized as "Rasis"), Arabian historian, was born at Cordova *ca.* 866 A.D. His history of the conquest of Spain by the Arabs survives in only fragmentary form, but in various translated and unauthorized forms it served as a source for several Spanish historians of the sixteenth and seventeenth centuries. See Ramon Menendéz Pidal, *Crónicas Generales de España Descritas*, 3rd ed. (Madrid, 1918). Pedro de Rojas was the author of *Historia de la Imperial . . . Ciudad de Toledo*, 2 vols. (Madrid, 1654–1663).

192.21 a galliot] A small galley, propelled by both sails and oars.

195.39 Morales, *Cronicon de España*] The *Cronica General de España* of Alonzo el Sabio (1221–1284), compiled by Florian de Ocampo as *Hispania Vincit. Los Cincos Libros Primeros de la Cronica General de España . . .* (Madrid, 1553), was extended between 1574 and 1586 by Ambrosio de Morales. The Ocampo portion brings the history of Spain up to within two centuries of the birth of Christ; the remainder, through the reign of King Bermudo III (1027–1037), is by Morales. The full work was known by the title *Corónica General de España* and was reprinted under that title in 1792.

196.5 atabals] Small kettledrums or tabors.

198.14 Alonzo the Third] Alfonso III (848–912), King of the Asturias and Leon 866–910, was surnamed "The Great" in recognition of his military successes.

198.36–40 * Judicio . . . —*Sebastianus Salmanticensis Episc.*] "* By the providence of God it happened that a part of that very mountain, engulfing its own base, flung sixty-three thousand soldiers with stupendous power into its raging current, and crushed them all. When the riverbed fills up now during winter, and erodes its banks, everywhere it reveals clearly the signs of their weapons and bones.—*Sebastian, Bishop of Salamanca.*"

200.6 his son Favila] Favila (d. 739) was King of Asturias and Leon, 737–739.

200.18–19 the hermitage or chapel of Santa Cruz, already mentioned] See above, 198.15.

201.23 the Sella]　A small river which flows northward into the Atlantic Ocean at Ribadesella in present-day Spain.

201.29 Alonzo the Catholic]　Alonzo I (693–757), King of Asturias 739–757, was surnamed "The Catholic" on account of his zeal in erecting monasteries and churches.

201.40 Sandoval, *El Rey Alonzo el Catholico*]　The historian Fray Prudencio de Sandoval wrote no work having this title. Probably the reference is to Sandoval's *Historias; de Idacio Obispo, que Escribio Poco Antes que se Perdio España ... De Sebastiano, Obispo de Salamanca, que Escriuio desde el Rey Don Pelayo, hasta Don Ordoño Primero Desto Nombre. De Sampiro ... De Pelagio ....* (Pamplona, 1615). Sebastian, Bishop of Salamanca, is one of Irving's sources for "The Chronicle of Pelayo," and Sebastian's work includes an account of the reign of Favila as well as of Alonzo the Catholic, King of Asturias 739–757.

202.9 the illustrious house of Omeya]　Founded by Mo'awiya, who reigned 661–680 A.D., the Omayyad or Ommiades dynasty remained in power until 750, when Marwan II, the reigning caliph, was killed and Abu-al-Abbas al-Saffah, the first Abassid caliph, usurped the throne.

202.24 the powerful dynasty of the Abbassides]　The Abassid caliphate, established in 750 A.D., continued until 1258.

202.33 Abderahman]　Abderahman or Abdurrahman (731–788 A.D.), was a son of Hixem ben Abdelmelic, an Ommiad monarch who reigned from 724 to 743 A.D., and a captive Berber named Rah. Abderahman was King of Cordova from 756 until his death.

203.30 The province of Barca]　East of the Gulf of Sirte, bounded on the north by the Mediterranean, in the northeastern portion of present-day Libya.

207.12 Alabdaries]　Inhabitants of Halep, or Aleppo, east of the Mediterranean Sea, a region occupied by Moslems.

207.23 Ocba the conqueror of Africa]　Uqba ben Al-Hachchach Al-Saduli, fifteenth Emir of al-Andalus, 734–741 A.D. In 739 the Berbers of Africa marched in rebellion against Tangier and were defeated with great slaughter by Uqba. Under his emirate the Moslems won dominion over all Spain except the region of Asturias, where King Pelayo reigned.

207.37 the battle of Beder]　Bedr, a village between Medina and Mecca, was the scene of the first victory of Mohammed over the Koreishites, in 624 A.D.

212.16–17 Tubal Cain]　Son of Lamech the Cainite and Zillah; said to be the inventor of the art of working in metals. See Genesis 4.22.

213.35 Cairvan]　Or Kairwan, a city in northern Africa about one hundred miles south of present-day Tunis.

217.9 Hixem]   Hixem Abul Walid (758–796 A.D.), the second King of
  Cordova in the Ommiades dynasty, reigned from 787 until his death.

219.12 Tadmir]   From the eighth to the twelfth century, a tributary
  Christian state in southeastern Spain, comprising Murcia with portions
  of Granada and Valencia. It was dependent on the caliphate.

220.33 Alphonso the Chaste]   Alfonso II (d. 842), King of Asturias
  791–842, was distinguished for his successful wars against the Moham-
  medans.

222.13   AH AD]   Anno Hegirae ("Year of the Hegira," 622 A.D.);
  Anno Domini.

222.17 Alhakem]   Alhakem (d. 822) was King of Cordova from 796
  until his death.

229.27 Musarabs]   Christians in Spain who, on condition of owning
  allegiance to the Moorish king, and conforming to certain Moorish
  customs, were allowed the exercise of their own religion.

229.44 the moon Ramazan]   The ninth month of the Mohammedan
  year.

231.10 the famous city of Candy]   Candia or Candy was originally a
  fortress built by the Moslems and called by them "Khandax." It not
  only rose to be the capital and chief city of Crete, a formidable nest
  for pirates and a great slave mart, but for a time it actually gave its
  name to the whole island. Crete was called in the official language
  of Venice "the island of Candia."

231.21 [A portion . . . lost.]]   The following is a translation of the passage in Conde's *Historia* (Part II, Chapter 37) for which Irving's
  adapted text has been lost: "In the year 203 and following, Abderahman [the son of Alhakem] went to the frontier of Galicia with the
  people of Merida, and defeated the Christians ·in many encounters
  of little importance; thence he departed for the frontiers of Afranc,
  and made the forays and assaults that had been intended: and in
  the year 205 (820) he returned to Cordova, since his father had no
  minister of state or war other than he. On passing through Tarragona he ordered the ships on the coast of Spain to depart, and they went
  against Gezira Sardinia, and fought with the Christians, and burned
  their fleet before the island, and captured eight of the enemies' ships.
    In reference to Abi Beeri ben Alcutia, Aben Hayan told that, after
  the slaughter of the suburb, King Alhakem was extremely tormented
  by severe melancholy and lost his color, so that he became pale and
  feeble, and through the force of his vehement sadness he contracted
  a fever, and the slaughter appeared to him, and he seemed to see
  people at war, and hear the clamour of arms and the outcries of
  soldiers and the dying; and this was most frequent when he was alone
  and walked through the rooms and on the roof of his citadel; many

times he would call at an untimely hour of the night to his slaves and servants"

233.17 the Duero]   A river in Spain and northern Portugal which flows westward into the Atlantic Ocean.

233.28 Ordoño II.]   Ordoño II, King of Leon 914–924, was the son of Alfonso III of Asturias, and during his father's lifetime he served as governor of Galicia. Upon the death of Alfonso III in 913 he continued in this office, but the next year, following the premature death of his elder brother King Garcia I, he was acclaimed the new king.

234.1–2 Cid Campeador]   Rodrigo Diaz de Bivar, "El Cid" (*ca.* 1040–1099), famous for his exploits in wars with the Moors.

236.34–35 the once flourishing city of Lara]   Lara, in the province of Burgos, was during the Middle Ages one of the most important cities of Castile. It included an extensive residential district and the monasteries of Silo and Arlanza, and it was protected by a strong castle.

237.26–27 the Vigil of St. John]   The evening of June 23.

243.18 Abderahman]   Abderahman III (891–961) was King of Cordova from 912 until his death. During his reign the Moslem power in Spain rose to its greatest height.

243.36 Seven Princes of Lara]   Members of a family belonging to the Castilian aristocracy of the tenth century. According to George Ticknor, the Laras are the subjects of some thirty traditionary ballads, in which the following story is told: "The Seven Lords of Lara, in consequence of a family quarrel, are betrayed by their uncle into the hands of the Moors, and put to death; while their father, with the basest treason, is confined in a Moorish prison, where, by a noble Moorish lady, he has an eighth son, the famous Mudarra, who at last revenges all the wrongs of his race" (*History of Spanish Literature* [Boston, 1849], I, 126).

245.25 the day of the Holy Cross]   May 3, commemorating the discovery of the True Cross by St. Helena.

247.8 Sancho II., King of Navarre]   Sancho II reigned from 970 until his death in 994. He was the son of Sancho I, King of Pamplona 905–925.

247.40 Sandoval, *The Five Bishops*. Mariana . . . . *Cron Gen. de España*]   For Sandoval's compilation, cited here and at 246.41, see Explanatory Notes 201.40. Juan de Mariana's *Historia General de España* first appeared in Spanish in 1601; augmented and corrected editions were published in 1617 and 1623, and the latter edition was often reprinted. For the *Cronica General de España* of King Alonzo el Sabio and others, see Explanatory Notes 195.39; Irving cites the same work at 269.38 below.

248.44 Garcia, surnamed the Trembler] Garcia II. (950–1000?) was King of Navarre from 994 until his death.

252.22 Cava] Cava, or Florinda (as she is called by Irving in the "Legend of Don Roderick"), was the daughter of St. Julian. It was the violation of Cava by Roderick the Goth that brought about the war between the Goths and the Moors. To avenge his daughter, St. Julian turned traitor to Roderick the Goth and induced the Moors to invade Spain.

256.19 Sylo] Sylo, Silos, or Silo was the site of a Benedictine abbey founded in the sixth century; the abbey was restored in the eleventh century. See Marius Férotin, *Histoire de l'Abbaye de Silos* (Paris, 1897).

260.19 the Cross of Calatrava] The insignia of an order of knights founded in 1158 by King Sancho III for the defense of the Spanish frontier against the Moors.

260.30 Ramiro the Second] Ramiro II (d. 950), King of Leon and Asturias *ca.* 930–950.

261.42–43 the *Chronicle* of Bleda] Fray Jaime Bleda, *Coronica de los Moros de España. Dividada en Ocho Libros* (Valencia, 1618).

262.29 Prince Ordoño] Later King Ordoño of Leon, 950–955. He was the son of King Ramiro II of Leon, whom he succeeded.

266.5 King Sancho I.] Sancho I of Castile, "The Great" or "The Fat," was also King of Navarre 970–1035. His dominions eventually included Castle, Leon, Navarre, and Aragon.

272.11–12 the words of the holy psalm: "Exaltabant ossa humilitata."] See Psalms 50.10 in the Vulgate Version of the Bible ("Exaltabunt ossa humiliata").

273.8 Fernando III.] Fernando III (*ca.* 1200–1252) became King of Castile on the death of his uncle, Henry I of Castile, in 1217; he succeeded his father, Alfonso IX of Leon, as King of Leon in 1230. He was canonized by Pope Clement X in 1671.

279.24–25 St. John de Acre] Acre, a seaport on the coast of Palestine, was captured by the Arabs in 638 A.D. and was recaptured by the Christians in 1104. It was named St. John de Acre by knights of a religious military order, the Knights of St. John of Jerusalem.

283.38 Aben Hud] Aben Hud (d. 1237) was descended from the family of Banú Hud, ancient Moslem kings of Saragossa.

283.40 Almohades] A Mohammedan dynasty in northern Africa and Spain, so called from the sect of the Almoahedrun ("worshippers of one god").

286.8 the Guadalete; that fatal river, sadly renowned in the annals of Spain] In 711 a mixed force of Arabs and Berbers, led by the Berber Taric, crossed from Africa and defeated Roderick, the last of the

Visigothic kings of Spain, in a battle beside the Guadalete River. Roderick was killed, his kingdom collapsed, and the Moslems took Cordova and its capital, Toledo.

289.9 Rodrigo, Archbishop of Toledo] Rodrigo Ximénez de Rada (*ca.* 1170–1247), Archbishop of Toledo, wrote an *Estoria de los Godos*, parts of which were available to Irving at second-hand in published works such as Alonzo Nuñez de Castro's *Vida de S. Fernando* (see Explanatory Notes 311.38) and perhaps also in manuscript form.

299.39 *Notas para la Vida*, p. 552] "Notas Para la Vida Del Santo/ Rey Don Fernando" is the running title of Miguel de Manuel Rodriguez, *Memorias Para la Vida de Santo Rey Don Fernando III. . . .* (Madrid, 1800). Irving's page-reference conforms to the material at that point in the *Memorias*.

300.17 Don Pelayo de Correa] Correa (d. 1275), from 1242 until his death Grand Master of an order founded in 1170 to protect the shrine of St. James at Santiago de Compostella against the Moors, was reputed the ablest captain of his time.

300.43 *Cronica del Rey Santo*] The anonymous *Crónica del Sancto Rey Don Fernando Tercero Desto Nombre* first appeared at Seville in 1516 and was reprinted at least ten times in the next century. Irving also refers to the work at 307.43.

306.10 Axataf] Upon the conquest of Cordova by the Spaniards in 1236, Seville came under the protection of the emir Aben-Raxid, who established there as his governor Abu-Faris, or Axataf.

307.18–19 "que . . . proteccion."] "for in this way he designated her [Seville] as his own in the native land, in the [episcopal] seat, and for protection."

307.42 Rodriguez, *Memorias del Santo Rey*] See Explanatory Notes 299.39.

308.23 Ramon Bonifaz] Bonifaz (d. 1256?) was probably of French descent. In 1227 he became alcalde of the district of San Lorenzo de Burgos, and he remained in this office until 1246. Following the capture of Seville, Bonifaz was given a house and fields within the conquered territory.

311.37 Zuniga, *Annales de Sevilla*] Lorenzo Baptista Zuñiga, *Anales Ecclesiásticos y Seglares de la Ciudad de Sevilla* (Sevilla, 1747).

311.38 Jacob Paranes, *Lib. de los Maestros de St. Iago. Corona Gotica . . .*] In a passage of Alonzo Nuñez de Castro's *Vida de S. Fernando El III . . .* (Madrid, 1787) relating to Don Pelayo Perez Correa's exploit narrated here, the footnote reads (p. 231): "Jacob. Parœnes *en el libro de los Maestros de Santiago . . . y otros Autores que escriben de esta Orden.*" However, the original of the work thus cited has not been identified. The first part of the *Corona Gothica, Castellana, y Austriaca*

..., by Diego de Saavedra Fajardo, was published in 1646 and was reprinted several times in the next two decades. Between 1671 and 1677 a continuation, parts two through four, was prepared and published by Alvar Nuñez de Castro. The completed work was frequently reprinted by itself and as part of the *Obras* of Saavedra Fajardo. See Antonio Palau y Dulcet, *Manual del Librero Hispaniamericano*, XVIII (Oxford and Barcelona, 1966), 192–97.

314.8 *herberos*] Soldiers with responsibility for finding pasturage for the cavalry's horses.

328.33 Pablo de Espinosa, *Grandesas de Sevilla*] Pablo Espinosa de los Monteros, *Primera Parte, de La Historia, Antigvedades, y Grandezas, de La Muy Leal Ciudad de Sevilla* (Sevilla, 1627). A *Segundo Parte* to this work was published at Seville in 1630.

328.34–35 Argoti de Molina, *Nobleza de Andaluzia.* ... Tomas Bocio, *Signales de la Iglesia.* . . . Don Rodrigo Sanchez, Bishop of Palencia] Gonzalo Argote de Molina, *Nobleza de Andalucia* (Sevilla, 1588). Bocio, *Signales* is unidentified. However, Irving's entire footnote is virtually identical in content to one in Alonzo Nuñez de Castro's *Vida de S. Fernando El III* ... (see Explanatory Notes 311.38), p. 338, where "Thomás Bocio, *en el lib*. 20. *de los señales de la Iglesia*" is mentioned. Rodrigo Sanchéz de Arevalo (1404–1470), bishop at various times of Zamora, Calahorra, and Palencia, was the author of a Latin history of Spain (Roma, 1470). The work, whose title-page begins *Incipit Compendiosa Historia Hispanica* ... and which is hence known as the *Compendiosa Historia Hispanica*, was reprinted in *Rerum Hispaniarum Scriptores* (Frankfurt, 1579) and in *Hispania Illustrata* (Frankfurt, 1603).

332.16 the Monument] Commemorating the Great Fire of 1666.

333.1–2 Murray's drawing room] The drawing room of John Murray II, Irving's English publisher during the 1820's, was a preferred place of resort for contemporary literary personalities.

333.11 the peace] Probably the Second Peace of Paris, concluded between France and other European nations in November 1815.

334.18 that of St. Thomas by Zurbaran] Francisco Zurbaran (1598–1662) painted his "Saint Thomas Aquinas" as an altar-piece for the church of the College of St. Thomas Aquinas in Seville.

334.24 General Palafox] José Palafox y Melzi (1780–1847), a Spanish general, in 1808 successfully defended the city of Saragossa during a two-month siege by the French.

335.20 Ceuta] A fortified town on the northern coast of Morocco, opposite Gibraltar. It was a Spanish military and penal station.

337.37 Boone's Lick] A settlement on the Missouri River, a few miles west of present-day Columbia, Missouri.

339.17 our little Frenchman Antoine] Antoine Deschetres (1791–*ca.* 1854). For details of his life history see John F. McDermott, ed. *The Western Journals of Washington Irving*, 2nd ed. (Norman, 1966), pp. 49–50 note 89.

342.3 It would appear that Eben Bonabben was mistaken] In the "Legend of Prince Ahmed al Kamel; or, The Pilgrim of Love" Eben Bonabben, tutor to the prince, is described as having "been instructed, when in Egypt, in the language of birds by a Jewish Rabbin, who had received it in lineal transmission from Solomon the Wise, who had been taught it by the queen of Sheba." Actually, in the published tale Eben Bonabben does not himself give this "mistaken" account of the origin of human knowledge of bird language.

343.39 Sale's Koran. De Herbelot] See *The Koran . . .* , trans. George Sale (London, 1734), Chapter XXVII, pp. 309–16; and Barthélemy Herbelot de Molainville, *Bibliotheque Orientale, ou Dictionnaire Universel . . .* (Paris, 1697), pp. 298, 396, 701–02, 819–21. Each of these works appeared in several later editions, and the ones Irving used are unknown.

TEXTUAL COMMENTARY

[ADVERTISEMENT OF AN ABRIDGEMENT OF *THE LIFE AND VOYAGES OF CHRISTOPHER COLUMBUS*]

Irving's public announcement of his intention to·make available an abridgement of the biography of Columbus, and so to frustrate an ambitious "literary pirate"[240] who had undertaken to do so without authorization, appeared on the editorial page of the New York *American* for April 4, 1829. So far as is known, it was not reprinted. Probably the author sent it from Seville, where he was then living, to his brother Ebenezer Irving, his agent in the United States, at about the same time he forwarded to Ebenezer the manuscript copy of the abridgement, in December 1828.[241] Because no manuscript version of Irving's public letter is known to survive, the newspaper text is the inevitable choice as copy-text.[242]

In the preparation of this edition a transcription of the New York *American* text owned by the New-York Historical Society (Newspapers/ New York City) has been collated with that in a second copy owned by the Library of Congress (Bound volume No. 8903).

See Discussions and Lists p. 538.

[REVIEW OF *A CHRONICLE OF THE CONQUEST OF GRANADA*]

Irving intended the review of his own *Conquest of Granada* (1829) to dispel doubts which had arisen as to the credibility of that work as a historical narrative—doubts resulting in large part from the unauthorized action taken by its English publisher, John Murray, of placing "By

240. Irving to Alexander H. Everett, Seville, December 13, 1828; PMI, II, 354–55.
241. See PMI, II, 355.
242. The letter was introduced in the New York *American* as follows:
The following notice from the author of the Life of Columbus, presents an appeal, that his countrymen will not, we are sure, be insensible to. If there be any abridgement of the work now in progress here, it will, we hope, be abandoned—or if not, and it is still persisted in, we are sure it should not, and think it would not, be patronised.—

Washington Irving" on the title-page.[243] Evidently recognizing that his tampering had interfered with the popular success of the *Conquest of Granada*, Murray had invited his annoyed author to prepare an anonymous statement of the ideas which had determined his methods in the work; and mollified, Irving had accepted. His essay duly appeared in the *Quarterly Review*, Murray's house organ, for May 1830.

Whether Irving assisted in preparing this work for publication beyond the stage of manuscript composition is uncertain. He was in London during the early months of 1830, so that it is possible he revised proofs; but since neither a manuscript version nor the proofs are known to survive, this must remain conjectural.[244] At any rate, the likelihood is that the *Quarterly Review* text of his self-review substantially represented his wishes. It was to the mutual interest of Murray and Irving that the latter's views concerning his recently published work should be made known. Moreover, Murray, recognizing his delinquency in the matter of unauthorized emendations and seeking to set to rights his relations with the author, was presumably on his good behavior. Finally, Irving appears to have been so far satisfied with the *Quarterly Review* text of the essay—a statement which he regarded as having a certain importance —as never to have revised it.

Interestingly, in his liberal quotations from his own *Conquest of Granada* he departs at many points in the review from the text of the work as originally published by John Murray. Some of the variant readings suggest freedoms taken with *Granada* in order to ensure an economical, unambiguous, visually pleasing text in the review itself. These include 18 additions or deletions of paragraph breaks, 17 condensations of passages of varying length, 6 omitted footnotes and footnote-references, and 1 virtually re-written "quoted" passage (see Pre-Copy-Text Rejected Variants 15.5–8). Other variants—see, for example, Pre-Copy-Text Rejected Variants 19.14, 22.1—appear to derive from stylistic

---

243. See Introduction, I, liv–lv.

244. For one of the other items he submitted for publication in the *Quarterly Review*, his notice of Alexander Slidell's *A Year in Spain* (see pp. 30–57), Irving played no part beyond submitting a manuscript to J. G. Lockhart, the editor of the magazine. On that occasion Lockhart published a text which differed at many points from the author's intention. Upon sending to Lockhart a third review essay six months after the Slidell piece had appeared, a notice of Henry Wheaton's *History of the Northmen* (see pp. 61–86), Irving urged him to treat it with more scrupulous care than he had "its predecessors." This admonition clearly referred to Lockhart's editorial changes, but the "predecessors" to the Wheaton article which Irving had in mind may or may not have included the review of the *Conquest of Granada*. He may, for example, have been thinking instead of volumes recently published by Murray, such as the *Voyages of the Companions of Columbus*, in the editing of which Lockhart possibly played a part. See Ben H. McClary, "Washington Irving's Amiable Scotch Friends: Three Unpublished Letters to the J. G. Lockharts," *Studies in Scottish Literature*, 4 (October 1966), 103.

preferences alone. In shaping his review the author evidently felt no compunction in, technically, misquoting himself.

In the American text of his Author's Revised Edition of the *Conquest of Granada* (1850), Irving wrote a further explanation of his conceptions of the work and the circumstances under which he had written it.[245] In that statement he drew upon parts of four paragraphs in the earlier, much fuller commentary (corresponding to T 4.38–7.11 inclusive). His re-utilizations of the *Quarterly Review* text are marked chiefly by substitution of "I" in references to himself for the "he" in the anonymous article, and by severe condensation.[246]

The *Quarterly Review* text was not reprinted during Irving's lifetime, but it was included, under the title "Conquest of Granada," in *Spanish Papers*, II, [378]–416. The accidentals of the *Spanish Papers* version reflect the imposition of the Putnam house style.[247] Except for the correction of 2 typographical errors in the *Quarterly Review* text (see Emendations 18.20, 19.2) and the introduction of a new one (see Rejected Variants 8.30), and also a note to the title presumably supplied by Pierre M. Irving (see Emendations 4.2–3), it includes only 2 substantive variants from the original version, both limited to single words (see

245. "Note to the Revised Edition," *Chronicle of the Conquest of Granada...* (New York, 1850), pp. xvii–xviii. Earl N. Harbert discusses the history of Irving's protracted experimentation with Fray Antonio Agapida as an unreliable yet accurate narrator in "Washington Irving's *Conquest of Granada*: A Spanish Experiment That Failed," *Clio*, 3 (1974), 305–13.

246. Word-for-word collation of the corresponding passages in the *Quarterly Review* and the *Conquest of Granada* (1850) is practicable at most but not all points. The single extended instance for which the procedure must be dispensed with will serve to exemplify Irving's method of shortening his earlier statement while retaining its essential purport. The following passage from the *Conquest of Granada* (1850), pp. xvii–xviii, may be compared with the corresponding *Quarterly Review*, text, 57.27–58.22 (see T 6.19–7.11):

In constructing my chronicle, I adopted the fiction of a Spanish monk as the chronicler. Fray Antonio Agapida was intended as a personification of the monkish zealots, who hovered about the sovereigns in their campaigns, marring the chivalry of the camp by the bigotry of the cloister, and chronicling in rapturous strains every act of intolerance towards the Moors. In fact, scarce a sally of the pretended friar, when he bursts forth in rapturous eulogy of some great stroke of selfish policy on the part of Ferdinand, or exults over some overwhelming disaster of the gallant and devoted Moslems, but is taken almost word for word from one or the other of the orthodox chroniclers of Spain.

The ironical vein also was provoked by the mixture of kingcraft and priestcraft, discernible throughout this great enterprise, and the mistaken zeal and self-delusion of many of its most gallant and generous champions. The romantic coloring seemed to belong to the nature of the subject, and was in harmony with what I had seen in my tour through the poetical and romantic regions in which the events had taken place. With all these deductions the work, in all its essential points, was faithful to historical fact, and built upon substantial documents.

247. See the Textual Commentary, I, 273–76.

Rejected Variants 12.21, 21.21). The *Spanish Papers* text thus includes no convincing evidence of authorial revision.

Because no manuscript version of the review is known to exist and Irving apparently did not revise it after its sole publication during his lifetime, the work as it appeared in the *Quarterly Review* is adopted here as copy-text. Certain regularizations are necessary to bring the copy-text into conformity with Irving's usual practice and with conventions followed elsewhere in this edition. Pairs of double quotation marks are substituted for single quotation marks enclosing quoted passages in the *Quarterly Review* (Emendations 4.4); to enclose quotations within quotations, single quotation marks are substituted for the double quotation marks employed in that text (Emendations 7.23–24); and at the beginning of the second and subsequent paragraphs of quoted passages a double quotation mark is substituted for the single quotation mark employed in the *Quarterly Review* (Emendations 18.20). In the copy-text only one of the quotations from the *Conquest of Granada* is given a page-reference (T 7.27), but this anomalous instance is allowed to stand even though it differs from otherwise consistent usage. Page-references to the remaining quotations from *Granada* are supplied at appropriate points in Discussions of Adopted Readings.

In the tables which follow this discussion an accounting is given of substantive variants, and accidental variants of particular interest, between John Murray's edition of the *Conquest of Granada* and the passages quoted from it in the copy-text. Variants between these two texts not recorded in Emendations are listed in a table of Pre-Copy-Text Rejected Variants. Substantive variants between the copy-text, passages adapted from it in the "Note to the Revised Edition" of the *Conquest of Granada*,[248] and the *Spanish Papers* text are also recorded in full. Variants between these texts not included in Emendations are set forth in a separate table of Rejected Variants. Full collation data is on file at the University of Texas.

In the preparation of this edition the following collations have been made:

1. A xerox copy of the text in a copy of the *Quarterly Review* owned by the University of Toronto (AP 4/ Q2) sight collated with the following additional copies: Princeton University (0901/ .Q 151); University of Virginia (AP 4/ .Q2); York University (AP 4/ Q2);

2. The above xerox copy collated twice and independently with the pertinent passages in a copy of the *Conquest of Granada* owned by the University of Toronto (Rare Books D-10/ 2984) and once with a second copy owned by the University of Toronto (HSp/ 1726c);

248. Variants between these two texts which are recorded in the tables pertain to T 4.25–5.14 (But . . . invention) and 6.10–19 (He . . . darkness.).

3. The xerox copy collated twice and independently with the pertinent passages in the *Conquest of Granada* (1850) owned by McMaster University (DP/ 122/ .I7) and once with a copy of the 1859 impression of the work in the possession of the editor (bookplate of L. P. Thompson pasted onto inside front cover);

4. The xerox copy collated twice and independently with the *Spanish Papers* text owned by the National Library of Canada;

5. A xerox copy of the above *Spanish Papers* text sight collated with additional copies owned by the New York Public Library and by Yale University (Iw/ Ir8/ 866).

See Discussions and Lists pp. 523, 538, 648, 678.

[REVIEW OF ALEXANDER SLIDELL'S
A YEAR IN SPAIN]

Irving's critical notice of *A Year in Spain* formed only a part of his stewardship on behalf of its author, Lieutenant Alexander Slidell. In the fall of 1830, upon receiving from Slidell a request for assistance in bringing out a British edition of his book of travels, he managed to place the work with his own publisher, John Murray, on condition that he edit it, correct the proofsheets, and finally review it in Murray's house organ, the *Quarterly Review*. Despite numerous claims already being made upon his time, he agreed. On December 18, 1830, he forwarded to Murray a first instalment of corrected pages of *A Year in Spain*, professing himself "quite delighted" with it thus far and requesting that proofs be returned "as fast as they can be furnished, that I may go on with a review of it, which I shall immediately commence." By December 26 he had completed a portion of his essay, which he sent along to Murray. He forwarded the final batch of copy for the book on January 18, 1831,[249] but owing to the tardy return of proofsheets he was unable to complete the review until several days later. Nevertheless, his article did appear in the *Quarterly Review* for February, pp. 319–42.[250]

Most of the manuscript Irving sent to Murray is extant in the archives

249. In "Washington Irving's British Edition of Slidell's *A Year in Spain*," *Bulletin of the New York Public Library*, 73 (June 1969), 369–74, Ben H. McClary lists the substantive variants between the 1830 and 1831 editions of *A Year in Spain* and discusses the editorial principles adopted by Irving as he prepared a text palatable to transatlantic taste. He notes that Irving's outright additions to the 1830 edition constitute "bits of himself placed in Slidell's work" and therefore "represent, in fact, new contributions to the Irving canon" (p. 372). These additions–seven passages totalling 204 words—are reprinted on pp. 372–73 of the article.

250. PMI, II, 450; STW, I, 468–69; Ben H. McClary, ed. *Washington Irving and the House of Murray* (Knoxville, 1969), pp. 142–46.

of John Murray Ltd., London. Written in dark brown ink on sheets of cream-colored paper approximately 4⅞₆ x 7½" in size, the manuscript text is arranged in two series of pagination, reflecting the two occasions on which parts of it were forwarded to the publisher. The first series, which corresponds to 319.1–329.14 in the *Quarterly Review* (T 30.13–42.6), is numbered by Irving 1–11, ⟨12⟩;[251] an unnumbered sheet following p. 2 includes a passage to be interpolated into that on p. 2 (see Discussions of Adopted Readings 30.22). The second series, corresponding to 329.15–342.10 in the *Quarterly Review* (T 42.7–57.41), is numbered by Irving 1–14, 16–21. A page or pages following p. 11 of the first series, and pp. 7, 15 of the second, are missing. The manuscript text includes a number of minor revisions by the author, but it reveals no evidence of revision by another hand. Five pencilled marks at successive points, indicating compositors' stints,[252] reveal that the manuscript was used as printer's copy. Probably the proofs included both the text of Irving's commentary and also the quotations from *A Year in Spain* which he wished to include in the review. However, he had not transcribed the latter passages into the manuscript but had simply jotted the first few words of each quotation, or its page-number in *A Year in Spain*, or both. He did not indicate the points at which the quotations were to conclude, evidently regarding each of his selections as self-contained and its point of termination self-evident.

Once he had forwarded the latter portion of his manuscript to Murray, Irving played no further part in preparing the review for publication. However, apparently at the proof stage, the text underwent revision by John Gibson Lockhart, the editor of the *Quarterly Review*. Lockhart's tamperings ranged throughout the piece and resulted in a text significantly at odds with the author's intention. Irving regarded the primary function of his review as to provide a forum for extensive and sympathetic quotation from Slidell's volumes. Accordingly, he indicated his intention to include several lengthy passages from *A Year in Spain*, keeping the text of his own commentary under comparatively strict control. Lockhart tipped the balance of emphasis in the opposite direction. Of the 21 instances in which he revised passages in Irving's text involving five words or more, 11 involve expansion of the manuscript version and only 3 compression or deletion; the passages of commentary added to Irving's version far exceed in length those dropped from it.[253] Ordinarily Lockhart wrote variations on the original text or else elaborations of it

251. Pages 9 and 10, first series, are written on sheets of the same paper which are, respectively, only 3 3/8" and 3 5/8" high.

252. The marks appear at the top of p. 9, first series; pp. 1, 10, 13, 14, second series.

253. For a representative instance of Lockhart's tendency to inflate the essay into a performance as much by the reviewer as the author under review, see Rejected Variants 30.13–16.

which employed some of Irving's phraseology; but at one point (see Rejected Variants 47.18) he added a passage entirely without precedent in the manuscript. As Ben H. McClary has remarked,[254] in the heavily revised final paragraph of the article Lockhart reveals his Tory bias by a condescending reference to Slidell as "our young American" (see Rejected Variants 59.19–37), a phrase also without precedent in the manuscript. Not only in his emendations of single words or brief phrases, but in punctuation, capitalization, and spelling as well, Lockhart revised Irving's article with a free hand.

Lockhart also took liberties with the quotations Irving had wished to include from *A Year in Spain*. Passages several sentences in length are at three points (*Quarterly Review* 323.39, 328.16–17, 330.41; corresponding to T 35.6, 41.3, 44.12) omitted from the quoted texts. In the latter instance Lockhart even re-wrote a portion of Slidell's text (*Quarterly Review* 330.42–331.4; corresponding to T 44.32–40) so as to render it intelligible after his omission of the paragraph preceding it. Futher, at one point he transposed a quoted passage and Irving's comments thereon (see Discussions of Adopted Readings 41.41–42.2). But the most striking evidence of the editor's concern for economy is his omission of an entire indicated quotation, with the author's introductory comments, which had formed part of the manuscript text (T 48.25–49.6). Finally, Lockhart—or at any rate someone other than Irving—made numerous changes to the accidentals in passages quoted from Slidell's book.

Because some pages of Irving's manuscript are missing, passages in the *Quarterly Review* text which correspond to the lacunae in the manuscript (the commentary at 325.17–32, 328.29–33, 335.37–40; see T 37.34–38.4, 41.41–42.1, 50.33–35; the quotations at 324.21–325.16, 325.33–328.28, 328.34–329.7, 335.41–339.21; see T 36.13–37.33, 38.5–41.40, 42.7–29, 50.36–55.17) cannot be collated against textual evidence of Irving's intention. However, the extant portions of the manuscript do indicate that the author wished each of the quotations to be included in his review.[255]

254. McClary, "Irving, Lockhart, and the *Quarterly Review*," *Bulletin of the New York Public Library*, 76 (1972), 232.

255. Although no specific reference to the passage quoted on 324.21–325.16 of the *Quarterly Review* occurs in the extant portion of Irving's manuscript, p. 11, first series in the latter text concludes with an introduction of a passage describing a Spanish diligence, followed by a citation of the appropriate page-number in *A Year in Spain* (see Emendations 35.5). Slidell's account of the diligence is in two parts, extending over 13 pages but separated by 6 pages of extraneous material; the second of these segments is the quotation without specific precedent in the manuscript. Since in editing Irving's article Lockhart consistently tended to condense or omit quoted material, it is reasonable to suppose on the basis of its appearance in the *Quarterly Review* that the second quotation—if not indeed the pages separating it from the first—was intended by Irving to be included; see Discussions of Adopted Readings 35.5.

For each of these quotations, passages at least 150 words in length are omitted from the *Quarterly Review* text; and since Irving indicated at no point in the manuscript that he wished portions of quotations not to be reproduced in the printed article, it is virtually certain that Lockhart made the deletions on his own.

The author's immediate reaction to the published review is not recorded, but it may easily be imagined. In this light it may be noted that Pierre M. Irving did not reprint the work in *Spanish Papers*, even though he was aware of its existence and did include Irving's other contribution to the *Quarterly Review*, the anonymous discussion of the *Conquest of Granada* (see pp. 4–30). Possibly Pierre had learned from his uncle that the published Slidell article did not represent his wishes; and because the manuscript of the work was unavailable—presumably then as now in the archives of John Murray, Ltd.—Pierre had no means of securing a satisfactory text. However this may be, the fact remains that as revised by Lockhart the review was printed only once, in the *Quarterly Review*; so that, as intended by Irving, the review is previously unpublished.

Because Irving edited *A Year in Spain* for publication by John Murray, it may be assumed that he intended passages quoted from that work to appear in the review as they stood in the Murray edition. Thus, the primary evidence of his intentions for the text of the article consists of the manuscript he submitted to Murray (the extant fragment of which represents approximately 90% of the commentary in the *Quarterly Review* text) and *A Year in Spain* itself. While the magazine text is useful in providing confirmation of Irving's wishes to quote certain material— wishes which would otherwise have had to be inferred from the manuscript—in affording some notion of his intentions for the commentary now missing from the manuscript, and in providing a format for quotations

---

The quotations on 325.33–328.28 and 328.34–329.7 of the *Quarterly Review*, recounting a robbery by highwaymen and its aftermath, together constitute one of a pair of such accounts quoted in the magazine, the second of which is introduced as "a comic account of another robbery" (335.39). Irving's manuscript text of the passage just quoted is missing, but p. ⟨12⟩, first series of the extant portion begins with a comment on events immediately following the earlier, brutal robbery; see T 42.3–6. Because the comment would be meaningless except in relation to the described event itself, it is clear that Irving intended Slidell's portrayal of it—easily the most memorable passage in *A Year in Spain*–to be included in the review.

The quotation on 335.41–339.21 of the *Quarterly Review*, recounting the second robbery, occurs at a point corresponding in Irving's manuscript to the missing p. 15, second series. However, it is followed on p. 16 by an observation as follows: "We have already exceeded our usual limits yet we cannot forbear making one more extract which shews the worthy lieutenant in a situation of more imminent jeopardy than any other of this his most eventful and adventurous land cruize" (T 55.18–21). The allusion to Slidell's "imminent jeopardy" in his "eventful" travels is clearly a reference to the passage previously quoted.

and citations, on the whole it clearly constitutes an adulteration. Accordingly, Irving's manuscript, supplemented by the appropriate passages from the Murray edition of *A Year in Spain*, is adopted in this edition as copy-text. In order to achieve continuity, passages of commentary missing from the manuscript are supplied in square brackets from the *Quarterly Review* (see Emendations 37.34–38.4, 41.41–42.2, 45.6–16, 50.33–35).

Although Irving specified only the beginnings of the passages for quotation from *A Year in Spain* (see Emendations 32.15, 33.21, 34.7, 35.5, 42.6, 43.34, 45.33, 46.39, 47.27, 48.26, 55.39), invariably their end-points are clear. In view of his wish "to exemplify our author's talent" (47.18) by quoting liberally from the book, it is assumed that he intended the passages to be quoted in full.

As a contributor to the *Quarterly Review* Irving tacitly approved its editorial styling of quotations; the magazine's format is accordingly followed here, with some modifications to bring it into line with conventions followed throughout this collection. As the Murray manuscript reveals, the author was content to adopt the *Quarterly Review*'s practice of indenting the first lines of quoted passages set off from the commentary, whether or not the quotations began in *A Year in Spain* with paragraph breaks. This procedure is hence adopted, and a list is given of the indented first lines which do not begin paragraphs in Slidell's book (Emendations 36.13). Single quotation marks were inserted in the *Quarterly Review* at the beginning of the first and subsequent paragraphs of quotations and at their conclusions. The practice is adopted here, but double quotation marks are instead supplied at the indicated points (Emendations 32.16). Thus, quotations within passages quoted from *A Year in Spain* are enclosed here within single quotation marks (Emendations 36.30). The *Quarterly Review* format for citing quotations is where possible directly adopted (Emendations 34.3, 37.33, 42.27, 46.22). However, because Lockhart's citations were often incorrect and not infrequently inconsistent with his own predominant format, some corrections of the magazine's citations are necessary (Emendations 33.17, 34.36, 36.12, 45.5, 47.17, 48.24, 55.17). At points where no citation whatever is provided in the published article, it is supplied within square brackets in the predominant *Quarterly Review* style (Emendations 41.40, 49.6, 50.32, 57.10).

Because Irving prepared his review rather hurriedly, the manuscript text includes various short-cuts and omissions which he would have wished corrected before the article was published. Thus, for example, punctuation is supplied where called for but omitted at the ends of lines in the manuscript (Emendations 31.11). Periods are supplied or substituted for inappropriate punctuation at the ends of sentences (Emendations 31.19), apostrophes are added to possessives (Emendations 31.40), and the ampersand is emended to "and" (Emendations 31.27). Words capitalized in the copy-text but not ordinarily capitalized elsewhere (invariably emended to lower-case in the *Quarterly Review*) are emended to lower-case (Emendations 30.24 *et al.*), but Spanish words capitalized apparently for emphasis (for example, "Ventas" 30.34, 48.26) are given as Irving wrote them. On occasion Irving underlines (32.15, 45.10, 49.8, 55.29–30), and on occasion he does not underline (43.34, 47.26) foreign words and phrases. *A Year in Spain* is equally inconsistent (for example, see 35.12, 36.14), and the *Quarterly Review* is only slightly more predictable. However, since no ambiguity is created by the absence of a consistent policy for foreign terms, no changes are made to the type-styles in any of the three texts.

Cancellations and revisions within Irving's manuscript are recorded in full in the list of Emendations; false starts immediately re-written are listed in a single entry (Emendations 30.14). Since Irving played no part in the final preparations of his article for publication, the accidental variants between the manuscript and the printed commentary shed no light on the author's developing intentions. Substantive variants only between the manuscript and the commentary sections of the *Quarterly Review* are ordinarily recorded in Emendations, unless of course the latter text is the source of an accepted accidental reading. Substantive variants between the two texts not listed in Emendations are given in Rejected Variants.[256] Catchwords at the bottoms of pages in the magazine are not noticed in the accounting of variants. Because it is assumed that Irving intended the text of *A Year in Spain* to be reproduced faithfully in the *Quarterly Review*, variants between Slidell's volumes and the quotations in the magazine are not recorded unless the latter text corrects an error in the original (for example, Emendations 40.33) or includes a passage which might possibly have been written by Irving (Rejected Variants 45.40).

In the preparation of this edition the following collations have been made:

1. A xerox copy of the *Quarterly Review* text owned by the University of Toronto (AP 4/ Q 2) collated by Professor Ralph M. Aderman against the original manuscript in the archives of John Murray, Ltd.;

2. A xerox copy of the Murray manuscript transcribed, and the transcription emended on the basis of the collation with the original manuscript;

3. The emended transcription collated twice and independently with a xerox copy of the University of Toronto *Quarterly Review* text;

4. The above xerox copy of the *Quarterly Review* text sight collated with the following additional copies: Princeton University (0901/ .Q 151);

---

256. In Rejected Variants the combined symbols "MSm, T" following the designation of an accepted reading mean "the manuscript as emended by the editor."

University of Virginia (AP 4/ .Q2); York University (AP 4/ .Q 2);
5. The xerox copy of the *Quarterly Review* text sight collated with appropriate passages in *A Year in Spain* owned by the following: New York Public Library (BXY); University of Toronto (HSp/ M 1561y); Yale University (Edg/ 826b).

See Discussions and Lists pp. 524, 539, 649.

[DEDICATORY LETTER IN
POEMS, BY WILLIAM CULLEN BRYANT,
AN AMERICAN]

The introduction to Bryant's *Poems* (1832), pp. [iii]–vi, is a result of Irving's efforts while in England to assist the poet in publishing for the first time in Europe a collected edition of his verse. The dedicatory letter to Samuel Rogers, which he composed as editor of the volume, was reprinted after his death in *Irvingiana*, p. xiii, and in PMI, II, 475–77. Alterations of a few accidentals and slight variations in format appear in each of these texts, but except for the correction of a single error no substantive variants are present. No evidence of authorial revision is discernible in either reprinting. Since no manuscript version of the work is known to exist, the text published in Bryant's *Poems* is adopted as copy-text. In the table which follows substantive variants between the three texts are recorded.

In the preparation of this edition the following collations have been made:
1. A xerox copy of the text in *Poems* owned by the New-York Historical Society (PS/ 1150/ .E32a) sight collated with the following additional copies: Princeton University (EX 3649/ 1832/ .11); Yale University (Iw/ B 841/ 832i);
2. The above xerox copy collated with the text in two copies of *Irvingiana*;
3. The above xerox copy collated with the text in three copies of PMI in the possession of the editor.

See Discussions and Lists p. 547.

[ADDRESS AT THE IRVING DINNER, MAY 30, 1832]

The text of Irving's remarks before the testimonial dinner in his honor survives in a single manuscript version, an eight-page holograph written on two sheets, each folded at the center so as to leave pages 5 x 6⅞″ in size. The manuscript, owned by the University of Virginia, is written in dark brown ink in a hurried hand. On the first page, written in pencil above Irving's text by an unknown person, is the heading "Original Address of/W Irving on his return from/Spain."[257] A second pencilled interpolation, possibly by the same person, appears on p. [6] (see Emendations 60.26–27). The manuscript includes a liberal sprinkling of authorial corrections in the same brown ink as the unrevised text.

It is possible that Irving used this manuscript as his notes for the speech at the testimonial dinner, but it is almost certain that he prepared it for the use of a person or persons delegated to write an official summary of the occasion. On May 31, 1832, the editors of the New York *American* professed to be "[p]ossessing ourselves in patience, until we receive the official account of the glowing festivities of yesterday" (p. 2 col. 1). And on June 5, the New-York *Spectator* prefaced its narrative of the proceedings by observing that the text had been "furnished for publication by the Committee" (p. 2 col. 3). Apparently the Committee on Arrangements for the dinner had responsibility for producing an account for publication.

As it was first published, in the New York *Morning Courier* for June 2, the report of the dinner occupied the full seven columns of fine print on the front page. It included transcripts of correspondence between Irving and the Committee on Arrangements, letters from persons unable to attend, the text of a florid inroductory address by Chancellor James Kent, toasts proposed by other dignitaries—all in addition to a description of the decorations, the menu, and the mood of those in attendance, and to the transcript of Irving's remarks. Since the *Morning Courier's* 15,000-word narrative was produced and set in type within only two days of the event, it is reasonable to asume that in piecing it together the Committee must have relied upon the assistance of various persons. Irving did his part by producing not only a text of his speech but also an introduction to it, cast in the journalistic third person (T 59.17–22),

Despite marks of haste such as the use of "Mr. I." for "Mr. Irving" and the liberal use of the ampersand for "and," Irving's 33 alterations within the manuscript reveal that he took pains to produce a text appropriate to the occasion. Aside from difficulties he encountered at the outset, in referring to himself in the third person, his revisions are ordinarily confined to matters of stylistic felicity—placement of words within a sentence, substitution of near-synonyms, adjustment of degrees

---

257. Although Irving had resided in Spain from 1826 to 1829, he had returned to the United States from England, not Spain. Slight though it is, the error in identifying the manuscript suggests that the notation was made either by a person unfamiliar with Irving's travels prior to 1832 or by one who confused his return to the United States in that year with his return in 1846, after completing his service as the United States Minister to Spain.

of emphasis or emotional impact. For example, having first written "country" in reference to the United States, he decided upon the emotively resonant "native place" (see Emendations 59.37), which phrase he was in a few sentences to echo in adapting the famous line from Scott's "The Lay of the Last Minstrel" (T 60.25): "This is my own, my native land!" Similarly, he toned down his reference to the welcoming dinner from "the happiest ↑the most overpowering↓ moment" to "the happiest moment" of his lifetime (see Emendations 59.27)—the identical phrase he had recently used in a letter accepting the invitation of the Committee on Arrangements to attend the affair.[258] Having completed the revisions, he evidently felt that he had embodied satisfactorily his perception that the return to the United States marked an epoch in his career.

The manuscript includes no printer's marks, but the close similarity at most points between it and the New York *Morning Courier* version suggests strongly that it, or possibly a fair copy derived from it, was employed in preparing the printed text. The *Morning Courier* account does include several substantive variants from the manuscript—comments on Irving's demeanor and on the reception of his remarks (see for example Rejected Variants 59.30), introductory phrases which smooth the jerky pace of the manuscript text (Emendations 59.21-22), an explanatory note (Rejected Variants 60.14), and briefer divergences.

Following its publication in the New York *Morning Courier*, Irving's speech appeared within the next few days in several other newspapers and weekly miscellanies. It was included, without indication of a source, in the New York *American*, an afternoon newspaper, for June 2, p. 2; the *American* text differs in substantives from the *Morning Courier* version at only 4 points (see Emendations 59.17–18, 60.40; Rejected Variants 60.17, 60.29), so that it may derive from the earlier newspaper text or else from a second copy of the official account made available by the Committee on Arrangements. Certainly there is no evidence that Irving played any part in the entire printing history of his speech beyond his submitting a manuscript. The 5 minor substantive variants between the *Morning Courier* text and that in the New-York *Spectator* for June 5, p. 2 —which purported to be "furnished . . . by the Committee"—are all of a sort which might proceed from a compositor's misreading of a manuscript text (see Emendations 60.41; Rejected Variants 59.30, 60.4–5, 60.8, 60.28). The 7 minor substantive variants between the text in the Boston *Daily Advertiser and Patriot* for June 5, p. 1, and the New York *American* text from which it was professedly taken were evidently the results of a printer's whim (see Rejected Variants 60.7, 60.8, 60.14, 60.28, 60.35, 60.37, 60.38), though it should be noticed that at some points readings are re-

---

258. The letter of invitation and Irving's reply are reprinted in STW, II, 336, note 41.

stored to those in Irving's manuscript. The *New-York Mirror* published on June 9, pp. 386–87, a version whose substantive readings differed at 5 points from the *Morning Courier* text (see Emendations 59.17–18, 59.21–22; Rejected Variants 59.28, 59.34–35, 60.2), the first variant reading of which nearly duplicates that in the New York *American*. The *Morning Courier* text was reprinted once more, in PMI, II, 488–90, where it is cited as "from . . . the Morning Courier." Except for a single substantive variant characteristic of Pierre M. Irving's editorship (see Rejected Variants 60.38), and alterations of accidentals, the PMI text is a faithful reprinting from the newspaper.

Irving's notable success as a public speaker at his homecoming dinner soon won him a place in a work by John Lauris Blake, a prolific compiler of textbooks, entitled *The Young Orator; Consisting of Prose, Poetry, and Dialogues for Declamation in Schools* (1833), pp. 83–85. Blake freely altered the report of the speech to his own purpose, omitting from it eight sentences including all references to the circumstances surrounding its presentation and the manner in which it was received, and making other adjustments as he saw fit. The text in *The Young Orator* is thus of historical interest but carries no textual authority.

It remains possible that the *Morning Courier* version and those which appeared subsequently were all derived from a manuscript prepared by Irving *after* he had written the hasty yet much-revised one at the University of Virginia. However this may be—and it is not likely—all contemporary printed versions but John L. Blake's include several sentences without precedent in the manuscript, and for which there is no warrant to assume Irving's authorship. Although the manuscript is not a fair copy and did not demonstrably serve as printer's copy, setting aside the interpolations in the printed texts it is largely consistent with them. It represents the last stage of composition which we can state with confidence to have been Irving's own, rather than his as combined with revisions by other persons; and it is hence adopted as copy-text.

Some regularizations are necessary in order to bring the copy-text into a form befitting a formal address. Thus "Mr I." is emended to "Mr. Irving," the ampersand is emended to "and" (Emendations 59.20–21), and question marks are when appropriate supplied or substituted for the indicated punctuation (Emendations 60.28). End-of-line punctuation omitted from the manuscript is supplied as required (Emendations 60.3).

All variants within the copy-text and all variants between it and the *Morning Courier* version are set forth in the tables which follow. Substantive variants between the copy-text and the New York *American*, New-York *Spectator*, Boston *Daily Advertiser*, *New-York Mirror*, and PMI texts are also given. In the list of Emendations only, the absence of a reference to any of these texts indicates that the missing reading is identical with that in the *Morning Courier*. The table of Rejected Variants includes all variants between the copy-text and that in the *Morning Courier*, and also substantive variants between the copy-text and the later reprinted versions, not set forth in the list of Emendations.[259]

In the preparation of this edition the following collations have been made:

1. A typed transcription of the manuscript, prepared from a xerox copy compared with the original, collated twice and independently with the *New-York Mirror* text owned by the University of Virginia (AP 2/ .N65);

2. A handwritten transcription of the above *New-York Mirror* text collated with the following additional copies: New York Public Library (*DA); Yale University (A 89/+48969);

3. A sight collation of three copies of the PMI text in the possession of the editor;

4. A xerox copy of the PMI text collated twice and independently with the text in a copy of the New York *Morning Courier* owned by the New York Public Library (*ZY);

5. The above xerox copy collated with the handwritten transcription of the *New-York Mirror* text;

6. The above xerox copy collated with a copy of the New York *American* owned by the New-York Historical Society (Newspapers/ New York City) and with a second copy owned by the Library of Congress (vol. no. 8903);

7. The above xerox copy collated with a copy of the New-York *Spectator* owned by the New-York Historical Society (Newspapers/ New York City);

8. The above xerox copy collated with a copy of the Boston *Daily Advertiser* owned by the New-York Historical Society (Newspapers/ Boston, Mass.);

9. The above xerox copy collated with a copy of *The Young Orator* owned by the Library of Congress (PN/ 4271/ .B77).

See Discussions and Lists pp. 526, 547, 652.

[REVIEW OF HENRY WHEATON'S
HISTORY OF THE NORTHMEN]

This essay probably grew out of Irving's exertions in 1831 to secure a publisher for his friend Wheaton's *History*. He managed to convince his own English publisher, John Murray II, to undertake the book, but

---

259. In Rejected Variants the combined symbols "MSv, T" following the designation of an accepted reading mean "the manuscript as emended by the editor."

Murray may well have exacted from him a promise of assistance in bringing the *History* before the public. A few months before, Murray had agreed in similar circumstances to publish Alexander Slidell's *A Year in Spain* (see pp. 30–57) provided that Irving edit it, correct the proofsheets, and then write a review of it, all unremunerated. In this case Irving appears not to have been called upon to perform editorial duties, but he did prepare an extended critical notice of the *History* for publication in Murray's house organ, the *Quarterly Review*. He sent a portion of the review to Murray on July 27, 1831, and the remainder to John Gibson Lockhart, the editor of the magazine, on September 1.[260] Shortly after forwarding the latter instalment, however, he became involved in a dispute with Murray which resulted in the suspension of their business dealings for many years. Ben H. McClary has speculated that in the midst of this falling-out Murray may have directed Lockhart to return Irving's manuscript.[261] However that may be, the essay did not appear in the *Quarterly Review* as originally planned. Irving must have had some form of the text in his possession when he returned to the United States, for the work was published in the *North American Review* for October 1832.

Because he spent the summer and fall of that year on an excursion through the United States, it is certain that Irving played no role in preparing the work for publication beyond submitting his text—a manuscript or, possibly, corrected *Quarterly Review* proofs. In the absence of a surviving manuscript or proofs of the article, it is thus impossible to state with certainty whether he authorized, or indeed was directly responsible for, a notable feature of the published text: its frequent departure from the text of Wheaton's *History* in "quotations" from that work. Certain classes of variants, such as the 10 changes to Wheaton's paragraphing (see Pre-Copy-Text Variants 64.26) and 14 omissions of footnote references and the notes themselves (Pre-Copy-Text Variants 64.35), may be owing to the imposition of the *North American Review's* editorial style. However, other deviations from the Wheaton volume—for example, a passage several sentences in length virtually re-written (Pre-Copy-Text Variants 71.6–13 inclusive)—cannot be accounted for on the basis of formal conventions alone. Probably Irving did intend the often loose quotations from the *History* to appear as they do in the *North American Review*. Unlike *A Year in Spain*—a work he had himself edited and "improved" prior to publication—the original passages in Wheaton's book were as their author had written them. As a professional man of letters, Irving may have felt that his sympathetic treatment of the *History* in the review

---

260. Ben H. McClary, "Washington Irving's Amiable Scotch Friends," p. 103. See also McClary, ed. *Washington Irving and the House of Murray* pp. 150–62.

261. McClary, ed. *Washington Irving and the House of Murray*, p. 162 note 9.

might properly include unobtrusive improvements of its style. The minor nature of a few revisions—for example, the substitution of "likewise" for "also" (see Pre-Copy-Text Variants 79.33)—seems to warrant this speculation. More certain is that Irving felt free to streamline Wheaton's text in order to smooth transitions between his own commentary and passages quoted from the *History*; see, for example, Pre-Copy-Text Variants 74.5–6. On the whole, his tampering with Wheaton's text was evidently intended not to misrepresent the *History* but to render passages from it economical, felicitous, and as harmonious as possible with the body of the review.

Unlike his article on *A Year in Spain*, wherein the text both of his own commentary and of the passages he had intended to quote were revised without his knowledge or approval, the published notice of Wheaton's *History* appears to have satisfied him. Pierre M. Irving, whose acquaintance with his opinions and wishes with regard to his published and unpublished writings was extensive and detailed, omitted the article on *A Year in Spain* from *Spanish Papers* but reprinted the *North American Review* text of the Wheaton essay with almost absolute faithfulness. Aside from an altered title (Emendations 61.2–3), an omitted footnote and footnote reference (Emendations 86.39), and four one-word substantive variants, all obvious errors (Rejected Variants 62.8, 63.22, 65.36, 67.36), the *Spanish Papers* text includes no deviations from the original printing other than the changes of accidentals associated with the Putnam house style.[262]

Thus, in the absence of a manuscript version and of evidence that Irving was dissatisfied with the work as it appeared in the *North American Review*, that text—the only one which appeared during his lifetime[263] —is adopted as copy-text.

In conformity with Irving's usual practice and conventions observed elsewhere in this edition, some regularizations of the copytext are made. Quotations are enclosed in pairs of double quotation marks rather than the single quotation marks used by the *North American Review* (Emendations 61.20–23), and quotations within quotations are enclosed within pairs of single quotation marks (Emendations 64.27). Pairs of double quotation marks are added when necessary (Emendations 66.11–14), and individual double quotation marks are substituted for single quotation marks at the beginning of the second and subsequent paragraphs within quoted passages (Emendations 64.36). A 5 points Irving quotes passages from the *History* which are quoted within that work itself, but he employs only one pair of quotation marks rather than two (see 67.5–68.2, 74.5–6,

262. See the Textual Commentary, I, 273–76.

263. The original text of the review was reprinted in *Essays from the North American Review*, ed. A. T. Rice (London, [1879]), pp. 215–54.

75.32–39, 81.30–33, 83.35–37). Although in these instances his practice is inconsistent with his usage elsewhere in the review, it creates no ambiguity and so is permitted to stand. Similarly, at 6 points he provides page-references to passages quoted from the *History* (see 69.38, 75.15, 76.34, 77.2, 79.34, 80.22), but his more prevalent practice, which he follows on 18 other occasions, is to leave page-references uncited. The citations he does include are permitted to stand—one error being corrected—but in preference to interrupting the text by a series of citations supplied in square brackets, page-references for uncited quotations are provided at appropriate points in the Discussions of Adopted Readings. At 2 points within a quoted prose passage, series of asterisks used in the copy-text to indicate hiatuses are altered to series of periods (see Emendations 71.7–8, 71.11); however, at another point where they mark an omission within quoted lines of verse in a manner identical with that used in the *History* (T 67.24), they are allowed to stand.

Substantive variants, and accidental variants of particular interest between quotations in the copy-text from Wheaton's *History* and the original passages in that work are recorded in the tables which follow.[264] Variants between the two texts not included in the list of Emendations are set forth in a separate table of Pre-Copy-Text Rejected Variants. Substantive variants, and accidental variants of interest, between the copy-text and the *Spanish Papers* version are recorded; variant readings not given in Emendations are listed in a separate table of Rejected Variants.

In the preparation of this edition the following collations have been made:

1. A xerox copy of the *North American Review* text owned by the University of Virginia (AP 2/ N 7) sight collated with the following additional copies: New-York Historical Society (E 171/ .N67); University of Toronto (AP 2/ .N7);

2. The xerox copy collated twice and independently with the *Spanish Papers* text in a copy owned by the National Library of Canada, and once with an additional copy owned by the New York Public Library;

3. The xerox copy collated three times and independently with the appropriate passages in a copy of Wheaton's *History* owned by the University of Toronto (HScan/ W 558h), and once with a copy owned by the Library of Congress (DL 65/ .W 55).

See Discussions and Lists pp. 527, 550, 654, 680.

---

264. A full accounting of substantive and accidental variants between the copy-text and the pertinent passages in Wheaton's *History* is on file at the University of Texas.

MATHEWS *NOT* AT HOME

The anecdote of Charles Mathews survives in a single manuscript version, owned by the University of Virginia. The text is written in dark brown ink, with remarkably few corrections, on both sides of two sheets of fair quality unlaid paper, each measuring 5 x 7⅝". The manuscript includes two notations not in the hand of Irving. The first, a pencilled "#9" in the upper right-hand corner of the first page, may be an editorial mark indicating the item's place in the sequence of articles in the *New-York Mirror* for March 1, 1834; the text was published anonymously in the issue of that date, p. 278. The second notation—the name "Washington Irving"— is written in brown ink in a feminine hand at the bottom of the fourth page, 4" below the last line of the author's text.

The variants between the manuscript and the printed text are minor— 20 of 29 involving alterations of punctuation, and only 2 involving substantive readings (see Emendations 87.26; Rejected Variants 87.23). It is unlikely that Irving was responsible for any of the emended readings. Probably he supplied this bit of anecdotage as a favor to his acquaintance, G. P. Morris, the editor of the *New-York Mirror*, and having supplied it saw no more of it until the work appeared in print.

The vignette has never been reprinted. Because the manuscript version shows some evidence of having been used as printer's copy and Irving likely played no part in preparing the printed text beyond submitting the manuscript, the University of Virginia manuscript represents the closest available approximation to his final intention for the work. Accordingly, it is adopted as copy-text.

In the tables which follow a full accounting is given of variants within the copy-text and between it and the *New-York Mirror* version. Variants not recorded in the list of Emendations are set forth in a separate table of Rejected Variants.

In the preparation of this edition the following collations have been made:
1. A typed transcription of the University of Virginia manuscript collated against the following copies of the *New-York Mirror* text: Los Angeles Public Library (fR/ 805); University of Virginia (*AP 2/ .N65); Yale University (A89/+N48969).

See Discussions and Lists pp. 552, 654.

NEWTON THE PAINTER

The brief account of Newton during the period of his "mental malady" was based, in part at least, upon a letter Irving received from Charles R.

Leslie, dated London, December 29, 1834.[265] A holograph manuscript of "Newton the Painter" is extant in the Berg Collection, New York Public Library. Written in dark brown ink on one side of three sheets of unlaid paper, each measuring 4¾ x 7⅝″, the manuscript is signed "Washington Irving" on the verso of the third sheet. The text includes a single notation not by Irving, a pencilled clarification of "consoling" at a point corresponding to T 88.23. Written in a fluent, somewhat hasty hand, the manuscript includes 12 minor cancellations and revisions.

The work was published anonymously in the *New-York Mirror* for March 21, 1835, p. 303. Andrew B. Myers has speculated that the brevity and transitory subject-matter of the item, and also its confidential nature, may have deterred Irving from permitting his authorship of it to be made known.[266] Certainly the *New-York Mirror*'s keen interest in painters and painting, and more particularly its recent expression of concern over the health of Newton,[267] made it an appropriate outlet for this bit of information concerning Irving's old friend. The published text of the vignette does not differ significantly from that in the manuscript: accidental variants occur at 15 points, substantive variants at 3 (see Rejected Variants 88.13, 88.23, 88.26). The manuscript includes no editorial marks (except possibly the pencilled clarification), but the close correspondence between it and the *New-York Mirror* text suggests that it, or a fair copy derived from it, served as printer's copy. Probably the extant manuscript, which is readily legible, was itself sent to George P. Morris, the editor of the magazine, who prepared the article for the printer. Irving's role in producing the printed text almost certainly did not extend beyond the stage of manuscript preparation.

"Newton the Painter" was not reprinted during the author's lifetime. Because the manuscript version constitutes the latest available evidence of his attention to the text, it is adopted as copy-text.

In the tables which follow a full accounting is given of variants within the copy-text and between it and the printed version. Variant readings

265. See *Autobiographical Recollections. By the Late Charles Robert Leslie, R. A.*, ed. Tom Taylor (Boston, 1860), p. 298. The fullest picture of the friendship between Irving, Leslie, and Newton is to be derived from correspondence included in this work; pp. 205–323. See also PMI, I, 406–II, 445 *passim*; STW, II, 431 (Index); McClary, ed. *Washington Irving and the House of Murray*, p. 241 (Index); Andrew B. Myers, "Washington Irving and Gilbert Stuart Newton: A *New-York Mirror* Contribution Identified," *Bulletin of the New York Public Library*, 76 (1972), 238–39.

266. Myers, "Irving and Newton," p. 238.

267. On August 23, 1834, a writer in the *New-York Mirror* had noted: "We have sought in vain among our files of English papers and periodicals for some notice of this gentleman's present state of health" (Myers, "Irving and Newton," p. 239 note 6). A portrait of Irving by Newton was reproduced in the *New-York Mirror* for December 30, 1837.

not included in the list of Emendations are set forth in a separate table of Rejected Variants.

In the preparation of this edition the following collations have been made:

1. A handwritten transcription of the manuscript collated twice and independently with the *New-York Mirror* text owned by the University of Delaware (AP 2/ N483) and once with the following additional copies: Los Angeles Public Library (fR/ 805); University of Virginia (*AP 2/ N65); New York Public Library (DA/ *A); Yale University (A 89/ +N48969).

See Discussions and Lists pp. 552, 655.

AN UNWRITTEN DRAMA OF LORD BYRON

The account of Lord Byron's plan for a "dramatic poem" was derived from knowledge Irving had gained from Thomas Medwin, an acquaintance of the late poet. Irving had often met Medwin in Paris in 1824 and 1825, and in his notebook for the latter year he transcribed an *"Unpublished note by Capt Medwin."* on this topic (reproduced in *Journals*, III, pp. 710–12).[268] Comparison of the transcribed note with "An Unwritten Drama of Lord Byron" partially confirms Irving's statement in the published work that he had received his information "nearly in the . . . words" he was subsequently using to summarize the play himself (T 90.5). Medwin's introductory paragraph, dealing with the manner in which Byron had supposedly become intrigued by a play attributed to Calderon, he shifted to a point later in his sketch (see T 90.3–8 Such . . . Spanish.); and the text following the material thus transposed is without precedent in Medwin's note. On the other hand, in his description of the play itself (T 89.1–90.2 The . . . passions.) Irving frequently drew almost word for word upon his transcription of the earlier sketch. Here, omitting material when possible (see Pre-Copy-Text Variants 89.30), and at a few points transposing sentences (for example, see Pre-Copy-Text Variants 89.8–11, 89.12–15), he distills from his source's more particularized and more explicitly interpretive account a faithful and evocative précis of what he terms "the story" (T 88.35).

No information is available as to the impetus which led Irving during

268. On the basis of Medwin's notes, in 1825 Irving even sketched out scenes for a play of his own. A thorough account of the circumstances surrounding Byron's unfinished drama, with a discussion of Irving's interest in it, is given by Charles E. Robinson in "The Devil as Doppelgänger in *The Deformed Transformed*: The Sources and Meaning of Byron's Unfinished Drama," *Bulletin of the New York Public Library*, 74 (March 1970), [177]–202; see especially pp. 189–93.

the summer of 1835 to prepare his sketch for publication in an elegant gift-book, *The Gift: A Christmas and New Year's Present for 1836*, pp. 166–71. Since he was extremely busy—revising and proofreading the second and third volumes of *The Crayon Miscellany*, purchasing and renovating a home, and overseeing the researches of his nephew Pierre for *Astoria*—it seems unlikely he would have written the work at this time unless solicited to do so. At any rate, given his crowded schedule, his dislike of proofreading, and the location of *The Gift's* publishers in Philadelphia, it is virtually certain that his own preparation of "An Unwritten Drama" for publication did not extend beyond the writing of a manuscript. However, no manuscript version of the text—other than the transcribed Medwin note—is known to survive.

Although submitted for publication in *The Gift*, "An Unwritten Drama" actually appeared first in the *Knickerbocker Magazine* for August 1835, pp. 142–44. This was as part of a pre-publication advertising campaign mounted by Messrs. Carey and Hart, the publishers. In a note appended to the sketch in the *Knickerbocker Magazine*, the editors of that popular monthly acknowledged its source:

> *We are indebted for this interesting sketch to the courtesy of Messrs. *Carey and Hart*, publishers of the forthcoming annual, 'The Gift,' in which it will appear. An extended notice of this beautiful gem of literature and art will be found in the original department of this Magazine.[269]

In short, the publishers of *The Gift* had made available to the *Knickerbocker Magazine* a bit of desirable copy in return for puffery. Only one substantive variant other than the added footnote occurs between the *Knickerbocker Magazine* version and that which appeared in *The Gift* (see Pre-Copy-Text Variants 90.36); indeed, accidental variants between the two texts are so few as to confirm that the magazine text was simply reprinted from *The Gift*. Thus, if Irving played any role in correcting proofs for the sketch, it was for the second, not the first published version. The appearance of the work in the *Knickerbocker Magazine* was a result of the enterprise of Carey and Hart alone.

"An Unwritten Drama" was again reprinted in the *New-York Mirror* for October 17, 1835, probably from *The Gift*. No substantive variants occur between those two texts. It may be that, like that in the *Knickerbocker Magazine*, the *New-York Mirror* version antedated publication of *The Gift*; however, in view of the *Knickerbocker Magazine* text's having appeared in the August issue of that journal—that is, in late July—it seems unlikely. Whether reprinted from an advance copy of *The Gift* or one already published, the *New-York Mirror* text reveals no evidence of authorial revision and possesses no textual authority.

269. *Knickerbocker Magazine*, 6 (August 1835), 144. For the critical notice of *The Gift*, in which that work is lavishly praised, see p. 164.

"An Unwritten Drama" was not reprinted again during Irving's life-time.[270] Because no manuscript text of the completed work is known to exist, and because Irving's latest probable attention to it was to the text which appeared in *The Gift*, where he intended it to be published, the version in *The Gift* is adopted as copy-text.

In the tables which follow an accounting is given of substantive variants between that portion of the copy-text which can be collated word-for-word with Medwin's transcribed note (T 89.1–90.2), and the note as published in *Journals*, III.[271] Variants between the texts not included in the list of Emendations are given in a separate table of Pre-Copy-Text Rejected Variants. The substantive variants between the copy-text and the *Knickerbocker Magazine* version are recorded in the table of Pre-Copy-Text Rejected Variants.

In the preparation of this edition the following collations have been made:

1. A xerox copy of the text in *The Gift* owned by the University of Virginia (AY 11/ G 49/ 1836) sight collated with an additional copy owned by Columbia University (Sp Coll B 810.81/ G 362);

2. The xerox copy collated twice and independently with the Medwin note as reproduced in *Journals*, III;

3. The xerox copy collated with the *Knickerbocker Magazine* text owned by the Legislative Library of Ontario (Periodicals/ First floor);

4. The xerox copy collated with the following copies of the *New-York Mirror* text: New York Public Library (*DA/+); New-York Historical Society (Periodicals).

See Discussions and Lists pp. 553, 682.

THE HAUNTED SHIP.
A TRUE STORY—AS FAR AS IT GOES

This brief tale first appeared in *Heath's Book of Beauty. 1836*, pp. [253]–57. The occasion of its composition was no doubt a request Irving had received either from the Countess of Blessington (1789–1849), the editor of that gift-book, or from a person acting on her behalf. On May 2, 1835, he forwarded the manuscript of the "nautical anecdote" to an intermediary, expressing the hope that "it may be acceptable to Lady

---

270. It has, however, been reprinted since Irving's death. In his edition of the work, *An Unwritten Drama of Lord Byron, by Washington Irving* (Metuchen, N. J.: Charles F. Heartman, 1925), T. O. Mabbott points out that the sketch may have served Edgar A. Poe as a source for his tale, "William Wilson."

271. A full record of substantive and accidental variants between the two texts is on file at the University of Texas.

Blessington, for her 'Annual.' "[272] Because *Heath's Book of Beauty* was published in London, it is certain that Irving's role in preparing "The Haunted Ship" for publication did not extend beyond the stage of manuscript preparation. However, no manuscript version of the work is known to survive.

The tale was first reprinted in the *New-York Mirror* for January 9, 1836, p. 218. The *New-York Mirror* text includes several accidental variants from the first printed version, but other than a slightly altered title (see Emendations 90.29–30) and an obvious error (see Rejected Variants 91.34), no substantive variants. Doubtless, as the heading under which it appeared—"Spirit of the English Annuals"—suggests, it was pirated from the Countess of Blessington's collection. A second pirated version appeared in *Friendship's Offering:—A Christmas, New Year and Birthday Present for MDCCCXLIX*, pp. 326–30. This text includes no substantive variants from the one in *Heath's Book of Beauty*, its apparent source. Presumably it was appropriated from that volume by publishers who, according to Ralph Thompson, "seem to have picked up material wherever they could find it . . . with a breezy disregard for the proprieties of copyright."[273]

Because no manuscript version of the work is known to exist and there is no evidence that Irving revised the text as first printed, the *Heath's Book of Beauty* version is adopted as copy-text. Substantive variants between it and the two reprintings are recorded in the tables which follow.

In the preparation of this edition the following collations have been made:

1. A xerox copy of the Yale University *Heath's Book of Beauty* text (Ia 107/ B644) sight collated with the following additional copies: New York Public Library (NCA–2 copies); University of Western Ontario (Accession no. 11803);

2. The xerox copy collated with the following copies of the *New-York Mirror* text: Yale University (A 89/ +N48969); a copy in the possession of the editor; New York Public Library (DA/ *);

3. The xerox copy collated with the text in the following copies of *Friendship's Offering*: Columbia University (Sp Coll B 810.81/ F 911); New York Public Library (NBA).

See Discussions and Lists pp. 553, 655.

272. R. R. Madden, *The Literary Life and Correspondence of the Countess of Blessington*, 3 vols. (London, 1855), III, 309. Irving's return address given in this work as "Newhall," was probably "New York" or "Newburgh."

273. Thompson, "Irving's 'Haunted Ship,'" *American Literature*, 6 (January 1935), 444. Other sources of information on the circumstances surrounding the various printings of the tale are Nelson F. Adkins, "An Uncollected Tale by Wash-

[LETTER TO THE EDITOR OF
THE NEW YORK *AMERICAN*]

The precipitating cause of Irving's letter was an observation he had made in "The Creole Village," a sketch published in *The Magnolia for 1837*, pp. 315–26. Discussing the Old World language and customs still traceable in various sections of the United States, he had written: "In the phraseology of New England might be found many an old English provincial phrase . . . with some quaint relics of the Roundheads; while Virginia cherishes peculiarities characteristic of the days of Elizabeth and Sir Walter Raleigh."[274] Coincidentally, *The Magnolia* was published at a time when a controversy was being aired in the New York *American* over the cultural peculiarities bequeathed by the original English settlers to the inhabitants of contemporary Virginia and North Carolina. One of the discussants quoted Irving's remark in favor of the claims of Virginia as the primary repository of surviving English customs. In response, an advocate of North Carolina's pretensions accused the Virginian of "blundering arrogance and ignorance" and, for good measure, attacked Irving as well.[275] The author's rejoinder, which appeared in the New York *American* for January 7, 1837, was prefaced by an editorial note that, "in order that there may be no misapprehension of the circumstances under which [Irving's] name has been introduced into this controversy, [Irving] has addressed the following letter to us."

The letter was once reprinted, with an acknowledgement of its source, in PMI, III, 100–01. The latter text includes only a single substantive variant from the original version; it reveals no evidence of authorial revision. Because no manuscript is known to survive, the New York *American* text of the letter is therefore adopted as copy-text. The substantive variant between it and the PMI text is reported in the table of Rejected Variants which follows.

In the preparation of this edition the following collations have been made:

1. The text in a copy of PMI in the possession of the editor sight collated with a copy owned by the New York Public Library;

2. The editor's PMI text collated with that in the following copies of the New York *American*: New-York Historical Society (Newspapers/

---

ington Irving," *American Literature*, 5 (Janaury 1934), 364–67; Aubrey Starke, "Irving's 'Haunted Ship'—A Correction," *American Literature*, 6 (January 1935), 444–45.

274. The sketch was reprinted in *Wolfert's Roost* (New York, 1855), pp. 38–48; the quoted passage is from pp. 38–39 in that work.

275. See Introduction, I, lx.

New York City); Yale University (Folio AN 33/ .N5/ .N469); New York Public Library (*AB).

See Discussions and Lists pp. 553, 655.

[LETTER TO THE EDITOR OF *THE PLAINDEALER*]

The stimulus for Irving's letter to *The Plaindealer* was a passage in the January 14, 1837 issue of that weekly magazine in which he found himself severely criticized for "deficiency of manliness" as an author.[276] Apparently he regarded this attack by William Leggett, the editor of *The Plaindealer*, as a genuine threat to his good name, for he immediately responded to Leggett's charges in a stern tone of offended dignity.[277] His statement, which appeared in *The Plaindealer* for January 28, effectively laid to rest—in print at least—the suspicions cherished by some persons concerning his integrity as an American writer long in favor among British readers and dealing regularly with British publishers.

The letter to the editor of *The Plaindealer* was once reprinted, with an acknowledgment of its source and an account of the incident of which it formed a part, in PMI, III, 104–09. As it appears in the biography the text includes only one substantive variant from the original version, the correction of a misprint (see Emendations 94.26). It includes a variety of accidental variants—notably the revision of "–k" spellings in "publick" and "criticks" in *The Plaindealer* to "public" and "critic"—but it reveals no evidence of authorial revision.

Because no manuscript version of the letter is known to exist, the version in *The Plaindealer* is adopted here as copy-text. The obsolescent spellings "publick" and "criticks," which *The Plaindealer* consistently employed, were uncharacteristic of Irving's practice; accordingly the copy-text spellings of the words are emended to those undoubtedly intended by the author (see Emedations 94.20, 95.11). In the tables which follow an accounting is given of substantive variants between the copy-text and the reprinting in PMI.

In the preparation of this edition the following collations have been made:

1. A xerox copy of the New York Public Library text of *The Plaindealer* (IAA/ +) sight collated with the Library of Congress copy (AP 2/ .P685);

---

276. *The Plaindealer*, 1, no. 7 (January 14, 1837), 102.

277. For an account of the circumstances surrounding Leggett's charges, see Introduction, I, lviii–lvix, lxi–lxii.

2. The xerox copy collated with two copies of the PMI text, one in the possession of the editor and one owned by the New York Public Library.

See Discussions and Lists p. 553.

[LETTER TO WILLIAM CULLEN BRYANT]

The public letter to Bryant was an outgrowth of Irving's spirited rebuttal of the accusation, by William Leggett of *The Plaindealer*, that he had betrayed a "deficiency of manliness" when, while preparing an English edition of Bryant's *Poems* in 1832, he had consented to altering a word which might have given offense to British readers.[278] Upon reading Irving's response to that claim in *The Plaindealer* for January 28, 1837, Bryant thought he discerned in a reference to the close association between himself and Leggett a suggestion that he was perhaps himself in some measure responsible for Leggett's comments. Accordingly, in a letter published in *The Plaindealer* for February 11 he firmly denied having instigated Leggett in any way. Referring to Irving's slight revision of his poem "Marion's Men," he wrote:

> . . . I had no doubt that it was made with the kindest intentions, and never complained of it to any body. If I had been disposed to complain of it privately, it would have been to himself; nor can I comprehend the disingenuous and pusillanimous malignity which would have led me to procure another to attack, in publick, what I had not even ventured to blame in private.[279]

Irving's shocked disclaimer of an intention to draw Bryant into a controversy between himself and Leggett was published in the New York *American* for February 17, 1837.[280] It was reprinted the next day, under the title "Washington Irving's Apology to William Cullen Bryant," in *The Plaindealer*. Except for the correction of a single typographical error (Emendations 98.17), the reprinted letter includes no substantive variants from that in the New York *American*, which is cited as the source of the text. Having pointedly sent his letter to a publication other than *The Plaindealer*, Irving obviously played no part in assisting its publication in that magazine. Indeed, his preparation of the letter for publication in the New York *American* almost certainly did not extend

278. See Introduction, I, lviii–lix, lxi–lxii.
279. "Mr. Irving's 'Poetick License,'" *The Plaindealer*, 1, no. 11 (February 11, 1837), 165–66.
280. In a brief introduction to Irving's letter setting forth the controversy with which it was associated, the editor of the New York *American* remarked (p. 2 col. 6) that the statement was "received too late yesterday afternoon for insertion" in the issue of February 16.

beyond the writing of a manuscript text, no copy of which is known still to exist.

One paragraph of the letter was subsequently included by Pierre M. Irving in PMI, III, 110. This passage, corresponding to T 98.23–30, forms part of an account of Irving's controversy in 1837 with William Leggett. It reveals no substantive variants nor any other evidence of authorial revision from the pertinent portion of the New York *American* text from which it is derived.

Because no manuscript version of Irving's letter is known to survive, and because apparently he did not revise it after preparing it for publication in the New York *American*, the newspaper version is adopted here as copy-text. The substantive variant between the copy-text and that in *The Plaindealer* is recorded in the table which follows.

In the preparation of this edition the following collations have been made:

1. A transcription of the New York *American* text owned by the New-York Historical Society (Newspapers/New York City) collated twice and independently with a copy owned by the New York Public Library (*AB);

2. The above transcription collated against the text in *The Plaindealer* owned by the New York Public Library (IAA/ +) and in a copy owned by the Library of Congress (AP 2/ .P685);

3. The above transcription collated against the text in two copies of PMI, one in the possession of the editor and one owned by the New York Public Library.

See Discussions and Lists p. 554.

[TOAST AT THE BOOKSELLERS' DINNER, MARCH 30, 1837]

Irving's comments formed part of the program at a "complimentary entertainment" organized by the booksellers of New York, Boston, and Philadelphia for the literary ladies and gentlemen of those cities. Held at the City Hotel in New York, this lavish exercise in public relations was attended by about three hundred persons. A report of the proceedings prepared by George P. Putnam, Irving's future publisher, occupied a full page in the New York *American* for April 3, 1837.[281]

281. "The Booksellers' Dinner," New York *American*, April 3, 1837, p. 1 col. 5– p. 2 col. 5. See also James Grant Wilson, *The Life and Letters of Fitz-Greene Halleck* (New York, 1869), pp. 397–400, where Irving's address is paraphrased (pp. 397–99); PMI, III, 114–15; STW, II, 53.

As he had for the dinner given him upon his return to the United States in 1832 (see pp. 59–60), on this occasion Irving prepared a manuscript report of his speech for the compiler of the newspaper account. The manuscript, which is extant at the Maine Historical Society, includes no non-authorial marks which might identify it as the copy actually used by the printer, but its close correspondence to the speech as it appeared in the New York *American*, and the fact that it was in the possession of George P. Putnam as late as 1861, indicate together that it was written for Putnam's use.[282] The text is in brown ink in a fluent and hurried hand, on all four sides of a sheet of blue stationery folded at the center to form four leaves, each 9⅔″ x 7⅞″. It includes only 9 cancelled passages, 4 of which are of single words.

As it appeared in the New York *American*, the speech includes 2 interpolated indications of the audience's response (see Rejected Variants 99.21, Emendations 99.24) and 5 other substantive variants from the manuscript, all pertaining to single words (Rejected Variants 99.12, 99.21, 99.21, 99.25, 99.27). The newspaper text alter Irving's "Mr" to "Mr." at 9 points and includes 20 other changes of his punctuation.

The New York *American* text of the address was reprinted in the New York *Albion*, a weekly miscellany, for April 8, 1837, (n.s. 5, no. 14, 111 col. 3). This version, which forms part of the *Albion*'s "extracts from the published proceedings," includes only 1 substantive variant from the *American* text—a correction of a misprint (Rejected Variants 99.12)—and has no textual authority. The address was reprinted once more, with an acknowledgment of the *American* as its source, in PMI, III, 115–16. The latter text includes 4 substantive variants from the first printed version, 3 limited to single words (see Emendations 99.15; Rejected Variants 99.12, 99.25) and the last more extensive—an omission of Irving's parenthetical reference to the advanced age of Samuel Rogers (Rejected Variants 99.27).[283]

Having turned over to George Putnam a manuscript account of his address, Irving was almost certainly not responsible for any alterations of it prior to publication. Because manuscript evidence of his intention is available, and there is no evidence that he revised the work once it had been published, the manuscript text at the Maine Historical Society

282. On February 28, 1861, Putnam wrote to a Dr. J. J. M. Fogg, proposing to exchange an Irving manuscript in his possession for four manuscript sheets of the *Life of Washington*, which Fogg then owned (Sleepy Hollow Restorations). Presumably the Booksellers' Dinner manuscript was added to the autograph collection of John S. H. Fogg, now at the Maine Historical Society, some time afterward. The surmise of Stanley T. Williams that the manuscript was an early draft by Irving (STW, II, 344 note 47) is unlikely.

283. Having quoted the remainder of Irving's remarks, Pierre M. Irving appended a comment in his own* person which included the information that had been omitted; see PMI, III, 116.

is adopted as copy-text. In the tables which follow a full accounting is given of variants within the copy-text and between it and the New York *American*. In the list of Emendations only, at points where the *Life and Letters* text is not cited its reading is identical with that in the *American*. Variants between the copy-text and the *American* not included in the list of Emendations, and substantive variants between it and the PMI text not included there, are recorded in a table of Rejected Variants.

In the preparation of this edition the following collations have been made:

1. A typed transcription of the manuscript, prepared on the basis of a xerox copy and a physical description of the original supplied by Mr. Thomas L. Gaffney, collated twice and independently against a copy of the *Life and Letters* text in the possession of the editor, and once with a second copy owned by the New York Public Library;

2. A xerox copy of the editor's PMI text collated twice and independently with the New York *American* text owned by the New York Public Library (*AB), and once with a copy owned by the New-York Historical Society (Newspapers/ New York City);

3. The above xerox copy collated with the *Albion* text in copies owned by the Toronto Public Library (M/ 051/ .A 47) and Yale University (AA 89/ Al 13).

See Discussions and Lists pp. 554, 655.

[LETTER OF "GEOFFREY CRAYON" TO THE EDITOR OF THE *KNICKERBOCKER MAGAZINE*]

Irving's letter on commencing his contributions to the *Knickerbocker Magazine* appeared in the March 1839 issue of that work, pp. 206–10, where it was supplied with a title, "The Crayon Papers." Lewis Gaylord Clark, the editor, caused this general title to precede all Irving's subsequent contributions under the pseudonym of "Geoffrey Crayon." No manuscript version of the text is known to survive.

One paragraph from the *Knickerbocker Magazine* article (T 103.26–104.6 I . . . pilgrimage.) was published in revised and condensed form as part of the "Introduction" to *A Book of the Hudson* (1849), a gathering of Irving's writings concerning the Hudson River and its historical and legendary associations.[284] The sketch was reprinted in full by Henry

284. The two editions of *A Book of the Hudson* are described in the Textual Commentary to "Communipaw," p. 412 note 299; see also *Washington Irving: A Bibliography*, pp. 39–40. Although they were set in type independently, the texts of the reprinted paragraph in the editions printed by R. Craighead and John F. Trow are identical.

T. Tuckerman in his essay on Irving in *Homes of American Authors* (New York, 1853), pp. 35–61. Tuckerman reproduced the *Knickerbocker Magazine* text almost exactly: he omitted the title "The Crayon Papers" (which appears never to have been specified by the author as to form part of the articles above which it appeared), and his text includes 5 other substantive variants from the first printed version (see Rejected Variants 100.39, 101.32, 102.4, 102.22, 103.22). There is no reason to suppose that Irving wished or authorized any of the variant readings to appear in Tuckerman's essay.

The sketch was not again reprinted until Pierre M. Irving included it in *Spanish Papers*, II, [417]–24. The *Spanish Papers* text includes numerous accidental variants from the first printed version, reflecting the imposition of the Putnam house style,[285] but aside from an altered title it includes only 2 substantive variants from the *Knickerbocker Magazine* text (see Rejected Variants 102.34, 103.12–13). It shows no sign of authorial revision.

In short, excepting his alterations of a single paragraph to render it suitable as part of *A Book of the Hudson*, Irving appears not to have revised the work once he had prepared it for publication in the *Knickerbocker Magazine*. In the absence of a manuscript, the first printed version is thus adopted as copy-text.

In accordance with the procedure adopted throughout this collection, pairs of double quotation marks are substituted for the single marks employed in the copy-text to enclose quotations (see Emendation 100.11). In the tables which follow an accounting is given of substantive variants between the copy-text and the three texts derived from it, the coverage for *A Book of the Hudson* being limited to the single adapted paragraph. Variant readings not recorded in the list of Emendations are given in a table of Rejected Variants.

In the preparation of this edition the following collations have been made:

1. A xerox copy of the *Knickerbocker Magazine* text owned by York University (AP 2/ K 64) sight collated with the following additional copies: University of Delaware (AP 2/ .F 64); Legislative Library of Ontario (Periodicals/ 1st floor);

2. The above xerox copy collated with the text in the Craighead edition of *A Book of the Hudson* owned by Columbia University (Sp Coll/ Park Benjamin Collection)' and with the following additional copies: University of Delaware (Spec Coll F/ 127/ .H8/ I86); Yale University (Za/ Ir8/ 849);

3. The above xerox copy collated with the text in the Trow edition of *A Book of the Hudson* owned by the Toronto Public Library (817.24/

---

285. See the Textual Commentary, I, 273–76.

.01) and with the following additional copies: Yale University (Za/ Ir8/ 849b); Sleepy Hollow Restorations (no identification number; bound in green cloth);

4. The above xerox copy collated with the text in *Homes of American Authors* owned by the University of Toronto (PS/ 141/ H6) and with an additional copy: New York Public Library (AB—bookplate of George Bancroft);

5. The above xerox copy collated twice and independently with the text in *Spanish Papers* owned by the National Library of Canada;

6. A xerox copy of the above *Spanish Papers* text sight collated with the following additional copies: New York Public Library; Yale University (Iw/ Ir8/ 866).

See Discussions and Lists pp. 555, 656.

SLEEPY HOLLOW

"Sleepy Hollow" was first published in the *Knickerbocker Magazine* for May 1839, pp. 404–11; no manuscript version is known to survive. The work was not reprinted during Irving's lifetime, but it was included by Pierre M. Irving in *Spanish Papers*, II, [425]–39. Accidental variants between the magazine and the *Spanish Papers* texts form a pattern consistent with the imposition of the Putnam house style in the latter work.[286] However, the reprinted version also includes several substantive variants from the original. While 4 of these are limited to one or two words (see Rejected Variants 106.43, 108.37, 113.9, 113.14), a further cluster extends over the greater part of a lengthy sentence (see Rejected Variants 107.27–29 inclusive). Who was responsible for these substantive changes? Tampering with Irving's works, except to correct errors, to clarify ambiguities, or on occasion—as he put it—to improve "by omissions,"[287] was uncharacteristic of Pierre M. Irving's editorial method. Nor would it have been consistent with his habits as a proofreader to permit a cluster of incorrect readings to be introduced into *Spanish Papers*.

The possibility thus arises that the alterations to the *Knickerbocker Magazine* text were made by Irving himself. His procedure in revising "Abderahman," which he first published in the *Knickerbocker Magazine* and later altered to form part of his projected "Chronicle of the Ommiades" (see pp. 202–32), affords a potential parallel to the present

286. See the Textual Commentary, I, 273–76.
287. Pierre M. Irving, Journal, February 28–November 30, 1859 (Berg Collection, New York Public Library). The quotation from the entry for March 10, pertains to revisions Pierre had made to the manuscript of Irving's *Life of George Washington*.

case. In preparing the manuscript of "Chronicle of the Ommiades" he did not re-use the manuscript text of "Abderahman" he had submitted to Lewis Gaylord Clark as copy; rather, he adopted the printed text as a basis for his revised version.[288] Thus in revising he simply cancelled the pertinent printed text and wrote the passages to be substituted in the margins. Although in the absence of a manuscript or corrected printed copy of "Sleepy Hollow" this suggested parallel must remain conjectural, the *Spanish Papers* texts of "Sleepy Hollow" and "Abderahman" do reveal a similar pattern of infrequent, scattered substantive revisions to the *Knickerbocker Magazine* texts. As Pierre M. Irving reported in his preface to *Spanish Papers*, Irving had once intended "to have brought together and published" his own miscellaneous writings, and before his death he had indeed made "some slight preparation towards this object."[289] Possibly Pierre had in hand a copy of the *Knickerbocker Magazine* text of "Sleepy Hollow" which included corrections by the author.

While the scanty textual evidence thus suggests that the *Spanish Papers* version may have incorporated authorial revisions of the original printed text, in the absence of the hypothesized corrected *Knickerbocker Magazine* text it is impossible to state with any certainty that the variant readings in *Spanish Papers* were introduced by Irving. Even if they were, it would remain in doubt which of the two texts includes accidentals which the more closely approximates Irving's wishes. Manuscript evidence for his other contributions to the *Knickerbocker Magazine* indicates that the printed texts often did include accidentals emended from what he had specified as his intention; but those printed versions are only a single step away from his manuscript, and they do incorporate a fair proportion of the readings he wished. The *Spanish Papers* text introduces a new set of accidentals, and unless, unrealistically, we assume that it was based upon a meticulously corrected copy of the *Knickerbocker Magazine* article, a further departure from Irving's original intention. It seems reasonable to suppose that a text derived immediately from his manuscript, and perhaps even approved by him prior to publication, incorporates a larger portion of his intentions than one derived from it and differing from it. Accordingly, in the absence of conclusive evidence to the contrary, the *Knickerbocker Magazine* version must be regarded as the closest available approximation to Irving's wishes for "Sleepy Hollow" in its original form; and it is adopted here as copy-text.

In accordance with the practice followed throughout this volume, pairs of double quotation marks are substituted for the single quotation marks employed in the copy-text to enclose quotations (see Emendations

288. For a more detailed discussion of Irving's revisions to "Abderahman," which had first appeared in the *Knickerbocker Magazine* for May 1840, see the Textual Commentary to "Chronicle of the Ommiades," pp. 477–79.

289. "Preface by the Editor," *Spanish Papers*, I, [iii].

106.13). In the tables which follow substantive variants, and accidental variants of particular interest, between the copy-text and that in *Spanish Papers* are reported. Variants not included in the list of Emendations are set forth in a table of Rejected Variants.

In the preparation of this edition the following collations have been made:

1. A xerox copy of the *Knickerbocker Magazine* text owned by York University (AP 2/ K 64) sight collated with the following additional copies: University of Delaware (AP 2/ .F64); New-York Historical Society (PS 1/ .K 7); Yale University (A 89/ 72);

2. The above xerox copy collated twice and independently with the *Spanish Papers* text owned by the National Library of Canada;

3. A xerox copy of the above *Spanish Papers* text sight collated with the following additional copies: New York Public Library; Yale University (Iw/ Ir8/ 866).

See Discussions and Lists pp. 556, 656.

[LETTER OF "HIRAM CRACKENTHORPE" TO THE EDITOR OF THE *KNICKERBOCKER MAGAZINE*]

This pseudonymous letter first appeared in the "Editor's Table" section of the *Knickerbocker Magazine* for May 1839, pp. 445–46. It formed a sequel to "The First Locomotive," an article published anonymously in the magazine the month before by Irving's friend Charles Augustus Davis.

Davis' account purported to be a "fragment of authentic history" written to perpetuate the memory of Jabez Doolittle, the "immortal progenitor" of the steam locomotive. "In the year 1808," the unnamed speaker of the piece recalled, while a passenger aboard the first steamboat ever to ascend the Hudson River from New York City, he happened to encounter Doolittle, an old acquaintance and an "ingenious worker in sheet-iron, tin, and wire." In the course of the voyage the inventor attentively studied the new vessel's steam engine for many hours, until he slyly confided to the speaker that he had "got a leetle notion on't"— and added that "if he didn't make a *wagon* go by steam . . . then he'd give up invention." Five years after that prediction, the speaker received an urgent request from Doolittle to visit him at his home "nigh Wallingford," in Connecticut. Hastening there, he learned that the prophesy was fulfilled and that he was now about to become the first outsider ever to set eyes on the completed *"steam-wagon."* Ushered into a long, dingy building, he caught sight of the masterpiece. Proudly the inventor boasted that he could accelerate the "hull scrape" to a speed "only a leetle slower than chain lightnin' " merely by connecting a single "trunnel-head"—which he pointed out—to the "main travelling wheel." The only riddle not yet solved, he said as he clambered atop the locomotive to make a few minor adjustments, was how to stop it once he had set it in motion. Thus suddenly left to himself, the speaker stood "amazed in contemplating the object," until an idea dawned in his mind and rose into a perverse desire: he must see the locomotive move off! Succumbing to temptation, he "pulled the crank that twisted the connecting trunnel-head into the travelling wheels"—and the machine crashed forward through the wall of the shed and out into the world. As it roared away, Doolittle was still to be seen perched atop his contrivance, "screwing down the valves, and oiling the piston-rod and crank-joints." Since that day, however, neither he nor his invention was even sighted again, "nigh Wallingford" or elsewhere.[290]

As Charles A. Davis recalled in a memoir of Irving, "The First Locomotive" had "amused him very much" and had led him to "*elongate* the story by way of verification."[291] The letter of "Hiram Crackenthorpe" was thus introduced in the *Knickerbocker Magazine* as follows:

> Since our last number, we have received letters from various parts of the country, respecting Jabez Doolittle and his Locomotive, by which it would appear, he has the gift of ubiquity; for he has been seen about the same time in a dozen different places, and a dozen different manners, but always under full speed; a kind of Flying Dutchman on land. '*Hic et ubique*' should be his motto. We subjoin one of these letters, as it may tend to set the Far West at ease on a matter that seems to have caused some consternation.

The letter was reprinted, under the title "The First Locomotive Again," in *The Knickerbocker Sketch-Book* (1845), a collection of articles from recent volumes of the *Knickerbocker Magazine*, pp. [27]–29. Besides the supplied title, the reprinted text includes 7 substantive variants from the original, 6 involving deletions to conceal the original format of the work as a letter to the editor (see Emendations 113.21; Rejected Variants 113.20, 113.21, 114.13, 114.20, 114.33–34), and 1 an obvious misprint (see Rejected Variants 114.7). Irving played no part in any of these revisions, for at the time *The Knickerbocker Sketch-Book* was published he was busily employed as the United States Minister to Spain; it is most unlikely that Lewis Gaylord Clark, who prepared the volume as

290. *Knickerbocker Magazine*, 13, no. 4 (April 1839), 343–48.

291. Charles A. Davis to Pierre M. Irving, New York, June 1863 (Berg Collection, New York Public Library). The background of Irving's sequel to "The First Locomotive" is discussed in further detail by Wayne R. Kime in "The First Locomotive to Cross the Rocky Mountains: An Unidentified Sketch in the *Knickerbocker Magazine*, May 1839, by Washington Irving," *Bulletin of the New York Public Library*, 76 (1972), 242–50.

a speculation on his own behalf, would have written him from New York to solicit revisions, or else approval of revisions already made, to the original text. Since no manuscript is known to survive, and since the work was reprinted only once during Irving's lifetime—and then under the supervision of someone else—the first printed version is clearly the appropriate choice as copy-text.

In accordance with the practice followed throughout this edition, pairs of single quotation marks enclosing quotations in the copy-text are emended to double quotation marks (Emendations 113.32); single quotation marks at the beginnings of successive paragraphs are deleted (Emendations 113.21). In the tables which follow an accounting is given of substantive variants and an accidental variant of interest between the copy-text and that in *The Knickerbocker Sketch-Book*; variants not included in the list of Emendations are set forth in a table of Rejected Variants.

In the preparation of this edition the following collations have been made:

1. A xerox copy of the *Knickerbocker Magazine* text owned by York University (AP 2/ K 64) sight collated with the following additional copies: University of Delaware (AP 2/ .F 64); Legislative Library of Ontario (Periodicals/ first floor); Yale University (A 89/ 72);

2. The above xerox copy collated twice and independently with *The Knickerbocker Sketch-Book* text in a copy owned by the University of Delaware (PS 645/ .C55);

3. A xerox copy of the above *Knickerbocker Sketch-Book* text sight collated with the following additional copy: New-York Historical Society (PS 525/ .C 363).

See Discussions and Lists pp. 556, 657.

NATIONAL NOMENCLATURE

Irving's longstanding interest in place-names came to fruition in "National Nomenclature," which appeared in the *Knickerbocker Magazine* for August 1839, pp. 158–62. The magazine text was not reprinted during his lifetime, but it was included by Pierre M. Irving in *Spanish Papers*, II, [440]–46. The reprint version includes one substantive variant from the original (see Rejected Variants 116.36) and various emended accidentals characteristic of the house styling of George Putnam, the publisher of *Spanish Papers*,[292] but it reveals no evidence of authorial revision. Since no manuscript is known to survive and there is no reason to

292. See the Textual Commentary, I, 273–76.

suppose that Irving revised the single version printed during his lifetime, the *Knickerbocker Magazine* text is adopted as copy-text.

In accordance with the practice followed elsewhere in this edition, pairs of single quotation marks enclosing quotations in the copy-text are emended to double quotation marks (see Emendations 115.9). In the list of Emendations which follows an accounting is given of the substantive variant and accidental variants of interest between the copy-text and that in *Spanish Papers*.

In the preparation of this edition the following collations have been made:

1. A xerox copy of the *Knickerbocker Magazine* text owned by York University (AP 2/ K 64) sight collated with the following additional copies: University of Delaware (AP 2/ .F 64); Legislative Library of Ontario (Periodicals/ first floor);

2. The above xerox copy collated twice and independently with the *Spanish Papers* text owned by the National Library of Canada;

3. A xerox copy of the above *Spanish Papers* text sight collated with the following additional copies: New York Public Library; Yale University (Iw/ Ir8/ 866).

See Discussions and Lists pp. 556, 657.

DESULTORY THOUGHTS ON CRITICISM

This work was first published in the *Knickerbocker Magazine* for August 1839, pp. 175–78. It was not reprinted during Irving's lifetime, but it was included by Pierre M. Irving in *Spanish Papers*, II [447]–52. Four substantive variants from the original text appear in *Spanish Papers*—a one-word adjustment characteristic of Pierre's editorial hand (Rejected Variants 122.23), an omitted concluding signature, and two corrected misspellings (see Emendations 120.36, 121.38). The *Spanish Papers* text also includes accidental variants from that in the *Knickerbocker Magazine*, reflecting the imposition of the Putnam house style,[293] but it affords no convincing evidence of authorial revision. Since no manuscript version is known to survive, and Irving appears not to have revised the work as first printed, the *Knickerbocker Magazine* text is adopted as copy-text.

In accordance with the practice followed elsewhere in this edition, pairs of single quotation marks enclosing material quoted in the copy-text are emended to double quotation marks (see Emendations 119.11–17). In the tables which follow an accounting is given of substantive

293. See the Textual Commentary, I, 273–76.

variants and an accidental variant of possible interest between the copy-text and that in *Spanish Papers*. Variants not included in the list of Emendations are set forth in a separate table of Rejected Variants.

In the preparation of this edition the following collations have been made:

1. A xerox copy of the *Knickerbocker Magazine* text owned by York University (AP 2/ K 64) sight collated with the following additional copies: University of Delaware (AP 2/ .F 64); Legislative Library of Ontario (Periodicals/ first floor); Yale University (A 89/ 72);

2. The above xerox copy collated twice and independently with the *Spanish Papers* text owned by the National Library of Canada;

3. A xerox copy of the above *Spanish Papers* text sight collated with the following additional copies: New York Public Library; Yale University (Iw/ Ir8/ 866).

See Discussions and Lists pp. 557, 657.

COMMUNIPAW

"Communipaw" was first published in the *Knickerbocker Magazine* for August 1839, pp. 257–62; a holograph manuscript of the article, which served as printer's copy, is extant in the Berg Collection, New York Public Library.[294] Written in dark brown ink with two different pens— one having a fine point, the other broader—the manuscript consists of twenty-one pages primarily of cream-colored paper, varying in width between $4\frac{7}{16}''$ and $5''$ and in length between $7\frac{11}{16}''$ and $7\frac{13}{16}''$. Pages 5, 7, 8, 9, and 20 include text written on additional slips pasted onto this paper; page 16 is only $6\frac{1}{2}''$ in length, its first few lines in an earlier version having been cropped (see Emendations 127.20). Pages 17–21 are renumbered from 14–18. Taken together, the pagination, the pastings, and the differing pen-strokes in the manuscript reveal that Irving prepared a complete version of "Communipaw" which he revised before submitting the work for publication. The earlier text, most of which forms part of the final version, consisted of seventeen numbered pages written with a fine-pointed pen and concluding at a point corresponding to T 128.35. In his later draft Irving cancelled some matter, made substitutions, and added a substantial amount of material.[295]

---

294. The manuscript is accompanied by two notes describing its origin and the early history of its ownership (it was in the possession of Lewis Gaylord Clark until 1864). That it served as printer's copy is indicated by two notations in ink on p. 13—a bracket to the left of the word "tainted," and a note in the left margin beside it ("35.–p. 261) indicating that the word occurs in the *Knickerbocker Magazine* text at that point (see T 126.38).

295. He wrote a new page 4 (T 123.34–39 traveller . . . turkey); pasted onto

The circumstances under which he partially rewrote "Communipaw" are unknown. Interestingly, however, a pasted portion of page 20 in the manuscript includes on its reverse side part of a legal document followed by the partial signature "Pierre/Notary." The signature is in the hand of Pierre M. Irving, who in 1839 was Notary to the Bank of Commerce in New York and who occupied an office near that institution where his uncle sometimes dropped in to visit. The possibility that in revising his manuscript Irving not only borrowed some of Pierre's stationery but made the changes while in Pierre's office is suggested by two considerations. First, the broad-tipped pen he used in preparing the new version was identical with the type ordinarily used by Pierre. Second, the revised manuscript includes numerous clarifications, editorial marks, and revisions made with a pen of this type, in ink of the same color, by Pierre M. Irving himself.[296]

That Irving should have permitted his nephew to insert revisions in his manuscript is not surprising. He was impatient of his "monthly recurring task" as a contributor to the *Knickerbocker Magazine*,[297] and he devoted no more pains to preparing copy than was absolutely necessary.[298] He may indeed have employed Pierre M. Irving on a fairly regular basis as his unofficial editor and liaison with Lewis Gaylord Clark. Certainly the "Communipaw" manuscript indicates that Clark held Pierre's editorial skills in esteem: the manuscript includes only 4 marks in Clark's sky-blue ink, only 1 of which involves a change to the text (see Emendations 128.37).

While Pierre M. Irving made only a single substantive change in the manuscript (see Rejected Variants 123.29), he freely altered its accidentals. He imposed on Irving's text a dense pattern of punctuation which approximated the *Knickerbocker Magazine* style. His deletions and alterations of Irving's punctuation were few, totalling 12, but he added

---

the top of page 7 a slip of paper including four lines of text (124.24–27 gardens . . . . notice and); discarded the original text from p. 9 to p. 12 in that version, substituting a new bottom of p. 9 and pp. 10–15 (125.25–127.19 Years . . . . Society); cropped the top of the original p. 13 and renumbered the remaining portion 16; renumbered the original pp. 14–17 as 17–20 (127.30–128.35 came . . . . VANDER DONK); pasted a postscript onto the bottom of p. 20 and added its continuation on a new p. 21.

296. The manuscript also includes a few pencil marks by Pierre M. Irving—clarifications of Irving's handwriting, "x" marks in the margins beside queried passages, instructions to the printer, carets, and 2 paragraph symbols added for clarification. See also Rejected Variants 123.29.

297. Irving to Pierre M. Irving, n.p., April 1840; PMI, III, 152.

298. The extant manuscripts of "[Anecdote of Admiral Harvey]," "The Empire of the West," and "[Anecdote of the French Revolution]" (see pp. 135–38) all show signs of Irving's casual habits of composition; and all include revisions of various kinds by Lewis Gaylord Clark to bring the works into publishable form.

84 commas, 4 semicolons, 4 periods, and 3 colons. He capitalized 5 words and added hyphens to compound words on 41 occasions. In short, probably with the tacit approval of his uncle, he significantly altered the text entrusted to him.

The Berg Collection manuscript does not represent the final stage in the preparation of "Communipaw" for magazine publication, for the printed text differed at several points from the manuscript version as revised by Pierre M. Irving. Easily the most important alteration is that the postscript to the work (T 128.36–129.6) was omitted; for some reason it was included, suitably revised, as a postscript to "The Conspiracy of the Cocked Hats" (pp. 129–33) which appeared in the *Knickerbocker Magazine* for September 1839. However, that Irving intended the passage to form part of "Communipaw" is clearly indicated by the cancelled signature on page 21 of the manuscript—"Hermanus Vander Donk," the name of the fictive author of the article. ("The Conspiracy of the Cocked Hats" purported to be a contribution by a different imaginary individual, "Roloff Van Ripper.") Substantive variants from the manuscript occur at 13 other points in the *Knickerbocker Magazine* text, and a variety of accidental variants is also present. Spelling is altered at 5 points, hyphenation is supplied to compound words at 12, commas are added at 30 and deleted at 7, and 16 other emendations of accidentals are made. In view of Irving's reluctance to linger over his magazine articles, and of Pierre M. Irving's having once revised the manuscript with care, these variants between the revised manuscript and the published text would seem to be the work of another person— probably Clark. There is no reason, at any rate, to suppose them the work of the author himself.

Following its publication in the *Knickerbocker Magazine*, "Communipaw" next appeared ten years later in *A Book of the Hudson*, a collection of Irving's writings about the Hudson River and its legendary history. Heavily revised and condensed, its original format as a letter to the editor having been dropped, it served as an introduction to a tale entitled "Guests from Gibbet Island."[299] In adapting the work to suit

299. "Guests from Gibbet Island" had first appeared in the *Knickerbocker Magazine*, 14 (October 1839), 342–50. After being reprinted in *A Book of the Hudson* it was reprinted again in *Wolfert's Roost* (New York, 1855), pp. 234–38.

A Book of the Hudson appeared in March 1849 in two separate editions: one printed by R. Craighead, one by George Putnam's regular printer, John F. Trow. The bewildering variety of bindings and degrees of illustration in which these works, whose contents were identical, were offered for sale is summarized in *Washington Irving: A Bibliography*, pp. 39–40. Research for this edition has not yielded further information as to the doubtful priority of the two editions. In the Craighead edition, "Communipaw" appears on pp. [11]–14; in the Trow, on pp. [9]–13. Subsequent page-references are to the Craighead edition, which Langfield and Blackburn believe may have been the earlier.

this new purpose Irving sought to combine passages in the earlier version with similar material from "The Conspiracy of the Cocked Hats." Both articles had affirmed the "romantic capabilities" of early Dutch colonial history, and both had given examples to demonstrate the principle they set forth: the former by recounting the erection of the "House of the Four Chimnies" and the miraculous generation of oysters and cabbages for which the village has since been renowned; the latter by describing the "in-and-in conspiracy" of the Dutch to overwhelm the Yankee invaders of New Amsterdam by sheer force of numbers. In re-shaping "Communipaw" as an introductory discourse he dispensed with these fabulous tales, combining the framing commentaries in the two articles into a single new affirmation that the sleepy Dutch villages along the Hudson River were regions of romance.

However, as it appeared in *A Book of the Hudson*, "Communipaw" was at least the second of Irving's efforts thus to coordinate the two related works. The fruit of his first attempt is a holograph manuscript, written in ink and at some points corrected in pencil on eleven sheets of blue laid paper 5 x 8″ in size unless cropped or comprised of pasted slips, which is in the Manuscript Division, New York Public Library.[300] This unpublished manuscript, whose contents are dominated by material from "The Conspiracy of the Cocked Hats," but which also includes passages adapted from "Communipaw," is untitled.[301] Although it was

---

300. Page 6 is 4 1/4″ high, and a fragment of a line of lost text is visible at its top; page 7 is 4 9/16″ high; page 8, consisting of three slips of paper pasted together, is 11 1/2″ high; and p. 9, consisting of two slips of paper pasted together, is 9″ high. Page 1 is numbered twice in pencil, pages 2–5 in ink over pencil, the fragmentary pages 6 and 7 in ink only, pages 8 and 9 in ink over pencil; page 10 is numbered in pencil but includes another partially erased pencilled number, 13; page 11 is also numbered in pencil and includes an illegible erased pencilled number. Except for a single cancellation in pencil on page 5, the manuscript text is written entirely in ink. The pencilled cancellation–deleting the final word of a sentence not present on the extant page 4, the multiple pagination, and the cropped pages 6 and 7 together show that Irving revised his sketch by cutting and splicing at various points; but the extant text is itself only cursorily revised.

301. The manuscript includes material adapted in the following sequence from the *Knickerbocker Magazine* texts of "Communipaw" and "The Conspiracy of the Cocked Hats":

Manuscript pages	*Knickerbocker Magazine*	
1–3	"Conspiracy,"	305.19–31
		305.13–19
		305.31–306.12
4	"Communipaw,"	258.16–18
		257.10–17
5		259.1–24
6–7		258.23–38
7		259.37–47
8	"Conspiracy,"	306.38–307.2, 308.16–28

written fluently, it includes minor cancellations in ink and pencil, cropped pages, and pastings which suggest at least some revision before Irving discarded it to begin a new version. It opens with a paragraph adapted from "The Conspiracy of the Cocked Hats":

Knickerbocker Magazine, October 1839	Manuscript, New York Public Library

Poetry and romance received a fatal blow at the overthrow of the ancient Dutch dynasty, and have ever since been gradually withering under the growing domination of the Yankees. They abandoned our hearths, when the old Dutch tiles were superseded by marble chimney-pieces; when brass and-irons made way for polished grates, and the crackling and blazing fire of nut-wood gave place to the smoke and stench of Liverpool coal; and on the downfall of the last gable-end house, their requiem was tolled from the tower of the Dutch church in Nassau-street, by the old bell that came from Holland. But poetry and romance still live unseen among us, or seen only by the enlightened few, who are able to contemplate this city and its environs through the medium of tradition, and clothed with the associations of foregone ages. (305.19–31)

It was the opinion of the venerable historian of the Manhattoes that poetry and romance received a fatal blow at the overthrow of the Dutch dynasty and have been gradually declining ever since under the growing domination of the Yankees. They abandoned our hearths when the glazed tiles pictured with scriptural story which once adorned our fireplaces were superseded by marble chimney pieces, when brass andirons made way for polished grates, and the crackling and blazing nut-wood fire gave place to the smoke and stench of Liverpool coal. Their downfall was complete when the last Dutch house, with ⟨cr⟩ crowstep gables, was pulled down and succeeded by a marble bank, and their requieum was tolled, from the tower of the Dutch church on Nassau Street, by an old bell that came from Holland.

With all due deference to the opinion of the Historian, however, I console myself with the idea that the elements of poetry and romance still linger among us⟨;⟩, ⟨clothed with the⟩ not, it is true, in the bustling ⟨highw⟩ streets of the monied metropolis nor in the palaces of its 'merchant princes;' but, like Kidd the pirates treasure, they must be sought for in out-of-the-way places, and digged for among the ⟨nun⟩ ruins and traditions of the past.

In a manner which likewise echoes the conclusion of "The Conspiracy of the Cocked Hats," the manuscript closes with a prophesy of the splendid future awaiting the New Netherlands.[302] Possibly Irving discarded the draft as unsuited to his purposes in *A Book of the Hudson* because, as a summary description of Communipaw, it was a self-contained work which purported to introduce nothing.

The incomplete holograph manuscript of the sketch eventually published in *A Book of the Hudson*, written in dark brown ink on one side of six sheets of light blue unlaid paper varying from 4¾₆″ to 4⅞″ in width and from 7⅜″ to 7⁹⁄₁₆″ in length, is also in the Manuscript Division, New York Public Library. Written in a fluent hand, it includes only a few corrections, almost all of which are deletions of false starts. The pages are numbered in pencil 1–5, 8, probably not by Irving but by the printer, whose name, "Whelpley," is written in pencil in the upper left-hand corner of the first page. As it appears in the manuscript, the title of the piece is "⟨Romantic Capabilities⟩ of/ ⟨The Manhattoes -⟩/ Communipaw -"[303] In characteristically resourceful fashion, Irving—in 1849 busily engaged in preparing a revised edition of his writings—selected and reworked a few passages from his *Knickerbocker Magazine* articles, putting them to a new purpose.[304]

Pierre M. Irving reprinted the *Knickerbocker Magazine* text of "Communipaw" in *Spanish Papers*, II, [453]–62. Except alterations of spelling

---

9	"Communipaw,"	261.27–45
10–11	"Conspiracy,"	307.18–45
11		308.1–8, 308.36–45

302. "The deliverance of the New Nederlands from Yankee domination will eclipse the redemption of Spain from the Moors and the oft sung Conquest of Granada will fade before the reconquest of New Amsterdam. Would that Peter Stuyvesant could rise from his grave to witness that day!" Compare *Knickerbocker Magazine*, 14 (October 1839), 308.40–45 (T 133.14–18).

Another manuscript which appears at one time to have formed part of this rejected draft is extant in the Manuscript Division, New York Public Library. It consists of two pages of laid paper 5 1/8 x 8″ in dimensions and including a text written in the same ink as the eleven-page untitled manuscript. The fragmentary text is adapted from the *Knickerbocker Magazine* version of "The Conspiracy of the Cocked Hats," 305.21–24, 305.28–29, 305.33–36, 307.2–4.

303. Pages 1 and 8 of the manuscript include slips of light blue unlaid paper pasted onto the sheets of cream-colored paper otherwise used. There is a single correction by Irving in a darker shade of ink, and a single cancellation in pencil and ink. The first word on page 1, "It," is thrice underlined in pencil, and in the left margin beside it what appears to be a Roman numeral "III" is written in pencil.

304. The manuscript includes material adapted in the following sequence from the *Knickerbocker Magazine* texts of "Communipaw" and "The Conspiracy of the Cocked Hats." For reference, corresponding page- and line-references to *A Book of the Hudson* are also given:

and punctuation reflecting imposition of the Putnam house style,[305] and 2 obvious misprints (see Rejected Variants 126.10, 128.9), the reprinted version includes only 1 substantive variant from the earlier one (Rejected Variants 123.37).

"Communipaw" was thus printed in full only once during the author's lifetime, in the *Knickerbocker Magazine*, and once thereafter, in *Spanish Papers*. Although he put portions of the sketch to a new use in *A Book of the Hudson*, Irving is not known to have revised the work as a whole. In some form, therefore, the text composed and published in 1839 must be selected as copy-text. The following are available as alternative choices:

1. The author's manuscript, excluding marks by Pierre M. Irving;
2. The author's manuscript, as revised by Pierre M. Irving;
3. The published text.

As has been pointed out, the *Knickerbocker Magazine* text is significantly at variance with the manuscript evidence of Irving's intention, and there is no indication that the changes were specifically authorized by him. Indeed, even as revised and "corrected" by Pierre, the manuscript in the Berg Collection is itself at variance with Irving's known intention. Pierre may well have been given the responsibility of putting the text into a final form suitable for use by Clark; but even if he was, it does not follow that Irving would have approved his every alteration. On the other hand, it is clear that the author had revised his own first draft with some care before he ever put it into the hands of his nephew.

Certainly, in view of the close working relationship becoming established in 1839 between Irving and Pierre, the latter's emendations of the manuscript cannot casually be dismissed as tamperings—or indeed, pronounced with certainty as misrepresentations of Irving's wishes. But at the same time, Pierre's marks are not those of his uncle; and once we depart from what the author himself wrote we enter a perilous area of speculation as to what he would, could, or should have wished. As the

Manuscript pages	*A Book of the Hudson*	*Knickerbocker Magazine*	
1	[11].4–13	"Conspiracy,"	305.9–18
1–2	[11].14–12.2		305.19–31
2–3	12.3–22		305.32–306.12
3	12.23–30	"Communipaw,"	257.10–17
3–4	12.30–34		258.13–18
4	12.35–13.9		258.19–46
4–5	13.10–24		259.1–24
[MS wanting]	13.25–36		261.46–262.2
[MS wanting]	14.1–7		262.3–9
[MS wanting]	14.10–16		259.33–36
8	14.16–27		261.32–40

305. See the Textual Commentary I, 273–76.

basis of the present edition, the manuscript of "Communipaw" which Irving himself completed must hence be selected as copy-text.

Reflecting the relative care with which it was produced for publication, the copy-text poses few editorial problems. Irving's spelling and capitalization are unusually accurate and self-consistent. Where two spellings of the same word are used, both are allowed to stand—*e.g.*, "weather cock" (128.19) and "weather-cock" (129.4)—except when a definite preference is evident. The various configurations of the abbreviated "Saint" are regularized to "St." (Emendations 125.13), but where Irving uses the full form it is permitted to stand. A few capitalizations of parts of proper names or pseudonyms are necessary to render the text self-consistent (*e.g.*, Emendations 123.11, 125.33, 126.5).

The two manuscript texts Irving prepared for publication in *A Book of the Hudson* are not analyzed in the tables which follow because, being tangential to the history of the work in its full and original form, they are not useful as sources of potential emendations. The list of Emendations includes all authorial cancellations in the manuscript; false starts re-written immediately afterward are listed in a single entry (Emendations 123.7). Substantive and accidental emendations to the copy-text by Pierre M. Irving are recorded in full. To facilitate comparison, the copy-text and Pierre's revision of it are analyzed in the tables as distinct texts; at points where the revised version is not cited it is to be presumed identical with the original.[306] Substantive and accidental variants between the copy-text and that in the *Knickerbocker Magazine* are given in full. At points in the list of Emendations where the *Spanish Papers* text is not cited its reading is to be presumed identical with that in the *Knickerbocker Magazine*. Substantive variants only between the copy-text and that in *Spanish Papers* are recorded. Variants not set forth in the list of Emendations are listed in a separate table of Rejected Variants.

In the preparation of this edition the following collations have been made:

1. A xerox copy of the *Knickerbocker Magazine* text owned by the University of Delaware (AP 2/ .F64) sight collated with the following additional copies: University of Virginia (AP 2/ K 64); Legislative Library of Ontario (Periodicals/ first floor); York University (AP 2/ K64);

2. The above xerox copy collated with the text in the Craighead edition of *A Book of the Hudson* owned by Columbia University (Special Collections/ Park Benjamin Collection) and with a copy of the Trow edition owned by Toronto Public Library (817.24/ .01);

3. A xerox copy of the Columbia University *A Book of the Hudson* text

---

306. Because Pierre M. Irving on 5 occasions added hyphens to end-of-line compound words, these emendations are reported in the list of Emendations even though the accepted forms of the words in question are listed as Hyphenated Compounds as well (see Emendations 123.39, 124.3, 124.4, 124.24–25, 129.1).

(see no. 2) sight collated with the following additional copies: Yale University (Za/ Ir8/ 849); New-York Historical Society (F 127/ .H8/ I 86 copy 1); University of Delaware (Spec. F 127/ .H8/ I 86);

4. A xerox copy of the Toronto Public Library *A Book of the Hudson* text (see no. 2) sight collated with the following additional copies: Yale University (Za/ Ir8/ 849b); Sleepy Hollow Restorations (no identification number; bound in green cloth);

5. The above xerox copy of the *Knickerbocker Magazine* text collated twice and independently with the *Spanish Papers* text owned by the National Library of Canada and once with the following additional copies: New York Public Library; Yale University (Iw/ Ir8/ 866);

6. A typed transcription of the author's manuscript in the Berg Collection, made from a xerox copy annotated on the basis of a comparison with the original, collated twice and independently with the xerox copy of the *Knickerbocker Magazine* text;

7. A xerox copy of the 11-page author's manuscript in the Manuscript Division, New York Public Library, collated twice and independently with the *Knickerbocker Magazine* texts of "Communipaw" and "The Conspiracy of the Cocked Hats" owned by the University of Delaware;

8. A xerox copy of the 2-page fragment of the above unpublished work, also in the Manuscript Division, New York Public Library, collated against the above *Knickerbocker Magazine* texts;

9. The 6-page author's manuscript in the Manuscript Division, New York Public Library, collated with the xerox copy from the Craighead edition of *A Book of the Hudson* (see no. 3) and with the xerox copy from the Trow edition (see no. 4);

10. The above manuscript collated twice and independently with the *Knickerbocker Magazine* texts of "Communipaw" and "The Conspiracy of the Cocked Hats" (see no. 7).

See Discussions and Lists pp. 528, 557, 657.

CONSPIRACY OF THE COCKED HATS

This sketch was first published in the *Knickerbocker Magazine* for October 1839, pp. 305–09, as a sequel to "Communipaw," which had appeared in the previous issue. Except for two minor fragments extant in the Berg Collection, New York Public Library, no manuscript version of "Conspiracy of the Cocked Hats" is known to survive. The holograph fragments, written in dark ink on opposite sides of a sheet of unlaid, unlined paper 5 x 8″ in size, are apparently rejected drafts of brief passages in the published text.[307] They are of almost no value for the purpose of establishing a critical text.

However, other manuscript evidence is extant which suggests that in an important respect the work did not appear in the *Knickerbocker Magazine* as Irving had intended it. The author's manuscript of "Communipaw," which served as printer's copy for the magazine text of that work,[308] includes a passage which for some reason was omitted from that sketch and was included instead, revised and expanded, as a postscript to "Conspiracy of the Cocked Hats."[309] As it appears in the *Knickerbocker Magazine* it does form an appropriate sequel to the latter work, serving as an ironic practical reversal of the Dutch schemes to extirpate the Yankees from their community. But on the other hand, in its original form it was a suitable addition to "Communipaw," a sketch which touched upon the exertions of the Yankees to gain a foothold in the Dutch village (see pp. 127–28). The complete holograph of "Communipaw" reveals clearly that, at least at one time, Irving intended his postscript to form part of that work. In view of his tendency as a contributor to the *Knickerbocker Magazine* to devote no more attention to the articles he submitted for publication than was absolutely necessary, it is unlikely that he would have seen fit to revise the manuscript of "Communipaw" once he, or his nephew Pierre, had sent it to Clark. Whatever the reason for shifting the postscript from "Communipaw" to "Conspiracy of the Cocked Hats"—whether to make up for an omision through oversight in the printing of "Communipaw," or possibly to fill out the comparatively brief "Conspiracy"—the shift, and the revisions it entailed, were likely made by Clark.

After he had published the work in the *Knickerbocker Magazine*, Irving drew upon "Conspiracy of the Cocked Hats" in preparing his introductory essay for *A Book of the Hudson* (1849), a gathering of his earlier writings about the Hudson River and its historical associations; but

307. The text on one side, which does not correspond closely to any part of the *Knickerbocker Magazine* version, is written beneath the number 3 at the upper right:

>   but you must ⟨co⟩ contemplate out city ⟨aside⟩
>   under another aspect, as connected with the
>   fortunes and achievements of its ancient
>   and heroic race, as connected with the

A transcription of the text on the verso of the sheet, written from the bottom upward above the number 5 at the lower left, appears below. The text corresponds to a passage which, much expanded, appears in the magazine on 306.13–22 (T 130.18–28):

>   Your Correspondent has professed to give
>   you an insight into the secret history of
>   Communipaw, but he has let you in to

308. For a detailed discussion of this manuscript see pp. 410–12.

309. For Irving's original postscript, see "Communipaw," 128.36–129.6 and the accompanying tables; for the revised version, see Emendations 133.20 for the present work.

except for this revision, wherein he joined portions of the sketch with segments from "Communipaw,"[310] he made no revisions of the work during his lifetime.

In *Spanish Papers*, II, [463]–70, Pierre M. Irving reprinted the work from the *Knickerbocker Magazine*. The *Spanish Papers* text includes no substantive variants from the original printing. It does reveal various alterations of accidentals, reflecting the imposition of the Putnam house style,[311] but there is no indication of authorial revision.

Since "Conspiracy of the Cocked Hats" was published only once during Irving's lifetime,[312] no manuscript evidence is of use for establishing a text of the entire work, and there is no evidence of authorial revision of the article as first published, the *Knickerbocker Magazine* version is adopted as copy-text. However, because Irving originally intended the postscript in the copy-text version of "Conspiracy of the Cocked Hats" to be appended instead to "Communipaw," and because there is no reason to suppose him responsible for the revisions made in order to render the passage suitable as a coda to "Conspiracy," that portion of the *Knickerbocker Magazine* version is omitted.

In accordance with the practice followed throughout this volume, pairs of single quotation marks enclosing quotations in the copy-text are emended to double quotation marks (see Emendations 130.5). In the tables which follow a single accidental variant of possible interest between the copy-text and that in *Spanish Papers* is recorded in the table of Rejected Variants.

In the preparation of this edition the following collations have been made:

1. A xerox copy of the *Knickerbocker Magazine* text owned by York University (AP 2/ K 64) sight collated with the following additional copies: University of Delaware (AP 2/ .F 64); Legislative Library of Ontario (Periodicals/ first floor); Yale University (A 89/ 72);

2. The above xerox copy collated with Irving's discarded manuscript draft for an introduction to *A Book of the Hudson* (Manuscript Division, New York Public Library—see pp. 413–15);

3. The above xerox copy collated with Irving's manuscript, entitled "Communipaw," published in *A Book of the Hudson* (Manuscript Division, New York Public Library—see p. 415);

4. The above xerox copy collated with "Communipaw" in the Craighead edition of *A Book of the Hudson* (see p. 412), using a copy owned by

310. For a discussion of Irving's two attempts to meld "Communipaw" and "Conspiracy of the Cocked Hats" into a single commentary, see pp. 412–15.

311. See the Textual Commentary, I, 273–76.

312. The statement by Williams and Edge in *Bibliography*, p. 142, that "Conspiracy of the Cocked Hats" was pirated from the *Knickerbocker Magazine* in *The Evergreen: A Monthly Magazine* during 1840 is incorrect.

Columbia University (Special Collections/ Park Benjamin Collection), and with the following additional copies: Yale University (Za/ Ir8/ 849); New-York Historical Society (F 127/ .H8/ 186 copy 1); University of Delaware (Spec. F 127/ .H8/ 186);

5. The xerox copy collated with "Communipaw" in the Trow edition of *A Book of the Hudson* (see p. 412), using a copy owned by the Toronto Public Library (817.24/ .01), and with the following additional copies: Yale University (Za/ Ir8/ 849b); Sleepy Hollow Restorations (no identification number; bound in green cloth);

6. The xerox copy of the *Knickerbocker Magazine* text collated twice and independently with pages 20 and 21 of the printer's copy manuscript of "Communipaw" (see pp. 412, 419–20);

7. The above xerox copy collated twice and independently with the *Spanish Papers* text owned by the National Library of Canada;

8. A xerox copy of the above *Spanish Papers* text sight collated with the following additional copies: New York Public Library; Yale University (Iw/ Ir8/ 866).

See Discussions and Lists pp. 528, 562, 660.

[LETTER ON INTERNATIONAL COPYRIGHT TO THE EDITOR OF THE *KNICKERBOCKER MAGAZINE*]

Irving's statement was first published in the "Editor's Table" section of the *Knickerbocker Magazine* for January 1840, pp. 78–79. He had recently received a letter from William H. Prescott urging him to prepare "a brief memorial" which would be signed by "the persons most interested in the success of the law,"[313] but he had not done so; nor had he signed a petition which had recently been set before him. Lest his failure thus far to commit himself publicly to the cause of international copyright be misconstrued, he prepared the statement to make clear his actual sentiments. The *Knickerbocker Magazine* text was not reprinted during the author's lifetime, but Pierre M. Irving reproduced it in full, with an acknowledgment of its source, in PMI, III, 149–51. As reprinted in the biography the work includes only a few accidental variants and no substantive variants from the earlier version, revealing no evidence of authorial revision. Because no manuscript text of the statement is known to survive, and Irving apparently did not revise it once it had been published, the *Knickerbocker Magazine* version is adopted as copy-text.

In the tables which follow two accidental variants of possible interest

---

313. Prescott to Irving, Boston, December 24, 1839; in George Ticknor, *Life of William Hickling Prescott* (Boston, 1864), pp. 170–72.

between the copy-text and that in PMI are listed in a table of Rejected Variants.

In the preparation of this edition the following collations have been made:

1. A xerox copy of the *Knickerbocker Magazine* text owned by York University (AP 2/K 64) sight collated with the following additional copies: University of Delaware (AP 2/.F 64); New-York Historical Society (PS 1/.K7); Yale University (A 89/ 72);

2. The xerox copy collated twice and independently with the PMI text in the possession of the editor and once with an additional copy owned by the New York Public Library (AN).

See Discussions and Lists pp. 563, 660.

[ANECDOTE OF ADMIRAL HARVEY]

This anecdote was published in the "Editor's Table" section of the *Knickerbocker Magazine* for February 1840, pp. 166–67, where it was presented as a proof that English persons do not invariably feel "decided hatred and repugnance" toward America and Americans. The vignette was introduced as follows: "An instance was recently related to us, by an illustrious American, known as well, and as highly honored, abroad as at home, which, without any infraction of social confidence, we shall here take the liberty to repeat, for the benefit of our readers." Lewis Gaylord Clark's reference to the circumstances of "social confidence" in which the anecdote was "related" to him suggests that the published text may originally have formed part of a letter addressed him by Irving. A holograph manuscript corresponding to the printed text, extent in the Manuscript Division of the New York Public Library, supports this speculation. Written hastily on two sheets of light blue laid paper,[314] the anecdote begins, as in the published text, with an extended dash between "Sir" and "Harvey"—a convention of discreet reference to an individual which Irving would presumably not have adopted had he been writing for Clark's private eyes alone.[315] Moreover, at the top of the first page he wrote two notations (both subsequently deleted by Clark): the number 6, and a short space after it, "By [?Webb?]." The "6" might naturally be assumed a page-number, suggesting that in its original form the manuscript formed part of a lengthier writing. Although on the basis of the scanty evidence the exact provenance of the manuscript text cannot be

---

314. The two sheets have been pasted onto a piece of cardboard: the first 5 x 8″, is pasted at its top left only, the second, 5 1/16 x 7″, is pasted on all four sides.

315. On the other hand, it is possible that Irving wrote the dash simply because he could not recall Admiral Harvey's unusual given name, Eliab.

specified with certainty, it likely formed part of a "private" letter, parts of which Irving assumed Clark would make public.[316]

However this may be, Clark carefully prepared the text for publication. Using sky-blue ink, he frequently clarified Irving's slurred handwriting by extending and crossing t's, dotting i's, re-writing words, and underlining capital letters to ensure they would be so interpreted by the printer.[317] He also made 5 substantive emendations of Irving's text and altered its accidentals in a variety of ways. In view of the brevity of the work, Clark's emendations constituted in all a significant revision.

Certain accidental readings in the printed text are without precedent in the manuscript as revised by Clark; this suggests that the work was revised once more prior to publication, probably by the printer or else by Clark himself at the proof stage. These later variants reveal an effort to make the work self-consistent, and consistent also with *Knickerbocker Magazine* styling.

The anecdote of Admiral Harvey was not reprinted during Irving's lifetime, and there is no reason to suppose he ever revised it once he had submitted it to Clark. The choice of a copy-text for this edition must thus be between the single printed version and some form of the single known manuscript. The manuscript version, as submitted by the author and without the alterations by Clark, is the necessary choice: it represents the only certain evidence of Irving's intention for the work. No doubt he assumed that the editor would revise his text somewhat, but there is no way of knowing which changes, as reflected either in the manuscript or in the printed text, would have met with his approval.

In the tables which follow a full accounting is given of variants within the copy-text and between it and the manuscript as revised by Clark, and also between it and the *Knickerbocker Magazine* text. Variants not included in the list of Emendations are set forth in a separate table of Rejected Variants. In both tables, unless specifically cited the reading of the manuscript as revised by Clark is identical with the original manuscript.

In the preparation of this edition the following collations have been made:

1. A typed transcription of the manuscript, prepared from a photostat annotated on comparison with the original, collated twice and independently with a xerox copy of the *Knickerbocker Magazine* text owned by York University (AP 2/ K 64);

316. Clark did not hesitate to draw upon Irving's "private" correspondence for use as *Knickerbocker Magazine* copy; see the Introduction, I, lxix–lxx.

317. The manuscript includes no direct evidence that it was used as printer's copy, but Clark's efforts to clarify Irving's scrawled text strongly suggest it, as do three guidelines he drew to indicate the sequence of the text at points where deletions had been made or possible ambiguities existed.

2. The xerox copy of the *Knickerbocker Magazine* text sight collated with the following additional copies: New-York Historical Society (PS 1/ K 7); University of Delaware (AP 2/ .F 64); Yale University (A 89/ 72).

See Discussions and Lists pp. 563, 660.

THE "EMPIRE OF THE WEST"

This review of an anonymous article in the *North American Review* for January 1840 was itself published anonymously in the "Editor's Table" section of the *Knickerbocker Magazine* for March of that year, pp. 260–61.[318] A fragment of the holograph manuscript of the article is extant at the University of Virginia. It consists of two sheets of cheap unlaid paper 5x8" in size and now torn at the edges, on which text is written in a hasty hand in dark ink, with few corrections. The first sheet, unnumbered but torn at the top right-hand corner where Irving usually numbered his pages, includes text corresponding to 260.1–10 in the *Knickerbocker Magazine* (T 135.25–136.3 The . . . traders.); the text on the second sheet, numbered 5, corresponds to 260.56–261.9 in the magazine (T 137.17–32 the rarity . . . purse.). On the reverse side of page 5 are six lines of cancelled text; see Discussions of Adopted Readings 136.6–7. Manuscript evidence of Irving's own intentions is thus available for about one-third of the published review.

The manuscript fragment includes several marks not made by Irving, most of them in dark ink by Lewis Gaylord Clark, the editor of the *Knickerbocker Magazine*. Several of these are clarifications of Irving's slurred handwriting, but the majority are emendations. Clark altered the accidentals of the text at many points and the substantives at 3, the chief of which is that he supplied a title.[319] This corrected manuscript was used as printer's copy,[320] but the corresponding passages in the published

318. The essay under review was entitled "Discovery Beyond the Rocky Mountains," *North American Review*, 50 (January 1840), 75–144. It purported to be a notice of the Rev. Samuel Parker's *Journal of an Exploring Tour beyond the Rocky Mountains, under the Direction of the American Board of Commissioners for Foreign Missions, Performed in the Years 1835, 1836, and 1837* . . . (Ithaca, 1838), and of John K. Townsend's *Narrative of a Journey Across the Rocky Mountains to the Columbia River* . . . (Philadelphia and Boston, 1839), but its range of subject-matter extended far beyond those two works. See Wayne R. Kime, "Washington Irving and *The Empire of the West*," *Western American Literature*, V, no. 4 (Winter 1971), 277–85.

319. Irving left a one-inch blank space at the top of page 1 of the manuscript, as if to make it convenient for Clark to insert whatever title he saw fit. For Clark's other substantive changes see Emendations 137.30; Rejected Variants 137.21.

320. Its use for this purpose is revealed by a notation in dark ink at the upper right-hand corner of page 1—"1st art[*torn*]/Eds Tab/————"—and by compositor's marks on page 5.

version include several variants from the text as revised by Clark. Some
of these, such as 3 substitutions of pairs of single for double quotation
marks, reflect the arbitrary imposition of *Knickerbocker Magazine*
styling; others are corrections of Irving's errors or else revisions of accidentals apparently made on the basis of editorial taste alone; and there
are 3 substantive variations from the revised manuscript text.[321] In view of
the casual haste with which he seems to have prepared this brief note,
it is virtually certain that Irving was responsible for none of the emendations to the manuscript reflected in the published version.

Because so small a proportion of the manuscript text is known to
survive, the extant manuscript clearly cannot serve as copy-text in
this edition. On the other hand, the version published in the *Knickerbocker Magazine*—the sole printing of the work during the author's lifetime—incorporates revisions by Clark and perhaps another person which
were almost certainly not authorized in an explicit manner by Irving.
While the *Knickerbocker Magazine* text is the only choice of copy-text
possible, for those passages which correspond to the manuscript fragment the authority of the printed version must be considered limited;
for as submitted by Irving, the manuscript provides firm evidence of his
intentions at the latest stage of the preparation of copy in which he
probably had a hand.

In accordance with the procedure followed throughout this edition,
pairs of double quotation marks are substituted for single quotation marks
enclosing quotations in the copy-text (Emendations 135.27–28). In the
tables which follow a full accounting is given of variants between the
copy-text and the extant portions of the printer's copy manuscript, both
as submitted by Irving and as revised by Clark. A full accounting of
variants within the manuscript fragment is also provided. Substantive
and accidental variants between the copy-text and the passages quoted
in it from the *North American Review* article—135.34–136.1, 136.18–
137.5, 137.8–11, 137.25–27—are also given. Variants not recorded in the
list of Emendations are given in a separate table of Rejected Variants.
In both tables, unless specifically cited the reading in the manuscript as
revised by Clark is identical with that in the manuscript as submitted
by Irving.

In the preparation of this edition the following collations have been
made:
1. A typed transcription of the manuscript, prepared using a xerox copy
annotated during a comparison with the original, collated twice and
independently with a xerox copy of the *Knickerbocker Magazine* text
owned by the University of Delaware (AP 2/ .F 64);
2. The above xerox copy of the *Knickerbocker Magazine* text sight col-

321. See Emendations 135.35–136.1, 137.23; Rejected Variants 137.19.

lated with the following additional copies: Legislative Library of Ontario (Periodicals/ first floor); Yale University (A 89/ 72); York University (AP 2/ K 64);

3. The above xerox copy collated twice and independently against the pertinent passages in the *North American Review* article, using a copy owned by the University of Toronto (AP 2/ N 7).

See Discussions and Lists pp. 528, 564, 661.

[ANECDOTE OF THE FRENCH REVOLUTION]

This brief narrative was published anonymously in the "Editor's Table" section of the *Knickerbocker Magazine* for April 1840, p. 351. It formed part of a commentary, written probably by Lewis Gaylord Clark, the editor of the magazine, on Irving's "A Time of Unexampled Prosperity," which sketch appeared in the same issue.[322] A two-page holograph manuscript of the anecdote is extant in the Beinecke Library, Yale University. Written with few authorial corrections in dark brown ink on unlaid paper, the unnumbered first page measures 4 15/16" x 6 13/16" and the numbered page 2, 4 15/16" x 10 13/16".[323] Apparently used as printer's copy,[324] the manuscript shows signs of careful editorial preparation by Clark. His revisions, made in sky-blue ink, include no substantive emendations, but they cover a wide range of changes to the accidentals in the text. Clark altered Irving's spelling at 2 points, added 24 commas, deleted 6 dashes—usually to substitute other punctuation, and made 18 other changes. Many of his revisions, especially the commas, appear to have been made on the basis of editorial taste alone, but others were corrections of Irving's oversights and odd usages. A few other emendations of Irving's text were made in pencil by an unknown person, possibly Clark.[325]

322. "A Time of Unexampled Prosperity," *Knickerbocker Magazine*, 15, no. 4 (April 1840), 303–24. This work was reprinted in *Wolfert's Roost* (New York, 1855), pp. 151–91.

323. Page 2 is made up of two sheets pasted together: one 4 15/16 x 7⅝" is pasted, with a ⅝" overlap, over a slip 4 15/16 x 2 15/16".

324. On the reverse side of the first page of the manuscript is the notation, written in pencil by an unknown person: "Printer's copy in the hand-/writing of Washington Irving,/originally printed in the Knicker/bocker Magazine./R.S.C" However, the manuscript includes no printer's marks or ink smudges. It is described by Barbara Damon Simison in "A Footnote to Washington Irving," *Yale University Library Gazette*, 40, no. 4 (April 1966), 194–96.

325. Pairs of double quotation marks were altered to single quotation marks at points corresponding to T 138.4–5, 138.15–17; a substantive change in pencil occurs at a point corresponding to T 138.22. In the tables which follow these emendations are treated as by Clark.

In the published version of the anecdote several readings occur which have no precedent in the revised manuscript. These include 10 changes of "Abbé" or "Abbe" to "abbé," and other minor emendations reflecting the imposition of *Knickerbocker Magazine* styling. There is no reason to suppose that Irving played any part in the preparation of his anecdote for publication beyond submitting the manuscript to Clark.

Because the work was not reprinted during the author's lifetime, the choice of copy-text for this edition must be between the published text and the manuscript, either as written by the author or as revised by Clark. The manuscript Irving sent to the editor almost certainly represents his final attention to the piece. In preparing it for publication, Clark made some refinements of which Irving may well have approved, but in doing so he imposed on it a dense style of punctuation consistent with the practices of the *Knickerbocker Magazine*. Which of Clark's revisions would have met with the author's approval? It is impossible to say. Accordingly, the manuscript in the form Irving submitted it to Clark is adopted as copy-text, affording as it does the soundest available basis for a text in line with his wishes.

In the tables which follow a full accounting is given of variants within the copy-text and between it and the *Knickerbocker Magazine* text. A full accounting of substantive and accidental variants between the copy-text and the same manuscript as revised by Clark is also given. Variants not reported in the list of Emendations are given in a separate table of Rejected Variants. In both tables, if the revised manuscript is not cited it is identical at that point with Irving's own version.

In the preparation of this edition the following collations have been made:

1. A typed transcription of a xerox copy of the manuscript, annotated on the basis of two comparisons with the original, collated twice and independently with a xerox copy of the *Knickerbocker Magazine* text owned by York University (AP 2/ K 64);

2. The above xerox copy of the *Knickerbocker Magazine* text sight collated with the following additional copies: Legislative Library of Ontario (Periodicals/ first floor); University of Delaware (AP 2/ .F 64); Yale University (A 89/ 72).

See Discussions and Lists pp. 565, 662.

[THE TAKING OF THE VEIL, AND THE CHARMING LETORIÉRES]

This work was first published in the *Knickerbocker Magazine* for June 1840, pp. 513–21, where it was untitled except for the running title

assigned by Lewis Gaylord Clark to each of "Geoffrey Crayon's" contributions, "The Crayon Papers." A fragment of the printer's copy manuscript is owned by the University of Virginia.[326] Written in dark brown
ink on one side of ten sheets of cheap, unlaid paper 5x8" in size, the
extant text corresponds to 519.5–521.32 in the magazine (T 145.10–
147.42)—that is, from the ruled line following "The Taking of the Veil" to
the conclusion. The manuscript includes two sets of pagination: the
first, from 1 to 10, is written and deleted in ink by Irving; the second,
from 22 to 31, is written in ink by Irving from 22 to 26, and by another
hand from 27 to 31. The deleted sequence may seem to suggest that
the surviving manuscript fragment was first written independently of
the material which eventually preceded it in the *Knickerbocker Magazine*;
but that was not the case. The first words on page ⟨1⟩/22—"So MUCH for
the beautiful . . ."—are clearly transitional, referring backward to "The
Taking of the Veil" just completed, and forward to its companion-piece
to come. Manuscript evidence reveals, therefore, that Irving never did
intend to publish the extant fragment as an autonomous work. No doubt
the series of pagination from 22 to 31 pertains to the completed manuscript he sent to Clark.

The manuscript is not a fair copy, but such authorial revisions as it
does include are minor. Because it is written in a clearer and less hasty
hand than some of Irving's manuscripts submitted for publication in the
Knickerbocker Magazine, the text shows few clarifying marks by Lewis
Gaylord Clark. Nevertheless, in preparing the fragment for publication
Clark did subject it to his usual close scrutiny. He made 2 substantive
changes (see Rejected Variants 146.22; Emendations 147.38), revised
Irving's spelling at 9 points, and made a variety of other alterations to
the accidentals. In short, Clark rendered the manuscript self-consistent
and approximately consistent with *Knickerbocker Magazine* styling; but
in doing so he emended a text which the author had not prepared with
careless inattention to detail.

Before the revised manuscript text was published it underwent further
revision, probably at the proof stage, which produced a pattern of
emendations similar to the one resulting from Clark's attentions to the
original text. These changes included only 2 substantive alterations (see
Emendations 147.22, 147.22) and 8 alterations of spelling, but it covered
a wide range of emendations to the accidentals in the revised text.
Certain of the emendations, such as wholesale substitution of single
for double quotation marks, simply reflect the imposition of the *Knickerbocker Magazine* styling, but others are more problematical. For ex-

---

326. The manuscript fragment includes no ink smudges or printer's marks, but on
pages 22, 23, 24, and 29 it does include notations and editorial marks by Lewis
Gaylord Clark which reveal that he intended it to serve as printer's copy.

ample, Clark already having added 16 commas to Irving's text, it does not seem reasonable for him at a later stage to add 6 more and delete 10 from the revised fragment. On the other hand, there is no evidence and very little likelihood that Irving revised his manuscript once he had submitted it to Clark. The pattern of re-revising the work specifically for publication in the *Knickerbocker Magazine,* yet of altering it according to principles somewhat different from Clark's, suggests that this final attention to the work was given it by a person in a position of some authority—either an especially trusted printer or else Clark's twin brother, Willis Gaylord Clark, who until his death in 1841 served from time to time as co-editor.

After its publication in the *Knickerbocker Magazine,* the double sketch was not reprinted during Irving's lifetime; nor, for some reason, was it included by Pierre M. Irving in *Spanish Papers.* It formed part of the contents of *The Crayon Papers* when that collection of reprinted miscellaneous writings appeared in 1883; but in none of the editions of *The Crayon Papers* does the text of this piece show any sign of authorial revision. Not a single substantive variant from the *Knickerbocker Magazine* text is present, and the several editions of *The Crayon Papers* carry no textual authority.

One is thus presented with an inevitable choice of copy-text: the *Knickerbocker Magazine* version. That text, the only one published during the author's lifetime, is the surest available indicator of his intentions for the entire work. While the extant manuscript corresponding to "The Charming Letoriéres" must exert considerable authority for that portion of the text, its authority for the greater portion of the work is almost nil, being limited to the force of the precedents it embodies for the treatment of accidentals.

In the tables which follow a full accounting is given of variants between the copy-text and the University of Virginia manuscript, both as submitted by Irving and as revised by Clark. Variants within the manuscript are recorded in full; false starts immediately re-written are listed in a single entry (Rejected Variants 145.15). Unless the revised manuscript reading is specifically cited in the tables it is to be presumed identical with the original. Certain regularizations of the copy-text have been undertaken. Chief among these are that pairs of double quotation marks are substituted throughout for pairs of single quotation marks in the copy-text (Emendations 139.37, 145.31 *et passim*), "Madamoiselle" is emended to "Mademoiselle" (Emendations 143.41), "De" within French proper names is emended to "de" (Emendations 138.36–37), and "tailor" is emended to Irving's "taylor" (Emendations 146.14).

In the preparation of this edition the following collations have been made:

1. A typed transcription of the University of Virginia manuscript, pre-

pared from a xerox copy annotated on the basis of a comparison with the
original, collated twice and independently with a xerox copy of the
Knickerbocker Magazine text owned by York University (AP 2/ K 64);
2. The xerox copy of the above *Knickerbocker Magazine* text sight collated with the following additional copies: University of Delaware (AP
2/ .F 64); Legislative Library of Ontario (Periodicals/ first floor); New-
York Historical Society (PS 1/ .K7); Yale University (A 89/ 72);
3. The above xerox copy of the *Knickerbocker Magazine* text sight
collated with the text in copies from four editions of *The Crayon Papers*
(see the Introduction to the Textual Notes, I, 260).

See Discussions and Lists pp. 566, 662.

LETTER FROM GRANADA

This article was first published in the *Knickerbocker Magazine* for July
1840, pp. 57–61.[327] Although there is no reason to doubt Irving's introductory explanation that in its original form the work was a letter
"scribbled to a friend" (T 148.4), no manuscript of such a letter is
known to survive, and its recipient is unknown.[328]

In a revised form, "Letter from Granada" was once reprinted during
Irving's lifetime. In preparing his Author's Revised Edition of *The
Alhambra* (1850), he drew upon the *Knickerbocker Magazine* text to
fashion an additional chapter in that work, entitled "Public Fêtes of
Granada," pp. 154–62. Whereas in the earlier text Irving had presented
his account of Spanish religious festivals as part of a letter to a friend,

327. The article appeared under the title "The Crayon Papers," which Lewis
Gaylord Clark used preceding Irving's acknowledged contributions as "Geoffrey
Crayon." This general title was followed by a rule, and then Irving's introductory
letter (T 148.4–10); the letter was followed by a rule and then a title to the body
of the work, "Letter from Granada." Because there is no evidence that Irving
ever intended "The Crayon Papers" to be the title of any of his contributions to
the *Knickerbocker Magazine*, "Letter from Granada" would seem to be the title
he intended to serve for this work as a whole.

328. In a letter to Peter Irving dated from the Alhambra on June 13, 1829,
published in part in PMI, II, 390–92, Irving does describe "the Marquis of Salar
(Hernando del Pulgar)," who is portrayed in "Letter from Granada" (see T
152.22–40). However, in the portion of the letter quoted in the biography there is
no indication that it had served Irving as a basis for his entire article. Stanley T.
Williams has suggested that he owed his account of *"el día de la toma"* in the
article (T 150.13–152.10) to a description of it he had heard from the Duke of
Gor, a cultivated young Spaniard whom he had met during his residence in the
Alhambra; see STW, I, 367, 498 note 52, Irving summarized his conversation with
Gor in his notebook for 1829, pp. [78–80, 85–86]; see *Journals*, IV, in the present
edition.

in *The Alhambra* he dispensed with that format. Instead, in a narrative essay he portrayed himself as an onlooker at the festival under the guidance of Mateo Ximenes, a figure who frequently appears in the revised edition of *The Alhambra* as a self-important cicerone. This change of format entailed in itself but little necessity for revision. For example, in the *Knickerbocker Magazine* Irving had introduced a paragraph as follows: "The next morning I revisited the square at sun-rise" (58.13; T 149.18). In *The Alhambra*, he wrote: "The next morning, accompanied by Mateo, I revisited the square at sunrise" (pp. 156–57). In fact, almost one-half of "Public Fêtes of Granada" is adopted nearly *verbatim* from passages in the magazine article (58.3–52 The...mind; 59.16–60.8 In ...Virgin–T 149.9–150.12, 150.27–151.24). However, besides supplying new first and final paragraphs in which the character of Mateo Ximenes is given prominence, Irving made several other changes to the earlier text. Two paragraphs (pp. 155–56) include material virtually identical to that in the magazine version (57.24–58.2 As...repose; 60.13–39 On ...extravagance–T 148.25–149.8, 151.29–152.10), but are thoroughly re-written; a paragraph describing "the actual lineal descendant of Hernando del Pulgar" (pp. 160–61) is shifted from the conclusion of the *Knickerbocker Magazine* text, where it comprises two paragraphs (60.40–61.13 To...glory!–T 152.11–34), to a point earlier in the work (corresponding to *Knickerbocker Magazine* 60.8; T 151.24); and no use is made of the note appended to the magazine text recounting briefly the marriage of the Marquis de Salar (61.15–19 Within . . . festivity–T 152.36–40). As it appears in *The Alhambra* of 1850, "Public Fêtes of Granada" fits neatly into a series of sketches portraying the development of Irving's familiarity with the Alhambra and its inhabitants, both past and present.[329]

The *Knickerbocker Magazine* text was reprinted by Pierre M. Irving in *Spanish Papers*, II, [471]–79. Except for a change of title and a single misprint (Rejected Variants 151.39),[330] the *Spanish Papers* text includes no substantive variants from the earlier one. It does reveal alterations of accidentals which reflect the imposition of the Putnam house style,[331] but it shows no signs of authorial revision. "Letter from Granada" also formed part of the contents of *The Crayon Papers*, a collection of Irving's fugitive writings which appeared in various editions beginning in 1883. Reprinted from the *Knickerbocker Magazine* or from the pre-

329. "Public Fêtes of Granada" forms a part of the contents of *The Alhambra* in the present edition.

330. Pierre M. Irving deleted "The Crayon Papers" from the title—as he did for all articles which had been preceded in the *Knickerbocker Magazine* by that designation—and moved "Letter from Granada" from its original position following Irving's introductory letter to the editor to a new position preceding it.

331. See the Textual Commentary, I, 273–76.

ceding editions of *The Crayon Papers*, these texts include no substantive variants from the original work except obvious typographical errors,[332] and they carry no textual authority.

"Letter from Granada" was thus published only once during Irving's lifetime, and there is no evidence that he ever revised the *Knickerbocker Magazine* text except to adapt it to be included in the Author's Revised Edition of *The Alhambra*. Since no manuscript is known to survive, the first printing of the work in its original, autonomous form, that in the *Knickerbocker Magazine*, is adopted as copy-text.

In accordance with the procedure adopted throughout this edition, pairs of single quotation marks in the copy-text are emended to double quotation marks (Emendations 150.14). In the tables which follow the substantive variants and two accidental variants of possible interest between the copy-text and that in *Spanish Papers* are listed in the table of Rejected Variants.

In the preparation of this edition the following collations have been made:

1. A xerox copy of the *Knickerbocker Magazine* text owned by York University (AP 2/ K 64) sight collated with the following additional copies: University of Delaware (AP 2/ .F 64); Legislative Library of Ontario (Periodicals/ first floor); Yale University (A 89/ 72);

2. The above xerox copy sight collated twice and independently with "Public Fêtes of Granada" in a copy of the Author's Revised Edition of *The Alhambra* owned by the New York Public Library (BXVN);

3. The xerox copy collated twice and independently with the *Spanish Papers* text in a copy owned by the National Library of Canada;

4. A xerox copy of the above *Spanish Papers* text sight collated with the following additional copies: New York Public Library; Yale University (Iw/ Ir8/ 866);

5. The xerox copy of the *Knickerbocker Magazine* text sight collated with the texts in copies from four editions of *The Crayon Papers* (see the Introduction to the Textual Notes, I, 260).

See Discussions and Lists pp. 568, 664.

---

332. The edition of *The Crayon Papers* published by J. H. Alden included a typographical error at a point corresponding to T 148.18: "every" for *Knickerbocker Magazine* "ever." The error is corrected in the other edition of *The Crayon Papers* published in 1883, that by J. B. Lovell. Since the pagination of the Lovell edition is identical with that in the two subsequent editions consulted in the preparation of this edition—New York: J. Millar, 1884, and New York: William L. Allison, n.d.— and the error is reproduced in neither of these, it appears likely that the first edition of *The Crayon Papers* was published by Alden, the second by Lovell. At any rate, the two subsequent editions appear to derive from Lovell.

AMERICAN RESEARCHES IN ITALY

This article first appeared in the *Knickerbocker Magazine for* October 1841, pp. 319–22. No manuscript version is known to survive, and the reason why the work should have been published seven months after the date when, according to Pierre M. Irving, Irving "brought . . . to an end"[333] his association with the *Knickerbocker Magazine* is unknown. Possibly he felt that in fairness he ought to submit to Lewis Gaylord Clark a further contribution in recompense for the generous payments he had received; or perhaps, actuated by other motives, he sent the work to Clark simply because he was sure the editor would print virtually any communication from him. At any rate, it does not seem likely that he offered the work to Clark prior to March 1841; more probably it appeared in the magazine soon after the editor had received it.

"American Researches in Italy" was not reprinted during Irving's lifetime, nor for some reason was it included by Pierre M. Irving in *Spanish Papers*.[334] However, it did form part of the contents of *The Crayon Papers*, a gathering of Irving's contributions to the *Knickerbocker Magazine* which appeared in various editions in 1883 and afterward. In this collection the text of the article was derived from the original printed version. None of the four editions of *The Crayon Papers* consulted in the preparation of this edition includes a single substantive variant from the *Knickerbocker Magazine* text. *The Crayon Papers* texts carry no textual authority.

Because "American Researches in Italy" was printed only once during Irving's lifetime, and there is no evidence that he revised the original version once it had appeared in the *Knickerbocker Magazine*, that text is adopted here as copy-text.

In accordance with the procedure adopted throughout this edition, pairs of single quotation marks in the copy-text are emended to double quotation marks (Emendations 153.20–21). Since only the copy-text carries textual authority, no variant readings are listed in the tables which follow.

In the preparation of this edition the following collations have been made:

1. A xerox copy of the *Knickerbocker Magazine* text owned by York University (AP 2/ K 64) sight collated with the following additional

---

333. PMI, III, 148.

334. Pierre M. Irving's statement of the date on which Irving gave up his role as a paid contributor to the *Knickerbocker Magazine* suggests that in gathering his uncle's uncollected writings for publication in *Spanish Papers* he may have overlooked this article. On the other hand, he omitted from *Spanish Papers* items, such as the review of Slidell's *A Year in Spain* (pp. 30–57), which he knew to be of Irving's authorship.

copies: University of Delaware (AP 2/ .F 64); Legislative Library of Ontario (Periodicals/ first floor); Yale University (A 89/ 72);

2. The above xerox copy collated with the texts in copies from four editions of *The Crayon Papers* (see the Introduction to the Textual Notes, I, 260).

See Discussions and Lists pp. 529, 569.

[MEMOIR OF THOMAS CAMPBELL]

The memoir of Thomas Campbell was published as an untitled portion of the introductory material in the first American edition of William Beattie's *Life and Letters of Thomas Campbell* (1850), I, xi–xvi. It was preceded by an undated letter to Irving from the publishers, Harper and Brothers (I, xi):

Dear Sir:—Thinking, from your early association with the reputation of Thomas Campbell in this country, that you may be gratified at this day in assisting in the amiable work of his recent biographer, Dr. Beattie, of presenting his memory in its better aspects to the world, we take the liberty of submitting the London proof-sheets to your inspection; and it would give us pleasure to publish any letter bearing on the subject, as an introduction of the work to the American people, you may find the leisure and inclination to write.

Yours very respectfully,

HARPER AND BROTHERS.

No manuscript version of Irving's generous response to this request is known to survive. In a second printing of the *Life and Letters of Thomas Campbell* by the Harpers in 1855, the text of the memoir was unchanged. The work was not reprinted elsewhere during Irving's lifetime.[335]

Pierre M. Irving included it in *Spanish Papers* as an addendum to Irving's biographical sketch of Campbell which had first appeared in an American edition of the poet's works he had edited in 1810 (see T I, 133–46).[336] As it appears in *Spanish Papers*, the later sketch shows no evidence of authorial revision. No substantive variants occur between it and the *Life and Letters* text; and while a few accidental variants are present, they are consistent with the imposition of the Putnam house style.[337]

---

335. Evert A. Duyckinck quoted one sentence from the memoir in his "Memoranda of the Literary Career of Washington Irving," *Irvingiana*, p. viii.

336. The *Spanish Papers* text is joined to Irving's earlier sketch by a brief commentary (II, 135) in which Pierre M. Irving summarizes the circumstances surrounding the preparation of the memoir in 1850.

337. See the Textual Commentary, I, 273–76.

Because no manuscript text of the work is known to exist, and Irving appears not to have revised the work after it had appeared as part of the first American edition of Beattie's *Life and Letters* of Campbell, the memoir in that work is adopted as copy-text.

In the preparation of this edition the following collations have been made:

1. A xerox copy of the text in Beattie's *Life and Letters* (New York, 1850) owned by Columbia University (Sp Coll/ Park Benjamin Collection) sight collated with the following additional copies: New York Public Library (Duyckinck/ AN/ (Campbell, T.)); Yale University (In/ C 154/ 848c);

2. The above xerox copy sight collated with the text in the 1855 printing of the *Life and Letters* owned by the University of Michigan (828/ C 1920/ B 37/ 1855);

3. The xerox copy collated twice and independently with the *Spanish Papers* text in a copy owned by the National Library of Canada and once with a copy owned by the New York Public Library.

See Discussions and Lists p. 569.

CORRECTION OF A MISSTATEMENT RESPECTING *ASTORIA*

Irving's response to a rumor made public by Henry Rowe Schoolcraft that he had received payment from John Jacob Astor for writing *Astoria* was first published in the *Literary World* for November 22, 1851, p. 408. No manuscript version is known to survive, but corrected galley proof of the work, owned by Sleepy Hollow Restorations, Inc., reveals that the author subjected his statement to careful revision and elaboration, even after he had sent a manuscript to his friend Evert A. Duyckinck, the editor of the *Literary World*.

The corrected galley, which is pasted full length on a single sheet of light cardboard or foolscap, indicates that the proofs underwent three stages of revision by the author. The first took the form of deletions at 7 points in the printed text, with substitutions or additions either indicated by editorial abbreviations or written in full in the right margin. Five of the marginal alterations were limited to single words, but 2 were lengthier. In the second stage of revision, using the same brown ink he had in the first, Irving wrote out revised or additional text on four tabs of paper which he then pasted at appropriate points beside the galley proof, two in the right margin and two in the left. The former tabs are pasted directly over the two extended passages he had written during the first stage of revision, but they are loosely hinged so that almost all the earlier text remains visible (see Pre-Copy-Text Variants 162.2–3, 162.13–14). The two tabs in the left margin are pasted down completely, and no text is visible beneath them (see Pre-Copy-Text Variants 161.25–32, 162.19–26). The evidence of the third and final stage of Irving's attention to the *Literary World* galley is a group of notations in pencil, obviously intended as reference marks either to indicate the points at which the four tabs were to be pasted,[338] or else to clarify the revisions already made in ink. Irving's meticulous revision of the letter bespeaks his determination that it should serve as a definitive rebuttal of the degrading rumor about himself that Schoolcraft had aired. However, there is no evidence that his attention to the work extended beyond his revision of the galley.

As published in the *Literary World* the text did incorporate the author's corrections to the galley proof, though not without introducing 3 substantive variants, 5 alterations of the spelling and 6 of the punctuation he had provided.[339] The text was not reprinted during Irving's lifetime, but Duyckinck included it in his "Memoranda of the Literary Career of Washington Irving," *Irvingiana*, pp. xvi–xvii. The *Irvingiana* text, which is presented "as it appeared in the *Literary World*," includes no substantive variants from the first printed version. A few accidental variants are present—6 spelling changes, and alterations owing to changes in styling such as the printing of book-titles in italic rather than roman type—but none of these suggests authorial revision.

Since Irving's latest known wishes for his letter to Schoolcraft are embodied in his corrections to the galley proof for the *Literary World*, the corrected galley is adopted here as copy-text. At points where he wrote more than a single revised text for a cancelled passage (*i.e.*, 162.2–3, 162.13–14), what appear to be the latest revised texts are considered to form parts of the copy-text.

In the tables which follow a full accounting is given of substantive and accidental variants between the copy-text and that published in the *Literary World*, and also between it and the galley proof in its uncorrected state. In the list of Emendations only, when the uncorrected galley is not specifically cited it is to be presumed identical with the corrected galley. Variants between the copy-text and the *Literary World* text not listed in Emendations are given in a separate table of Rejected Variants. Variants between the two forms of the galley not listed in Emendations are given in a separate table of Rejected Pre-Copy-Text Variants. In that

338. Above and to the left of the two tabs in the right margin the letters "A" and "B" are written in the right margin. Directly above the first tab in the left margin the letter "C" is written in pencil; above and to the right of the fourth tab, "D" is written in pencil.

339. For the substantive variants see Emendations 161.27; Rejected Variants 162.12–13, 162.20.

table the symbols "MStc, 1A" cited as the source of an accepted reading denote that the present text is derived from the copy-text as emended from the *Literary World* version in the manner described in the list of Emendations.

In the preparation of this edition the following collations have been made:

1. A xerox copy of the corrected galley compared with the original, and its doubtful holograph passages transcribed, by Professor Andrew B. Myers;

2. A typed transcription of the xerox copy collated twice and independently with a xerox copy of the *Literary World* text owned by the New-York Historical Society (PS 1/ .L 6) and once with a copy owned by Yale University (A 89/ +L71285);

3. The above xerox copy of the *Literary World* text collated with the text in two copies of *Irvingiana* (see the Introduction to the Textual Notes, I, 259).

See Discussions and Lists pp. 529, 569, 664, 684.

THE CATSKILL MOUNTAINS

This article was first published in 1851 as a contribution to *The Home Book of the Picturesque*, a collection of essays on American scenery, pp. [71]–78. According to Pierre M. Irving, his uncle was at work on the essay as early as July 1851, and at that time he intended to include in it an account of his first voyage up the Hudson River to Albany, in 1800. This extended passage he subsequently discarded; but the transcription of it which Pierre provided in PMI—see below, pp. 344–45— reveals that a few sentences from the earlier account did survive, slightly revised, in the final draft.[340] The completed manuscript draft of the essay, which served as printer's copy for the *Home Book* text, is owned by Sleepy Hollow Restorations, Inc.[341] Written in brown ink on sixteen

340. Compare Home Book 72.27–73.6 I . . . . it. (T 164.3–11), 74.2–13 All . . . . since. (T 164.37–165.7) to PMI, I, 40.16–24 (T 344.3–10), 42.20–43.2 (T 345.16–26). What appears to be a preliminary sketch for "The Catskill Mountains" is included in *Journals*, III, under "Notes, 1825," pp. 660–61.

341. The pages of the manuscript, some pasted onto sturdier sheets of paper and some not, are laid loose in an unidentified book cover with a brown leather spine and marbled covers. The manuscript is accompanied by a pencilled note dated "Brooklyn April 2. 1859" and signed "F. Saunders." In this note Frederick Saunders (1807–1902) certified that the manuscript was the one Irving had written for the *Home Book;* he added, "I received it from the Printer after it had been printed." Two reference marks within the manuscript, apparently indicating printers' stints, strengthen the identification of it as printer's copy. The description of the manu-

sheets of white laid paper which have been cropped to measure a uniform 7¾″ x 4¾″, the manuscript pages are numbered in ink by Irving except for pages 2, 3, 4, 6, 15, and 16, where the original pagination has apparently been cropped away and new page-numbers are supplied in pencil by another hand. The text includes numerous cancellations and substitutions in brown ink by Irving, but no revisions by any hand other than his.[342] While by no means a fair copy, the manuscript does appear to be the author's final copy.

Irving's attentions to the manuscript did not include a careful attempt to correct lapses or errors in punctuation, to regularize inconsistent spellings, or in general to prepare it for printing without further editorial attention. Omissions and other errors through oversight occur at several points—see, for example, Emendations 72.25, 75.4, 75.6, 75.10, 75.19, 75.29, 76.28–29, 77.10—but easily the most notable instance of the loose ends in the manuscript is the inconsistent spelling of the name "Catskill." The manuscript text is entitled "The Katskill Mountains," but its first sentence begins as follows, as if to indicate that "Catskill' is the preferred spelling: "The Catskill, Katskill, or Cat River Mountains . . . ." Of the 11 other occasions on which Irving uses the name, he adopts the spelling "Catskill" on 6 and "Katskill" on 5, alternating between the two apparently at random.[343] In view of eccentricities such as this, one is inclined to wonder whether, having written out the manuscript text, he proofread it at all. The publisher of the *Home Book* was George P. Putnam, who had prepared the Author's Revised Edition of his works, and in the practices of whose firm he had come to place faith. Perhaps, as he had when a contributor to the *Knickerbocker Magazine*, Irving left the final determination of accidentals to the editor or the printer. In any case, there is no evidence to suggest that Irving paid any further attention to the text of his article once he had sent it along to Putnam.

Prior to its publication, however, the work underwent careful revision by an unknown person. In addition to a supplied subtitle, "By Washington Irving," as it appeared in the *Home Book* the essay included 42 substantive variants from the manuscript—31 limited to substitutions of single words, but 4 pertaining to passages more than five words in length. Clearly more than a touching up of blemishes in the manuscript was involved in this revision. For example, the substitutions of "chains" for

---

script in this Textual Commentary is based upon an examination of it by Professor Andrew B. Myers.

342. However, beneath the title on page [1], "By Washington Irving" is written in pencil and then erased; see also Discussions of Adopted Readings 164.4–5.

343. "Catskill" occurs in the manuscript at points corresponding to T 163.15, 163.37, 164.41, 166.20, 166.33, 167.13; "Katskill" occurs at points corresponding to 164.19, 165.41, 166.38, 166.43, 167.17.

"sierras" (T 163.21) or "Rotterdam" for "Holland" (166.29) were made from considerations of lexical taste rather than in order to impose appropriate editorial styling. Besides the revised substantives the printed text includes a variety of deviations from the accidentals in the manuscript, including 65 added commas, 40 spelling changes, and 30 changes of initial lower-case letters to capitals.[344]

The Home Book of the Picturesque was advertised for sale in the weekly *Literary World* for November 8, 1851. However, obviously as a part of his pre-publication advertising campaign, the enterprising George Putnam had authorized the editor of the *Literary World*, Evert Duyckinck, to print "The Catskill Mountains" in the issue of the magazine for November 1, vol. 9, no. 248, pp. 350–51.[345] The *Literary World* text of the article differs in substantives from that in the *Home Book* at only two points—one an obvious misprint, the other an omitted footnote;[346] and the close correspondence between the accidentals of the two texts confirms than an advance copy of the *Home Book* formed the basis of the magazine version. The *Literary World* text was itself reprinted in *Littell's Living Age* for November 29, 1851, vol. 31, no. 393, pp. 408–10, where the same substantive variants from the *Home Book* text are reproduced; the *Literary World* is acknowledged in *Littell's Living Age* as the source of the reprinted text.

A portion of a single paragraph in the *Home Book* version, or possibly in one of the two magazines, was reprinted once more during Irving's lifetime. The passage, which corresponds to 74.20–75.19 in the *Home Book* (And here . . . . knowledge."–T 165.14–40), appeared under the title "Our Changing Sky and Climate./ By Washington Irving," in *The Ladies' Repository*, 12, no. 2 (February 1852), 75. The text in this magazine is an obvious, though unacknowledged, piracy;[347] it carries no textual authority.

344. The extent of the divergence between the manuscript and the *Home Book* text renders desirable some further inquiry into the possibility that Irving was responsible for the alterations to the manuscript. However, in the absence of further information we can only speculate as to the manner in which the work was revised prior to publication. Possibly the *Home Book* text incorporates two distinct revisions of the author's manuscript: one, by the printer, limited to the correction of errors, the regularization of accidentals, and the imposition of a house style; the other, by an unknown hand, resulting in most of the substantive changes.

345. Accordingly, the article was preceded in the *Literary World* by a bit of puffery, wherein "Mr. Putnam's Holiday Season publication" was praised as a "well conceived and liberal enterprise."

346. The substantive variants between the *Home Book* and *Literary World* texts occur at points corresponding to T 167.17 (Catskill) and 164.41–43 ([*omitted*]); the parenthesized readings are those from the magazine.

347. The substantive variants between the *Home Book* and *Ladies' Repository* texts occur at points corresponding to T 165.14 (¶ Let me, reader, say), 165.18 (o the); the parenthesized readings are those from the *Ladies' Respository*. The latter

Pierre M. Irving included "The Catskill Mountains" in *Spanish Papers*, II, [480]–87. The *Spanish Papers* text includes 4 substantive variants from that in the *Home Book*—a deletion of the subtitle and of a footnote and footnote reference, a misprint, and a minor alteration of diction characteristic of Pierre's meticulous editorial hand (see Rejected Variants 166.40). It includes 2 instances in which single sentences in the *Home Book* have been divided into two, and numerous other alterations of accidentals reflecting imposition of the Putnam house style;[348] but there is no evidence to suggest that Irving had played a part in any of these changes to the original printed text.

The textual situation for "The Catskill Mountains" is thus that in 1851 Irving completed a manuscript which, revised by an unknown person or persons, was set in type for publication in *The Home Book of the Picturesque*. The *Literary World* text of the article antedated publication of the *Home Book* but was clearly derived from the printed *Home Book* text. There is no evidence to indicate conclusively that the author was responsible for any of the emendations to the manuscript text embodied in the *Home Book* version. His somewhat casual treatment of accidentals in the manuscript does suggest that he assumed his article would be revised during the printing process, either by an editor or by a printer familiar with the styling to be adopted for the volume. Nevertheless, the author's manuscript represents the most reliable evidence at present available as to the author's final intention for the original version of "The Catskill Mountains"; and thus it is adopted as copy-text.

Certain regularizations of the accidentals in the copy-text are necessary to correct Irving's oversights and to render the text reasonably self-consistent. Chief among these are that periods are supplied where omitted by the author at the ends of sentences (Emendations 164.5); end-of-line commas omitted from the manuscript are inserted (Emendations 163.9); "mountains" is capitalized when used as part of a proper name (Emendations 163.21–22); "Katskill" is (except when employed deliberately as a variant spelling) emended to "Catskill" (Emendations 163.2), and Irving's attempts to spell "Rensselaerswyck" are emended to that form (Emendations 166.41–42).

In the tables which follow a full accounting is given of variants within the copy-text; false starts immediately rewritten and misspellings immediately corrected are listed in a single entry (Emendations 164.23). Substantive and accidental variants between the copy-text and the

---

text has been reprinted as an autonomous work; see Daniel R. Barnes, "Washington Irving: An Unrecorded Periodical Publication," *Studies in Bibliography*, 20 (1967), 260–61.

348. See the Textual Commentary, I, 273–76.

Home Book version are recorded in full. In the list of Emendations only, the absence of a specific citation of the *Spanish Papers* text indicates that its reading is identical with that for the *Home Book*. Variants between the copy-text and the *Home Book* not recorded in the list of Emendations are set forth in a table of Rejected Variants. In the latter table are listed substantive variants and a few accidental variants of possible interest between the copy-text and the *Spanish Papers* text.

In the preparation of this edition the following collations have been made:

1. A typed transcription of the manuscript, prepared from a xerox copy, collated against the original by Professor Andrew B. Myers;

2. The typed transcription collated twice and independently with a *Home Book* text owned by the New York Public Library (NBY+ copy 1—Bryant Collection);

3. A xerox copy of the above *Home Book* text sight collated with the following additional copies: New York Public Library (NBY+ copy 2—Duyckinck Collection); Yale University (Za/ C 786/ 852);

4. The above xerox copy collated with the *Ladies' Repository* text in copies owned by the University of Virginia (*AP 2/ .L 32/ 1852) and the New-York Historical Society (PS 1/ .L35);

5. The above xerox copy collated with the *Literary World* text owned by the University of Texas (051/ L 713) and with a second copy owned by the New-York Historical Society (PS 1/ .L6);

6. The above xerox copy collated with the *Littell's Living Age* text owned by the Legislative Library of Ontario (Periodicals/ first floor);

7. The above xerox copy collated twice and independently with the *Spanish Papers* text owned by the National Library of Canada;

8. A xerox copy of the above *Spanish Papers* text sight collated with the following additional copies: New York Public Library; Yale University (Iw/ Ir8/ 866).

See Discussions and Lists pp. 529, 570, 664.

[REMARKS AT THE COOPER MEMORIAL MEETING, FEBRUARY 24, 1852]

Irving's introductory comments in his role as Chairman of the Committee on Arrangements for the meeting to honor the memory of James Fenimore Cooper was published in *Memorial of James Fenimore Cooper* (1852), p. 23. No manuscript text of the remarks is known to survive. Certainly Irving played no part in the preparations for publishing the speech in the *Memorial* beyond writing out a manuscript—if he did that much. The remarks were not reprinted during Irving's lifetime and have not been reprinted since; the *Memorial* text is hence adopted as copy-text.

In the preparation of this edition a xerox copy of the *Memorial* text owned by the New-York Historical Society (PS/ 1431/ .M4) has been sight collated with a second copy owned by the University of Toronto (PS/ 1435/ .M4).

See Discussions and Lists p. 574.

CONVERSATIONS WITH TALMA

This article was first published in *The Knickerbocker Gallery: A Tribute to the Editor of the Knickerbocker Magazine from its Contributors* (1855), pp. [15]–22. A holograph manuscript text which almost certainly served as printer's copy is extant in the Henry E. Huntington Library. Written in black ink on one side of eighteen sheets of pale blue lined paper, most 5 x 8″ in size but some of slightly varying lengths and consisting of scraps of paper pasted together,[349] the manuscript text is in a fluent hand and includes only minor authorial corrections. Insight into Irving's procedure in preparing his contribution to *The Knickerbocker Gallery* may be gained through study of two other holograph manuscripts from which he pieced together parts of the article.

The first of these manuscripts, five hurriedly written pages comprising a summary of his activities on April 25, 1821, describes a visit he paid to Talma at the French tragedian's home in Paris.[350] These notations provided a basic sequence of action and abbreviated bits of dialogue which Irving expanded into the account of his meeting with the actor (*Knickerbocker Gallery* [15].4–16.32; T 168.4–169.13). The following parallel texts typify the process of expansion from sketchy notes to the published narrative:

349. The sheets are mounted at their left edges in a volume which includes as well the text as published in the *Knickerbocker Gallery* and a holograph letter from Irving to Robert Balmanno, Sunnyside, April 15, 1850. The manuscript is paged in ink by the author 1–8, 8/2, 9–17. It includes only one mark not by Irving: a pencilled partial right bracket to the right of "has" at a point corresponding to 18.22 in the *Knickerbocker Gallery* (T 170.28). Since in that printed version "has" occurs at the end of a line, it is virtually certain that the notation is a printer's reference mark.

350. Irving's notes, owned by the Beinecke Library, Yale University, are written on two sheets of unlaid paper folded at the center to form four sides, each 4⅝ x 7⅜″ in size. The notes appear on the first, third, and fourth sides of the first sheet and on the first and second sides of the second. On the third and fourth sides of the latter sheet Irving wrote a summary of his activities on April 26, 1821, the day after he had met Talma.

Irving's Notes

Talma is about 5 feet ⟨8 Inches⟩ 7 or 7½ Inch/ English—rather inclined to fat—with large/ face & thick neck—His eyes are bluish &/ have a peculiar cast in them at times—He/ speaks English well, and is very frank,/ ⟨and⟩ animated and natural in conversa-/tion—a fine, hearty, simplicity of manners -/

Asked me if this was my first visit to Paris, told/ him that I had been here once before—about/ 14 years since—⟨but that I saw ⟨P⟩ a great/ change⟩ "Ah! that was in the time of the/ Emperor" said he— He remarked that/ Paris was very much changed—thinks the/ french character greatly changed—more/ grave—You see the young men from the/ colleges said he—How grave they are—⟨walking⟩/ They walk together—conversing incessantly/ on ⟨Subect⟩ politics—& other grave ⟨subjetis⟩ ↑subjects↓/ Says the nation has become as grave as the/ English—

Knickerbocker Gallery
[15].14–16.12

Talma is about five feet seven or eight inches, English, in height, and somewhat robust. There is no very tragic or poetic expression in his countenance; his eyes are of a bluish gray, with, at times, a peculiar cast; his face is rather fleshy, yet flexible; and he has a short thick neck. His manners are open, animated, and natural. He speaks English well, and is prompt, unreserved, and copious in conversation.

He received me in a very cordial manner, and asked if this was my first visit to Paris. I told him I had been here once before, about fourteen years since.

"Ah! that was the time of the Emperor!" cried he, with a sudden gleam of the eye.

"Yes—just after his coronation as King of Italy."

"Ah! those were the heroic days of Paris—every day some new victory! The real chivalry of France ralled round the Emperor; the youth, and talent, and bravery of the nation. Now you see the courts of the Tuileries crowded by priests, and an old, worn-out nobility brought back by foreign bayonets."

He consoled himself by observing, that the national character had improved under its reverses. Its checks and humiliations had made the nation more thoughtful. "Look at the young men from the colleges," said he, "how serious they are in their demeanor. They walk together in the public promenades, conversing always on political subjects, but discussing politics philo-

> sophically and scientifically. In fact,
> the nation is becoming as grave as
> the English."

Although by expanding his acerbic notes of Talma's comments into complete "quoted" sentences Irving laid claim to an accuracy of transcription which his material did not fully warrant, nonetheless his aim in "Conversations with Talma" was clearly not to misrepresent but rather to flesh out the bare bones of his narrative notes. No early manuscript account of his second interview with Talma (*Knickerbocker Gallery* 16.33–18.11; T 169.18–170.18) is known to survive, but the published text was likely the result of a similar expansion and regularization.

"Conversations with Talma" was in fact a collection of Irving's previously unpublished writings associated with the actor. The second manuscript item which sheds light on the genesis of the article is, presumably, what he characterizes in the published work as "some desultory observations made at the time, and suggested by my conversations with Talma" (T 170.20–21). This manuscript, owned by Yale University, is written in dark brown ink on thirteen sheets of white, unlined paper 5x8" in size,[351] and is entitled "French Romance." The notation "(rough sketch)" is conspicuous on the first page beneath and to the right of the title, but the deletions and substitutions in a darker shade of ink throughout the manuscript reveal that at some point Irving took pains to improve it. Probably the relative fluency with which he drafted the final manuscript text of this portion of "Conversations with Talma" was owing to the care he had taken with the earlier draft. At any rate, his claim in the published article that the extended comments on contemporary French taste in the arts were "given very much in the rough style in which they were jotted down, with some omissions and abbreviations, but no heightenings nor additions" (T 170.23–25) requires qualification. The *Knickerbocker Gallery* text may have included no "heightenings," but the author was by no means content for it to appear in a "rough style."

To enhance the continuity of "Conversations with Talma" Irving shifted his discussion in "French Romance" of the success of *Hamlet* in the Théâtre Français from a point immediately preceding the final paragraph to the outset, where it followed closely upon Talma's quoted comments on Shakespeare (*Knickerbocker Gallery* 17.24–18.11; T 171.5–20). Moreover, within this passage he compressed two paragraphs into one, transposing the material of the second paragraph into the second and third sentences of the first:

351. Except pages 8, 9, and 13, which include brief false starts on their reverse sides, the text of "French Romance" is written on one side of each sheet only.

"French Romance"

This tragedy may be considered as one of the/ great ⟨footholds⟩ ↑triumphs↓ of the romantic style—/ ⟨but his⟩ but it has gained another still/ greater in the success of Marie Stuart;/ imitated from the ⟨Ge⟩ german tragedy of/ Schiller⟨;⟩. ⟨In vain have t⟩ The critics thundered/ their tirades against this drama; ⟨and⟩ ↑they↓ ex-/ claimed against ↑the apostacy of↓ their countrymen, that, having/ from their infancy ⟨had their⟩ been accustomed/ to the touching beauties and harmonious verses/ of Athalie, Polyeucte & Merope, they should/ receive with transport the barbarous ⟨rhym⟩/ productions of a german muse. All in vain;/ the nightly receipts ⟨at the⟩ are the most/ eloquent critiques on a piece, and Marie Stewart maintains triumphant possession/ of the boards.

⟨How far this new taste may be carried it/ is impossible to say—and whether it may ↑in fact↓ emanci-/ pate the french stage from the rigorous Shackles/ of Aristotle.⟩ The Amateurs of the Old School/ are sadly alarmed at these foreign innovations;/ they tremble for the ancient decorum and/ pompous proprieties of their drama, and ⟨make/ sad [?ontacies?] about the⟩ notwithstanding Hamlet/ & Marie Stuart have both been put in the/ Straight Waistcoat of Aristotle, yet they are/ terribly affraid they will do mischief and/ set others madding.

Knickerbocker Gallery 19.10–25

The success of this tragedy may be considered one of the triumphs of what is denominated the romantic school; and another has been furnished by the overwhelming reception of Marie Stuart, a modification of the German tragedy of Schiller. The critics of the old school are sadly alarmed at these foreign innovations, and tremble for the ancient decorum and pompous proprieties of their stage. It is true, both Hamlet and Marie Stuart have been put in the strait waistcoat of Aristotle; yet they are terribly afraid they will do mischief, and set others madding. They exclaim against the apostasy of their countrymen in bowing to foreign idols, and against the degeneracy of their taste, after being accustomed from infancy to the touching beauties of Athalie, Polyeucte, and Merope, in relishing these English and German monstrosities, and that through the medium of translation. All in vain! The nightly receipts at the doors outweigh, with managers, all the invectives of the critics, and Hamlet and Marie Stuart maintain triumphant possession of the boards.

"Conversations with Talma" includes a second passage wherein two paragraphs from "French Romance" are compressed into one (*Knickerbocker Gallery* 21.23–35; T 172.42–173.9); here, however, Irving deleted several sentences of the earlier text. Elsewhere, at a point in the published text following the discussion of Shakespeare's "triumphs over transla- tion" (*Knickerbocker Gallery* 20.11; T 171.36), a deletion of an entire paragraph occurs. Excepting these revisions of relatively lengthy passages, however, the process of transforming "French Romance" into the latter portion of "Conversations with Talma" was straightforward: it involved frequent recastings of sentences and substitutions of words and phrases, but it did not include the insertion of new material. It seems probable that no manuscript draft intervened between "French Romance" and the final manuscript of the article.

Comparison of the latter manuscript of the *Knickerbocker Gallery* text reveals that the work underwent a variety of minor changes prior to publication. Substantive variants between the two texts occur at 11 points, and Irving's accidentals were revised extensively. Many of the latter emendations were necessary refinements of his casually pointed manu- script, but an even greater number reflected the imposition of an editorial styling akin to that of the *Knickerbocker Magazine*. For example, commas were deleted at 5 points but added at no less than 116, resulting in a noticeably dense pattern of punctuation. There is no reason to suppose that the author himself played any part in the preparation of "Conversa- tions with Talma" beyond the drafting of the final manuscript. In 1855, when the *Knickerbocker Gallery* appeared, his literary energies were directed almost exclusively toward the *Life of George Washington*, and it is unlikely that he would have been willing to correct proofsheets. As had been his practice when a regular contributor to the *Knickerbocker Magazine*, he probably left the final preparation of copy to someone else.

After its publication in the *Knickerbocker Gallery*, the article was reprinted once during Irving's lifetime, in *The Atlantic Souvenir* (1859), pp. [33]–40. Except that it lacks a part of the concluding dateline, the *Atlantic Souvenir* text is identical with the original version. The pagina- tion and running heads are altered, and a signature "3" appears on the first page of the *Atlantic Souvenir* article which has no counterpart in the *Knickerbocker Gallery*; but in all other respects—page-sige, type- style, lineation—the two texts appear to be successive printings from the same stereotype plates. Possibly in 1859 the printers of the *Atlantic Souvenir* purchased the plates and altered them minimally before pub- lishing the compilation as a gift-book of their own. At any rate, the text of the article underwent no authorial revision before being reprinted in the *Atlantic Souvenir*.

Pierre M. Irving reprinted "Conversations with Talma," acknowledged as from the *Knickerbocker Gallery*, in *Spanish Papers*, II, [151]–60. The latter text includes 2 substantive variants and numerous variants in spelling, capitalization, and punctuation from the original printing, but all these may readily be ascribed to printer's error, to Pierre M. Irving's editorial preparation of the text, or to the imposition of the Putnam house style.[352] There is no evidence that Irving revised the work once he had completed the printer's copy manuscript for the *Knickerbocker Gallery*.

Despite the ample textual evidence pertaining to its genesis, the textual situation for "Conversations with Talma" is thus quite straight-forward. Irving prepared a manuscript whose text, revised by a meticulous hand, was published in the *Knickerbocker Gallery*. This text was reprinted once during his lifetime and, with further revisions chiefly of accidentals, once afterward. Because the printer's copy manuscript for the original published text is extant, and because there is no evidence that Irving revised the article once he had completed the manuscript, that text constitutes the closest available approximation of his intention for the article in its original form. Even though it betrays some signs of inattention or haste which render its authority less firm than that of a manuscript to which he had devoted minute care, the Huntington Library manuscript is clearly the proper choice as copy-text.

Several varieties of emendation are undertaken to correct errors and oversights in the copy-text. Pairs of double quotation marks are supplied when necessary (Emendations 168.24), individual double quotation marks are supplied when necessary to complete pairs (Emendations 168.22), and commas are added at appropriate points to separate Irving's commentary from direct quotations introduced within it (Emendations 168.33). Periods are inserted at the ends of sentences where the author neglected to include them, or they are substituted for indicated inappropriate punctuation which he neglected to delete (Emendations 168.40). Apostrophes are added to possessives (Emendations 169.10), and commas are supplied where appropriate but omitted at the ends of lines in the manuscript (Emendations 168.19).

In general the accidentals in the copy-text are permitted to stand unless clearly in error. "Boulevards" (169.27) and "boulevards" (172.29) are both present because Irving's preference is uncertain, but "Revolution" is emended to lower-case form at 172.2 in accordance with his practice elsewhere in the article. "Theatre Francaise" is corrected to "Théâtre Français" (Emendations 168.41).

Irving's revisions to his notes on Talma and "French Romance" were so extensive as to preclude tabulation of variants between them and the copy-text. However, at some points of close correspondence between the latter manuscript and the copy-text, "French Romance" is useful in clarifying his intention; readings from that text are thus incorporated from time to time in the tables which follow (*e.g.*, Emendation 170.40, 172.40; Rejected Variants 172.8). All cancellations and revisions within the copy-text itself are recorded in the list of Emendations; false starts

352. See the Textual Commentary, I, 273–76.

immediately rewritten are reported in a single entry (Emendations 169.24). Substantive and accidental variants between the manuscript and the *Knickerbocker Gallery* text are given; unless otherwise noted, the latter text and the article as reprinted in the *Atlantic Souvenir* are identical. In addition to accidental readings from the *Spanish Papers* text included in the list of Emendations so as to provide a full accounting of the textual alternatives available, substantive variants between the copy-text and the posthumous version are recorded. In the list of Emendations only, the *Spanish Papers* reading is to be regarded as identical with that in the *Knickerbocker Gallery* unless it is specifically cited. The table of Rejected Variants includes all variants between the copy-text and the *Knickerbocker Gallery* and *Atlantic Souvenir* versions not included in the list of Emendations, and substantive variants between it and the *Spanish Papers* version not included in the list of Emendations. A few rejected accidental readings from *Spanish Papers*, of possible interest, are included as well.

In the preparation of this edition the following collations have been made:

1. A typed transcription of Irving's final manuscript text, prepared on the basis of a xerox copy checked twice against the original, collated with a xerox copy of the preliminary notes on Talma;

2. The above typed transcription collated twice and independently with a typed transcription of "French Romance," prepared on the basis of a xerox copy checked against the original;

3. The transcription of the final manuscript collated twice and independently with the *Knickerbocker Gallery* text owned by the University of Virginia (*PS/ 535/ K5);

4. A xerox copy of the above *Knickerbocker Gallery* text sight collated with the following additional copies: New York Public Library (NBF); Yale University (Is 50/ t 855);

5. The xerox copy of the *Knickerbocker Gallery* text sight collated with the *Atlantic Souvenir* text in copies owned by the New York Public Library (NBF) and Yale University (Ia 107/ At 63);

6. The xerox copy of the *Knickerbocker Gallery* text sight collated twice and independently with the *Spanish Papers* text owned by the National Library of Canada;

7. A xerox copy of the above *Spanish Papers* text sight collated with the following additional copies: New York Public Library; Yale University (Iw/ Ir8/ 866).

See Discussions and Lists pp. 530, 574, 666.

[MEMOIR OF WASHINGTON ALLSTON]

Irving's recollections of Washington Allston were first published in 1855 as part of the entry on the artist in Evert A. and George L. Duyckinck's *Cyclopædia of American Literature* II, 14–16.[353] A holograph manuscript which almost certainly served as printer's copy for the *Cyclopædia* text is extant in the Manuscript Division, New York Public Library.[354] Written on one side of fifteen sheets of light-weight laid paper 5x7″ in size and bearing the watermark "Moirier, London," its pages are numbered consecutively in ink by Irving.[355] It includes only 21 cancellations, none exceeding a few words in length. The scarcity of cancellations, and the presence of only a single correction by another hand—an oversight corrected by Pierre M. Irving (see Emendations 178.2–3)—suggest that in preparing the manuscript Irving was copying from an earlier draft, revising minimally as he proceeded.[356] The neatness of the manuscript also indicates that the copy submitted for publication in the *Cyclopædia* had been prepared with some care and in general represented the author's wishes. This impression seems consistent with the stipulation Irving had earlier made to Evert Duyckinck upon consenting to prepare the article— that his text should be printed entire and unmutilated.[357] Nothing is known of the manner in which the manuscript text was altered after it left Irving's hands, but there is no reason to suppose that his own par-

353. The sketch was introduced in the *Cyclopædia* as follows: "Of the moral harmony of Allston's daily life, we have been kindly favored with a picture, filled with incident, warm, genial, and thoroughly appreciative, from the pen, we had almost said the pencil, of the artist's early friend in Italy, Washington Irving. It is taken from a happy period of his life, and our readers will thank the author for the reminiscence:—"

354. The manuscript includes two pencilled notations, vertical marks between sentences, which appear to be printers' reference marks: one, at a point corresponding in the *Cyclopædia* text to 16.1.40 (T 177.7 pencil. He); the other, at a point corresponding to 16.2.12 in the *Cyclopædia* (T 177.34 America. I). The manuscript is bound in a volume which also includes illustrations and three letters from Irving to Evert A. Duyckinck, dated November 23, 1854, December 26, 1854, and May 4, 1855.

355. Page 11 of the manuscript consists of two slips of paper pasted together. The first scrap includes the latter portion of a quotation from a letter of Allston's which concludes at 16.1.24 in the *Cyclopædia* (T 176.39 there."); the second scrap includes the continuation of the text.

356. At the time when Irving prepared the manuscript, in late 1854, Pierre M. Irving was serving him full-time as proofreader, co-researcher, critic, and general literary factotum. It would thus have been natural for Pierre to have glanced through his uncle's account of Allston, perhaps even collating it with an earlier version, before it was passed along to the Duyckincks.

357. Washington Irving to Evert A. Duyckinck, Sunnyside, November 23, 1854 (Manuscript Division, New York Public Library).

ticipation in the final preparation of the work for publication extended beyond submission of the manuscript.

The person who saw the work into print, probably Duyckinck, did correct certain of the author's oversights. Most notably, Irving had been inconsistent in his spelling of Allston's surname: in his first 11 uses of the name, he had spelled it erroneously as "Alston"; in the latter 3 references he spelled it accurately. In the *Cyclopædia* text the name appeared consistently as "Allston." The published text includes many other alterations of the manuscript version besides corrections of errors, however. In addition to a slightly revised initial sentence wherein Irving is identified as the author of the account, it includes 11 substantive variants from the original text—8 limited to substitutions for single words (or misreadings of them), 1 a printer's error, 1 an added footnote reference, and 1 a rewritten footnote.[358] It reveals as well a wide variety of alterations to the accidentals of the manuscript, including 32 spelling changes in addition to the regularization of "Allston." In short, at numerous points the *Cyclopædia* text of the memoir was at variance with Irving's expressed intention.

The article on Allston was not reprinted during the author's lifetime, but in his "Memoranda of the Literary Career of Washington Irving," a contribution to *Irvingiana*, Duyckinck reprinted four paragraphs from the *Cyclopædia* text (p. vi). The reprinted passage, which corresponds to T 174.25–175.16 (We . . . . painter.), reveals no evidence of authorial revision. Except for a slightly adapted first sentence to indicate the source of the quoted paragraphs, and a single other substantive variant from the first printing,[359] the *Irvingiana* text—which was probably prepared using the *Cyclopædia* version as printer's copy—includes no variants whatever from its predecessor.

Under the title "Washington Allston," the *Cyclopædia* text was reprinted in full by Pierre M. Irving in *Spanish Papers*, II, [143]–50. Except for a revised introductory sentence in which the reading of Irving's manuscript was restored, a misprint, and a deleted footnote and footnote reference (see Rejected Variants 172.42–43), the *Spanish Papers* text includes no substantive variants from the earlier one. Emendations of accidentals were made in a manner consistent with the imposition of

358. In the order cited above, the substantive variants are listed at the following points in the tables which follow: Emendations 146.10; Rejected Variants 173.32, 174.26, 175.16, 175.39, 176.40, 177.7, 177.7; Rejected Variants 177.34; Rejected Variants 175.31; Rejected Variants 177.42–43.

359. The *Irvingiana* text begins: " 'We had delightful rambles together,' he writes, 'about Rome . . . .' " The corresponding *Cyclopædia* text is as follows: "We had delightful rambles together about Rome . . . ." The other substantive variant occurs at a point corresponding to T 175.14: in *Cyclopædia* the word "prospect" was used; in *Irvingiana* it appeared as "prospects."

the Putnam house style,[360] but there is no evidence of authorial revision. The available textual evidence thus indicates that Irving left the memoir of Allston untouched once it had appeared in print.[361]

Because a full manuscript is extant which almost certainly served as printer's copy for the first published text, and because it is unknown whether Irving approved the numerous minor alterations of the manuscript incorporated in the *Cyclopædia* text, the manuscript constitutes the best available evidence of his final intention for the memoir in its original form. Accordingly, the manuscript is adopted as copy-text.

Certain regularizations have been undertaken to correct errors and, when Irving's prevailing intention is clear, to render the copy-text self-consistent. Periods are supplied at the unpunctuated ends of sentences (Emendations 173.27), apostrophes are added to possessive forms (Emendations 173.34), end-of-line commas omitted from the copy-text are supplied (Emendations 174.5), words capitalized in a manner uncharacteristic of Irving's practice are emended to lower-case forms (Emendations 174.27), "Alston" is corrected to "Allston" (Emendations 173.23), the necessary punctuation is added to incomplete pairs of double quotation marks (Emendations 174.13), and for quotations within quotations pairs of single quotation marks are substituted for the double quotation marks Irving used (Emendations 176.32–33).

In the tables which follow a full accounting is given of variants within the copy-text; false starts immediately rewritten and misspellings immediately corrected are gathered into a single entry (Emendations 174.13). Substantive and accidental variants between the copy-text and the *Cyclopædia* version are reported in full. In the list of Emendations only, unless the *Spanish Papers* text is specifically cited its reading is to be presumed identical with that in the original printing. Variants between the copy-text and the *Cyclopædia* not included in the list of Emendations are set forth in a separate table of Rejected Variants. The latter table includes a full reporting of substantive variants only between the manuscript and the *Spanish Papers* text; however, a few accidental variants of possible interest between the two texts are listed as well.

In the preparation of this edition the following collations have been made:

1. A typed transcription of the copy-text, prepared on the basis of a xerox copy and corrected after comparison with the original, collated twice and independently with the *Cyclopædia* text owned by the University of Virginia (R/ PS85/ .D6/ 1856);

360. See Textual Commentary, I, 273–76.

361. Irving's sketch of Allston was reprinted in full from *Spanish Papers* (or the later edition of the miscellaneous works, *Biographies and Miscellanies*), in Jared B. Flagg, *The Life and Letters of Washington Allston* (New York, 1892), pp. 68–75.

2. A xerox copy of the above *Cyclopædia* text sight collated with the following additional copy: Victoria College (PS/ 85/ D8/ 1855);

3. The xerox copy of the *Cyclopædia* text collated with the text in two copies of *Irvingiana* (see the Introduction to the Textual Notes);

4. The xerox copy of the *Cyclopædia* text collated twice and independently with the *Spanish Papers* text owned by the National Library of Canada;

5. A xerox copy of the above *Spanish Papers* text sight collated with the following additional copies: New York Public Library; Yale University (Iw/ Ir8/ 866).

See Discussions and Lists pp. 530, 579, 668.

[THE CHRONICLE OF PELAYO]

Irving began work on "The Chronicle of Pelayo" in the fall of 1827, and almost two years later, while a resident of the Alhambra, he completed a first draft. In 1835 he planned to include "Pelayo" in *The Crayon Miscellany*, a serial publication designed, as he told his brother Peter, to "form a kind of gallery of varied works," none of which were "of sufficient importance to stand by themselves."[362] In July of that year he reported to Peter that the third and concluding volume of *The Crayon Miscellany*, entitled *Legends of the Conquest of Spain*, had been stereotyped and would include "The Legend of Don Roderick," "Legend of the Subjugation of Spain," "Legend of Count Julian and His Family," and "Pelayo." However, possibly in order to avoid swelling the *Legends* to a length disproportionate with its predecessors, at the last moment he withheld the latter work,[363] returning the manuscript to its place in his trunks among the literary material he had accumulated and planned to draw upon at some appropriate time. A substantial proportion of the "Pelayo" manuscripts now extant probably formed part of the narrative he had thus prepared for publication in 1835; some passages may derive from the still earlier stages of composition.

Irving's agreement in 1839 with Lewis Gaylord Clark, the editor of the *Knickerbocker Magazine*, to furnish articles to that publication in return for an annual fee, provided him a convenient outlet for writings he had already prepared but had not yet published. Accordingly, his contributions to the *Knickerbocker Magazine* included two works derived from his studies of the early conflicts between the Spaniards and the Moors, one of which appeared in January 1840 under the title "Pelayo

362. Irving to Peter Irving, New York, January 8, 1835; PMI, III, 65.
363. PMI, III, 75–76.

and the Merchant's Daughter," pp. 65–70.[364] The manuscript which served as printer's copy for this article is extant at the Beinecke Library, Yale University.

The Yale University manuscript reveals that prior to submitting it to Clark the author adhered to a principle which he followed throughout his two-year interlude as a magazinist: to devote no more trouble to the writing of articles than was absolutely necessary. On the first four pages of the twenty-page manuscript, corresponding to 65.1–66.12 in the published text, he supplied an introductory comment on the obscurity of the historical record pertaining to early Spain, a brief account of the parentage and early years of his protagonist, and a sketch of the Gascon marauders in Spain—one of whom was to figure in Pelayo's encounter with the merchant of Bordeaux. It appears likely that these initial pages, which are written with few corrections in a single shade of dark brown ink and are numbered in a single series of pagination,[365] are a condensed re-casting of part of that "unpublished work" which Irving specified in his subtitle as the immediate source of the anecdote.

At any rate, beginning with the fifth page of the manuscript four separate series of pagination appear, three cancelled. Two of these— 29–44 and 12–27, both written in ink by Irving—suggest that at one time the sheets formed part of a complete draft of "Pelayo" which was subsequently either shortened or lengthened. A third cancelled sequence, written in pencil by an unknown hand, runs from page 354 to page 369. Probably this series pertained not to "Pelayo" alone but to the combined manuscript copy Irving had submitted in 1835 for publication as *Legends of the Conquest of Spain*. It is at least clear from the multiple pagination that for the *Knickerbocker Magazine* article he was adapting a manuscript, portions of which he had previously drafted more than once. But except for pages 1–4, the Yale manuscript reveals no evidence of extensive authorial revision at the time the magazine copy was prepared.[366]

364. The second was "Abderahman: Founder of the Dynasty of the Ommiades in Spain," *Knickerbocker Magazine*, 15 (May 1840), 427–40; see the Textual Commentary to "Chronicle of the Ommiades," pp. 474–77.

365. The first page, from which a portion at the upper right has been torn away, is numbered "1" in pencil at the top center. This page consists of two slips of unlaid, unlined paper pasted together to form a sheet 4½ x 7 7/16" in size. The remainder of the manuscript, which includes no pastings, is written on what appears to be the same variety of paper. Its pages range in width from 4 7/16 to 4 ¾" and in length from 7¼ to 7½". The manuscript text is written on one side of a page throughout.

366. On page 4, 2 substitutions above the line do appear; and at 10 points on the pages that follow Irving used pencil to encircle problematical words and insert alternative readings, some of which he subsequently copied over in ink. These cursory attentions suggest the casual manner in which he prepared the selection from his

Almost as a matter of necessity, therefore, Lewis Gaylord Clark went over the article with care. Besides entering frequent clarifications of Irving's slurred hand, guidelines to indicate the sequence of the text at points where cancellations made it ambiguous, and marks to indicate the proper placement of interlineated material, using bright blue ink he rather extensively altered the accidentals in the manuscript copy,[367] and in addition he made 3 substantive changes. He deleted the subtitle "(from an unpublished work)"; clarified an unusual expression by adding a single word;[368] and at another point added a word obviously omitted through oversight.[369] Clark's pervasive minor revisions of the work Irving had submitted to him seem somewhat cavalier, but they were not. At the same time as he was imposing on the manuscript a dense *Knickerbocker Magazine* style of pointing, he was also rendering the text presentable—indeed legible—to the printer, something Irving had neglected to do.

In all probability Irving played no part in the preparation of "Pelayo and the Merchant's Daughter" for publication once he had turned over the manuscript to Clark. Numerous accidental readings in the printed article have no precedent in the manuscript, but they probably derive from the printer, to whom Clark gave a free hand, or else from the revision of proofsheets by the editor himself.[370] Only 2 substantive

more extensive manuscript. He wrote the number "5" in the upper right-hand corner of the first page in the adapted fragment, but he did not bother to continue the series. Chores of this kind he left to Clark—who duly added page-numbers from 6 to 19 on the leaves that followed. In doing so, however, Clark wrote "7" on two consecutive pages, so that the revised pagination is 1–7, 7–19.

367. He inserted 93 commas, altered 11 commas to semicolons, made 9 changes in capitalization, added 2 pairs of single quotation marks, deleted 3 pairs of double quotation marks, added 6 paragraph breaks not indicated by Irving and clarified many others which were so indicated, and made 9 other emendations of the accidentals, besides those of spelling. Irving's spelling he altered 15 times, 10 of which instances involved adding hyphens to compound words, 4 supplying apostrophes.

368. At a point corresponding in the *Knickerbocker Magazine* to 69.1–2 Then Pelayo obtained from the holy father consent that the merchant's wife and daughter should pass the night within his cell . . . , Irving wrote "from the holy father that . . ."; Clark added the word "consent."

369. At a point corresponding in the *Knickerbocker Magazine* to 78.48–49 . . . she would take the book, and would read it . . ., Irving wrote "and would it"; Clark added "read."

370. Revisions of accidentals include the substitution of 19 pairs of single for double quotation marks, the insertion of 1 complete and 2 incomplete pairs of single quotation marks, the addition of 12 commas and the deletion of 2, 2 changes in capitalization, and 6 other emendations of punctuation. The printed text incorporates 20 spelling changes from the revised manuscript—3 involving the addition of apostrophes to possessives, 4 the addition of hyphens to compound words, 7 the substitution of -or for Irving's -our spellings, 2 the substitution of -ise for Irving's

variants from the corrected manuscript appear in the *Knickerbocker Magazine* text, one an obvious printing error, the other a correction of an authorial error.[371] The final stage of revision thus consisted primarily of bringing the accidentals of the revised manuscript fully into line with *Knickerbocker Magazine* styling. Relying as much as possible on the cooperation of other persons, Irving had once more completed his onerous "monthly recurring task" as a magazine writer.[372]

"Pelayo and the Merchant's Daughter" was not incorporated as a whole into the final manuscript draft of "Pelayo," which Irving compiled in the spring of 1847. However, the *Knickerbocker Magazine* text almost certainly did serve him as a basis for two rewritten passages in the later version.[373] It is thus proper to summarize here the manner in which he adapted the printed text in his later draft, which eventually provided copy for *Spanish Papers*.

Almost the whole of the latter manuscript, which was originally 62 pages in length (pages 52–55 are now missing), is extant at the University of Virginia. Pages 1–22, written in a clear, fluent hand on sheets of unlaid, unlined paper uniform in quality, evidently represent the latest period in the author's attention to "Pelayo." These pages are written in a single shade of ink and include (for Irving) remarkably few cancellations and substitutions. Evidently in part a copied or rewritten version of an earlier manuscript draft now lost, the text on pages 1–22 also incorporates rephrased passages from "Pelayo and the Merchant's Daughter"—specifically, the initial two paragraphs of the article describing the "mere wilderness of dubious facts" which confronts the inquirer into Spanish history (*Knickerbocker Magazine* 65.5–21 It . . . . interwoven.), and parts of the two following paragraphs, characterizing the Gascon hidalgos whom Pelayo encountered (65.42–66.10 The Gascons . . . . them.). With a single exception, the divergences between the corresponding passages in the two texts proceed from considerations of

---

-ize spellings, the substitution of "inquired" for "enquired," "burgher" for "burger," and 2 corrections.

371. At a point corresponding to 66.46–47 in the *Knickerbocker Magazine,* Irving wrote "for he was always prepared . . ."; in the printed version the word "was" was omitted. At a point corresponding to 70.28–29 in the printed text, Irving wrote "hoped that she had awaken some tenderness . . ."; in the *Knickerbocker Magazine* the verb was corrected to "awakened."

372. Irving to Pierre M. Irving, n.p., April 1840; PMI, III, 152. The *Knickerbocker Magazine* text was reprinted in *The Evergreen* for February 1840 (vol. 1, pp. 100–02). *The Evergreen,* a short-lived periodical whose subtitle "A Monthly Magazine of New and Popular Tales and Poetry" blandly indicated its identity as a medium for pirated magazine articles, published a text of "Pelayo and the Merchant's Daughter" which included no substantive variants from that in its original printed form.

373. It is possible though unlikely that the printer's copy manuscript served this

verbal taste alone. The exception is that, whereas in the *Knickerbocker Magazine* Irving began his discussion of the Gascon marauders with a general reference to an "old chronicler" whose opinions he was summarizing, in the 1847 version he specifies "the worthy Agapida" as his source. Fray Antonio Agapida, the monkish chronicler and zealous adherent of the Christian cause whom he had originally intended to serve as the fictive narrator for all his chronicles of early Spain, had not appeared in "Pelayo and the Merchant's Daughter." In the 1847 draft he is present, not indeed as the narrator but as one of the several sources from whose testimony the work is purportedly drawn.[374]

As Irving's recurrence to the magazine article suggests, the manuscript he pieced together in 1847 was a conglomerate of pages written and revised at intervals since 1835, if not earlier. As indicated, pages 1–22 of the manuscript, corresponding in *Spanish Papers* to 209.1–223.17 THE . . . . couched (T 180.2–188.10), bear evidence of a late stage of composition.[375] Pages 23–36, which recount essentially the same material as had been included following 66.11 of the *Knickerbocker Magazine* text, corresponding in *Spanish Papers* to 223.17–229.19 his . . . . c. 101 (T 188.10–191.42), clearly derive from an earlier period. Written on sheets of paper poorer in quality and smaller in size than those which precede them,[376] they include a series of page-numbers cancelled in order to arrange them in sequence with pages 1–22; prior to 1847 they had been pages 9–22. We thus have two manuscript texts describing Pelayo's

---

purpose. The casual manner in which Irving consistently prepared copy for Clark suggests unconcern as to what the editor might do with his manuscripts. Moreover, the manuscript of "Communipaw," which Clark apparently retained until years after Irving's death (see above, p. 410), reveals that he was not punctilious about returning manuscript copy to Irving. Even if he did return the manuscript of "Pelayo and the Merchant's Daughter," it would have been simpler for the author to revise the article using the clear printed text as his reference than to refer to the manuscript. For example, in revising the "Chronicle of the Ommiades" in 1847, Irving used the *Knickerbocker Magazine* text of "Abderahman" rather than the printer's copy manuscript for that work.

374. "Some parts of these Chronicles run into a quiet, drolling vein, especially in treating of miracles and miraculous events; on which occasion Fray Antonio Agapida comes to my assistance, with his zeal for the faith, and his pious hatred of the infidels" (Irving to Pierre M. Irving, Sunnyside, April 14, 1847; PMI, IV, 15–16).

375. With the exception of page 21, which includes 3 lines of cancelled text on its reverse side, pages 1–22 are written on one side of a sheet, each measuring approximately 5 x 7½". Pages 8 and 9 are written on the first and third sides of a sheet folded at the center so as to form a booklet of 4 pages. Pages 18 and 22 are similarly arranged, as are 20 and 21; the latter were apparently intended to fit inside the fold following page 18. Page 19 is written on a single sheet 4 15/16 x 7 9/16" in size.

376. Pages 23–36 are written on sheets of unlaid, unlined paper approximately 4½ x 6⅝" in size. Except for page 25, which includes 4 lines of cancelled material on its reverse side, Irving's text appears on one side of each sheet only.

encounter with the merchant of Bordeaux and his daughter.[377] However, while a part of the manuscript fragment used for "Pelayo and the Merchant's Daughter" apparently formed part of the draft Irving had intended to publish in 1835, the date at which pages 23–36 of the 1847 version were first composed, and the immediate purpose for which Irving composed them, is undeterminable. All that can be affirmed with certainty is that, as demonstrated below, these pages were at one time part of a complete draft of "Pelayo" which, condensed and also superseded at points where in 1847 the author wrote out a fresh text, nonetheless comprised the greater part of that final version.

Pages 37–41 of the latter manuscript, corresponding in *Spanish Papers* to 230.4–233.3 Pelayo . . . . defiance (T 192.3–193.36), were written at the same time as pages 1–22; they constitute the only passage besides the introductory pages wherein Irving wrote out a fresh text. It may be noted that, whereas in the later revisions he freely refers to Fray Antonio Agapida (for example, see T 192.26, 192.37), the chronicler goes unmentioned in the passages drafted prior to 1847. Like pages 1–22, pages 37–41 are numbered in a single series.

The five pages which follow page 41 of the University of Virginia manuscript, corresponding in *Spanish Papers* to 233.4–235.15 Such . . . . c. 2. (T 193.37–195.12, 195.39), include three sets of pagination; they are heavily revised, though the colors of ink and breadths of pen-point indicate that the revisions were not made in 1847. The first series of pagination, 8–12, Irving no doubt used at an early stage of composition when, characteristically, he paged each chapter separately. The second series, 59–63, evidently pertains to a completed draft of the work which (as will presently appear) ran to 79 pages in 10 chapters. In that version, these pages concluded Chapter Eight. The third series of pagination, from 41 to a page designated "45 to 63," clearly derives from a condensation of a preceding draft from which 18 pages before the extant page 8/59/41 had been cut. These five pages are uniform in quality and (with a few exceptions owing to the addition of pasted slips) in size with pages 23–36 in the 1847 sequence. As an instance of Irving's inattention to detail it may be noticed that, having written out a new text on pages 37–41, he did not bother to re-number pages 41–"45 to 63" in the series which followed them; the manuscript thus includes two pages numbered 41.

The remainder of the draft Irving prepared in 1847 consists of two chapters, the only instances where his chapter-numbers (9 and 10) and synoptic chapter-headings survive. The first chapter, which corresponds in *Spanish Papers* to 236.1–241.9 CHAPTER V . . . . victory. (T 195.13–

---

377. Even though they follow the same narrative line, at most points the two accounts cannot be collated word-for-word.

198.16), is written on pages 64–74, of which pages 69–72 are now missing; the second, which corresponds in *Spanish Papers* to 242.1–244.8 CHAPTER VI . . . . Pelayo. (T 198.17–199.36), is on pages 75–79. Excepting 2 instances on page 66 where brief emendations are made with ink and pen apparently identical with those Irving employed in preparing his 1847 draft, these chapters reveal no evidence of authorial revision at that time.

Irving's technique of composition in 1847 can thus be characterized as a sort of hasty joinery; and as the absence of consistent sequences of chapter-numbers and pagination suggests, he made no effort to prepare the narrative for early publication. The reshaping of his old material was a therapeutic exercise—or as he put it to Pierre M. Irving, "an amusing occupation." His claim that for "two or three fragmentary Chronicles" he had been "filling up the chasms, rewriting parts" was an accurate summary of his attention to the manuscript of "Pelayo"—which, as he said, was "now complete, though not thoroughly finished off."[378]

Between 1847 and his death in 1859, Irving did not return to the work to "finish it off." It thus remained for Pierre M. Irving, his literary executor, to smooth away its rough edges and prepare it for publication. Probably Pierre began his task in earnest shortly after completing the fourth and final volume of the *Life and Letters,* which appeared in December 1863. When he did set to work, he did so with characteristic deliberation, first annotating the manuscript in pencil with proposed corrections and other insertions, and after further consideration going over some of these in ink. Probably since *Spanish Papers* was to be published by George Putnam, Irving's publisher from 1848 until his death, and was to be set in type by the firm of John F. Trow, whose printers were familiar with the Putnam house style and the curiosa of the author's manuscript copy, Pierre did not bother to insert directions at every point which might require emendation or clarification. Nevertheless, his pencilled notations in the manuscript are quite frequent. The pencilled markings which he did not subsequently re-write in ink were primarily to correct Irving's oversights and clarify his handwriting. They included numerous crossed t's, dotted i's, and carets, a spelling correction, queries, a series of double quotation marks clearly intended to signify that all quoted passages were to be so punctuated (see Discussions of Adopted Readings 185.36–42), and four cancellations of brief passages, usually associated with false starts not fully deleted by Irving. The more critical emendations to the manuscript Pierre wrote in both pencil and ink. Among these were a revised and regularized pagination of Irving's pages 41–79 (to 42–62); inserted chapter-numbers and headnotes; a spelling change; a deletion of a word he had earlier added in pencil;

---

378. Irving to Pierre M. Irving, Sunnyside, April 14, 1847; PMI, IV, 15–16.

and 5 other substantive emendations, each involving 1 or 2 words. During this second review of the manuscript he added a few marks in ink—including another spelling correction and 2 substantive changes—at points he had not marked in pencil. Finally, in ink, on a blank page preceding the author's text, Pierre supplied a title, "The Legend of Pelayo," and on its reverse side he wrote a terse editorial note for publication in *Spanish Papers*:

> [The Legend of Pelayo, a fragment of which was printed in "The Spirit of the Fair" in 1864, and another, entitled "Pelayo & the Merchant's Daughter" in "The Knickerbocker" in 1840, is now first published entire—Ed]

In this clarified, corrected, and partially regularized state Pierre turned over the manuscript to the printer—planning, as he had often done during Irving's lifetime, carefully to read the proofsheets against the copy he had submitted.

The Spirit of the Fair, a magazine published as an adjunct to the New York Metropolitan Fair of 1864 had, as Pierre indicated, published a brief portion of the narrative. "The Story of Pelayo. A Fragment, by Washington Irving. (*Now published for the first time.*)" appeared in the eleventh number of that publication (April 16, 1864), p. 126; and, continued, in the twelfth (April 18, 1864), pp. 138–39. The passages which were thus first published correspond in *Spanish Papers* to 210.19–219.5 (T 181.1–186.2); that is, omitting the first 4 paragraphs, they include the whole of the first 2 chapters, describing the hero's origins and youth. Which manuscript served as printer's copy for the *Spirit of the Fair* text is not known. The corresponding pages of the manuscript text subsequently published by Pierre—pages 3–17—include marks by two printers who regularly set Irving's works in type for Putnam,[379] but they reveal no evidence that the manuscript served as copy for *The Spirit of the Fair*. While there is a possibility that another author's manuscript, now lost, served that purpose, this was almost certainly not the case. Probably Pierre, upon being approached with a request for a contribution, either wrote out a transcript of the appropriate passages or else authorized another person to perform the task. The pattern of variants

---

379. In the left margin of page 7 the name "Nelson" is written in pencil; in the upper left margin of page 14 the name "Hall" is written in pencil. The pencilled signature of "Nelson" also occurs on page 31; of Hall, on renumbered page 50. The initials "J. S. S." are written in pencil in the left margin of pages 23 and renumbered page 43, and also, in blue crayola, above a bracket on page 26 marking a stint. The pencilled signature "C. E. Allen" is written at the upper left of renumbered page 58. Smudged printer's fingerprints appear throughout the manuscript. On the reverse side of page 3 the notation "Irving/ 210–224" is written in pencil; similar notations appear on the reverse side of renumbered pages 42 and 57. These are printers' marks indicating the portions of manuscript set in type to make up the designated pages of *Spanish Papers*, I.

between the 1847 manuscript and the magazine text suggests the latter possibility as the more likely. Pierre's transcriptions of much-revised passages in the "Chronicle of the Ommiades" reveal that in copying Irving's texts he tended to be scrupulously faithful, ordinarily emending only in cases of error or oversight by the author.[380] On the other hand, the *Spirit of the Fair* text includes several variants from the manuscript which suggest a less than rigid interpretation of the importance of faithfulness to Irving's wishes.[381] Without diverging from the 1847 manuscript so far as to warrant speculation that it was based upon a different document, the *Spirit of the Fair* text is clearly uncharacteristic of Pierre M. Irving's editing. It is of no use for defining a critical text of "Pelayo."

The proofsheets for *Spanish Papers* have not survived, but marks in the manuscript reveal both that Pierre kept an anxious eye on the length of the work as a contribution to his crowded collection of Irving's miscellaneous writings,[382] and also that he collated proofsheets against the manuscript.[383] The readings in the published text which differ from the author's manuscript were thus authorized, if they were not indeed dictated by him. The *Spanish Papers* text derives from no manuscript other than the corrected one Pierre turned over to the printer, but it

380. See the Textual Commentary to "Chronicle of the Ommiades," pp. 484–85 below.

381. The substantive variants between the manuscript and *Spirit of the Fair* texts appear below:

Irving's Manuscript	*Spirit of the Fair*	*Spanish Papers* Page, line	T
son to	son of	210.29	181.9
hope	hopes	211.10	181.20
In the	In	211.14–15	181.24
writer	author	212.6	182.2
lists	list	212.28	182.21
prepared	proposed	215.29	184.18
caparisoned for him in	caparisoned in	216.7–8	184.26
He left	He had left	217.5	184.38

On 6 other occasions, statements which Irving had written as single sentences are converted into two in the published version.

382. At the bottom of the title-page of the manuscript, Pierre wrote in pencil the following notation:

$$1581—$$
$$920—$$
$$\overline{}$$
$$661 \qquad 37 \text{ pages print.}$$

Probably the figures in the subtraction were associated in some way with the number of lines in the proofs.

383. On the reverse side of renumbered page 47 of the manuscript, Pierre wrote in pencil: "p. 236." Since the printed text of "Pelayo" includes on its page 236 the material on that page of the manuscript, Pierre's notation seems quite possibly a reference mark written when proofreading.

does differ at numerous points from that text, reflecting in its accidentals the imposition of the Putnam house style.[384] Collation of the manuscript as revised by Pierre (excepting the title, chapter-numbers, and chapter-headings he added) against the printed text—*Spanish Papers*, I, [209]–44—reveals extensive emendations of Irving's accidentals. No less than 218 commas were added, 20 deleted; 9 dashes were added, 3 deleted; and 3 semicolons, 1 colon, 3 periods, 1 exclamation mark, 8 pairs of double quotation marks, and 2 unpaired double quotation marks were added (one erroneously). The Putnam text reveals numerous changes to Irving's pointing besides simple insertions of punctuation. These include the alteration of 7 commas to semicolons and 1 to a period; 27 semicolons to commas, 1 to a colon, 3 to commas followed by double dashes, 5 to periods; 3 colons to semicolons, 2 to periods; 1 period to a comma, 3 to semicolons, 1 to a colon, and 1 to a question mark; 1 dash to a period; and 1 question mark to a comma.

The often inconsistent spelling in the manuscript was modified at 84 points in the *Spanish Papers* text. Only 2 of these changes involved proper names, and each was clearly made in order to achieve consistency (see Emendations 181.3, 196.9). The most common variety of spelling change, which occurred at 29 points, was to hyphenate compound words which Irving had left unhyphenated.[385] Irving's –our spellings were 9 times changed to –or; internal –z– spellings were 4 times modified to –s– (an internal –s– was once altered to –z–); 13 corrections of obvious misspellings were made, and 26 other spelling changes occurred, many involving the Americanization of Irving's "English" usages and the modernization of his slightly obsolescent ones.[386] Initial lower-

384. See the Textual Commentary, I, 273–76.

385. The hyphenations in *Spanish Papers* of compound words unhyphenated in the manuscript are listed here. In each entry Irving's spelling is given, preceded by the appropriate page-line reference or references to *Spanish Papers*: 243.29 after times, 234.10 battle axes, 243.27 blood/red, 224.24 boar/spears, 221.6 broken down, 210.2 bye ways (to by-ways), 230.22 cockleshell, 215.13 cross bow, 231.3 ever blessed, 217.10 first born, 220.13 foster/father, 215.20 foster father, 224.24 hunting dresses, 224.18 hunting horn, 224.24 hunting swords, 219.5 long/lost, 221.22, 222.8 money bags, 232.20 never/failing, 215.13–14 play/things, 234.1–2 rallying point, 230.21 safe keeping, 221.8 scamper grounds, 223.22 scull cap (to skull-cap), 243.16 sea breeze, 215.21 serving men, 237.19 silver tongued, 221.10 tomorrow (to tomorrow), 221.29 well fed.

386. As enumerated above, the emendations of Irving's spelling in *Spanish Papers* were as follows. In each entry, a page-line reference to *Spanish Papers* appears first, followed by the author's spelling and that adopted in the published text: 230.21 armour/ armor, 224.10 demeanour/ demeanor, 226.17 dishonour/ dishonor, 240.24 favour/ favor, 238.1 honour/ honor, 237.21 honours/ honors, 221.24, 225.17, 228.11 valour/ valor; 233.15 enterprize/ enterprise, 221.21 merchandize/ merchandise, 215.21 orizons/ orisons, 214.13 surprized/ surprised; 212.8 baptised/ baptized; 211.28 born/ borne, 235.7 kingg/ king, 222.20 224.30, 226.9, 226.12 merchants/

case letters were emended to capitals on 24 occasions, 4 of which pertained to words at the beginning of quoted statements or to words beginning sentences; 10 to words associated with the Christian religion
and 1 with the Moslem religion; 3 to titles of nobility which formed parts
of proper names; 2 to adjectives which formed parts of personal names
or pseudonyms; 2 to designations of nationality; and 2 to what were
interpreted as parts of place-names.[387] Irving's initial capitals were 16
times emended to lower-case letters. Of these, 5 pertained to words which
he had written at the beginnings of sentences but which in the printed
text were amalgamated into the sentences preceding them; 8 to titles of
nobility used to denote individuals but not as parts of their proper
names; and 2 to common nouns within sentences.[388] In short, the
Spanish Papers text regularized, modernized, and made self-consistent
the accidentals of Irving's manuscript, imposing on it a pattern of punctuation and spelling consistent with the format adopted in works published by George Putnam during the author's lifetime under the supervision of himself and Pierre.

This process of regularization included the six footnotes wherein
Irving cited authorities from which details of the narrative were drawn.
In his later manuscripts—for example, that for *The Life of George Washington*—the author had tended to specify his sources hastily and in no
particular form, obviously expecting his notes to be made presentable by
the printer. (On occasion he even delegated the writing of footnotes to

---

merchant's, 232.2 parlty/ partly, 222.25–26 percieved/ perceived, 243.6 reccollected/
recollected, 234.5 seazed/ seized, 240.14 showerd/ showered, 235.5 sovreign/
sovereign, 240.28 wricks/ wrecks; 211.7 bans/ banns, 212.14, 228.30 befel/ befell,
227.23 carrolled/ carolled, 225.1 chace/ chase, 236.1 Chap:/ Chapter, 237.2 chil-
ren/ children, 222.31 despatched/ dispatched, 243.24 encreasing/ increasing, 225.6
enquired/ inquired, 220.22 every thing/ everything, 210.7, 210.14–15 extravagancies/
extravagances, 224.17 forbad/ forbade, 223.23 gallopped/ galloped, 217.23 past/
passed, 231.25 renegade/ renegado, 241.5 relique/ relic, 240.29 reliques/ relics,
243.2 sea/board/ seaboard, 231.23 sea bord/ seaboard, 236.6 sea/ board/ seaboard,
225.10 skreen/ screen, 234.20 strong/hold/ stronghold, 221.26 waylaid/ waylayed.

387. As enumerated above, the emendations of lower-case letters to capitals in
Spanish Papers were as follows. In each entry a page-line reference to *Spanish Papers*
appears first, followed by the manuscript reading: 226.20 arise, 225.7 they, 226.23,
243.28 this; 215.22, 243.7 church, 215.4, 221.24, 226.26 heaven, 212.29 holy virgin,
209.14 jesuit, 231.4 knighthood, 226.30 lord, 242.9 providence; 232.19 moslem;
210.26 duke, 210.28, 213.13 prince; 241.7 third, 210.30 wicked; 210.20, 234.7 gothic;
213.19 golden Tagus, 231.21 mountains.

388. As enumerated above, the emendations of capitals to lower-case letters in
Spanish Papers were as follows. In each entry a page-line reference to *Spanish Papers*
appears first, followed by Irving's manuscript reading: 226.23, 229.13 And; 218.14
Joyful; 218.31 Who; 228.26 Yet; 210.28, 211.9, 218.8 Duke; 218.6, 218.18, 218.23,
218.29, 219.2 Duchess; 224.31 Boar; 226.18 Hermit; 242.13 Renegado.

Pierre.)[389] Putnam had obliged by adapting his notations to a fairly consistent footnote form: an asterisk or other reference mark followed by the name of the author of the work cited, followed by a comma and the italicized title of the work. If a page-number, chapter-number, or other division was specified, the title was usually followed by a comma. If not, by a period. Since in the "Pelayo" manuscript the citation of sources was done in no less irregular a fashion than Irving had adopted in his other works published by Putnam, the recasting of his footnotes for *Spanish Papers* constituted what might be called a traditional editorial attention to the manuscript.

Only 11 substantive variants, all minor, occur between the revised manuscript text and that in *Spanish Papers*. Of the latter readings, 2 are clearly less appropriate in their contexts than the corresponding ones in the manuscript. Quite possibly these variants, each involving only a single letter, represent misprints overlooked by Pierre when proofreading (see Rejected Variants 188.26, 195.37). The remaining substantive variants, presumably inserted by him at the proof stage, are thoroughly characteristic of his meticulous habits as an emender of his uncle's works. However, it cannot be said that any of Pierre's final adjustments to the manuscript text represent significant improvements over what Irving had written. For example, the change of "him" to "himself" at 226.21 (T 190.5), while it produces a reading more idiomatic in nineteenth-century American usage and thereby achieves an end which Pierre appears to have regarded as desirable, divests the statement in which it occurs of the archaic flavor Irving had intended should characterize his "legendary" narrative of Old Spain. At any rate, Pierre's substantive alterations were few, modest, and motivated only by the wish to hit upon the right word or tense which, in his casual revision of 1847, the author himself had failed to find.

The *Spanish Papers* text was thus produced under the best of possible auspices, given the circumstances of its posthumous publication. It was prepared for the printer by Pierre, who knew his uncle's literary instincts and intentions better than anyone else then or since, and who was committed to bringing his unrealized aims for the work to fruition. It was published by George Putnam, whose house styling he had approved and with whose firm he had enjoyed a remarkably smooth working relationship. Probably it is safe to say that Pierre and Putnam prepared the text with more care than Irving would himself have devoted to the same tasks. The *Spanish Papers* version is of more than historical interest, therefore;

389. See the following manuscript of the *Life of Washington*, V: Chapters 5 (Manuscript Division, New York Public Library), 12 (Buffalo and Erie Public Library), 16–25 (Berg Collection, New York Public Library), and 31 (Manuscript Division, New York Public Library). Footnotes added by Pierre M. Irving to this volume appear on pp. 7, 19, 260, 261, and 262 of the 1859 duodecimo edition.

it represents a creditable attempt by the late author's closest associates to publish a work of which he would have approved.

Nevertheless, the fact remains that the *Spanish Papers* text of "Pelayo" was prepared for publication, and in its accidentals significantly revised from the manuscript, by persons other than Irving himself. The author may well have approved, in part or as a whole, of the printed result of the collaboration between his nephew and Putnam; but he did not so approve it. He had given his final effective attention to the manuscript in April 1847, when, upon setting it aside to pursue other duties, he left it "complete, though not thoroughly finished off." In this same state the manuscript passed to Pierre in 1859. Divested, therefore, of the revisions made to it after Irving's death, the manuscript which eventually served as printer's copy for *Spanish Papers* represents Irving's final expressed intention for the text of "Pelayo": and it must serve in this edition as copy-text. For that portion of the manuscript no longer extant—the pages renumbered by Pierre 52–55, corresponding in *Spanish Papers* to 238.14–240.12 So . . . . clamber (T 196.36–197.40)—the published version is necessarily adopted to fill the hiatus.[390]

The twentieth-century editor of "Pelayo" is accordingly placed in a position similar though not identical to that of Pierre M. Irving in 1859. The chief difference is that, whereas Pierre interpreted his responsibility as to carry out Irving's imperfectly realized plans, in this edition a greater emphasis is placed upon accurately representing Irving's own achievement. If the relatively conservative approach to emending the manuscript which is implicit in this bias produces a text somewhat less regular and self-consistent than the one published in *Spanish Papers*, adherence to the approach yields a result which represents more accurately than Pierre's the final expressed wishes of the author.

Textual and other evidence does justify certain classes of emendations. Clearly the author's general intention was to produce in "The Chronicle of Pelayo" a work fit to range beside *Legends of the Conquest of Spain* and his other narratives of early Spanish history such as the *Conquest of Granada*. Thus, for example, he intended to include at the beginning of each chapter a chapter-number and a chapter-summary. As has been noted, the two final chapters in the manuscript do include this material. Moreover, for each of the four chapters preceding them he included a blank space at the top of the initial page, in which that information could conveniently be entered. The latter procedure was one he was regularly to adopt in volumes four and five of the *Life of Washington*; and in those instances, one of Pierre's duties as his uncle's literary fac-

---

390. The same procedure is necessarily adopted from briefer passages in which the manuscript has been torn and the text lost; see Emendations 180.34.

totum was to supply the chapter-numbers and headnotes.[391] In light of this previous working relationship, it is reasonable to suppose that Irving would have expected Pierre to interpret the blank spaces preceding the first four chapters of the manuscript text as the points at which, in the usual fashion, preliminary material was to be inserted. In fact, Pierre did so, and his chapter-numbers and headnotes formed parts of the *Spanish Papers* text. It thus seems proper at present to regard the four blank spaces in the manuscript (on pages 1, 14, 18, and 37) as clear expresssions by Irving of a partially realized intention—one which it was Pierre's duty to realize in full. Accordingly, except as modified to conform with the styling adopted at these points throughout the *Complete Works*, the chapter-numbers and headnotes are included as they appeared in *Spanish Papers*. They are enclosed in brackets to indicate that they were not written by the author and cannot strictly be said to form parts of the copy-text (see Emendations 180.4–7).

A second class of regularizations is likewise warranted by analogy between the "Pelayo" manuscript and the *Life of Washington*, in preparing which Irving regularly delegated certain housekeeping chores to Pierre and to George Putnam. Because the author expected his documentation of source material routinely to be regularized in the printing process, it may be supposed that he expected the notes in "Pelayo" to receive the same treatment by the publisher as they did in his other works. Pierre seems to have made the same assumption, for in the manuscript he made no revisions to the notes. It thus seems plausible to suppose that Irving regarded the very raggedness of his footnotes as a sign of a partially realized intention for them which, as usual, it was the publisher's part to fulfill. For this reason, the citations of sources are reproduced here from *Spanish Papers* rather than from the manuscript; Irving's own notes are reproduced in the list of Emendations (Emendations 180.38).

A third class of regularization is the enclosing all direct quotations within pairs of double quotation marks. Twenty-one pairs of double quotation marks scattered throughout the manuscript reveal that Irving intended quoted passages to be so designated, but it was again necessary for Pierre and later the printer to impose this convention consistently. Supplying punctuation of the sort was a duty Irving was content during his later career to delegate to others.[392] Pierre correctly interpreted such quotation marks as did appear in the manuscript as indications of an

391. See the following manuscript fragments of the *Life of Washington*: Volume IV, Chapters 4 (Yale University) and 15 (Berg Collection, New York Public Library); Volume V, Chapters 16–25 (Berg Collection, New York Public Library).

392. For example, see the immediately preceding Textual Commentaries for "Washington Allston" (1855) and "Conversations with Talma" (1855).

intention to publish the work in a manner consistent with Irving's other historical narratives, and he saw to it that in *Spanish Papers* the text regularly included the appropriate punctuation. It seems proper to follow his procedure here (see Emendations 185.12), for it constituted the fulfillment of a wish Irving had already realized in part, not a revision contrary to his expressed intention or his practice in other works.

Justified as it may be in the cases of chapter-headings, footnote style, and quotation marks, the notion that an imperfect manuscript text constitutes a warrant to underake wholesale emendaions of all kinds is of course questionable at the best. In general, the safest course is to respect the copy-text, even in its inconsistencies.[393] In the present text some of Irving's mild eccentricities of pointing—for example, his use of the colon simply to mark a pause (191.25), or the semicolon to perform the introductory function of a colon (199.26), or itself merely to mark a pause (188.34)—have thus been preserved. However, the author's casually produced text has not been permitted to assume an authority beyond its intrinsic merit. Commas are supplied to separate the text from direct quotations within it (Emendations 183.23), apostrophes are added to possessive forms (Emendations 187.29), periods and one question mark are inserted at the ends of unpunctuated or inappropriately punctuated sentences (Emendations 183.34, 188.3). Irving tended to neglect punctuating at the ends of lines in the manuscript, apparently observing a kind of mental pause as he prepared to begin the next line but leaving no written record of it; end-of-line punctuation is thus supplied when necessary (Emendations 181.33). Other insertions—most frequently, of commas to complete pairs or to dispel the ambiguities created by Irving's often vague antecedents of pronouns—are reported as they are made. Unless the author's preferences between alternative spellings are clear and decided, variant forms are allowed to stand—thus, "armor" (187.35) and "armour" (192.18). In accordance with his usual practice, civil or religious titles are capitalized if employed as parts of proper names (Emendations 181.7, 181.9) but are given in lower-case forms if used alone, in reference to specific persons (Emendations 181.9, 196.12) An exception to this rule is "Duchess," which on the five occasions when it is used (285.20–43) is invariably capitalized; here Irving's capitalization is permitted to stand.

Where useful, the pre-copy-text sources have been drawn upon as providing early indications of the author's wishes (for example, see Dis-

---

393. The principle operates in reverse for the portion of the "Pelayo" text in which it is necessary to draw upon *Spanish Papers*. The accidentals in the interpolated passage are thoroughly "Putnamized," but being derived from the author's lost manuscript, they do incorporate some of the readings he intended. The number of such readings may well not be increased in the emending of suspicious accidentals in the printed text.

cussions of Adopted Readings 186.20–23). Throughout, the *Spanish Papers* text affords useful evidence of what well informed persons regarded as the author's probable wishes for the completed work. However, even though *Spanish Papers* is often cited in the tables which follow as the textual source for emended readings, each such emendation is made not on the derived authority of *Spanish Papers* but as a responsibility of the present editor.

Limitations of space render it impracticable in the tables which follow to list all of Irving's cancellations and corrections within the copy-text or in general to distinguish between his marks in ink or in pencil. The handwriting of the author is ordinarily easy to distinguish from that of Pierre M. Irving, but the authorship of marks such as pencilled deletions or commas (both especially numerous on pages 23–36 of the copy-text) is often difficult to specify with confidence. Thus all substantive and accidental readings in the manuscript are assumed to be Irving's unless there is at least a distinct possibility that they are Pierre's. All emendations to the copy-text probably or certainly by Pierre are pointed out, but owing to limitations of space their being in pencil, ink or both is not ordinarily noted.[394] Cancellations within the manuscript are set forth if they reveal in an economical manner the textual situation necessitating an editorial decision (for example, Emendations 188.11, 192.8), provide the textual basis for Discussions of Adopted Readings (Emendations 190.18), or pertain to revisions by Pierre.[395] A full list of cancelled passages within the copy-text is on file at the University of Texas.

Unless recorded in the list of Emendations, substantive variants and accidental variants of particular interest between the copy-text and passages in the manuscript and printed texts of "Pelayo and the Merchant's Daughter"—*Knickerbocker Magazine* 65.5–21 It . . . . interwoven. (T 180.8–32) and *Knickerbocker Magazine* 65.42–66.10 The . . . . them. (T 186.20–36)—are set forth in a separate table of Rejected Pre-Copy-Text Variants. Unless recorded in the list of Emendations, substantive variants and accidental variants of particular interest between the copy-text and that in *Spanish Papers* are given in a separate table of Rejected Variants.

In the preparation of this edition the following collations have been made:

1. A typed transcription of the Yale University manuscript of "Pelayo and the Merchant's Daughter," prepared from a xerox copy annotated

394. Pierre M. Irving's handwritten chaper-numbers and chapter-headings, which served as the original copy for the *Spanish Papers* material drawn upon here, are not recorded in the tables which follow as not technically forming parts of the copy-text.

395. Substantive and accidental readings inadvertently left uncancelled in the copy-text are listed in single entries (Emendations 181.2, 188.19).

on the basis of comparisons with the original made twice and independently, collated twice and independently with the text in the *Knickerbocker Magazine* owned by the Legislative Library of Ontario (Periodicals/ first floor);

2. A xerox copy of the above *Knickerbocker Magazine* text sight collated with the following additional copies: University of Delaware (AP 2/ .F 64); New-York Historical Society (PS 1/ .K7); York University (AP 2/ F 64);

3. The xerox copy of the *Knickerbocker Magazine* text collated with the text in *The Evergreen* owned by the New-York Historical Society (PS 1/ .E5);

4. A typed transcription of the University of Virginia manuscript prepared from a xerox copy annotated on the basis of comparisons with the original made twice and independently, collated twice and independently with a xerox copy of a *Spanish Papers* text owned by the University of Texas (Ir8/ SP1/ 1866) and once with a copy owned by the National Library of Canada;

5. The typed transcription of the University of Virginia manuscript collated twice and independently with the text in a copy of *The Spirit of the Fair* owned by Yale University (CC/ 44/ 025) and once with an additional copy: New York Historical Society (E 632/ .N66);

6. The xerox copy of the University of Texas *Spanish Papers* text collated with the xerox copy of the *Knickerbocker Magazine* text (see no. 1);

7. The typed transcription of the University of Virginia manuscript text collated with the above xerox copy of the *Knickerbocker Magazine* text.

See Discussions and Lists pp. 530, 582, 670, 684.

[THE SUCCESSORS OF PELAYO. FAVILA]

The manuscript of Irving's sequel to "The Chronicle of Pelayo" is owned by the University of Virginia. Adopting the format he regularly employed in 1827 for the first drafts of his suite of narratives of early Spain, the author wrote the text on six sheets of cream-colored paper folded at the center so as to form booklets of four pages, each 4⁹⁄₁₆ x 6¾" in size. Pages 1–6 of the ten-page sketch are written on the first sides of the six booklets, which were tucked consecutively within each other at the fold; pages 7–9 and the unnumbered page [10] are written on the third sides of the sixth, fifth, fourth, and third booklets respectively.[396]

396. The reverse side of page 9 includes 6 lines of rejected but uncancelled text; page [10] includes the following 4 lines of cancelled text which pertain not to this narrative but to the one following it—now lost—in Irving's projected series of chronicles: ⟨On the untimely death of/ Favila he was succeeded by/ the husband of his sister Herma-/ -sinda -⟩

All ten pages are written on the right-hand five-eighths of the sheets, leaving wide margins at the left for corrections and insertions.

Because Irving's ink throughout the manuscript is a uniform dark brown and his handwriting reveals no clear evidence of revision at a later date, such alterations as occur were apparently made when the work was first drafted. The scarcity of interlineated corrections—of 32 authorial emendations, only 9 are written above the lines—suggests that Irving revised as he proceeded, entering most of his changes beside rather than above or below the rejected readings. Thus, in one of the lengthiest revisions in the manuscript, he cancelled two sentences totalling 32 words, but then, shortly after beginning a new paragraph, he re-inserted them in slightly revised form.[397] Aside from shiftings and recastings of entire statements such as this, his adjustments were confined to cancellations of false starts at the beginnings of sentences, deletions of superfluous words, as "fresh ⟨and beautiful⟩" (T 201.26), or substitutions of near-synonyms, as "⟨age⟩ ↑time↓" (201.25).

In the process of editing *Spanish Papers* after his uncle's death, Pierre M. Irving made a few additional revisions to the manuscript text, with an eye toward including it in the collection. Using pencil, he re-numbered Irving's pages 1–9 to 63–71, bringing them into sequence with the printer's copy manuscript of "Pelayo." Also in pencil he added the title and subtitle in a blank space at the top of the first page. With characteristic concern for detail, at one point he indicated by underlinings his concern that the word "seen" should be used twice within a single sentence (see 201.34). This supposed problem he did nothing further to solve, but at 2 points elsewhere he wrote brief substantive emendations in pencil (Emendations 200.5, 201.15). And finally, this time in ink, he restored one further word which had been deleted by Irving (Emendations 201.14). The manuscript shows no evidence that it was ever sent to the printer, however; and the absence of re-writings in ink by Pierre over his few pencilled emendations is a clear indication that at some point he decided to withhold it from publication. Probably this change of intention was owing to the bulk of other material already to be included in *Spanish Papers*—for example, the "Chronicle of the Ommiades"—which in his opinion possessed a better claim to the limited space available.

As distinct from Pierre M. Irving's emendations to it, the University of Virginia manuscript is thus adopted as copy-text, being the sole evidence of the author's latest wishes for this work which he did not live to see in print. Owing to limitations of space, in the table which follows

---

397. The following cancelled passage, which occurs in the manuscript at a point corresponding to T 200.18, preceding the new paragraph, may be compared to 200.22–25 It . . . . Moors: ⟨The Moors had made an/ inroad into his territories and/ were retreating with the plun-/ der of the valleys. Favila inst/ -antly took the field with his/ cavaliers, pursued, over-/ took and routed the enemy⟩

cancellations within the copy-text are not ordinarily recorded. Those only are set forth which reveal in short space a textual situation requiring an editorial decision (for example, Emendations 200.40), or which pertain to revisions made by Pierre M. Irving. Pierre's emendations are noted in full, though their being in ink or pencil is not reported. A full list of cancelled passages within the copy-text is on file at the University of Texas.

In general, the accidentals of Irving's manuscript text are respected, with the result that a few slightly unorthodox readings—for example, a long sentence fragment (see Discussions of Adopted Readings 200.10–14) —are reproduced. However, a few emendations of capitalization are made when clearly appropriate (for example, Emendations 200.27, 201.4), end-of-line punctuation omitted in the copy-text is supplied (Emendations 201.7), and other changes are made as required. A single footnote is cast in the Putnam house styling (Emendations 201.40), in conformity with Irving's intention eventually to publish "Favila" as part of the more extensive collection of Spanish narratives which appeared in *Spanish Papers*.

See Discussions and Lists pp. 531, 588.

CHRONICLE OF THE OMMIADES

The "Chronicle of the Ommiades" is the lengthiest of the narratives of early Spanish history which Irving "roughly sketched out" while in Spain in 1827, revised twenty years later, and left unpublished at his death. It is also the one for which his research was least extensive and his subsequent revisions least thorough. Although he mentioned it in April 1847 to Pierre, as among the chronicles which he had in recent weeks made "complete, though not thoroughly finished off," his statement was in this case an exaggeration. In his earliest attentions to the narrative he had not prepared a complete account of the period of history he planned eventually to summarize—the reign of the Ommiades dynasty in Spain from 752 to 1030 A.D.—and in his later revision he gave close attention to only a fraction of the first draft. To have corrected the whole of that work, and then to add the further chapters necessary to realize his original intention, would have entailed hard and continuous labor of a kind quite different from the "amusing occupation" Irving enjoyed when revising his Spanish writings in 1847.[398]

The surviving textual evidence of Irving's earliest work on the "Chronicle of the Ommiades" consists of 313 manuscript pages, bound in three

398. Irving to Pierre M. Irving, Sunnyside, April 16, 1847; PMI, IV, 14–16.

volumes owned by the Columbia University Library; 2 unbound pages
also owned by Columbia University; and an additional page owned by
the University of Virginia. In all, these represent about 85% of the first
draft of the chronicle. Irving's pagination of the manuscript, though
apparently congenial to his working methods, was extremely irregular;
and because after his death the work was set (almost) in order by Pierre,
it will be useful to list here, for reference, the partial scheme of page-
numbering adopted by the author in correlation with the complete one
imposed by his nephew:

Irving's Pagination	Pierre M. Irving's Pagination	Location of Manuscript
[missing]	[1–31 missing]	
1–17	32–49	Columbia Volume I
[missing]	[50–63 missing]	
16–30	64–78	"
31	[no number]	Virginia
32–40	81–89	Columbia Volume I
[missing]	[90, 91 missing]	
3, 4	92, 93 [subsequently renumbered 62, 63]	Columbia Special Collections
No pagination	94–153	Columbia Volume I
No pagination	154, 155, 156/7/8– 229	Columbia Volume II
1–25	230–255	"
26	256	Columbia Volume III
No pagination	257–367	Columbia Volume III

Except as noted, in further references to the early draft Pierre M. Irving's
system of pagination is employed.[399]

Irving wrote his first draft in brown ink on pages of heavy, cream-
colored paper 4⅞″ x 7⅞″ in size. He filled only the right five-eighths of each
page, leaving the wide left margin blank so as to facilitate subsequent
insertions and corrections. This procedure was customary with him at
the time, as was his leaving blank spaces of about 1½″ at the top of pages
which either signified new chapters in his sources or were reserved as
free space where his own chapter-numbers and chapter-headings might

---

399. Irving did adopt a supplementary system not reflected in the above table.
At intervals he wrote an ascending sequence of numbers conspicuously in pencil
in the upper left-hand corners of the manuscript pages. This method of assigning a
single reference number to a gathering of pages—for example, designating pp. 94–102
in Pierre's series by simply writing "18" on the first page—is similar to the one he
employed to arrange his notes for "Fernando the Saint"; see below, pp. 501, 504.

be inserted, or both. The blank spaces occur on 17 pages in the extant fragment.[400]

The composition of the 1827 draft was a smooth process, as is revealed by the infrequency and brevity of cancellations and marginal notes and insertions. Irving had before him Jose Antonio Conde's authoritative *Historia de la Dominación des Arabes en España* (1820–21), and his procedure was essentially to write out a selective translation–paraphrase of appropriate passages in this work.[401] Ordinarily he excluded the portions of Conde's encyclopedic account which detailed events occurring contemporaneously throughout Spain, focusing instead upon passages which traced the careers of the Ommiades themselves. He was faithful to Conde in translating accounts of conversations, although he regularly recast the indirect discourse of the *Historia* into "quoted" interchanges.[402]

400. In the original pagination pp. 32, 64, 70, 75, 31, 94, 139, 146, 159, 180, 194, 200, 220, 227, 254, 292, 298. Pages 94, 146, and 180 also include pencilled identifying numbers, as described in note 399, in their upper left corners.

401. The inclusive pages drawn upon by Irving in Conde's *Historia* are I, 124–494. The Columbia University manuscript of the 1827 draft indicates that in preparing it he did have recourse to other sources besides Conde. For example, in a note concerning the suppression by King Muhamad I of a rebellion by a Moor named Lobea ben Muza, he wrote (p. 116): "This rebel leader of Toledo is called Lobo by/ Mariana, Loth by Bleda; Lope King of Toledo by/ Ambrozio Morales and Lobea ben Muza by the Ara-/ bian writers consulted by Conde." Some of Irving's study notes, consisting chiefly of extracts and digests of narratives, with notations of important names and dates, are extant at Columbia University and in the Berg Collection, New York Public Library.

402. The following parallel texts, recounting an interview between King Hixem, the second of the Ommiades kings, and an astrologer, afford a representative instance of Irving's rendering conversations from the Spanish:

Conde, *Historia*, I, 229	Irving
El año ciento setenta y ocho estando el Rey Hixêm en Cordoba recreándose en sus Almunias y amenos huertos, donde se entretenía en cultivar por su mano algunas floras y plantas, un célebre astrólogo de su corte le dijo: Señor, trabaja en estos breves dias para el tiempo de la eternidad: el Rey le dijo, que por qué le decia aquella sentencia: y el astrólogo le pidió que no le mandase decir otra cosa, que sin pensar lo habia dicho: instóle el Rey que no le ocultase su pensamiento, seguro de que por nada del mundo se disgustaría de lo que le dijese. Entonces el astrólogo le dijo, que estaba escrito en el cielo que Hixêm debia morir antes de dos años.	Hixem was one day ⟨in his gar-/ -den near Cordova⟩ recreating him-/ -self in his pleasant garden near/ Cordova and attending to some/ favorite plants and flowers. A/ famous Astrologer whom he main-/ -tained at his court approached/ him with a gloomy aspect. "Senior/ said he time is short, work/ rather for eternity." The King demanded why he/ addressed to him that sentence./ "I entreat your majesty," replied/ the astrologer to ask me no farther,/ what I have already said was/ uttered in an unguarded moment./ Hixem insisted, upon knowing/ his secret meaning, assuring/ him that nothing he ⟨should⟩ ↑might↓ say/ should cause displeasure. Then/ said the astrologer "Prepare Oh/ Hixem for thy latter

The passages he adapted from the Spanish historian as sayings of his own "Arabian chronicler" were also straightforward translations (for example, see T 232.4–5); but as these supposed quotations suggest, he placed no premium on literal fidelity to his source.

As he wrote out a text in this manner, Irving added four brief notes to himself, one for general reference and three as reminders of material eventually to be inserted. The first, on p. 120, was a pencilled reference to "The rebel family of Hassan" that had played a part in the reign of Muhamad I (852–886 A.D.) which was then under discussion. Perhaps he judged it necessary to include further notice of the rebellion against the king led by Omar Aben Hassan (Conde, Part II, Chapters L, LI, LVI, LXI); but if so, he never did so. The first two of the notations which certainly did serve as reminders of material to be added appear in his account of the later career of Abderahman III (911–963 A.D.). Here, on p. 228, he made a note—"(insert verses)"—that certain lines presented by Conde as addressed to that king, and also verses written by him, should be taken in.[403] On the following page, having narrated the death of Abderahman III, he added a second self-reminder:

> See Compendium
> v. 1 P 251
> review of his reign

The reference is to Jean Baptiste Duchesne's *Abregé de l'histoire d'Espagne* (1741), a popular work which by 1827 had appeared in at least nine Spanish translations, as *Compendio de la Historia de España*. Irving's final note to himself appears on p. 367, the final page. Having recounted the brief reign of Hixem II (976 A.D.), he wrote below:

> See subsequent reigns
> to Hixem III deposed AH 422
> D 1030. He was the last of the
> Ommiades

For some reason, probably owing to other interests, early in 1828 he set aside his incomplete sketch.[404] An account of the Ommiades caliphs whose reigns he had not yet added to the series summarized in the manu-

---

end, for it / is written in the heavens
that/ thou shalt die before two years."
Irving's translation may be further compared to his revised version of the passage, made in 1847 (see T 221.22–32).

403. See Conde, *Historia*, I, 452–53.

404. PMI, II, 277. The date "*Jany 1. 1828*" written on the reverse side of p. 323 of the manuscript, possibly as a dateline for an unwritten letter, indicates approximately the period of Irving's final attentions to the manuscript while in Spain.

script was readily available in Conde, and no doubt he intended at some time to draw further on this convenient authority. However, his occupations during the remainder of his stay in Europe and the first seven years of his renewed residence in the United States precluded a return to the interrupted project. The "Ommiades" manuscript lay in his trunk, as he was later to put it, "like waste paper."[405]

Irving's agreement in 1839 to become a regular contributor to the *Knickerbocker Magazine* afforded him a ready opportunity to supply original articles to Lewis Gaylord Clark, the editor, using bits of his material set aside in this way. The task of supplying copy was not always so easily accomplished, but he took advantage of the situation as fully as he could. Thus "Pelayo and the Merchant's Daughter," a portion of a larger Spanish narrative he had first drafted in 1827, appeared in the *Knickerbocker Magazine* for January 1840. Similarly, a second article entitled "Abderahman: Founder of the Dynasty of the Ommiades in Spain," appeared in the issue for May of the same year (XV, 427–40).

The magazine text of "Abderahman" was introduced by a letter to the editor, signed "G.C.," in which Irving compared the protagonist of his sketch to "our own WASHINGTON" and acknowledged that in recounting the career of the monarch he had "conformed to the facts furnished by the Arabian chroniclers, as cited by the learned Conde." The fact that the first pages of the 1827 draft of the "Chronicle of the Ommiades"—pages 1–31 in Pierre's pagination—are missing from the extant manuscript suggests that in preparing his article Irving made practical use of the original narrative he had written concerning Abderahman.[406] At any rate the printer's copy manuscript of the article, which is owned by the Hispanic Society of America, clearly never formed part of the author's early draft. It seems likely that, as he was to do in 1847 with chapters of the "Chronicle" recounting reigns subsequent to that of Abderahman, Irving first entered revisions in the left margins of the missing pages, then used the revised manuscript as a basis for a new draft written on fresh sheets of paper. Notations on several pages in the Hispanic Society manuscript, such as "Greenburgh Jany 29th 1840/ Dear Sir," on the reverse side of p. 42, lend weight to this speculation. The text is written in a consistent shade of dark brown ink, ordinarily on one side of 49 sheets of paper, chiefly of two varieties: light blue woven linen, and white, lightly lined unlaid paper. However, 3 pages (12, 23, 37) consist of pasted slips of paper of other varieties, and 3

405. Irving to Pierre M. Irving, Sunnyside, April 16, 1847; PMI, IV, 15.
406. At least, he must have had it at hand. Pierre's subsequent numbering of the extant portions of the 1827 draft, beginning at p. 32, seems to indicate that pp. 1–31 of the original version were available to him then.

others (37, 38, 39) are written on the reverse sides of mailing envelopes.[407] In short, the completed manuscript was an inelegant patchwork of the spare paper Irving had on hand.

Yet however motley the varieties of paper he used, the author did not prepare the *Knickerbocker Magazine* text of "Abderahman" in an especially casual manner. On the contrary, the pattern of cancellations and revisions within the manuscript reveals that he wrote his text with reasonable care. The great majority of his adjustments were minor, such as the addition of modifiers or the substitution of alternative words or phrases. A representative instance occurs at a point corresponding to 439.9–10 in the *Knickerbocker Magazine* (T 216.17): he altered "great and persevering magnanimity" to "noble and repeated magnanimity." In his more extensive revisions a pattern is evident, of cancelling extraneous matter when feasible and of condensing the text that remained. Thus, although 10 sentences were entirely recast, without especial regard to their length, in 11 other instances a desire for economy was clearly a motivation.[408] In revising the manuscript text he added only a single sentence—see *Knickerbocker Magazine* 431.37–38 Abderahman . . . Zenetes (T 207.3–5)—but he deleted 2, one of them of considerably greater length than the insertion.[409] In its substantive readings at least, the "Abderahman" manuscript Irving turned over to Lewis Gaylord Clark represented his matured intentions for the text; not, that is, as a fragment of an unpublished work, but as a biographical narrative complete in itself.

407. Most but not all of the blue and beige pages vary only slightly in size between 4 7/8 x 7 3/4" and 4 7/8 x 8": pages 16, 16 [2], and 25 are written on shorter slips of paper. Irving neglected to assign numbers to the pages following pp. 16 and 25 in the manuscript; he also omitted a p. 45 from his series.

408. For example, introducing the melancholy verses said to have been addressed by Abderahman to a palm-tree—see Conde, *Historia*, I, 169–70—he first wrote, "The following/ is ⟨The⟩ a ⟨rude⟩ ↑rude but literal translation↓ of them/ as they have been rendered from the Arabic/ into the Spanish"; but he subsequently added a colon after "translation" and deleted the remainder of the statement as unnecessary. See *Knickerbocker Magazine* 434.20–21; T 210.42.

409. This cancelled passage is of particular interest, for by drawing attention to the birth of Abderahman's successor, Hixem, it opens up the dimension of the future course of the Ommiades dynasty in an explicit way not evident elsewhere in the article. It may thus have been a passage derived from Irving's original draft of the "Chronicle" but omitted from the *Knickerbocker Magazine* article as not pertaining to it. The cancelled passage occurs at a point preceding 433.49 in the magazine text (T 210.20):

⟨Fortune appeared willing to make/ amends to the youthful sovreign for all his past afflictions. The Sultana Howara,/ whom he had espoused shortly after his arriv/ arrival in Spain, and whom he loved with/ impassioned tenderness, gave birth to a/ son, whom he named Hixem. Rejoiced/ at an event that promised prosperity to/ his line and honors, he dispensed/ bounteous gifts to the people on the occasion,/ and the whole nation testifyed their/ sympathy in his public rejoicings⟩

By May 1840, it is true, Irving and Clark had developed a working relationship which entailed the entensive revision by the editor of the accidentals in the author's manuscripts—even on occasion of the substantive readings. However much care Irving might devote to a major article such as "Abderahman," he was already fatigued with his duties as a magazinist, and he invariably left to Clark the final editing of his contributions. Accordingly, using his accustomed sky-blue ink on pages 1–17 and 30–47 of the manuscript and dark brown ink on pages 18–29,[410] Clark prepared the article for the printer. In addition to writing clarifications of Irving's handwriting, paragraph divisions, carets, guidelines to indicate the placement of interlineated material, and marginal notations as to type-styles, he rendered the accidentals in the manuscript more complete and consistent, imposing on the text a partial overlay of the *Knickerbocker Magazine*'s dense style of punctuation. Thus he regularized the erratic quotation marks in Irving's text and made 161 other emendations of punctuation. Of the latter, fully 130 were added commas; 13 others were commas converted to semicolons, and only 1 comma was deleted. Clark freely altered Irving's accidentals in other ways, including 11 changes in capitalization, 2 in paragraphing, and 27 in spelling. In revising the substantives, however, he was much less cavalier. Besides supplying a general title, "The Crayon Papers," which linked the article to others published by Irving in the *Knickerbocker Magazine*, he made only 9 substantive emendations, all but 1 of which involved single words in the manuscript.[411] Clark's revisions were consistent in character with his attentions to the manuscript copy for Irving's other *Knickerbocker Magazine* articles.

Clark did not mark the manuscript text of "Abderahman" exhaustively but left further revisions, identical in kind with those he had entered, to be made either by the printer, or possibly by himself at the proof stage. Thus the *Knickerbocker Magazine* text of the article includes numerous readings without precedent in the printer's copy manuscript.[412] These changes included further insertions and adjustments of quotation marks and 154 other changes of punctuation. Of those, 71 were added commas and 3 were semicolons converted to commas; only 11 commas were deleted. Other emendations of accidentals included 17 changes in

410. Clark's editorial revisions on pp. 18–29 are difficult to distinguish from Irving's own text. Notations of doubtful authorship are ascribed here to Irving.

411. For Clark's substantive emendations of the manuscript text, all of which were incorporated in the *Knickerbocker Magazine* version, see Emendations 205.42, 206.34, 215.41; Rejected Variants 202.17, 202.21, 203.32, 209.32, 212.29, 212.31.

412. The use of the manuscript as printer's copy is indicated by a pencilled bracket to the left of the word "There" on p. 19, followed by the notation "p. 433–57"; p. 433 of the printed article begins at this point. Faint smudge marks appear throughout the manuscript at intervals.

capitalization, 58 in spelling, and 1 alteration of type-style. Substantive revisions of the printer's copy were relatively few and minor. Eleven substantive variants appeared, all limited to single words.[413] The *Knickerbocker Magazine* text of "Abderahman," which incorporated most but not all of Clark's revisions to the manuscript, represented a pervasive but often necessary departure from Irving's accidentals and a cautious and on the whole responsible revision of the substantive readings in his text. The published article thus represented his own imperfectly expressed wishes for the work as realized, yet also modified, by at least one other hand.[414]

Having expended considerable effort in preparing "Abderahman" for publication in 1840, with characteristic resourcefulness Irving made use of the published text when he began revising the "Chronicle of the Ommiades" as a whole, in 1847. Rather than drafting a new account of Abderahman's reign on the basis of the manuscript he had submitted to Clark (which may or may not have been returned), or of the portions of the 1827 version pertaining to that monarch, so far as possible he prepared the introductory portion of the revised "Chronicle" using printed copy. The evidence of his revision of the magazine text survives in 20 pages, in part emended sheets and in part freshly written manuscript pages, owned by the Berg Collection, New York Public Library. In this draft Irving divided the article into three chapters, each of which he prepared in a somewhat different way. It will thus be useful to review his changes chapter-by-chapter.

After ripping the appropriate pages from a copy of the *Knickerbocker Magazine*, Irving revised his first chapter by writing cancellations, substitutions, and additions in ink on pages 427–31 of the printed text, which he did not bother to renumber. He deleted the introductory letter from "G.C." (427.1–17) and in addition the title of the article, supplying in its place the general title "Chronicle of the Ommiades." In the pages that followed he added a comma, corrected 2 spellings, and made

413. For the substantive variants between the manuscript text as corrected by Clark and the *Knickerbocker Magazine* text see Emendations 202.14, 203.21, 212.21; Rejected Variants 202.22, 202.23, 209.14, 211.3, 211.39, 213.17, 214.44, 217.37.

414. The *Knickerbocker Magazine* text of "Abderahman" was reprinted in the various editions of *The Crayon Papers* which appeared beginning in 1883. The text in the edition published by J. B. Alden (New York, 1883), pp. 299–324, reveals no substantive variants from the magazine version except the deletion of a line, "BY THE AUTHOR OF THE SKETCH-BOOK," and an obvious misprint (434.34 facillty for facility). Spot-collations of the Alden text with those in later editions of *The Crayon Papers* published by J. Lovell (New York, [1883]), pp. 161–79, by Millar (New York, 1884), pp. 161–79, and by William L. Allison (New York, n.d.), pp. 161–79, reveal no substantive variants. However, spellings altered in the Alden edition from the *Knickerbocker Magazine* are reproduced in the later editions. No edition of *The Crayon Papers* carries textual authority.

substantive changes—2 of which involved single words, 1 the insertion of 8 words, and the fourth the recasting of 4 sentences at the beginning of a paragraph.[415] Although it is clear he intended the first revised chapter to conclude with "lamentations" at 431.36 in the *Knickerbocker Magazine text* (T 206.43), he did not bother to cancel either the remainder of that page or the greater part of p. 432, which was also to be superseded.

In writing his second chapter, which was to substitute for the passages from 431.37 to 432.26 in the *Knickerbocker Magazine* (T 207.1–208.27), Irving revised the printed text more thoroughly than he had the passages preceding it. This chapter he wrote out in ink on one side of sheets of unlaid, unlined paper 5½ x 8⅜″ in size, numbered 1–5. Except for a single condensation of a sentence and a single transposition of two others,[416] in the portions of the revised chapter which do include material derived from the magazine text Irving simply rephrased his statements. For example, in the *Knickerbocker Magazine* he had written: "A civil war was the consequence, and Spain was deluged with blood" (431.52–432.1). The corresponding statement in the revision (see T 207.40–41) is "↑An insurrection and↓ ⟨A⟩a civil war was the consequence; and ↑the country↓/ ⟨Spain was deluged with blood⟩ ↑⟨the country⟩ was laid waste with fire and sword↓." The fluency with which Irving re-wrote this chapter—the 5 manuscript pages include only 16 cancellations, all pertaining to minor adjustments of syntax and word choice—was no doubt owing in part to his adopting a narrative sequence virtually identical to that in the magazine text. However, at 3 points he did interpolate new material gleaned from a fresh inspection of Conde's *Historia*: a paragraph detailing the strange portents observed by the Arabs at about the time of Abderahman's landing in Spain (T 208.3–7), and 2 expanded discussions of the political dissensions amongst the Arabs during that period.[417] The second chapter of the revised "Abderahman" provided a considerably more thorough account of the civil order in Spain at the outset of the Ommiades dynasty than Irving had included in his magazine article.

Although he did not write a chapter-number or chapter-heading at the top of the manuscript page beginning his description of the exploits

415. For Irving's substantive emendations see Emendations 202.9–10, 202.18–19, 204.3–10 (inclusive), 205.28.

416. For the condensation, compare *Knickerbocker Magazine* 431.52–432.5 with T 207.40–208.2; for the transposition, compare *Knickerbocker Magazine* 432.10–15 with T 208.11–15.

417. The corresponding original and expanded passages may be compared in the following texts: *Knickerbocker Magazine* 431.40–42, T 207.6–16; *Knickerbocker Magazine* 431.48–52, T 207.21–39. The source of the interpolations is Conde, *Historia*, I, 137–45.

of Abderahman after his arrival in Spain (*Knickerbocker Magazine* 432.27–440.35—corresponding to T 208.33–218.2), Irving left a two-inch blank space above his text, indicating an intention eventually to do so. On this unnumbered page, identical in size and variety of paper with those which comprised the second chapter, he wrote out 10 lines almost duplicating the corresponding magazine text (432.27–33 Abderahman . . . . Spain!—corresponding to T 208.33–39). However, tiring of needless transcription, on the next line he wrote out the first seven words of the succeeding paragraph in the magazine article and beneath them the direction: "Take in at printed page 432 * –." He then wrote another asterisk in the left margin of printed page 432, added a guideline to make clear the point at which the printed text was to resume its function as copy for the revised "Chronicle," and used the *Knickerbocker Magazine* article, whose pages he again did not renumber, as his text for the remainder of the chapter. He made only one further substantive emendation, a deletion of a single word (see Emendations 209.24), before turning his attention to the lengthy manuscript which followed, recounting the deeds of Abderahman's successors.

Irving's revision of the original account of Hixem, Abderahman's son, may have included 2 one-word changes to the 1827 draft, but these were only preliminaries (if indeed he had not written them in 1827). The final version of this chapter, extant at Johns Hopkins University, is a thorough re-writing of the original, not one sentence of which went unrevised. The Johns Hopkins manuscript, which consists of 11 pages numbered by Irving 21–31, is written in ink on one side of sheets of unlaid, unlined paper identical in size and texture with those which had comprised the second chapter and the first page of the third in the revised version of "Abderahman." At the center of a 2-inch blank space on p. 21 it includes as a chapter title the name "*Hixem.*" Although at one point the revised text indicates a recurrence to Conde and at another to a different source— or possibly to Irving's general knowledge,[418] the 1827 version of this chapter, pp. 32–49 as renumbered by Pierre, is otherwise identical in substance with the revision. One difference in conception is that, whereas in the early draft Irving had simply translated certain philosophical reflections in the *Historia*, at 3 points in the 1847 version he explicitly cites "the Arabian chronicler" as the source of the comments. One of these citations forms part of a passage which typifies the variety of revision

---

418. The phrases "in the seventh year of his reign" have no precedent in the first draft; see Conde, *Historia*, I, 231. The brief paragraph identifying "Alphonso the Chaste" (T 220.32–35) has no precedent either in the 1827 draft or in Conde. However, Irving had written an unpublished narrative dealing in part with this individual, entitled "Alonzo the Chaste and Alonzo the Catholic." The manuscript of that early draft is owned by the University of Virginia.

he made most frequently—on 18 occasions—to his early draft, a simple recasting or rephrasing of a sentence:

1827 Manuscript Text	1847 Manuscript Text
During the civil wars among the/ true believers the Christians had/ regained possession of many cities/ formerly taken from them in/ the north of Spain and the/ Southern provinces of France. To/ reconquer these and restore them/ to the dominion of the true faith,/ Hixem ordered in the fifth year/ of his reign that an algihed/ or holy war should be publish/ -ed throughout his dominions.	During these lamentable wars and dissensions/ among true believers, says the Arabian/ chronicler, the Christians had regained possession/ of many cities in the north of Spain and the/ southern provinces of France. To regain these/ Hixem ⟨ordere⟩ ordered that an Algihed or holy/ war should be proclaimed, ⟨throughout his/ dominions⟩ on the same day and the same hour/ from the Khatib or pulpit of every mosque/ throughout his dominions.[419]

At 3 points Irving added new sentences,[420] but on 5 others he deleted sentences in the early draft, parts of whose contents were implied or made explicit in their immediate contexts,[421] and on 5 more he considerably abbreviated his original statements.[422] His 1847 account of King Hixem was a leaner, more incisive narrative than the one from which it was derived.

The following chapter, which recounts the beginning of the reign of Alhakem, successor to Hixem, is also extant in revised form at Johns Hopkins University. Its subject-matter probably corresponds closely to Irving's original account, but comparison between the two versions is impossible since pp. 50–63 of the 1827 draft—those superseded by the revision—are missing. The physical similarity between the manuscript of

419. See T 220.14–19. The two other citations of "the Arabian chronicler" in the 1847 manuscript correspond to T 218.8, 218.22.

420. These three sentences correspond to T 218.26–27 Hixem . . . war, 219.34 Seek . . . distinction, and 220.32–35 The . . . it.

421. For example, describing in the early draft a ferocious attack upon the city of Narbonne, Irving wrote: "Terror was ⟨sp⟩/ spread throughout the southern/ regions of france at this sudden/ irruption from the mountains./ The affrighted inhabitants aban-/ doned their habitations and/ fled into the interior or hid/ themselves in caves and/ secret places." In the revision the entire first sentence was omitted; see T 220.39–40. Irving's four other deletions occurred at points in the 1847 manuscript corresponding to T 219.8 following "Tagus."; 219.42 preceding " 'Hard!'"; 220.6 preceding "Hixem"; and 220.24 preceding "The."

422. The condensed sentences in the revised version correspond to T 218.18–19 The . . . tempests; 218.30–34 Seeing . . . surrender; 219.22–24 The . . . mountains; 219.40–41 He . . . fugitives; 221.12–14 He . . . gardens.

this revised chapter and the one preceding it suggests nonetheless that Irving was guided by principles similar to those evident in his preparation of the Hixem chapter. The text, which includes only 12 cancellations, involving adjustments in syntax, substitutions of near synonyms, and the placement of 2 passages, 32 and 34 words in length, is written in ink, invariably on one side of 9 pages identical in size and variety of paper with those in the preceding revised chapter. Irving numbered the first page 50, as if to follow p. 49 in the 1827 draft, but then he substituted 32, bringing it into sequence with his revised pagination; but he neglected to assign numbers to the next 8 pages. He did not write a chapter-title or chapter-number on page 32, but a blank space of almost 3″ at the top of that page reveals his intention eventually to do so. A reference to "the Arabian chronicler" in the first sentence of the new chapter suggests a return to Conde,[423] but the manuscript affords no further evidence of the manner in which it was altered from the missing earlier version.

Thus far in rewriting his "Chronicle" Irving had worked with smooth assurance. As his fitful numbering of pages, his providing no footnotes and only occasional chapter-titles, and his indicating material to be inserted from the *Knickerbocker Magazine* merely by writing a conspicuous asterisk in his copy of that magazine article all suggest, he cut corners wherever he could. He now adopted a method of revision still less time-consuming than the one he had followed for the two previous chapters: using the same dark brown ink he had employed in making those revisions, beginning on p. 64 of the original draft he simply emended that text rather than writing out a new version. Pages 64–78, the unrenumbered p. 31, and pp. 81–89, 92–93 of the 1827 manuscript are therefore dense with cancellations, substitutions, and additions. The greater part of these changes are condensations of the earlier text, which are made at 28 points, or outright deletions, which occur at 12. In contrast, only 11 statements are expanded from the earlier draft, and only 6 are without any precedent there. However, despite his effort to streamline the passages to be retained, Irving's additions to the manuscript easily exceeded in length his deletions. At five points he drew further upon Conde to insert passages 15, 24, 39, 131, and 146 words in length, containing material not included in the earlier version;[424] the latter of these occupied the entire left margin of one manuscript page and spilled over onto the next (pp. 68, 69). Irving wrote his revisions in the left margins

423. See T 222.15–16; however, a Spanish equivalent of the saying does not occur in the corresponding passage of the *Historia*, I, 232.

424. In the order specified, the five inserted passages correspond to T 228.39–40 That . . . city; 230.21–22 The . . . rebuilt; 231.34–36 At . . . recreation; 228.12–23 but . . . account; 226.18–30 Soon . . . opposition. In the same order, the pages in Conde's *Historia* from which the inserted passages are derived are as follows: I, 246, 255, 256, 245, 242.

at 16 other points, often but not always supplying guidelines to indicate their proper placement. The result was a patchwork of original and re-worked material comprising a new version prepared according to the same principles he had followed in writing new drafts of the two previous chapters, but revised in a less thoroughgoing manner.[425] Blank spaces at the tops of pages 64, 70, and 75 indicate the author's intention to begin new chapters at these points, and it is virtually certain that the missing page 90 was also blank at the top.[426]

Having completed his revised accounts of Abderahman, Hixem, and Alhakem, the first three monarchs of the Ommiades line, Irving revised the remainder of the 1827 manuscript in a much more cursory fashion. Between pages 94 and 153 only 22 pages in the manuscript include re-visions in their left margins, and not all these changes clearly derive from 1847. The three pages subsequently numbered by Pierre M. Irving 154, 155, 156/7/8 are written across their full width in dark ink, as are pp. 168 and 169; these are all presumably revised versions of discarded portions of the original draft.[427] After p. 169, however, Irving wrote in-sertions in the left margins of only 37 pages; and of those, 14 were probably added in 1827 rather than twenty years later. In sum, he gave careful attention to slightly less than one-third the length of the original "Ommiades" narrative, revised the next one-sixth only cursorily, and the remaining one-half almost not at all. Whatever the specific reasons for his setting the work aside in 1847, however, Irving must have recognized in doing so that the revision, research, and composition still before him would require far more time and energy than he then had to spare. Quite likely he left the "Chronicle" with the thought that, as he wrote to Pierre, it could be "put ... by to be dressed off at leisure."[428]

During the remainder of his lifetime Irving did not return to the "Chronicle of the Ommiades," and thus, as his literary executor, Pierre inherited in 1859 a mass of manuscript, some of which it would possibly

425. It should be noted, however, that in the absence of pp. 50–63 in the early draft, a thorough comparative analysis of Irving's processes of revision is not possible.

426. Page 89 of the 1827 manuscript includes only 6 lines of text, its bottom three-quarters being left blank, as to end a chapter. Pierre M. Irving subsequently re-numbered the narrative unit ending on p. 89 "Chap VIII"; at the top of p. 94 of the early draft he wrote in pencil "Chap X-" It follows that the mising p. 90 must have begun a new chapter which Pierre numbered "IX." Since Pierre wrote a chapter-number and chapter-heading on no other page which did not include a blank space at its top, it seems likely that p. 90 would have included such a space.

427. Pages 154, 155, 156/7/8 describe the results of a rebellion against King Almondhir, who reigned 275–300 A.H. (891–916 A.D.). Pages 168–69 recount a victory in battle by his successor, King Abdallah, who reigned 300–350 A.H. (916–966 A.D.); page 170, which is cancelled, includes information which overlaps with that on the two preceding pages.

428. Irving to Pierre M. Irving, Sunnyside, April 14, 1847; PMI, IV, 16.

be his responsibility to prepare for the press. One of his first undertakings, therefore, was in all probability to renumber in ink the surviving
portions of the 1827 manuscript (see above, pp. 470–72). As was customary
with him, in the course of reviewing Irving's early draft he made various
notations on it in pencil. From these pencilled markings it would appear
that he studied the portions of the narrative up to p. 93 with much
greater care than those which followed. Quite possibly, indeed, he read
through the initial segment of the work with a copy of Conde at hand,
for his 7 alterations of proper names as spelled by Irving all bring them
into conformity with the usages of the Spanish historian. On pp. 64, 70,
and 75 Pierre added chapter-numbers and chapter-headings, and finally
he wrote several of the minor emendations that consistently characterized
his activities as an editor. For example, on p. 93 he added pairs of asterisks and daggers at points in the text where Irving had included footnotes, and he slightly revised the format of a citation in one of the notes
(see Emendations 231.36, 231.38–39, 232.5, 232.6).

Pierre's pencilled marks in the manuscript following p. 93 are few,
but the notation *"Almondhir - / Chap XV"* at the top of p. 146 suggests
that, having taken the trouble to count the chapters thus far, he may at
one point have considered including about one-half of the narrative. If
so, he soon dismissed the idea. The further evidence of his review of
these later passages, pp. 94–367, is a scattered assortment of carets, clarifications of Irving's handwriting, 7 spelling changes, and 8 changes of
substantive readings. Pierre's study of the early draft from beginning
to end was probably done for the sake of thoroughness alone.

Since, as he put it in an editorial note written for publication in
Spanish Papers, the accounts of Abderahman, Hixem, and Alhakem were
"all that would seem to bear the impress of/ ⟨a final⟩ ↑some↓ preparation
for the press,"[429] Pierre edited this segment of the "Chronicle" for the
printer. He began with the corrected copy of the *Knickerbocker Magazine* "Abderahman" by assigning the numbers 1–6 to the pages of Irving's
first chapter,[430] 7–11 to the second, and 13–20 to the third (the first page
of the third chapter he left unnumbered). As usual, he first read through
these chapters entering marks in pencil, then wrote over the more important of them in ink, at the same time adding further emendations in
ink. His editing of the revised article consisted primarily of correlating
the printed and the handwritten texts as Irving had indicated an intention
to do, entering corrections of spelling identical with those Irving had

429. Pierre M. Irving, "The Chronicle of the Ommiades" (Special Collections,
Columbia University).

430. Later, having pasted a portion of p. 432 of the *Knickerbocker Magazine* into
the position Irving had indicated as his wish, Pierre cancelled the remainder of the
printed page, cancelled its page-number "6," and renumbered the preceding page
of revised magazine copy "5–6."

made once, correcting misprints, and writing a chapter-number and chapter-headings.

His preparation of the revised account of King Hixem was even less elaborate; and his revisions of the following chapter (the first of those dealing with King Alhakem and the latter of the two which in 1847 Irving had rewritten) were also minor. Readying the first five chapters of the "Chronicle" for the printer had thus been a simple process; but when Pierre reached the passages Irving had revised by entering his often extensive and nearly illegible emendations directly onto the manuscript of the first draft, he faced a more challenging task. He decided that instead of attempting to use these already confusing pages as printer's copy by adding to them marks and directions of his own, the wiser course was to prepare fresh texts. Accordingly, using laid paper 5½ x 8¼" in size, he wrote out in ink a transcription of pages 64–89 of Irving's revised first draft. The greater part of Pierre's transcribed pages has survived, some owned by Johns Hopkins University, some by the Berg Collection, New York Public Library. For convenient reference, the page-numbers of the extant portions of this manuscript are listed below as they correspond to those in the early version:

Revised 1827 Draft	Pierre M. Irving's Transcription	Location
64–69	Chapter VI, 41–45	Johns Hopkins
70–74	Chapter VII, 46–48	Johns Hopkins
75–78	Chapter VIII, 49–51	Berg Collection
31	″ , [pages 52, 53 are missing]	
81–89	″ , 54–58	Johns Hopkins
	″ , 59	Berg Collection.[431]

Pages 41–51 and 54–59 in Pierre's recopied text reveal numerous variants from Irving's manuscript. These include 41 emendations of spelling—18 of which are impositions of "Alhakim" for the name which, following Conde, Irving had usually spelled "Alhakem"; 15 changes of capitalization, and 56 of punctuation.[432] The transcribed passages incorporate all the

431. It should be noticed that the unrenumbered p. 31 in the early draft includes material not present in Pierre's transcription, but that p. 54 of the latter manuscript begins in mid-sentence (T 229.15 by) continuing a statement obviously begun on p. 31. This may suggest that pp. 52, 53 of the transcribed manuscript, listed above as "missing," were in fact never written: that Pierre, recognizing a hiatus between the renumbered pp. 78 and 81 of the early version, estimated its length as 2 pages, and hence in his transcription left an appropriate space between pp. 51 and 54. Page 31 in the 1827 draft fits neatly between 78/51 and 81/54; perhaps it was overlooked by Pierre when he attempted to set the manuscript in order.

432. As an indication of the divergence between his own habits of punctuating and the styling in *Spanish Papers*, it is interesting to note that while Pierre added

emendations Pierre had entered in pencil on the first draft, with the sole exception of an erroneous one-word "correction" he evidently recognized to be ill-advised (see Emendations 230.28). Finally, the recopied chapters include 6 substantive variations from Irving's text. Of these, 5 involve changes to single words, and all 5 are of at best questionable necessity.[433] The sixth, on the final page of the transcription, represents for Pierre a departure from his habitual practice of permitting passages to stand when they could be mended by the alteration or insertion of a word or two. Irving had written that, having demolished the southern suburb of Cordova, Alhakem "left to/ his successors a solemn prohibi/ -tion to restore it, but to suffer/ it to remain an open field" (see T 231.15–16). Pierre first copied this statement exactly, but on second thought he revised it as follows: ". . . left to his successors a solemn prohibi-/ tion to restore it, ⟨but to suffer it to remain an⟩ ↑commanding that it should remain an↓/ ⟨open field⟩ ↑open field↓." Though unusual in its length, the six-word substitution is a characteristic expression of Pierre's concern for clarity and his consequent distrust of elliptical and possibly ambiguous expressions.

Irving had not extensively revised the two extant pages of the ninth chapter in the early draft, relating the horrible death of Alhakem; and so to prepare them for the press Pierre merely re-re-numbered them in ink 62 and 63 (from 92 and 93), adding no further revisions to those he had already made in pencil. The nine chapters of the revised "Chronicle of the Ommiades"—the three of "Abderahman," the two rewritten ones pertaining to Hixem and Alhakem, the three transcribed ones recounting the further career of Alhakem, and the final brief account of the death of that king—were thus ready for publication in *Spanish Papers*. As an explanatory introduction to the narrative thus pieced together, Pierre wrote an editorial note which began and ended as follows:

[Th⟨is⟩e ↑following Chronicle↓ is a fragment, including only the reigns/ of Abderahman, the Founder of the Dynasty/ of the Om-

---

13 commas, he also deleted 13, producing a text considerably less dense in punctuation than those published by George Putnam. It may also be pointed out, as an indication of Irving's carelessness in punctuating his revised manuscript, that 13 of Pierre's emendations of accidentals involved supplying periods at points where the author had included either inappropriate punctuation or none at all.

433. Irving's own readings, the substantive emendations in Pierre's transcriptions, and the corresponding T page-line numbers appear below:

Washington Irving	Pierre M. Irving	T
harrassing	by harassing	226.10
of the	of	229.1
depths	depth	230.8
one	sole	230.20
seas	deep	230.41

miades in Spain, and his successors/ Hixem and Alhakim./ .../
The three reigns here presented take in a/ period of 66 years from
755 to 821, and/ give pictures of the foundation of the Moorish/
empire in Spain, when Cordova use [sic]/ to be the capital, and its
famous mosque/ was commenced and completed — In these/
Memoirs the author "has conformed to the/ facts furnished by the
Arabian chroniclers, as/ cited by the learned Conde." Ed][434]

A conspicuous pencilled "III" on the manuscript indicates that the
"Chronicle" was to appear as the third item in *Spanish Papers*, following
the contents of *Legends of the Conquest of Spain* and "The Legend
of Pelayo."

Printers' signatures, smudges, and reference marks scattered throughout the extant portions of the manuscript submitted by Pierre to Putnam
indicate that the work was set in type—at least through Pierre's page 58,
where the last such mark appears.[435] Pencilled notations by Pierre on the
reverse sides of pp. 31 and 40 indicate that, perhaps while reading proofs,
he was keeping an anxious eye upon the length of the "Chronicle." The
first of these, "7 in print," is probably an indication of the length in
print of the chapter just completed. The second note is a calculation:

$$20$$
$$26$$
$$\overline{}$$
46 print thus far

As it appeared in *Spanish Papers*, I, [247]–73, "Abderahman" was 26
pages in length. The above sum thus included that text plus the two
chapters following it in the page-proofs Pierre had before him. Probably
the figure, which did not include the four latter chapters of the fragment
—the complete text would have run to at least 70 pages—was not at all
satisfactory. At any rate, when *Spanish Papers* was published the "Chronicle" did not include accounts of the reigns of Hixem and Alhakem, parts
of which Pierre had given himself such trouble to prepare.

Introduced by a suitably revised editorial comment on its relation to
the unfinished "Chronicle,"[436] the *Spanish Papers* text of "Abderahman"

434. Pierre M. Irving, "The Chronicle of the Ommiades" (Special Collections,
Columbia University). The remainder of Pierre's introduction consists almost entirely of a quotation from Irving's introduction to the account of Abderahman published in the *Knickerbocker Magazine*.

435. In addition to ink smudges and various reference marks, the "Abderahman"
copy includes pencilled signatures by two printers—"Nelson" and "Hall" (2), and
the initials in blue pencil of a third, "J. S. G." Irving's revised chapters IV and V
include smudge marks and two signatures, one by "Nelson" and one by "J.S.G."
Pierre's transcriptions include ink smudges and two signatures, one by "J.S.G." and
one on p. 57 by "Hall."

436. See *Spanish Papers*, I, [245]. Pierre's pencilled notes for this new preface are
extant on 2 pages owned by Columbia University.

was an essentially faithful reproduction of the printer's copy, except as modified by the Putnam house style.[437] For example, among the changes of punctuation, 45 commas were added, 65 deleted (the *Knickerbocker Magazine* style of punctuating was even more dense than that of Putnam), and 2 were altered to semicolons. Initial lower-case letters were on 11 occasions altered to capitals, and initial capitals were emended to lower-case on 14; spelling was altered 31 times. Setting aside the regularization of chapter-numbers and chapter-headings, only 5 substantive variants occurred between the revised "Abderahman" text and that in *Spanish Papers*: the deletion of Irving's general title and 4 emendations of single words.[438] The *Spanish Papers* text was clearly derived from no copy other than Irving's extant revision of the *Knickerbocker Magazine* text.

Having traced the textual history of the "Chronicle of the Ommiades," it is now necessary, first, to specify those passages among the manuscripts which, though in Irving's phrase "not thoroughly finished off," may yet be considered sufficiently "complete" to warrant being included in an edition of his writings; second, to specify for those sections the appropriate copy-text. The "complete" sections of the fragmentary narrative are clearly those to which the author gave close attention when he revised a part of his early draft in 1847: the accounts of Abderahman, Hixem, and Alhakem. After p. 93 of the early draft Irving's revisions in dark ink were infrequent, and excepting the re-written pages 154, 155, 156/7/8 and 168–69, cursory. Whether he lost interest, or felt hurried after laboriously re-working the first one-third of the narrative, his subsequent revisions reveal neither the persistent concern for streamlining nor the attempts to render the narrative more detailed which characterize the revisions through p. 93.

The combined details of his study of the "Ommiades" manuscripts and preparation of a portion of them for the press reveal that, on the whole, Pierre M. Irving performed his duties as Irving's literary executor with perspicuity and tact, displaying a sure sense of his uncle's wishes. However, in selecting a copy-text for the present edition it is fundamental that, as transcribed or revised by Pierre after the death of the author, manuscript texts possess no independent textual authority. It follows that the fragmentary "Chronicle" presented here must be based upon Irving's own latest attentions to the work: in general, that is, those of 1847, regarded as distinct from the additions subsequently made to them by Pierre.

In the case of the "Abderahman" section (T 202.2–218.2), the result of Irving's latest effort is of course his revision, elaboration, and division into three chapters of the *Knickerbocker Magazine* article, extant as a

437. See the Textual Commentary, I, 273–76.
438. See Emendations 208.10, 208.10, 213.24; Rejected Variants 208.10.

combination of corrected printed copy and holograph manuscript in the Berg Collection, New York Public Library. The *Spanish Papers* text, which is derived solely from this document as corrected by Pierre, is of interest as the product of an enlightened collaboration between Irving's nephew and trusted publisher, but it carries only a secondary, derived authority. But on the other hand, the printer's copy manuscript of "Abderahman" submitted by Irving for publication in the *Knickerbocker Magazine* is of primary importance for establishing a critical text of the first and third of these chapters. As distinct from the two stages of revision, by Lewis Gaylord Clark and perhaps another person, which resulted in its publication in 1840, the Hispanic Society manuscript embodies the latest evidence in the author's own hand of his actual intentions for the greater part of the text he incorporated into the "Chronicle of the Ommiades." While it is true that Irving relied upon the printed *Knickerbocker Magazine* text as his basis for revisions in 1847, it does not follow from this practice that he thus placed a tacit seal of approval upon the numerous revisions of his manuscript version which were included in the *Knickerbocker Magazine.* His use of the printed pages indicates in itself only that he found it convenient to proceed in that way.

For Chapters I and III of the "Abderahman" section (T 202.2–206.43, 208.28–218.2), in order to represent Irving's own wishes as fully as possible the copy-text must thus be a mixed or composite one, combining the Hispanic Society manuscript of 1840 as a textual basis, together with the scattered manuscript changes made by Irving in 1847 to the printed *Knickerbocker Magazine* pages. The result conjoins his original intentions for these portions of the work with his later wishes for them as forming part of a longer narrative in a way that no single copy-text can do. In line with this approach, for the first few sentences of Chapter III (T 208.33–40 sovereign), Irving's recopied but slightly altered lines in the Berg Collection manuscript thus assume precedence as copy-text over the printed lines from which they were taken. For Chapter II of the "Abderahman" section (T 207.1–208.27) the situation is simpler: the Berg Collection's expanded holograph text must serve as copy-text because it is significantly revised by the author from the earlier manuscript and printed passages roughly corresponding to it.

For Chapters I and III substantive and accidental variants between the Hispanic Society manuscript, that text as revised by Clark, the *Knickerbocker Magazine* version, and that printed text as revised by Irving in 1847 are recorded; those variants not set forth in the list of Emendations are noted in a table of Rejected Variants. In any entry in the tables the absence of a reference to MShc (the Hispanic Society manuscript as revised by Clark) indicates that no revision was made by the editor to Irving's original (MSh); and the absence of a reference to MSn (the Berg Collection manuscript) indicates that its reading is identical with the one in the *Knickerbocker Magazine* (1A). Substantive variants and a few accidental variants of particular interest between the copy-text for Chapters I–III and the *Spanish Papers* text are recorded.

Of the two versions of the chapter pertaining to Hixem (T 218.3–222.6), that on pp. 32–49 of the 1827 manuscript and the thoroughly rewritten narrative on pp. 21–31 of the Johns Hopkins manuscript, the latter is the necessary choice as copy-text, representing as it does the author's later intentions. Since pp. 50–63 of the first draft are missing, for the first chapter describing the career of Alhakem (T 222.7–225.14) the sole version extant, the rewritten one whose first page Irving numbered 32 and whose succeeding pages Pierre numbered 33–40, is adopted as copy-text. Substantive and accidental variants between the two drafts of Chapter IV are noted in the list of Emendations only selectively, when the pre-copy-text version sheds helpful light on problems posed by the copy-text (for example, see Emendations 221.20).

Chapters VI–VIII (T 225.15–231.18) exist in two forms: first, as drafted in 1827 and revised twenty years later by Irving; second, as transcribed by Pierre. The former pages clearly represent the author's latest expressed wishes for the text and are adopted as copy-text. They consist of pp. 64–78 in the first draft owned by Columbia University, the lone p. 31 owned by the University of Virginia, and pp. 81–89 in the Columbia University draft. As posthumously prepared texts derived from the author's manuscripts, the edited transcriptions by Pierre possess a textual authority analogous to the *Spanish Papers* text of "Abderahman"; but they are not represented in the tables which follow because with regard to substantive readings they virtually reproduce Pierre's emendations in the copy-text itself. Chapter IX (T 231.19–232.6) is extant in only a single version, and that fragmentary. Pages 92 and 93 of the early draft, which Irving revised in 1847 and Pierre later renumbered 62 and 63 as part of a new sequence, are adopted as copy-text.

Owing to limitations of space, cancellations within the copy-text are ordinarily not recorded.[439] In most cases those only are set forth which provide bases for Discussions of Adopted Readings (for example, Emendation 228.29) or which describe revisions by Pierre M. Irving. Irving's changes to the *Knickerbocker Magazine* text in Chapters I and III of the "Abderahman" section are noted in full, however, and Pierre's emendations to the copy-text are all identified, though their being in ink or pencil is not noted, and the unregularized forms of chapter-numbers and chapter-headings introduced by him are not ordinarily recorded, as not in a strict sense forming parts of the copy-text (see Emendations 202.3–4, 218.4–6).

---

439. Substantive and accidental readings inadvertently left uncancelled in the copy-text are listed in Emendations 204.24, 206.36.

Textual and other evidence warrants certain varieties of regularization to the copy-text. Irving intended the narrative units in his manuscript to be printed as chapters, each with a chapter-number and chapter-heading. He indicated this by the chapter-number he inserted, along with a title, on the first page of the rewritten second chapter of "Abderahman"; he also indicated it by the blank spaces he left at the tops of the pages beginning the chapters numbered by Pierre III, IV, V, VI, VII, and VIII. In preparing the *Life of Washington* it was frequently Irving's practice to leave the drafting of chapter-numbers and chapter-headings to Pierre, who did so as part of his full-time assistance to his uncle.[440] It is thus natural to presume that the author would have expected Pierre to interpret the blank spaces in the present manuscript as clear signs of a general intention which it would be his duty to fulfill. As we have seen, Pierre did so; he added the appropriate data, and when *Spanish Papers* appeared this introductory material formed an integral part of the text of "Abderahman." Since Irving's wish was clearly to publish the "Chronicle of the Ommiades" in a format consistent with his other Spanish narratives, and since by the close of his career it had become customary for Pierre to supply chapter-numbers and chapter-headings, it is appropriate to include here the material prepared by Pierre for publication in *Spanish Papers*. For Chapters I–III, the chapter-headings are reprinted from *Spanish Papers* but modified to conform with the styling adopted by Twayne at these points throughout the *Complete Works*; for Chapters IV–VIII, Pierre's manuscript interpolations are regularized to conform to the Twayne house style; and for Chapter IX the preliminary material is supplied by the present editor (Emendations 231.19–20).

A second variety of regularization undertaken here is the supplying of double quotation marks to enclose direct quotations. Throughout the manuscripts associated with the "Chronicle" Irving indicated in a fitful way his intention to observe this convention, which with the help of his editors he followed in his published works;[441] but in this instance he fulfilled his intentions erratically. Pairs of double quotation marks are thus added (Emendations 202.26) and made complete (Emendations 202.5, 219.41) as necessary.

Provided they were in contemporary use, Irving's spellings are permitted to stand even if somewhat unusual (219.37 risqued, 224.3 scymetar). Alternative spellings are also both admitted if no clear preference between them is evident (225.23 entrusted, 225.27 intrusted), but if a spelling is not in conformity with Irving's predominant practice it is emended (for example, 218.33 visier to vizier). Ampersands are thus ex-

440. See the Textual Commentary to "The Chronicle of Pelayo," pp. 464–65.
441. See the Textual Commentary to "The Chronicle of Pelayo," pp. 465–66.

panded to "and" (Emendations 226.26). Names are made consistent in spelling, according to the author's preferred usages (for example, Emendations 219.16 Alhakem, Emendations 228.19 Casim). The capitalization in the copy-text is allowed to stand unless it is erroneous or uncharacteristic of Irving's habits and prevailing intention in the work (Emendations 203.15). Thus, for example, words from foreign languages capitalized in the manuscript, perhaps so as to be read clearly, are often emended to lower-case on the authority of his practice in the Author's Revised Editions of *Mahomet and His Successors*, the *Conquest of Granada*, and the *Columbus*. An exception is "Alcazar," which is invariably capitalized on the 13 occasions where it appears in the copy-text, and also in Irving's other writings such as the 1850 *Granada* 444.19; it is left unchanged. Perhaps from literally translating the Spanish "cristianos," Irving sometimes wrote "Christian" or "Christians" with a lower-case "c"; the word and its derivatives are capitalized (Emendations 225.26). On the other hand, as a rule civil, military, and religious titles are not capitalized unless they form parts of proper names (Emendations 204.21).

Some of the author's mildly unusual practices of punctuation—for example, his use of the semicolon simply to enforce a distinct pause (218.32, 224.6)—are permitted to stand. Other eccentricities, such as his tendency not to punctuate at the end of lines, are in fact lapses and are corrected. A single entry (Emendations 203.29) lists the instances in which end-of-line commas or other indicated punctuation are supplied; periods are added or substituted for indicated punctuation at the ends of sentences (Emendations 203.41); commas are inserted to separate direct quotations from the commentary enclosing them (Emendations 203.32).

In the preparation of this edition the original manuscripts have in all cases been consulted and xerox copies of them annotated on the basis of the examination. The following collations have also been made:

1. A xerox copy of the *Knickerbocker Magazine* of "Abderahman" owned by York University (AP 2/ F64) sight collated against the Hispanic Society manuscript; a second collation of the photocopied magazine text against a microfilm copy of the manuscript;

2. The xeroxed *Knickerbocker Magazine* text compared with the following additional copies: University of Delaware (AP 2/ .F64); Legislative Library of Ontario (Periodicals/ first floor); Yale University (A 89/ 72);

3. The xeroxed *Knickerbocker Magazine* text sight collated against the "Abderahman" texts in four editions of *The Crayon Papers* (see the Introduction to the Textual Notes, I, 260);

4. The xeroxed *Knickerbocker Magazine* text collated twice and independently against the revised "Abderahman" text in the Berg Collection, New York Public Library;

5. A xeroxed copy of the Berg Collection manuscript collated twice and independently with the corresponding text in a copy of *Spanish Papers*

owned by the National Library of Canada, and twice and independently with an additional *Spanish Papers* text owned by the University of Texas; 6. Irving's original account of Hixem (Columbia University, pp. 32–49) collated twice and independently with his revised version (Johns Hopkins University, pp. 21–31);

7 Pages 64–78 in the Columbia University manuscript, p. 31 owned by the University of Virginia, and pp. 81–89 in the Columbia University manuscript, collated twice and independently against Pierre M. Irving's transcriptions owned by Johns Hopkins University and the Berg Collection, New York Public Library.

See Discussions and Lists pp. 532, 590, 671.

CHRONICLE OF
FERNAN GONZALEZ, COUNT OF CASTILE

When, early in 1847, Irving decided to amuse himself by revising the series of Spanish "Chronicles" he had "roughly sketched out" while in Madrid twenty years before, the "Chronicle of Fernan Gonzalez" was the first of these narratives he looked over. "I took it up," he later informed Pierre M. Irving, "was amused with it, and found I had hit the right vein in my management of it. I went to work and rewrote it, and got so in the spirit of the thing, that I went to work, *con amore*, at two or three fragmentary Chronicles, filling up the chasms, rewriting parts." The "Chronicle of Fernan Gonzalez" was in fact the only one of the group which was rewritten from beginning to end. Although at Irving's death it remained in his own words "complete, though not thoroughly finished off,"[442] the work was unique among the Spanish chronicles as being a thorough revision of an earlier draft.

That draft is no longer known to exist, but the manuscript of the 1847 text, which eventually served as printer's copy for the *Spanish Papers* version, is extant at the University of Virginia. Written in dark brown ink almost without exception on one side of sheets of unlaid, unlined paper approximately 4⅞″ x 7⅝″ in size, the manuscript is comprised of 111 pages, numbered by Irving 1–93, 94/94, 94/94/94, 95, 95/95, 96–108.[443] While it does include numerous cancellations several words in length, often representing minor false starts as Irving revised his earlier

---

442. Irving to Pierre M. Irving, Sunnyside, April 14, 1847; PMI, IV, 14, 15.

443. Two pages in the manuscript, pp. 15, 31, include lines of cancelled or superseded text on their reverse sides. At three points Irving wrote his text on the first and third sides of sheets folded at the center to form booklets: the pages are pp. 11–12, 44–45, 61–62. The multiple numeration of pages 94 and 95 was necessary to correct repeated oversights in paging.

copy, the manuscript text suggests that, having "hit the right vein" in preparing it, he found the process of composition a smooth one. Only 9 pages consist of slips of paper pasted together—often indications of major insertions, transpositions, or other revisions by the author,[444] and none of these includes cancelled text or other marks near the pastings which would confirm a suspicion that serious problems had arisen at those points. Two interlineations in a darker shade of ink on page 40, 2 and 3 words in length respectively, suggest that, having completed the new draft of "Fernan Gonzalez," he may have given the work a casual review before passing on to his other narratives; but he made no attempt fully to prepare it for the press. For example, on page 1 he had written out a general title, and on 19 of the pages which followed he had left blank spaces at breaks in the narrative where chapter-numbers and chapter-headings were to be inserted; but he did not bother to fill in that information. Such details might wait until the chronicles were to be given a last look prior to publication, and at that point the headnotes could as easily be attended to by some other person as by himself. Irving's interlude of "amusing occupation" on the chronicles gave him the "pleasure" it did precisely because it permitted him to indulge his "literary vein" without being obliged to perform all the uninspiring editorial drudgery he associated with publication.[445]

Between 1847 and 1859 the author gave no further attention to the manuscript. It thus remained for Pierre M. Irving, his literary executor, to make the necessary preparations to publish "Fernan Gonzalez" in a presentable form. Since *Spanish Papers* was to be published by George Putnam, Irving's publisher from 1848 until his death, and hence was to be set in type by the firm of John F. Trow, Inc., Pierre knew that it would not be necessary elaborately to emend the work by way of editorial direction. However, in keeping with his cautious and methodical habits, before submitting the manuscript to Putnam Pierre went over it at least twice, first marking it at various points in pencil, and later in ink.

444. The pages consisting of slips of paper pasted together are 1, 10, 13, 23, 46, 48, 94, 94/94/94, 105. The pastings on pages 94 and 94/94/94 may appear to be associated in some way with Irving's odd numbering system at that point, but this does not seem to be so. Page 94 consisted first of two slips of paper pasted together to form a sheet of the usual size; a new paragraph (corresponding to T 265.30) begins immediately below the pasting, but there is no evidence to suggest that including the paragraph was an afterthought by Irving. At the bottom of the same page, another sheet is pasted so as to fold upward and thereby maintain consistent dimensions among the sheets of the manuscript as a whole. This pasted sheet is itself comprised of two slips of paper; it measures 4 7/8 x 4 1/2" and includes the footnote corresponding in T to 265.35–42. Irving appears simply to have wished to include his footnote on the same manuscript page as the reference to it in the text. Page 94/94/94 shows no sign of revision at points adjacent to the pasting of the two slips which comprise it.

445. WI to PMI, Sunnyside, April 14, 1847, and April 15, 1847; PMI, IV, 16, 17.

The pencilled notations which Pierre did not subsequently write over in ink were infrequent. Besides a single query as to the spelling of a proper name (see Discussions of Adopted Readings 262.25), he wrote 17 emendations of Irving's accidentals, 8 of which were changes in spelling, 9 in punctuation. The latter revisions included the addition of 6 pairs of double quotation marks to a single passage early in the chronicle, almost certainly as a sign to the printer that all direct quotations were to be so punctuated (see Discussions of Adopted Readings 245.8–17). He also made 11 substantive emendations, chiefly deletions of words contiguous to Irving's cancellations and erroneously allowed by him to stand, and other brief corrections of oversights.

The greater number of Pierre's pencilled emendations of the manuscript text he later re-wrote in ink. These included the added word "Introduction" beneath Irving's general title (T 233.4), and the chapter-numbers and chapter-headings in the blank spaces provided for the purpose. In addition to a single change of spelling he made 5 further substantive emendations, 4 of which involved supplying 1 or 2 words at points where text had obviously been omitted by Irving, and the fifth correcting an obvious error. Pierre wrote a few additional corrections in ink only, consisting of 2 spelling changes and 3 substantive emendations, each involving a single word. In short, his revisions to the manuscript were neither numerous nor major. They were intended to correct Irving's errors, to supply routine material he had neglected to prepare himself, and at a few points to indicate general principles according to which the text was to be set in type.

The process of transforming Irving's manuscript as corrected by Pierre into the version which appeared in *Spanish Papers*, I, [277]–350, involved extensive revision of its accidentals but few changes to its substantive readings. The emended accidentals reflected the imposition of the Putnam house style.[446] Although Irving had been careless in supplying punctuation to his fluently written text, the changes to it in the published version indicate not so much the degree of his remissness in that regard as the relative density of the Putnam style of pointing. A collation of the corrected manuscript against the published text reveals that a total of 547 commas were added in *Spanish Papers*, 34 deleted, 18 altered to semicolons, and 2 to other marks of punctuation; 7 semicolons were added, 98 altered to commas, 10 to commas followed by double dashes, and 6 to other punctuation; 1 colon was added, 4 were altered to commas, 7 to semicolons, 3 to commas followed by dashes, and 3 to periods; 33 periods were added, 1 deleted, and 5 altered to other punctuation; 8 dashes were added and 2 dashes were altered to

446. See the Textual Commentary, I, 273–76.

commas; 1 exclamation mark was added, 1 altered to a comma; 63 pairs of double quotation marks were added; 4 double quotation marks were added to incomplete pairs, 1 deleted; roman letters were altered to italics on 2 occasions, italics to roman on 1. Other emendations included 6 paragraph divisions added, 1 deleted; 8 combinations of statements which Irving had written as two sentences into one, and 5 divisions of single sentences into two; and the regularization of 9 citations in footnotes into a consistent form.

Setting aside changes of capitalization, the spelling in the corrected manuscript was altered 211 times. Of these, 42 were confined to adding hyphens to compound words; 26 were emendations of –our to –or spellings; 28 pertained to proper names; 13 were rectifications of Irving's perpetual confusions between –ie– and –ei– spellings; 12 were limited to the addition of apostrophes to possessives; 10 were altered spellings of compounds wherein a hyphen was not added in *Spanish Papers*; 7 were revisions of internal –z– to –s– spellings, 7 were adjustments at points where Irving had adopted the correct spellings of words which, though similar to those he intended, he did not mean to employ; 5 were revisions of en– to in– spellings; and 38 others, involving corrections of outright errors and substitutions of preferred forms. Finally, Irving's "S^{t}" was 23 times emended to "St." The *Spanish Papers* text regularized, corrected, and made reasonably self-consistent the spellings in Irving's manuscript, although at many points it departed from his legitimate wishes as he had expressed them in the manuscript.

The patterns of capitalization in the manuscript of "Fernan Gonzalez" were altered in *Spanish Papers* in almost as sweeping a manner as those of spelling. Initial capitals were altered to lower-case letters on 140 occasions, only 6 of which were necessitated by the conversions of two sentences into one. The most numerous emendations of this sort were made to military, civil, or religious titles which Irving had used to refer to persons but not as parts of proper names; these occurred 118 times. Other emendations of initial capitals to lower-case letters occurred in the following situations: 6 changes of military or civil titles, used with reference to no person; 4 changes of words which Irving had used in connection with proper names or as parts of them; 3 alterations of the word "Cortes"; 2 alterations of foreign words capitalized immediately prior to definitions of the terms; and 1 correction to a word which originally began a sentence but whose placement was changed by an interlineated substitution. Emendations of lower-case letters to capitals were made 33 times, 4 of which pertained either to the first words of quoted statements or to statements written as one sentence in the manuscript but rendered as two in the published version. Words which the printers apparently interpreted as parts of proper names were capitalized at 13 points; words associated with the Christian religion were capitalized 14 times; and words denoting nationality were twice capitalized.[447]

Only 12 substantive variants, all limited to 1 or 2 words, occur between the revised manuscript text and that in *Spanish Papers*. Of these, 3 are obvious misprints, and the remaining 9, certainly authorized and probably introduced by Pierre, are characteristic of his painstaking meticulousness. They are evidently motivated by a desire to eradicate errors and infelicities (for example, see Rejected Variants 242.13), ensure consistency (Rejected Variants 257.6), and adhere to idiomatic usage (Rejected Variants 253.36). The number and the on the whole finical character of the substantive variants between these two texts indicate that the printers of "Fernan Gonzalez" had access to no other manuscript copy than the one which remains extant at the University of Virginia.[448]

Pierre M. Irving collated the proofsheets of the printed text against the manuscript copy,[449] and as the pattern of substantive variants between the two versions reveals, he did so with care. The *Spanish Papers* text of "Chronicle of Fernan Gonzalez, Count of Castile" was thus prepared under the best of possible auspices, given the circumstances of its posthumous publication: it was edited by Pierre, who knew his uncle's literary instincts and aims better than anyone else then or since, and it was published by Putnam, of whose house style the author had approved. Pierre and Putnam collaborated to produce a creditable approximation of what they assumed from experience would have been Irving's wishes for the final text.

However, while the *Spanish Papers* version is of more than historical interest on account of its genesis, it possesses only a secondary, derived authority as a source for the present critical text of "Fernan Gonzalez." Irving may (or may not) have approved of the emendations to the 1847 manuscript made on his behalf by Pierre and the printers, but the fact

447. A classified list of the emendations made in *Spanish Papers* to the spelling and capitalization of the corrected manuscript is on file at the University of Texas together with the collation data.

448. Ink smudges throughout the manuscript reveal in themselves that it served as printer's copy, but various printers' reference marks are also present. These include 15 pencilled brackets or short vertical bars scattered throughout, marking stints, and printers' signatures on the following pages: "Allen," pp. 1, 29; "Nelson," pp. 9, 11, 36, 57, 93; "Hall," pp. 17, 43, 63, 67, 84, 93; "Cummings," pp. 52, 86; "Adams," p. 98. On the reverse sides of pages 10 and 66 are written notations of the printed pages in *Spanish Papers* derived from the sections of the manuscript text just completed; the name "Irving" is written in blue crayola on the reverse side of p. 83.

449. Pierre M. Irving left two pencilled marks in the manuscript which indicate that he collated it against the proofs. The first was the notation "p 319" beneath Irving's text on p. 66; this point corresponds to the bottom of p. 319 of the text in *Spanish Papers*. The second mark was "p 331" beneath Irving's text on p. 83; the point at which he wrote this reference mark corresponds to 331.20 in *Spanish Papers*.

is that he had no opportunity to pass judgment. The sole indication we possess of his explicit wishes for the text of this chronicle is the manuscript he prepared in 1847 and left at his death to Pierre. That manuscript, divested of the marks in pencil and ink later added to it by Pierre, must serve as the copy-text for this edition.[450]

The twentieth-century editor of "Fernan Gonzalez" is accordingly placed in a position similar though not identical to that of Pierre M. Irving in 1859. The chief difference is that, whereas Pierre interpreted his responsibility as to carry out Irving's imperfectly realized plans, in this edition a greater emphasis is placed upon accurately representing the author's own achievement. If the relatively conservative approach to emending the manuscript text which is implicit in this bias produces a result somewhat less regular and self-consistent than the one published in *Spanish Papers*, adherence to the approach yields a narrative which represents more accurately than Pierre's the final expressed wishes of the author.

Textual and other evidence does, however, justify certain classes of regularization. For example, the blank spaces at appropriate points in the manuscript reveal that Irving did intend chapter-numbers and chapter-headings to be included as parts of his work, as they were in the cognate narratives which had comprised *Legends of the Conquest of Spain* (1835). Moreover, on the basis of his working relationship with Pierre in preparing *The Life of George Washington*,[451] it is reasonable to suppose that he would have regarded the spaces as clear signals to his nephew of the variety of material which was to be inserted in them. In fact, Pierre did so; and his chapter-numbers and chapter-headings for "Fernan Gonzalez" formed parts of the *Spanish Papers* text. It thus seems proper to include in this edition the preliminaries to the several chapters as they appear in *Spanish Papers* except as modified to conform with the styling adopted by Twayne at these points throughout the *Complete Works* (see Emendations 233.4). However, the interpolated passages are enclosed within brackets to indicate that they were not written by Irving and cannot in a strict sense be said to form parts of the copy-text.

A second class of regularization undertaken here is likewise warranted by analogy between the manuscript of "Fernan Gonzalez" and the collaborations during Irving's lifetime metween himself, his nephew, and Putnam.[452] Because the elderly author evidently expected his citations of source material to be regularized during the printing process, it is natural to suppose that he would have expected the footnotes in this

450. The *Spanish Papers* text is necessarily drawn upon at points where copy-text readings have been lost owing to damage to the manuscript; see Emendations 237.37.

451. See the Textual Commentary to "The Chronicle of Pelayo," pp. 464–65.

452. See the Textual Commentary to "The Chronicle of Pelayo," p. 465.

manuscript to be treated by Putnam as they had been for his other writings. Acting on his behalf, Pierre evidently did so, too; for though he cancelled one footnote and parts of two others, he made no notations in the manuscript to indicate the manner in which the remaining citations were to be set in type. It seems reasonable to presume that Irving would have expected the very unevenness of his method of citing authorities to be interpreted by Pierre and the printer as signs of a partially realized intention which it was their part, as usual, to fulfill. For this reason, citations of sources in the footnotes are reproduced here from *Spanish Papers* rather than from the manuscript; Irving's own notes are reproduced in the list of Emendations (see Emendations 240.38).

A third variety of regularization warranted by Irving's practice within the manuscript and elsewhere is enclosing all direct quotations within pairs of double quotation marks. The 6 instances in which such punctuation was included in the manuscript (5 of which pairs are incomplete) reveal an intention to signify quoted passages in this manner. However, as often occurred during Irving's later career, it proved necessary for Pierre and the printers to impose the convention on the full text.[453] Pierre saw to it that quotation marks were included at appropriate points in *Spanish Papers,* and it seems reasonable to follow his procedure, which constituted the fulfillment of a wish Irving had realized in part— not an emendation to the manuscript according to a principle at odds with the author's expressed intention or his practice in other works (see Emendations 239.24, 248.27–28).

Of course, the notion that an imperfect manuscript text is a warrant to undertake wholesale emendations of all kinds is questionable at the best. In general, the aim of representing Irving's wishes for the text in its final stage is more likely to be realized by respecting the copy-text, even in its inconsistencies. Hence, many of the author's characteristic though somewhat unusual practices are in evidence here—spellings, for example, such as "traytor" (T 254.2), "superceded" (234.15), and "Beside" as an adverb (237.30). If a word is spelled in two ways, and no clear preference between the alternatives is evident, both spellings are allowed to stand (235.26 enterprize, 235.42 enterprise); however, if a clear bias is evident, variant readings are emended to conform to the prevailing form ("skilful" to "skillful," Emendations 265.21). Unorthodox features of Irving's punctuation which appear to proceed from authorial design rather than oversight are permitted to stand. Among these are Irving's practice of omitting the comma following the second item in a series of three (263.22–23, 265.9), inserting a comma between subject and verb (235.2), and employing the semicolon to conclude a specifically introductory statement (269.17), the colon simply to mark a pause (246.19).

453. See the Textual Commentary to "The Chronicle of Pelayo," pp. 465–66.

On the other hand, since Irving was far from scrupulous in pointing his manuscript, his casually produced text has not been permitted to assume an authority disproportionate to its character. For example, it is often necessary to capitalize words at the beginnings of sentences (Emendations 242.21), to supply periods or other appropriate punctuation at the ends of sentences (Emendations 236.6, 250.6–7, 252.16), to add apostrophes to possessives (Emendations 237.37), and to insert commas separating the commentary from direct and indirect quotations within it (Emendations 242.21). Because in the hurry of composition the author often neglected to punctuate at the ends of lines in the manuscript, end-of-line punctuation is supplied as required (Emendations 233.11). Other emendations of punctuation, often relating to incomplete pairs of commas, adjustments necessitated by interlineations and cancellations, and run-on statements, are reported as they occur. In accordance with Irving's usual practice, civil and religious titles are capitalized when used as parts of proper names (Emendations 234.30), but they are given in lower-case forms when used alone, in reference to specific persons (Emendations 234.5). Thus "Count," employed alone in reference to Count Fernan Gonzalez, is emended to "count," in conformity with the majority usage in the manuscript (Emendations 235.23).

Irving was inconsistent in his spelling of several proper names. For example, he alternated between "San," "Saint," and some configuration of the abbreviation "S^t" (regularized here to "St.," Emendations 236.21) in reference to the same individual. Thus one encounters "St Pedro de Arlanza" (corresponding to T 237.32), "St Peter" (245.15–16), "San Pedro" (246.22), and "St Pedro of Arlanza" (260.15). No serious ambiguity is created by these several usages, and all (excepting the regularized "St.") are allowed to stand. Similarly, alternative names such as "Sancho I." (266.5), "Sancho the First" (266.42) and "Sancho the Fat" (267.1) are left unemended, though portions of proper names or pseudonyms left uncapitalized in the copy-text are emended to capitals (Emendations 240.12). For certain names, the divergence between Irving's usages is not limited to conventions of abbreviation, and regularization becomes necessary to prevent confusion. One individual, whose name is most frequently rendered "Don Gonzalo Gustios," is referred to in five different and not mutually recognizable forms (see Discussions of Adopted Readings 243.34); and similar though less vexing problems arise for other persons (see Emendations 235.22, 243.6). Probably these difficulties arose from Irving's reliance on multiple sources not in agreement on the names, and also from his own carelessness.

Limitations of space render it impracticable to list in the tables which follow all Irving's cancellations and corrections within the copy-text. The author's handwriting is ordinarily easy to distinguish from that of

Pierre M. Irving, but the authorship of marks such as deletions or commas is often difficult to specify with confidence. Thus all readings are assumed to be Irving's unless there is at least a distinct possibility that they are Pierre's. All emendations to the copy-text probably or certainly by Pierre are pointed out, but owing to limitations of space their being in pencil, ink, or both is not ordinarily noted.[454] Cancellations within the copy-text are set forth if they reveal in an economical manner the textual situation necessitating an editorial decision (for example, Emendations 258.9), provide the textual basis for Discussions of Adopted Readings (Emendations 262.25), or pertain to revisions by Pierre.[455]

Unless recorded in the list of Emendations, substantive variants and accidental variants of particular interest between the copy-text and that in *Spanish Papers* are set forth in a separate table of Rejected Variants. The *Spanish Papers* text is frequently cited in the list of Emendations as the source of emended readings. It should be emphasized, however, that while *Spanish Papers* does provide a useful indication of what well informed persons regarded as the author's probable wishes, it possesses no textual authority deriving directly from Irving. Each emendation to the copy-text is made as a responsibility of the present editor rather than on the derived authority of *Spanish Papers*.

In the preparation of this edition the following collations have been made:

1. A typed transcription of the University of Virginia manuscript, prepared from a xerox copy annotated on the basis of comparisons with the original made twice and independently, collated twice and independently with the text in a copy of *Spanish Papers* owned by the University of Texas (Ir8/ SP1/ 1866), and once with an additional copy owned by the National Library of Canada.

See Discussions and Lists pp. 533, 600, 675.

CHRONICLE OF FERNANDO THE SAINT

The "Chronicle of Fernando the Saint," the lengthiest of the narratives of medieval Spain which Irving left unpublished at his death, is unique among these works for the degree of insight it affords into the author's methods of composition. 87 pages of manuscript notes and early drafts

---

454. Pierre M. Irving's handwritten chapter-numbers and chapter-headings, which served as the original copy for the *Spanish Papers* material interpolated here, are not recorded in the tables which follow as not technically forming parts of the copy-text.

455. Accidental readings inadvertently left uncancelled in the copy-text are listed in Emendations 238.4.

extant at the University of Virginia include material which corresponds in various ways to the subject-matter of Chapters I, II, VI–XI, and XIII of the 21-chapter work as it eventually appeared in *Spanish Papers*, I, [353]–451. These working papers shed helpful light on the genesis of the "Chronicle" in 1827.

The textual evidence from what was probably the earliest stage of Irving's active interest in the life of Fernando is slight. It consists of a single half-sheet, folded at the center so as to form pages approximately 5x7¾" in size, and including on its first three pages summarized genealogical data, character sketches, and notations of major events, all of which details were later to form the contents of the first chapter (T 273.8–276.23). This gathering of information no doubt served as a convenient reference as Irving sought to fix in his mind the persons and circumstances associated with the beginning of King Fernando's reign.

The remainder of the manuscript material pertaining to the early history of the "Chronicle" was probably written at about the same time as the genealogical data, but it was intended to serve a different purpose. These notes were prepared as the bases for the narrative itself. They comprise part of a larger collection of information, some of which Irving actually did use in 1847 as copy for Chapters XIV–XXI in the final draft. Much of the early research data for Chapters I–XIII does not correspond closely to the final text, but some does. Approximately one-half of this material represents the state of composition immediately preceding the author's latest version of "Fernando the Saint."

Irving's procedures in writing his early notes were not entirely consistent. He did regularly employ half-sheets of heavy unlaid, unlined paper, folded at the center so as to form pages about 5 x 7" in size; and for his more extended groupings of notes he ordinarily slipped these within each other at the fold, to form unbound booklets. In the upper-left-hand corner of the first page of a booklet he sometimes wrote a capital letter, probably to indicate its place in a sequence of information; but he did not always do so. Neither did he consistently write page-numbers nor attempt to arrange all his pages in a single sequence. His two consistent practices as a researcher were, first, to leave a blank space of about 1¼" at the top of each page beginning a new narrative unit (often corresponding to a new chapter in one of his sources); second, to leave a wide left margin, writing on only the right five-eighths of each page.

The 84 pages of manuscript notes thus prepared are as follows:

1. 11 pages, numbered 1–10, 11/12, including material which corresponds to parts of Chapters I and II (T 276.21–281.38). Further details are summarized on the reverse sides of pp. 3, 9, which are unpaged.

2. 8 pages, unnumbered, including text and reference notes corresponding to parts of Chapter I (273.36–276.7).

3. 3 pages, numbered 23–25, including material some of which was incorporated in Chapter VI (285.16–31).

4. 10 pages, unnumbered, including text which corresponds to parts of Chapter VI (285.31–287.26).

5. 32 pages, numbered 1–12, 12–24, 24/24, 25–30, including text which corresponds to parts of Chapters VII–IX (289.15–294.8, 294.32–296.14).

6. 10 pages, unnumbered, including text and reference notes which corresponds to parts of Chapter IX–XI (296.10–299.27).

7. 3 pages, unnumbered, including text a small proportion of which corresponds to part of Chapter XI (299.33–36).

8. 4 pages, unnumbered, including text and reference notes corresponding to parts of Chapters XI and XIII (303.8–30, 303.35–305.10, 307.27–35).

9. 3 pages, unnumbered, including text which corresponds to part of Chapter XIII (306.6–307.1).

The notes are in general summary-translations, with occasional extracts, from printed Spanish sources. At 10 points Irving included references to the specific works drawn upon,[456] but he was by no means consistent in doing so. The left margins of the manuscript pages he used to insert new or revised material or to write himself brief queries or reference notes.[457]

The 32-page fragment listed above as Item 5 exemplifies the manner in which, much as he had done in preparing a manuscript of *Mahomet* in 1831,[458] in 1847 Irving prepared portions of this "Chronicle" by simply revising his research notes on it. In working up passages to be included to Chapters VII–IX of his final version, he simply entered 8 substitutions and additions in the left margins of these research notes, then wrote out a fresh draft of the narrative segment, incorporating the changes and introducing other adjustments of style. The absence from the later version of historical details not included in the first draft suggests strongly that, in preparing the revision, Irving had before him no authority other than his own notes. In short, the process of revision in 1847 was for these pas-

---

456. These include 2 references to "Bleda"—that is, Fray Jaime Bleda, *Coronica de los Moros de España* (Valencia, 1618); 3 references to "Cronica de Rey Don Fernando" (once, "Chronica")—that is, *Cronica del Sancto Rey Don Fernando . . .* (Sevilla, 1516); 3 references to "Chron. Gen. de Esp." (twice, "Cronica General")— that is, an unspecified version of Alfonso el Sabio's much-lengthened and often-recopied manuscript history, *Coronica General de España*; and 2 references to an unidentified work, "Cronica Gotica por Don Alonzo Nuñez de Castro" (once, "Corona"). This latter work may possibly have been Don Alonzo Nuñez de Castro's *Vida de S. Fernando El III, Rey de Castillo Y Leon . . .* (Madrid, 1787).

457. Marginal additions were made at 26 points in the early draft. An instance of the sort of reference note Irving wrote himself is in the left margin of p. 1, Item 1: summarizing there the activities of Queen Berenguela upon the death of the young King Enrique (corresponding roughly to T 275.39–40 The . . . Castile), he noted an associated detail: "King Fernando 1⟨5⟩⟨0⟩ ↑18↓ years/ of age." See T 276.21.

458. See the Textual Commentary to *Mahomet and His Successors*, ed. Henry A. Pochmann, pp. 563–65.

sages limited to re-structuring and pervasive re-phrasing. The same may be said for the research notes designated above as Items 1 and 2, though the relationships between the remaining segments of the early draft and the sections of the final narratives to which they correspond are much less close and continuous. It is thus clear that, while the early manuscripts are of interest as a whole for the insight they afford into Irving's quite straightforward processes of composition, they are of virtually no value for establishing a critical text of the completed work.

The manuscript of the final version of "Chronicle of Fernando the Saint," prepared in 1847, survives in almost complete form. The text corresponding to Chapters I–XIII and the first two paragraphs of Chapter XIV (T 273.2–309.5 CHRONICLE . . . church.) is owned by the University of Virginia;[459] the manuscript text including the third paragraph of Chapter XIV through a part of the first paragraph of Chapter XVII (309.6–316.31 At . . . armour) is owned by the Berg Collection, New York Public Library; and the remainder—excepting 4 missing pages in Chapter XX (326.15–327.13 security . . . Laudamus.) and probably 2 missing pages in Chapter XXI (328.15–36 sweetest . . . 146.)—is owned by the University of Virginia.

The 1847 manuscript text of "Fernando the Saint" consists in effect of two parts: one which Irving entirely rewrote at that time, and one which he merely revised using manuscripts which dated from 1827, the period of his initial researches in Spain. The text corresponding to Chapters I–XIII and the first two paragraphs of Chapter XIV comprises the portion rewritten in 1847. These 99 manuscript pages are written in dark brown ink across the full width of sheets of unlaid, unlined paper numbered by Irving [1], [2], 3–31, 32/33, 34–42, 44–52, 52 [2]–80, 80 [2]–92, 92 [2]–98.[460] Cancellations and substitutions are neither lengthy nor, for Irving, very frequent. He may have intended to make further minor revisions, however, for he clearly did not regard his labors on this portion of the narrative as quite complete. Besides following his usual practice

459. Filed together with this portion of the "Fernando the Saint" manuscript at the University of Virginia is a page numbered 100 and including 4 lines of text which constitute a rejected version of lines in the "Chronicle of Fernan Gonzalez, Count of Castile." The page is in fact a false start for p. 100 in Irving's manuscript of that work.

With a single exception, the "Fernando the Saint" text is written on one side of each sheet only; and with 9 exceptions—pp. 14, 22, 23, 27, 34, 39, 66, 82, and 87—sheets 5 x 7 5/8" in size are used, rather than ones pieced together by pasting smaller slips. With two exceptions, pp. 46–47 and 68–69, Irving wrote these pages on individual sheets of paper rather than folded half-sheets.

460. The upper-right-hand corners of the first two pages of the manuscript, where Irving ordinarily wrote page-numbers, have been shredded away. In paging his text the author skipped from 42 to 44 and at 3 points later used the same numbers (52, 80, 92) for successive pages.

of leaving blank spaces at the top of the first pages of successive narrative units, where chapter-numbers and chapter-headings might be inserted, he also wrote two notes to himself regarding material which was wanting in the work as it then stood (see Emendations 284.9, 289.11). There is little likelihood that he ever performed the further research necessary to supply the information thus indicated.

Beginning with p. 99, the 1847 manuscript text is a revision of the notes Irving had compiled while in Spain. Like the portion of the early draft superseded by the 1847 version, these pages are not numbered by him in a single series; some are not numbered at all. After Irving's death Pierre M. Irving renumbered the entire sequence following page 98; and since his arrangement is far simpler to use for purposes of reference than the near-chaos left by his uncle, the two series are listed here side-by-side:

Washington Irving	Pierre M. Irving
3–46	99–142
[Not numbered]	143–47
1–14	148–61
[Not numbered]	162–70
1–4	171–74
1–4	175–78
[Missing]	[179–82 missing]
9–12	183–86
[Missing]	[Final pages missing].[461]

Pierre M. Irving's pp. 99–178 and 183–86 of the manuscript are written on sheets of paper identical in size and texture to that on which the extant sections of the early draft are written; and with the exception of p. 133, which includes text written across its full width,[462] all include text at the

461. As a supplement to his several incomplete series of pagination, Irving's manuscript included an alphabetical sequence of capital letters written in the upper-left-hand corners of the following pages, all of which also include blank spaces at the top: pp. 109 (B), 135 (⟨3⟩C), 143 (D), 148 (E), 172 (G), 175 (H). In the final manuscript only pp. 102–03, 141–42, and 154–57 are written on folded half-sheets still intact. Probably as Irving revised this portion of the text he separated successive pages which had originally been written on the first and third sides of folded half-sheets, neglecting to do so only for the few pages noted.

462. Despite its deviation in format from the pages in the latter portion of the manuscript which had first been drafted in 1827, p. 133 was probably also written at that time. Irving left a 1 3/4″ blank space at its top and hence regarded it as the first page of a future chapter. Probably when he began to write out this new narrative unit he momentarily departed from the format he had adopted in the pages preceding it (3–36), but then, recognizing his oversight, he returned to that format on the pages which followed (38–46). The pen he used to write p. 37/133 appears to have been the same as he used for the rest of the series.

right five-eighths of each page, with extended substitutions or interpolations added when necessary at the left.[463]

This latter portion of the manuscript does not show evidence of thorough revision in 1847; the author made fewer and less extensive alterations to the concluding chapters than he had to the early draft corresponding to pp. 1–98 in the final version. Pages 99–186 include only 16 substantive revisions in the left margins in Irving's hasty, nervous later hand, and no revisions of accidentals only. Of the 16, all but 5 changes are very brief, ranging in length from 1 to 7 words. Irving introduced no new facts which would suggest a recurrence to his sources, and his revisions were confined mainly to the adjustments of phraseology he had once referred to as his "filigree work."[464]

Having passed once through the entire manuscript of "Fernando the Saint," Irving looked over the narrative pen in hand before turning his attention to other topics. This last perusal was not a close reading in which he sought to supply necessary finishing touches and correct his own numerous oversights. Rather, his tinkerings, in a very dark shade of brown ink, were miscellaneous and minor: none of the 22 substantive emendations he made at this point ran to more than a few words. Irving's cursory review of the text reflected the desultory attitude he was frankly adopting toward it in 1847. Like the other Spanish chronicles, "Fernando the Saint" was providing him an "amusing occupation." He was not interested in "muddling" over these unpublished works with too close a care; and as he told Pierre, he was content to leave them "complete, though not thoroughly finished off," ready at a suitable time "to be dressed off at leisure."[465]

Irving did not live to take up the manuscript again, of course, and at his death in 1859 the imperfect work passed into the hands of his literary executor, Pierre M. Irving. After a quick survey of all the papers pertaining to the "Chronicle,"[466] at some time afterward Pierre thus began to edit the 1847 text for publication in *Spanish Papers*. Using ink over pencil he renumbered the pages following Irving's p. 98, and he also inserted chapter-numbers and chapter-headings in the blank spaces Irving had

463. Except for pp. 171, 186, which include cancelled text on their reverse sides, the latter section of the 1847 manuscript is written on one side of each sheet only. It includes no pages comprised of slips of paper pasted together.

464. See Henry L. Ellsworth, *Washington Irving on the Prairie; or, A Narrative of a Tour of the Southwest in the Year 1832*, ed. Stanley T. Williams and Barbara D. Simison (New York, 1937), p. 71.

465. Irving to Pierre M. Irving, [Sunnyside], April 14, 1847; PMI, IV, 15–16.

466. On p. [4], Item 6 of the early draft, Irving had identified one Diego Perez as "... the person who/ had ⟨effected⟩ wrought such acts of/ prowess in the battle of [*blank space*]/ with the branch of an olive...." Pierre inserted the name "Xeres" in the blank space. See T 297.33–35.

left for the purpose. Using ink, he wrote explanatory notes and pasted them onto the manuscript at the two points where the author had indicated material as wanting. In his usual way, Pierre read through the entire text, entering corrections and noting various problems in pencil. After further thought and research, he went over the work again, ordinarily writing over his more substantial pencilled emendations in ink and making further changes in ink only. However, he made no attempt to include in the manuscript an exhaustive set of directions to the printers. Having worked with Irving's manuscript copy since 1848, they could be relied upon to make whatever minor adjustments of spelling and punctuation were necessary. Moreover, Pierre would have an opportunity to review their work when he collated the proofsheets against the manuscript text. Accordingly, his emendations of the manuscript more often involved substantives than accidental readings.

The marks made in pencil only by Pierre represent only a small fraction of those he first entered in pencil; the greater number were subsequently written over in ink. In addition to 6 alterations of spelling and a variety of guidelines, clarifications, and insertions of punctuation, he wrote 10 substantive emendations in pencil, 7 of which are clearly corrections of Irving's errors. At the 3 other points, however, Pierre's brief changes proceed from an apparent wish to improve readings which, though not incorrect, Irving himself might have preferred to see changed.[467] These latter alterations bespeak Pierre's just impression that the manuscript had been prepared in somewhat careless fashion, without close attention to verbal detail.

Pierre's emendations to the manuscript in ink over pencil, or a combination of the two, included 24 substantive changes besides simple deletions of rejected passages Irving had failed to cancel. Only 5 of the former alterations were necessary to correct outright errors; the remaining 19 were substitutions for the author's text of readings which, again, Pierre apparently presumed he would have preferred.[468] A pattern is evident throughout Pierre's revisions, of removing what he regarded as unnecessary matter, either by deleting it or by substituting a condensed version. His additions, invariably as brief as possible, were made only to supply text where Irving had omitted it or to correct his errors of grammar or

467. In the order specified, Pierre M. Irving's pencilled substantive emendations to the manuscript are listed in Emendations 283.37, 295.14, 301.24–25, 302.26, 305.3, 313.36, 316.15; 285.22, 287.35, 313.43.

468. In the order specified, Pierre's substantive emendations to the manuscript in ink over pencil, or a combination of the two, are listed in Emendations 288.8–9, 297.20, 300.38, 320.39, 325.8; 278.19–20, 284.30–31, 285.16–17, 289.29, 293.26–27, 293.28–30, 293.31–33, 294.2–4, 294.6, 294.24, 295.9–11, 295.28–31, 298.16–19 *inclusive*, 299.4, 299.5–6, 299.26, 299.37.

logic. His few emendations in ink only, which include substantive revisions at 3 points, are of a piece with his other changes.[469]

It is noteworthy that the majority of Pierre's substantive emendations of the manuscript text occur in the portion which Irving thoroughly rewrote in 1847. His alterations to the first 98 pages are not only more numerous but more lengthy than those to the pages which follow; and none of his changes following p. 99 involves more than 5 words in Irving's text. Even though the author had not extensively revised his early draft on pages 99 and following, Pierre evidently had the impression that the latter portions of the text were marred by errors and infelicities less frequently than those which Irving had drafted for amusement in 1847.

When he turned over the revised manuscript to George Putnam,[470] Pierre had reason to expect that his late uncle's intentions for "Chronicle of Fernando the Saint" would be realized in the printing process, since Irving had approved the Putnam house style. As he anticipated, the *Spanish Papers* text was characterized by Putnam's distinctive styling[471] and revealed a considerably more dense pattern of punctuation than that in the manuscript version. Commas were added at no less than 805 points, deleted at only 58; 31 commas in the manuscript were emended to semicolons and 20 to other punctuation. Semicolons were added at 8 points, deleted at 3; they were converted to commas at 117, to commas followed by dashes at 18, and to other punctuation at 13; 1 colon was deleted, 7 were altered to semicolons, and 3 were altered to periods. Reflecting the casualness of Irving's pointing in the manuscript, in the *Spanish Papers* text 44 periods were added, only 1 deleted; 14 periods were altered to other punctuation. Dashes were added 14 times, and Irving's dashes were deleted or emended to different punctuation at 26. Pairs of double quotation marks were added 49 times, and 9 other emendations of punctuation were made.

The great majority of the 271 spellings of words other than proper names altered in *Spanish Papers* from the revised manuscript text of "Fernando the Saint" reflected Putnam styling. These changes included 60 hyphens added to unhyphenated compounds, and 20 other emenda-

469. Pierre's substantive emendations to the manuscript in ink only are listed in Emendations 294.17–18, 314.8, 325.26.

470. Printers' smudges, signatures, and other marks throughout the manuscript reveal that it was used as printer's copy for the *Spanish Papers* text. The name "Cummings" is written in pencil in the left margin or at the top of pp. 1, 21, 46, 86, 104, 122, 143, and 171; the name "Hall" is written in pencil on pp. 14, 37, 55, 65, 74, 79, 92, 133, 158, 183; the name "Nelson" is written in pencil on pp. 7, 12, 28, 47, 67, 80 [2], 98, 133, 150. Pencilled notations of the page-numbers in *Spanish Papers* corresponding to various segments of the manuscript appear on the reverse sides of pp. 36, 54, and 78.

471. See the Textual Commentary, I, 273–76.

tions of compound words. On 37 occasions the –our spellings usually (though not always) employed in the manuscript were altered to –or; words spelled by Irving with an internal –e– were 19 times altered to the –i– forms preferred by Putnam; and internal –z– spellings were 10 times altered to –s–. Contractions in the manuscript were 29 times either spelled out or spelled differently, and the *Spanish Papers* text included 36 other spellings changed by editorial preference where the author had not been in error. The 56 remaining changes in spelling were corrections of errors.

The emendations of capitalization from manuscript to published version were hardly less frequent than those of spelling; and like them, most were made according to consistently applied principles. Thus, of the 61 initial lower-case letters altered to capitals, 33 pertained to words associated with Christianity. 19 words designating title or rank and used as parts of proper names were capitalized, in accordance with Irving's own customary usage, and the remaining 9 capitalizations were also consistent with the Putnam styling. Initial capitals in the revised manuscript were emended to lower-case letters in *Spanish Papers* on 170 occasions. Titles or ranks denoting individuals but not used as parts of proper names were 55 times printed with lower-case letters, and a similar change was made at 23 points, where Irving signified individuals or groups of persons by referring to their occupations or their social status (for example, cavalier, gamester). Words apparently used by him as parts of proper titles, pseudonyms, or place-names were 23 times printed without the initial capitals he had employed.[472] In many of the 53 other instances in which capitals in the manuscript are emended to lower-case letters, Irving appears to have capitalized for emphasis, or, indeed, for no obvious reason. Statements written in the manuscript as two sentences were 12 times printed as one in *Spanish Papers*; and statements written as one sentence were 6 times divided into two.

The *Spanish Papers* text included 39 substantive variants from the printer's copy manuscript as revised by Pierre. Most of these emended readings were no doubt introduced, as they were certainly approved by him, during the printing process; they are characteristic of the concerns for economy, clarity, and adherence to contemporary idiom he had displayed in his earlier revisions. The closeness of Pierre's attention to "Fernando the Saint" as it went through the press is indicated by the detail that all but one of the substantive variants between the manu-

472. Irving was evidently more inclined to capitalize nouns than were Putnam's printers. However, lest the practices of either be made to seem absolutely consistent, it is to be noted that, whereas some words associated with Christianity are written in the manuscript with lower-case initial letters which are capitalized in *Spanish Papers*, 16 others associated with Christianity or other faiths are initially capitalized in the manuscript but printed with lower-case initial letters.

script and *Spanish Papers* were limited to 1 or 2 words. No evidence suggests that the published version was derived at any point from manuscript copy other than the extant revised version of 1847.

Prepared under the supervision of the author's literary executor, and published by his own publisher, George Putnam, the *Spanish Papers* text of "Fernando the Saint" was a creditable attempt to realize Irving's unfulfilled wishes as fully as possible under the circumstances of its posthumous publication. However, the fact remains that the published "Fernando the Saint" was not the product of Irving's own enterprise; it resulted from the good offices of Pierre and Putnam, and it thus possesses only a secondary, derived authority as a source for the present critical text of the work. The most authoritative source of information available to us regarding Irving's intentions for the final version of "Fernando the Saint" is the manuscript which he revised and partially re-wrote in 1847 and left at his death "complete, though not thoroughly finished off." So far as possible, the manuscript must thus serve in this edition as copy-text.[473]

The twentieth-century editor of the narrative is accordingly placed in a position similar though not identical to that of Pierre M. Irving in 1859. The chief difference is that, whereas Pierre interpreted his responsibility as to carry out Irving's imperfectly realized plans, in this edition a greater emphasis is placed on accurately representing the author's own achievement. If the relatively conservative approach to emending the manuscript text which is implicit in this bias produces a result somewhat less regular and self-consistent than the one published in *Spanish Papers,* adherence to the approach yields a narrative which represents more faithfully than Pierre's the final expressed wishes of the author.

Textual and other evidence does, however, justify certain classes of regularization. Irving clearly planned at some time for chapter-numbers and chapter-headings to be inserted in the blank spaces at the top of the pages beginning successive narrative units. During the preparation of the *Life of George Washington* it had often been part of Pierre's duties on behalf of his uncle to write this prefatory material on his own,[474] so it is virtually certain that Irving would have expected him to interpret the blank spaces in the "Fernando the Saint" manuscript as indications of a partially realized intention which it was proper for him to fulfill. In fact, Pierre did so: chapter-numbers and chapter-headings supplied by him appeared as integral parts of the

473. Owing to the absence from the manuscript copy-text of pp. 179–82 and 187 and following, corresponding to T 326.16–327.13 and 328.15–36, the printed version necessarily serves as copy-text for these passages. The same procedure is followed for a few brief passages where the copy-text has been torn or worn away (see Emendations 273.10).

474. See the Textual Commentary to "The Chronicle of Pelayo," pp. 464–65.

Spanish Papers text. In view of the collaboration between the two Irvings during the lifetime of the author, it seems proper to regard the material added by Pierre at the heads of chapters as a legitimate extension of Irving's intention. The chapter-numbers and chapter-headings in *Spanish Papers* are thus incorporated in this text, modified in accordance with the styling adopted by Twayne at these points throughout the *Complete Works,* and enclosed in brackets as an indication of their authorship by Pierre rather than by Irving (see Emendations 273.2–7).

A second class of regularization undertaken here is the supplying of double quotation marks to enclose quotations. This is a practice Irving followed in the Author's Revised Edition of his works, even though in the manuscripts of his later writings he tended to supply quotation marks only irregularly; clearly he assumed that the editor or the printer would attend to such details. In the manuscript of "Fernando the Saint" he did include 24 pairs of double quotation marks and 4 incomplete pairs. Pierre, evidently confident that the printers would supply the necessary punctuation at other points where it was appropriate, did not pencil quotation marks into the printer's copy as he had for "The Chronicle of Pelayo" and "Chronicle of Fernan Gonzalez."[475] And in fact, direct-quotations are ordinarily enclosed in quotation marks in the *Spanish Papers* text. In view of Irving's expectation in his later career that other persons would supply quotation marks for him, and his clear intention in the present work to punctuate quoted material in the conventional manner, it seems proper here to supply double quotation marks at points where they were not included in the manuscript (see Emendations 276.17, 312.35).

A third class of regularization is also warranted by the history of Irving's collaboration with Pierre and with George Putnam. In preparing manuscript copy the elderly author cited his sources in footnotes in a hasty and irregular manner; indeed, in the *Life of George Washington* he not infrequently left the drafting of citations themselves to Pierre. He seems to have regarded the recasting of his (or Pierre's) references into a consistent footnote form as a normal part of the styling to be imposed on his manuscripts by the printers.[476] Having assisted his uncle on a regular basis in preparing the *Washington* and in seeing it through the press, Pierre knew that the regularization of footnotes by the printer formed a part of the well established working relationship between Irving

---

475. See above, pp. 466, 498. Since "Fernando the Saint" was to follow "The Chronicle of Pelayo," "Chronicle of the Ommiades," and "Chronicle of Fernan Gonzalez" in the contents of *Spanish Papers,* and since enclosing direct quotations within quotation marks was standard Putnam practice, Pierre no doubt assumed it would not be necessary in this work to remind the printers by inserting his own punctuation.

476. See the Textual Commentary to "The Chronicle of Pelayo," p. 465.

and Putnam. Accordingly, he made no revisions to the 24 footnotes in the manuscript of "Fernando the Saint," and in *Spanish Papers* they appeared in a format consistent with Irving's other works published by Putnam. On the basis of the prior cooperation between Irving, Pierre, and Putnam, it seems natural to assume that the author would have expected the footnotes in this work to be regularized as a matter of course. Hence the citations in footnotes are reproduced here as they appeared in *Spanish Papers* (see Emendations 279.36).

In the cases of the two passages in "Fernando the Saint" for which text must be supplied from *Spanish Papers* owing to the absence of manuscript copy-text, emendations are made sparingly. Even though these interpolated texts reflect the Putnam house style and perhaps Pierre M. Irving's editorial tastes as well, there is no feasible method of extracting from them the readings actually intended by the author. Derived as it is from the missing manuscript, the published version does incorporate at least some of the readings Irving intended, and it seems safest as a general rule to leave the interpolated passages as they stand.

In determining the accidentals of the present text several of Irving's mild eccentricities of pointing, such as the placing a comma between subject and verb (301.11) or using a colon simply to mark a full stop (325.16) are preserved. Similarly, if authorized by contemporary usage his somewhat unusual spellings, such as 288.14 scull, 279.25 Marocco, are permitted to stand. If no clear preference is evident between alternative spellings of the same word—for example, 278.6 afterward, and 279.25 afterwards—both forms are preserved; but if a particular form is clearly predominant it is adopted throughout. The ampersand is automatically emended to "and" when used alone in place of that word (see Emendations 285.39).

Irving was far from scrupulous in pointing his manuscript, and his casually produced text has thus not been permitted to assume an authority incommensurate with its character. Owing to the only partially completed state of the copy-text, several other classes of emendations are necessary to correct Irving's errors and omissions and to dispel ambiguities. Periods, exclamation marks, and question marks are when necessary inserted or substituted for other indicated punctuation (Emendations 274.6, 276.17, 313.31); apostrophes omitted from possessives are supplied (Emendations 284.11); end-of-line punctuation omitted from the copy-text is supplied (Emendations 273.16); capitals are supplied at the beginnings of sentences (Emendations 286.34); semicolons are substituted for commas to prevent run-on constructions (Emendations 286.16); and commas are supplied to separate the text from direct quotations within it (Emendations 280.34).

Proper names are in general made consistent in spelling, in accordance with Irving's majority usage (for example, Emendations 291.8 Xuarez, Emendations 318.35 Tello Alonzo). On occasion this procedure is painfully necessary. The author made some effort to be consistent in spelling the names of four prominent characters in the "Chronicle"— King Alfonso III of Leon, King Alfonso IX of Castile, Prince Alonzo (brother to King Fernando) and Prince Alfonso (son to King Fernando) —but he was not successful in his attempt. The spellings "Alonzo," "Alfonso," "Alonso," or "Alfonzo" all occur in reference to one or other of these figures, although only the first two represent his predominant intentions (see Emendations 273.8, 273.38, 300.1, 300.29). Irving often spelled the names of saints in more than one way, as for example 307.13 Saint Isidro and 307.22 San Isidro, or 309.44 St Iago and 279.4 Santiago. In these cases the different spellings are allowed to stand, but the author's various configurations of "S" and "t" are regularized to a consistent "St." (Emendations 279.21).

Words not ordinarily capitalized by Irving are emended to lower-case forms (Emendations 273.24); and conversely, other words are capitalized in accordance with his usual practice (Emendations 285.23). In general, the author adhered in "Fernando the Saint" to his accustomed practice of capitalizing civil, military, and religious titles only when using them as parts of proper names or titles. In accordance with this usage, some emendations are made to render the text self-consistent (see Emendations 273.12, 275.43). However, in a few instances Irving suspended his own rule, using the capitalized titles themselves as names or parts of nicknames; and when his intention to capitalize is clear, the copy-text is left unemended (see Discussions of Adopted Readings 297.24, Emendations 309.33, 318.17).

Limitations of space render it impracticable to list in the tables which follow all Irving's cancellations and corrections within the copy-text. The author's handwriting is readily distinguishable from that of Pierre M. Irving, but the authorship of marks such as deletions or commas is often difficult to specify with confidence. Thus all readings are assumed to be Irving's unless there is at least a distinct possibility that they are Pierre's. All emendations probably or certainly by Pierre are pointed out, but their being in pencil, ink, or both is not ordinarily noted.[477] Cancellations within the copy-text by Irving himself are set forth only if they reveal in an economical manner a situation presenting an editorial problem (for example, Emendations 278.32–33), provide the textual

---

477. Pierre M. Irving's handwritten chapter-numbers and chapter-headings, which served as the original copy for the *Spanish Papers* material interpolated here, are not recorded in the tables which follow, as they do not technically form parts of the copy-text.

bases for Discussions of Adopted Readings (Emendations 301.11), or pertain to revisions by Pierre.[478]

Unless recorded in the list of Emendations, substantive variants and accidental variants of particular interest between the copy-text and that in *Spanish Papers* are set forth in a separate table of Rejected Variants. The *Spanish Papers* text is frequently cited in the list of Emendations as the source of emended readings; but it should be emphasized that, while the published version does provide a useful indication of what well informed persons regarded as the author's probable wishes, it does not possess textual authority deriving directly from Irving. Emendations to the copy-text are made as a responsibility of the present editor rather than on the derived authority of *Spanish Papers*.

In the preparation of this edition the following collations have been made:

1. A typed transcription of the copy-text prepared from a xerox copy annotated on the basis of comparisons with the original made twice and independently, collated three times and independently with the text in *Spanish Papers* owned by the University of Texas (Ir8/ SP1/ 1866) and once with an additional copy owned by the National Library of Canada.

See Discussions and Lists pp. 534, 614, 676.

[MY UNCLE]

The manuscript of this work, which is owned by Yale University,[479] consists of text written on twelve unnumbered pages of unlined, unlaid paper. All the pages are 4 1/16" wide; pages [2]–[5] and [7]–[12] are 5 15/16", page [6] 4" in length; page [1] consists of two slips pasted together and is 8 1/8" long. The slip at the top of page [1], 2 9/16" high, includes ten lines of cancelled text which possibly portray another relation of the nameless narrator of the piece. The fact that it is pasted to the bottom slip, a sheet identical in size with pages [2]–[5] and [7]–[12], clearly suggests that in its original form the extant manuscript formed part of a larger projected work.[480] With the single exception of a cancelled four-word false start on page [12], which corresponds

478. Substantive and accidental readings inadvertently left uncancelled in the copy-text are listed in Emendations 297.3, 301.14.

479. A text of the sketch, omitting cancellations and substitutions, is included by Barbara D. Simison in her "Washington Irving's 'My Uncle,'" *Yale University Library Gazette*, 38 (October 1963), 86–91.

480. For a hypothetical discussion of its genesis, see Introduction, I, lxxxiii–lxxxix.

to no passage in the extant sketch,[481] Irving's text is written on one side of each sheet only.

The manuscript text includes numerous minor cancellations, ranging from a fraction of a word to 25 words, which suggest that in writing it Irving was composing as he went. From the neatness of the manuscript and the character of the author's corrections within it the process of composition appears to have been rather fluent. For example, the four lengthiest revisions are simple cancellations or parts of sentences, and the great majority of the substituted readings are not interlineated but follow cancellations of false starts immediately along the line. The text is written in a single shade of ink, suggesting that, once having drafted it, Irving left it unrevised. It includes no marks in a hand other than his.

In the list of Emendations which follows all variants within the manuscript, which necessarily serves as copy-text, are set forth. False starts immediately re-written are gathered in a single entry (Emendations 330.28). Recurrent varieties of emendation include conversion of ampersands to "and" (Emendations 330.23), adding apostrophes to possessives (Emendations 331.17), supplying periods at the ends of sentences (Emendations 332.28), and altering to lower-case form words capitalized in a manner not consistent with Irving's usual practice (Emendations 330.33).

See Discussions and Lists p. 635.

[SIR DAVID WILKIE IN SPAIN]

What is almost certainly the English text of the sketch of Wilkie in Spain which Irving prepared for publication, in Spanish, in a Seville newspaper[482] is extant in manuscript form at Yale University. Written in ink on six pages of plain, now yellowed paper 5⅛ x 8⅜″ in size,[483] the first five pages are numbered 1–5; the sixth is unnumbered (see Emendations 334.13). Three flamboyant ink flourishes utterly uncharacteristic of Irving, at the top of page 1 and the bottom of pages 3 and 4, may have been made by a copyist, or by Irving's translator, as indications of his progress

481. The cancelled words are: "⟨and a very thorough⟩".
482. See Introduction, I, lxxxix–xc.
483. The manuscript is accompanied by a sheet of paper folded at the center so as to form a booklet of four pages, on the first page of which is a notation in ink in an unknown hand: "Unpublished Essay by/ Washington Irving/ on/ Sir David Wilkie/ ———." Pages 1 and 2 of the manuscript are written on the first and third sides of a sheet folded as above; page 4 is written on the first side of such a sheet. Pages 3, 5, and [6] are written on loose sheets identical in size with the folded pages.

through the manuscript. Two other marks, a pencilled "x" in the left margin of page 3 opposite the beginning of a paragraph (T 334.21) and another at the top of the following page, were almost certainly made by Pierre M. Irving. While at work on the *Life and Letters* he habitually made reference marks of this sort in his uncle's papers; and a passage in the biography which, though not explicitly acknowledged, is clearly drawn from Irving's manuscript,[484] demonstrates that he was familiar with it.

Despite Irving's claim to Wilkie that his article was "hastily done,"[485] the manuscript suggests that he devoted some care to its composition. It includes 30 cancelled passages, ranging in length from a fragmentary word to 39 words. One of the longer cancellations, 27 words in length, Irving at once re-wrote after drafting a new clause introductory to it (see Emendations 333.25–27); but two other sentences, one 24 words characterizing "Mr Wilkies style of painting" and the other of 37 words and describing the "strong sensation" in England in response to Wilkie's productions upon his return from Spain, are simply deleted (see Emendations 334.26, 334.29). The Author was bringing his article into focus by excising material which did not touch immediately upon the attitudes of Wilkie and other Englishmen toward the painters of Spain. Besides these alterations reflecting a refined definition of the aims of the piece, the revisions in the manuscript are of a sort routine in Irving's miscellaneous writings—notably, substitutions of near-synonyms (for example, see Emendations 333.22) and deletions of false starts (Emendations 333.21).

Since the Yale University manuscript is the only version of Irving's essay located or known to exist, it is necessarily adopted as the copy-text. In the list of Emendations a full accounting is given of variants within the manuscript; false starts immediately rewritten are listed in a single entry (Emendations 333.21).

See Discussions and Lists pp. 537, 637.

THE VILLAGE CURATE

The manuscript of this work is owned by the Olin Library, Washington University. It consists of four sheets of woven rag paper, each sheet $9\frac{13}{16}$ x $7^{13}⁄_{16}''$ in size but folded in half on its long side so as to form a booklet. The fourth sheet is slipped within the fold of the third, the third within the second, and so on, and all four sheets are stitched together with

484. Compare T 334.13–20 with Pierre's interpolated comment on an extract from Irving's diary entry for April 18, 1828, describing his visit in company with Wilkie to the Chapel of St. Thomas at Seville; PMI, II, 311.

485. Irving to David Wilkie, Alhambra, Granada, May 15, 1829 (Yale).

string at the center of the fold. Irving's text, written in brown ink across the full width of each page, consists of eight numbered pages, written on the first and third sides of each folded sheet. His revisions to the text are with two exceptions written in the same color of ink.[486] The physical configuration of the manuscript, with its text on the first and third sides of folded sheets of paper, is characteristic of the author's works written or first drafted while in Spain between 1827 and 1829. Probably "The Village Curate" was intended at one time to form part of *The Alhambra* (1832), one of the works which Irving began during this period.[487]

The text is in an unhurried hand, somewhat more readily legible than most of Irving's manuscripts, and it reflects careful though not extensive revision. Of 57 cancellations and substitutions only 9 of the substitutions are interlineated, indicating that the author wrote the greater number of his revisions as he proceeded. Of the interlineated passages, all but one are very brief, from 1 to 4 words in length.

Since the Washington University manuscript is the only version of "The Village Curate" known to exist, it is necessarily adopted as copy-text. Some regularizations of the text have been made, including conversion of the ampersand to "and" (Emendations 335.9), addition of periods at the unpunctuated ends of sentences (Emendations 335.23), supplying end-of-line punctuation omitted from the manuscript (Emendations 335.14), and altering a few initial capitals to lower-case (Emendations 335.33, 336.9). In the list of Emendations which follows a full accounting is given of variants within the copy-text; false starts immediately rewritten and misspellings immediately corrected are gathered into a single entry (Emendations 335.10).

See Discussions and Lists p. 639.

THE LOG HOUSE HOTEL

The manuscript of this sketch, written in brown ink on eight numbered pages of woven rag paper, is owned by the Olin Library, Washington University. The pages are $7\frac{11}{16}$ x $4\frac{15}{16}''$ in size, except for page 5, which has an additional slip pasted across the bottom, forming a flap and

---

486. A six-line passage on page 4, cancelled in ink, is cancelled a second time by a series of diagonal lines in pencil (see Emendations 336.6); almost immediately above, Irving used pencil to write two angle brackets (⟨⟨) to indicate a paragraph break (T 336.5). The physical description of the manuscript is from information provided by Holly Hall, Acting Chief, Rare Books and Special Collections, Olin Library, Washington University.

487. For further discussion of the circumstances under which Irving composed the sketch, see Introduction, I, xc.

making the page when folded 10½ x 5″ in size, and page 8, which is 7$\frac{15}{16}$″ x 5¼″. Irving's text is on one side of each sheet only, except that on the reverse side of page 5 is a fragment of a discontinued letter: "Washington. Jan. 18th, 1833/ Gentlemen,/It is with."[488] Evidently the sketch, which describes an incident in the author's trip to the West in the fall of 1832, was written at some time after his return to the East in December of that year.[489]

His revisions to the work, made in a shade of ink identical with that in the remainder of the manuscript, reflect careful attention to syntax and word-choice but not to punctuation. The text is clearly not a fair copy with whose details Irving began tinkering but a revised draft. It includes 22 cancellations of 1 or 2 words, usually with substitutions above the line. Many of these reflect his wish to refine his caricature of "Sambo," the black servant. Thus, for example, he made adjustments to this character's speeches in dialect (see Emendations 337.34) and to the portrayal of his amusing behavior (Emendations 339.25). At four points he wrote interlinear revisions of passages a sentence or more in length, sometimes adding or deleting details but more frequently re-arranging the syntax of his statements. No marks by any hand other than Irving's are present in the manuscript.[490]

Because the Washington University manuscript is the only version of the work known to exist, it is necessarily adopted as copy-text. Several varieties of regularization are necessary to correct Irving's oversights and omissions. Pairs of double quotation marks are supplied to enclose direct quotations (Emendations 337.34), and commas are inserted to separate quotations from the authorial commentary (Emendations 338.15). Periods are supplied at the unpunctuated ends of sentences (Emendations 338.40), or more frequently, they are substituted for Irving's hasty dashes at those points (Emendations 337.35). End-of-line commas neglected by the author are inserted (Emendations 337.35), apostrophes are added to contractions (Emendations 337.35), question marks are supplied at appropriate points (Emendations 338.3), ampersands are converted to "and" (Emendations 338.3–4), and a few words capitalized for no apparent reason and in a manner inconsistent with Irving's usual practice in the copy-text are emended to lower-case forms

488. The physical description of the manuscript is based on information supplied by Holly Hall, Acting Chief, Rare Books and Special Collections, Olin Library, Washington University.

489. For a more particular discussion of the place of the incident in Irving's 1832 tour, and of the circumstances under which his sketch was written, see Introduction, I, xc–xci.

490. This sketch has been edited and published by John F. McDermott, "An Unpublished Washington Irving Manuscript," *Papers on English Language and Literature*, 1, no. 4 (Autumn 1965), 369–73.

(Emendations 338.29). In the list of Emendations a full accounting is given of variants within the copy-text.

See Discussions and Lists p. 642.

[HISTORY OF THE CONQUEST OF MEXICO]

A single manuscript page of Irving's uncompleted history exists in fac-simile form. It was published in 1915 by Joseph F. Taylor as an illustra-tion to his article, "Washington Irving's Mexico," wherein a printed text six times the length of the manuscript specimen, a portion corresponding to it, is also given. Taylor claimed to be presenting this "most interesting fragment" in its entirety, and he suggested that it "probably formed a part of the introductory chapter." The present whereabouts of the manuscript fragment, which in 1915 had "recently come to light,"[491] is unknown.

On the basis of the facsimile, the only description of the original manu-script page that can be given with confidence is that it was written and carefully revised in ink across the full width of a sheet of paper. This configuration may suggest that it derives from a period subsequent to Irving's residence in Madrid in 1827 and 1828, when his interest in the conquest of Mexico led him to undertake a partial translation of Padre Sahagún's *Historia* and to perform work of some kind on another manu-script he designated as "Montezuma."[492] At that time he tended to write his drafts of narratives on Spanish subjects on the right-hand five-eighths of pages, leaving ample space for recasting and adding new material. The facsimile page is clearly not an early draft. Its 13 cancelled readings bespeak close attention to the shaping of phrases and to nice distinctions in word-choice characteristic of a later stage of composition. The re-visions are minor—deletions of false starts, or else substitutions for single words (for example see Rejected Variants 340.5). Probably the text pub-lished by Taylor does represent a portion of an early chapter in the draft Irving was writing in December 1838, when he was "dismounted from [his] *cheval de bataille*" by William H. Prescott.[493]

The text published by Taylor is Irving's adapted translation of a pas-sage in Don Antonio de Solis y Ribadeneyra, *Historia de la Conquista de Mexico . . .* (1771), I, 147–49.[494] In the Solis text, which the author

491. Taylor, "Washington Irving's Mexico: A Lost Fragment," *The Bookman*, 41 (1915), 665–69.

492. Andrew B. Myers, ed. "Washington Irving's Madrid Journal 1827–1828 and Related Letters," *Bulletin of New York Public Library*, 62 (1958), 410.

493. Irving to Pierre M. Irving, Madrid, March 24, 1844; PMI, III, 143.

494. The passage is in a chapter of Book II of the *Historia*, entitled "Refierense Diferentes Prodigios, y señales que se vieron en Mexico, antes que llegase Cortés, de que aprehendieron los Indios, que se acercaba la ruína de aquel Imperio."

had studied repeatedly while living in Spain,[495] an Aztec laborer is portrayed as presenting himself at the palace of Montezuma and demanding an audience with the emperor. Upon being admitted into the presence of his sovereign, the peasant tells a story of being grasped by the *"garres"* of *"un Aguila de extraordinaria grandeza,"* of being flown to its distant eyrie, and of being told there by the eagle of men coming from another part of the world to destroy Montezuma's kingdom and also his religion. In adapting this strange fable, Irving simply altered the laborer's tale from a quoted speech to a third-person narrative. The only detail in the Taylor text which Irving did not glean from Solis was the name of the peasant, who in the *Historia* is referred to simply as "un Labrador."

A collation of the single page of manuscript facsimile accompanying Taylor's printed text with that edited version yields the unhappy conclusion that the published fragment is probably not very true to Irving's original. Taylor includes none of the variants on the page of manuscript text; he silently makes 3 substantive emendations (see Emendations 340.8, 340.12–14, 340.14), he twice alters Irving's spelling, and he introduces 10 other accidental readings not authorized by the manuscript. Probably the remainder of the published text differs in similar ways from the remainder of the manuscript.

Nevertheless, in spite of its possible corruption the Taylor version is the sole authority we have for the fragment in its entirety, and there is no choice but to adopt it as copy-text. Naturally, for those portions of the copy-text which correspond to the manuscript facsimile—T 340.1–14 He .... water—the latter version assumes overriding authority. In the tables which follow a full accounting is given of variants between the copy-text and the facsimile page, and of variants within the manuscript facsimile. Variants of the latter variety not set forth in the list of Emendations appear in a separate table of Rejected Variants; false starts immediately rewritten in the manuscript are listed in a single entry (Rejected Variants 340.4).

In the preparation of this edition a typed transcription of the manuscript facsimile has been collated twice and independently with the corresponding portion of the printed text.

See Discussions and Lists pp. 537, 645, 676.

---

495. See *Washington Irving Diary. Spain 1828–1829*, ed. Clara L. Penney (New York, 1926), pp. 75, 76. As a possible indication that the text published by Joseph F. Taylor was based upon a manuscript written in 1828 rather than ten years later, it may be noticed that on October 21, 1828 Irving recorded in his diary reading "Solis Hist. Mexico," and began the next day's entry: "Write at Mexican Story." Quite possibly he began at that time a narrative derived in some way from Solis.

ILLUSTRATION TO THE LEGEND OF
PRINCE AHMED

The manuscript of this appendage to "The Legend of Prince Ahmed al Kamel; or, The Pilgrim of Love," a tale which appeared in the Author's Revised Edition of *The Alhambra* (1850), is extant in the Princeton University Library.[496] The text is written fluently in ink on one side of eight numbered sheets of medium weight unlaid paper, each 4⅜″ x 6¼″ in size.[497] It may have been omitted from the revised edition of *The Alhambra* because Irving's extensive additions to that work had swollen it to a size precluding the insertion of further material. As he indicates at the conclusion of the "Illustration," the work is chiefly an adaptation and condensation of a passage in *The Koran*, as translated and annotated by George Sale (1697?–1736).[498] The *Bibliotheque Orientale* ... of Barthélemy de Herbelot, who is also mentioned in the concluding note, was Irving's authority for the comment that "Arabian traditions" recount "several miracles" as occurring in the course of the visit between Solomon and Balkis (T 343.35).[499]

The manuscript includes several cancelled passages, ranging from a fragment of a word to 12 words in length. As one might expect in so straightforward a process of adaptation as resulted in the "Illustration," Irving's alterations were minor, not once including changes to the whole of a sentence. They included simple deletions and substitutions of a word or two (for example, see Emendations 343.19), cancellations of false starts (Emendations 343.7), and adjustments of syntax (Emendations 342.5). The revisions are in the same shade of ink as the unrevised text.

In the list of Emendations all variants within the manuscript, which necessarily serves as copy-text, are set forth; false starts immediately rewritten are listed together in a single entry (Emendations 342.14). Classes of multiple emendations include supplying pairs of double quotation marks (Emendations 342.31), adding quotation marks to incomplete

---

496. The manuscript text has been edited and published by Howard C. Horsford, "Illustration to the Legend of Prince Ahmed[:] An Unpublished Sketch by Washington Irving," *Princeton University Library Chronicle*, 14 (1952–53), 30–36.

497. Written in pencil from the bottom upwards in the left margin of the first page is the notation: "7–29–38. Philip A Rollins '89 — Friend — gift."

498. The first edition of Sale's translation was published at London in 1734; in that edition see Chapter XXVII "*Intitled*, The Ant; revealed at MECCA," pp. 309–16. Sale's *Koran* was reprinted many times, and which edition Irving used is not known.

499. In the *Bibliotheque Orientale, ou Bibliotheque Universel, contenant générale-ment tout ce qui regarde la connaissance les peuples des Orient. Leurs histoires et traditions fableuses* .... (Paris, 1697), see especially the article entitled "Soliman ben Daoud," pp. 819–21; see also "Div ou Dive," p. 298; "Gian," p. 396; and "Peri," pp. 701–02. The *Bibliotheque Orientale* appeared in five editions during the eighteenth century; which one Irving used is unknown.

pairs (Emendations 343.1), supplying end-of-line commas omitted from the manuscript (Emendations 342.12), and altering words not ordinarily capitalized by Irving to lower-case forms (Emendations 342.16).

See Discussions and Lists p. 646.

[A VOYAGE UP THE HUDSON RIVER IN 1800]

According to Pierre M. Irving, Irving's account of his youthful voyage formed "part of an unfinished article commenced in June, 1851" as a contribution to *The Home Book of the Picturesque* (1852); it was "thrown aside" to give place to "The Catskill Mountains," the article of his which did appear in that work.[500] As published for the first time in PMI, the reminiscence does reveal in two brief passages its common origin with "The Catskill Mountains," but at both points the *Home Book* text is thoroughly revised from the earlier version.[501] The two passages which represent sections of text reworked in "The Catskill Mountains" constitute less than one-sixth the length of the fragmentary essay included in PMI. Pierre M. Irving was thus accurate when, introducing the latter text, he remarked that "with this exception [*i.e.*, the two overlaps] the extract is new, and affords a curious picture of some of the features of the river travel of bygone days." The manuscript from which he transcribed portions to be included in the biography has since been lost. Of necessity, then, the PMI version is adopted as copy-text.

In the preparation of this edition the texts in three copies of PMI in the possession of the editor (see the Introduction to the Textual Commentary) have been sight collated.

See Discussions and Lists pp. 537, 647.

[A JOURNEY TO SACKETT'S HARBOR IN 1814]

These four paragraphs were first published in PMI, I, 317–18, where they served as a first-hand account of a part of Irving's military mission to Sackett's Harbor. According to Pierre M. Irving the manuscript text, which has since been lost, was written on four sheets of paper, numbered 10–13, and "evidently form[ed] pages of an article, which [Irving] had prepared for the press" but for some reason had not seen into print. Introducing the passage, Pierre quoted a few phrases apparently taken

---

500. PMI, I, 40; for "The Catskill Mountains," see pp. 163–67 above.
501. Compare "[A Voyage]," PMI, I, 40.16–24 My . . . now (T 344.3–10), 42.20–43.2 But . . . . landscape (T 345.16–26) with "The Catskill Mountains," *Home Book*, 72.27–73.6 I . . . . it (T 164.4–11), 74.2–13 All . . . . since (T 164.37–165.7).

from a fragmentary statement on the first page: "The narrative begins on the second day after [Irving] had left Utica, when he was proceeding on his way amid such 'general stillness' that 'the fall of an acorn among the dry leaves would resound through the forest'" (I, 316–17).

In light of its autobiographical subject-matter, its emphasis upon the panoramic beauty of the wilderness landscape, and its having been at Irving's death (according to Pierre) in a state ready for publication, quite possibly the text formed part of the autobiographical reminiscences the author had prepared as his contribution to *The Home Book of the Picturesque* (1852) but had set aside in favor of "The Catskill Mountains." If so, then the fragment derives from the same rejected essay as his account of a voyage up the Hudson River in 1800.[502]

In the absence of an alternative choice, the PMI version of the work is necessarily adopted as copy-text. In the preparation of this edition the texts in three copies of PMI in the possession of the editor (see the Introduction to the Textual Commentary) have been sight collated.

See Discussions and Lists p. 647.

---

502. See "The Catskill Mountains," pp. 163–67; "[A Voyage up the Hudson River in 1800]," pp. 344–45.

DISCUSSIONS OF ADOPTED READINGS

These commentaries describe textual problems at the points signified in the tables by asterisks; and in addition they include explanations of decisions whether to emend at other problematical points not recorded in the tables. Each discussion is preceded by a page-line reference and key word or words for the passage under consideration; a bracket separates this information from the editorial comments which follow.

A key to identifying symbols used in referring to manuscript and printed texts is given on pages 348–54.

[REVIEW OF *A CHRONICLE OF THE CONQUEST OF GRANADA*]

4.2–3 [REVIEW ... *GRANADA*]] The asterisk following the title in 2A refers to a footnote, probably adapted by Pierre M. Irving from one Washington Irving had included in his "Note to the Revised Edition" of the *Conquest of Granada,* p. xv. The note in 2A is as follows: "*Note by the Author.* This review, published in the *London Quarterly Review* for 1830, was written by the author at the request of his London publisher, to explain the real nature of his work, and its claim to historic truth."

11.29–30 "I ... one,"] See C, I, 17: " 'I will pick out the seeds one by one of this pomegranate,' said the wary Ferdinand."

12.38–13.9 "This ... Zahara."] The quotation is from C, I, 19–20.

15.5–8 "This ... Granada."] A loose adaptation of the original in C, I, 30–31.

15.29–43 "He ... foot."] The quotation is from C, I, 61.

16.12–26 "They . . . friends."] The quotation is from C, I, 68–69. In C a paragraph break and two sentences intervene between "mountains" and "It" (16.20); the hiatus is indicated in 1E by a series of dots.

17.3–21 "The ... enemy."] Lines 17.3–15 (The ... defiance) are quoted from C, I, 76–77; at that point Irving skips to C, I, 80 for the remainder of the quotation.

18.3–31 "Boabdil ... victory."] Lines 18.3–19 (Boabdil .... sorrow ....) are quoted from C, I, 137–38. The series of dots following "sorrow" denotes a hiatus of one paragraph in the quotation (see C, I, 138–39), whose latter portion, 18.20–31, is from C, I, 139–40.

18.39–19.42 "The . . . flight."] The quotation is from C, I, 151–53.

20.3–39 "The ... Atar."] The quotation is from C, I, 163–65.

21.31–23.32 "Great ... behold.' "] The quotation is from C, I, 326–32. The series of dots following "followers" (21.43) signifies a hiatus of ten sentences (see C, I, 327).

23.38–24.32 "At . . . premeditated."] The quotation is from C, I, 354–57. However, following "hearts" (24.23) five sentences in the original are omitted (see C, I, 355–56).

24.39 his versatile subjects] The word "versatile" seems odd in this context. Irving has characterized the Moorish populace as continually shifting its opinions of its rulers in a manner "changeful as the wind" (21.21), and since the declining reputation of El Zagal is being discussed in the present passage, the changefulness of the citizenry would seem to be what he intends to signify by "versatile." "Mercurial" or "volatile" seem more appropriate. However, since "versatile" does imply diversity of potential, it is sufficiently suitable as not to require emendation.

25.4–40 "While . . . sepulchre."] The quotation is from C, II, 208–11.

26.27–27.23 "Having . . . Moor.' "] The quotation is from C, II, 379–82.

[REVIEW OF ALEXANDER SLIDELL'S *A YEAR IN SPAIN*]

30.22 The frightful stories] This sentence begins a passage (30.22–28 that the) Irving wrote on an unnumbered sheet as an interpolation in the text on p. 2, first series of MSm.

32.15 *impayable.*] Irving's parenthetical reference identifies the page in Y, volume I, on which the passage to be quoted at this point (32.16–33.17) begins.

33.21 end of it.] Irving's quoted phrase and page-reference identify . the beginning of the passage in Y, volume I, to be introduced at this point (33.22–34.3).

34.7 the individual.] Irving's quotation and page-reference identify the beginning of the passage in Y to be introduced at this point (34.8–36).

35.5 earthquake.] Irving's quotation and page-reference identify the beginning of the passage in Y to be introduced at this point (35.6–36.12). In 1E the quotation introduced here is followed by another, on a closely related topic (36.13–37.33), which is given without intervening commentary. Because at least a page is missing from MSm following p. 11, first series (which concludes with the introduction to the initial quotation discussed here), we have no indication whether Irving wrote a transitional statement connecting the two quoted discussions of a *diligence*. However, in view of Lockhart's habit of condensing or omitting quoted material whenever possible, we may at least assume on the basis of their presence in the magazine text that Irving intended to include both passages concerning the *diligence*.

37.34–38.4 [We . . . him.]] This passage, for which the copy-text is missing, is adopted from 1E text (325.17–32).

41.41–42.2 [The . . . . cares is]] In 1E (328.29–33, 329.8–9), from which the bracketed passage is taken in the absence of a copy-text, a quotation from Y is introduced following the first of the two sentences interpolated here. However, the extant portion of MSm makes clear Irving's intention to insert the quotation at the point where it appears in this edition, 42.7–27.

42.3 wonderfully] The word "Wonderfully" is the first on page ⟨12⟩, first series, in MSm, following a hiatus of at least a page. The "w" is capitalized, if not boldly so, but Irving's intention was nevertheless not for the word to begin a sentence. Divested of the phrases interpolated here from 1E ("This picture . . . is," 42.1–2), the statement is simply an incomplete comparison, not a deliberately fragmentary sentence of the sort which follows it. The extant conclusion of the sentence ("wonderfully . . . son," 42.2–4) is hence spliced together with the phrases preceding it in the corresponding sentence in 1E.

42.6 master hand.] Irving's page-reference indicates the beginning of a passage in Y to be introduced at this point (42.7–27).

43.34 impurificado.] Irving's fragmentary quotation identifies the beginning of the passage in Y to be introduced at this point (43.35–45.5). In 1E Slidell's description of Don Diego is divided into two separate sections and is considerably revised from Y; Irving's intention was presumably to present the passage as it appears in the work under review. On the reverse side of p. 8, second series in MSm are two lines of cancelled text which Irving adapted from a portion of the Y passage quoted here (see 44.32–33): "⟨coat, whose colour, of the falling leaf,/seemed indicative of his fortunes.⟩"

45.6–16 [We . . . . sent]] Owing to the absence of a copy-text for this passage—p. 7, second series is missing from MSm—it is necessary to fill the hiatus by drawing upon 1E (331.5–17).

45.33 mass.] Irving's quotation and page-reference identify (erroneously as to the latter; see Emendations 46.22) the beginning of the passage in Y to be introduced at this point (45.34–46.22).

45.39 beauty.] The asterisk in 1E corresponds to an explanatory footnote, without precedent in Y, at the bottom of the page (331.41–46):
*So it has usually been in countries where the dark complexions predominate[.] Witness the blue eyes and golden tresses of the classical poets of antiquity— and the yellow periwigs which the Roman ladies of the imperial times used to import from the banks of the Rhine and the Danube. See Professor Bottiger's 'Sabina, or Scenes from the Toilette of a Roman Dame,'—one of the most valuable works of that equally learned and amusing author.

The copy-text gives no indication that the note is by Irving; it is hence omitted as probably by Lockhart.

46.31 girl. Frank] The 1E reading is an appropriate emendation of MSm, causing the first sentence to serve specifically as an introduction

to the second, which is fragmentary. However, the practice of employing a fragmentary sentence for summary characterization is typical of
Irving; see for example 42.4–6.

46.39 creation.] Irving's brief quotation and page-reference identify
the beginning of the passage in Y to be inserted at this point (47.1–17).

47.18 As our object] Although this phrase, which begins page 12,
second series in MSm, is written beginning at the left margin, Irving
clearly intended it to begin a paragraph. It is preceded by a quotation from Y (47.1–17) on an entirely different topic, and the manuscript
page preceding it is only two-thirds filled, indicating the end of an
expository unit.

47.27 Panza.] Irving's brief quotation and page-reference identify (the
latter inaccurately; see 48.24) the beginning of the passage in Y to be
inserted here (47.28–48.24).

48.26 oil.] Irving's brief phrases and page-reference together identify
the beginning of a passage in Y to be inserted at this point (48.27–
49.6).

49.14 happily.] Irving's brief phrases and page-reference identify (the
latter inaccurately; see 50.32) the beginning of a passage in Y to be
inserted at this point (49.15–50.32).

50.33–35 [We . . . Cordova.]] Owing to the absence of a copy-text
for this passage—p. 15, second series is missing in MSm—it is necessary
to fill the hiatus by drawing upon 1E (335.37–40). Because it is clear
from the extant portion of MSm that Irving did intend to quote the
passage from Y introduced by this sentence in 1E—see 55.19–21 and
the Textual Commentary, note 255—the quotation (50.36–55.17) is
not enclosed in brackets.

54.40–44 "*A ratcatcher . . . rateros."] Slidell's explanatory footnote
and the asterisk referring to it (54.8) are omitted from 1E but are
included here, despite the absence of manuscript evidence of Irving's
intention. From his summary references in MSm to the passages for
quotation, Irving appears to have wished them given whole rather
than in the mutilated form at times imposed by Lockhart.

55.39 story.] Irving's brief phrases followed by a citation identify the
beginning of a passage in Y to be inserted at this point (55.40–57.10).

[ADDRESS AT THE IRVING DINNER, MAY 30, 1832]

59.17–18 Mr. Irving . . . hailed.] Clearly the journalists handled the
transition from the events preceding Irving's address to the speech
proper in slightly different ways. Irving may have deleted his sentences
in MSv so as to enable the reporters to devise whatever transitions
they chose. His cancelled sentence is restored here as forming an
integral part of his own introduction, which is necessary to set the scene.

60.40 —As long as I live!"]   The similarity between the sentence added
in the published texts and the pencilled insertion in MSv by an
unknown person (see Emendations 60.26–27) suggests that the individual either copied inaccurately from a published account or quoted
from memory. It seems possible that Irving's address did at some point
include a statement similar to the interpolation in the manuscript and
at this point in the published texts, but the copy-text affords no
indication that he wished it to appear in print. It is rejected from this
text, which represents not his speech itself but his account of it for
the use of the journalists.

[REVIEW OF HENRY WHEATON'S
HISTORY OF THE NORTHMEN]

63.35–38 "The . . . island."]   The quotation is from H, p. 50.

63.40–43 "it . . . tongue."]   The loose quotation is from H, p. 50, where
Wheaton cites as authority for his comment on Icelandic language
a study by the Danish philologist Rasmus Rask (1787–1832).

64.26–65.43 "The . . . . heart."]   The quotation is from H, pp. 54–55,
58–59. Following "people" (65.13) Irving omits five paragraphs in H.

66.11–16 "Vid . . . . looked;"—]   The specimen of Icelandic verse and
the English original are quoted—the former inaccurately—from Ebenezer
Henderson's *Iceland; or the Journal of a Residence in the Island,
during the Years 1814–1815*, 2 vols. (Edinburgh, 1818), II, 368.

67.5–68.2 "O . . . . rings."] The quotation is from H, I, 85–86, where the
verses are acknowledged as by "The Hon. W. Spencer."

68.6–12 "are . . . land."] The quotation is from H, p. 88.

68.17–21 "The . . . departed."] The quotation is from H, p. 80.

71.6–15 "The . . . . art."]   This loose quotation is from H, p. 121.

74.5–6 "they . . . fire."]   The adapted quotation is from H, p. 135.

74.11–18 "sometimes . . . . isle."]   The quotation is from H, p. 139.

75.33–40 "Cease . . . . !"]   The quotation is from H, p. 54.

76.37–77.2 "The . . . . incursions."]   Although, as Irving indicates, the
quotation is from H, pp. 189–90, following "father" (76.39) a sentence
and fifteen lines of verse in H are omitted.

77.27–30 "the . . . history."]   The quotation is from H, pp. 162–63.

77.42–79.3 "The . . . . France."]   The quotation is from H, pp. 165–67.

79.15–21 "Under . . . . them."]   The quotation is from H, pp. 245–46.

81.30–33 "Par . . . successeur."]   The quotation is from H, p. 350, where
it is cited as from "Thierry, tom. 1, p. 221."

82.14–18 "The . . . arrow."]   The quotation is from H, p. 358.

83.35–37 "Fight . . . yours."]   This quotation is from H, p. 363, in which
the speech continues for five more sentences.

83.40–85.29 "The . . . . knights."]   The quotation is from H, pp. 364–67.

85.33–38 "Years . . . curfew,"] The passage is quoted accurately from Francis Palgrave, *History of England. Volume I. Anglo-Saxon Period.* . . . (London, 1831), p. 389.

86.33–39 "All . . . . antiquary."] The quotation is in fact a loose adaptation of Palgrave's *History of England*, p. 387: "But all this pomp and solemnity has passed away like a dream. The 'perpetual prayer[']' has ceased for ever—the roll of Battle is rent.—The shields of the Norman lineages are trodden in the dust.—The abbey is levelled with the ground—and a dank and reedy pool fills the spot where the foundations of the quire have been uncovered, merely for the gaze of the idle visiter, or the instruction of the moping antiquary."

COMMUNIPAW

123.16 and its] The 1A reading, "from whence its," is an appropriate emendation, making explicit a spatial point of view only implied in Irving's statement, and also rendering parallel two coordinated clauses which are not parallel in MSn; but the 1A reading is not a correction of an outright error and so is rejected.

124.26–27 worthy . . . record] In MSn the cancellation is written on the first line of page 7 in Irving's first draft. The "worthy of" superseding it is on a slip of paper, also numbered 7, pasted to the top of the sheet.

127.24 highway; endeavored] The 1A emended reading, in restoring Irving's deleted connective, does not relate the verb phrase to the tandem series of phrases in the manner the author clearly intended. Irving's parallel phrases are connected by semicolons, not commas followed by "and"; hence the emendation.

CONSPIRACY OF THE COCKED HATS

133.2 Many is the time] An unusual but not unprecedented use of "many" construed as singular; see OED, "many," def. 1E. No emendation is made.

THE "EMPIRE OF THE WEST"

136.6–7 how . . . citizens] On the verso of p. 5 in MSv are six cancelled lines which constitute a draft of this passage: "¶⟨itself at the mouth of the Columbia/ how a mere trading company has seated/ itself at the ↑that great western↓ ⟨great⟩ portal of our empire/ on the Shores of the Pacific, and has/ virtually locked it against our own/ citizens⟩"

136.18 ¶We] In N, the quoted passage begins in mid-sentence in a paragraph describing "some defects" in "the practical working of the political institutions of the United States." The beginning of the sentence is: "Among these, we . . ." (pp. 100–01).

AMERICAN RESEARCHES IN ITALY

154.26 are drawn forth] The present tense is somewhat surprising at this point in Irving's summary of Wilde's past researches and their results. Probably he is referring to an as yet unpublished writing by Wilde; see 156.36.

CORRECTION OF A MISSTATEMENT RESPECTING *ASTORIA*

161.25–32 The work . . . . known.] This passage comprises the contents of Tab "C" in MStc; see Textual Commentary, note 338. At its conclusion Irving wrote in pencil: "I never asked nor received &c"; see 161.32.

162.2–3 the amount . . . exaggerated.] The accepted reading comprises the contents of Tab "A" in MStc; see Textual Commentary, note 338. Before pasting the tab onto the copy, Irving first deleted the pre-copy-text reading and wrote beside it, in ink: "the amount, as stated to him, was greatly exaggerated." Tab "A" is pasted over that intermediate version.

162.13–14 when, . . . obliged to seek] The accepted reading comprises the contents of Tab "B" in MStc; see Textual Commentary, note 338. The words "to seek," necessary to connect the interpolation and the portion of the sentence retained from the earlier draft (162.14–16 accommodations . . . declined), are in pencil. Irving neglected to delete the text superseded by Tab "B." Below the tab is written another, intermediate version: "when, by investing my very moderate means in wild lands [I?] was straitened and obliged [to?] seek"

162.19–26 The only . . . . investment.] This passage comprises the contents of Tab "D" in MStc; see Textual Commentary, note 338. At its conclusion, Irving began a new paragraph: "My intimacy with Mr A. &c &c"; see 162.27.

162.39–40 who, . . . regarded him] Irving first wrote "who" and "ed" in the right margin, but to ensure clarity he drew a line to the bottom of the sheet, where he copied the phrase as revised: "who, like Malte Brun, regarded him/ &c &c"

THE CATSKILL MOUNTAINS

163.24–27 In many . . . . mighty forest] On the reverse side of page 12 in MSt, partially obscured by the heavy paper on which the sheet is mounted, are a few deleted phrases which appear to comprise an early version of this passage: "In this great [*ten words unrecovered*] Here are vast rocky ridges clothed with primeval forests"

164.4–5 I . . . mountains.] In MSt this sentence is underlined in pencil by an unknown hand. Similar markings occur at points corresponding to 164.12–14 I . . . marvellous, 165.6–7 host . . . since. Following "perished" at a point corresponding to 166.30–at the end of a paragraph–a spiral flourish in written in pencil across the blank remaining space in the line.

CONVERSATIONS WITH TALMA

170.10–11 for . . . and natural outbreaks] The 1A reading fulfills Irving's intention of specifying the varieties of "familiar touches" achieved by Shakespeare. Because he neglected to delete the semicolon following "touches," in MSh the sentence appears to be dominated by a series of three poorly coordinated phrases characterizing aspects of Shakespeare's talents; in fact, only two such qualities are cited–"the individuality of his characters" and "the varied play of his language."

170.18 strangers."] Irving's extended dash, a flourish he made upon completing the initial portion of the MSh text, was perhaps first intended to separate the section just concluded from the transitional note which follows (170.20–25). However, the purpose is specifically served by a short rule he wrote on the first line of a slip of paper pasted to the bottom of p. 8 in MSh, and including the first four lines of the bracketed note (170.20–22 [To . . . were). The first dash is hence omitted as serving no purpose.

[MEMOIR OF WASHINGTON ALLSTON]

177.9 on the subject.] Irving's slurred "re" in MSn may in fact be "on," the 1A and 3A reading, which suits the context. Since the word occurs at the end of a line in MSn, it may also be the beginning of "re/garding," the latter portion of which Irving neglected to add on the next line. In any case, "re" or "re." is not characteristic of his practice in his journals and letters, much less in his published writings; "on" is hence adopted as a reasonable alternative which may in fact represent his intention.

[THE CHRONICLE OF PELAYO]

180.2 [THE CHRONICLE OF PELAYO] The title supplied to MSv by Pierre M. Irving duplicates the one employed by the author when he thought of including a version of the narrative in *Legends of the Conquest of Spain*; see PMI, III, 74. It also echoes the concluding line of the final draft (see T 199.36). However, in 1847 Irving referred to the work as "The Chronicle of Pelayo," just as he referred to all the narratives he revised at that time as "a series of Chronicles" (PMI, IV, 14–15). In 1859, when he showed his Spanish manuscripts to Pierre M. Irving, the latter designated the works as "his Spanish chronicles in manuscript" (Journal, 1859, p. [21]—Berg Collection, New York Public Library), quite possibly reproducing the term Irving had used. "CHRONICLE" is thus employed in the title as apparently representing the author's latest intention.

185.36–42 "What . . . . child?"] In MSv the quotation marks in this passage are supplied in pencil by Pierre M. Irving.

186.20–23 The Gascons . . . dared.] Although the phrase "says the worthy Agapida" suggests that the present passage and its continuation (186.23–27) constitute a direct quotation, Irving apparently intended to present it as an indirect summary of Agapida's opinion rather than a reproduction of his exact words. The punctuation in the pre-copy-text versions, which are both cast as indirect quotations, lends weight to this view. Hence quotation marks are not supplied. Similar situations, with similar precedent in MSy and 1A, occur at 189.22–29, 191.20–22, 191.32–41.

190.18 harbouring . . . beasts] Below the line, to the left of the tear on page 30 in MSv, Pierre M. Irving wrote in pencil: "? herding with/ harboring with." Later, preceding Washington Irving's "ha," he inserted in ink above the line, "harbo⟨u⟩ring with." In the roughly corresponding passage in MSy, Washington Irving had employed the locution "harbour with," which in 1A is emended to "harbor with." The evidence thus indicates "harbouring" as likely his intention in MSv.

192.8 Don Roderick] Probably on the precedent of Irving's having on several occasions in the preceding chapter deleted the "Don" before "Pelayo" (see Emendations 188.11), Pierre M. Irving deleted the title here. However, the author's intention in referring to Pelayo was not necessarily the same as to Roderick the Goth; the title is restored.

196.21–23 with . . . . accept] Two or perhaps three lines of text at the bottom of renumbered page 50 in MSv are lost; the word "accept" begins page 51. For this passage, the T text is drawn from 4A, 237.28–30.

196.36–197.40 So . . . . clamber] The 4A text, 238.14–240.12, is adopted to fill the hiatus created by the missing renumbered pages 52–55 of MSv.

[THE SUCCESSORS OF PELAYO. FAVILA]

200.10–14 Of . . . faith.] Irving drafted and revised this fragmentary sentence with sufficient care that his intention seems clearly to have been to separate it from the preceding sentence, perhaps in order to render its contents more distinct as illustrations of the general characteristics mentioned immediately before. His locution is permitted to stand.

201.22 prince of the apostles] Irving appears to intend this epithet referring to St. Peter as a descriptive term rather than a title; his clearly written lower-case "p" and "a" are left unemended.

CHRONICLE OF THE OMMIADES

208.10 camels, he] The inserted "he" in 2A dispels some of the ambiguity in Irving's sentence, wherein any of three individuals might be supposed the subject of "set out . . . Cordova"; the "he" reduces the figure to two: Yusuf, Irving's intended reference, and Amer ben Amru.

208.24 Amru, his son, and secretary] The MSn reading leaves it unclear whether "his son and secretary" denotes one person or two. The ambiguity is compounded by an earlier reference (208.9) which admits of either interpretation. Conde, Irving's source, makes it clear (Part II, Chapter 4) that "son" and "secretary" are two different persons; hence the comma inserted here to distinguish them.

208.40 sovereign] Irving's note in MSn designating the sequence of the text to follow is deleted by Pierre M. Irving. Below the cancelled note Pierre then copied 8 lines onto the manuscript from the appropriate passage in 1A (432.34–40 saw . . . . where), pasting the remainder of the printed page 432 onto the bottom of the manuscript page.

218.4–6 [CHAPTER IV . . . . HIXEM.]] Pierre M. Irving's preliminary material for this chapter and Chapters V–VIII is emended to conform to the Putnam house style as modified throughout this edition of the *Complete Works* by Twayne Publishers.

221.1–3 "The . . . slain."] The beginning of the passage purportedly quoted from an "Arabian chronicler" is readily identifiable; the conclusion is less so. The quotation may possibly extend through the remainder of the paragraph, to 221.10, but because Irving ordinarily quotes only single sentences from his fictional sources, it is presumed to conclude as indicated here.

222.13–14 AH AD/ 180 796] The reference dates are deleted in pencil by Pierre M. Irving, and are hence restored. They are written in the left margin slightly above the first line of Washington Irving's text.

228.29 return immediately] The cancellation is by Pierre M. Irving and was made in order to avoid repeating "immediately" within a single sentence. Though awkward, Washington Irving's reading is restored.

231.10 Candy] Pierre M. Irving underlined the name and in the left margin of MSc wrote "Candia?" Conde spells the name "Candax." Washington Irving's spelling was obsolescent but had not been entirely supplanted by Pierre's modern alternative, and so it is permitted to stand.

231.19–20 [CHAPTER IX . . . ALHAKEM.]] The chapter-number and chapter-heading are supplied in the absence of a copy-text. The chapter-heading is a rough translation of the title of Irving's source at this point, Conde's *Historia*, Part II, Chapter 37.

CHRONICLE OF FERNAN GONZALEZ, COUNT OF CASTILE

234.4 Gonzalo Nuño] In MSv, Irving refers to this individual by two different names: in the present passage he is "Gonzalez Nuño"; at 234.22, "Gonsalvo Nuñez." The inconsistency is perhaps explainable by Irving's reliance on various sources as he wrote out his narrative. In Mariana's *Historia General*, his source for the genealogical sketch, the name is spelled "Gonzalo Nuño" (Book III, Chapter 2); however in Bleda's *Coronica* the name is given as "Gonçalo Nunez" (Book III, Chapter 18), which approximates the reading at 234.22. Mariana's spelling is adopted in both instances.

235.32 wars.*] Using pencil, Pierre M. Irving deleted the asterisk in MSv and also the footnote to which it refers (235.43). Probably he did so because the reference to "Sandoval ut supra" ("Sandoval as above") is meaningless within this chronicle in itself, as being the first footnote in the work. However, Washington Irving intended to publish "Fernan Gonzalez" as one of a group of narratives, and he may well have planned to include a reference to Sandoval in a work which preceded "Fernan Gonzalez" in the series. The note is hence restored, regularized according to the Putnam house style.

239.16 ¶His] The word is written at the left margin on the top line of page 18 in MSv, but the bottom line of the preceding page includes only 2 words; the paragraph break is clearly intended. Similar situations occur in MSv at points corresponding to 255.14, 261.27, 262.6, 263.43, 266.20, 270.3.

243.34 Don Gonzalo Gustios, of Lara,] The name of this individual is spelled in five different ways in MSv: Gonzalo Gustios, of Lara, the prevailing usage; Gustios Gonzalez (237.15); Gustio Gonzalez (259.18); Gustio Gonzalo de Salas (259.37, 259.41), Gustios Gonzalez of Salas (258.32–33). Probably some of the confusion was owing to disagreement among Irving's sources. For example, Mariana consistently refers to the person as "Gustio Gonzalez"; Bleda, as "Gonçalo Gustios." Irving himself, in his uncompleted sketch "The Seven Sons of Lara," explains that the individual was known not only by the name "de Lara" but also "was likewise called de Salas from having his estates in a place of that name" (University of Texas). In accordance with Irving's predominant usage in MSv and almost invariable usage in "The Seven Sons of Lara," and another uncompleted work, "Ruy Velazquez" (University of Virginia), "Gonzalo Gustios" is adopted here as the name of the individual. Either "Salas" or "Lara" appears to be proper as an indication of his residence.

245.8–17 "Of . . . here."] The quotation marks in this paragraph are added in pencil to MSv by Pierre M. Irving.

257.23–24 "which . . . blazon."] Whether Irving intended these phrases to be interpreted as a direct quotation from Agapida is impossible to tell with certainty, though "says Agapida" certainly suggests it. In light of the conspicuous reference to the friar earlier in the paragraph (257.16), a direct quotation seems likely as the intention.

262.25 Urraca,] The cancellation, substitution, and asterisk are by Pierre M. Irving. Below the text on this page of MSv, p. 85, Pierre M. Irving added a note, subsequently deleted: "⟨*Urraca? see next page⟩." The spelling he supplied is Irving's majority usage, and it duplicates the spelling of the name by two of the author's chief sources, Bleda and Mariana.

262.33–37 For . . . Sancha] Despite the phrase "says Fray Antonio Agapida," this introductory sentence gives no clear indication (except the rather stilted "edifying and praiseworthy") that a direct quotation from Agapida is intended. This is in contrast to more obviously mannered passages such as 257.23–24, which are enclosed here within quotation marks. The present sentence is treated as a paraphrase or indirect quotation. A similar situation (preceding a quotation from Agapida) occurs at 263.19–26.

263.39 "This] In MSv Agapida's speech does not begin a paragraph in the conventional manner, indented on a line below the immediately preceding word. Irving's intention is indicated, however, by double angle brackets (⟨⟨) written conspicuously between "Estevan" and "This."

CHRONICLE OF FERNANDO THE SAINT

275.30–31 two of her confidential cavaliers] This statement is confusing because it precedes a list of three names, not two. The second of the three individuals, Don Gonzalo Ruiz Giron, was Queen Berenguela's major-domo, and perhaps he would not properly be called a "cavalier"; but the context does suggest that Irving was referring to him as one of the queen's "confidential cavaliers." Probably the name of the third individual in the list, Don Alonzo Tellez de Meneses, was added as an afterthought.

282.13 Agapida] The asterisk, by Pierre M. Irving, corresponds to an explanatory note written by him at the bottom of p. 28 in MSv: "*Fray Antonio Agapida, an imaginary chronicler—See Review of the Con-/quest of Granada in Vol II. Ed." The note was omitted from *Spanish Papers*.

284.9 ☞ (Something is wanting here.)] The asterisk following Irving's parenthetical comment is by Pierre M. Irving and corresponds to an explanatory note he pasted at the bottom of p. 34 in MSv. As it appeared in *Spanish Papers*, I, 372–73, the note follows:

       * The hiatus, here noted by the author, has evidently arisen from from the loss of a leaf of his manuscript. The printed line which precedes the parenthesis concludes page 32 of the manuscript; the line which follows it begins page 34. The intermediate page is wanting. I presume the author did not become conscious of his loss until he had resorted to his manuscript for revision, and that he could not depend upon his memory to supply what was wanting without a fresh resort to authorities not at hand. Hence a postponement and ultimate omission. The missing leaf would scarce have filled half a page of print, and it would seem from the context must have related the invasion of Andalusia by Fernando and the ravages committed by his armies.—ED.

Before writing this explanation, Pierre had attempted on p. 32 of the manuscript to fill the hiatus himself. Following "King Fernando" at the bottom of that page (T 284.8), he wrote: "[who invaded Andalusia, sacking cities &] laying waste fields of grain/ The line in brackets is by the Editor to supply a hiatus in the [*illegible*]"

289.11 chronicle.]   The deleted asterisk probably referred to a reference note Washington Irving wrote himself at the page in MSv, p. 47, which concludes this chapter: "(notice death of Queen Beatrix about this time —/ see Mems para la Vida &c — P 60)" In *Spanish Papers*, I, 381, Pierre M. Irving included the following comment:

    NOTE BY THE EDITOR.—A memorandum at the foot of this page of the author's manuscript, reminds him to "notice death of Queen Beatrix about this time," but the text continues silent on the subject. According to Mariana, she died in the city of Toro in 1235, before the siege of Cordova. Another authority gives the 5th of November, 1236, as the date of the decease, which would be some months after the downfall of that renowned city. Her body was interred in the nunnery of Las Huelgas at Burgos, and many years afterwards removed to Seville, where reposed the remains of her husband.

Irving's own note is cancelled in MSv by Pierre M. Irving.

290.38 flouting]   Irving's usage is preserved here even though "flouting" (jeering, scoffing) seems unusual as applied to a flag. It may represent a half-conscious amalgamation in meaning between "floating" and "flouting."

292.44 The death]   These words are written beginning at the left margin at the top of p. 57 in MSv, but Irving's intention to begin a new paragraph is indicated by the bottom line of the preceding page, which includes only a single word. A similar situation occurs at 297.23.

295.9–11 King Fernando . . . concurred]   Through "he," the cancellations
are made by Pierre M. Irving, probably because they almost duplicate
an earlier passage, 280.31–34. The comma following "Fernando" in
MSv suggests that Washington Irving may have intended to cancel
"was always"; but the evidence is inconclusive and the passages deleted
by Pierre M. Irving are therefore restored.

295.28–31 In the . . . . issuing]   The text of this passage left by Irving
at his death was awkward at two points: the comma following "Cordova" suggested a continuation of the sentence which the author did
not intend; and "The king" identified Fernando in a redundant manner
as the subject of the new sentence. Pierre M. Irving revised the
passage by converting its two sentences into one. He interlineated the
word "hearing," deleted "received intelligence" and "The . . . sending,";
in place of the latter construction he supplied "he sent" and "to that
city,"; and finally, to render the verbs in the new sentence parallel, he
converted "issued" to "issuing." Washington Irving's text is restored
here, but with the comma following "Cordova" altered to a period.

297.24 Countess]   On the five occasions when he employs this title by
itself in reference to the Countess Doña Yrenia, wife of Don Alvar
Perez de Castro (297.24–299.3), Irving capitalizes it. Because this
deviation from his usual practice of capitalizing titles only as parts
of proper names apparently represents his fixed intention, it is preserved.

299.37 orders.*]   The asterisk and the footnote to which it corresponds,
299.38–39, were deleted in MSv by Pierre M. Irving. The restored
footnote is regularized here in conformity with the Putnam house style.

301.11 Lara.†]   Having added a second footnote to his text on p. 79 of
MSv (see 300.43), Irving altered to daggers the asterisks at this point
and at the beginning of the footnote corresponding to it, at the bottom
of the page. However, his precaution proved in *Spanish Papers* to be
unnecessary, for the two notes were published on separate pages (I,
401, 402), enabling the printers to use asterisks, the preferred footnote
symbol, in booth instances without ambiguity. Irving's revised symbols,
the daggers, are employed here and in the corresponding note, 301.42.
In similar circumstances his asterisks in MSv were converted to daggers
in 1A 307.35, 307.43; the daggers are reproduced here.

309.23 While]   The new paragraph is indicated in MSn not by indentation but by a 1½-inch blank space at the top of MSn p. 101; the preceding page is only three-quarters filled. Similar situations occur at
312.19, 319.21, 323.1, 325.24.

309.33 Admiral]   In reference to Admiral Bonifaz, Irving almost invariably capitalizes the title, apparently as a kind of nickname. His
uncharacteristic practice of capitalizing a title even when not employed as part of a proper name is preserved in this instance.

313.12 from him.]   The cancelled lines are written in the left margin of pages 119, 120 of MSn. They represent an experimental attempt, quickly abandoned, to shift some material used earlier (see 312.41– 313.8) to this point and to economize space. The tentative revision is cancelled by Pierre M. Irving, who also wrote "st"—that is, "let it stand"—between the two texts near the beginning of the original passage.

318.17 Stout Prior]   Irving uses this epithet as a nickname and hence almost invariably capitalizes it; for example, at 316.22. His usage is preserved here. He also employs "Prior" alone in capitalized form; and although it differs from his usual practice of not capitalizing civil or religious titles unless they form parts of proper names, his usage is also preserved here.

327.37 ornaments and insignia]   Irving wrote "ornaments" in a position above the line slightly before "insignia," as if to caret it in rather than to substitute it for the latter word. The word "ornaments" is a natural supplement to the statement and is hence included here; "and" is supplied as the connective Irving presumably intended.

[SIR DAVID WILKIE IN SPAIN]

334.13 visitors.]   Irving's reference marks in MSy correspond to a similar one at the top of a separate sheet, on which is also written "(vide Page 3)." The separate sheet, p. [6], includes two sentences to be interpolated at this point: T 334.13–20.

[HISTORY OF THE CONQUEST OF MEXICO]

339.33 attested by too]   Irving's meaning is that the force of the testimony by numerous Spanish historians is so strong as to preclude the possibility of doubting the anecdote. The syntax of 1A, "attested too by," bears no logical relation to the preceding portions of the sentence. The words "too by" are thus transposed.

341.36 palace. His]   The run-on 1A reading is uncharacteristic of Irving. "His" begins a statement distinct in content from the one preceding it, which recounts Iztupulcan's timely escape from the palace.

[A VOYAGE UP THE HUDSON RIVER IN 1800]

344.31 * * * At length]   Series of asterisks are employed throughout PMI to signify editorial omissions within quoted material. At this point and at 345.4, 345.16, they indicate either deliberate omissions by Pierre M. Irving or, possibly, hiatuses within the fragmentary original text.

LIST OF EMENDATIONS

In this list are summarized all emendations of the original copy-texts. The numbers before each entry indicate the page and line. Chapter numbers, chapter or section titles, epigraphs, chapter-summaries, texts, quotations, and footnotes are included in the line count. Only running heads and rules added by the printer to separate the running heads from the text are omitted from the count.

The reading to the left of the bracket is the portion of the text under discussion and represents an accepted reading that differs from the copy-text. The source of that reading is identified by symbol after the bracket. The readings after the semicolon include the rejected reading of the copy-text and any other text in which it appears, together with further alternatives which may occur. The swung (wavy) dash ∼ represents the same word, words, or characters that appear before the bracket, and is used in recording punctuation variants. The caret ∧ indicates that a mark of punctuation is omitted. T signifies that a decision to emend or not to emend has been made on the authority of the editor of this edition.

If explanatory comment is needed, editorial remarks follow the entry in italics. If more explanation is required than can conveniently be inserted in the List of Emendations, the entry is preceded by an asterisk * and the necessary comments appear following the same page-line reference in the Discussions of Adopted Readings.

A key to identifying symbols used in referring to manuscript and printed texts is given on pages 348–54.

[ADVERTISEMENT OF AN ADBRIDGEMENT OF *THE LIFE AND VOYAGES OF CHRISTOPHER COLUMBUS*]

3.2–3   [ADVERTISEMENT . . . *COLUMBUS*]] T; [*omitted*] 1A.

[REVIEW OF *A CHRONICLE OF THE CONQUEST OF GRANADA*]

*4.2–3   [REVIEW . . . *GRANADA*]   ] T; Art. II.—*A Chronicle of the Conquest of Granada, from the MSS. of Fray Antonio Agapida. By Washington Irving. 2 vols. post 8vo. 1829* 1E; CONQUEST OF GRANADA. *Review of a Chronicle of the Conquest of Granada, from the MSS. of Fray Antonio Agapida.** 2A.

4.4   There] T; There 1E, 2A.

4.4   "working-day world"] 2A; '∼ - ∼ ∼' 1E. *Pairs of double quotation marks are substituted for single quotation marks at the following additional points*: 4.8, 4.42, 5.1, 5.6, 5.40, 5.40, 5.40–43, 6.37–38, 6.44–7.1, 7.19–26, 10.11–12, 10.13–14, 11.29–30, 12.38–13.9, 15.5–8, 15.14, 15.29–43, 16.12–26, 17.3–21, 18.3–31, 18.39–19.42, 20.3–39, 21.31–23.32, 23.38–24.32, 25.4–40, 26.27–27.23, 29.8–9.

5.10   hare-brained]   T; hair-brained 1E, 2A; harebrained 1A. *A common misspelling of Irving's.*

5.11   forays]   1A; forages 1E, 2A. *1A reading more appropriate to context, which emphasizes excitement, adventure.*

7.23–24   'Tell your sovereigns,']   2A; "~ ~ ~," 1E. *Quotations within quotations enclosed in 1E by pairs of double quotation marks are enclosed by single quotation marks at the following additional points*: 7.24–26, 15.7–8, 18.8–9, 18.9–13, 19.6, 19.7–12, 19.19, 19.24, 19.24–25, 19.31, 19.32, 20.26, 20.26, 20.28, 20.28–29, 20.34, 20.34–35, 20.36, 20.37, 22.34, 22.35–23.32, 24.17, 24.18–20, 24.21, 25.25, 25.25–30, 27.8–9, 27.11–12, 27.12–13, 27.14, 27.14–16, 27.18, 27.18–19, 27.22–23.

9.13   crowd.*]   2A; ~†. 1E.

14.25–34   " 'Behold . . . . inflict.' "]   T; ‸' ~ . . . . ~.' ‸1E; "‸~ . . . . ~.‸" 2A. *The extended quotation includes a quoted speech within it.*

14.35   marquis]   2A; Marquis 1E. *Emendation reflects Irving's usual practice for titles not used as parts of proper names; see 14.17.*

17.17   downfall]   C, 2A; downfal 1E.

17.36   Hassan]   2A; Hassen 1E. *See 7.14.*

18.7   cimeter]   C; cimetar 1E, 2A. *No authority in dictionaries for 1E spelling.*

18.20   "At Loxa,]   2A; '~ ~, 1E; ‸~ ~‸ C. *Beginning of second quoted paragraph. Single quotation marks at the beginning of second and subsequent paragraphs of quoted passages in 1E are converted to double quotation marks at the following additional points*: 19.13, 19.21, 20.10, 20.16, 20.26, 20.30, 20.36, 20.38, 22.20, 24.24.

19.2   standards]   C, 2A; [*blank type*]tandards 1E.

20.1   rout]   2A; route 1E. *1E spelling is obsolescent.*

[REVIEW OF ALEXANDER SLIDELL'S *A YEAR IN SPAIN*]

30.11–12   [REVIEW . . . *SPAIN*]]   T; A Year in Spain. By a

Young/ American. Murray. 1831. MSm; ART. I.—*A Year in Spain.* By a Young American. London, 2 vols. 12 mo. 1831. 1E.

30.13 ¶This] ₐ~ MSm; ₐIn this 1E.

30.13 books] T; book MSm; [*1E wanting*]. *Obvious error.*

30.14 country] T; ⟨count⟩/ ~ MSm; [*1E wanting*]. *The incated false starts immediately re-written occur in MSm at the following additional points*: 30.27 ⟨ven⟩, 31.16 ⟨dou⟩, 31.18 ⟨fortn⟩, 31.30 ⟨microsc⟩, 31.32 ⟨be/becom⟩, 32.5 ⟨ports of⟩, 35.4 ⟨a⟩—for "and is," 43.15 ⟨battl⟩, 45.27 ⟨the⟩.

30.16 "far wandering" foot] T; "~ ~" ~ ⟨'⟩ MSm; '~ ~ₐ ~' 1E.

30.17 stream of] 1E; ⟨flood⟩ ↑stream↓ of/ of MSm.

30.18 burly] 1E; burley MSm.

30.19 poet-ridden daughters] 1E; ⟨daughters⟩ ~-/ ~ ~ MSm.

30.19–20 portfolios] 1E; port/ folios MSm. *No authority in dictionaries.*

*30.22 The frightful stories] 1E; ⟨Never is the⟩ ↑Take in the extra leaf # # ↓/ / ~ ~ ~ MSm.

30.24 rugged] 1E; ⟨drea⟩ ~ MSm.

30.24 inns] 1E; Inns MSm. *Besides those listed in separate entries, the following words capitalized in MSm but not ordinarily capitalized elsewhere by Irving are emended to lower-case, as in 1E*: 30.30 (Southern), 30.31 (Beefsteak), 31.24 (Second), 35.2 (Starting), 35.4 (Mountain), 42.33 (Mother), 42.34 (Mayoral), 42.40 (Zagal), 43.14 (Yore), 43.20 (Scenes), 43.24 (Genius), 45.19 (Lodgings), 46.24 (Sailor), 46.29 (Single), 46.36–37 (Landsman), 48.26 (Eggs), 49.9 (Seventeenth), 55.28 (Inn), 55.31 (Barber).

30.26 simple tourist] T; Simple ⟨traveller⟩ ↑tourist↓ MSm; [*1E wanting*].

30.28 well balanced] T; ~ ballanced MSm; ~ hung 1E.

30.30 Pyrenees,] T; ⟨Peninsula⟩ ↑~,↓ MSm; ~; 1E.

30.31 Cockney . . . civilization,] T; ⟨English travel⟩ ↑Cockney Comfort,↓/ and Cockney ⟨Comfort,⟩ ↑civilization,↓ MSm; cockney comfort and cockney domination, 1E.

30.32–33 and have . . . unknown] T; ↑and have been introduced even in Greece and ↓ ⟨are as yet⟩/ ↑ the Holy Land, are as yet↑ unknown MSm; and have been introduced into Greece and Holy Land, are as yet unknown 1E.

30.34 Ventas] T: ⟨Spanish⟩ ~ MSm; ventas 1E.

30.35   ¶We] 1E; ∧~ MSm. *Word begins a page in MSm; last line on preceding page is only one-third filled.*

30.36   unhackneyed country] 1E; ⟨land⟩ ~ ~ MSm.

31.1   recorded ... work] T; ⟨described by⟩ ↑recorded in↓ the/ ⟨author⟩ ↑present work↓ MSm; ~ ... volumes 1E.

31.2–3   before-mentioned disinclination] T; ⟨disinclination of/ travellers to⟩ ~∧~ disincli-/-nation MSm; ~-/~ ~ 1E. *Unhyphenated form of compound not authorized in dictionaries.*

31.3   comfort loving] T; comfort⟨ab⟩ loving MSm; ~-~ 1E.

31.5   this, . . . production.] 1E; ⟨his volumes.⟩ ↑this, his maiden production.↓ MSm.

31.11   Lieutenant,] 1E; ~∧/ MSm. *End-of-line commas are supplied after the parenthesized words at the following additional points*: 31.17 (undertaking), 31.20 (second), 32.13 (companion), 43.29 (master), 45.23 (person), 47.25 (ragged), 57.16 (Sevillanas).

31.16   ¶There were] 1E; ¶<The lieutenant, as his work abundantly/ testifies>/ ¶~ ~ MSm.

31.17   regarded] 1E; ⟨looked⟩ ↑~↓/ upon MSm. *Irving neglected to complete the cancellation.*

31.19   possesses.] T; ~∧ MSm. ~: 1E. *Periods are supplied or substituted for indicated punctuation at the following additional points*: 31.26 (hotels,), 32.4 (Panza—), 32.15, 34.7, 35.5, 45.29 (embroidered —), 46.39, 55.31.

31.20   received but] 1E; ⟨been but⟩ ~ ~ MSm.

31.21   upon his] 1E; ~ ⟨the⟩/ ~ MSm.

31.26   solitude] T; Solitude MSm; lordly and sullen solitude 1E.

31.27   scenes and characters] T; ⟨pictures⟩ ↑scenes & characters↓ MSm; ~ ~ character 1E. *The ampersand is replaced by "and" at the following additional points*: 31.44, 31.44, 35.1, 42.34, 42.38, 45.22, 45.23, 45.24, 45.30, 47.19, 55.32, 55.36, 57.23.

31.27   life, taken] 1E; ~, ⟨such as the / is⟩ ↑⟨beheld it,⟩↓ ~ MSm.

31.28   of what] 1E; ~ ⟨the Scenes⟩ ↑~↓ MSm.

31.30   the persevering] 1E; a ~ MSm. *Phrase is parallel to preceding one, in which "the" is employed.*

31.31   touch] T; ⟨effect⟩ ↑~↓ MSm; [*1E wanting*].

31.36   Throughout] 1E; ⟨His work⟩ Through/ out MSm.

31.38   running] 1E; ⟨[dispend?]⟩ ~ MSm.

31.40   Lieutenant's] 1E; Lieutenants MSm. *Apostrophes are added to possessives at the following additional points*: 32.15, 43.20, 43.27, 47.18, 55.27, 55.34.

31.42   the facility] 1E; ⟨and the keen midshipman/ relish⟩
         ~ ~ MSm.

31.43   experience] 1E; ⟨set⟩ ~ MSm.

31.43   put up] 1E; ⟨wi⟩ ~ ~ MSm.

32.1   sea-faring] 1E; ⟨midshipman⟩ ↑~_∧~↓ MSm. *No au-*
         thority in dictionaries for unhyphenated form.

32.5   ourselves] 1E; ⟨to be able⟩ ~ MSm.

32.6   proof, having] T; ~. ⟨Ha⟩ ~ MSm; knowledge: having
         1E. *Irving neglected to alter punctuation on deciding*
         to continue the sentence.

32.9   more completely] 1E; ⟨in better⟩ ~ ~ MSm.

32.10   presenting a few of] 1E; ⟨extracting⟩ ↑~↓ ~ ~ ~ ⟨such
         of⟩ MSm.

32.13   fair travelling companion] 1E; ⟨compan⟩ ~ ~ ~ MSm.

32.14   Diligence] T; Dilligence MSm; diligence 1E. *Emen-*
         dation reflects usual practice; see 35.2, 35.3, 42.40.

*32.15   *impayable.*] 1E; *impayable*_∧ (vide Page 9) MSm.

32.16   "My attention] T; [*MSm wanting*]; _∧~ ~ Y; '~ ~ 1E.
         Double quotation marks are supplied at the beginning
         of paragraphs and at the conclusions of passages
         quoted from Y at the following additional points:
         32.32, 33.17, 33.22, 34.3, 34.8, 34.36, 35.6, 35.14, 36.12,
         36.13, 37.33, 38.5, 38.8, 38.33, 39.15, 39.40, 40.16, 40.37,
         41.28, 41.40, 43.35, 44.13, 44.32, 45.5, 45.34, 46.5, 46.17,
         46.22,47.1, 47.17, 47.28, 48.24, 48.27, 49.6, 49.15, 49.38,
         50.19, 50.32, 50.36, 51.6, 51.17, 51.42, 52.31, 53.30, 54.9,
         54.27, 54.40, 54.44, 55.16, 55.40, 56.15, 56.29, 57.10.

33.17   pp. 9–11] T; [*MSm. wanting; but see Emendations*
         32.15]; p. 9–11 1E.

33.18   *sabreur* seems] 1E; *Sabreur*⟨appears⟩/ ~ MSm.

33.19   *Utiliser*] T; *Utili*⟨z⟩*ser* MSm; *utiliser* 1E. *See 33.6.*

33.19   but to] 1E; ~ ⟨seems⟩ ~ MSm.

*33.21   end of it.] 1E; ~ ~ / ~. / ¶"As soon as ⟨the⟩ we drove
         &c. p. 20) MSm.

34.3   —vol. 1. pp. 20, 21.] 1E; [*MSm wanting; but see Emenda-*
         tions 33.21.

34.5–6   it . . . *interieurs*] 1E; ⟨which⟩ it is one/ of those charac-
         teristic ⟨sketches that let⟩ ↑scenes, those↓ ⟨one in to
         the interior⟩ *interieurs* MSm.

*34.7   the individual.] T; ~ ~_∧/ ¶"Before separating – – vide
         P 34) MSm; ~ ~:– 1E.

34.36   pp. 34, 35.] T; [*MSm wanting; but see Emendations*
         34.7]; p. 35. 1E. *Error.*

34.40	scenes] 1E; ⟨personal anecdotes and⟩ ~ MSm.
34.40	which] 1E; ~/ ⟨~⟩ MSm.
34.41–35.1	characteristic] 1E; ⟨living information concerning the nation.⟩/ ~ MSm.
35.2	it from] 1E; ~/ ⟨from Barcel⟩ ~ MSm.
35.3	many a] 1E; ⟨the⟩ ↑~ ~↓ MSm.
*35.5	earthquake.] 1E; Earthquake∧/ ¶"By the time – see Page 54) MSm.
36.12	pp. 54–57] T; [*MSm wanting; but see* Emendations 35.5]; pp. 55, 56 1E.
36.13	¶"The manner] 1E; [*MSm wanting*]; ∧∧~ ~ Y. *The first lines of quoted passages not beginning paragraphs in Y are indented at the following additional points*: 38.5, 43.35, 45.34, 55.40.
36.30	'That other one!'] T; [*MSm wanting*]; "~ ~ ~!" Y, 1E. *Quotations within passages from Y are enclosed within single quotation marks at the following additional points*: 38.40–41, 46.13–14, 46.15–16, 50.6, 50.27, 50.27–28, 51.19–20, 51.23, 52.13, 52.13, 52.31, 52.31, 52.32–33, 52.33–34, 52.34, 52.34–36, 53.2–3, 54.4–5, 54.6–8.
37.33	–pp. 64–67.] 1E; [*MSm wanting*.]
*37.34–38.4	[We . . . him.]] T; [*MSm wanting*]; ∧~ . . . ~∧ 1E.
37.38	Diligence] T; [*MSm wanting*]; diligence 1E. *Invariably capitalized in extant portions of MSm. The same emendation is made at 38.4, 41.43.*
40.33	butts] 1E; [*MSm wanting*]; buts Y. *Probably a misprint.*
41.40	[–pp. 88–96]] T; [*MSm wanting*]; [*omitted*] 1E.
*41.41–42.2	[The . . . . cares is]] T; [*MSm wanting*]; ~∧ . . . . ~ ~∧ 1E.
*42.3	wonderfully] T; Wonderfully MSm; singularly 1E.
42.4	fisherman's wife] 1E; Fisherman ~ MSm. *Copy-text usage is awkward and uncharacteristic.*
42.5	mighty] T; ⟨powe⟩ ~ MSm; [*1E wanting*].
*42.6	master hand.] T; ~ ~./ ¶See P. 101 MSm; [*1E wanting*].
42.27	–pp. 101, 102.] 1E; [*MSm wanting; but see* Emendations 42.6].
42.30–31	From information] 1E; ⟨Poor Pepe⟩ ~ ~ MSm.
42.37	Pepe,] 1E; ~∧ MSm. *Comma necessary for clarity.*
42.40	spot. The] 1E; ~⟨,⟩. ⟨and the⟩/ ~ MSm.
42.40	the successors] 1E; ⟨successors to pointed out them/ out to us pointed⟩ ~ ~ MSm.
42.44	On our] 1E; ⟨On my a⟩ ~ ~ MSm.

43.4   Sir, to shoot] T; $\sim_\wedge$ ⟨[2 *words illegible*]⟩/ $\sim$ $\sim$ MSm;
            sir, $\sim$ $\sim$ 1E. *Comma marks pause following direct
            address.*

43.5   blunderbuss] 1E; ⟨p⟩ $\sim$ MSm.

43.7   mayoral's] T; Mayorals MSm; [*1E wanting*].

43.8   it was] T; ⟨but⟩ $\sim$ $\sim$ MSm; It $\sim$ 1E. *See* Rejected Vari-
            ants 43.7–8.

43.10   his dismal affair] 1E; ⟨this⟩ $\sim$ ⟨advent⟩ $\sim$ ⟨adventure⟩
            $\uparrow\sim\downarrow$ MSm.

43.11   to Madrid] 1E; ⟨through Valencia to Mad⟩/ $\sim$ $\sim$ MSm.

43.13   happy] 1E; ⟨great⟩ $\sim$ MSm.

43.13   In traversing] 1E; ⟨It is true he is⟩/ $\sim$ $\sim$ MSm.

43.14   for giants] 1E; ⟨by Don Quixote for⟩ $\uparrow$for$\downarrow$ Giants MSm.

43.17   once graced] 1E; ⟨the⟩ $\sim$/$\sim$ MSm.

43.19   grove] 1E; Grove ⟨of/ tr⟩ MSm.

43.19   Sancho] 1E; ⟨his⟩ $\sim$ MSm.

43.22   the central provinces] 1E; ⟨La Mancha/ and⟩ $\sim$ ⟨other⟩
            $\sim$ $\sim$ MSm.

43.27   account] 1E; ⟨description⟩ $\uparrow\sim\downarrow$ MSm.

43.29   extracting] T; ⟨giving⟩ $\sim$ MSm; [*1E wanting*].

43.29   his language master] T; ⟨D⟩ $\sim$ $\sim$ $\sim$ MSm; $\sim$ $\sim$–/ $\sim$
            1E.

43.30   who . . . representative] 1E; ⟨for the/ accuracy of which
            we can vouch,/ and which may serve as a specimen/
            of a numerous class in Spain for/ the accuracy of
            which we can vouch,/ and which⟩ $\uparrow$who$\downarrow$ may serve
            as ⟨a specimen⟩ $\uparrow$the representative$\downarrow$ MSm.

*43.34   impurificado.] T; $\sim$./ ¶"The reader MSm; *impurificado.*
            1E.

45.5   –pp. 167–169.] T; [*MSm wanting*]; –p. 169 1E. *Error.*

*45.6–16   [We . . . . sent]]   T; [*MSm wanting*]; $_\wedge\sim$ . . . . $\sim_\wedge$ 1E.

45.17   leaf] 1E; ⟨y⟩ $\sim$ MSm.

45.21   frequent reverses] 1E; ⟨change freq⟩/ $\sim$ $\sim$ MSm.

45.22   amusing and characteristic . . . history,] T; $\uparrow$amusing &$\downarrow$
            characteristic sketch is given of his/ history, ⟨which
            gives an amusing/ peep into Spanish life⟩ MSm; amus-
            ingly characteristic . . . $\sim$, 1E.

45.23   tall,] 1E; $\sim_\wedge$ MSm. *Emendation reflects Irving's usual
            practice.*

45.23   bony] 1E; bon⟨e⟩y MSm.

45.24   thin, wrinkled,] 1E; $\sim_\wedge$ $\sim_\wedge$ MSm. *Pauses indicated by
            deliberate pace.*

45.25   Lieutenant] 1E; lieutenant MSm. *Ordinarily capitalized.*

The same emendation is made at 46.38–39, 55.19, 55.26, 55.27, 57.16.

45.29   embroidered. His] T; embroidered − ⟨In a word⟩/ his MSm; ∼: his 1E. *Irving neglected to capitalize "his" after making the cancellation.*

45.29–30   determines] 1E; ⟨determines not⟩ ∼ MSm.

45.32–33   ∼ Florencia,] 1E; ∼ₐ MSm. *Second comma of a pair.*

*45.33   mass.] 1E; ∼./ ¶"She might be nineteen vide p. 199. MSm.

45.40   *basquiña*] 1E; *basquina* Y.

46.22   —pp. 190, 191.] 1E; [*MSm wanting; but see* Emendations 45.33].

46.25   Doña] 1E; Dona MSm. *The same emendation is made at 46.30.*

46.28   whole of] 1E; ⟨re⟩ ∼/ ∼ MSm.

46.30   Don Valentin] 1E; ∼ Valantin MSm. *Thus Y; see also 45.20.*

46.31   disinterested,] 1E; ⟨and⟩ ↑∼,↓ MSm.

46.35   when we] 1E; ⟨we have a⟩ ∼/ ∼ MSm.

46.36   our author] 1E; ⟨the/ lieutenant⟩ ↑∼ ∼↓ MSm.

46.37   and the thorough] 1E; ⟨who by the tone⟩ ∼/ ∼ ∼ MSm.

46.38   sudden burst] T; ⟨enthu⟩ ∼ ∼ MSm; [*1E wanting*].

46.39   of the goddess] T; ∼ ⟨his own⟩ ∼ ∼ MSm; [*1E wanting*].

*46.39   creation.] T; creationₐ/ ¶"The Madrilena &c P. 302 MSm; [*1E wanting*].

47.17   pp. 300, 301.] T; [*MSm wanting; but see Emendations 46.39*]; pp. 302, 303. 1E. *Error.*

*47.18   ¶As our object] T; ₐ∼ ∼ ∼ MSm; ¶∼ ∼ ∼ 1E. *For the context in 1E see* Rejected Variants 47.18.

47.18   chiefly] 1E; ⟨more⟩ ↑∼↓ MSm.

47.20   his discussions of] 1E; ⟨all⟩ ∼ ⟨remarks on⟩ ↑∼ ∼↓ MSm.

47.21   which] 1E; ⟨of⟩ ∼ MSm.

47.24   description] 1E; ⟨picture⟩ ∼ MSm.

47.27   sallies] 1E; salleys MSm. *Emendation reflects Irving's usual spelling.*

*47.27   Panza.] T; ∼./ ¶"After being detained" P 24 v 2. MSm; Squires. 1E *See* Rejected Variants 47.27.

47.42   everywhere] 1E; every/ where Y. *Irving's, Slidell's usual practice.*

48.24   pp. 15–17.]   T; [*MSm wanting; but see* Emendations
                 47.27]; p. 15–17 1E.
*48.26   oil.]   T; ~./ ¶The eggs were soon emptied − v. 2. p.
                 ⟨27⟩ 29 MSm; [*1E wanting*].
49.6   [−pp. 20, 21.]]   T; [*MSm, 1E wanting; but see* Emen-
                 dations 48.26].
49.11   travelling companions]   1E; ⟨fellow⟩ ~ ~ MSm.
*49.14   happily.]   1E; ~./ ¶(I was not the sole occupant. v 2
                 P 49 MSm.
50.32   [−pp. 50–53.]]   T; [*MSm wanting; but see* Emenda-
                 tions 49.14]; [*omitted*] 1E
*50.33–35   [We . . . Cordova.]]   T; [*MSm wanting*]; ∧~ . . . ~∧
                 1E.
55.17   pp. 65–74.]   T; [*MSm wanting*]; p. 70–74 1E. *Error.*
55.18   limits, yet]   T; ~, ~ MSm; [*1E wanting*]. *Comma
                 marks pause between independent clauses.*
55.24   Among]   1E; ⟨In the course/ of his journey he had
                 formed an acquain-/ -tance with a fellow traveller, a
                 curate⟩/ ~ MSm.
55.25–26   age, with whom]   1E; age⟨.⟩, ⟨He and the⟩ ↑with whom↓
                 MSm.
55.29   recommended]   1E; reccommended MSm.
55.32   craft,]   1E; ~∧ MSm.
55.37   windows]   1E; ⟨balcon⟩ ~ MSm.
55.38   shaded by striped]   1E; shaded striped MSm. *1E an ap-
                 propriate correction of the oversight.*
*55.39   story.]   T; ~./ ¶There were few ornaments here &c.
                 V2. P. 161. MSm; ~:− 1E.
57.10   [−pp. 161–164.]]   T; [*MSm wanting; but see* Emenda-
                 tions 55.39]; [*omitted*] 1E
57.13   mischievous]   1E; mischevious MSm.
57.17–18   vehemently suspect]   1E; ⟨sus⟩ ~/ ~ MSm.
57.18   a Mentor]   1E; ~/ ⟨the⟩ ~ MSm.
57.20–21   travelling sketches]   T; ⟨familiar⟩ ~ ~ MSm; [*1E
                 wanting*].
57.22   to the]   T; ⟨and⟩ ~ ~ MSm; [*1E wanting*].
57.24   work.]   T; ⟨volumes⟩ ↑work↓. MSm; [*1E wanting*].
57.26   in the latter part of]   T; ⟨towards the⟩ ↑~ ~ ~ ~↓/
                 ⟨and⟩ ~ MSm; [*1E wanting*].
57.29   we have therefore]   T; ⟨but⟩ ~/ ~ ↑~↓ MSm; [*1E
                 wanting*].
57.29   those features]   T; ⟨such⟩ ~ ~ MSm; [*1E wanting*].
57.32   do . . . advise]   T; ⟨do him a give him better⟩ ↑do him

better service than to↓/ ⟨advise than⟩ advise MSm; [*1E wanting*].

57.32   make another essay]   T; ⟨continue⟩/ ~ ~ ~ MSm; [*1E wanting*].

57.34   give us]   T; ⟨trust as much as/ abandon himself without reserve, to the⟩/ ~ ~ MSm; [*1E wanting*].

57.38   that he may have]   T; ⟨wishing him⟩ ↑~ ~ ~ ~↓ MSm; [*1E wanting*].

57.39   them, that]   T; ~, ⟨and⟩ ~ MSm; [*1E wanting*].

[DEDICATORY LETTER IN *POEMS, BY WILLIAM CULLEN BRYANT, AN AMERICAN*]

58.2–3   [DEDICATORY . . . *AMERICAN*]]   T; [*omitted*] 1E, 1A, 2A.

58.4–5   TO/ SAMUEL ROGERS, ESQ.]   T; ~/ ~ ~, ~./ [rule] 1E; "TO SAMUEL ROGERS, ESQ. 1A; [*To Samuel Rogers, Esq.*] 2A.

58.7   During]   1A, 2A; DURING 1E.

58.7   years']   1A, 2A; years 1E. *Possessive.*

[ADDRESS AT THE IRVING DINNER, MAY 30, 1832]

59.16   [ADDRESS . . . 1832]]   T; Original Address of/ W Irving on his return from/ Spain MSv; [*1A wanting*]. *In MSv the title is written in pencil by an unknown hand.*

*59.17–18   ¶Mr. Irving . . . hailed.]   T; ∧⟨Mr I. rose greatly agitated by the/ warm cheering with which he was/ hailed.⟩ MSv; ¶Mr. IRVING on rising was greatly agitated by the warm cheers with which he was hailed. 1A [*6A prints the name as "Irving"*]; When the applause, with which this toast was received ceased, Mr. IRVING rose, greatly agitated by the warm cheers with which he was hailed. 2A [*4A adds a comma after "received"; 5A omits comma after "applause," prints the name as "Irving"*].

59.18   He observed]   6A; ⟨You all⟩ ~ ~∧ MSv; ~ ~, 1A.

59.19–20.   speaking: . . . wanting]   T; ~: ⟨this however said he is a scene⟩ ↑but he↓/ ⟨that I⟩ should be wanting ↑⟨however⟩↓ MSv; ~, . . . ~ 1A.

59.20   nature, if he were]   5A; nature ⟨if I said he⟩, ↑if he↓ ⟨if I⟩ were MSv; ~, ~ ~ was 1A.

59.20–21   and excited]   1A; & ~ MSv. *Ampersands are emended*

to "and," as in 1A, at the following additional points:
59.30, 60.2, 60.8, 60.14, 60.16, 60.17, 60.18, 60.21, 60.21,
60.23.

59.21–22   He . . . . after a]   T; ↑He proceeded in as nearly as can
be reccollected↓ ⟨I find myself, after a⟩/ ↑the following words. "I find myself, after a↓ MSv; —After renewed cheering he proceeded in, as nearly as can be
recollected, the following words:—"I find myself, after
a 1A [*6A adds comma after "cheering"*]; After renewed cheering he proceeded in, as nearly as can be
recollected, the following words: ¶"Mr. President and
gentlemen—I find myself, after a 5A.

59.23   surrounded]   1A; ⟨when⟩/ ~ MSv.

59.23–24   whom in]   1A; ~ ⟨I⟩ ~ MSv.

59.25   recognize as]   1A; ⟨re know to⟩ ↑recognize↓/ ⟨by⟩ ↑as↓
MSv; recognise ~ 5A.

59.27   received by them]   T; ⟨welcomed home after my/
wandering⟩ ~ ~ ~ MSv; ~ ~ ~, 1A.

59.27   the happiest moment]   1A; ~ ~ ↑⟨the most overpower-
ing⟩↓ ~ MSv.

59.29   led at times to doubt]   T; ~∧ ↑~ ~↓∧ ~ ~ ⟨at times⟩
MSv; ~, ~ ~, ~ ~ 1A.

59.31   kind]   1A; ⟨kind⟩/ ~ MSv.

59.32   Gentlemen,]   1A; ~∧ MSv. *Comma marks slight pause.*

59.33   have alluded]   1A; ⟨ever⟩ ~ ~ MSv.

59.35   overpowering testimonial]   T; ⟨in⟩ over-/ -powering ~
MSv; ~ testimonials 1A; testimonials 5A.

59.37   Never, certainly,]   1A; ~∧ ~∧ MSv. *Commas necessary to mark deliberate pace.*

59.37   native place]   1A; ⟨country⟩ ↑~ ~↓∧ MSv; ~ ~, 5A.

59.38–60.1   changes, it is true,]   1A; changes∧ ⟨in the scenes of my
early⟩ ↑it is true↓/ ⟨resort⟩, MSv.

60.1   the changes of]   1A; ↑the↓ changes ⟨from the⟩/ of MSv.

60.1–2   prosperity. Even]   T; ~; ⟨and if years have wrought/
any change for the worse in the ⟨cont⟩/ countenances
of my old associates, the⟩/ ~ MSv; ~; even 1A. *Irving
neglected to emend punctuation on deciding to begin
a new sentence.*

60.3   years,]   1A; ⟨time⟩ ↑years↓∧/ MSv. *End-of-line comma
omitted from MSv is also supplied after 60.19 nation,
as in 1A.*

60.4   glow . . . welcome,]   T; ⟨expression⟩ ↑glow↓/ ⟨of ancient⟩

↑of ancient↓ friendship ↑⟨of former scenes⟩↓ and heart-
felt welcome, MSv; ~ ... ~∧ 1A.

60.6	the time] 1A; ~ ⟨first⟩/ ~ MSv.
60.11–12	bay, ... associations,] 1A; ~∧ ... ~, MSv.
60.11	recollections] 1A; reccollections MSv.
60.12	to see its] 1A; ~ ~ ⟨this⟩ ~ MSv.
60.14	which] T; ⟨wh⟩ ~ MSv; [*omitted*] 1A.
60.15	sight, seated] 1A; ~∧ ⟨with⟩ ~ MSv.
60.16	watery domain; and stretching] T; watry domain;/ ⟨with⟩ ↑&↓ stretching MSv; ~ ~, stretching 1A.
60.16–17	extent; when] 1A; ~,/ ⟨with spires & domes, some familiar to/ memory, others⟩ When MSv; ~–~ 6A. *Capitalized "when" in MSv begins continuation of a single question.*
60.17–18	domes, ... memory,] 1A; ~∧ ... ~, MSv.
60.19	reach?] 5A; ~. MSv, 1A.
60.21	ineffectual,] 1A; ~∧ MSv. *Comma marks pause before subordinate clause.*
60.22	property in] 1A; ⟨interest in⟩ ~/ ~ MSv.
60.24	before me—] T; ~ ~- ⟨"This w⟩ MSv; ~ ~: 1A.
60.25	'This ... land!'] T; "~ ... ~!" MSv; "~ ... ~." 1A; "~ ... Land!" 2A, 3A, 4A; '~ ... ~.' 5A.
60.26	has been asked,] 1A; ⟨is⟩ ~ ~ ~∧ MSv. *Comma separates quotation from commentary.*
60.26	'Can ... country?'] 5A; ∧can ... ~?∧ MSv; "~ ... ~?" 1A; '~ ... ~?∧ 6A. *"Can" begins a quoted sentence.*
60.26–27	Whoever] 1A; ↑Whoever asks that question must know but little of me or of my heart.↓ ~ MSv. *Interlineation is in pencil by an unknown hand.*
60.27	inadequate] 1A; ⟨feeble⟩ ~ MSv.
60.27–28	its blessings and delights.] 1A; ⟨the⟩ ↑its↓ blessings/ and delights. ⟨which surround him./ to what of this favored land.⟩ MSv.
60.28	sacrifice] 1A; ⟨chan⟩ sacrafice MSv.
60.28	to?] 1A; ~. MSv. *Question marks are also supplied, as in 1A, at 60.36, 60.37; see in addition* Emendations 60.19, 60.39.
60.33–34	exultation;] 1A; ~, MSv. *Series of parallel phrases requires semicolon.*
60.34	triumph,] 1A; ~; MSv. *Series of parallel phrases requires comma.*
60.35	glowing] 5A; ⟨glowing ↑signs↓⟩ / ~ MSv; growing 1A.

60.36   community in which]   1A; ⟨country⟩ ↑⟨commun⟩ com-
                 munity↓ ⟨in which⟩ ↑in↓ ⟨among⟩/ which MSv.
60.36–37   by which]   1A; ⟨of⟩ ↑~↓ ~ MSv.
60.38   happy to]   1A; ⟨eager to⟩ ~ ~ MSv.
60.39   name?]   6A; ~. MSv; ~?" 1A; ~?' 2A.
*60.40   ——As long as I live!"]   T; —— ~ ~ ~ ~ ~!ₐ MSv;
                 They know but little of my heart or my feelings who
                 can ask me this question. I answer, as long as I live."
                 1A; They know but little of my heart or of my feel-
                 ings who can ask me this question!—As long as I live."
                 2A, 4A.

60.41   ¶Mr. Irving . . . toast:]   T; ¶Mr I. concluded by proffer-
                 ing as a/ toast. MSv; The roof now rung with bravos,
                 handkerchiefs were waved on every side, "three
                 cheers" again and again, and plaudit upon plaudit
                 following in such quick succession, begun, ended and
                 begun again, that it was some time before the toast
                 with which Mr. Irving concluded, could be heard.
                 It was as follows— 1A [3A *duplicates 1A except that
                 it adopts "waved" rather than "were waved"; 5A dupli-
                 cates 1A except that it concludes with a colon rather
                 than a dash; 6A duplicates 1A except that it includes
                 a comma after "ended"*].

                 [REVIEW OF HENRY WHEATON'S
                 HISTORY OF THE NORTHMEN]

61.2–3   [REVIEW . . . *NORTHMEN*]   T; Aʀт. III.—*Wheaton's
                 History of the Northmen, or Danes and Normans.*
                 London. 8vo. 1831. 1A; WHEATON'S HISTORY OF
                 THE NORTHMEN. *History of the Northmen, or
                 Danes and Normans.* London. 8vo. 1831. 2A.
61.20–23   "Why . . . day?"]   2A; '~ . . . ~?' 1A. *Quotations are en-
                 closed within pairs of double quotation marks at the
                 following additional points*: 63.35, 63.36–38, 63.40–43,
                 64.26–65.43, 66.15–16, 67.5–22, 67.25–68.2, 68.6–12,
                 68.17–18, 68.18–21, 71.6–15, 74.5–6, 74.11–18, 74.27,
                 74.28, 74.37–75.15, 75.23, 75.24, 75.32–39, 76.13–34,
                 76.37–77.2, 77.27–30, 77.42–79.3, 79.15–21, 79.30–34,
                 80.16, 80.16–22, 81.30, 81.30–33, 82.14–18, 82.28, 82.33,
                 82.33–34, 83.35–37, 83.40–85.29, 85.33–34, 85.35–38,
                 86.22, 86.23, 86.24–26, 86.33, 86.33–39.
64.27   'very short.']   2A; "~ ~." H, 1A. *Quotations within*

quotations are enclosed within pairs of single quotation marks here and at the following additional points: 64.28–32, 75.4–6, 75.13–14, 76.19–20, 84.13, 84.14, 84.25, 84.32, 85.18–20, 85.25, 85.25–26.

64.36　　　　"Thus]　2A; ∧~ H; '~ 1A. *A double quotation mark is supplied at the beginning of second and subsequent paragraphs within quotations at the following additional points:* 65.14, 67.25, 76.24, 76.26, 76.30, 76.40, 78.32, 84.7, 84.15, 85.4

66.11–14　　"Vid .... á."]　T; ∧~ .... â.∧ 1A, 2A. *Double quotation marks supplied here and at* 69.29–38 *in accordance with Irving's practice elsewhere in 1A; see Emendations* 61.20–23.

66.13　　　　Bölverk]　T; Böloerk 1A, 2A. *See Discussions of Adopted Readings* 66.11–16.

66.14　　　　vitis á]　T; ~ â 1A, 2A. *See Discussions of Adopted Readings* 66.11–16.

69.31　　　　Freyr]　H; Freyn 1A, 2A. *See also H, p. 114 et passim.*

71.7–8　　　complexion. ... The]　T; complexion, as well as the squalid poverty and misery in which they were condemned to live. The H; ~ * * * * *. The 1A; ~ ..... ~ 2A. *Emendation reflects procedure for indicating omissions followed elsewhere in this collection. The same emendation is made at* 71.11.

71.11　　　　race ...—while the]　T; race, is in a like manner personified in a vivid description of a single family. Then comes the H; ~ * * *—~ ~ 1A; ~, ... ~ ~ 2A.

71.12　　　　Herser]　H; Hersen 1A, 2A.

76.36　　　　King Ella]　2A; king ~ 1A. *See* 76.11.

77.35　　　　Björn]　2A; Biorn 1A. *See* 76.8. *Emended spelling regularly used in H.*

79.34　　　　p. 257]　T; p. 252 1A; *p. 252 2A. Error.*

80.16　　　　minstrels]　H; minstrel 1A, 2A. *Irving's error; see "they,"* 80.17.

81.31　　　　plâit]　H; plait 1A, 2A.

81.32　　　　Choisissez-le dès à présent]　T; choisissez-le des ~ ~ H; Choisisez le dès ce présent 1A, 2A.

82.15　　　　mast-head]　H, 2A; mast/ head 1A.

86.9–10　　　"Hic ... infelix."]　T; ∧~ ...~.' 1A; ∧~ ... ~." 2A.

86.20　　　　William the Conqueror]　2A; ~ ~ conqueror 1A. *Epithet is ordinarily used as a proper name; see by way of analogy* 81.35.

86.39　　　　antiquary."†]　T; ~.'* 1A; ~."∧ 2A. *The concluding* *citation of Palgrave's* History (*see* Discussions of Adopted Readings 371.33–39), *to which the dagger refers, is also omitted from 2A, probably as redundant; see* 82.2, 40.

MATHEWS *NOT* AT HOME

87.2	MATHEWS *NOT* AT HOME] T; MATHEWS *not* AT HOME. MSv; ~ *NOT* ~ ~. 1A *In MSv the title is written on the same line as the first sentence of the anecdote. The format is altered to conform to the practice observed throughout T.*
87.3	¶Those] 1A; ∧~ MSv. *See* Emendations 87.2.
87.6	city,] 1A; ~∧ MSv.
87.8	Mathews, . . . budget,] 1A; ~∧ . . . ~∧ MSv. *Commas separate relative clause from main statement.*
87.14	travel] 1A; ⟨tavel⟩ ~ MSv.
87.15	covering,] 1A; ~∧ MSv.
87.17	landmark] 1A; land mark MSv. *No authority in dictionaries.*
87.18	for him; and] T; ↑for↓ ⟨to⟩ him; ⟨which done⟩ and∧ MSv; ~ ~, ~, 1A.
87.21	vain: . . . himself] T; ~:/ ↑and he now began to worry himself↓ ⟨As he is one of the most fidgetting and⟩ MSv; ~; . . . ~ 1A.
87.26	Knight of the Woful Countenance,] T; ~ ~ ~ ~ countenance, MSv; knight of the rueful countenance∧ 1A.
87.30	his dramatic] 1A; ~ ⟨[ap?]⟩ ~ MSv.

NEWTON THE PAINTER

88.2	NEWTON THE PAINTER] T; Newton the Painter./ ——— MSn; ¶*Newton, the painter.*— 1A. *In 1A the title is immediately followed on the same line by the first sentence of the text proper.*
88.3	¶Letters] T; ∧~ MSn, 1A. *See* Emendations 88.2.
88.4	Gilbert Stuart Newton.] W; ~ ~ ~, ⟨the/ painter⟩ MSn; *Gilbert Stuart Newton.* 1A.
88.6–7	His hours . . . regular,] 1A; ⟨He is⟩ ↑His hours and habits are perfectly regular,↓ MSn.
88.7–8	like . . . dream, and] 1A; ⟨more⟩ like one in a pleasant dream,/ ⟨than⟩ and MSn.
88.10	early . . . morning;] 1A; ⟨at an early hour of⟩ ↑early

in↓ the/ morning, MSn. *Semicolon corrects awkward run-on construction.*

88.14   own. For]   T; ∼; ∼ MSn; ∼; for 1A. *Irving neglected to revise punctuation on deciding to begin a new sentence.*

88.16   remembers]   1A; remember⟨ed⟩s MSn.

88.18–19   and they]   1A; ⟨and th⟩ ∼ ∼ MSn.

88.19–20   acquits himself]   1A; ⟨talks⟩ ↑∼↓ ∼ MSn.

88.20   ever]   1A; ⟨eer⟩ ↑∼↓ MSn.

88.22   Dr. Sutherland]   T; Dr∧ ∼ MSn; ∼ Southerland 1A.

88.24   from the world]   1A; from ⟨society⟩/ the wor⟨d⟩ld MSn.

88.25   genius,]   T; ∼⟨.⟩, MSn; ∼; 1A.

88.27   it may]   1A; ⟨and⟩ ∼ ∼ MSn.

AN UNWRITTEN DRAMA OF LORD BYRON

88.30–31   AN . . . BYRON]   T; AN UNWRITTEN DRAMA OF LORD BYRON./ BY WASHINGTON IRVING. 1A, 2A.

88.32   ¶The]   T; ¶THE 1A; ∧THE 2A.

THE HAUNTED SHIP. A TRUE STORY—AS FAR AS IT GOES

90.29–30   THE . . . GOES]   T; ∼ . . . ∼./ BY THE AUTHOR OF "THE SKETCH-BOOK." 1E, 2A; A . . .∼./ [*rule*]/ BY WASHINGTON IRVING./ [*rule*] 1A.

90.31   ¶The]   T; ∧THE 1E; ¶THE 1A, 2A.

[LETTER TO THE EDITOR OF THE NEW YORK *AMERICAN*]

93.2–3   [LETTER . . . *AMERICAN*]]   T; [*omitted*] 1A, 2A.

[LETTER TO THE EDITOR OF *THE PLAINDEALER*]

94.14   [LETTER . . . *PLAINDEALER*]]   T; [*omitted*] 1A, 2A. *In 1A the article within which Irving's letter is quoted is entitled "Mr. Washington Irving."*

94.20   public]   2A; publick 1A. *The same emendation is made at the following additional points:* 94.36, 95.6, 95.11, 95.20, 96.24, 96.35, 96.43, 97.7.

94.26   reputation]   2A; repu-/ation 1A.

94.30   London (I think in 1832),]   2A; ∼, (∼ ∼ ∼ ∼)∧ 1A. *Parenthetical comment is extension of adverbial phrase and belongs together with it.*

94.31   from some friend (I now forget from whom),]   2A; ∼ ∼ ∼, (∼ ∼ ∼ ∼ ∼)∧ 1A. *Parenthetical comment*

*is elaboration of preceding phrase and belongs to-
gether with it.*

95.11   critics] 2A; criticks 1A. *Emendation reflects Irving's
           usual practice.*

96.21   "Tour on the Prairies"] T; ∧~ ~ ~ ~∧ 1A, 2A. *See*
           95.13, 96.15.

[LETTER TO WILLIAM CULLEN BRYANT]

98.2   [LETTER . . . BRYANT]] T; [*omitted*] 1A, 2A. *For
           the title of the article in 2A within which the letter
           was quoted see Textual Commentary, p. 399.*

98.17   innuendo] 2A; inuendo 1A.

[TOAST AT THE BOOKSELLERS' DINNER, MARCH 30, 1837]

99.1   [TOAST . . . MARCH 31, 1837]]   T; [*omitted*] MSm,
           1A.

99.2   ¶Mr. Washington Irving] T; ∧Mr ~ ~ MSm; ¶Mr.
           WASHINGTON IRVING∧ 1A; ¶~ ~ ~, 3A.

99.4   honor—of Samuel Rogers,] 3A; honor – of ⟨Mr⟩ Samuel
           Rogers ∧ / MSm; ~–~ *Samuel Rogers,* 1A.

99.4   Mr. Irving] 1A; Mr∧ ~ MSm. *The same emendation
           is supplied, as in 1A, at the following additional
           points:* 99.2, 99.5, 99.14, 99.15, 99.17, 99.18, 99.27, 99.29.

99.4   Rogers,] 1A; ~∧ MSm.

99.5   in a long] 1A; ⟨in a Mr. Rogers had⟩ ~ ~ ~ MSm.

99.9   he had] 1A; ⟨being considered in/ fact the⟩ ~ ~ MSm.

99.10   encouraging,] 1A; ~∧/ MSm. *Irving neglected to add
           end-of line punctuation.*

99.12   warmest sympathy in] 1A; ⟨greatest⟩ warmest sympa-/
           thy ⟨with⟩ in MSm.

99.13   I am] 1A; ⟨He was⟩ ↑~ ~↓ MSm.

99.13–14   "I . . . remarks,"] T; ~ . . . ~∧ MSm, 1A. *Irving is
           quoting himself. A pair of double quotation marks is
           also supplied at* 99.14–17.

99.14   added Mr. Irving] 3A; ⟨Mr Irving added⟩ ↑added Mr
           I↓ MSm; ~ ~ I. 1A. *The same pattern of variant
           spellings and abbreviations of "Irving" occurs at* 99.17,
           where the same emendation is made.

99.14   yesterday] 1A; ⟨the/ day previously⟩ ↑~↓ MSm.

99.15   Halleck's] 1A; Hallecks MSm. *The same correction is
           made, as in 1A, at* 99.18.

99.16   which I had sent to him; and] T; ↑which I had ⟨I⟩↓
           sent to him; ⟨by Mr I,/ and the remarks passage

related to⟩/ and MSm; ~ ~ ~ ~ ~ ~, ~ 1A; ~
~ ~ sent him, and 3A.

99.17   merits.]   1A; ~— MSm. *End of sentence; Irving bore down heavily on his dash, as in a pause for thought.*

99.17   letter:]   1A; ~ – MSm. *Hasty dash simply marked a pause before Irving began transcribing quoted passage.*

99.18–27   "'With . . . . grave.'"]   T; "ₐ~ . . . . ~ₐₐ" MSm; "ₐ~ . . . . ~.ₐ" 1A. *Irving is quoting himself quoting the letter.*

99.18   acquainted–]   1A; ~ – MSm; ~, 3A.

99.19   volume,]   3A; ~ₐ MSm; ~; 1A. *Comma marks pause between independent clauses.*

99.20   always.]   1A; ~ – MSm. *Irving's "dash" is a hurried slur at end of line.*

99.20   any thing]   1A; ~ ~/ ⟨thing⟩ MSm; ~-/ ~ 3A.

99.23   once–]   1A; ~ – MSm; ~, 3A.

99.24   acquaintance.—I]   T; ~ₐ – ~ MSm; ~ (Cheers.)ₐ ~ 1A; ~ [Cheers].ₐ ~ 3A. *Irving apparently intended the dash to mark a pause rather than to serve in lieu of a period.*

99.28   much out of health.]   1A; ↑much↓ ⟨infirm⟩/ ↑out of↓ ⟨in⟩ health –) MSm; [3A *wanting*].

99.29   Mr. Irving]   1A; ⟨Mr I concluded by/ pro giving "The health of Samuel/ Rogers, the friend of American/ Genius." The company all rose,/ and drank it standing with the greatest/ enthusiasm⟩/ ¶Mr ~ MSm.

99.29   toast: "Samuel Rogers – the]   T; ~. "~ ~ – ~ MSm; ~: ¶*Samuel Rogers*—The 1A; ~: ₐ~ ~—~ 3A. *Irving's period not specifically introductory, as context requires.*

99.29–30   "Samuel . . . genius."]   T; "~ . . .~ₐ" MSm; ₐSamuel . . . ~.ₐ 1A; ₐ~ . . . ~.ₐ 3A.

99.32   enthusiasm.]   1A; ~ – MSm.

[LETTER OF "GEOFFREY CRAYON" TO THE EDITOR OF THE *KNICKERBOCKER MAGAZINE*]

100.2–3   [LETTER . . . *MAGAZINE*]]   T; THE CRAYON PAPERS./ [*rule*] 1A; [*title wanting*] 3A; LETTER TO THE EDITOR OF "THE KNICKERBOCKER."/ ON COMMENCING HIS MONTHLY CONTRIBUTIONS. 4A.

100.11   "bore,"]   4A; '~,' 1A, 3A. *Pairs of double quotation marks are substituted for single quotation marks at the following additional points*: 100.25, 101.22, 101.23, 102.27, 103.6, 103.31–32, 103.32–33.

SLEEPY HOLLOW

104.35   SLEEPY HOLLOW] T; ~ ~./ [*rule*]/ BY GEOFFREY
CRAYON, GENT./ [*rule*] 1A; SLEEPY HOLLOW./ BY
GEOFFREY CRAYON, GENT. 2A *Indication of authorship
omitted in conformity with Irving's practice of signing
"Geoffrey Crayon" or "G.C." at the close of acknowledged contributions to the* Knickerbocker Magazine;
see 113.16.

104.36   Having] T; HAVING 1A, 2A.

106.13   "bee,"] 2A; '~,' 1A. *Pairs of double quotation marks
are substituted for single quotation marks in 1A at the
following additional points:* 106.41, 107.15–16, 108.17,
112.5, 112.5–6, 112.25, 112.27.

107.41   Christian] 2A; christian 1A. *Emendation reflects Irving's
usual practice.*

109.20   coincided] 2A; cöincided 1A. *Emendation reflects Irving's usual practice.*

[LETTER OF "HIRAM CRACKENTHORPE" TO THE EDITOR OF THE *KNICKERBOCKKER MAGAZINE*]

113.18–19   [LETTER ... *MAGAZINE*]] T; [*omitted*] 1A; THE
FIRST LOCOMOTIVE AGAIN./ [*rule*]/ BY WASH-
INGTON IRVING./ [*rule*] 2A.

113.21   SIR:] T; 'SIR: 1A; [*omitted*] ∧ 2A. *Single quotation
marks at the beginning of paragraphs in 1A (where the
entire letter is presented as a quotation) are deleted
at the following additional points:* 114.6, 114.13, 114.33.

113.22   "The First Locomotive."] T; '~ ~ ~.' 1A; 'THE FIRST
LOCOMOTIVE.' 2A. *Pairs of double quotation marks are
substituted for single quotation marks in 1A at the
following additional points:* 113.27, 114.2–3, 114.14,
114.15, 114.16, 114.22–23, 114.30.

114.4   Black Hills] T; ~ Hill 1A, 2A. *Almost certainly a misprint; see* 113.25.

NATIONAL NOMENCLATURE

115.2   NATIONAL NOMENCLATURE] T; ~ ~./ [*rule*]
1A; ~ ~. 2A.

115.9   "Nicodemused into nothing."] 2A; '~ ~ ~.' 1A. *Pairs
of single quotation marks in 1A are emended to
double quotation marks at the following additional
points:* 115.11, 115.38, 116.23, 117.14, 117.40, 118.2–3,
118.10, 118.39, 118.42.

115.28	second-hand] T; second/ hand 1A; second-/ hand 2A. *See* 117.6.
117.26	Duke of York] 2A; duke ~ ~ 1A. *Emendation reflects Irving's usual practice for titles used as parts of proper names.*
117.32	Empire State] 2A; empire state 1A. *Irving is apparently employing the term as a pseudonym.*

DESULTORY THOUGHTS ON CRITICISM

119.10	DESULTORY . . . CRITICISM] T; ~ . . . ~. 1A, 2A.
119.11–17	"Let . . . . 'em!"] 2A; [*rule*]/ 'Lᴇᴛ . . . .'em!' 1A. *Pairs of single quotation marks enclosing quoted material in 1A are emended to double quotation marks at the following additional points:* 119.25, 120.4, 120.4–5, 120.36–37.
119.19	All] T; [*rule*]/ Aʟʟ 1A; Aʟʟ 2A.
120.36	ejaculation] 2A; ejeculation 1A.
121.38	canonized] 2A; cannonized 1A. *No authority in dictionaries.*

COMMUNIPAW

122.34	COMMUNIPAW] T; Communipaw/ [*rule*] MSn; ~./ [*rule*] 1A; ~. 4A.
122.35	ᴛᴏ . . . ᴋɴɪᴄᴋᴇʀʙᴏᴄᴋᴇʀ.] 1A; To the Editor of the Knickerbocker‿ MSn; *To the Editor of "The Knicker-bocker"*‿ 4A.
122.36	Sɪʀ: I] 1A; Sɪʀ,/ ¶I MSn; Sɪʀ:,/ ¶I MSnp; Sɪʀ,– 4A. *Format adopted consistent with Irving's other* Knickerbocker Magazine *contributions.*
123.1	in following] 1A; ⟨in gleaning/ the scattered facts concerning the/ early history of⟩ ~ ~ MSn.
123.7	according] 1A; ⟨accord⟩/ ~ MSn. *Indicated false starts re-written immediately afterward occur at the following additional points in MSn:* 124.33 ⟨band⟩, 125.2 ⟨depend⟩, 125.7 ⟨er⟩, 126.16 ⟨progenitor⟩, 126.20 ⟨mysti⟩, 126.40 ⟨b⟩—for "burgher," 127.8 ⟨pro⟩.
123.8	Diedrich, and] 1A; ~, ⟨is⟩/ ~ MSn.
123.9	ever-to-be-lamented] 1A; ever-to-be‿/ lamented MSn.
123.9	planted their standard,] 1A; ⟨founded⟩ ↑planted↓/ their ⟨colony⟩ ↑⟨plant⟩ standard,↓ MSn.
123.11	Dreamer] MSnp, 1A; dreamer MSn. *See* 124.1. *Irving's lower-case "d" is thrice underlined, probably but not certainly by Pierre M. Irving.*

123.11   landed]   1A; ⟨founded⟩, ⟨on the opposite side of the⟩/
                ∼ MSn.
123.14   Communipaw, therefore, may truly]   1A; ∼, ↑∼,↓ ∼
                ∼ ⟨therefore⟩ MSn.
123.14   parent]   1A; ∼ ⟨city⟩ MSn.
123.15   immediately opposite]   1A; ⟨immediately but a few
                miles distant/ from merely on the opposite side of the/
                bay⟩ ∼ ∼ MSn.
*123.16   and its]   T; ∼ ↑⟨[all?]⟩↓ ∼ MSn; from whence its 1A.
123.17   are . . . descried,]   T; ↑are↓ actually/ ⟨peering ↑was it
                visible↓ above the from among the/ cabbage gardens
                and⟩ ↑to be descried,↓ MSn; can actually be descried∧
                1A.
123.18   orchards, it]   1A; ∼, ⟨and cabbage gardens/ in the midst
                of which it lies nestled,⟩/ ∼ ⟨It⟩ MSn.
123.21   ramble and research]   1A; ∼ ⟨, ransack⟩ ∼ ∼ MSn.
123.22   antiquity-hunting]   1A; ⟨ransacking every/ corner of the
                world, in quest of⟩ ∼-/-∼ MSn.
123.23   our worthy burghers]   1A; ⟨such of⟩ ∼ ∼ ∼ MSn.
123.25   abroad]   1A; ⟨to⟩ ∼ MSn.
123.32   while the]   1A; ∼ ⟨it⟩ the MSn.
123.32   begotten,]   T; ⟨produced⟩/ ∼, MSn; ∼∧ 1A.
123.34   astonishment—not, Sir,]   T; ∼ – ∼∧/ ∼, MSn; ∼; ⟨–⟩
                ∼,/ ∼, MSnp; ∼; ∼, ∼, 1A; ∼; ∼, sir, 4A. *End-of-*
                line comma neglected.
123.39   long legged]   T; long/ legged MSn; long-/ legged MSnp;
                long-legged 1A.
123.40   remarkable—Sir, it]   T; ∼ – ∼∧ ↑∼↓ MSn; ∼. ⟨–⟩ ∼,
                ↑∼↓ MSnp; ∼. ∼, ↑∼↓ 1A. *Irving intends pause in*
                mid-sentence, as at 123.33, 123.34.
124.3   the same]   1A; ⟨the same/ quilted caps and linsey
                woolsey short/ gowns and petticoats;⟩ ∼ ∼ MSn.
124.3   knee buckles]   T; ∼/ ∼ MSn; ∼-/ ∼ Msnp; ∼-∼ 1A.
124.4   close quilled caps]   T; ⟨qui⟩ ∼ ∼ ∼∧ MSn; ⟨qui⟩ ∼-∼
                ∼, MSnp; ∼ ∼ ∼, 1A.
124.4   linsey woolsey]   T; ∼/ ∼ MSn; ∼-/ ∼ MSnp; ∼-∼ 1A.
124.4–5   the same implements]   1A; ⟨in/ a word he⟩ ∼ ∼ ∼
                MSn.
124.5–6   in a word Communipaw,]   T; ∼ ∼ ∼∧ ⟨the⟩ ∼, MSn;
                ∼ ∼ ∼, ⟨the⟩ ∼, MSnp; ∼ ∼ ∼, ∼, 1A; ∼ ∼
                ∼, ∼∧ 4A.
124.6   day,]   MSnp, 1A; ∼∧ MSn, 4A.
124.7–8   aforesaid, as . . . streets,]   1A; ∼∧/ ↑∼ . . . ∼∧↓ MSn;
                ∼,/ ↑∼ . . . ∼,↓ MSnp. *Commas necessary for clarity.*

124.10	in the way] 1A; ⟨f⟩ ~ ~ ~ MSn.
124.12	and windows] 1A; and/ ~ ~ MSn.
124.12	large ones] 1A; ~ ⟨windows⟩ ↑~↓ MSn.
124.20	Pompeii remain,] 1A; Pompeie ~∧ MSn; Pompei⟨e⟩i ~, MSnp.
124.20	in . . . unaffected] T; in/ statu quo; ⟨as⟩ unaffected MSn; unaffected 1A. *1A emended reading probably to avoid repetition of "in statu quo" at 123.44.*
124.21	buried by] 1A; ~ ⟨in⟩ ~ MSn.
124.22–23	wonderful little] 1A; ⟨little⟩ ~ ~ MSn.
124.24	universe?—Has] T; ~?/ – ⟨The reply is involves a point of history⟩/ ~ MSn; ~?∧ ~ 1A.
124.24–25	cabbàge gardens] T; ~/ ~ MSn; ~-/ ~ MSnp; ~-~ 1A.
*124.26–27	worthy . . . record] T; worthy of notice and/ ⟨worthy of⟩ record∧ MSn; ~ . . . ⟨worthy of⟩ ~, MSnp; ~ . . . ~, 1A.
124.32	Acker,] MSnp, 1A; ~∧ MSn. *Second comma of a pair.*
124.35	fructification and perpetuity] 1A; ⟨reward and⟩ ~,/ ~ ⟨perpetuate⟩ ~ MSn. *Deletion of "perpetuate" eliminates need for comma.*
124.36	These] 1A; ⟨These robust e⟩/ ~ MSn.
124.36	gigantic] 1A; ⟨tall⟩ ~ MSn.
124.38	among the] 1A; ⟨in the⟩ ~ ~ MSn.
124.42	true Dutchmen] T; ⟨devoted⟩/ true Dutchmen MSn; true Nederlanders 1A.
124.43–44	A strict non-intercourse] 1A; ⟨All⟩ ~ ~ non∧ inter-/ course MSn; ⟨All⟩ ~ ~ non-inter-/ course MSnp.
124.44	observed] 1A; ⟨enforced⟩ ↑~↓ MSn.
125.1	crossed to] 1A; ~ ⟨from⟩ ~ MSn.
125.1	and the English] 1A; ⟨nor could a boat/ land upon the shores of⟩ ~ ~/ ~ MSn.
125.7	mansion,] MSnp, 1A; ~∧ MSn.
125.9	aristocratical] 1A; ⟨lordly and⟩ ~ MSn.
125.13	St.] 1A; St∧ MSn; Saint 4A. *The various configurations of Irving's abbreviation are emended thus at 125.40, 126.3, 126.19, 128.5.*
125.17	Van Horne . . . compeers] 1A; Van Horne ⟨assemble⟩ ↑and↓ his compeers, MSn. *Revision eliminates necessity for comma.*
125.18	councils of war] T; ⟨deliberations⟩ ~ ~ ~∧ MSn; ⟨deliberations⟩ coun⟨c⟩↑s↓ils ~ ~, MSnp; ~ ~ ~, 1A.
125.18	re-conquering] MSnp, 1A; re conquering MSn.

125.22	persuading themselves] 1A; ⟨regarding with evil eye, the British/ flag⟩ ~ ~ MSn.
125.23	arrive,] 1A; ~∧/ MSn.
125.24	broom which] 1A; ~/ ⟨that⟩ ~ MSn.
125.24	mast-head.] 1A; ~∧ ~∧ MSn; ~-~∧ MSnp.
125.25	rolled] 1A; ⟨cont⟩ ~ MSn.
125.32	deliberating. In] 1A; ~; ~ MSn; ~. ⟨;⟩ ~ MSnp.
125.33	Bergen Hills] 4A; ~ hills MSn, 1A. *See* 260.38 *and* 258.10 (Bergen Heights).
125.40	miracle worked . . . St. Nicholas] T; ~∧ ~ . . . St∧/ ~∧ MSn; ~, ~ . . . S⟨t⟩aint/ ~, MSnp; ~, ~ . . . Saint ~, 1A.
125.42	in the course] 1A; ⟨a⟩ ~ ~ ~ MSn.
126.3	blessed St. Nicholas] T; Blessed St∧ ~ MSn; good Saint ~ 1A. *For "blessed" see* 125.40.
126.3	kept] 1A; ⟨g⟩ ~ MSn.
126.4	wrought] 1A; ⟨gifted them with miraculous qualities⟩/ ~ MSn.
126.5	The hat] 1A; ~ ⟨broad brimmed⟩ ~ MSn.
126.5	Doubter] MSnp, 1A; doubter MSn. *See* 124.1, 126.1.
126.14–15	hardened . . . concreted . . . barnacles,] T; ~∧ . . . ~∧ . . . ~∧ MSn; ~, . . . ~, . . .~, MSnp, 1A. *Comma marks pause between independent clauses.*
126.15	length, turned] T; ~, ⟨by⟩/ ~ MSn; ~∧ ~ 1A.
126.17	Foot] 1A; foot MSn; ⟨f⟩Foot MSnp.
126.19	saw] 1A; ⟨read⟩ ↑~↓ MSn.
126.19	St. Nicholas] T; St∧ ~ MSn; S⟨t⟩aint ~ MSnp; Saint ~ 1A. *The same emendation is made from the identical pattern of variants at* 128.5.
126.22	gubernatorial] 1A; Gubernatorial MSn.
126.25–26	Ever since that time] T; ⟨From⟩ ↑~ ~↓ ~ ~∧ ⟨forward⟩ MSn; ⟨From⟩ ↑~ ~↓ ~ ~, ⟨forward⟩ MSnp; ~ ~ ~ ~, 1A.
126.26	has been] 1A; ⟨was⟩ ↑~ ~↓ MSn.
126.29	cabbages,] MSnp, 1A; ~∧/ MSn.
126.33	¶As these] 1A; ¶⟨Out of these sources of abundance a trade/ gradually/ ¶The superabundance of these two⟩/ ¶~ ~ MSn.
126.33	hands,] MSnp, 1A; ~∧ MSn. *Comma marks pause following long introductory clause.*
126.35–36	produced once more an intercourse] T; ⟨softened their brought them⟩ ↑~↓ ~ ~/ ⟨into⟩ ~ ~ MSn; ⟨softened their brought them⟩ ↑~,↓ ~ ~,/ ⟨into⟩ ~ ~ MSnp; ~, ~ ~, ~ ~ 1A.

126.38	to visit] 1A; ⟨visit⟩ ~ ~ MSn.
126.41	you . . . one] 1A; ⟨and⟩ you may/ be sure he is ⟨one of the former⟩ one MSn.
126.42	of the "bitter blood" who] T; ↑~ ~ "~ ~"↓ ~ ⟨that⟩ MSn; ↑~ ~ "~ ~," ~↓ ⟨that⟩ MSnp; ~ ~ '~ ~,' ~ 1A; ~ ~ "~ ~," ~ 4A.
127.1–2	source of] 1A; ⟨object of subject of⟩/ ~ ~ MSn.
127.2–3	wide spreading irruptions] T; ⟨all/ pervading invasions⟩ ↑~ ~ ~↓ MSn; ⟨all/ pervading invasions⟩ ↑~- ~ ~↓ MSnp; ~-~ ~ 1A.
127.3	Word] 1A; ⟨The⟩ ~ MSn.
127.5–6	of the alarming power] 1A; ⟨and⟩ ~ ~/ ~ ⟨ascendancy⟩ ~ MSn.
127.7	elbowing] 1A; ⟨monopolizing/ all civic posts of honor and profit;⟩ el-/ bowing MSn.
127.8	bargaining . . . hereditary] 1A; ⟨and⟩ ~ . . . ⟨old⟩/ ↑~↓ MSn.
127.12	vestige] 1A; ⟨du Dutch⟩ ~ MSn.
127.13	¶In consequence] 1A; ⟨In consequence/ of In consequence of the hostile feelings/ awakened by this⟩ ¶~ ~ MSn.
127.13	traders] 1A; ⟨fr⟩ ~ MSn.
127.20	But,] T; ⟨insomuch that the people of Communipaw/ look upon the once Nay⟩ ↑But↓, MSn; ~∧ 1A. *The cancellation, at the top of p. 16 in MSn, forms a part of Irving's first draft; the fragmentary sentence preceding it is lost.*
127.20	this] 1A; th⟨eir⟩is MSn.
127.21	made by] 1A; ↑~↓ ⟨of⟩/ ↑~↓ MSn.
127.22	Yes, Sir—] T; ⟨During⟩ ~∧ ~ – MSn; ⟨During⟩ ~, ~; ⟨–⟩ MSnp; ~, ~; 1A; ~, sir; 4A.
127.22	land] 1A; Land MSn.
127.23	company . . . before] 1A; ⟨band⟩ ↑company↓ of Yankee projectors/ ⟨made an⟩ landed ⟨upon⟩ before MSn.
127.24	stopped] 1A; ⟨bewildered⟩ ~ MSn.
*127.24	highway; endeavored] T; ~, ↑⟨&⟩↓ endea-/ vored MSn; ~, and endeavored 1A.
127.32	rout] T; route MSn; rout⟨e⟩, MSnp; rout, 1A.
127.32	and have] 1A; ⟨the/ House of the Four Chimnies⟩ ~ ~ MSn.
127.34	they know nothing] 1A; ⟨to hold banks⟩ ~ ~/ ~ MSn.
127.36	the family] 1A; ⟨their⟩/ ~ ~ MSn.
127.37	grandfathers] 4A; grand/ fathers MSn; grand-fathers 1A.

127.40   quaintly]   1A; ⟨curio⟩ ~ MSn.
127.41   thick,]   1A; ~ₐ MSn. *Comma clarifies.*
128.5   forgotten,]   MSnp, 1A; ~ₐ MSn. *Comma clarifies.*
128.13   older persons]   1A; ⟨older branches⟩ ~ ~ MSn.
128.16–17   this venerable mansion]   1A; ⟨it in tradition⟩ ↑~ ~ ~↓
              MSn.
128.19   blown off]   1A; ~ ⟨down⟩ ↑~↓ MSn.
128.21   historic pile,]   1A; ⟨fated mansion,⟩ ↑~ ~,↓ MSn.
128.21   .   say,]   MSnp, 1A; ~ₐ MSn. *Second comma of a pair.*
128.23–24   increase and multiply]   1A; ⟨maintain continue and⟩/
              ~ ⟨the⟩ ~ ~ MSn.
128.24   His wife has]   1A; His wife, ⟨who is⟩/ has MSn. *Can-*
              cellation eliminates necessity for comma.
128.26   grandchildren]   4A; grand/ children MSn; grand-chil-
              dren 1A.
128.26   great grandchildren]   T; ~ grand children MSn; ~
              grand-children 1A; great-grandchildren 4A.
128.32   Saint Nicholas!]   1A; ~ ~!/=== MSn. *The double*
              rule, which separates the letter from the concluding
              salutation, is a flourish without textual import.
128.33   With great respect, Mr. Editor,]   4A; with ~ ~ – Mrₐ
              Editorₐ MSn; with ~ ~, ⟨–⟩ Mr. Editor, MSnp; With
              ~ ~; Mr. Editor, 1A. *Irving's dash was probably a*
              slurred comma.
128.34   Your obt. servt.,]   T; ~ obtₐ servtₐ, MSn; ~ ob'tₐserv'tₐ,
              MSnp; ~ ob'tₐ servant, 1A.
128.37   with concern]   T; ~ ↑great↓ ~ MSn; [*1A wanting*].
              The interlineation is by L. G. Clark.
128.37–38   Mr. Editor?–In]   T; Mrₐ ~?–~ MSn; Mrₐ ~?–i⟨I⟩n
              MSnp; [*1A wanting*].
129.1   cabbage garden]   T; ~/ ~ MSn; ~-/ ~ MSnp; [*1A*
              wanting].
129.6   village!]   T; ~!/ ⟨Yours Mr Editor, in extreme haste/
              Hermanus Vander Donk.⟩ MSn; [*1A wanting*].

CONSPIRACY OF THE COCKED HATS

129.8   CONSPIRACY . . . HATS]   T; ~ . . .~./ [*rule*] 1A; ~
              . . . ~. 2A.
130.5   "Academies," "Seminaries," and "Institutes,"]   2A; '~,'
              '~,' ~ '~,' 1A. *Pairs of double quotation marks are*
              substituted for single quotation marks in 1A at the
              following additional points: 130.29–34, 131.8, 131.33,
              131.33, 131.40–41, 132.21, 132.22, 132.22–23, 132.23,
              132.24, 132.30–31.

133.20   RIPPER.]   T;   ~./   ¶P.S. Just as I had concluded the
            foregoing epistle, I received a piece of intelligence,
            which makes me tremble for the fate of Communipaw.
            I fear, Mr. Editor, the grand conspiracy is in danger
            of being countermined and counteracted, by those
            all-pervading and indefatigable Yankees. Would you
            think it, Sir! one of them has actually effected an entry
            in the place by covered way; or in other words, under
            cover of the petticoats. Finding every other mode
            ineffectual, he secretly laid siege to a Dutch heiress,
            who owns a great cabbage-garden in her own right.
            Being a smooth-tongued varlet, he easily prevailed on
            her to elope with him, and they were privately married
            at Spank-town! The first notice the good people of
            Communipaw had of this awful event, was a litho-
            graphed map of the cabbage-garden laid out in town
            lots, and advertised for sale! On the night of the
            wedding, the main weather-cock of the House of the
            Four Chimnies was carried away in a whirlwind! The
            greatest consternation reigns throughout the village!
            1A; [2A *includes only accidental variants from 1A*].
            Omitted as probably not intended by Irving to form
            part of the article; see the Textual Commentary.

[LETTER ON INTERNATIONAL COPYRIGHT TO
THE EDITOR OF THE *KNICKERBOCKER MAGAZINE*]

133.22–23   [LETTER . . . *MAGAZINE*]]   T; [*omitted*] 1A, 2A.
            In 1A the letter forms the greater part of an article
            by the editor entitled "International Copy-Right Law."

[ANECDOTE OF ADMIRAL HARVEY]

135.2   [ANECDOTE . . . HARVEY]]   T; [*omitted*] MSn, 1A.
135.4   midshipman,]   MSnc;   ~∧ MSn, 1A. *Comma clarifies.*
135.5   Liverpool, . . . February,]   T; ~∧ . . . ~∧ MSn; '~,'
            . . . ~, MSnc, 1A. *Commas mark slight pauses.*
135.5   Rockaway]   1A; ⟨I⟩ ~ MSn.
135.6   crew]   1A; ⟨crew⟩ ~ MSn.
135.8   supper.]   MSnc, 1A; ~∧ MSn.
135.8   They]   1A; ⟨He/ was with several others was quartered/
            in the family of ⟨the⟩ ↑one↓ Hicks a quaker,⟩/ ~
            MSn.
135.11   family, who]   1A; ~∧ ↑~↓ MSn; ~, ↑~↓ MSnc.

135.13   pleasantly among]   1A;   ~ -/ ~ MSn. *Probably a slip of the pen.*

135.14   Quaker]   1A;   quaker MSn. *See* 135.11, 135.22. *The same emendation is made at* 135.15 (Quakers).

135.16   The good]   MSnc, 1A; the ~ MSn. *Oversight.*

135.17   King's]   MSnc; Kings MSn; king's 1A.

135.18   they. "We]   T; ~. "we MSn; ~⟨.⟩; "~ MSnc; ~; '~ 1A. *Period and space following it in MSn suggest Irving intended a new sentence.*

135.20   words,]   T; ~ₐ MSn; ~; MSnc, 1A. *Comma marks pause between independent clauses.*

135.20   but if]   1A; ~ ⟨of⟩ ~ MSn.

THE "EMPIRE OF THE WEST"

135.25   THE . . . WEST"]   T; [*omitted*] MSv; THE 'EMPIRE OF THE WEST.'— MSvc, 1A. *In 1A the title appears on the same line as the beginning of the article proper; in accordance with the format adopted elsewhere in this edition it is raised here to a separate line.*

135.26   ¶We]   MSv; ₐ~ MSvc, 1A. *See Emendations* 135.25.

135.27–28   "Discovery . . . Mountains."]   MSv; '~ . . . ~.' 1A. *Pairs of single quotation marks in 1A are emended to double quotation marks at the following additional points:* 135.25, 135.34–136.1, 137.8–9, 137.10–11, 137.25–27.

135.34   ¶The Reader]   MSv; ₐ~ ~ MSvc, 1A.

135.35–136.1   degrees . . . (Pacific) Ocean]   MSv; degrees of latitude along the great ⟨⟨⟩Pacific⟨⟩⟩ Ocean MSvc; degrees of latitude, along the great ocean? N; degrees along the great Pacific Ocean, 1A.

136.1   nullified]   MSv; ~, MSvc, 1A.

136.2   statesmen]   MSv; ~, MSvc, 1A.

136.18–137.4   "We . . . energy."]   T; "~ . . . . ~.ₐ 1A.

137.10   a considerable]   N; considerable 1A.

137.18   ¶By the way]   T; ₐ⟨I⟩ ~ ~ ~ MSv; ₐ ~ ~ ~ 1A. *An incomplete line above the phrase in MSv makes clear Irving's intention to begin a new paragraph.*

137.19   salt water]   MSv; ~-~ MSvc, 1A.

137.23   ¶We]   MSv; ₐ~ 1A.

137.23   tribute of praise]   MSv; tribute 1A.

137.24   Mr. Nathaniel J. Wyeth]   T; Mrₐ/ ~ ~ ~ MSv; Mr. NATHANIEL J. WYETH 1A.

137.25   enterprizing]   MSv; enterprising 1A.

137.29   foothold]   MSv; foot-hold 1A.

137.30   energy and a]   T; ∼, & a MSv; ∼⟨, & a⟩& MSvc; energy
               and 1A.
137.31–32   Mr. Astor; all]   MSvc; Mr∧ ∼; ∼ MSv; Mr. Astor. All
               1A

[ANECDOTE OF THE FRENCH REVOLUTION]

137.34   [ANECDOTE . . . REVOLUTION]]   T; [*omitted*]
               MSy, 1A.
137.35   ¶Before]   T; ∧∼ MSy, 1A; (∧∼ MSyc. *Clark's par-
               enthesis at the left margin was apparently to indicate
               that a paragraph break was not to be included.*
137.38   who might]   1A; ⟨that⟩ ↑∼↓ ∼ MSy.
138.3   port-cochéres]   MSyc, 1A; port cocheres MSy.
138.4   inquiring . . . porters]   1A; ⟨e⟩↑i↓nquiring . . .
               ⟨P⟩↑p↓orters MSy.
138.4–5   "Is . . . table?"]   T; "∼ . . . ∼." MSy; ⟨'⟩'∼ . . . ∼?⟨'⟩'
               MSyc; '∼ . . . ∼?' 1A. *Deletions are in pencil.*
138.7   ¶An Abbé]   T; ¶ ∼ abbé MSy; ⟨¶⟩ ∼ abbé MSyc; ∧ ∼
               abbé 1A. *Capitalized "Abbé" reflects Irving's usual
               practice.*
138.7   seated]   1A; ⟨dor⟩ ∼ MSy.
138.10   persons]   1A; ⟨victims⟩ ↑∼↓ MSy.
138.11   Abbé]   MSyc; Abbe MSy; abbé 1A. *The same emenda-
               tion is made from the same pattern of variants at
               138.14, 138.15 (MSy Abbè), 138.17, 138.23; see also
               Emendations 138.7, 138.21, 138.22.*
138.12   man, tried]   T; ∼∧∼ MSy; ∼,∼, MSyc, 1A. *Added
               comma is second of a pair.*
138.12   tip-toe]   T; tip toe MSy; ∼-∼, MSyc, 1A.
138.13   port-cochére]   1A; port/ cochere MSy; port/ cochére
               MSyc.
138.15–17   "What!" . . . "you . . . . him!"]   T; "∼! . . . "∼ . . . . ∼-"
               MSy; ⟨'⟩'∼!⟨'⟩' . . . ⟨'⟩'∼ . . . ∼!⟨-'⟩' MSyc; '∼!' . . .
               '∼ . . . . ∼!' 1A. *Deletions are in pencil.*
138.16   thinking!–]   T; ∼∧-" MSy; ∼! ⟨-"⟩ MSyc; ∼! 1A.
               *Irving's quotation mark is misplaced; context requires
               exclamation mark.*
138.17   traytor–]   T; ∼∧- MSy; tra⟨y⟩ ↑i↓tor!⟨.ff MSyc; traitor!
               ∧ 1A. *Context requires exclamation mark.*
138.18   guillotine]   1A; gullotine MSy.
138.21   "Where . . . . Abbé–?"]   T; ∧∼ . . . . Abbe -?∧ MSy;
               ∧∼ . . . . ∼ -?∧ MSyc; '∼ . . . . abbé ∧ ?' 1A.
138.22   Alas!]   1A; "∼! MSy; ⟨'⟩'∼! MSyc. *Quotation mark mis-
               placed; see 138.21.*

[THE TAKING OF THE VEIL, AND THE
CHARMING LETORIÉRES]

138.25–26   [THE . . . LETORIÉRES]] T; THE CRAYON
PAPERS./ [*rule*] 1A.

138.35   One] T; ONE 1A. *Similar emendations are made to the
following display capitals in 1A:* 139.24 ALL, 145.5
SO MUCH (MSv SO MUCH). *See also Emendations*
145.11–12, 147.38.

138.36–37   de Froulay de Tessè, Marchioness de Créqui] T; ~ ~
De ~, ~ De ~ 1A. *In accordance with Irving's usual
practice, "De" within French proper names is emended
to lower-case at the following additional points:* 140.30,
143.4, 143.13, 143.21, 143.26.

139.8   Tuileries] T; Tuilleries 1A.

139.37   "Heaven . . . grace,"] T; '~ . . . ~,' 1A. *Pairs of single
quotation marks in 1A are converted to double quota-
tion marks at the following additional points:* 139.38–
39, 139.40, 139.41, 139.42, 140.1–2, 140.3–4, 140.9,
140.9–11, 140.12, 140.12–16, 140.22, 140.22–25, 140.31–
36, 140.44, 141.16, 141.18–24, 142.12, 142.12–14, 143.24,
143.25, 143.26, 143.28, 143.30, 143.31, 143.32, 143.33,
143.33–37, 143.40.

139.41   "What . . . you?"] T; ∧~ . . . ~?∧ 1A. *Direct quotation.*

140.3   aunt De Rupelmonde] T; ~ de ~ 1A. *Emendation
reflects Irving's usual practice for "de" not preceded
by given name or title.*

140.31–32   "My prince,"] T; ∧~~,' 1A.

143.33   vehemently. "In] T; ~./ ¶'In 1A. *Paragraph break inappropriate; the speech is a single statement, interrupted only momentarily by the commentary.*

143.40–144.4   "there . . . proximis: 'Adjutorium nostrum in nomine
Domini!'"] T;'~ . . . .~:' '~~~~~!'∧ 1A. *In 1A
the quotation mark following* proximis *is misplaced;
the archibishop's quotation forms part of a single
speech in which he is himself quoted.*

143.41   Mademoiselle] T; Madamoiselle 1A. *The unusual, obsolescent spelling is emended at the following additional points:* 144.27, 144.32, 144.38.

145.1–2   "Countess of Hevouwal," etc.] T; ∧~ ~ ~,' ~ 1A. *As-
suming that the lone quotation mark was not included
by mistake in 1A, it forms part of a pair left incomplete. The point preceding "Countess" is selected as
that where the missing punctuation was to be included,*

since this character has previously been known by her given name rather than by a title.

145.11–12   THE CHARMING LETORIÉRES./ ¶ "A good] T; THE
            CHARMING LETORIÉRES. ∧∧ 'A GOOD MSv; THE CHARM-
            ING LETORIÉRES./ ∧ 'A GOOD MSvc; ~ ~ ~./ ¶'~ GOOD
            1A.

145.12   "A . . . recommendation,"] T; '~ . . . reccommendation,'
            MSv; '~ . . .~,' 1A.

145.15   phraze] MSv; phrase 1A.

145.22   humour; it is true, he] T; ⟨taste⟩ ↑humour↓; it is true,/
            ⟨he was sc himself scantily⟩ he MSv; ⟨taste⟩ ↑humour.↓
            ⟨;⟩ ⟨i⟩It is true,/ ⟨he was sc himself scantily⟩ he MSvc;
            humor. It ~~,~ 1A.

145.23   that?–He] MSv; ~?⟨–⟩~ MSvc; ∧~ 1A.

145.28   and, if] MSv; ~∧~ 1A. *Commas are added, as in MSv,
            after the indicated words in 1A at the following ad-
            ditional points:* 146.1 and, 146.6 and, 146.11 was,
            146.11 afterward, 146.37 way, 146.38 facility, 147.3
            theatre, 147.23 yet, 147.26 arcade.

145.29   looks] MSv; ~, 1A. *Commas are deleted, as in MSv,
            after the indicated words in 1A at the following ad-
            ditional points:* 146.3 himself, 146.12 Sophia, 146.22
            home, 147.15 hearted, 147.35 assistance.

145.29   demeanour] MSv; demeanor 1A.

145.31   "charming."] MSv; '~.' 1A. *In addition to substitutions
            noted in separate entries, pairs of double quotation
            marks are supplied, as in MSv, to replace single quo-
            tation marks in 1A at the following points:* 146.2,
            146.2–4, 146.8, 146.8–10, 146.20,. 146.26, 146.27–28,
            146.29, 146.29–31, 146.33–36.

145.34   a gateway] T; ⟨an⟩ ~ ~ MSv; ⟨an⟩ ~ gate-way MSvc;
            ~ gate-way 1A.

145.35   up and] MSv; ~,~ MSvc, 1A. *Commas are deleted,
            as in MSv, after the indicated words in MSvc and
            1A at the following additional points:* 147.5 breeding,
            147.7 forward, 147.31 morning, 147.39 life.

145.38–39   "To . . . over."] T; ∧~ . . . ~.∧ MSv; ∧~ . . . ~.' 1A.

145.40   ¶"And why so?"] T; ∧"~~~?∧ MSv; ¶"~~~?∧
            MSvc; ¶'~~~?' 1A.

145.41   ¶"Because, I've no money;—do let me be quiet."] T;
            ∧"~, ~ ~ ~;/ - ~ ~ ~ ~ ~." MSv; ¶"~,
            ~ ~ ~;/ ⟨-⟩~ ~ ~ ~ ~." MSvc; ¶'~∧ ~
            ~ ~; ∧~ ~ ~ ~ ~.' 1A.

146.3   twenty four] MSv; ~-~ MSvc, 1A.

146.14   taylor] MSv; ta⟨y⟩↑i↓lor MSvc; tailor 1A. *The same*
                emendation is made from the same pattern of variants
                at 146.15, 146.17, 146.32.
146.17   tone.–He] MSv; ~. ⟨-⟩~ MSvc; ~. ∧ ~ 1A.
146.20   spirit!] 1A; ~, MSv; ~, ↑!↓ MSvc.
146.20–24   "you . . . . speeches."] T; "~ . . . . ~ -∧ MSv; "~ . . . .
                ~. ⟨-⟩" MSvc; '~ . . . ~.' 1A.
146.21   shew] MSv; show 1A.
146.24   won't] MSvc; wont MSv; wo n't 1A.
146.27   'charming'] T; "~" MSv; '~∧ 1A. *Quotation within*
                quotation.
146.29   alone,] MSv; ~! 1A.
146.32   "And . . . note?"] T;-"~ . . .~?∧ MSv; '~ . . .~?' 1A.
                Dash in MSv appears to be a slip of the pen.
146.33   you'll] MSv; you↑#↓'ll MSvc; you 'll 1A.
146.33   moment: "Faith,"] T; ~ -"~∧" MSv; ~: ⟨-⟩ "~∧"
                MSvc; ~: '~,' 1A.
146.34   him.–The] MSv; ~. ⟨-⟩ ~ MSvc; ~.∧~ 1A.
146.35   –but–] MSv; ∧~– 1A.
147.2   that,] MSv; ~⟨,⟩ MSvc; ~∧ 1A.
147.15   simple hearted] MSv; ~-~ MSvc, 1A.
147.22   fiery] MSv; fiëry MSvc, 1A.
147.22   relatives] MSv; relations 1A. *Compositor's misreading.*
147.22   sword wounds] MSv; sword-thrusts 1A.
147.27   fidelity;] MSv; ~, 1A.
147.29   the princess reentered] T; ~ Princess ~ MSv; ~
                Princess rëentered MSvc; ~ ~ rëentered 1A. *Emen-*
                dation to "princess" reflects Irving's usual practice for
                titles not used as parts of proper names.
147.34   reopened] MSv; rëopened MSvc, 1A.
147.36   any one to aid him;] T; any/ [*MS torn*] him; MSv;
                ~~~~~, 1A.
147.38   Of] T; Of MSv; ⟨Of⟩ With MSvc; With 1A.

                LETTER FROM GRANADA

148.2   LETTER FROM GRANADA] T; THE CRAYON
                PAPERS./ [*rule*] 1A; ~~~. 2A. *Adopted title prob-*
                ably represents Irving's intention, as 1A reading
                almost certainly does not; see Textual Commentary,
                notes 327, 330; *Emendations* 148.11.
148.5   1829] T; 1828 1A, 2A. *Irving misremembered: his ex-*
                tended stay in the Alhambra was in 1829. The same
                emendation is made at 148.12.
148.11   [*rule*]] 2A; [*rule*]/LETTER FROM GRANADA. 1A.

150.14	"The day of the Capture:"] T; '~~~~~:' 1A; "~~~~~;" 2A. *Pairs of double quotation marks are substituted for single quotation marks in 1A at the following additional points*: 150.40, 152.32–33, 152.33–34.
150.17	Torre] T; Terre 1A, 2A. *Misprint for Spanish "tower."*
152.18	hare-brained] T; hair-brained 1A, 2A. *A frequent Irving error.*
152.35	[*rule*]/¶Within] T; [*rule*]/¶Wɪᴛʜɪɴ 1A; ¶Within 2A.

AMERICAN RESEARCHES IN ITALY

153.2	AMERICAN . . . ITALY] T; THE CRAYON PAPERS./ [*rule*]/ ~ . . . ~. 1A. *The general title in 1A is omitted as not pertaining to this work in particular.*
153.17	poet's] T; poets 1A.
153.20–21	"vexed questions"] T; '~ ~' 1A. *Pairs of single quotation marks in 1A are emended to double quotation marks at the following additional points*: 154.18–19, 156.9, 156.10, 156.24.
154.39	Villani] T; Villari 1A. *Perhaps the result of confusion with "Vasari" preceding.*

[MEMOIR OF THOMAS CAMPBELL]

157.2	[MEMOIR . . . CAMPBELL]] T; [*omitted*] 1A, 2A.
157.11	Lies Bleeding] 2A; lies bleeding 1A. *As parts of a title whose other words, except connectives, are capitalized, these words seem properly capitalized as well.*
159.28	"Literary . . . Ages,"] 2A; ᴧ~ . . . ~,ᴧ 1A. *Probably a printer's oversight; see* 157.11.

CORRECTION OF A MISSTATEMENT RESPECTING *ASTORIA*

161.2	CORRECTION . . . ASTORIA] T; ~ . . . "ASTORIA," BY WASHINGTON IRVING. MStc, 1A. *Latter portion of title omitted as unnecessary.*
161.24	"Astoria."] T; ᴧ~.ᴧ MStc, 1A. *See* 161.22, 162.9.
161.26	In the] 1A; ⟨During⟩ ~ ~ MStc; [*MSt wanting*].
161.26	seen] 1A; ⟨been⟩ ~ MStc; [*MSt wanting*].
161.27	magnates of the North West Company] T; ↑magnates of↓ North West Company MStc; ~ ~ ~ ~ ~ ~, 1A; [*MSt wanting*]. *Article omitted from MStc through oversight.*
161.27	trappers] 1A; ⟨traders⟩ ~ MStc.

161.33   the work]   1A; that work MSt; th⟨at⟩↑e↓ work MStc.
161.35   collating]   1A; collecting MSt; coll⟨ec⟩↑a↓ting MStc.
161.36   Halleck,]   T; ~ₐ MStc, 1A. *First comma of pair prob-
             ably omitted for lack of space at end of printed line.*
162.22   Mr. Astor]   1A; Mrₐ ~ MStc; [*MSt wanting*].
162.25   years']   1A; years MStc; [*MSt wanting*].
162.27   Mr. Astor]   T; him MSt; ⟨him⟩ ↑Mrₐ A.↓ MStc; Mr. A.
             1A. *The full name is used in accordance with Irving's
             practice elsewhere in the article.*
*162.39–40 who, . . . regarded him]   1A; like Malte Brun, regard-
             ing him MSt; ↑who_ₐ↓ like Malte Brun, regard⟨ing⟩↑ed↓
             him MStc.

THE CATSKILL MOUNTAINS

163.2   THE CATSKILL MOUNTAINS]   T; The Katskill
             Mountains/ [*rule*] MSt; ~ ~ ~./ BY WASHINGTON
             IRVING. 2A; ~ ~ ~. 5A. *Irving's "Katskill" is emended
             to "Catskill" at* 164.19, 165.41 (Catskills), 166.38 (Cats-
             kills), 166.43, 167.17 (Catskills).
163.3–4   name, . . . domination,]   2A; ~ₐ . . . ~, MSt.
163.5   which, . . . deer,]   2A; ~, . . . ~ₐ MSt.
163.9   beetling]   2A; ⟨impending⟩ ↑beatling↓ MSt.
163.9   cliffs,]   2A; ~ₐ/ MSt. *End-of-line commas omitted from
             MSt are supplied, as in 1A, after the indicated words
             at the following points*: 164.9 present, 164.27 sky,
             164.30 after flake, 164.35 hunters, 164.36 morasses,
             166.10 Montagne, 166.22 Montagne, 166.44–167.1 sub-
             stance, 167.6 flashed.
163.9   tumbling as it were]   2A; ⟨tumbling seeming to⟩ ↑~ ~
             ~ ~↓/ ⟨tumble⟩ MSt.
163.10   hunter. With]   2A; ~;/ ⟨Yet with all this rude interior
             their aspect/ Towards the Hudson however their
             aspect/ is ⟨for⟩ full of grace and beauty⟩ ~ MSt. *Irv-
             ing neglected to revise punctuation.*
163.10–11   rudeness,]   2A; ~ₐ MSt.
163.12   a country]   2A; ~ ⟨wide⟩ ~ MSt.
163.14   Apennines]   2A; Appenine MSt.
163.15   The Catskills]   2A; ⟨These mountains⟩ ↑~ ~↓ MSt.
163.17   Southwest to Northeast]   2A; South west to North east
             MSt; southwest to northeast 5A.
163.18   Maine, for nearly fourteen hundred miles,]   2A; ~,/
             ↑~ ~ ~ ~ ~ₐ↓ MSt. *See* Emendations 163.19.
163.19   confederacy]   T; ~ ⟨for nearly fourteen hundred miles,⟩
             MSt; ~, 2A.

163.21–22   such as the Cumberland Mountains,] 2A; ↑such as t↓ the Cumber[*MS cropped*]/ mountains∧ MSt. *"Mountains" is also capitalized when used as part of a proper name at 163.37, 164.20, 164.41, 166.20, 166.33 (Mountain), 167.13.*

163.22   Alleganies] 2A; Allganys MSt; Alleghanies 5A. *See* 71.17.

163.22   Lehigh] 2A; LeHigh MSt.

163.25–26   their . . . defiles teem] T; ⟨Here are forests for the along these⟩ ↑their↓/ rocky ridges ⟨and in⟩ their rugged clefts and/ defiles ⟨are a [? d?] mighty forests that/ have never been all⟩ teem MSt; ~ . . . ~, ~ 1A.

163.29   streams flowing] 2A; ⟨untasked⟩ ~ ⟨that/ have never flowing on⟩ ~ MSt.

163.31   Country; resisting] T; ~; ⟨retaining⟩/ ~ MSt; country; ~ 2A.

163.32   and maintaining] 2A; ~/ ⟨destined to preserve us⟩ ~ MSt.

163.35   all controlling] T; ~ controling MSt; ~-~ 2A.

163.38–39   connected. Their . . . region] T; ~⟨;⟩. Their detached ⟨situation⟩ ↑position↓,/ overlooking a ⟨region of⟩ ↑wide↓ lowland ↑region↓ MSt; ~. ~ . . . ~, 2A.

163.40   through it, has] 2A; ~ ⟨h⟩ ~,/ ha⟨ve⟩s MSt.

164.1   which in my mind constitute] T; ~ on ~ ~ ~ MSt; which constitute 2A. *Irving's "on my mind" is not idiomatic in the context; "in" is supplied as closer to what he wrote than "to."*

164.2   scenery.] 2A; ~;/ MSt. *Irving neglected to revise punctuation after deciding to end the sentence.*

164.5   mountains.] 2A; ~∧ MSt. *Periods are supplied, as in 1A, at the unpunctuated ends of sentences in MSt at the following additional points*: 164.7, 166.29, 166.30, 167.6, 167.20, 167.28.

164.11   My] 2A; ⟨It was my first voyage and⟩/ my MSt. *First word of sentence.*

164.15   trader,] 2A; ~∧ MSt.

164.17   telling] 2A; ⟨cram⟩ ~ MSt.

164.18   river, such as Spuyten Devil Creek,] 2A; ~∧ ~ ~ ~ ~ devil/creek∧ MSt; ~, —~ ~ ~ ~ ~, 5A. *Context indicates pause following "river."*

164.18–19   The Tappan Sea, The Devil's] T; ~ ~ ~, ~ Devils MSt; the ~ ~, the ~ 2A.

164.19   other hobgoblin places.] 2A; ⟨the like⟩ ↑~ ~ ~.↓ MSt.

164.22–23   me, . . . belief,] 2A; ~, . . . ~∧ MSt.

164.23   treasury]   2A; ⟨treasury⟩/ ∼ MSt. *False starts immedi-*
            ately rewritten and misspellings immediately cor-
            rected occur in MSt at the following additional points:
            164.27 ⟨sky⟩, 164.35 ⟨kinds⟩, 165.7 ⟨brain⟩, 165.14 ⟨w⟩—
            for "which," 165.21 ⟨refresh⟩, 165.34 ⟨shake⟩, 166.1
            ⟨Direct⟩, 167.10 ⟨lif⟩, 167.25 ⟨whether⟩.

164.26   wigwam,]   2A; ∼ₐ MSt. *Pause precedes concluding*
            phrase.

164.28   Manitou, or Master Spirit,]   T; ∼ₐ ∼ ∼ ∼, MSt; ∼,
            ∼ master spirit, 2A; ∼ ∼ master-spirit 5A.

164.30   gossamers and morning dew,]   T; ∼ ∼ ∼/ ∼ₐ MSt;
            ∼, ∼ ∼ ∼, 2A. *Comma marks pause following series*
            of three.

164.36   morasses]   2A; merasses MSt.

164.37   these were]   2A; ∼ ⟨and ⟨m⟩ many more f⟩ ∼ MSt.

164.38   summer's day,]   2A; summers dayₐ MSt. *Comma marks*
            pause before participial phrase.

164.38   mountains,]   2A; ∼ₐ MSt. *Comma precedes relative*
            clause.

164.39–40   question. Sometimes]   5A; ∼ - ∼ MSt; ∼—sometimes
            2A. *New sentence clearly intended.*

164.40   they seemed]   2A; ∼ ⟨were⟩ ∼ MSt.

164.42   postscript]   2A; post script MSt.

164.42   Winkle,]   2A; ∼ₐ MSt; [5A *wanting*]. *Comma marks*
            pause within long series of prepositional phrases.

164.43   Sketch Book]   2A; Sketchbook MSt; [5A *wanting*]. 2A
            reading approximates actual title, The Sketch-Book,
            more closely than MSt.

165.3   and later]   2A; ∼/ ⟨when he had sank⟩ ∼ MSt.

165.6   trader,]   2A; ∼ₐ MSt. *Comma continues pattern estab-*
            lished earlier in sentence.

165.7   brain,]   2A; ∼ₐ MSt. *Comma precedes relative clause.*

165.8   As to]   2A; ⟨The Indian⟩ ∼ ∼ MSt.

165.9   sunshine]   2A; sun/ shine MSt. *See* 75.4.

165.9   spirits,]   2A; ∼ₐ ⟨of these/ mountains⟩ MSt.

165.9   been suggested]   2A; ⟨ar⟩ ∼ ∼ MSt.

165.10   mountains; the clouds]   T; ∼; ⟨which indicate the
            changes of/ wreathe their aereal changes⟩; ∼ ∼ MSt;
            ∼, ∼ ∼ 2A.

165.11   their summits]   2A; ⟨them⟩ ∼ ∼ MSt.

165.11   aerial effects]   T; ∼ ⟨changes⟩ ∼ MSt; aërial ∼ 2A.

165.14   vicissitudes,]   T; ∼ₐ MSt, 2A. *Comma clarifies.*

165.16   cold, . . . dry,]   2A; ∼, . . . ∼ₐ MSt.

165.18–19	They float] 2A; ⟨They float our/ Our summer sky instead of being like⟩/ ~ ~ MSt.
165.22	poetical;] 2A; ~, MSt. *Semicolon eliminates run-on construction.*
165.25	sunshine,] 2A; ~ₐ MSt.
165.25–26	snow clad earth gives] T; snow ⟨clad⟩ ↑clad↓/ gives MSt; ~-~ ~ ~ 2A. *Though cropped at the left margin, MSt shows no sign that an entire word has been cut away. The 2A "earth" is a plausible correction of the apparent oversight.*
165.32	purifying gusts] T; ⟨sublime/ and⟩ ~ ~ MSt; gusts of tempest 2A.
165.32	grandeur] 2A; ⟨sublimity⟩ ↑~↓ MSt.
165.34–35	the sublime . . . autumn] 2A; ⟨the⟩ ↑the sublime melancholy of↓ our Autumn MSt. *The 2A "autumn" reflects Irving's usual practice; see 165.23, 165.28.*
165.36	a woodland] 2A; ⟨the⟩ ↑~↓ ~ MSt.
165.37	yellow] 2A; ⟨gold⟩ ~ MSt.
165.38	the glory of the Lord] T; ~ ~ ~ ⟨God⟩ ↑~ ~↓ MSt; ~ ~ ~ God 2A.
165.39	firmament sheweth] T; fermament ~ MSt; ~ showeth 2A.
165.40	sheweth forth] T; setheth forth MSt; showeth 2A.
165.41	the Indians only] 2A; ⟨only⟩ the Indians ↑only↓ MSt.
165.43	themes] 2A; ⟨a⟩/ ~ MSt.
166.6	them] 2A; thesm MSt.
166.6	pigment,] 2A; ~ₐ MSt. *Comma precedes relative clause.*
166.11	Huguenot] 2A; ↑huguenot↓ MSt.
166.11	Councillors] T; ⟨huguenots who had⟩ ~ MSt; counsellors 2A.
166.12	supposed ore] 2A; ⟨ore⟩ ~ ~ MSt.
166.14	gold] 2A; Gold MSt. *See 166.19, 166.23.*
166.19	expedition, nor of its whereabouts,] 2A; ~ₐ ~/ ~ ⟨the⟩ ↑~↓ ~ₐ MSt. *Context suggests pauses intended.*
166.21	Like] 2A; ⟨It was⟩ ~ MSt.
166.23	Van der Donk,] 2A; Vander Donkₐ MSt. *See 166.4. Comma precedes relative clause.*
166.26	agent, . . . Corsen,] 2A; ~ₐ . . . ~, MSt.
166.35	ship in which] 2A; ship which MSt. *Oversight.*
166.36	away, and] 2A; ~ₐ ~ MSt. *Comma separates independent clauses.*
166.39	In 1649, about two] 2A; ↑In 1649ₐ about↓ Two MSt. *Comma is first of a pair in the sentence as revised.*

166.39	shipwreck] 5A; Shipwreck MSt; ship-/wreck 2A. *Emendation reflects Irving's usual practice in MSt.*
166.41–42	Slechtenhorst, . . . Rensselaerswyck,] 2A; ~∧ . . . Rennsellaerwick∧ MSt. *Commas enclose appositive. The indicated spellings of "Rensselaerswyck" are similarly emended at 167.2 Rensellaerwick, 167.12 Rennsellaerwick.*
166.42	had purchased on behalf of] T; ⟨pu⟩ had purchased ⟨on/ in the name⟩ ↑on behalf↓ of MSt; ~ ~ in ~ ~ 2A.
167.4	at the farmer's house] T; a ~ farmers ~ MSt; in ~ ~ ~ 2A. *To correct the oversight "at" is adopted as idiomatic and closer to what Irving wrote than "in."*
167.14	taken captive] 2A; ⟨arrested⟩ ↑~ ~↓ MSt.
167.16	no record] 2A; ~ ⟨further⟩ ~ MSt.
167.17	Catskills; adventurers] 2A; Katskills; ⟨which seem to⟩ ~ MSt; ~. Adventurers 5A.
167.18	to attend] 2A; ~ ⟨meddle with⟩ ↑~↓ MSt.
167.21	from these] 2A; from th⟨o⟩ese ↑⟨this⟩↓ MSt.
167.22	to prove,] 2A; ~ ~∧ MSt. *Comma clarifies.*
167.24	there,] 2A; ~∧ MSt. *Comma follows long conditional clause.*

[REMARKS AT THE COOPER MEMORIAL MEETING, FEBRUARY 24, 1852]

167.29–30	[REMARKS . . . 1852]] T; [*omitted*] 1A.

CONVERSATIONS WITH TALMA

168.2–3	CONVERSATIONS . . . . BOOK.] T; Conversations with Talma./ From rough notes in a common place book∧/ [*rule*]/ By the author of the Sketch Book. MSh; Conversations with Talma./ FROM ROUGH NOTES IN A COMMON-PLACE BOOK./ [*rule*]/ by the author of the sketch-book./ [*rule*] 1A; CONVERSATIONS WITH TALMA./ from rough notes in a common-place book. 3A. *Acknowledgment of authorship omitted as unnecessary.*
168.4	Paris, *April* 25th, 1821.] T; ~∧ ~ 25ʰ∧ ~. MSh; ~, ~ 25, ~. 1A; ~, April 25, ~. 3A. *Abbreviated ordinal reflects Irving's usual practice.*
168.4	call] 1A; ⟨visit⟩ ↑~↓ MSh.
168.5	Talma,] 1A; ~∧ MSh. *Comma separates appositives.*
168.6	des Petites Augustines] T; ~ petites/ ~∧ MSh; Des

~ ~, 1A; Des ~ Angustines, 3A. *"Petites" capitalized as part of proper name.*

168.12 John Kemble,] T; ~ ~ₐ MSh; ~ Philip ~, 1A. *Comma marks pause before relative clause.*

168.15 countenance; his eyes] 1A; ~; ⟨which⟩ ~ ~ 1A.

168.19 received] 1A; recieved MSh.

168.19 manner,] 1A; ~ₐ/ MSh. *End-of-line punctuation omitted in MSh is supplied, as in 1A, after the indicated words at the following additional points:* 168.41, Français, 171.31 phrases, 172.10 moustaches, 172.10 tobacco, 172.30 unaffected, 173.14 diet, 173.17 drama, 173.17 literature.

168.22 Emperor!"] 1A; ~!ₐMSh. *Individual double quotation marks are supplied, as in 1A, after the indicated words at the following points:* 169.1 revolution, 170.18 strangers.

168.24 "Yes . . . Italy."] 1A; ~ - ~ MSh; ~, ~ 3A. *1A reading was Pairs of double quotation marks are supplied—unless otherwise noted—as in 1A at the following points:* 168.25–29, 168.38, 168.38–169.1, 169.20–21, 169.21–24 *(second quotation mark omitted in 1A),* 169.25, 169.25–28.

168.24 Yes—just] 1A; ~-~ MSh; ~, ~ 3A. *1A reading was Irving's probable intention; for his use of the single dash, see* 168.26.

168.26 Emperor—the youth] T; emperor - ~ ~ MSh; ~; ~ ~, 1A; ~,—~ ~ 3A. *Capitalized in accordance with contemporary usage; see also* 168.22.

168.27 Now] 1A; ⟨Ah, Paris is⟩/ ~ MSh.

168.27 Tuileries] 1A; Tuilleries MSh.

168.33 said he,] 1A; ~ ~ₐ MSh; ~ ~; 3A. *Comma marks pause separating commentary from quotation. Further commas are supplied in this situation, as in 1A, at the following points:* 168.38, 169.1, 169.6, 169.37, 172.2.

168.34 always] 1A; ⟨incessantly⟩ ~ MSh.

168.36 is becoming] 1A; ⟨was⟩ ↑~↓ ~ MSh.

168.39 life, . . . people,] 1A; ~; . . . ~ₐ MSh. *Irving neglected to revise punctuation after deciding to add the parallel phrase.*

168.40 classic antiquity.] 1A; ⟨the⟩ ~ ~ₐ MSh. *Periods are supplied or substituted, as in 1A, at the ends of sentences or footnotes at the following additional points:* 169.35, 170.42, 171.1, 172.34 (MSh vulgar:), 173.9, 173.11, 173.35.

168.41   never . . . Théâtre Français] 1A; ⟨seldom⟩ ↑~↓ . . .
              Theatre Francaise MSh. *The emendation to "Théâtre
              Français," the 1A reading, is also made at 170.7,
              170.27.*

168.41–42   actors, while] 1A; ~, While MSh. *Capital "W" is only
              barely large enough to be so classified and was prob-
              ably intended by Irving as lower-case.*

169.1   scenes] 1A; ~ ⟨of real life⟩ MSh.

169.5   revolution, and that] 1A; ~∧ ~ ~ MSh. *Pause seems
              necessary between compound objects not grammati-
              cally parallel.*

169.6   "The] 1A; 'The MSh.

169.8   sheep."] 1A; ~." ⟨He spoke of the vehement⟩ MSh.

169.9   away, he] 1A; ~∧ ⟨Talma⟩ ↑~↓ MSh. *Comma clarifies.*

169.10   I pointed to] 1A; ~ ⟨noticed⟩ ↑~ ~↓ MSh.

169.10   children's] 1A; childrens MSh. *Apostrophes are sup-
              plied, as in 1A, to possessives at the following addi-
              tional points:* 169.15, 169.33, 170.9, 170.31, 170.33,
              170.39, 171.39.

169.11   Ah!] 1A; ~∧ MSh. *Context indicates exclamation in-
              tended.*

169.12   nowadays] 3A; now/ adays MSh; now-a-days 1A.

169.16   by turns,] 1A; ~ ~∧ MSh. *Pause seems necessary to
              separate carefully balanced phrases.*

169.24   France] 1A; ⟨fr⟩ ~ MSh. *False starts immediately re-
              written occur in MSh at the following additional
              points:* 169.40 ⟨cours of⟩, 169.41 ⟨ali⟩, 170.1 ⟨Sill⟩,
              170.38 ⟨trans⟩, 171.38 ⟨His⟩, 172.27 ⟨ben⟩, 172.28
              ⟨ghosts⟩, 172.39 ⟨wa⟩.

169.27   Boulevards,] 1A; ~∧ MSh. *Comma marks pause fol-
              lowing long   adverbial construction.*

169.32   exhausted,] 1A; ~∧ MSh. *Comma marks pause between
              independent clauses.*

169.36   but he declined it] 1A; ⟨He⟩ ↑~ ~↓/ ~ ~ MSh.

169.37   value,] T; ⟨use⟩ ~, MSh; ~; 1A.

169.38   circumstance] 1A; ⟨anec⟩ ~ MSh.

169.42   He spoke of] 1A; ⟨He had studied/ endeavored, he
              said, to⟩ ~ ~ ~ ⟨the⟩ MSh.

169.43   tragedians, and of] T; ~,/ ⟨but⟩ ↑~ ~↓ MSh; ~; ~
              ~ 1A.

169.44   encountered] 1A; ⟨had⟩ ~ MSh.

170.3   expressed] 1A; ⟨possesses/ affirmed⟩ ~ MSh.

170.4   said] 1A; ⟨felt as if⟩ ↑~↓ MSh.

170.5   being able] 1A; ⟨his⟩ ~ ~ MSh.

170.6   He had]   1A; ⟨He had of/ late⟩ ~ ⟨adverted to⟩ ~ MSh.

170.9   Shakespeare's]   T; ⟨his⟩ ↑Shakespears↓ MSh; Shaks-
             peare's 1A.

*170.10–11   for . . . and natural outbreaks]   1A; for ⟨natural and⟩
             familiar touches; ⟨and⟩/ of pathos and tenderness and
             ⟨for bursts of/ passion⟩ natural outbreaks MSh; ~
             . . . , ~ ~ ~ 3A.

*170.18   strangers."]   1A; ~.ʌ------- MSh.

170.23   which were]   1A; ⟨but were⟩ ~ ~ MSh.

170.27   success]   1A; success⟨ful⟩ MSh.

170.30   pseudo-classic]   1A; ~ʌ~ MSh. *No authority in dic-
             tionaries for unhyphenated form.*

170.34   it . . . hover]   1A; ⟨he hovers in idea⟩ ↑~ . . . ~↓ MSh.

170.38   boxes,]   1A; ~ʌ MSh. *Comma marks pause preceding
             modifying phrase.*

170.40   grand theatre]   MSy, 1A; ⟨Theatre Franc⟩ Grand ~
             MSh. *Irving momentarily continued to capitalize, but
             "grand theatre" is not a proper designation.*

170.41   rule.]   1A; ~. ⟨it⟩ MSh.

171.7   a modification]   1A; ⟨a German an⟩ ~ ~ MSh.

171.12   afraid]   1A; affraid MSh.

171.14–15   after being accustomed]   1A; ⟨in relishing⟩ ~ ~ ~
             MSh.

171.17   monstrosities,]   1A; ~ʌ MSh. *Comma marks pause pre-
             ceding modifying phrase.*

171.18   in vain. The]   T; ~ ~./ the MSh; ~ ~! ~1A; ~ ~!
             the 3A. *"The" begins a sentence at the top of a new
             page in MSh; Irving probably lost track of what pre-
             ceded it.*

171.21   assures me]   1A; assure ~ MSh. *Error; for the tense see
             172.3.*

171.25   feel]   1A; ⟨read⟩ ~ MSh.

171.27–28   thought, . . . passion,]   T; thought⟨, that are/ most
             likely⟩ of character and passionʌ MSh; thought, of
             character, and passion, 1A. *Comma following
             "thought," partially deleted by cancelling stroke, is
             necessary for clarity; comma following "passion" is
             second of a pair.*

171.31   expression,]   1A; ↑expression ⟨language⟩,↓ ⟨expression⟩,
             MSh.

171.35   beauties]   1A; ⟨merits⟩ ↑~↓ MSh.

171.35   translated]   1A; ⟨re⟩ ~ MSh.

171.36   tongue?]   1A; ~. MSh.

171.36–37   His . . . exuberant]   1A; ⟨He can afford to be stripped

of all the magic/ of his style; for⟩ His ⟨pages⟩ ↑scenes↓
are so exhubrant MSh.

171.37   and masterly strokes] 1A; ⟨that he/ who can in any
                degree⟩ ~ ⟨in⟩ ~/ ~ MSh.

171.37–38   nature, . . . can] 1A; nature∧ . . . ⟨who⟩ can MSh.
                Comma is second of a pair.

171.39   are like . . . Aladdin] 1A; ~ ~ ⟨Alladins⟩ . . . Alladin
                MSh.

171.42   Shakespeare] T; Shakespear MSh; Shakspeare 1A.
                Emended spelling reflects Irving's usual practice.

172.2   revolution] 1A; Revolution MSh, 3A. *See 169.5, 171.44,
                172.16. The single instance of the word in MSy is
                lower-case.*

172.3   who are] 1A; ⟨are tot⟩ ~ ~ MSh.

172.4   a different people] 1A; ⟨totally⟩ ~/ ~ ~ MSh.

172.6–7   tact, . . . feelings,] 1A; ~, . . . ~∧ MSh.

172.12   in dress] 1A; ~ ⟨his⟩ ~ MSh.

172.13   perfumes] 1A; ⟨[?sw   lte?] poetry and⟩ ~ MSh.

172.18   Though these realities] 1A; ⟨When such realities⟩/ ~
                ~ ~ MSh.

172.22–23   every thing; in their] T; ~ ~; ↑~↓ ⟨In⟩ ~ MSh; ~/
                ~: ~ ~ 1A; everything; ~ ~ 3A.

172.32   consoled] 1A; ⟨persuaded⟩ ↑~↓ MSh.

172.34   have grown up] 1A; ⟨that read the romances⟩ ↑⟨de-
                lighted in⟩↓ ~/ ~ ~ MSh.

172.40   French,] 1A; french, MSy; ~∧ MSh. *Comma clarifies.*

172.44   envelop] 1A; envellope MSh. *In roughly corresponding
                MSy passage, "envelloping."*

173.8   misanthropy] MSy, 1A; manthropy MSh.

173.10–11   way, . . . literature,] MSy, 1A; ~∧ . . . ~∧ MSh. *Irv-
                ing wrote hurriedly; the period at the end of sentence
                is also missing.*

173.12–13   Nations, . . . individuals,] 1A; ~∧ . . . ~∧ MSh. *Commas
                avoid ambiguity and alter pace to suit deliberate
                manner of passage.*

173.13   refinements,] 1A; ~∧ MSh. *Comma marks pause be-
                tween independent clauses.*

173.14   a change] 1A; ⟨the stimulus⟩ ~ ~ MSh.

173.16   away . . . from] 1A; away ⟨entirely⟩ from rigid rule;
                ⟨to descending⟩ ↑from↓ MSh.

173.16   narrative,] 1A; ~∧ MSh. *Semicolon in roughly cor-
                responding passage of MSy suggests intention for
                pause.*

173.18   glowing,] MSy; ~∧/ MSh; ~∧ 1A.

173.20   Paris, 1821.]   1A; Paris∧ 1821. MSh; Paris, ∧∧ 2A. *Date-*
                line emended to reflect consistent 1A style; see Emen-
                dations 168.4.

[MEMOIR OF WASHINGTON ALLSTON]

173.22   [MEMOIR . . . ALLSTON]]   T; [*omitted*] MSn, 1A;
                WASHINGTON ALLSTON. 3A.

173.23   I first became acquainted]   MSn; "I ~ ~ ~," writes
                Washington Irving to us, 1A; ~ first ~ ~ 3A.

173.23   Allston]   3A; Alston MSn; Allston, 1A. *"Alston" is*
                emended to "Allston," as in 1A, at the following addi-
                tional points: 173.27, 174.32, 174.44, 175.7, 175.9,
                175.16, 175.17, 175.21, 175.24, 176.23.

173.27   Allston.]   1A; Alston∧ MSn. *Periods are supplied at the*
                unpunctuated ends of sentences in MSn at the follow-
                ing points: 175.9, 175.21, 177.21, 177.22, 178.14, 178.16.

173.32   benevolence,]   1A; ~∧ MSn. *Slight pause accentuates*
                careful balance of sentence.

173.34   man's]   1A; mans MSn. *Apostrophes are supplied to*
                possessives, as in 1A, at the following additional
                points: 174.8, 174.20, 176.11, 176.38, 177.8. 177.10,
                177.20, 177.38, 178.13.

173.34   us, and]   1A; ~∧ ~ MSn. *Comma separates inde-*
                pendent clauses.

174.4   paintings,]   1A; ~∧ MSn. *Comma separates indepen-*
                dent clauses.

174.4   most]   1A; ⟨best⟩ ↑~↓ MSn.

174.5   masterpieces,]   1A; master pieces∧/ MSn. *End-of-line*
                commas omitted from MSn after the indicated words
                are supplied, as in 1A, at the following additional
                points: 176.36 weeks, 176.41 colossal.

174.6   collection,]   1A; ~∧ MSn. *Comma separates direct*
                quotation from commentary. A comma is also sup-
                plied for this purpose, as in 1A, at 174.41.

174.9   succession, even]   1A; ~∧ ~ MSn. *Context suggests*
                pause.

174.11   distinctly;]   1A; ~, MSn. *Semicolon eliminates run-on*
                construction.

174.13   will]   1A; ⟨wi⟩ ~ MSn. *The indicated false starts im-*
                mediately rewritten, and misspellings corrected im-
                mediately afterward, occur in MSn at the following
                additional points: 174.26 ⟨ne⟩, 174.26 ⟨been⟩, 175.9
                ⟨studio⟩, 176.12 ⟨terriffic⟩, 177.11 ⟨Egrmont⟩.

174.14   memory."]   3A; ~.ʌ MSn; ~.' 1A. *Oversight. Incom-*
              plete pairs of double quotation marks in MSn are
              completed at the following additional points: 174.42,
              177.2.
174.17   recollect]   1A; reccollect MSn.
174.19   Angelo, and his]   1A; ~ʌ ~ ⟨the⟩ ↑~↓ MSn. *Comma*
              clarifies.
174.20   St. Peter's]   1A; Sᵗ Peters MSn.
174.27   villa,]   1A; Villaʌ MSn. *Emendation to lower-case re-*
              flects usual practice in MSn; comma enhances deliber-
              ate pace intended. The following additional words
              capitalized in MSn are emended to lower-case, as in
              1A: 174.28 *statues,* 174.38 *sublime.*
174.28   terraced gardens]   1A; ⟨gard⟩ ~ ~ MSn.
174.36   masterpieces]   1A; master pieces MSn; master-/pieces
              3A.
174.37   tastes,]   1A; ~ʌ MSn. *Comma clarifies and marks slight*
              pause before dependent clause.
174.44   Allston]   T; Alston MSn; ~, 1A.
175.1   feasible]   1A; feasable MSn.
175.7   connected with]   1A; ~ ⟨back⟩ ~ MSn.
175.10–11   society, . . . acquainted,]   1A; ~ʌ . . . ~ʌ MSn. *Com-*
              mas separate independent clauses and pace long, un-
              punctuated statement.
175.12   rainbow]   1A; rain bow MSn. *The same correction is*
              made at 175.14.
175.15   reality. So]   T; ~, ~ MSn; ~, so 1A; ~; so 3A. *The*
              "S" is written boldly; Irving clearly intended to
              begin a new sentence.
175.17   after he]   1A; ~ ⟨his return from Italy⟩/ ~ MSn.
175.18   but, . . . cities,]   T; ~, . . . ~ʌ MSn; ~ʌ . . . ~ʌ 1A.
175.18–19   we saw each other only]   1A; ~ ⟨only⟩/ ~ ~ ~ ↑~↓
              MSn.
175.21–22   was dejected]   1A; ⟨was in delicate health⟩ ~ ~ MSn.
175.24–25   Allston, . . . company,]   1A; ~, . . . ~ʌ MSn.
175.29   papers,]   1A; paperʌ MSn. *Obvious oversight; comma*
              clarifies.
175.32   from his]   1A; ⟨of⟩ ~ ~ MSn.
175.32   to me, relating]   1A; ~ ~ʌ ~ MSn. *Comma clarifies.*
175.33   first, dated May 9th 1817,]   T; ~ʌ ~ ~ 9ᵗʰ 1817, MSn:
              ~, ~~ 9, ~, 1A.
175.37   about, &c.,]   1A; ~ʌ &cʌʌ MSn.
175.41   beginning, the Prophet]   T; ~,/ The ~ MSn; ~: ~ ~

1A; ~; ~ prophet 3A. *Since the proper title is not being given, a capitalized "The" serves no purpose.*

175.42   handwriting]   T; *hand/ writing* MSn; *hand-writing* 1A.

176.6   Don't]   1A; Dont MSn.

176.7   sovereign]   1A; sovreign MSn.

176.8   state]   T; ~⟨-⟩ MSn; ~, 1A. *What appears to be Irving's heavy deleted dash may be his cancellation of a comma.*

176.9   preternatural]   1A; perternatural MSn.

176.19   destruction]   1A; distruction MSn.

176.24   London, 13 March 1818]   T; ~∧ ~ ~ ~ MSn; ~, 13th ~, ~ 1A.

176.26   a study]   1A; ⟨the⟩ ~ ~ MSn.

176.30   I asked, 150 guineas]   1A; ~ ~∧ ~ ~ MSn.

176.32–33   'as . . . evinced.' &c.]   1A; "~ . . . ~∧" &c∧ MSn; ∧~ . . . ~,∧ &c. 3A. *Quotation within quotation. In similar circumstances pairs of single quotation marks are substituted, as in 1A, for double quotation marks in MSn at the following points: 177.16, 177.20–21, 177.24.*

176.38   Jacob's Dream.]   1A; Jacobs dream. MSn; '~ ~.' 3A. *Emendation reflects usual practice in MSn for picture-titles.*

176.43   successful,]   1A; ~∧ MSn. *Comma separates independent clauses.*

177.1   picture,]   1A; ~∧ MSn. *Comma marks pause between independent clauses.*

177.3   a "decided hit"]   T; ~ "~/ ~∧ MSn; '~ ~ ~,' 1A; "~ ~ ~," 3A.

*177.9   on the subject.]   T; [re?]/ ~ ~. MSn; ~ ~ ~:– 1A.

177.14   it. Indeed]   1A; ~: ~ MSn.

177.16   back'–]   T; ~"– MSn; ~, ' 1A. *See* Emendations 176.32–33.

177.24–25   picture, and I have not]   1A; picture. ⟨I⟩ and I have ⟨no doubt⟩/ not MSn. *Irving neglected to revise punctuation.*

177.28   Petworth,]   1A; ~∧ MSn. *Comma precedes subordinate clause.*

177.30   Allston;]   1A; ~, MSn. *Semicolon eliminates run-on construction.*

177.32   he had]   1A; ⟨he had made his arrangements to return to/ America⟩ ~ ~ MSn.

177.33   affliction, and . . . prospects,]   1A; ~; ~ . . . ~∧ MSn. *Irving apparently neglected to revise semicolon after deciding to add a phrase parallel to the one preceding it.*

177.39   Some of]   1A; ⟨Several⟩ ∼ ∼ MSn.

177.40   urgent. He]   1A; ∼⟨,⟩. ⟨and⟩ ∼ MSn.

177.42   in the possession of]   T; in possession of MSn; [*1A, 3A wanting; see* Rejected Variants 177.42–43]. *Hone was the possessor of the picture, not vice-versa.*

177.42   Philip Hone, Esq.,]   T; ∼ ∼ₐ Esqₐₐ MSn; [*1A, 3A wanting; see* Rejected Variants 177.42–43].

178.2–3   companionship of such a man]   1A; companion ship of ↑such↓ a man MSn. *Interlineation is by Pierre M. Irving; it is a reasonable correction of Irving's oversight.*

178.3   invaluable.]   1A; ∼./ ⟨in every point of view.⟩ MSn.

178.8   After]   1A; ⟨The⟩ ∼ MSn.

178.9   Royal Academy]   1A; ∼ academy MSn. *Proper name.*

[THE CHRONICLE OF PELAYO]

*180.2   [THE CHRONICLE OF PELAYO]   T; The Legend of Pelayo. MSv; THE LEGEND OF PELAYO./ [*rule*] 4A.

180.3–7   [CHAPTER I. . . . *Grafeses.*]   4A; [*omitted*] MSv. *Chapter-numbers and chapter-headings supplied from 4A occur at 184.35–36, 186.3–6, 192.1–2.*

180.10   country,]   4A; ∼ₐ MSv. *For MSy, 1A, see* Precopy-Text Rejected Variants 180.10–11. *Comma is second of a pair.*

180.14   Jesuit]   MSy, 1A, 4A; jesuit MSv. *Emendation reflects Irving's usual practice.*

180.21   labyrinth]   4A; labyr⟨y⟩↑i↓nth MSv. *MSy, 1A wanting. The correction is by Pierre M. Irving.*

180.24   bye-ways]   T; ∼ₐ∼ MSv; by-ways 4A. *MSy, 1A wanting. OED lists "bye-way" but no unhyphenated form. Hyphens are added to other compounds unhyphenated in MSv at 184.9–10, 184.19, 186.13, 192.41.*

180.34   chronicle]   4A; chron[*torn*] MSv. *Additional readings supplied from 4A in place of text lost or truncated owing to tears in MSv occur at the following points, where the 4A interpolations are shown within brackets:* 192.16 Descen[d]ing, 192.17 t[hrough], 193.24 within t[he], 193.24 cavern [was], 196.21 canst th[ou]. *See also* Emendations 190.18, 196.21–23.

180.38   *Abarca, . . . § 2.]   4A; *Padre Pedro Abarca. Anales de Aragonₐ Anti Regnoₐ § 2. MSy; *Padre Pedro

ABARCA. Anales de Aragon, Anti Regno, § 2. 1A;
*Abarca∧ Anales de Aragon∧ Ante Regno § 2. MSv.
*Footnote citations are adopted from 4A at the follow-
ing additional points; the MSv readings are given in
parentheses:* 182.43 (*El Moro Rasis, (*La Destruycion de Espana/ ⟨Roj⟩ Rojas Hist. Toledo P2. L. 4 C.
1.); 191.42 (*El Moro Rasis. Destruycion de Espana/
Part 2. C. 101.); 195.39 (*Morales. ⟨Chronicon⟩ ↑Croni-
con↓ de Espana/ L. 13. C. 2.); 198.40 (Sebastianus
Salmanticensis Episc.); 199.37 (La Destruycion de
Espana Part 3.). *However, see* Emendations 182.43.

181.2	Gothic] 4A; gothic MSv. *See* 183.9, 192.9. *The same emendation is made at* 194.23.
181.2	The chronicle] 4A; ; ~ ~ MSv. *Semicolon forms part of a cancelled passage and was inadvertently allowed by Irving to stand. Punctuation thus left uncancelled in MSv occurs before or after the indicated words as shown:* 191.6 (; but), 195.1 (sons,), 198.36 (- Judicio), 198.36 (* actum).
181.3	court] 4A; Court MSv. *See* 184.18.
181.3	Ezica] 4A; Ezeca MSv. *The "e" in MSv appears to be an undotted "i"; see* 184.15.
181.4–5	at Toledo] 4A; ⟨of⟩ ↑~↓ ~ MSv. *The correction is by Pierre M. Irving.*
181.7	Duke] 4A; duke MSv. *Usual practice for proper titles; see* 182.27.
181.9	duke] 4A; Duke MSv. *Usual practice for the title used alone in reference to an individual. The same emendation is made at* 181.19, 185.23, 185.21.
181.9	Prince Witiza] 4A; prince ~ MSv. *Usual practice for proper names; see* 181.28, 182.11. *The same emendation is made at* 182.33.
181.11	Witiza the Wicked] 4A; ~ ~ wicked MSv. *Capitalized as part of a proper name, or pseudonym.*
181.11–12	prince, . . . rival,] 4A; ~∧ . . . ~∧ MSv. *Commas set off the infinitive phrase.*
181.12–13	not, however,] 4A; ~∧ ~, MSv. *Emendation reflects Irving's usual practice; see* 181.14. *The same emendation is made at* 183.44, 198.27.
181.19	duke,] 4A; Duke∧ MSv. *Comma separates introductory phrase from unpunctuated compound statement which follows.*
181.26	apartment,] 4A; ~∧ MSv. *Comma clarifies.*
181.33	garments,] 4A; ~∧/ MSv. *Pause precedes participial*

*phrase. End-of-line commas or other indicated punc-
tuation omitted from MSv is also supplied after the
words shown at* 182.21 doubtful, 182.29 more, 185.10
request, 185.30 attendance, 185.40 adoption;, 185.42
count, 186.9 Cantabria, 186.21 Agapida, 186.24 algo,
187.28 posted, 189.1 merchant, 189.14 sun; 190.5 son,
191.17 (friend), 193.23 molested; 196.30 end, 196.33
thee, 199.25 kingdom, 199.34 warfare, 199.35 queen.

181.34   brocade,]   4A; ~ₐ MSv. *Comma is second of a pair.*
181.36   borne]   4A; born MSv. *Misspelling in the sense used.*
181.39   air,]   4A; ~ₐ MSv. *Comma necessary for clarity.*
182.13   him,]   4A; ~ₐ MSv. *Second comma of a pair.*
182.15   was granted]   4A; was/ ⟨was⟩ ~ MSv. *The deletion is in
              pencil, possibly by Pierre M. Irving.*
182.16   or if]   4A; ⟨of⟩or ~ MSv. *The correction is by Pierre
              M. Irving.*
182.17   overcome,]   4A; ~ₐ MSv. *Second comma of a pair.*
182.19   made,]   4A; ~ₐ MSv. *Comma marks a pause, as in the
              first half of this carefully balanced sentence.*
182.22   Holy Virgin]   4A; holy virgin MSv. *Irving's usual prac-
              tice; see* 181.24, "Fernando the Saint" 311.14–16.
182.24   slain,]   4A; ~; MSv. *Irving neglected to revise punctu-
              ation after deciding to extend the statement.*
182.32   magnificence,]   4A; ~ₐ MSv. *Comma precedes long
              subordinate clause.*
182.35   chronicle,]   4A; ~ₐ MSv. *Comma marks pause follow-
              ing long introductory clause.*
182.41–42   night, it]   4A; ~ₐ ~ MSv. *Second comma of a pair.*
182.43   c. 1.]   T; Cₐ 1. MSv; cl. 4A. *Misprint.*
183.21   gold,]   4A; ~ₐ MSv. *Comma lends directness to Irving's
              enumeration.*
183.23   written,]   4A; ~ₐ MSv. *Comma marks a pause between
              commentary and quotation. Further commas are sup-
              plied for this purpose at* 188.31, 189.2, 189.3, 190.4,
              191.5, 191.5, 194.15, 194.16, 196.17, 196.17, 196.27.
183.30   witnessed,]   4A; ~ₐ MSv. *Comma marks pause follow-
              ing long introductory construction.*
183.34   affliction. The count]   4A; ~: ~ ~ MSv. *Irving thought
              better of continuing sentence. Periods are also sup-
              plied or substituted for indicated punctuation at*
              184.22, 185.12, 187.3, 196.27 *semicolon,* 199.10 *semi-
              colon.*
184.4   playthings]   T; play/ things MSv; play-/ things 4A.
184.18   rest,]   4A; ~ₐ MSv. *Second comma of a pair.*

184.28	Tagus, or] 4A; ~; ~ MSv. *Irving neglected to revise his punctuation after deciding to extend the clause.*
184.32–33	too, . . . palfrey,] 4A; ~_∧ . . . ~_∧ MSv. *Commas necessary for clarity.*
184.37	¶Among] T; _∧~ MSv; ¶Among 4A. *Irving clearly intended to begin the chapter with a paragraph break.*
185.4–5	throbbed, . . . why,] 4A; ~_∧ . . . ~_∧ MSv. *Commas necessary for clarity and to mark pauses.*
185.7	him, and] 4A; ~_∧ ~ MSv. *Comma separates independent clauses.*
185.10	¶The count] 4A; _∧~ ~ MSv. *Sentence begins a new page in MSv; bottom line of preceding page includes only 1 word.*
185.12	"For . . . part,"] 4A; _∧~ . . . ~,_∧ MSv. *Pairs of double quotation marks are also supplied at 185.12–15, 185.25, 185.25–28, 188.31–32, 189.2, 189.3–4, 190.4–5, 191.34–35.*
185.13	passed] 4A; past MSv. *Misspelling in the sense used.*
185.20	castle,] 4A; ~_∧ MSv. *Comma follows the introductory clause; see 185.16.*
185.21	sovereigns] 4A; sov↑e↓reigns MSv. *The insertion is by Pierre M. Irving. MSv "sovreign" is emended to the correct spelling at 195.4.*
185.29	day, . . . state,] 4A; ~_∧ . . . ~_∧ MSv. *Commas enclose a subordinate clause.*
185.42	agitation,] 4A; ~_∧ MSv. *Comma is second of a pair.*
186.8	Pelayo,] 4A; ~_∧ MSv. *Comma necessary for clarity.*
186.9	dead,] 4A; ~_∧ MSv. *Comma necessary for clarity.*
186.13	foster-father] 4A; foster/ father MSv. *See 215.20.*
186.34	Spain,] MSy, 1A, 4A; ~_∧ MSv. *First comma of a pair.*
186.34	harassing] 4A; harrassing MSv. *For MSy, 1A see* Pre-copy-Text Rejected Variants 186.33–36.
186.38	border,] 4A; ~_∧ MSv. *Comma marks pause following long introductory clause.*
187.2	traded,] 4A; ~_∧ MSv. *Irving neglected to add punctuation to replace semicolon in cancelled passage immediately following.*
187.7	waylaid] 4A; waylayed MSv. *No authority in dictionaries.*
187.10	wife,] 4A; ~_∧ MSv. *First comma of a pair.*
187.12	nephew, . . . clerk,] 4A; ~_∧ . . . ~_∧ MSv. *Commas necessary for clarity.*
187.29	merchant's] 4A; merchants MSv. *The same emendation is made at 188.39, 189.40, 189.42.*
187.31	terms,] 4A; ~_∧ MSv. *Comma clarifies.*

187.33   perceived]   4A; percieved MSv.

187.42   page,]   4A; ~∧ MSv. *Comma marks pause following*
              long introductory construction.

187.42   prize,]   4A; ~∧ MSv. *Comma separates independent*
              clauses.

188.3   land?]   4A; ~. MSv. *Context warrants emendation.*

188.10   He . . . lance,]   4A; He hastily couched/ ⟨was totally
              unprepared.⟩ ⟨He hastily couched⟩/ his lance, MSv.
              The second cancellation is by Pierre M. Irving, cor-
              recting Irving's oversight.

188.11   Pelayo]   4A; ⟨Don⟩ ~ MSv. *The same cancellation*
              occurs in MSv at 188.18, 188.23, 189.10, 189.19, 189.23,
              189.26, 189.30, 189.42, 190.3, 190.5, 191.2, 191.11,
              191.14, 191.23, 191.31, 191.35.

188.15   galloped]   4A; gallopped MSv.

188.19   others,]   4A; ~∧ MSv. *First comma of a pair.*

188.19   seeing]   4A; for ~ MSv. *The "for" Irving inadvertently*
              left uncancelled. At 191.22 he similarly failed to cancel
              a "He" before "Yet."

188.28   with difficulty]   4A; ↑with↓ ⟨~⟩/ ~ MSv. *The second*
              "with" is written in pencil and deleted in ink, both
              by Pierre M. Irving.

188.37   hunting horn,]   T; ~ ~∧ MSv; ~-~, 4A. *Comma pre-*
              vents confusion later in sentence.

189.5   boar]   4A; Boar MSv. *Emendation reflects Irving's*
              usual practice; see 187.28, 188.43.

189.19   merchant,]   4A; ~∧ MSv. *Second comma of a pair.*

190.3   hermit]   4A; Hermit MSv. *Irving's usual practice. See*
              189.37, 189.41.

190.4   Arise]   4A; arise MSv. *First word of a sentence.*

190.11   sway,]   4A; ~∧ MSv. *Comma clarifies.*

190.13   Lord]   4A; lord MSv. *Ordinarily capitalized; see* 192.23.

*190.18   harbouring . . . beasts]   T; ha[*torn*]ith the beast[*torn*]
              MSv; harboring with the beasts 4A.

190.25   country."]   4A; ~.∧ MSv. *Second quotation mark of a*
              pair.

190.36   carolled]   4A; carrolled MSv.

191.1   eyes,]   4A; ~∧ MSv. *Comma necessary for clarity.*

191.12   abashed,]   4A; ~∧ MSv. *Comma clarifies.*

192.5   pilgrimage]   4A; pilgrim↑age↓ MSv. *Interlineation is by*
              Pierre M. Irving.

*192.8   Don Roderick]   T; ⟨Don⟩ Roderick MSv; Roderick 4A.

192.12   stable,]   4A; ~∧ MSv. *Comma is second of three, each*
              following a verb phrase.

192.18   safe keeping, he] T; ~ ~_∧ ~ MSv; ~-~, ~ 4A. *Pause separates compound participial expression from main statement.*

192.19   cockleshell,] T; ~_∧ MSv; cockle-shell, 4A. *Second comma of a pair.*

192.33   Spain,] T; ~_∧ MSv, 4A. *Second comma of a pair.*

192.35   grave, and] 4A; ~_∧ ~ MSv. *Careful pacing of earlier portions of sentence suggests a pause is intended here.*

192.39   Gijon,] 4A; ~_∧ MSv. *Comma marks pause separating the name from the geographical description.*

192.40   Mountains] 4A; mountains MSv. *Irving's usual practice for place-names.*

193.8   and partly] 4A; ~ parlty MSv.

193.17   story,] 4A; ~_∧ MSv. *Second comma of a pair.*

193.21   chapel,] 4A; ~_∧ MSv. *Comma necessary for clarity.*

193.23   Moslem] 4A; moslem MSv. *Emendation reflects Irving's usual practice; see 196.14, 198.10.*

193.30   removed,] 4A; ~_∧ *Second comma of a pair.*

193.44   inaccessible] 4A; inaccess⟨a⟩↑i↓ble MSv. *The correction is by Pierre M. Irving.*

194.17   kings,] 4A; ~_∧ MSv. *Second comma of a pair.*

194.20   seized] 4A; seazed MSv.

194.38   heart,] 4A; ~_∧ MSv. *Second comma of a pair.*

194.40   sword,] 4A; ~_∧ MSv. *Comma separates the accounts of two distinct actions.*

195.4   shield,] 4A; ~_∧ MSv. *Usual practice; see 181.39.*

195.6   king] 4A; kingg MSv.

195.6   with their] 4A; ↑~↓ ~ MSv. *The interlineation, by Pierre M. Irving, corrects Irving's oversight.*

195.13   CHAPTER V . . . . Covadonga.] 4A; Chap: ⟨9.⟩ ↑V↓/ The battle of Covadonga. MSv. *The deletion and interlineation are by Pierre M. Irving. Format follows styling adopted for preceding chapters; see Emendations 180.4–7.*

195.17   Tuerto,] 4A; ~_∧ MSv. *Second comma of a pair.*

195.18   sea-bord] T; sea ⟨board⟩/ bord MSv; seaboard 4A. *See 231.23.*

196.9   Alcamar] 4A; Acamar MSv. *See 195.20, 198.29.*

196.12   bishop] T; Bishop MSv, 4A. *Irving's usual practice for titles not used as parts of proper names. The same emendation is made at 196.36, 197.36.*

196.13   its entrance] 4A; his ~ MSv. *Probably Irving absent-mindedly repeated the "his" earlier in the sentence, referring to Oppas.*

*196.21–23   with . . . . accept]   4A; with th[*torn*]/ thy [*torn*]/
                accept MSv.

196.33   Oppas,]   4A; ~∧ MSv. *Comma is second of a pair.*

196.33   men; false]   T; ~; False MSv; ~, ~ 4A. *The capital is*
                an error.

ᵛ196.36–197.40 So . . . . clamber]   4A; [*wanting*] MSv.

197.15   heaven]   T; [*MSv wanting*]; Heaven 4A. *See* 226.26,
                243.8.

197.41   showered]   4A; showerd MSv.

198.9   wrecks]   4A; wricks MSv.

198.13   church of Oviedo]   4A; Church ~ ~ MSv. *Irving's*
                usual practice; See 198.15.

198.14   Third]   4A; third MSv. *Part of a proper name.*

198.16   Pelayo,]   4A; ~∧ MSv. *Second comma of a pair.*

198.17–18   CHAPTER VI. . . . *death.*]   4A; Chap ⟨10⟩ VI./ Pelayo
                becomes King of Leon – His/ death – MSv. *The*
                cancellation and the "VI" are by Pierre M. Irving.
                Format follows styling adopted in preceding chapters;
                see Emendations 180. 4–7.

198.19   destroyed,]   4A; ~∧ MSv. *Comma marks pause follow-*
                ing long introductory clause.

198.26   troops,]   4A; ~∧ MSv. *Second comma of a pair.*

198.27   renegado]   4A; Renegado MSv. *Irving's usual practice;*
                See 196.36.

199.1   was the slaughter]   4A; ↑was the↓ ⟨a⟩/ slaughter MSv.
                The interlineated "was" is by Pierre M. Irving, cor-
                recting Irving's oversight.

199.5   sea-board]   T; sea/ board MSv; seaboard 4A. *See*
                "Ommiades" 254.7.

199.6   victories,]   4A; ~∧ MSv. *Comma clarifies.*

199.8   recollected]   4A; reccollected MSv.

199.9   a scourge]   4A; ↑~↓ ~ MSv. *The interlineation, by*
                Pierre M. Irving, corrects Irving's oversight.

199.28   the lion was]   4A; ~ ~ ~ ⟨was⟩ MSv. *The cancella-*
                tion is in pencil, probably by Pierre M. Irving.

199.35   Gaudiosa,]   4A; ~∧ MSv. *Comma is second of a pair.*

[THE SUCCESSORS OF PELAYO. FAVILA]

200.2   [THE . . . . FAVILA]]   T; The Successors of Pelayo./
                [*rule*]/ Favila/ [*rule*] MSv. *Title supplied by Pierre*
                M. Irving.

200.3   ¶The good]   T; ∧~ ~ MSv. *Indentation at beginning*
                of paragraph.

200.5	died, as has been noted,] T; ~⟨, ~ ~ ~ ~,⟩ MSv. *The cancellation is by Pierre M. Irving.*
200.5	737, and] T; ~∧ ~ MSv. *Comma separates independent clauses.*
200.7	hardy,] T; ~∧ MSv. *Emendation reflects Irving's usual practice in series of three.*
200.27	chapel] T; Chapel MSv. *See 200.19, 201. 30.*
200.28	spirits,] T; ~∧ MSv. *Comma marks pause following introductory phrases.*
200.31	seized] T; siezed MSv. *The same correction is made at 201.12.*
200.31	foreboding] T; forboding MSv. *The same correction is made at 200.38.*
200.40	gay air] T; ⟨a light heart⟩ ↑~ ~↓ MSv. *The accepted reading would be more idiomatic if preceded by "a"; but it is not awkward as it stands, and Irving's cancellation is clearly indicated in MSv.*
201.4	valley] T; Valley MSv. *See 200.22, 200.27.*
201.7	king,] T; ~∧/ MSv. *Comma precedes subordinate participial phrase. End-of-line commas omitted from MSv are supplied after the indicated words at 201.9–10 dismounting, 201.20 deplored, 201.30 church.*
201.8	prowess,] T; ~∧ MSv. *Second comma of a pair.*
201.14	Thus,] T; Thus ⟨vainly⟩ ↑vainly↓, MSv. *The cancellation is by Irving, the interlineation by Pierre M. Irving.*
201.15	Don Favila] T; ⟨Don⟩ ~ MSv. *The cancellation is by Pierre M. Irving.*
201.20	temerity.] T; ~∧ MSv.
201.30	St.] T; Sᵗ MSv. *The abbreviation is similarly regularized at 201.30 (MSv Sᵗ).*
201.22	Peter,] T; ~∧ MSv. *Comma separates appositives.*
201.28	queen] T; Queen MSv. *Irving's usual practice for titles not used as parts of proper names.*
201.29	Catholic; but] T; ~∧ ~ MSv. *Semicolon marks distinct pause following the list.*
201.31	hidalgos] T; hidalgoes MSv. *No authority in dictionaries.*
201.32	story] T; Story MSv. *Emendation reflects Irving's usual practice.*
201.40	*Sandoval . . . Catholico.] T; *Sandoval. El Rey Alonzo el Catholico. MSv. *Adopted reading reflects Putnam house style.*

CHRONICLE OF THE OMMIADES

202.2   CHRONICLE . . . OMMIADES] T; Abderahman./
founder of the Dynasty of the Ommiades/ in Spain/
By the Author of the Sketch-Book/—— MSh; ABDER-
AHMAN./ FOUNDER OF THE DYNASTY OF THE OMMIADES/
IN SPAIN./ BY THE AUTHOR OF THE SKETCH-BOOK/——
MShc [*1A duplicates MShc except that a colon follows
"ABDERAHMAN" and a period follows* "SKETCH-
BOOK"]; ABDERAHMAN./—— 2A.

202.3–4   [CHAPTER I. . . . *Abderahman.*]] T; [*omitted*] MSh,
1A; Of the youthful fortunes of Abderaham - ⟨Founder
of the Dynasty of/ the Ommiades/ in Spain -⟩/ ——
MSn; ₍~ ~. . . . ~.₎ 2A. *The MSn text is supplied
by Pierre M. Irving. Chapter-numbers and chapter-
headings are also adopted from 2A at 207.1–2 and
208.28–32.*

202.5   "Blessed be God!"] T; "~ ~ ~!₍ MSh; "BLESSED
BE GOD!" MShc; 'BLESSED ~ ~!' 1A; "BLESSED ~
~!" 2A. *Double quotation marks are also added to
complete pairs in Chapters I-III at* 202.5, 203.7, 204.39,
205.2, 205.6, 205.26, 205.37, 206.13, 206.22, 206.23,
206.26, 206.37, 206.37, 213.28, 213.29, 215.1, 217.39.

202.9–10   Omeya, . . . Mahomet,] 2A; Omeya₍ MSh, 1A; Omeya₍
↑one of the two lines descended from Mahomet₍↓
MSn.

202.11   Abu al] 2A; Aboul MSh, 1A; ⟨Aboul⟩ ↑~ ~↓ MSn. *At*
202.22–23, 203.1, *and* 211.7 *Pierre M. Irving made
the same changes to MSn as the one here by Washington Irving. The emended readings, as in 2A, are also
adopted at those points.*

202.13   Meruan] 2A; Marvau MSh, 1A; ⟨Marvau⟩ ↑~↓ MSn.

202.14   Omeya,] MShc, 1A, 2A; ~₍ MSh. *Second comma of
a pair.*

202.14   proscription] 1A, 2A; prescription MSh.

202.18–19 bodies . . . were] 2A; bodies, covered with cloths, and
MSh; bodies covered with cloths, and MShc, 1A;
bodies, covered with cloths, ↑were↓ ⟨and⟩ MSn.

202.24   Abbassides] 1A, 2A; Abassides MSh. *The same correction is made at* 202.28, 216.32.

202.26   "Blessed be God!"] 2A; ₍~ ~ ~!₍ MSh; '~ ~ ~!'
MShc, 1A. *Pairs of double quotation marks are also
supplied at* 204.13, 204.13–15, 204.21–23, 204.24–25,
204.25–27, 204.37, 204.37–39, 205.2–5, 207.32, 207.32–

33, 208.25, 208.26–27, 208.38–39, 213.29, 218.8, 218.8–10, 218.22, 218.22–25, 219.31, 219.31–38, 219.41, 219.41–42, 220.14–15, 220.15–31, 221.1, 221.2–3, 221.25, 221.25, 221.26, 221.27, 221.27–28, 221.30, 221.30–32, 222.15, 222.15–16, 232.4, 232.5.

202.33   Abderahman,]   MShc, 1A, 2A; ∼₍∧₎ MSh. *Second comma of a pair.*

203.15   shepherds]   1A, 2A; Shepherds MSh. *The indicated words not ordinarily capitalized by Irving are emended to lower-case at 204.11 stranger; 204.15 emissaries; 205.40 empire; 206.12 ambassadors; 206.40 venerable; 207.11 peninsula; 207.32 sage; 207.36 standard; 208.34 supreme; 211.19 castle; 213.43 camp; 214.17 empire; 219.7 vega; 220.17 algihed; 220.19 khatib; 220.26 country; 221.15 court; 221.33, 221.44 astrologer; 221.38 astrologer's; 222.15 chronicler; 223.37 cavalry; 226.19 eastern; 228.19 cousin; 228.30 empire; 229.10 mountains; 229.14 state; 229.28 eunuchs.*

203.21   shepherd's]   1A, 2A; shepherds MSh. *An apostrophe is also added to a possessive at 203.25.*

203.29   Bedouins,]   MShc, 1A, 2A; ∼₍∧₎/ MSh. *End-of-line commas or other indicated punctuation omitted from the copy-text are supplied after the words cited at 203.31 Habib, 204.1 carriage, 204.17 Abderahman, 204.25 they, 205.4 door, 206.16 lived, 206.32 feelings, 207.28 suppressed, 208.38 shouted, 213.1 family, 213.7 apparently, 214.26 government, 215.28 valley, 218.35 granted, 219.3 manner, 219.19 prince, 219.27 triumph, 220.2 course, 220.17 these, 220.18 hour, 221.6 gates, 222.32 landing, 223.37 Suleiman, 224.25 arrow, 226.19 provinces, 226.19 Abderahman, 226.27 rebellion, 227.20 vizier;, 228.19 Casim, 229.23 sexes, 230.9 arms, 230.11 rage, 230.12 multitude, 230.17 prisoners, 230.21 ground, 230.44 this, 231.1 fleet;.*

203.32   "Surely,"]   2A; "∼₍∧₎" MSh; '∼,' 1A. *Commas are also inserted to separate quotations from commentary at 204.18, 204.37, 204.39, 205.2, 205.26, 206.22, 215.14, 221.27, 221.37, 224.27, 231.3, 231.28.*

203.32   "I]   MShc, 2A; '∼ MSh, 1A. *Single quotation marks are similarly emended at 204.18, 204.18, 211.3, 211.9.*

203.34   my]   1A, 2A; his MSh. *Irving's oversight.*

203.39   ¶The]   1A, 2A; ₍∧₎∼ MSh. *The word begins a page in MSh; the bottom line of the preceding page is only one-third filled. Paragraph-breaks are also inserted when clearly intended by Irving at* 208.33, 213.16, 226.18, 227.6, 228.6, 229.8.

203.41   hospitality.]   MShc, 1A, 2A; ~ₐ MSh. *Periods are also added or substituted for indicated punctuation at the ends of sentences at* 204.2, 205.22 *comma,* 206.3, 208.4, 209.9 *dash,* 209.35, 211.12, 211.36 *semicolon,* 212.43 *comma,* 213.13 *comma,* 216.3, 216.26 *comma,* 216.39 *dash,* 217.16, 219.27, 219.38 *colon,* 221.3 *dash,* 221.43, 224.11, 224.29, 224.38, 225.9 *comma,* 225.23 *semicolon,* 225.25 *semicolon,* 225.30, 225.36 *dash,* 226.10, 226.14, 227.15 *comma,* 228.21, 228.40, 229.44, 231.14.

204.3   In . . . time the]   2A; One night, when all were buried in sleep, they were roused by the tramp of horsemen. The MSh, 1A; ⟨One night, when all were buried in sleep, they were roused by the tramp of horsemen⟩. ↑In the mean time↓ ⟨T⟩the MSn.

204.3   like]   2A; who ⟨had⟩ like MSh; who, ⟨had⟩ like MShc; who, like 1A; ⟨who⟩, like MSn. *Comma in MSn is redundant.*

204.4   posts,]   2A; ports↙ MSh; ports, MShc, 1A; po⟨r⟩sts, MSn. *Irving also wrote "posts" in the margin of MSn.*

204.5   prince. Hearing]   2A; prince, had heard MSh, 1A; prince⟨,⟩. ⟨had heard⟩ ↑Hearing↓ MSn.

204.7   travel, he sent]   2A; ~: He had immediately sent MSh; ~. He had immediately sent 1A; ~⟨.⟩, he ⟨He had immediately⟩ sent MSn.

204.9   traced]   2A; had traced MSh, 1A; ⟨had⟩ traced MSn.

204.9–10   coming . . . demanded]   T; demanded MSh, 1A; ↑⟨and⟩ coming upon the encampment in the dead of the night↓ demanded MSn; coming upon the encampment in the dead of the night, demanded 2A.

204.11   tribe.]   MShc, 1A, 2A; ~? MSh.

204.12   description]   1A, 2A; discription MSh.

204.20   errand,]   MShc, 1A, 2A; ~ₐ MSh. *Pause separates independent clauses.*

204.21   prince]   1A, 2A; Prince MSh. *The indicated ranks or titles, or parts thereof, capitalized in the copy-text are also emended to lower-case in similar circumstances at* 205.43 prince; 207.16 wali; 208.13 emir; 213.36 caliph; 218.33 commander; 221.41–42 wali alhadi; 223.8 alcaydes; 227.8, 227.10, 227.16, 227.18 vizier. *See also* Emendations 205.28.

204.24   Six]   1A, 2A; Th⟨en⟩ ~ MSh. *Irving neglected to complete the cancellation. At* 223.23 "and . . . the . . . the" *preceding "During" form parts of cancelled passages and were inadvertently allowed to stand; at 227.17 he similarly neglected to cancel "to" before "The prince"; at 230.7, "to the" before "to the."*

204.39 none!] 1A, 2A; ~,! MSh. *The exclamation mark appears to be Irving's latest choice.*

205.7 Africa; never] T; ~, ~ MSh; ~. ~ MShc; ~. Never 1A, 2A. *Semicolon eliminates run-on construction.*

205.10 Tahart,] MShc, 1A, 2A; ~∧ MSh. *Comma separates appositives.*

205.28 One . . . xeques then] T; Then one of the noblest Xeque's MSh; Then one of the noblest Xeques 1A; ⟨Then o⟩One of the noblest Xeques ↑then↓ MSn; One of the noblest, Xeques, then 2A. *The word "xeques," a variant spelling of "sheikh," is also emended to lower-case at 206.40 xeque.*

205.31 recollection] 1A, 2A; reccollection MSh. *The same emendation is made at 210.33–34 recollections.*

205.42 needs to be] MShc, 1A, 2A; needs ⟨to be⟩ MSh. *Irving neglected to rewrite his cancelled words after deciding against an interlineation that would have superseded them.*

206.8 sovereignty] 1A, 2A; sovreignty MSh. *Irving's "sovreign" is similarly corrected at 208.40, 216.20.*

206.34 They] MShc, 1A, 2A; The MSh. *Oversight.*

206.36 noble house] 1A, 2A; ⟨house⟩" ↑~ ~ MSh. *Punctuation inadvertently allowed to stand by Irving occurs as shown before or after the indicated words in the copy-text: 208.11 (Cordova;.); 210.43 (stranger;;); 226.31 (; At night); 228.7 (him.; Instead); 228.28 (plans;.); 230.4 (immediately,); 230.11 (frenzy.); 230.13 (foot..).*

206.39 desart,] MShc; ~∧ MSh; desert, 1A, 2A. *Comma necessary for clarity.*

206.41 tears] MShc, 1A, 2A; ~ -/ MSh. *Probably an inadvertent mark at the end of the line.*

207.1 CHAPTER II.] 2A; Abderahman ben Omeya -/ —-/ Chap 2ᵈ MSn. *The chapter-title is omitted as redundant; the chapter-number is emended to conform to the Putnam house style.*

207.3 Andalusia] 2A; Andalucia MSn. *The same emendation is made to "Andaluzia" at 229.27.*

207.4 Almunecar, or Malaga,] 2A; ~∧ ↑~ ~∧↓ MSn. *Clarity requires commas.*

207.23	Africa,] 2A; ~ – MSn. *The dash is probably a slurred comma.*
207.27	Alabdaries] T; Alabdarides MSn, 2A. *See* Rejected Variants 207.12.
207.35–37	Amru, . . . Beder,] 2A; ~∧ . . . ~∧ MSn. *Commas enclose long modifying phrase.*
208.9	Saragossa,] 2A; ~∧ MSn. *Comma precedes relative clause.*
208.10	putting] 2A; pulling MSn. *Irving forgot to cross his t's.*
*208.10	camels, he] 2A; camels MSn.
208.16	valley,] 2A; ~ – MSn. *Slurred comma.*
208.17	Samael] 2A; Samail MSn.
*208.24	Amru, his son, and secretary] 2A; ~, ~~∧ ~~ MSn.
208.34	tranquility] MSh; tranquillity 1A, 2A; tranquil↑l↓ity MSn. *The spelling change in MSn is by Pierre M. Irving.*
208.37	beauty,] MSh, 1A, 2A; ~; MSn. *Second comma of a pair.*
208.38	Long] MShc, 1A, 2A; long MSh, MSn. *First word of a quoted exclamation; an emendation to a capital is also made at the beginning of a sentence at 222.38.*
208.38	Abderahman, Miramamolin] 2A; Abderahman ben Moavia, Miramamolin MSh; Abderahman ben Moavia Meramamolin 1A; ~∧ ~ MSn. *In MSn a cancellation intervenes between the two parts of the appositive.*
208.39	Spain!] MSh, 1A, 2A; ~. MSn. *An exclamation mark is also supplied at 209.16.*
*208.40	sovereign] 1A, 2A; sovreign MSh; sovreign/ ⟨Take in at printed page 432 * –⟩ MSn.
209.24	zeal] 2A; desperate zeal MSh, 1A; ⟨desperate⟩ zeal MSn.
209.38	Allah] 1A, 2A; allah MSh.
209.42	uncontrolled] 1A, 2A; uncontrouled MSh.
210.2	Yusuf,] MShc, 1A, 2A; ~∧ MSh. *First comma of a pair.*
210.25	reconstructed] 2A; re constructed MSh; re-constructed MShc, 1A.
210.26	Guadalquivir] 2A; Guadalquiver MSh, 1A.
210.32	youth;] 1A, 2A; ~, MSh. *Emendation necessary for clarity.*
210.43–211.10	"Beauteous . . . . tears!"] 2A; '~ . . . . ~!' MSh, 1A.
210.43	Palm!] 1A, 2A; ~ –! MSh. *The dash is written over by the new punctuation.*
211.2	branches.] 1A, 2A; ~.' MSh. *See below,* 211.10.
211.10	recall] 1A, 2A; recal MSh.

211.19   seized] 1A, 2A; Siezed MSh. *Irving's "siezed" is sim-*
            ilarly corrected at 211.35, 212.19, 213.17, 213.42.

212.20   Casim, . . . Yusuf,] 1A, 2A; ~∧ . . . ~∧ MSh; ~∧ . . .
            ~, MShc. *Commas enclose appositive.*

212.21   Muhamad,] T; Muhamed∧ MSh; unharmed, 1A, 2A.
            The same correction of the MSh spelling is made at
            215.17, 215.32.

213.5   laid by] MShc, 1A, 2A; lay ~ MSh.

213.24   chieftains] 2A; chieftans MSh; chieftain 1A.

213.34   caliph,] MShc, 1A, 2A; ~∧ MSh. *Second comma of a*
            pair.

213.35   commander,] MShc, 1A, 2A; ~∧ MSh.

213.44   Abderahman,] 1A, 2A; ~∧ MSh. *First comma of a pair.*

214.5   inscription:] MShc, 1A; ~. MSh; ~,— 2A.

214.20   peace,] MShc, 1A, 2A; ~∧ MSh. *Comma follows intro-*
            ductory phrase.

214.21   Suleiman, . . . eldest,] MShc, 1A, 2A; ~∧ . . . ~∧ MSh.
            Commas enclose appositive.

214.22   Toledo;] MShc, 1A, 2A; ~∧ MSh. *Emendation elim-*
            inates confusing syntax.

214.22   Abdallah, . . . second,] MShc, 1A, 2A; ~∧ . . . ~∧ MSh.
            Commas enclose appositive.

214.23   Hixem,] MShc, 1A, 2A; ~∧ MSh. *Second comma of a*
            pair.

214.32   Yusuf,] MShc, 1A, 2A; ~∧ MSh. *Second comma of a*
            pair.

214.33   resigned,] MShc, 1A, 2A; ~∧ MSh. *Comma dispels*
            some of the confusion caused by Irving's awkward
            phrasing.

215.18   in the] 2A; on the MSh, 1A; ⟨o⟩in the MSn.

215.29   harassing] 1A, 2A; harrassing MSh.

215.32   Muhamad,] 1A, 2A; Muhamed∧ MSh. *Comma is first*
            of a pair.

215.41   to the time] MShc, 1A, 2A; to time MSh. *Irving's over-*
            sight.

216.22   accessible] MShc, 1A, 2A; accessable MSh.

216.22   subjects;] MShc, 1A, 2A; ~, MSh. *Emendation elimin-*
            ates run-on construction.

217.5   Moslem] 1A, 2A; moslem MSh.

217.11   Suleiman] 2A; Soleiman MSh, 1A.

217.21   authority,] MShc, 1A, 2A; ~∧ MSh. *Comma concludes*
            long introductory clause.

217.28   exorbitant] 1A, 2A; exhorbitant MSh.

217.32   consists the] 1A, 2A; ~ th[*torn*] MSh.

217.35   their fields]   2A; [*torn*]lds MSh; [*torn*]lds, MShc; ∼ ∼,
                1A.

217.38   government;]   1A, 2A; ∼, MSh. *Emendation eliminates*
                run-on construction.

217.40   counsel]   1A, 2A; council MSh.

218.3   *HIXEM*]   T; *Hixem* MSb.

*218.4–6   [CHAPTER IV . . . . *Hixem.*]]   T; *Chap. IV.*/ Rebellion
                of the brothers of Hixem — A holy war proclaimed —/
                Completion of the great mosque — Death of Hixem —
                MSb. *The chapter-number and chapter-heading are*
                supplied by Pierre M. Irving. Material supplied by him
                at the beginnings of chapters is also regularized and
                enclosed in brackets at 222.7–12, 225.15–17, 227.3–5,
                228.4–5. *See also* Emendations 231.19–20.

218.9   he giveth]   T; He giveth MSb.

218.14   Miramamolin]   T; Miramomilin MSb.

218.22   grievous]   T; gri↑e↓v⟨i⟩ous MSb. *The corrections are by*
                Pierre M. Irving.

218.23   brethren]   T; breth⟨e⟩ren MSb. *Correction probably by*
                Pierre M. Irving .

218.28   mountains,]   T; ∼ₐ MSb. *Comma separates indepen-*
                dent clauses.

218.32   of holding]   T; of -/holding MSb. *Probably a slip of*
                the pen.

218.33   vizier]   MSc; visier MSb. *Emendation reflects usual*
                spelling.

218.33   army,]   T; ∼ₐ MSb. *Comma clarifies.*

218.36   disguise,]   T; ∼ₐ MSb. *Comma necessary for clarity.*

218.36   undiscovered,]   T; ∼ₐ MSb. *Comma separates inde-*
                pendent clauses.

219.3   toward him,]   T; towards him, MSc; toward himₐ MSb.
                Comma clarifies.

219.10   favor,]   T; amnesty and favour, MSc; ∼ₐ MSb.

219.16   Alhakem]   T; Al Hakem MSb. *Emendation reflects*
                Irving's usual spelling. Other variant spellings of the
                name are regularized as follows: 221.41, 222.5, 228.36
                Alhakim; 228.31 AlHakim; 222.7 ALHAKIM (*Pierre M.*
                Irving's chapter-title—to ALHAKEM); 222.9, 222.11,
                227.4 ALHAKIM (Pierre M. Irving's headnotes); 222.38
                Alhakim (*Pierre M. Irving's insertion*); *see also* Emen-
                dations 228.22.

219.19   himself,]   MSc; ∼ₐ MSb. *Comma follows introductory*
                construction.

219.26   conqueror,]   MSc; ∼ₐ MSb. *First comma of a pair.*

219.31   war,]   T;   ~$_\wedge$ MSb. *Comma separates independent clauses.*

219.36   upon him]   T;   ~ ⟨the⟩h⟨e⟩im MSb. *The correction of "he" to "him" is by Pierre M. Irving.*

219.41   "All]   T; $_\wedge$~ MSb. *Double quotation marks are also added in order to complete pairs at 231.3, 231.3.*

219.44   Valencia]   T; Valentia MSb. *See 224.37.*

220.1   harassed]   T; harrassed MSb. *A similar emendation to "harassing" is made at 226.10.*

220.4   forgiveness]   T; forgiv↑e↓ness MSb. *Addition by Pierre M. Irving.*

220.12   subdued,]   T;   ~$_\wedge$ MSb. *Comma separates independent clauses.*

220.25   Abdelwahid, . . . King,]   T;   ~$_\wedge$ . . . ~$_\wedge$ MSb. *Commas enclose appositive.*

220.31   Abdelwahid]   T; Abdelwahed MSb. *Thus Conde.*

220.33   Chaste,]   T;   ~$_\wedge$ MSb. *Comma precedes relative clause.*

220.34   resigned]   T; resignd MSb.

220.36   force, . . . Abdelmelic,]   T;   ~$_\wedge$ . . . Abdelmelec$_\wedge$ MSb. *Commas enclose modifying phrase. The emended spelling duplicates MSc and Conde.*

220.38   Narbonne, . . . sword,]   T;   ~$_\wedge$ . . . ~$_\wedge$ MSb. *Commas enclose element of compound verb.*

220.44–221.1   Abdallah]   T; Abdalla MSb. *See 220.36, 221.3.*

221.11   war,]   MSc;   ~$_\wedge$ MSb. *Comma separates independent clauses.*

221.20   chains;]   MSc;   ~$_\wedge$ MSb. *Semicolon separates independent clauses and maintains pacing of sentence.*

221.23   Cordova,]   T;   ~$_\wedge$ MSb. *Comma marks pause following long introductory clause.*

221.26   sentence?]   T;   ~ - MSb. *Clearly a question.*

221.39   life,]   T;   ~$_\wedge$ MSb. *Comma follows introductory clause.*

222.1   year,]   MSc;   ~$_\wedge$ MSb. *Comma separates independent clauses.*

222.2   received]   MSc; recieved MSb. *The same emendation is made at 225.3.*

222.4   interred]   MSc; enterred MSb.

222.5   oration,]   MSc;   ~$_\wedge$ MSb. *Comma separates independent clauses.*

*222.13–14   AH AD/ 180 796]   T; ⟨~~/ ~~⟩ MSb.

222.17   Hixem,]   T;   ~$_\wedge$ MSb. *Second comma of a pair.*

222.21   Abderahman]   T; abderahman MSb. *The same correction is made at 227.21.*

222.28   sovereignty]   T; sovreignty MSb.

222.33   Miramamolin,] T; ~_∧ MSb. *Comma separates appositives.*

223.14   career] T; car⟨r⟩eer MSb. *Correction is in pencil, almost certainly by Pierre M. Irving.*

223.25   flames of revolt] T; ~, ~~ MSb. *Evidently Irving neglected to cancel the comma after changing his plans for continuing the sentence.*

223.25   Valencia] T; Valen⟨t⟩↑e↓ia MSb. *The deletion and substitution are by Pierre M. Irving, who probably intended a "c." Conde spells the name correctly, and see 224.37.*

224.2   time,] T; ~_∧ MSb. *Second comma of a pair.*

224.7   other's] T; others MSb. *Possessive.*

224.10   success,] T; ~_∧ MSb. *Second comma of a pair.*

224.26   Alhakem by] T; ~;~ MSb. *Apparently Irving neglected to revise his punctuation after deciding to continue the statement.*

224.42   victory, and] T; ~;/ and MSb. *MSb marks a fuller pause than the context indicates Irving intended; possibly after writing the semicolon he changed his plans for the continuation of the sentence.*

224.42   softened] T; softend MSb.

225.3   Alkinza] T; Alkenza MSb. *Emended spelling is Conde's; see also 227.31.*

225.4   eldest,] T; ~_∧ MSb. *Comma necessary for clarity.*

225.6   every] T; evry MSb.

225.9   Thus,] T; ~_∧ MSb. *First comma of a pair.*

225.19   Murcia,] T; ~_∧ MSc. *Comma follows long introductory construction.*

225.20   general,] T; ~_∧ MSc. *Comma clarifies.*

225.26   Christians] T; christians MSc. *Emendation reflects Irving's usual practice—see Granada (1850) 320.6—and is also made at 228.11 Christian.*

225.30   contrary,] T; ~_∧ MSc. *Second comma of a pair.*

226.5   command;] T; ~, MSc. *Emended punctuation avoids run-on statement.*

226.8   son;] T; ~.; MSc. *Period forms part of a cancelled passage and was inadvertently allowed to stand by Irving. Punctuation thus left uncancelled in the copy-text occurs before or after the indicated words as shown: 226.31 (; At night); 228.7 (him.; Instead); 228.28 (plans;.); 230.4 (immediately,); 230.11 (frenzy ..); 230.13 (foot ..).*

226.11   apparently] T; apparanty MSc.

226.18   five thousand]   T; 5000 MSc. *Irving's usual practice;
                see 209.8.
226.26   and dangerous]   T; & ∼ MSc. *The ampersand is also
                emended to "and" at 227.40, 228.15, 228.23, 229.41,
                231.26.*
226.42   king,]   T; ∼∧ MSc. *Second comma of a pair.*
227.23   rage, and]   T; ∼∧∼ MSc. *Comma separates indepen-
                dent clauses.*
227.24   admission to]   T; ⟨to admit⟩/ ↑∼∼↓ MSc. *The inter-
                lineated "to" is by Pierre M. Irving.*
228.6   Merida,]   T; ∼∧ MSc. *Comma follows introductory
                clause.*
228.9   sternness]   T; sterness MSc.
228.16   king, therefore,]   T; ∼∧∼∧ MSc. *Commas clarify.*
228.17   Yahye, . . . council,]   T; Yayhe ↑Yuhye↓∧ . . . ∼∧ MSc.
                *Commas enclose appositive. Pierre M. Irving trans-
                posed the "y" and "h" of Irving's misspelled name;
                but then, above the line, he misspelled it himself. The
                emended spelling is Condé's.*
228.19   Casim]   T; Cas⟨s⟩im MSc. *The correction is almost
                certainly by Pierre M. Irving. The same correction
                is made by him at 228.32, 228.35, 229.17.*
228.22   Alhakem]   T; Al⟨H⟩hakem MSc. *Pierre M. Irving wrote
                "h" over the capital.*
*228.29   return immediately]   T; ∼ ⟨∼⟩ MSc.
228.39   terrific]   T; terrific MSc.
229.3   place,]   T; ∼∧ MSc. *Comma separates independent
                clauses.*
229.4   written:]   T; ∼. MSc. *Inappropriate punctuation to
                introduce a quotation.*
229.5   spectacle;]   T; ∼, MSc. *Emended punctuation avoids
                run-on construction.*
229.17   foremost]   T; for↑e↓most MSc. *The interlineation is by
                Pierre M. Irving.*
229.29   made,]   T; ∼∧ MSc. *Comma necessary for clarity.*
229.41   seized]   T; siezed MSc. *The same emendation is made
                at 231.26.*
229.42   decrees,]   T; ∼∧ MSc. *Comma marks pause following
                introductory construction.*
230.5   to . . . multitude.]   T; to ⟨take/refuge with the⟩ ↑the↓
                city guard;/ ↑pursued by the multitude.↓ MSc. *The
                interlineated "the" before "city guard" is by Pierre
                M. Irving; it corrects Irving's oversight.*
230.15   slaughter]   T; slaughtre MSc. *Irving's usual spelling.*

230.28   in the villages]   T; ⟨in⟩ ↑on↓/ ~~ MSc. *Cancellation and interlineation by Pierre M. Irving, probably to avoid repetition of "in the" in the same sentence.*

230.37   Crete,]   T; ~∧ MSc. *Comma necessary for clarity.*

230.41   Grecian Sea]   T; Grecian Seas MSc. *Later in sentence this body of water is referred to as "it"; see also* 230.35.

231.2   youth,]   T; ~∧ MSc. *Second comma of a pair.*

⁕231.10   Candy]   T; *Candy* ↑Candia?↓ MSc.

⁕231.19–20   [CHAPTER IX. . . . *Alhakem.*]]   T; [*MSc wanting*].

231.21   [A portion . . . lost.]]   T; [*MSc wanting*]. *Editorial insertion.*

231.24   Jacinto,]   T; ~∧ MSca. *Comma separates appositives.*

231.36   recreation.†]   T; ~.↑†↓ MSca. *The dagger is added by Pierre M. Irving; see also* Emendations 231.38–39.

231.38–39   ⁕ . . . . (See Conde, 1, 257.)]   T; † . . . . ⟨(⟩ See *Conde,* 1.257∧ ⟨)⟩ MSca. *Dagger added, parentheses deleted, "Conde" underlined, and comma following it added by Pierre M. Irving.*

232.5   change."⁕]   T; ~.∧↑⁕↓ MSca. *The asterisk added by Pierre M. Irving corresponds to another preceding a footnote in the left margin of MSca; see* Emendations 232.6.

232.6   ⁕Loado . . . contrariedades.—Conde, C. 37.]   T; ⁕Loado . . . contrariedes./*Conde,* C. 37. MSca. *Irving transcribed Conde's "contrariedades" incorrectly; the asterisk and the underlining of "Conde" are by Pierre M. Irving.*

CHRONICLE OF FERNAN GONZALEZ, COUNT OF CASTILE

233.2–3   CHRONICLE . . . CASTILE]   T; Chronicle of/ ⟨Don⟩ Fernan⟨do⟩ Gonzalez/ Count of Castile. MSv; ~ . . . ~. 1A.

233.4   [INTRODUCTION.]]   T; [*rule*]/Introduction./ [*rule*] MSv; [*rule*]/ INTRODUCTION. 1A. *The MSv reading is supplied by Pierre M. Irving. Chapter-numbers and chapter-headings added to MSv by Pierre M. Irving are adopted here from 1A and further regularized at* 234.7–10, 236.29–31, 239.1–3, 240.5–8, 241.1–3, 243.1–5, 245.19–20, 247.1–3, 249.1–3, 250.32–35, 252.32–34, 255.20–22, 256.1–3, 257.11–15, 260.20–23, 262.30–32, 266.1–4, 268.1–2, 269.25–26.

233.11   cliffs, in]   1A; ~∧/~ MSv. *Comma clarifies antecedent. Commas and other indicated punctuation omitted at*

the ends of lines in MSv are supplied after the words
shown at the following points: 234.26 Duke, 234.40
arms, 236.17 soldiery, 236.40 sacked, 239.16 Xeriz,
239.23 peace, 240.15 Montaneses, 241.7 heights, 241.31
ambush, 241.39 conviction, 241.42 proceed, 242.8
stratagem, 243.10 son, 243.29 danger, 243.37 Velazquez, 244.2 however, 244.4 sheep, 244.22 altar, 245.8
truth, 247.17 acquisitions, 248.3 enemy, 248.25 chieftain, 248.37 victory, 248.43 Abarca, 249.10 Castilians,
251.4 Gonzalez, 251.17 count, 251.18 hermitage, 252.13
times, 252.15 bravest, 252.24 alone, 254.22 way, 254.25
mountains, 254.30 alighted, 254.32 mountains, 254.36–
37 astonishment, 255.31 count, 255.40 honor, 256.29
remorse, 256.32 knees, 257.1 told, 257.32 Piedrafita,
257.32 When, 257.33 him, 258.13 angels, 258.18 divisions; 258.35 Biscaya, 258.38 himself, 259.1 sleep,
259.3 air, 259.5 thither, 259.18 long, 259.19 stanched,
259.24 sounded, 259.40 shields, 260.10 forces, 260.38
Ramiro, 261.12 morning, 261.32 staff, 261.35 king;
264.34 finished, 264.38 count, 264.41 however, 265.5
known, 265.5 wonder, 265.28 warrior, 266.5 throne,
266.30 necessary, 267.12 Abderahman, 267.18 miramamolin, 267.20 Cordova, 267.34 physicians, 268.10
declared, 268.14 councillors, 268.40 payment, 270.34
heaven, 271.12 pageants, 271.16 friars, 271.39 grave.

233.19	They] 1A; ⟨t⟩They MSv. *The capitalization is prob-* *ably by Pierre M. Irving.*
233.21	Latin] 1A; latin MSv. *Usual practice for designations* *of nationality.*
233.28	II., who] 1A; II∧∧~ MSv. *Comma is the first of a* *pair. Period is added in conformity with Irving's usual* *practice in published works and is also added follow-* *ing roman or arabic numerals at 235.4, 247.8, 250.36,* *262.39, 263.10, 265.30, 266.5, 267.26, 267.36.*
234.1	latter,] 1A; ~∧ MSv. *Comma dispels ambiguity.*
*234.4	Gonzalo Nuño] T; Gonzalez Nuño MSv, 1A.
234.4	Doña Ximena,] 1A; ↑Donna ~∧↓ MSv. *Irving's pre-* *ferred spelling; see 253.16. Comma separates ap-* *positives.*
234.5	counts] 1A; Counts MSv. *Not used as part of proper* *name nor simply as a title. The emendation to "count"* *is also made at 247.31, 250.7, 250.21, 250.23, 251.39;* *see also Emendations 235.23. The indicated denomina-* *tions of other ranks or titles capitalized in MSv but*

not used as parts of proper names are similarly
emended at 271.10 abbot; 258.12 apostle; 253.44,
254.8, 254.20, 254.30–31 archpriest; 236.25 bishop;
260.25 captain; 237.21, 249.35 cavaliers; 255.36, 261.9,
261.11, 261.20, 261.27, 261.31, 261.34, 261.38 countess;
252.29, 253.3 emperor; 264.22, 264.31 esquire; 248.41,
253.3, 254.3 king; 261.11 lord; 268.35 (MSv Mayor
Domo), 268.37, 268.40 (MSv Mayor Domo) major
domo; 267.18, 267.33 miramamolin.

234.13   Charlemagne,]   1A; ∼ᴧ MSv. *Second comma of a pair.*

234.14   granddaughter]   1A; grand daughter MSv. *No authority
in dictionaries; Webster prescribes emended reading.*

234.14   sovereign]   1A; sovreign MSv. *The same emendation
is made at 269.21, 269.22 (sovereignty); see also* Emendations 234.31.

234.22   Gonzalo Nuño]   T; Gonsalvo Nuñez MSv. Gonzalvo
Nuñez 1A. *See* Discussions of Adopted Readings
234.4.

234.23   904,]   1A; ∼ᴧ MSv. *Comma clarifies.*

234.25   age,]   T; ∼ᴧ MSv, 1A. *Second comma of a pair.*

234.30   Sebastian, . . . Bishop of Oca,]   1A; ∼ᴧ . . . bishop∼∼ᴧ
MSv. *Commas enclose appositive; "Bishop" forms
part of proper title. The indicated titles used as parts
of proper names but uncapitalized in MSv are similarly
emended at 257.25, 260.30 King; 262.27 Prince; 251.41,
253.16, 255.24 Princess.*

234.31   sovereign]   1A; sov↑e↓reign MSv. *Correction is by
Pierre M. Irving; the same correction is made by him
at 243.19, 258.6 (sovereigns).*

234.40   Castile,]   T; ∼ᴧ MSv, 1A. *Second comma of a pair,
necessary for clarity.*

235.7   poverty,]   1A; ∼ᴧ MSv. *Second comma of a pair.*

235.15   count,]   1A; ∼ᴧ MSv. *Comma necessary for clarity.*

235.18   troops,]   1A; ∼ᴧ MSv. *Comma separates independent
clauses.*

235.22   Velazquez]   1A; Velasquez MSv. *In accordance with
Irving's usual practice in MSv and in "Ruy Velazquez,"
an unpublished sketch owned by the University of
Virginia, the same emendation is made at 237.12,
243.37, 258.34.*

235.23   count,]   1A; Countᴧ MSv. *Title used in reference to
Fernan Gonzalez but not as part of his proper name.
The same emendation is made at 236.15, 237.25, 238.12,*

238.25, 238.30, 239.15, 240.14, 240.32, 241.20, 241.40,
243.12, 243.13, 243.18, 244.41, 245.3, 247.31, 247.39,
248.12, 248.28, 249.23, 249.28, 249.37, 251.10, 251.13,
251.15, 251.33, 253.1, 253.9, 253.12, 253.26, 253.30,
253.40, 253.43, 254.3, 254.14, 255.1, 255.4, 255.18,
255.31, 255.32, 255.38, 256.39, 257.4, 257.9, 257.18,
258.6, 258.23, 258.37, 258.38, 258.39, 259.15, 259.23,
259.28, 259.33, 260.2, 260.4, 261.4, 261.8, 261.28, 261.29,
261.33, 261.35, 261.38, 262.10, 262.19, 262.24, 263.6,
264.24, 264.28, 264.42, 266.11, 266.26, 268.6, 268.19,
268.29, 268.33, 268.37, 269.5, 269.12, 269.19, 271.33.
See also Emendations 234.5.

235.27	saying,] 1A; ∼ₐ MSv. *Comma marks pause following summary phrase.*
235.29	heaven,] T; ∼ₐ MSv; Heaven, 1A. *Irving failed to substitute punctuation after cancelling a semicolon in order to extend the statement.*
*235.32	wars.*] T; ∼.⟨*⟩ MSv; ∼.ₐ 1A.
235.43	* Sandoval, *ut supra*, p. 298.] T; ⟨* Sandovalₐ ut supraₐ p. 298.⟩ MSv; [*omitted*] 1A. *The note is cancelled by Pierre M. Irving.*
236.6	armour.] T; ∼ₐ MSv; armor. 1A. *Periods are supplied or substituted for indicated punctuation at the ends of sentences at the following additional points*: 237.34, 239.41, 241.28, 242.11, 243.29, 244.3 *semicolon*, 244.6, 244.10, 245.12 *semicolon*, 245.28, 246.22, 246.42, 247.37, 248.3, 248.16, 250.31, 251.6, 253.19 *colon*, 253.37, 254.14 *colon*, 254.27 *semicolon*, 254.31 *semicolon*, 255.9, 256.37, 258.9, 258.37, 259.32, 260.9 *colon*, 261.33, 262.21, 264.44, 265.2 *comma*, 265.12, 266.16, 268.15, 268.19, 271.35, 272.5.
236.9	fight,] 1A; ∼ₐ MSv. *Second comma of a pair.*
236.21	St.] 1A; Sᵗ MSv. *Abbreviations of "Saint" consisting of various configurations of "S" and "t" are emended to this form at* 237.21, 237.27, 237.38, 237.39, 243.11, 245.15, 251.29, 256.32, 258.12, 258.20, 258.21, 259.11, 259.35, 260.6, 261.17, 271.15, 271.30, 271.34, 271.34, 271.40.
236.21	16th] 1A; 16*th* MSv.
236.27	church] T; Church MSv, 1A. *Not ordinarily capitalized; see* 236.18. *In accordance with Irving's usual practice, the indicated words capitalized in MSv are emended to lower-case*: 238.25, 239.22 alcayde; 237.17 alfarez;

268.10, 268.20, 268.25 cortes; 264.1 fortress; 244.33 hermit; 267.27 his; 238.2 the; 250.18 xemete; 240.3 xeriz.

236.31   *Alonzo the Great*]   T; Alonzo the/ Great MSv; ALFONSO THE GREAT 1A. *Pierre M. Irving's spelling reflects Irving's preferred usage (see 234.27, 238.29), which was usually emended in 1A to "Alfonso." The same emendation is made in a 1A headnote at 243.2; see also* Emendations 243.6.

236.33   Quircé]   1A; Quircé MSv. *Irving's "accent" may well be a slip of the pen; emended reading reflects usual spelling, as at 237.18.*

236.34   town,]   1A; ~∧ MSv. *Comma separates appositives.*

237.15   Gonzalo Gustios]   T; Gustios Gonzalez MSv, 1A. *The same emendation is made at 258.32–33; see* Discussions of Adopted Readings 243.34.

237.20   day,]   1A; ~∧ MSv. *Second comma of a pair.*

237.29   perceived]   1A; percieved MSv. *The same emendation is made at 244.22, 270.3.*

237.37   morrow.]   1A; morro[*MS torn*] MSv. *Additional readings supplied from 1A in place of text lost owing to tearing in MSv occur at the following points, where the interpolations are shown within brackets:* 237.43 gat[es], 238.1 distan[ce], 250.25 warriors[,], 266.20 wh[ich], 266.27 equal[ly], 268.15 cavalier[s.].

237.37   midsummer's]   1A; midsummers MSv. *Apostrophes are added to possessives at* 238.37, 241.11, 243.41, 248.12, 249.17, 249.42, 257.6, 257.8, 259.13, 261.32, 264.5, 266.36, 271.21. *See also* Emendations 252.29.

237.42   castle,]   1A; ~∧ MSv. *First comma of a pair.*

238.4   castle.]   1A; ~, . MSv. *Comma forms part of a cancelled passage and was inadvertently allowed by Irving to stand. A similar oversight occurs at 244.22, where a semicolon intervenes between "place" and the period.*

238.8–9   castle, . . . walls,]   1A; ~∧ . . . ~∧ MSv. *Commas necessary for clarity.*

238.12   castle,]   1A; ~∧ MSv. *Comma marks pause following long introductory construction.*

238.21   capitulated;]   1A; ~∧ MSv. *Semicolon marks pause between independent clauses distinct in subject-matter.*

238.25   fortress,]   1A; ~∧ MSv. *Comma separates independent clauses.*

238.29   Leon,]   1A; ~∧ MSv. *Second comma of a pair.*

238.31   relatives,]   1A; ~∧ MSv. *Comma clarifies.*

238.38	affection, and] 1A; ~ —/ ~ MSv. *Dash is almost a lot and was quite possibly intended as a comma.*
239.6	Muñon] T; Mugnon MSv, 1A. *See* 243.31, 260.27. *The same emendation is made in a headnote at* 239.2 (*Muñon*).
239.13	wall; and] 1A; ~∧ ~ MSv. *Elsewhere Irving carefully paced his sentence (see preceding semicolon), but he neglected to separate its two main clauses.*
239.17	castle,] 1A; ~∧ MSv. *Second comma of a pair.*
239.22–23	Abdallah, . . . fortress,] 1A; ~∧ . . . ~∧ MSv. *Commas enclose appositive.*
239.24	"God,"] 1A; ∧~,∧ MSv. *Pairs of double quotation marks are supplied at the following additional points:* 239.24–26, 242.21, 244.3, 244.3–6, 246.5–7, 246.9, 246.28, 246.28–33, 246.44, 246.44–45, 247.24–29, 247.31, 247.32–37, 248.3–7, 248.17, 248.17–23, 248.25, 248.26–27, 249.25, 249.26–27, 249.28, 249.28–34, 252.6, 252.6–7, 252.8, 252.9–29, 253.3–4, 253.4, 253.4–7, 253.15, 253.15–25, 254.2, 254.2–3, 254.13, 254.13–14, 254.27, 254.27–29, 254.31, 254.32–33, 254.33, 254.34–36, 254.39, 254.39, 254.42, 254.42–44, 256.40, 256.40–41, 257.23, 257.23–24, 258.9–10, 258.10–15, 259.35, 261.25, 261.25–26, 262.11, 262.11–14, 262.15, 262.15–17, 263.27, 263.27–30, 263.39, 263.39–40, 265.38, 265.38–39, 270.28, 270.28–29, 271.44, 271.44–272.1, 272.12.
239.30	Abdallah] 1A; Abdalla MSv. *See* 239.22, 239.33.
239.33	Almondir,] 1A; ↑~∧↓ MSv. *First comma of a pair.*
239.39	restored,] 1A; ~∧ MSv. *Comma follows long introductory expression.*
240.38	* Sandoval, p. 301.] 1A; ∧Sandoval∧ P. 301. MSv. *Regularized 1A readings for Irving's footnote citations are adopted at the following additional points; the MSv readings are given in parentheses:* 247.40–41 (* Sandoval. The 5 Bishops. Mariana Lib. 8 C. 5 p 367/ Chron Gen de España Part 3 Cap. 18 fol 53.), 247.42 (* ⟨Chron⟩ Cron. Gen de España ut supra), 250.40 († Mariana⟨na⟩ Lib 8 Cap. 5. P 367), 257.39 (Sandoval P. 313.), 261.40 (Cronica General de España), 261.42–43 (the Chronicle of Bleda, L. 3. C. 19.), 269.38 (* Cronica de Alonzo el Sabio P. 3 C. 19), 272.15 (* Sandoval p. 334.). *See also* Emendations 250.39.
240.10	stable,] 1A; ~∧ MSv. *Comma separates independent clauses.*
240.12	Great] 1A; great MSv. *Part of proper name; see* 234.27.

The indicated portions of proper names, titles, or pseudonyms are similarly emended at 258.12 Most High, 258.36 Old, 263.7 Trembler, 266.42 First, 267.25 Fourth, 267.25 Bad, 272.2 Third.

240.13 achievements,] 1A; ~∧ MSv. *Comma separates independent clauses.*

240.17 bands,] 1A; ~∧ MSv. *Comma clarifies.*

240.18 country,] 1A; ~∧ MSv. *Comma precedes modifying participial phrase.*

240.23 capital] 1A; capitol MSv. *Misspelling in sense used.*

240.33–34 surrounded,] 1A; ~∧ MSv. *Second comma of a pair.*

241.11 recollected] 1A; reccollected MSv. *A similar emendation to MSv "reccollection" is made at* 255.33.

241.12 Carazo] 1A; Corazo MSv. *Preferred spelling; see* 237.31, 238.20. *The same emendation is made at* 241.21.

241.23 enterprize,] T; ~∧ MSv; enterprise, 1A. *Comma necessary to avoid ambiguity.*

241.27 Lara,] 1A; ~∧ MSv. *Comma marks pause before subordinate clause.*

241.37 seized] 1A; siezed MSv. *The same emendation is made at* 246.4 (seize), 248.39, 265.31, 266.24.

242.12 music,] 1A; ~∧ MSv. *Comma is second of a pair.*

242.16 deceived] 1A; decieved MSv. *The same emendation is made at* 267.31.

242.21 voice,] 1A; ~∧ MSv. *Commas are also inserted to separate commentary from direct or indirect quotations at* 235.23, 242.22, 244.3, 246.5, 246.9, 246.28, 246.44, 246.44, 247.31, 248.17, 248.17, 248.25, 248.27, 249.16, 249.16, 249.25, 252.8, 252.9, 254.13, 254.39, 254.42, 262.15, 262.15, 263.27, 263.27, 263.39, 266.32, 266.32, 270.28, 271.40, 271.44. *See also* Emendations 252.1.

242.21 The foe!] 1A; the ~! MSv. *Words at the beginning of exclamations or sentences are also capitalized at* 244.3, 245.12, 246.5, 254.13, 254.27, 254.31.

242.21–22 count, followed . . . cavaliers,] 1A; ~∧ ↑~ . . . ~ -↓ MSv. *Commas clarify, enclosing modifying phrase.*

242.38 success,] 1A; ~∧ MSv. *Second comma of a pair.*

243.6 Alonzo] T; Alfonzo MSv; ALFONSO 1A. *Emendation reflects Irving's usual spelling; see* Emendations 236.31. *The same change is made at* 243.9, 243.14.

243.7 feebleness,] 1A; ~∧ MSv. *Second comma of a pair.*

243.8 compel] 1A; compell MSv. *No authority in dictionaries.*

243.12 malady,] 1A; ~∧ MSv. *Second comma of a pair.*

243.14   reconciliation]   1A; recconciliation MSv. *The same correction is made at 263.35.*

243.19   sovereign,]   T; sov↑e↓reign∧ MSv; ∼∧ 1A. *Comma is second of a pair; for the interlineation see* Emendations 234.31.

243.30   arms,]   T; ∼∧ MSv, 1A. *Second comma of a pair.*

*243.34   Don Gonzalo . . . Lara,]   1A; Don Gonzalo ↑Gustios,↓ of Lara∧ MSv. *Comma is second of a pair.*

243.39   enemy,]   1A; ∼∧ MSv. *Comma clarifies.*

243.41   Diaz,]   1A; ∼∧ MSv. *Second comma of a pair.*

244.5   Almanzor,]   1A; ∼∧ MSv. *Comma marks pause following introductory phrase.*

244.23   brave,]   1A; ∼∧ MSv. *Comma marks pause following introductory phrase.*

244.27   monk,]   1A; ∼∧ MSv. *Comma clarifies.*

244.28   knight,]   1A; ∼∧ MSv. *Comma marks pause following modifying phrase.*

244.32   recently,]   1A; ∼∧ MSv. *Second comma of a pair.*

245.9   thee, but]   T; ∼∧ ∼ MSv; ∼; ∼ 1A. *Comma separates independent clauses.*

245.16   Peter,]   1A; ∼∧ MSv. *Comma separates appositives.*

245.17   interred]   1A; enterred MSv. *No authority in dictionaries.*

245.17   Receiving]   1A; Recieving MSv. *The same emendation is made at 262.19 (receive), 263.36 (received), 269.9.*

245.22   absence,]   1A; ∼∧ MSv. *Comma marks pause following introductory construction.*

245.27   cymbals,]   1A; ∼∧ MSv. *Comma separates independent clauses.*

245.32   ground,]   1A; ∼∧ MSv. *Comma marks pause before subordinate clause.*

245.33   cavalier,]   1A; ∼∧ MSv. *Comma precedes modifying phrase.*

245.35   vainglorious]   1A; vain/ glorious MSv.

245.37   bitt]   T; bit⟨t⟩ MSv; bit 1A. *The cancellation is by Pierre M. Irving.*

246.4   them,]   1A; ∼∧ MSv. *Comma separates independent clauses.*

246.6   lord,]   1A; ∼∧ MSv. *Comma precedes subordinate clause.*

246.7   So saying,]   1A; ∼ ∼∧ MSv. *Comma marks pause after summary phrase; see 348.21,* Alhambra *(1850) 454.9.*

246.17   horse,]   1A; ∼∧ MSv. *Comma necessary for clarity.*

246.20   refreshed,]   1A; $\sim_\wedge$ MSv. *Comma marks pause follow-*
                ing introductory construction.

246.32   rock,]   1A; $\sim_\wedge$ MSv. *Comma necessary for clarity.*

247.4   inspirited]   1A; enspirited MSv.

247.8   Sancho II.,]   1A; $\sim$ II$_{\wedge\wedge}$ MSv. *Comma separates ap-*
                positives.

247.18   Rioxa,]   1A; $\sim_\wedge$ MSv. *Comma clarifies.*

247.22   matters,]   1A; $\sim_\wedge$ MSv. *Second comma of a pair.*

247.23   come, Señor,"]   T; $\sim$," $\sim_{,\wedge}$ MSv. *Misplaced quotation*
                mark.

247.25   Castile,]   1A; $\sim_\wedge$ MSv. *Comma separates independent*
                clauses.

247.34   counsel]   1A; council MSv. *Misspelling in sense used.*
                The same emendation is made at 257.36, 267.9.

247.40   Sandoval,]   T; $\sim$. MSv, 1A. *Emendation reflects the*
                usual Putnam style.

248.27   pitiless]   1A; pit⟨y⟩↑i↓less MSv. *The correction is by*
                Pierre M. Irving.

248.27–28   "that . . . country."]   T; $_\wedge\sim$ . . . $\sim$." MSv; $_\wedge\sim$ . . .$\sim_\wedge$
                1A. *Quotation marks are supplied in order to com-*
                plete pairs at the following points: 249.21, 250.5,
                250.7, 264.40, 271.40.

248.39   Navarre,]   1A; $\sim_\wedge$ MSv. *First comma of a pair.*

248.43   Navarre,]   1A; $\sim_\wedge$ MSv. *Second comma of a pair.*

249.17   night,]   1A; $\sim_\wedge$ MSv. *Second comma of a pair.*

249.22   cavalier, . . . Laynez,]   1A; $\sim_\wedge$ . . . $\sim_\wedge$ MSv. *Commas*
                enclose appositive.

249.28   spoken,]   1A; $\sim_\wedge$ MSv. *Pause seems intended preceding*
                the address by name.

249.35   cavaliers,]   1A; Cavaliers$_\wedge$ MSv. *Comma marks pause*
                following introductory construction.

250.1   stream,]   1A; $\sim_\wedge$ MSv. *Comma necessary for clarity.*

250.4   galloped]   1A; gallopped MSv. *The same emendation*
                is made at 259.20.

250.6–7   combat!]   1A; $\sim$. MSv. *Context warrants the emenda-*
                tion. Exclamation marks are also supplied or sub-
                stituted for indicated punctuation at 252.17, 252.18
                semicolon.

250.14   dead,]   1A; $\sim_\wedge$ MSv. *Second comma of a pair.*

250.18   value,]   1A; $\sim_\wedge$ MSv. *Comma clarifies.*

250.20   nails,]   1A; $\sim_\wedge$ MSv. *Comma separates independent*
                clauses.

250.23   count,]   1A; Count$_\wedge$ MSv. *Comma precedes relative*
                clause.

250.25   an array]   1A; a↑n↓ ⟨shining⟩ array MSv. *The change to the article is by Pierre M. Irving; an adjustment Irving had overlooked.*

250.31   Asturias.†]   1A; Asturias_∧* MSv. *In 1A Irving's asterisk was emended to the dagger here and in the corresponding footnote (250.40) to avoid duplicate sets of asterisks for footnotes printed on the same page.*

250.37   father,]   1A; ~_∧ MSv. *Second comma of a pair.*

250.39   * Cron. Gen. de España, ut supra.]   T; * Cron Gen de Espana ⟨ut supra⟩. MSv; * *Cron. Gen. de España.* 1A. *Deletion is by Pierre M. Irving. Restored note is emended in accordance with Putnam house style.*

251.2   foreseeing]   1A; forseeing MSv.

251.17   cap-a-pie]   T; ~_∧ ~_∧ ~ MSv; *cap-a-pie* 1A. *No authority in dictionaries for unhyphenated form.*

251.18   treachery,]   1A; ~_∧ MSv. *Second comma of a pair.*

251.20   nightfall]   1A; night fall MSv. *See 261.11.*

251.29   Compostella,]   1A; ~_∧ MSv. *Second comma of a pair.*

251.37   rank,]   1A; ~_∧ MSv. *Comma necessary for clarity.*

251.41   Sancha,]   1A; ~_∧ MSv. *Comma precedes relative clause.*

252.1   surely,]   1A; ~, MSv. *Comma, probably by Pierre M. Irving, separates indirect quotation from commentary.*

252.6   this,]   1A; ~_∧ MSv. *Comma clarifies.*

252.7   Christendom]   1A; christendom MSv. *Ordinarily capitalized; see 252.10.*

252.9   Behold,]   1A; ~_∧ MSv. *Pause follows initial command. The same emendation is made at 252.21.*

252.10   Spain,]   1A; ~_∧ MSv. *Comma follows first item in series of three.*

252.11   dungeon]   1A; dungen MSv.

252.13   will it tell]   1A; ~↑~↓ ~ MSv. *Interlineation is by Pierre M. Irving, a necessary correction.*

252.15   inveigled]   1A; inviegled MSv.

252.16   dungeon?]   1A; ~. MSv. *Context warrants emended punctuation. Question marks are inserted or substituted for the indicated punctuation at 253.5 period, 258.10 comma, 258.17 period, 267.7 period.*

252.29   woman's]   1A; woman↑'↓s MSv. *Apostrophe added by Pierre M. Irving. The same correction is made by him at 253.4.*

253.12   count saw]   1A; ~ ↑~↓ MSv. *Interlineation is by Pierre M. Irving, a necessary correction.*

253.18   instead,]   1A; ~_∧ MSv. *Comma is second of a pair.*

253.21   one word,]   1A; ~ ↑~_∧↓ MSv. *Interlineation is by*

	Pierre M. Irving, a plausible correction of Irving's oversight; comma separates clauses.
253.27	oath,] 1A; ~∧ MSv. *Comma precedes subordinate clause.*
253.29	way,] 1A; ~∧ MSv. *Comma separates independent clauses.*
253.32	night,] 1A; ~∧ MSv. *Comma separates independent clauses.*
254.4	in vain,] 1A; ~ ~∧ MSv. *Comma precedes subordinate clause.*
254.28	escape, for] 1A; ~∧ ~ MSv. *Comma precedes subordinate clause.*
254.37	he saw] T; ↑~ ~↓ MSv; ~ ~, 1A. *The interlineation, a plausible correction of Irving's oversight, is by Pierre M. Irving.*
254.40–41	Nuño Laynez] 1A; Nuno ~ MSv.
255.7	leader,] 1A; ~∧ MSv. *Comma clarifies.*
255.8	chivalry,] 1A; ~∧ MSv. *Second comma of a pair.*
255.26	him,] 1A; ~∧ MSv. *Comma separates independent clauses.*
255.27	routed,] 1A; ~∧ MSv. *Comma separates independent clauses.*
255.34	imprisonment,] T; ~∧ MSv, 1A. *Second comma of a pair.*
256.4	Gonzalez] 1A; Gonzales MSv. *The same emendation is made at 267.23.*
256.10	Gormaz] T; Ormaz MSv, 1A. *See 263.43, 264.1.*
256.13–14	Madrid, . . . village;] T; ~; . . . ~, MSv; ~, . . . ~, 1A. *Irving neglected to revise his punctuation after deciding to add modifying phrase.*
256.15	Burgos.] 1A; ⟨Madrid.⟩ ~. MSv. *Pierre M. Irving corrected his uncle's error.*
256.24	career] 1A; car⟨r⟩eer MSv. *Cancellation probably by Pierre M. Irving.*
256.30	tears,] T; ~∧ MSv, 1A. *Second comma of a pair.*
256.38	made,] 1A; ~∧ MSv. *Comma marks pause following long introductory construction.*
256.40	church;] 1A; ~∧ MSv. *Irving intended a significant pause before the quotation.*
257.3	Prudencio] T; Prudencia MSv, 1A. *Misspelling.*
257.16–17	Agapida, . . . extracted,] 1A; ~∧ . . . ~∧ MSv. *Commas enclose relative clause.*
257.18	which crowd] 1A; ↑⟨of⟩↓ which ⟨ancient⟩ ↑crowd↓ MSv.

	The cancellation of "of," by Pierre M. Irving, corrects Irving's oversight.
257.19	ever] 1A; ⟨n⟩ever MSv. *Pierre M. Irving corrected the error.*
257.30	Andalusia] 1A; Andaluzia MSv. *Emendation reflects usual spelling.*
257.34	forebodings] 1A; forbodings MSv.
257.35	occasion,] 1A; ∼∧ MSv. *Pause seems necessary following long subordinate clause.*
258.4	never,] 1A; ∼∧ MSv. *First comma of a pair.*
258.9	vision,] 1A; ∼∧ MSv. *Comma clarifies.*
258.9	Why sleepest] 1A; ↑Why↓ Sleepest MSv.
258.15	say,] 1A; ∼∧ MSv. *Second comma of a pair.*
258.17	hence; why] 1A; ∼∧ ∼ MSv. *A blank space in MSv indicates intention for a pause.*
258.19	division,] 1A; ∼∧ MSv. *Second comma of a pair.*
258.27–28	counsellors] 1A; councillors MSv. *The same correction is made at 270.44.*
258.31	mountaineers] 1A; mountainiers MSv.
258.32–33	Gonzalo Gustios] T; Gustios Gonzalez MSv, 1A. *See* Discussions of Adopted Readings 243.34.
258.34	Gonzalo Diaz] T; ∼ Dias MSv, 1A. *The name is spelled "Diaz" at 243.41. Mariana refers to this person as "Gonçalo Diaz."*
258.40	knights,] 1A; ∼∧ MSv. *Second comma of a pair.*
259.8	people,] 1A; ∼∧ MSv. *Comma precedes subordinate clause.*
259.16	had not] 1A; ⟨but⟩ ⟨for the⟩ ∼ ∼ MSv. *The first cancellation, extending Irving's, is by Pierre M. Irving.*
259.18	Gonzalo Gustios] T; Gustio Gonzalez MSv; Gustios Gonzalez 1A. *See* Discussions of Adopted Readings 243.34.
259.19	Fernan,] 1A; ∼∧ MSv. *First comma of a pair, preceding subordinate clause.*
259.23	count,] 1A; Count∧ MSv. *First comma of a pair.*
259.35	Iago! St. Iago] T;∼! Sant⟨;⟩Iago MSv; ∼! San ∼ 1A. *See* Emendations 236.21.
259.37	Gonzalo Gustios] T; Gustio Gonzalo MSv; Gustios Gonzalo 1A. *The same emendation is made at 259.41. See* Discussions of Adopted Readings 243.34.
259.37	de Salas,] 1A; ∼ ∼∧ MSv. *First comma of a pair.*
260.6	and of] 1A; ∼ ⟨to⟩ ∼ MSv. *Deletion is probably by Pierre M. Irving.*

260.30   Second,]   1A; ~∧ MSv. *First comma of a pair.*
261.5   tears,]   1A; ~∧ MSv. *Comma precedes subordinate*
            clause.
261.21   chains,]   1A; ~∧ MSv. *Space in MSv suggests Irving*
            intended a pause.
261.34   portal, thinking . . . countess,]   1A; ~∧ ↑~ . . .
            Countess∧↓ MSv. *Commas enclose subordinate con-*
            struction.
261.35   count,]   1A; Count∧ MSv. *First comma of a pair.*
261.42   Ramiro,]   1A; ~∧ MSv. *Comma separates clauses.*
262.8   king,]   1A; ~∧ MSv. *Comma distinguishes the keeper's*
            two actions.
262.16   lady,]   1A; ~∧ MSv. *Comma separates independent*
            clauses.
262.25   Urraca,]   1A; ⟨Uracca⟩ ↑Urraca∧↓ MSv. *Comma is*
            first of a pair. Indicated variant spellings of the name
            are similarly emended at 267.27 Urracca, 267.39 Ur-
            racca; the spelling "URACCA" in Pierre M. Irving's
            chapter-heading at 260.23 is also emended.
262.37   countess,]   1A; ~∧ MSv. *Comma separates appositives.*
263.1   stepbrother]   T; step brother MSv; step-brother 1A.
            Thus Webster.
263.2   Navarre,]   1A; ~∧ MSv. *Comma marks pause between*
            the alternative names.
263.6   Nay,]   1A; ~∧ MSv. *Usual practice following mild intro-*
            ductory exclamations; see Granada *(1850) 411.26.*
263.9   son-in-law]   1A; son in law MSv. *No authority in dic-*
            tionaries; the same emendation is made at 263.13.
263.9–10   Ordoño III., for]   1A; ~ III∧∧ for MSv. *Comma pre-*
            cedes long subordinate clause.
263.18   effecting]   1A; affecting MSv. *Misspelling in the sense*
            used.
263.19   time,]   1A; ~∧ MSv. *First comma of a pair.*
263.24   Zamora, consuming]   1A; ~∧ ~ MSv. *Comma precedes*
            participial phrase.
263.24   Xeriz]   T; Xerez MSv, 1A. *See 239.16, 240.3.*
263.25   likewise, and]   1A; ~∧ ~ MSv. *Comma clarifies.*
263.32   discord,]   1A; ~∧ MSv. *Second comma of a pair.*
263.34   Gonzalez, . . . danger,]   1A; ~∧ . . . ~∧ MSv. *Commas*
            enclose modifying phrase.
263.43   Estevan]   1A; Esteban MSv. *Irving's usual spelling; see*
            263.38.
264.16   Pascual]   1A; Pasqual MSv. *See 264.6–7.*
264.17   custom,]   1A; ~∧ MSv. *Second comma of a pair.*

264.25   stood,]   1A; ~_∧ MSv. *Second comma of a pair.*

265.1   knight, . . . him,]   1A; ~_∧ . . . ~_∧ MSv. *Commas enclose*
                subordinate clause.

265.9   arms, device and steed,]   T; ~_∧ ~ ~/ ~_∧ MSv; ~,
                ~, ~ ~, 1A. *Emendation reflects Irving's usual*
                practice for series of three.

265.14   fought on,]   1A; ~ ~_∧ MSv. *Comma separates inde-*
                pendent clauses.

265.21   skillful]   T; skil⟨l⟩ful MSv; skilful 1A. *Cancellation prob-*
                ably by Pierre M. Irving. See 267.16, 269.23.

265.27   explained,]   1A; ~_∧ MSv. *Comma marks pause follow-*
                ing summary introduction.

265.28   admiration,]   1A; ~_∧ MSv. *Comma necessary for clarity.*

265.35   kind]   1A; king MSv. *Obvious error.*

267.4   and had rather]   1A; ~ ↑~↓ ~ MSv. *Interlineation, a*
                necessary correction, is by Pierre M. Irving.

267.17   beforehand]   1A; before hand MSv.

267.30   ever,]   1A; ~_∧ MSv. *Second comma of a pair.*

267.38   terror,]   1A; ~_∧ MSv. *Comma separates independent*
                clauses.

267.39   Urraca,]   1A; Urracca_∧ MSv. *Second comma of a pair.*

268.13–14   therefore,]   1A; ~_∧ MSv. *Second comma of a pair.*

268.40   figures,]   1A; ~_∧ MSv. *Second comma of a pair.*

269.23   horse dealing,]   T; ~ ~_∧ MSv; ~-~, 1A. *Second*
                comma of a pair.

269.27   ¶The]   T; _∧~ MSv; ¶Thε 1A. *First word of a chapter.*

270.3   Gonzalez,]   1A; ~_∧ MSv. *First comma of a pair.*

270.5   castles,]   1A; ~_∧ MSv. *Second comma of a pair.*

271.6   humility,]   1A; ~_∧ MSv. *Comma precedes subordinate*
                clause.

271.7   Christendom,]   1A; Christiandom_∧ MSv. *Comma is*
                second of a pair.

271.10   Arlanza,]   1A; ~_∧ MSv. *Comma separates independent*
                clauses.

271.18   men,]   1A; ~_∧ MSv. *Second comma of a pair.*

271.23   faith,]   1A; ~_∧ MSv. *Balanced sentence calls for pause*
                following first independent clause.

271.31   Arlanza]   T; Arlanzas MSv, 1A. *See 246.29, 269.36.*

271.32   repose,]   T; ~_∧ MSv; ~; 1A. *Comma separates inde-*
                pendent clauses.

271.33   convent:]   T; ~_∧ MSv; ~,– 1A. *Colon supplied to fol-*
                low the specifically introductory phrases.

271.35   Hazinas]   1A; Hazenas MSv. *Emendation reflects usual*
                spelling; see 257.22.

271.38   Gothic letters,]   1A; gothic letters   MSv. *Designation*
          of nationality; comma is second of a pair.

271.40   Awake, . . . sleepest,]   1A; ~∧ . . .~∧ MSv. *Commas*
          separate personal address from command.

272.7   Fernando]   1A; Ferdinand MSv. *Emendation reflects*
          Irving's usual spelling.

CHRONICLE OF FERNANDO THE SAINT

273.2   CHRONICLE . . . SAINT] T; Chronicle of Fernando
          the Saint. MSv; ~ . . . ~./ [*rule*] 1A.

273.3–7   [CHAPTER I. . . . *Fernando.*]]   T; [*rule*]/ Chap. 1/
          [*rule*]/ The parentage of Fernado – Queen Berenguela
          –/ The Laras – Don Alvar conceals the death of King
          Henry –/ Mission of Queen Berenguela to Alfonso IX
          – She renounces the / crown of Castile in favor of her
          son Fernando/ [*rule*] MSv; ∧~ ~ . . . . ~.∧ 1A. *MSv*
          reading supplied by Pierre M. Irving. Chapter-numbers
          and chapter-headings added to the copy-text by Pierre
          M. Irving are also adopted and regularized at 276.24–
          26, 280.1–5, 282.9–12, 283.32–36, 285.11–15, 289.13–14,
          291.1–3, 294.29–31, 296.15–19, 299.16–20, 303.31–34,
          306.1–5, 308.29–33, 311.33–34, 314.22–24, 316.10–13,
          318.18–22, 322.23–24, 324.18–20, 327.14–15.

273.8   III.,]   1A; ~.∧ MSv. *First comma of a pair.*

273.8   Alfonso]   1A; Alfon⟨z⟩so MSv. *Indicated variant spell-*
          ings of this individual's name are emended to Irving's
          usual spelling adopted here at 275.33, 276.27, 276.31,
          276.34, 277.15, 277.24, 284.14 Alfonzo; 284.24 Alonzo.

273.8   III.]   1A; III∧ MSv. *Periods are also supplied following*
          roman numerals at 273.12, 273.16, 273.19, 273.20,
          280.14, 285.16.

273.9   Berenguela,]   1A; ~∧ MSv. *Comma separates apposi-*
          tives.

273.10   parentage]   1A; paren[*torn*]/ -age MSv. *Additional*
          readings supplied from 1A in place of text lost owing
          to damage in the copy-text occur at the following
          points, where the 1A interpolations are shown within
          brackets: 273.11 befo[re], 273.18 interd[ict], 279.14
          abandon[ed], 279.17 recoun[t], 279.18 leng[th], 279.19
          Christia[ns].

273.12   Alfonso III.]   1A; ↑1189↓ ~ III∧ MSv. *The date, appar-*
          ently for Irving's own reference, is written in the left
          margin. Other marginal dates not reproduced here

	occur in the copy-text as follows: 299.21 1240.; 301.25 1243; 302.5 1244.
273.12	King] 1A; king MSv. *Part of a proper title. The same emendation is made at* 273.13, 282.16, 282.27. *The indicated titles and other words used as parts of proper names but uncapitalized in the copy-text are similarly emended at* 289.9 Archbishop; 295.5 Count; 280.12 Emperor; 294.12 Frontier; 300.17, 301.27, 304.17 Grand; 283.20, 301.27, 304.17, 309.43, 310.6, 311.18 Master; 285.27, 285.29, 316.16, 317.42 Prince; 273.14, 273.21, 280.11, 295.13 Princess; 275.40, 280.23 Queen; 299.2 Rock; 307.13 Saint. *See also* Emendations 309.33, 318.17.
273.13	Leon,] 1A; ~∧ MSv. *First comma of a pair.*
273.14	Teresa] T; Theresa MSv, 1A. *Usual spelling; see* 284.40, 285.1 *The same emendation is made at* 284.34.
273.16	consanguinity,] 1A; ~∧/ MSv. *End-of-line commas or other indicated punctuation omitted from the copy-text are supplied after the following words:* 273.25 resisted, 274.12 point;, 274.30 poor, 275.15 palace, 275.31 Biscay, 275.39 about, 276.1 connexions, 276.10 throne, 276.14 place, 276.40 days, 278.26 others, 278.43 brothers, 279.2 excursions, 279.16 miramamolin, 279.25 Acre, 280.12 Philip, 281.6 Fernando, 281.26 gates, 281.31 Andujar, 281.35 made, 283.11 Pudiello, 283.13 himself, 285.35 destroying, 285.39 Xerez, 286.11 ravage, 286.33 battalions, 287.5 field, 287.17 peril, 287.19 Alvar, 287.44 Vargas, 288.11 tree, 289.17 guarded, 289.19 Perez, 289.20 ladders, 289.23 ramparts, 291.12 accepted, 291.30 Señor, 291.40 enterprise, 292.21 Zaen, 292.26 counsellors, 292.38 water, 292.40 asunder, 293.28 repair, 294.27 joy, 295.33 multitudes, 297.8 Alhamar, 297.12 standard, 299.1 therefore, 299.10 value, 299.36 usual, 300.17 Correa, 300.26 more, 300.35 chroniclers, 301.6 daughter, 302.7 fatigues, 303.12 journey, 303.27 weeks, 303.28 frontier, 304.17 Correa, 304.37 cavalry, 305.5 resolution, 305.6 camp, 305.33 learning, 306.30 Seville, 307.12 mother, 307.37 Toledo, 307.39 years, 308.12 marry, 308.26 Biscay, 309.4 lance, 309.26 land, 309.27 Tangier, 310.1 friars, 310.2 Niebla, 310.4 peril, 310.9 Gelbes, 310.16 ruins, 310.16 day, 310.31 Triana, 310.40 latter, 311.25 thirst, 311.26 fountain;, 311.26 soldiers, 311.29 Virgin, 312.5 camp, 312.7 armed, 312.13

arrived, 312.16 pavilions, 312.36 forward;, 312.39 horse,
312.42 tent, 313.4 Xuarez, 313.9 tranquilly, 313.15 by,
313.25 capellina, 313.44 exclaimed, 314.11 confused,
314.31 soldiers, 314.37 combustibles, 314.38 shore, 315.7
wild, 315.39 daily, 315.44 vessels, 316.8 provisions,
316.31 kindled, 317.2 them, 317.4 foot, 317.10 friars,
317.10 leader, 317.11 aid, 317.17 Sietefilla, 317.27
Garcia, 317.33 and, 320.7 across, 320.15 dismayed,
321.2 remained, 321.7 tent, 321.28 side, 321.36 Seville,
322.17 Admiral, 322.19 ships, 322.22 Triana, 323.3 Infanzon, 323.4 vassals, 323.7 cavaliers, 323.14 exclaimed,
323.24 after, 324.21 Orias, 324.38 Guzman, 325.3 Triana, 325.17 cooperation, 325.18 passed, 325.28 success,
326.7 made, 327.19 Alua,   327.37 Sacrament, 327.40
kingdom.

273.24 church] T; Church MSv, 1A. *Emendation reflects Irving's usual practice and is also made at 274.31, 276.18,
281.42, 294.2, 316.31. In accordance with Irving's usual
practice, the indicated words capitalized in the copy-
text are emended to lower-case*: 289.28 adalid; 328.2
angels; 325.9 army; 303.37 autumn; 321.34 bold;
291.17, 292.6 camp; 294.12, 297.44, 298.3, 310.28 castle; 284.37, 293.38, 305.23 cathedral; 285.33 cavalry;
293.19, 293.27, 293.38, 304.33, 308.35, 325.8 city; 284.8
collision; 326.1 commander; 294.33, 299.36 conquest;
290.37 convents; 305.17 cortes; 304.19 council; 299.9
courier; 295.4 court; 276.30 crown; 307.38 crusade;
275.14 episcopal; 283.13 esquires; 312.20 foragers;
317.16 friar; 318.9 friars; 318.26 gamester; 325.14 garrison; 312.30 genetes; 327.12 heaven [*manuscript copy-
text wanting*]; 318.9, 319.2 knights; 307.5 metropolis;
291.20 montero; 294.23 mosque; 294.23 muezzin;
283.15, 283.27 peña; 283.16, 298.40 rock; 300.36 saintly;
323.10 scutcheon; 309.32 sea; 314.19 secret; 325.30
seeing; 325.18 sentinels; 289.38 several; 315.37 ships;
324.3 since; 309.44 sixty; 315.29 slain; 327.32 son; 309.6
spring; 318.7, 318.14 suburb; 309.13 succours; 311.13
supplicated; 309.22 surrendered; 325.3 surround; 318.3
sword; 321.29 the; 307.16 vision; 292.41 whereupon;
305.31 yoke; 314.1 your; 323.3 youthful.

273.34 Fernando,] 1A; ~∧ MSv. *First comma of a pair.*
273.38 Alfonso IX.] T; Alfonzo III. MSv; Alfonso III. 1A.
Irving confused Berenguela's father with her husband.

274.1   eleventh]   1A; 11*th* MSv. *Irving's usual practice.*

274.1   ex-Queen]   1A; ex Queen MSv. *No authority in diction-*
               aries. Hyphens are also added to compound expres-
               sions at 275.23, 284.42, 285.18, 289.26, 293.29–30, 322.2.

274.6   Nuñez.]   1A; ~∧ MSv. *Periods are inserted or supplied*
               in place of indicated punctuation at 276.18, 277.26
               comma, 277.33, 277.43 *comma,* 278.27, 284.9, 284.15
               284.25 *semicolon,* 284.33, 285.37 *dash,* 286.6 *colon,*
               288.26 *dash,* 289.7, 289.29, 289.38, 291.39, 292.10,
               292.26, 293.6, 295.18, 295.27 *comma,* 295.34, 296.14,
               297.6, 302.37, 303.7, 304.27, 304.31, 305.4 *dash,* 305.9,
               306.16 *dash,* 307.6, 307.23, 307.27, 309.7, 309.35, 310.12,
               310.14, 310.28, 310.44, 311.16, 311.32 313.29 *comma,*
               313.35 *comma,* 314.7, 314.17 *dash,* 316.2, 316.7 *dash,*
               317.18 *dash,* 317.40 *comma,* 318.5 *colon,* 320.1 *semi-*
               colon, 321.1 *comma,* 321.31, 322.36, 323.3 *comma,*
               323.36 *dash,* 323.42, 324.10 *dash,* 324.12, 324.24,
               325.23, 325.25 *comma.*

274.13   commotions,]   1A; ~∧ MSv. *Second comma of a pair.*

274.19   counsel]   1A; council MSv. *Inappropriate in sense used.*
               The same emendation is made at 285.16, 307.31,
               324.27; 280.6, 304.23 counsels; 280.10 counsellors.

274.41   receiving]   1A; recieving MSv. *The same emendation*
               is made at 281.37, 284.38, 292.43 received; 284.37
               receive.

275.16   companions,]   1A; ~∧ MSv. *Second comma of a pair.*

275.26   crown,]   1A; ~∧ MSv. *Comma separates independent*
               clauses.

275.29   her]   1A; hir MSv.

275.32   Gonsalvo Ruiz Giron]   T; Gonzalo ~ ~ MSv, 1A.
               Variant forms of this name are regularized to the
               reading adopted here at 278.40 Gonsalvo Ruyz Giron;
               281.2–3 Ruy Gonsalvo Giron.

275.33   Alfonso III.]   T; Alfonzo IX. MSv; Alfonso IX. 1A.
               Irving confused Queen Berenguela's father with her
               former husband.

275.33   Fernando,]   1A; ~∧ MSv. *Second comma of a pair.*

275.40   Tello, the bishop,]   1A; ~∧ ~ Bishop∧ MSv. *Commas*
               enclose appositive.

275.43   queen]   1A; Queen MSv. *Not used as part of proper*
               name. The same emendation is made at 276.13, 278.31,
               303.16, 303.28. *The indicated ranks and titles capital-*
               ized in the copy-text but not useful as parts of proper

names are similarly emended at 281.43, 282.6 archbishop; 275.40, 277.39 bishop; 276.17–18, 284.36, 293.25,
317.35, 327.32 bishops; 287.43, 302.39 cavalier; 290.4,
290.25–26, 298.30, 298.42, 316.14 cavaliers; 278.29
count; 304.25 grand master; 278.31, 291.28, 294.4,
297.43, 299.6, 302.39, 303.28, 303.29, 304.27, 307.37,
309.29 king; 310.36 master; 279.15–16 miramamolin
(*from* Miramolin); 286.41, 287.5, 287.19, 287.33,
300.16, 301.25, 326.9 prince; 303.25 queen mother's
(*from* Queen Mothers); 307.10, 307.16 saint; 313.25,
313.29, 314.5 squire; 317.18 squires; 299.8 viceroy
(*from* Vice Roy).

275.43–44   reconciliation] 1A; recconciliation MSv.

276.15   immediately,] 1A; ~ₐ MSv. *First comma of a pair.*

276.15–16   nobles, prelates and people,] T; ~ₐ ~ ~ / ~, MSv;
~, ~, ~ ~, 1A. *Emendation reflects Irving's usual
practice for lists of three.*

276.17   "Long ... Castle!"] 1A; ₐ~ ... ~·ₐ MSv. *Pairs of double quotation marks are also supplied at* 282.19, 282.20–
21, 287.20, 287.21, 287.38, 288.5, 288.5–6, 288.14–15,
288.15–16, 288.44, 288.44–289.4, 289.4, 289.5–7, 290.18,
292.4–7, 292.14, 292.14–18, 293.18, 293.19–22, 293.26–
27, 293.27–31, 293.32–33, 294.6, 294.7–8, 294.24,
294.25–28, 297.19–20, 298.22, 298.22–31, 298.32,
298.32–34, 301.31, 301.32–33, 305.7, 305.7–9, 307.18–19,
307.19, 307.19–20, 307.27–28, 307.28–32, 307.33–35,
311.15, 312.36–37, 313.5–8, 318.7, 320.19, 320.19–22,
328.9, 328.9–11.

276.17   Castile!] 1A; ~. MSv. *1A clearly more appropriate.
Exclamation marks are inserted or supplied in place
of indicated punctuation at* 288.15, 290.18 *period,*
320.20 *dash.*

276.19   31st of August, 1217,] 1A; 31. August/ 1217, MSv.
*Emendation reflects Irving's usual though not in-
variable practice; see* Columbus (*1848*), I, 250.9; Granada (*1850*), 504.10. "4ᵗʰ April" *is emended to* "4th
of April" *at* 300.4.

276.31   Alfonso,] 1A; Alfonzoₐ MSv. *Second comma of a pair.*

276.33   deceive] 1A; decieve MSv. *The same emendation is
made at* 298.8–9 deceived.

276.37   conceived] 1A; concieved MSv. *The same emendation
is made at* 300.34, 321.4.

277.7   appointed,] 1A; ~ₐ MSv. *Second comma of a pair.*

277.11   father,] 1A; ~∧ MSv. *Comma precedes modifying phrase.*

277.18   Leon,] 1A; ~∧ MSv. *Comma separates independent clauses.*

277.29–30   Lope Diaz de Haro] T; ~ Diez ~ Faro MSv, 1A. *See 275.31, 281.2.*

277.30   perceiving] 1A; percieving MSv.

277.34   Fernando,] 1A; ~∧ MSv. *First comma of a pair.*

277.41   Nuñez] 1A; Nunez MSv. *See 277.4. Tildes are also added at 301.6 Doña, 311.20 Señora; also see Emendations 312.32.*

278.7   on their way] 1A; in ~ ~ MSv. *MSv reading not idiomatic.*

278.8   Count] 1A; Cound MSv.

278.13   near,] 1A; ~∧ MSv. *Comma necessary for clarity.*

278.15   cavaliers,] 1A; ~∧ MSv. *Comma follows long introductory construction.*

278.19–20   drew . . . drawn] T; ⟨drew⟩ ↑came↓ / nigh ⟨they⟩ their attention was ⟨drawn⟩ ↑attracted↓ MSv; came nigh, their attention was attracted. 1A. *The two deletion-interlineations are by Pierre M. Irving.*

278.32–33   harshness, however,] 1A; ~; ⟨beyond safe exacting⟩ ↑~∧ MSv. *Irving neglected to emend punctuation as part of his changes to the sentence.*

278.39   fulfilled,] T; ~∧ MSv, 1A. *Second comma of a pair.*

278.41   months,] 1A; ~∧ MSv. *Comma separates independent clauses.*

278.43   possessions,] 1A; ~∧ MSv. *Comma follows introductory phrase.*

279.3   melancholy,] 1A; ~∧ MSv. *Comma follows introductory phrase.*

279.5   indulgences] 1A; indulgencies MSv.

279.5   order,] 1A; ~ – MSv. *The dash was likely intended as a comma. Similar emendations of Irving's often-slurred "dashes" are made at 288.17, 292.42, 300.18, 305.13, 313.11, 313.12, 318.6.*

279.14   Fernan,] T; Fernando∧ MSv; Fernando, 1A. *Comma is second of a pair. The same emendation of spelling is made at 279.22, 279.24, 301.5, 301.11.*

279.17   Moors,] 1A; ~∧ MSv. *Comma necessary for clarity.*

279.21   St.] 1A; Sᵗ MSv. *Various configurations of this abbreviation are regularized to "St." at 279.24, 293.15, 293.15,*

293.39, 294.2, 294.22, 309.44, 310.6, 310.30, 311.8, 311.18, 311.32, 315.22, 317.5, 317.9, 317.12, 317.12, 317.20, 317.20, 317.24, 318.7, 318.7, 319.33, 321.30, 326.1.

279.36   * *Cronica* . . . p. 17.]   1A; * Cronica Gotica – por Don Alonzo Nuñez de Castro/ P. 17. MSv. *Irving's footnotes and indicated parts of footnotes are adopted from the regularized 1A text at 279.37, 282.39, 283.41, 293.43, 300.43, 301.42 (but see Discussions of Adopted Readings 301.11), 304.43, 305.36 Note.–, 305.39–40 Notas . . . &c., 305.42, 306.35, 307.42, 307.43, 311.37, 311.38–39, 312.43, 316.38–39 (but see Emendations 317.43), 317.43, 320.42–43, 322.39, 324.39, 324.40, 325.43, 326.38.*

279.23   granted,]   1A; $\sim_\wedge$ MSv. *Comma separates independent clauses.*

279.25   de Acre]   1A; d'Acre MSv. *See 279.21.*

279.28   Gonzalo]   T; Gonsalvo MSv, 1A. *See 274.6.*

279.28   brothers,]   1A; $\sim_\wedge$ MSv. *Second comma of a pair.*

279.29   seized]   1A; siezed MSv. *The same correction is made at 288.13, 289.34, 299.14.*

279.30   Baeza,]   1A; $\sim_\wedge$ MSv. *Comma necessary for clarity.*

280.2–3   *Aben Mohamed*]   T; Aben Mohamed MSv; $\sim$ MOHAMMED 1A. *A part of Pierre M. Irving's headnote; see 281.5, 281.30.*

280.6   Fernando, . . . mother,]   1A; $\sim_\wedge$ . . . $\sim_\wedge$ MSv. *Commas enclose modifying phrase.*

280.7   quietness,]   1A; $\sim_\wedge$ MSv. *Comma precedes modifying phrase.*

280.32   inclinations,]   1A; $\sim_\wedge$ MSv. *Comma separates independent clauses.*

280.34   "God,"]   1A; "$\sim_\wedge$" MSv. *Commas are also inserted to separate the commentary from direct quotations within it at 294.6, 294.7, 297.20, 307.19, 307.19, 307.28, 307.32, 307.33, 311.14, 313.30, 313.34, 317.20, 323.11.*

280.39   Rodrigo]   1A; Roderigo MSv. *Usual spelling.*

281.3   de Meneses,]   1A; $\sim$ $\sim_\wedge$ MSv. *Comma precedes modifying phrase.*

281.5   Mohamed,]   1A; $\sim_\wedge$ MSv. *Comma separates appositives.*

281.7   Fernando]   1A; Ferdinand MSv. *The same correction is made at 295.22, 300.21.*

281.9   tower,]   1A; $\sim_\wedge$ MSv. *Second comma of a pair.*

281.11   leapt]   T; leap⟨t⟩ed MSv; leaped 1A. *Pierre M. Irving*
                emended Irving's "leapt."

281.13   tower,]   1A; ∼∧ MSv. *Comma follows introductory*
                phrase.

281.28   city,]   1A; ∼∧ MSv. *Comma precedes modifying*
                phrase.

281.30   Mohamed, . . . Baeza,]   1A; ∼∧ . . . ∼∧ MSv. *Commas*
                enclose appositive.

281.33   Calatrava,]   1A; ∼∧ MSv. *Second comma of a pair.*

281.33   Meneses, . . . Tellez,]   1A; ∼∧ . . . ∼∧ MSv. *Commas*
                necessary for clarity.

282.7   Toledo,]   1A; ∼∧ MSv. *Comma precedes relative clause.*

282.13   Agapida]   1A; Agapida MSv.

282.19   reward it]   1A; ∼ ⟨they⟩ ↑it↓ MSv. *Deletion and in-*
                terlineation are by Pierre M. Irving; a necessary cor-
                rection.

282.27   Seville,]   1A; ∼∧ MSv. *Second comma of a pair.*

282.32   Mohamed]   1A; Mohammed MSv. *See 282.16.*

282.34–35   Moors, . . . movements,]   1A; ∼∧ . . . ∼∧ MSv. *Com-*
                mas necessary for clarity.

283.1   sovereign]   1A; sovreign MSv. *The same correction is*
                made at 284.10, 285.9–10, 296.2; 295.25 sovereigns.

283.1   Seville,]   1A; ∼∧ MSv. *Second comma of a pair.*

283.4   Martos,]   1A; ∼∧ MSv. *Comma precedes relative*
                clause.

283.4–5   Yrenia, . . . Castro,]   1A; ∼∧ . . . ∼∧ MSv. *Commas en-*
                close appositive.

283.12   Alonzo,]   1A; Alfonso∧ MSv. *Second comma of a pair;*
                for the spelling see 283.6.

283.19   Ybañez,]   1A; ∼∧ *Comma separates appositives.*

283.37   sheik named]   T; ∼ ⟨of/ the⟩ ⟨lineage of Aben Alfange
                name of⟩ ↑∼↓ MSv; ∼, ∼ 1A. *The first cancellation*
                is by Pierre M. Irving, correcting Irving's oversight.

284.9   ☞ (Something is wanting here.)]T; ☞ (∼ ∼ ∼ ∼∧)
                MSv; ☞ (∼ ∼ .∼ ∼.)* 1A.

284.11   year's]   1A; years MSv. *Apostrophes are added to pos-*
                sessives at 287.40, 303.25, 303.27, 305.10, 315.29.

284.17   Jaen,]   1A; ∼∧ MSv. *Comma necessary for clarity.*

284.22   Martos,]   1A; ∼∧ MSv. *Second comma of a pair.*

284.26   Fernando,]   1A; ∼∧ *Second comma of a pair.*

284.29   cities,]   1A; ∼∧ MSv. *Second comma of a pair.*

284.30–31   By . . . her,]   T; ⟨By the advice of his sagacious and in-
                trepid/ mother therefore, and a⟩Accompanied by

⟨her,⟩ ↑his mother,↓ MSv; Accompanied by his mother, 1A. *The cancellations and substitutions in MSv are by Pierre M. Irving. Irving's text is restored here.*

284.37   cathedral,]   1A; Cathedral⋀ MSv. *Comma precedes subordinate clause.*

284.38   king,]   1A; ∼⋀ MSv. *Comma necessary for clarity.*

284.39   *Te Deums*]   1A; Te Deums MSv. *Usual practice; see 327.13 (manuscript copy lacking), 450.13–14. "Te deum laudamus" is emended to "Te Deum Laudamus" at 293.25; "deum" is emended to "Deum" at 328.6.*

285.5   Merlio]   1A; Menlio MSv. *Misspelling; Irving's "n" was perhaps intended as an "r."*

285.7   Benevente,]   1A; ∼⋀ MSv. *Comma necessary for clarity.*

285.16–17   having, . . . mother   the   queen   Berenguela,]   T; ∼⋀ . . . ∼ ⟨∼ ∼ ∼⟩, MSv; ∼, . . . mother, 1A. *Cancellation by Pierre M. Irving, probably to avoid repetition.*

285.22   now called himself]   T; ⟨now⟩ ∼ ∼ MSv; called himself 1A. *Cancellation is by Pierre M. Irving.*

285.23   seignorial]   1A; senorial MSv.

285.23   Christian]   1A; christian MSv. *The same emendation is made at 311.31, 318.23, 318.32, 319.15, 323.2, 325.18; also at 288.24, 289.36, 315.29, 318.5, 323.25 Christians. Other words emended to capitalized form in accordance with Irving's usual practice are 293.31 Catholic; 293.15 Incarnation; 292.20 Moorish; 327.31, 327.36–37 Sacrament; 293.36 Virgin.*

285.30   Castilian,]   1A; ∼⋀ MSv. *Second comma of a pair.*

285.35   country]   1A; countrey MSv.

285.39   Xerez]   1A; Xeres MSv. *Emendation reflects more frequent spelling and is also made at 286.15, 286.16, 297.34, 306.12, 327.19.*

285.39   and sheep]   1A; & sheep MSv. *The same emendation is made at 288.35, 305.26, 305.41, 311.2, 312.39, 313.29, 314.2, 314.5, 318.4, 318.10, 323.29, 325.16, 325.26.*

286.6   Mohamed,]   1A; ∼⋀ MSv. *Comma separates appositives.*

286.11   soldiers,]   1A; ∼⋀ MSv. *Comma necessary for clarity.*

286.12   gave them up]   T; ∼ them↑selves↓ ∼ MSv; ∼ themselves ∼ 1A. *Interlineation is by Pierre M. Irving.*

286.15   sea-bord]   T; sea/ bord MSv; seaboard 1A. *See "Pelayo" 192.41*

286.16   call;]   1A; ∼, MSv. *Emended punctuation eliminates*

	run-on construction. Semicolons are also substituted for commas for this purpose at 298.40, 300.20, 312.33, 313.35, 313.40, 313.43, 315.24, 319.18, 320.27, 321.40, 322.4, 323.15, 327.20.
286.17	Gazules] T; Azules MSv, 1A. *Emendation reflects usual spelling; see* 288.3, 312.24. "Ganzules" *is similarly emended at* 325.14.
286.20	distance,] 1A; ~∧ MSv. *Comma necessary for clarity.*
286.23	reconnoitre] 1A; recconnoitre MSv.
286.32	wherewith] 1A; w↑h↓erew⟨h⟩ith MSv. *The correction is by Pierre M. Irving.*
286.33	battalions] 1A; battallions MSv.
286.34	With] 1A; with MSv. *Words at the beginnings of sentences are also capitalized at* 298.9, 305.10, 309.29, 316.7, 320.4, 320.20, 323.14, 325.29.
286.37	on either flank] 1A; in ~ ~ MSv. *Not idiomatic.*
286.43	and look] 1A; an ~ MSv. *Error.*
287.3	Garci Perez] T; Garcia ~ MSv. *Emendation reflects usual spelling; see also* Emendations 287.44.
287.5	exhorted] 1A; ex↑h↓orted MSv. *The correction is by Pierre M. Irving.*
287.10	purpose,] 1A; ~, MSv. *Comma is by Pierre M. Irving and is the second of a pair.*
287.22	embrace,] 1A; ~∧ MSv. *Comma precedes subordinate clause.*
287.31	him,] 1A; ~∧ MSv. *Comma follows introductory construction.*
287.33	prince,] 1A; ~∧ MSv. *First comma of a pair.*
287.35	to join] T; ⟨to⟩ ~ MSv; join 1A. *The cancellation is by Pierre M. Irving.*
287.44	Garci Perez] T; Garci↑a↓ ~ MSv. Garcia ~ 1A. *The interlineation is by Pierre M. Irving.*
288.1	battle,] 1A; ~∧ MSv. *Second comma of a pair.*
288.8–9	not been pardoned by] 1A; not ↑been↓ pardoned/↑by↓ MSv. *The interlineations, correcting Irving's error, are by Pierre M. Irving.*
288.15–16	—"So . . . them!"—] T; ∧∧~ . . . ~!∧∧ MSv; —(∧~ . . . ~!∧)— 1A. *Dashes supplied to mark pauses and prevent ambiguity.*
288.15–16	them, Smash] T; ~ – smash MSv; ~! smash 1A. *Emended to conform to Spanish original,* 288.15.
288.20	slain,] 1A; ~∧ MSv. *Comma separates independent clauses.*

288.27   lances,]   1A; ~∧ MSv. *Comma separates independent clauses.*

288.34   overturning,]   1A; ~∧ MSv. *Comma precedes subordinate clause.*

288.38   nowhere]   1A; no where MSv.

288.39   Moors,]   1A; ~∧ MSv. *Second comma of a pair.*

289.9   Rodrigo,]   1A; ~∧ MSv. *Comma separates appositives.*

289.11   chronicle.]   1A; ~.⟨⟩ MSv.

289.25   sleep,]   1A; ~∧ MSv. *Comma precedes subordinate clause.*

289.27   Some, . . . place,]   1A; ~∧ . . . ~∧ MSv. *Comma enclosing modifying phrase are necessary for clarity.*

289.28   Muñoz,]   1A; ~∧ MSv. *First comma of a pair.*

289.29   together ladders of wood] T; ⟨together⟩ ladders ⟨of wood⟩ ↑together↓ MSv; ladders together 1A. *Emendations in MSv are by Pierre M. Irving.*

289.30   length,]   1A; ~∧ MSv. *Comma follows long introductory construction.*

289.35   battlements,]   1A; ~∧ MSv. *Comma is second of a pair.*

289.37   ladder,]   1A; ~∧ MSv. *Comma separates independent clauses.*

289.40   horse,]   1A; ~∧ MSv. *Comma separates independent clauses.*

290.1   Axarquia,]   1A; ~∧ MSv. *Second comma of a pair.*

290.5   one,]   1A; ~∧ MSv. *Comma necessary for clarity.*

290.10   Perez, . . . Martos,]   1A; ~∧ . . . ~∧ MSv. *Commas clarify.*

290.13   letter]   1A; letters MSv. *Error; see 290.14.*

290.20   letter,]   1A; ~∧ MSv. *Second comma of a pair.*

291.8   Xuarez] T; Xuares MSv. *Emendation reflects usual spelling; see 313.4, 313.38. "Suarez" is similarly emended at 318.28, 318.34, 319.28–29, 320.12.*

291.9   name,]   1A; ~∧ MSv. *Second comma of a pair.*

291.14   companions]   1A; ~∧ *Comma separates clauses.*

291.16   with him,]   1A; ~ ~∧ MSv. *Comma precedes modifying phrase.*

291.27   king, . . . sleeping,]   1A; ~∧ . . . ~∧ MSv. *Commas necessary for clarity.*

291.29   wroth]   1A; wrath MSv.

291.30   replied, "Señor] T; ~. "~ MSv; ~,–"~ 1A. *Inappropriate punctuation to introduce the quotation; the same emendation is made at 323.43.*

291.30   your majesty]   1A; Your ~ MSv. *The same emendation is made at 291.32, 314.1; also at 291.42 your Majesty.*

292.8   done,]   1A; ~∧ MSv. *Comma separates independent clauses.*

292.9   bridge,]   1A; ~∧ MSv. *Comma helps diminish confusion created by elliptical syntax.*

292.13   alarm,]   1A; ~∧ MSv. *Comma precedes modifying phrase.*

292.15   scouts,]   1A; ~∧ MSv. *Comma separates independent clauses.*

292.21   Valencia,]   1A; Valentia∧ MSv. *Comma necessary for clarity. Emended spelling reflects usual practice; the same emendation is made at 292.29, 292.32.*

292.21   Jayme]   T; James MSv, 1A. *See 308.6, 308.10.*

292.21   Aragon]   1A; Arragon MSv. *Emended spelling reflects usual spelling in the copy-text; the same emendation is made at 297.13, 308.6, 308.8.*

292.22   army,]   1A; ~∧ MSv. *Comma necessary for clarity.*

292.25   Hud, . . . objects,]   1A; ~∧ . . . ~∧ MSv. *Commas enclose modifying phrase.*

292.33–34   Arramin, . . . favorite,]   1A; ~∧ . . . ~∧ MSv. *Commas relieve awkwardness.*

292.35   time,]   1A; ~∧ MSv. *Comma precedes modifying phrase.*

292.42   Fernando,]   1A; ~∧ MSv. *Comma precedes relative clause.*

292.44–293.1   and . . . Andalusia.]   1A; (~ . . .~). MSv. *The parentheses are almost certainly by Pierre M. Irving, to mark a passage for possible deletion.*

293.2   army,]   1A; ~∧ MSv. *Second comma of a pair.*

293.10   famine,]   1A; ~∧ MSv. *Comma separates independent clauses.*

293.15   Paul,]   1A; ~∧ MSv. *Second comma of a pair.*

293.26   faith.*]   1A; ~.∧ MSv. *Irving neglected to include an asterisk corresponding to the one beginning a footnote at the bottom of the same page in MSv (293.43).*

293.26–27   pious king," says Agapida,]   T; ⟨pious⟩ king∧∧ ⟨says Agapida⟩, MSv; king, 1A. *The cancellations are by Pierre M. Irving.*

293.28–30   which . . . greatest]   T; ⟨which had been built with unparallelled/ splendor, in honor of the Arch imposter Mahomet,/ and was⟩ the greatest MSv; the greatest 1A. *The cancellations are by Pierre M. Irving.*

293.30   Spain,] 1A; ∼ₐ MSv. *Comma is the second of a pair.*
293.31–33   No pains . . . abominations."] T; ⟨No pains were
               spared, ₐ/ continues he, ₐto cleanse it from every
               trace/ or taint of its former abominations.ₐ⟩ MSv;
               [*omitted*] 1A. *The cancellation is by Pierre M. Irving.*
293.37   fervor] 1A; favor MSv. *Obvious lapse.*
294.2–4   and . . . that] T; and ⟨⟨Fray Antonio Agapida cites as/
               an instance of even handed justice on the/ part of
               this excellent King, that⟩⟩ MSv; and 1A. *The paren-*
               theses and the deletion are by Pierre M. Irving.
294.5   shoulders,] 1A; ∼ₐ MSv. *Second comma of a pair.*
294.6   triumph," continues the worthy Agapida, "when] T;
               ↑popular↓ triumph ∧∧⟨continues/ the worthy Aga-
               pida⟩∧∧ when MSv; popular triumph when 1A. *The*
               interlineation and cancellation are by Pierre M. Irving.
294.12   Frontier,] T; frontierₐ MSv; frontier, 1A. *Comma*
               necessary for clarity.
294.17–18   had been thronged] 1A; ↑had↓ been thronged MSv.
               The interlineation, by Pierre M. Irving, is a necessary
               correction.
294.22   Fernando, . . . Iago,] 1A; ∼ₐ . . . ∼ₐ MSv. *Commas*
               enclose modifying phrase.
294.24   infidels] T; ⟨∼⟩ ↑Moslems↓ MSv; Moslems 1A. *The*
               emendation in MSv is by Pierre M. Irving.
294.35   queen, however,] 1A; ∼ₐ ∼, MSv. *Emendation re-*
               flects Irving's usual practice.
*295.9–11   King Fernando . . . concurred] T; King Fernando,
               ⟨was always⟩ a mirror of/ obedience to his mother,
               ⟨excepting when she en-/ deavored to dissuade him
               from his wars with/ the Moors; he⟩ readily⟨, there-
               fore⟩ concurred MSv; King Fernando, a mirror of
               obedience to his mother, readily concurred 1A.
295.13   Juana,] 1A; ∼ₐ MSv. *Comma separates appositives.*
295.14   Pothier] 1A; ⟨Poictiers and a descendant of Pothier⟩
               ↑Pothier↓ MSv. *The interlineation, by Pierre M. Irv-*
               ing, fills a gap created by Irving's cancellation.
295.15   Pothier] 1A; Po⟨u⟩thier MSv. *Cancellation probably*
               by Pierre M. Irving.
295.19   subjects,] 1A; ∼ₐ MSv. *Second comma of a pair.*
*295.28–31   In the . . . . issuing] T; In the course of his progress,
               ↑hearing↓ while at Toledo/ ⟨arrived Don Alvar Perez,
               whom he had left as/ Adelantado or military gover-
               nor of the frontier⟩ he/ ⟨received intelligence⟩ of a

severe famine which pre-/-vailed at Cordova, ⟨The king thought readily to relieve/ the city by sending⟩ ↑he sent↓ a large supply of money ↑to that city,↓, and at/ the same time issu⟨ing⟩ed MSv; In the course of his progress, hearing while at Toledo of a severe famine which prevailed at Cordova, he sent a large supply of money to that city, and at the same time issued 1A.

295.39   Perez, . . . frontier,]   1A;   ~∧ . . . ~∧ MSv. *Commas necessary for clarity.*

296.25   Nasar,] 1A;   ~∧ MSv. *Second comma of a pair.*

296.26   years,]   1A;   ~∧ MSv. *Comma follows introductory phrase.*

296.30   territories,]   1A;   ~∧ MSv. *Comma precedes modifying phrase.*

296.33   everywhere]   1A;   every where MSv. *No authority in dictionaries.*

297.3   Granada]   1A;   ~, MSv. *Comma forms part of a cancelled passage and was inadvertently allowed to stand. Similar oversights occur as shown before or after the indicated words at 300.23 (; of); 303.5 (himself,); 309.8 (, some); 310.18 (– and saw); 310.31 (– a Moorish); 315.12 (, waited); 325.29 (city.).*

297.12   Moors,]   1A;   ~∧ MSv. *First comma of a pair, necessary for clarity.*

297.18   Moors,]   1A;   ~∧ MSv. *Second comma of a pair.*

297.20   from the pen]   1A;   ↑~ ~ ~↓ MSv. *The interlineated phrase is by Pierre M. Irving, restoring text cancelled by Irving through oversight.*

297.28   Martos]   1A;   Arcos ↑~↓ MSv. *Pierre M. Irving wrote Irving's usual spelling above the line. See 282.36.*

297.43   king, Aben]   1A;   King∧ Ben MSv. *"Aben" reflects usual practice; comma separates appositives.*

298.16–17   sight, . . . attempt]   T;   ~ – ⟨for it seemed hopeless/ to attempt⟩ MSv; sight,– 1A. *The dash and the cancellation are by Pierre M. Irving; comma precedes subordinate clause.*

298.17   force]   T;   ~ ↑seemed hopeless↓ MSv;   ~ seemed hopeless 1A. *Interlineation is by Pierre M. Irving. See previous entry.*

298.18   at thinking]   T;   ⟨~ ~⟩ ↑when they thought↓ MSv. *Cancellation and interlineation are by Pierre M. Irving.*

298.18–19   donzellas, exposed . . . warfare.]   T;   ~ – ⟨~ . . . ~.⟩

MSv; donzellas. 1A. *Cancellation and dash are by Pierre M. Irving.*

298.20 Machucha] T; Machuca MSv; Machacha 1A. *Usual spelling; see 288.17.*

298.33 death,] 1A; ~‸ MSv. *Comma separates independent clauses.*

298.39 fortress,] T; ~‸ MSv; ~; 1A. *Comma separates independent clauses.*

298.41 knights,] 1A; ~‸ MSv. *Comma necessary for clarity.*

299.4 otherwise called] T; ⟨~ ~⟩ ↑surnamed↓ MSv; surnamed 1A. *The cancellation and interlineation are by Pierre M. Irving.*

299.5-6 had . . . king, . . . found] T; ⟨had accomplished his mission to the king‸ whom/ he found⟩ ↑arrived in presence of the King↓ MSv; arrived in presence of the king‸ 1A. *Cancellation and interlineation are by Pierre M. Irving; comma following "king" clarifies.*

299.14 him,] 1A; ~‸ MSv. *Comma precedes subordinate clause.*

299.26 supply in person] T; ~ ⟨~ ~⟩ MSv; supply 1A. *The cancellation is by Pierre M. Irving, to avoid repetition of "person" in the sentence.*

299.30 regulate] 1A; regulate⟨d⟩ MSv. *The correction is by Pierre M. Irving.*

299.37 orders.] T; ~. ⟨*⟩ MSv; ~.‸ 1A.

299.38-39 * During . . . . p. 552.] T; [*rule*]/ ⟨* During this time there was an insurrection of/ a Moorish adventurer – See Notas para la Vida P 552⟩ MSv; [*omitted*] 1A. *See* Discussions of Adopted Readings 299.37.

300.1 Alonzo] T; Alfonso MSv, 1A. *Emended spelling reflects usual practice; see 284.26, 285.27. The same emendation is made to 302.11, 302.43; also at 302.14 Alonso.*

300.5 Hudiel,] 1A; ~‸ MSv. *Comma separates appositives.*

300.9 Alhamar,] 1A; ~‸ MSv. *Comma separates appositives.*

300.11 situated,] 1A; ~‸ MSv. *Comma follows introductory phrase.*

300.17 state,] 1A; ~‸ MSv. *Comma necessary for clarity.*

300.22 revenues;] T; ~‸ MSv; ~, 1A. *Cancelled passage immediately preceding indicates Irving's intention.*

300.29 Alfonso] 1A; Alonso MSv. *Emendation reflects usual spelling; see 300.15, 316.16. The same emendation is made at 304.20, 308.3; also at 326.6, 327.39 Alonzo.*

300.38 convent of las Huelgas] 1A; ↑convent of↓/ las Huelgas

	MSv. *The interlineation, by Pierre M. Irving, corrects an omission by Irving.*
*301.11	Lara.*] T; ~. ⟨*⟩† MSv; ~.* 1A.
301.14	Aben Alhamar] 1A; the ⟨King⟩/ ~ ~ MSv. *Irving neglected to cancel "the." He also neglected to include "be engaged." in a cancellation preceding 305.16 for; the two words were cancelled by Pierre M. Irving.*
301.14	Granada,] 1A; ~∧ MSv. *Second comma of a pair.*
301.24–25	son and heir] 1A; ~ an↑d↓ ~ MSv. *The "d," a necessary correction, is by Pierre M. Irving.*
301.31–32	"Thus," ... Agapida,] 1A; ∧~,∧ ... ~, MSv. *Commas are probably by Pierre M. Irving.*
301.37	truce,] 1A; ~∧ MSv. *Second comma of a pair.*
301.38	Fernando] 1A; Fer⟨di⟩nando MSv. *Deletion is probably by Pierre M. Irving.*
302.3	Fernando,] 1A; ~∧ MSv. *Comma clarifies.*
302.13	force,] 1A; ~∧ MSv. *Comma clarifies.*
302.24	Castro,] 1A; ~∧ MSv. *Comma separates appositives.*
302.26	Aben ... Granada,] 1A; ⟨the King of⟩/ ⟨Granada⟩ Aben Alhamar, the King of Granada, MSv. *The first cancellation and the commas are by Pierre M. Irving.*
302.29	place,] 1A; ~∧ MSv. *First comma of a pair.*
302.37	came, . . . chronicles,] MSv; ~, . . . chroniclers, 1A. *Commas are probably by Pierre M. Irving.*
302.41	harassing] 1A; harrassing MSv. *Similar emendations to "harassed" are made at 304.28, 314.25.*
302.42–43	Alhamar, . . . vega,] T; ~∧ . . . ~∧ MSv; ~, . . . Vega, 1A. *Commas enclose modifying phrase.*
303.1	king, however,] 1A; ~, ~; MSv. *Irving probably neglected to revise the semicolon after changing his intention for continuing the sentence.*
303.2	valor into] 1A; valor to MSv. *Irving probably lost track of what he had written as he began a new page in MSv.*
303.4–5	place, contenting himself] T; place, ↑he↓ content⟨ing⟩ ↑ed↓ himself MSv; place, he contented himself 1A. *The comma following "place" is by Pierre M. Irving and is necessary after the introductory clause. The interlineated "he" and the alteration of Irving's "contented" are also by Pierre M. Irving.*
303.6	effected,] 1A; ~∧ MSv. *Second comma of a pair.*
303.10	other,] 1A; ~∧ MSv. *Comma marks pause between independent clauses.*

303.14   sides,] 1A; $\sim_\wedge$ MSv. *Comma precedes subordinate clause.*

303.21   support,] 1A; $\sim_\wedge$ MSv. *Second comma of a pair.*

303.27   society,] 1A; $\sim_\wedge$ MSv. *Comma necessary for clarity.*

303.38   near Ciudad Real,] 1A; nr $\sim$ $\sim_\wedge$ MSv. *Comma clarifies.*

304.1   campaigns,] 1A; $\sim_\wedge$ MSv. *Comma necessary for clarity.*

304.5   Granada,] 1A; $\sim_\wedge$ MSv. *Comma precedes modifying phrase.*

304.7   collect,] 1A; $\sim_\wedge$ MSv. *Comma separates independent clauses.*

304.14   gained,] 1A; $\sim_\wedge$ MSv. *Comma follows introductory clause.*

304.20   tranquilization] T; tranquil↑l↓ization MSv; tranquil-lization 1A. *The spelling change is by Pierre M. Irving.*

304.31   holds] 1A; $\sim_\wedge$ MSv. *Pause clearly intended between independent clauses.*

304.33   king,] 1A; $\sim_\wedge$ MSv. *Second comma of a pair.*

304.36   Omar,] 1A; $\sim_\wedge$ MSv. *Comma necessary for clarity.*

305.3   saw] 1A; $\sim$ ⟨saw⟩ MSv. *The cancellation is by Pierre M. Irving.*

305.14   Aben] 1A; Abu MSv. *Usual spelling.*

305.16   revenues;] 1A; $\sim_\wedge$ MSv. *Irving neglected to punctuate after making a deletion which necessitated it.*

305.20   king,] 1A; $\sim_\wedge$ MSv. *Comma necessary for clarity.*

305.22   mosque,] 1A; $\sim_\wedge$ MSv. *Comma necessary for clarity.*

305.26   place,] 1A; MSv. *Irving neglected to add comma after cancelling a passage immediately following, which rendered it necessary.*

305.29   Alhamar,] 1A; $\sim_\wedge$ MSv. *Comma follows introductory phrase.*

305.40–41   31st December . . . 26th February.] 1A; 31 Dec'r . . . 26 Feb. MSv. *Emendation reflects Irving's occasional practice in contemporary works, as* Granada *(1850),* 444.11; *however, see* Emendations 276.19.

306.9   fear:] 1A; $\sim$, MSv. *Emendation eliminates run-on construction.*

306.10   Axataf,] 1A; ↑$\sim_\wedge$↓ MSv. *Comma separates appositives.*

306.12   Xerez,] 1A; Xeres$_\wedge$ MSv. *Comma follows long introductory construction.*

307.3   genial] 1A; geneal MSv.

307.5   highway] 1A; high way MSv. *No authority in dictionaries.*

307.11–12   in deep affliction] 1A; ↑in↓ deep affliction MSv. *The interlineation, a necessary correction, is by Pierre M. Irving.*

307.24   Berenguela,] 1A; ∼∧ MSv. *First comma of a pair.*

307.26   told,] 1A; ∼∧ MSv. *Second comma of a pair.*

307.35   cavaliers,] 1A; ∼∧ MSv. *Comma necessary for clarity.*

307.37   Rodrigo, the great adviser] 1A; ∼. The ∼ ∼ MSv. *Emended reading correlates appositives and eliminates sentence fragment.*

308.1   ¶These] 1A; ∧∼ MSv. *A one-inch space at the bottom of the preceding page in MSv indicates Irving's intention to begin a new paragraph.*

308.6   Aragon,] 1A; ∼∧ MSv. *First comma of a pair.*

308.10   daughter,] 1A; ∼∧ MSv. *Comma separates appositives.*

308.18   saintly] 1A; sainlty MSv.

308.23   Burgos,] 1A; ∼∧ MSv. *Comma separates appositives.*

308.24   Boniface, by name] 1A; ∼./ ∼ ∼ MSv. *Irving perhaps decided to continue his sentence after concluding it.*

308.35   Seville,] 1A; ∼∧ MSv. *Comma follows long introductory clause.*

308.39   king,] 1A; ∼∧ MSv. *Comma precedes modifying construction.*

*309.33   Admiral] T; admiral MSn, 1A. *The same emendation is made at 327.27.*

309.33   in no ways] T; ∼ ∼ way⟨s⟩ MSn; ∼ ∼ way 1A. *Cancellation is by Pierre M. Irving.*

309.34   prizes,] 1A; ∼∧ MSn. *Comma necessary for clarity.*

310.1–2   Aznal Farache] 1A; ∼/ farache MSn. *The indicated variant spellings of the name are similarly emended at 310.14 Asnal Farache, 326.1 Asnal farache.*

310.6   reinforced,] 1A; ∼∧ MSn. *Irving neglected to replace comma at close of cancelled extension of introductory phrase.*

310.10   hand,] 1A; ∼∧ MSn. *Comma clarifies.*

310.30   after,] 1A; ∼∧ MSn. *Comma necessary for clarity.*

310.39   horse, . . . example,] 1A; ∼∧ . . . ∼∧ MSn. *Commas necessary for clarity.*

310.40   latter,] 1A; ∼∧ MSn. *First comma of a pair.*

311.1   back,] 1A; ∼∧ MSn. *Comma necessary for clarity.*

311.4   galloped] 1A; gallopped MSn. *The same correction is made at 316.32, 317.2.*

311.8   Correa, . . . St. Iago,] T; ~ₐ . . . Stₐ ~ₐ MSn;
             ~, . . . Santiago, 1A. *Commas enclose appositive.*
311.14   words,] T; ~. MSn; ~: 1A. *MSn clearly inappropri-*
             ate; only a slight pause seems intended.
311.32   St. Iago,] T; Sᵗ Iagoₐ MSn; Santiago, 1A. *Comma sep-*
             arates appositives.
312.7   also,] 1A; ~ₐ MSn. *Comma necessary for clarity.*
312.32   Señor] 1A; Senior MSn. *The same emendation is made*
             at 442.13, 442.25.
312.34   duello] T; duelo MSn; *duello* 1A.
312.35   odds."] 1A; ~.ₐ MSn: *Quotation marks are also sup-*
             plied in order to complete pairs at 313.34, 313.36,
             313.42.
312.36   Señor,] 1A; Se⟨g⟩ñorₐ MSn. *The cancellation and the*
             tilde are by Pierre M. Irving.
313.5   let] T; ⟨~⟩ ↑leave↓ MSn; leave 1A. *The cancellation*
             and interlineation are by Pierre M. Irving.
313.11   road,] 1A; ~ₐ MSn. *Comma necessary for clarity.*
313.11   on each side] 1A; in ~ ~ MSn. *Unidiomatic.*
313.12   separate] 1A; seperate MSn.
*313.12   from him.] 1A; ~ ~./ ↑⟨and deliberately laced/ on
             his capellina, he/ ⟨couched⟩ grasped his/ spear and
             again set/ forward, with his/ squire close after him./
             "What madness is this"/ said the King "does he/
             think to ⟨set⟩ cope with/ the whole seven." We/ shall
             see replied Don/ Lorenzo/ When ⟨the Garci⟩ Garci/
             Perez arrived ⟨near⟩ ↑opposite↓ the/ Moors ⟨he⟩ MSn.
313.16   Garci Perez] 1A; ⟨~ ~⟩ ↑he↓ MSn. *Deletion and in-*
             terlineation are by Pierre M. Irving.
313.31   copia?] T; copia. MSn; capa? 1A. *Question marks are*
             substituted for indicated punctuation at 313.34 dash,
             323.12 comma, 323.12 period.
313.36   alluding] 1A; allud⟨ed⟩ing MSn. *The emendation of*
             "alluded," a correction of Irving's oversight, is by
             Pierre M. Irving.
313.39   king: "Behold! . . . how] 1A; king. "~! . . . "how MSn.
             Period inappropriate; quotation mark preceding "how"
             unnecessary.
313.42   Garci] 1A; Garci⟨a⟩ MSn. *Cancellation is by Pierre*
             M. Irving.
313.43   them; they] T; ~, ⟨they⟩ ↑and↓ MSn; them, and 1A.
             Deletion and interlineation are by Pierre M. Irving,
             made to avoid run-on sentence.

313.43	off,] 1A; ~∧ MSn. *Comma precedes modifying phrase.*
314.1	majesty,] 1A; ~∧" MSn. *Comma follows personal address; see 313.39. Quotation mark unnecessary; another needless quotation mark is deleted at 314.2 after "him."*
314.6	up, and] 1A; ~. ~ MSn. *Comma clearly appropriate.*
314.8	herberos,] T; ⟨herberos⟩ ↑foragers↓∧ MSn; foragers, 1A. *Comma necessary for clarity. Cancellation and substitution are by Pierre M. Irving, for consistency with 314.6–7.*
314.13	withal] 1A; withal⟨l⟩ MSn. *Cancellation in pencil, probably by Pierre M. Irving.*
314.21	discovered.] 1A; ~./ ⟨Cap – 48./ Medina del Campo 1567/ written by Rodrigo Archbp of Toledo.⟩ MSn. *Irving's reference note is cancelled by Pierre M. Irving.*
315.12	Bonifaz] 1A; Boniface MSn. *Usual spelling; see 315.35.*
317.43	part 4.] T; P 4. MSn; p. 4. 1A. *Emendation dispels ambiguity and brings note into conformity with Putnam style; see 293.43.*
316.15	making . . . the] 1A; ⟨making/ foraging the⟩ ↑making cavalgadas about the↓ MSn. *The final "the" is by Pierre M. Irving, a necessary restoration.*
316.22	brethren] 1A; breth⟨e⟩ren MSn. *Cancellation is by Pierre M. Irving and is also made by him at 317.19, 328.1.*
316.23	foraging] 1A; for⟨r⟩aging MSn. *Correction is by Pierre M. Irving.*
316.27	camp,] 1A; ~∧ MSn. *Comma necessary for clarity.*
316.33–34	The Moors . . . kine,] 1A; ↑~↓ ~ . . . ~∧ MSv. *Interlineation is by Pierre M. Irving, restoring a word mistakenly cancelled by Irving.*
317.16	burly] 1A; burley MSv.
317.18	cavaliers, . . . twenty,] 1A; ~∧ . . . ~∧ MSv. *Commas necessary for clarity.*
317.23	friars,] 1A; ~∧ MSv. *Comma is second of a pair.*
317.27	Cordova,] 1A; ~∧ MSv. *Second comma of a pair.*
317.29	foot,] 1A; ~∧ MSv. *Comma necessary for clarity.*
317.35	bishops,] 1A; Bishops∧ MSv. *Comma is first of a pair.*
318.5	Prior] 1A; ⟨F⟩Pri⟨a⟩or MSv. *The correction of "Friar" to "Prior" is by Pierre M. Irving.*
318.11	suburb,] 1A; ~∧ MSv. *Comma follows long subordinate construction.*

318.14	afterwards,] 1A; ~ᴀ MSv. *Second comma of a pair.*
*318.17	Stout Prior] T; stout Prior MSv; stout prior 1A.
318.35	Tello Alonzo] T; Alfonso Tello MSv; Alfonzo Tello 1A. *Emendation reflects usual spelling; see 281.33, 283.6. At 319.9 "Alonzo Tello" is emended to "Tello Alonzo."*
319.6	Moors,] 1A; ~ᴀ MSv. *First comma of a pair.*
319.27	The defence] 1A; This ~ MSv. *Irving's oversight.*
320.5	orders,] 1A; ~ᴀ MSv. *Second comma of a pair.*
320.14	round,] 1A; ~ᴀ MSv. *Comma necessary for clarity.*
320.39	The city] 1A; ↑The↓ city MSv. *The interlineation is by Pierre M. Irving.*
321.21	towards] 1A; ~ -/ MSv. *Probably an unintentional mark.*
321.24	sprung] 1A; sprang MSv.
321.25	anchor, spread] 1A; ~ᴀ ⟨and⟩ ~ MSv. *Deletion necessitates comma.*
321.30	St. Iago, . . . Correa,] T; Sᵗ Iagoᴀ . . . ~ᴀ MSv; Santiago, . . . ~, 1A. *Commas enclose appositive.*
322.31	Moors,] 1A; ~ᴀ MSv. *First comma of a pair.*
322.33	Christians, their] 1A; ~ᴀ ~, MSv. *Misplaced.*
323.31	Moors, . . . pursuers,] 1A; ~ᴀ . . . ~ᴀ MSv. *Commas enclose subordinate expression.*
323.39	scarcely] 1A; scarcly MSv.
323.43	eyeing] 1A; eying MSv.
324.16	amity,] 1A; ~ᴀ MSv. *Comma separates independent clauses.*
324.30	stealth,] 1A; ~ᴀ MSv. *Comma clarifies.*
324.36	proposals,] 1A; ~ᴀ MSv. *Comma follows introductory construction.*
324.37	towers,] 1A; ~ᴀ MSv. *Comma separates independent clauses.*
325.8	bringing] 1A; bring↑ing↓ MSv. *Correction is by Pierre M. Irving.*
325.19	a detachment] 1A; the ~ MSv. *Emendation suits the context.*
325.20	shore,] 1A; ~ᴀ MSv. *Comma separates independent clauses.*
325.22	messenger,] 1A; ~ᴀ MSv. *Second comma of a pair.*
325.26	many slain] 1A; ⟨some/ slain⟩ ↑~ ~↓ MSv. *The interlineated "slain" is by Pierre M. Irving, correcting Irving's oversight.*
325.35	Axataf] T; Ajataph ↑~↓ MSv; Ajataf 1A. *Alternative spelling, which reflects Irving's usual practice, is*

	written above the line by Pierre M. Irving here and at 326.3. *The same emendation is made at* 325.30, 326.3
326.8	desired] 1A; disired MSv.
327.13	*Laudamus.*] T; ~. * 1A; [*MSv wanting*]. *Asterisk omitted because no footnote was printed which corresponds to it.*
327.31	to be administered] 1A; to/ ⟨be brought⟩ administered MSv. *The "be" was cancelled through oversight.*
327.32	clergy,] 1A; ~∧ MSv. *Comma precedes relative clause.*
327.33	Philip, Archibishop] 1A; ~∧ ~ MSv. *Comma separates appositives.*
*327.37	ornaments and insignia] T; ↑ornaments↓ insignia MSva; ornaments 1A.
328.14	heard,] 1A; ~∧ MSva. *Comma separates independent clauses.*

MY UNCLE

330.2	[MY UNCLE]] T; [*omitted*] MSy.
330.3	¶My uncle] T; ⟨You nothing of moment. His character had/ no striking trait, but many pleasant ones/ that won upon his friends. He was a kind,/ easy, indolent ⟨sort⟩ ↑fanciful being↓, humourous at times, but/ his humour always tinged with a vein of/ melancholy. He often made you laugh and/ yet there was a sadness that came over you/ while you laughed. He had his whims and/ peculiarities, but they were harmless, and/ we all loved him ⟨heartily⟩ heartily.⟩/ ¶ ~ ~ MSy.
330.5	something] T; ⟨a little⟩ ↑~↓ MSy.
330.9	for a livelihood] T; ⟨and⟩ ~ ~ ~ MSy.
330.14	dilettante] T; dilletante MSy.
330.16	gentlemanlike] T; gentleman like MSy. *MSy suggests Irving may have intended to write the word as emended. At any rate, "like" as a combining form not ordinarily written separately in contemporary usage.*
330.19	dined with] T; ~ ⟨at his⟩ ~ MSy.
330.23	and] T; & MSy. *The same emendation is made at* 330.30, 330.39, 332.12, 332.36.
330.24	detail; they] T; ~,/ ~ MSy. *Irving probably re-shaped sentence in his mind before beginning a new line, then neglected to revise punctuation and eliminate run-on construction.*
330.26	His vanity] T; ⟨His buoyancy was⟩ ~ ~ MSy.

330.28   commonly]   T; ⟨commo⟩/ ∼ MSy. *The indicated false
              starts immediately rewritten occur at the following
              points in MSy:* 330.27 ⟨Tho⟩, 331.41 ⟨meetings⟩, 332.20
              ⟨fairies⟩, 332.30 ⟨Aft⟩.

330.28   sentiment. It]   T; ∼ –. ⟨He never got over/ got⟩ ∼ MSy.
              *Irving's dash apparently inadvertent, made during a
              pause for thought.*

330.29   was so]   T; ⟨mingled so⟩ ∼ ∼ MSy.

330.33   banking house]   T; Banking ∼ MSy. *Other words not
              ordinarily capitalized by Irving are emended to lower-
              case at the following points:* 331.26 your, 331.32 story,
              331.36 post, 332.15 great.

330.35   town. My]   T; ∼, ∼ MSy. *Irving neglected to revise
              punctuation after deciding to begin new sentence.*

330.40   straiten]   T; straighten MSy. *Misspelled for the sense
              used.*

330.41   gratuities]   T; ⟨presents⟩ ↑∼↓ MSy.

330.42   lived on]   T; ⟨we⟩ ∼ ∼ MSy.

331.1   poverty, while]   T; ∼, ⟨without an idea how it was to
              be/ avoided. When he could no longer afford to go to/
              He⟩ ∼ MSy.

331.4   o'clock]   T; oclock MSy. *Irving's spelling not in con-
              temporary use.*

331.6   crumbling into morsels]   T; ∼ ⟨with⟩ ↑∼↓ ∼ MSy.

331.9   portfolios]   T; portfolio's MSy. *Not a possessive.*

331.9   musical instruments]   T; ⟨splendid⟩/ ∼ ∼ MSy.

331.10   poetry. His very dress betrayed]   T; ∼⟨,⟩. ⟨He⟩ His
              very/ dress, ⟨though he⟩ betrayed MSy. *Irving ne-
              glected to delete comma following "dress."*

331.11   in all]   T; ∼ ⟨his⟩ ∼ MSy.

331.13   he . . . cameo]   T; ⟨a rich cameo a brilliant ring sparkled⟩
              ↑∼ . . . ∼↓ MSy.

331.17   uncle's]   T; uncles MSy. *Apostrophes are added to pos-
              sessives at the following additional points:* 332.1, 333.1.

331.20   commonplace]   T; common placed MSy. *Irving's spell-
              ing not in contemporary use.*

331.25   Brother," said he]   T; ∼ˇ" ∼ ∼ MSy. *Comma separates
              interrupted quotation from commentary.*

331.27   until fortune]   T; unti⟨f⟩l ∼ MSy.

331.30   books, which]   T; ∼ˇ/ ∼ MSy. *Comma necessary for
              clarity.*

331.33   recollect]   T; reccollect MSy.

331.35   sports. When]   T; sports⟨,⟩. ⟨make our/ playthings, and

	tell us stories about/ fairies and giants. I reccollect w)When MSy.
331.36	we scrambled] T; ⟨and⟩ ~ ~ MSy.
331.39	Uncle?" said he, and] T; Uncle,∧ said he?"/ and MSy. *Question mark and quotation mark misplaced.*
331.44	sensitiveness . . . spirit] T; ⟨tender sensitive⟩/ sensitive-ness of of ⟨saddened heart⟩ ↑proud yet delicate spirit↓ MSy.
332.4–5	books; and] T; ~; ⟨in⟩ ~ MSy.
332.6	Such] T; ⟨Travellers⟩/ ~ MSy.
332.10	or as] T; ~ ⟨writing⟩ ~ MSy.
332.11	though he] T; ~ ⟨my uncle⟩ ↑~↓ MSy.
332.12–13	and handled] T; ⟨his⟩ ~ ~ MSy.
332.20	Hall] T; ⟨great⟩ ~ MSy.
332.21	glided] T; ⟨danced⟩ ↑~↓ MSy.
332.22	great kitchen] T; ⟨kitchen⟩ ~ ~ MSy.
332.27	exclaim, "Ah] T; ~. "~ MSy. *Irving clearly did not intend a full stop.*
332.27	let them] T; ⟨"⟩~ ~ MSy.
332.28	possible. They'll] T; ~∧/ ~ MSy. *A period is also supplied at the end of a sentence at 4.27.*
332.30	literary inclinations] T; ~ ⟨la⟩ ~ MSy.
332.34	It is said] T; ⟨He disliked/ to be interrupted at his avocations; grew a little/ impatient of noise, and testy if intruded/ upon; and though a gallant old bachelor⟩/ ~ ~ ~ MSy.
332.43	set up] T; ⟨opened/ took a⟩ ~ ~ MSy.
332.44	lounged at] T; ⟨resorted to⟩ ~ ~ MSy.
333.1	bookshops, and] T; ⟨exhibitions;⟩ bookshops; ⟨was a member of/ the royal institutions, and what is more,/ attended all the courses of lectures. He⟩/ and MSy.
333.3	authors.] T; ~⟨,⟩. MSy.
333.4	musical amateur] T; ⟨dille⟩/ ~ ~ MSy.
333.6	music; and] T; ~; ⟨his house was⟩ ~ MSy.
333.11	¶Not long] T; ¶⟨He was in a fair way of⟩/ ¶~ ~ MSy.
333.11	recommended] T; reccommended MSy.

[SIR DAVID WILKIE IN SPAIN]

333.17	[SIR . . . SPAIN]] T; [*omitted*] MSy.
333.18	¶The inconveniences] T; ∧~ ~ MSy.
333.19	its roads] T; ⟨the⟩ ↑its↓ roads ⟨in this country⟩ MSy.
333.19	a country] T; ⟨the⟩ ~ ~ MSy.
333.20	visited or known] T; ⟨known/ or⟩ ~ ~ ~ MSy.

333.21   seldom]   T; ⟨sed⟩ ∼ MSy. *False starts immediately*
               rewritten occur at the following additional points in
               MSy: 333.21 ⟨Pyr⟩, 333.24 ⟨visited Se⟩, 334.10 ⟨urban⟩.
333.22   made a tour of]   T; ⟨visited⟩ ↑∼ ∼ ∼ ∼↓ MSy.
333.25–27   and . . . . engravings]   T; ↑and is one of the very few
               painters of the present↓ ⟨and is known/ throughout
               Europe by the presents that have been⟩ ↑day who
               appear to have inherited the genius of the old mas-
               ters.↓/ ⟨made of his works by the King of England
               to⟩ ↑He is known throughout Europe by the ⟨presents
               that have been⟩↓/ ⟨other sovreigns and by the admir-
               able⟩ engra / -vings MSy.
333.27–28   his works.]   T; ↑∼ ∼↓ ⟨these⟩. MSy.
333.28   excels]   T; excells MSy. *Obsolescent spelling.*
333.29   His works]   T; ⟨The natur/ and⟩ ∼ ∼ MSy.
333.32   more free in style,]   T; ↑∼ ∼ ⟨from⟩ ∼ ∼,↓ MSy.
333.33   scope]   T; ⟨range⟩ ∼ MSy.
333.35   Italy, France and Germany,]   T; ∼∧ ∼/ ∼ ∼, MSy.
               Emended punctuation reflects Irving's usual practice
               in series of three.
333.36   buried]   T; ⟨lost⟩ ∼ MSy.
334.2   Velasquez]   T; ⟨Of Murillo in particular he observed
               that/ much as he is admired abroad, it is necessary/
               to visit Spain to know the variety and⟩/ ∼ MSy. *See*
               334.3–6.
334.3   Mr. Wilkie]   T; Mr∧ W MSy. *Emendation to full name*
               reflects Irving's invariable usage elsewhere in MSy.
               Periods are added following "Mr" at 334.14, 334.21,
               334.30, 334.38.
334.5   and when]   T; & ∼ MSy. *The same emendation is made*
               at 334.36.
334.9–10   It is but]   T; It/ but MSy. *Obvious oversight at end of*
               line.
334.11   whose attention]   T; ∼ ⟨[ink smear]le to kind attention
               to the/ strangers of taste, who⟩ attentions MSy. *Plural*
               "attentions" fails to agree with the repeated singular
               "has been" later in sentence.
334.13   mentioned]   T; ⟨noticed⟩ ↑∼↓ MSy.
*334.13   visitors.]   T; ∼. # # MSy.
334.18   such as]   T; ⟨San⟩ ∼ ∼ MSy.
334.18   St. Thomas]   T; S^t ∼ MSy.
334.22   a scene in]   T; ⟨the⟩ ↑a scene↓ / ⟨interior of⟩ ↑in↓ MSy.
334.24   To these]   T; to ∼ MSy. *New sentence begins at this*
               point.

334.26	In these] T; ⟨Mr Wilkies style of painting great/ merit lies in his fidelity to nature, and/ the truth with which he depicts scenes from/ real life.⟩ ~ ~ MSy.
334.27	painters,] T; ~∧/ MSy. *Irving neglected to punctuate at end of line.*
334.29	The King of England, who] T; ⟨His/ paintings has Spanish pain Since his return/ to England his observations on the Spanish school/ and the exhibition of his paintings have produced/ a strong sensation, and have turned the/ attention of English amateurs to Spain.⟩ The/ King of England, ⟨who has a high opinion for/ the talents of Wilkie, and⟩ who MSy.
334.30	Mr. Wilkie] T; ⟨the artist⟩ ↑Mr∧ Wilkie↓ MSy.
334.32	with him] T; ~ ⟨Wilkie⟩ ↑~↓ MSy.
334.36	style of] T; ⟨paintings of⟩ ~ ~ MSy.
334.36	Velasquez] T; Velasques MSy. *See* 334.2, 334.29.
334.37	who are] T; ⟨of whose works the/ King possesses several excellent specimens and/ for whose⟩ ~ ~ MSy.
334.38	¶As] T; ⟨Wilkie is the first great English painter that⟩/ ¶ ~ MSy.
334.38	English] T; english MSy.
334.38–39	who . . . it is] T; ⟨has visited this country, and⟩ ↑who . . . it↓ ⟨It⟩ is MSy.
334.39–40	liberal spirit] T; ~ ⟨and⟩ ~ MSy.
334.40	is disposed] T; ⟨has dis⟩ ~ ~ MSy.
334.42	paintings;] T; ~∧/ MSy. *Punctuation supplied to continue pattern established by preceding item in series of three.*
334.43	made,] T; ~∧/ MSy. *End-of-line comma marks slight pause following measured series of three phrases.*

THE VILLAGE CURATE

335.2	THE VILLAGE CURATE] T; THE VILLAGE CURATE MSw.
335.3–4	hamlets;] T; ~, MSw. *Emendation eliminates run-on construction.*
335.4	are without] T; ~ ⟨in⟩ ~ MSw.
335.5	often at] T; ⟨at⟩ ↑~ ~↓ MSw.
335.5	dwellings.] T; ~⟨,⟩. MSw.
335.7	huts . . . and rushes] T; ⟨cabins⟩ ↑huts↓, ⟨built of branches, and⟩/ of straw & rushes MSw.
335.8	men are] T; ~ ⟨pat⟩ ~ MSw.
335.9	musket and] T; ~ & MSw. *The ampersand is also*

emended to "and" at 335.7, 335.14, 336.35, 336.41, 337.19, 337.23, 337.24.

335.10 follow an] T; ~ ⟨and⟩ ↑~↓ MSw. *Misspellings immediately corrected or false starts immediately rewritten occur at the following additional points:* 335.14 ⟨w⟩—for "whither," 335.25 ⟨h⟩—for "his," 335.28 ⟨loiter⟩, 336.1 ⟨meana⟩, 336.12 ⟨ri⟩, 336.17 ⟨the⟩.

335.14 courage,] T; ~∧/ MSw. *End-of-line commas omitted in MSw are supplied after the indicated words at the following additional points:* 3.15 curate, 8.17 thee.

335.16 at some] T; ~ ⟨no great⟩ ~ MSw.

335.18–19 condemned . . . murder] T; ⟨confined a galley slave at Ceuta⟩ ↑~ . . . ~↓ MSw.

335.22 Spain,] T; ~∧ MSw. *Comma marks pause between independent clauses.*

335.23 safe.] T; ~∧ MSw. *Periods are supplied at the ends of sentences at the following additional points:* 336.33, 337.12, 337.24.

335.23 a short] T; ⟨he a⟩ ~ ~ MSw.

335.25 woollen] T; wollen MSw.

335.26–27 and he] T; ⟨made more⟩ ~ ~ MSw.

335.30 remained there] T; ⟨when there⟩ re-/ mained there MSw.

335.33 steward] T; Steward MSw. *Emendation reflects conventions of capitalization ordinarily followed in MSw. Initial capitals are also emended to lower-case at* 335.34 seventeen, 336.22 scoundrel; *see also* Emendations 336.9.

335.33 where] T; ⟨of which⟩ ~ MSw.

335.35–36 in . . . towards] T; ⟨towards⟩/ ~ . . . ~ MSw.

335.37 to plead] T; ~ ⟨win⟩ ~ MSw.

335.37–38 young girl] T; ⟨solitary situation of the⟩ ~ ~ MSw.

335.39 violent] T; ⟨fierce⟩ ~ MSw.

335.39 counsel] T; council MSw. *The same emendation is made at* 336.9 (counsels), 336.19.

335.42 discharge] T; ⟨performance⟩/ ~ MSw.

335.42 office.] T; ~– MSw. *Irving's dash is a slurred period.*

336.2 integrity, my child,"] T; ~," ~ ~∧∧ MSw. *Punctuation misplaced.*

336.3 nor regard] T; ⟨an⟩/ ~ ~ MSw.

336.4 threats. Thy] T; ~. ⟨" The⟩ ~ MSw.

336.5 thou mayst] T; ~ ⟨hast nothing⟩ ~ MSw.

336.6 young . . . advice,] T; young/ ⟨girl departed but in a

few days returned/ again. "Ah,⟨"⟩ my father," said
she, "it is all/ in vain; I have endeavoured in every
way to/ discourage him, but he gives me no rest,/
and defe promised to was strengthened/ by his council
and⟩ ↑girl↓ promised to be guided/ by ⟨it⟩ his ⟨coun-
cil⟩ ↑advice↓, MSw.

336.9	curate] T; Curate MSw. *Emendation reflects Irving's usual practice in MSw. The same emendation is made at 336.11, 336.32.*
336.9	but she] T; ~ ⟨her⟩ ~ MSw.
336.14	mildly, however,] T; ~∧ ~, MSw. *Emendation reflects Irving's usual practice of enclosing "however" within two commas or none; see 336.7, 337.3.*
336.14	thee!"] T; ~!∧ MSw. *Double quotation marks are supplied to complete pairs at 336.34 after "should," 336.35 before "I."*
336.15	Thy tears] T; thy ~ MSw. *Beginning of sentence.*
336.16	recollect] T; ⟨Jesus/ the shepher⟩ reccollect MSw.
336.16–17	brings . . . lamb] T; ⟨bears the lost⟩ ↑brings back the wandering↓ lamb MSw.
336.17	fold."] T; ~." ' MSw.
336.18	blushing] T; ⟨"tis not⟩ ~ MSw.
336.18–19	good counsel] T; ⟨council⟩ ~ council MSw.
336.22	'Well,'] T; ∧~,∧ MSw. *A pair of single quotation marks is also supplied at 336.22–25.*
336.22	thy] T; th⟨e⟩y MSw.
336.22	is at] T; ⟨has⟩ ~/~ MSw.
336.25	go,' said he,] T; ~∧∧ ~ ~, MSw.
336.26–27	'this . . . it.'] T; ∧~ . . . ~." MSw.
336.27	he left me] T; ⟨he threw his gun on his shoulder and⟩ ~/ ~ ~ MSw.
336.29	the frightful things] T; ⟨what he is capable of, and⟩ ~ ~ ~ MSw.
336.29	him. What] T; ~; What MSw. *Irving apparently neglected to revise punctuation after deciding to begin new sentence.*
336.31	head?"] T; ~." ⟨With these words she burst/ forth again into a flood of tears —⟩ MSw.
336.32	all?" said] T; ~," ~ MSw. *Context indicates question mark.*
336.32	curate. "Then] T; Curate, ⟨with/ an intrepid air.⟩ 'then MSw. *Spacing in MSw indicates "then" is to begin new sentence.*

336.32   God] T; god MSw.

336.33   Be not alarmed] T; ⟨I feared for thee my child; for my-
self/ be not alarmed.⟩ ~ ~ ~ MSw.

336.33   The threats] T; ⟨I feared⟩ ~ ~ MSw.

336.35   the curate] T; ~ ⟨little⟩ ~ MSw.

336.37   would give] T; ~ ⟨be/ to⟩ ~ MSw.

336.38   Notwithstanding that] T; ~ ⟨all⟩ ~ MSw.

336.42   acts . . . from] T; acts ⟨in moments of r⟩ of vengeance,
⟨and⟩ ↑from↓/ ⟨the facility with which they escaped
from pun⟩ ↑the natural violence of their passions and↓/
⟨to fly to the⟩ from MSw.

337.2   waylay] T; way lay MSw. *No authority in dictionaries.*

337.2   fortified himself] T; ⟨comforted him⟩ ~ ~ MSw.

337.3   thought] T; thoughts MSw. *Despite the plural, Irving
mentions only a single thought. Perhaps he neglected
to revise after deciding in mid-sentence to conclude it
differently from what he had first intended.*

337.6   ¶He was] T; ¶⟨He was⟩/ ¶⟨One⟩ ~ ~ MSw.

337.9   on his shoulder] T; ⟨in his hand⟩ ↑~ ~ ~↓ MSw.

337.9   and to turn] T; ⟨the steep banks on either side hemmed/
in the deep hollow road⟩, ~ ~ ~ MSw. *Comma redundant.*

337.10   As the ruffian] T; ⟨The⟩ ~ ~ ⟨robber⟩ ↑~↓ MSw.

337.12   Christian] T; christian MSw.

337.15   notwithstanding,] T; ⟨with fumbling⟩ ↑~↓/ ⟨steps and
[fumblin spirits?]⟩, MSw

337.17   held it] T; ⟨cocked it⟩, ~ ~ MSw. *Comma redundant.*

337.18–19   with . . . where] T; ⟨but his⟩ ↑with a↓ mild ⟨serene⟩
countenance, ⟨his⟩ ↑and a serene &↓ lofty ⟨&/ un-
wrinkled⟩ brow, ⟨on which a sober conscience⟩/ where
MSw.

337.20   scowl of] T; ~ ⟨of and⟩ ~ MSw.

337.21–22   also; he] T; also∧ ⟨beneath the⟩ he MSw. *Semicolon
supplied to separate independent clauses, as in preceding portion of sentence.*

337.23   father,"] T; ~∧" MSw.

337.24   struck off] T; ⟨turned⟩ ↑~↓ ~ MSw.

337.24   forest] T; ⟨woods⟩ ~ MSw.

THE LOG HOUSE HOTEL

337.26   THE . . . HOTEL] T; The Log house Hotel/—— MSw.

337.27   St. Charles, . . . sun,] T; S^t∧ ~, . . . ~∧ MSw. *Comma
is second of a pair.*

337.28 o'clock]   T; O'clock MSw. *"Capital" letter owing to hasty penmanship.*

337.29 Hotel, kept . . . couple;]   T; ~. ↑~ . . . ~; MSw. *Irving neglected to revise punctuation after deciding to continue the sentence. See also* Emendations 1.5–7.

337.29–30 the husband . . . negro]   T; the husband↓ ⟨Immediately/ there was turmoil and consternation⟩ ↑was absent on a deer hunt; but we were received↓/ ↑by a tall↓ ⟨throughout the establishment. A tall⟩/ long sided negro MSw.

337.30–31 negro, . . . trowsers,]   T; ~, . . . ~∧ MSw.

337.31 streaming]   T; ⟨fr st⟩/ ~ MSw.

337.34 "Massa, . . . style,"]   T; ∧~∧ ⟨they⟩ . . ./ ~∧∧ MSw. *Initial comma marks pause following direct address. Pairs of double quotation marks are supplied at the following additional points*: 337.34–35, 337.35–38, 338.1–2, 338.15, 338.15–16, 338.24, 338.24–25, 338.30, 338.31–32, 338.41, 338.44, 338.44, 339.1, 339.7–10, 339.26, 339.26–27.

337.35 also, Sambo.]   T; ~∧ ~ – MSw. *Comma marks slight pause; Irving's dash is a slurred period. Similar dashes at ends of sentences are converted to periods at the following points*: 338.4, 338.5, 338.15, 338.16, 338.21, 338.25, 338.30, 338.32, 338.34, 338.39, 338.41, 338.44, 339.4, 339.8, 339.10, 339.15, 339.24, 339.27.

337.35 fear,]   T; ~∧/ MSw. *Comma marks pause before direct address. End-of-line commas are supplied after the indicated words at the following additional points*: 338.10 stableyard, 338.14 him, 338.33 himself, 339.14 negro.

337.35 you'll]   T; ⟨dis house is famous for good/ eating.⟩ youll MSw. *Apostrophes are suppled to contractions at the following additional points*: 338.2, 338.24, 338.25, 338.31, 339.7.

337.36–38 Dis . . . . it.]   T; ¶⟨In a little while the whole establishment⟩ ↑dis house is famous all↓/ ↑along the road, They talk of it in Illinois and↓ ⟨was in an uproar the long negro, a little⟩/ ↑Boones lick — and reccommend travellers to it —↓ ⟨negro, a strapping negress & two or three/ little girls all on the⟩ MSw. *"They" begins a sentence; "lick" is part of a proper name; final dash is a slurred period.*

338.1 with . . . authority –]   T; ⟨out to some –⟩ ↑with a tone↓/ ⟨–body behind the barn, whom we could⟩ ↑of absolute authority $-\downarrow/$ ⟨not see⟩ — MSw. *Second dash redundant.*

338.2 house?] T; ~ — MSw. *A question mark is also supplied—in the absence of any punctuation—at 338.41.*

338.3–4 and out] T; & ~ MSw. *The ampersand is emended to "and" at the following additional points:* 338.7, 338.8, 338.15, 338.35, 338.43, 339.13.

338.4 We looked] T; ⟨I⟩ ~ ~ MSw.

338.5 old, . . . trowsers,] T; ~, . . . ~$_\wedge$ MSw.

338.5 ragged linen] T; ⟨linen⟩ ~ ~ MSw.

338.8–9 barn, . . . barn,] T; ~, . . . ~$_\wedge$ MSw.

338.10 orchard] T; ⟨peach⟩ ~ MSw.

338.10 the little] T; ⟨a⟩ ↑~↓ ~ MSw.

338.14 seized] T; siezed MSw. *The same emendation is made at* 339.17

338.14 whirled . . . neck] T; ⟨run wrung⟩ whirled him round by/ the ⟨head⟩ neck MSw.

338.15 "There," cried he,] T; $_\wedge$there$_{\wedge\wedge}$ ~ ~$_\wedge$ MSw. *Beginning of a sentence. Commas separate quotation from commentary and are added in similar situations at the following points:* 338.24, 338.24, 338.30, 338.30, 339.26, 339.26.

338.25 d——d] T; d— d MSw.

338.25 stick! Dere's] T; ~$_\wedge$ deres MSw. *Spacing in MSw indicates "deres" is to begin a new sentence whose subject matter is distinct from the preceding one*

338.26 captured, slain] T; ~$_\wedge$ ⟨and⟩/ ~ MSw.

338.26–27 cook: and] T; ~: ⟨While our/ dinner was preparing we had some conver/ conversation with the negro⟩ ~ MSw.

338.28 ¶While the repast] T; ¶⟨The house was kept by a decent couple/ who had re⟩/ ¶While ⟨our dinner⟩ ↑the repast↓ MSw.

338.29 water,] T; ⟨cold⟩ ~$_\wedge$ MSw. *Comma reflects Irving's usual practice following first item in series of three.*

338.29 whiskey] T; ⟨g⟩whiskey MSw.

338.29 sugar; and] T; Sugar; ⟨Gentleman⟩ and MSw. *Lowercase "sugar" reflects Irving's usual habits of capitalization in MSw. The following additional words are emended from capitalized forms:* 338.33 whiskey, 339.15 whiskey.

338.35 ¶He] T; ⟨H⟩/ ¶~ MSw

338.36 Missouri; each change,] T; ~, ~ ⟨place⟩ ↑~$_\wedge$↓ MSw. *Semicolon eliminates run-on construction.*

338.36   said,]   T; ~ₐ MSw.
338.37   for the best,]   T; ⟨best⟩ ~ ~ ~ - MSw. *Dash is a*
                slurred comma.
338.37   One lived so]   T; ⟨It was so⟩/ ~ ~ ~ MSw.
338.38   said. There]   T; ~, ~ MSw. *Irving neglected to revise*
                punctuation upon deciding to begin a new sentence.
338.40   buy himself free.]   T; ⟨make his⟩ ~ ~ ~ₐ MSw. *A pe-*
                riod is also supplied at the end of a sentence at 339.6
339.1   dress!"]   T; ~!ₐ - MSw. *Dash made, probably by ac-*
                cident, as Irving paused before beginning new para-
                graph.
339.5   ¶Sambo]   T; ¶⟨Dinner was announced -⟩ / ¶~ MSw.
339.5   long gone]   T; ⟨gone⟩ ~ ~ MSw.
339.13   heard]   T; ⟨An⟩/ ~ MSw.
339.13–14   with another]   T; ~ ⟨a buck⟩ ~ MSw.
339.15   inflamed by]   T; ~/ ⟨with⟩ ~ MSw.
339.21   saddled,]   T; ~ₐ MSw. *Comma marks pause between*
                clauses in complex sentence.
339.23   put]   T; ⟨slipped⟩ ↑~↓ MSw.
339.25   gave a glance at]   T; ⟨eyed⟩ ↑~ ~ ~ ~↓ MSw.
339.27   gentlemen."]   T; ~ –ₐ/—— MSw. *Irving's line is a con-*
                cluding flourish.

[HISTORY OF THE CONQUEST OF MEXICO]

339.29   [HISTORY . . . MEXICO]]   T; [*omitted*] 1A.
*339.33   attested by too]   T; ~ too by 1A.
340.1   He]   MSt; ¶~ 1A.
340.4   air and,]   MSt; ~ ~ₐ 1A.
340.7–8   hut, . . . maize,]   T; ~, . . . ~ₐ/ MSt; ~ₐ . . . ~ₐ 1A.
340.8   vast]   MSt; lost 1A.
340.9   lakes]   MSt; ~, 1A.
340.12–14   the vast . . . a mere]   T; a ↑the↓ vast ⟨extent⟩ ↑vally↓/
                ⟨of country, to the distant city of Mexico⟩ ↑of Mexicoₐ
                the great lake shining in the midst & the city↓/ ⟨and
                a of Mexico⟩ a mere MSt; the vast valley of Mexico,
                the great lake shining, in the midst the city, a mere 1A.
                Irving neglected to delete the initial "a"; comma
                following "Mexico" precedes modifying clause; Irv-
                ing's "&" is converted to "and."
340.14   island]   MSt; expanse 1A.
*341.36   palace. His]   T; ~, his 1A.

ILLUSTRATION TO THE LEGEND OF PRINCE AHMED

342.2   ILLUSTRATION . . . AHMED]   T; Illustration to the/
           Legend of Prince Ahmed./—— MSp.
342.3   ¶It would]   T; ∧~ ~ MSp.
342.3   Eben Bonabben]   T; Ebn ~ MSp. *Emendation reflects
           consistent spelling in ARE "Legend of Prince Ahmed."*
342.5   he knew]   T; ~ ⟨was⟩/ ~ MSp.
342.7   it was through]   T; ~ ⟨was⟩ ↑~ ~↓ MSp.
342.8   that he first]   T; ⟨which first⟩ ~ ~/ ~ MSp.
342.9   Lapwing]   T; lapwing MSp. *Invariably capitalized
           elsewhere in MSp.*
342.11   Jerusalem,]   T; ~∧ MSp. *Second comma of a pair.*
342.12   Yemen,]   T; ~∧/ MSp. *Comma separates appositives.
           End-of-line commas are supplied after the indicated
           words at the following points:* 342.22 sagacious, 343.2
           David.
342.14   of genii]   T; ⟨g of⟩ ~ ~ MSp. *Indicated false starts
           immediately rewritten in MSp occur at the following
           additional points:* 2.8 ⟨and⟩—*preceding* "delights,"
           342.39 ⟨subject⟩, 343.24 ⟨their⟩.
342.16   courtiers]   T; Courtiers MSp. *The following words not
           ordinarily capitalized by Irving are also emended to
           lower-case forms:* 342.40 sun, 343.1 effect, 343.19
           ambassadors.
342.18   elevated]   T; ⟨lif⟩ ~ MSp.
342.26   Lapwing]   T; ~⟨,⟩ MSp.
342.31   "Be not]   T; ⟨Oh Son of David said⟩/ ∧~ ~ MSp.
342.31   "Be . . . David,"]   T; ∧~ . . . ~,∧ MSp. *Pairs of double
           quotation marks are supplied at the following addi-
           tional points:* 342.32–40, 342.41, 342.42, 343.27, 343.28–
           32.
342.34–35 such wonders of Saba]   T; ⟨of a⟩ ~ ~ ~ ⟨thee city/
           and country of⟩ ~ MSp.
342.37   queen]   T; ⟨sovriegn⟩~ MSp.
342.38   stones,]   T; ~∧ MSp. *Comma eliminates run-on con-
           struction.*
342.39   sovereign:]   T; sovriegn: ⟨princess⟩ MSp.
342.40   worshipped]   T; worshiped MSp.
342.41–42 "We shall see," said he,]   T; ∧we ~ ~∧∧ ~ ~∧ MSp.
           Commas separate quotation from commentary; "We"
           begins a quoted sentence.
343.1   "From]   T; ∧~ MSp. *First quotation mark of a pair.*

*Individual quotation marks are also supplied at
343.7 after "bird," 343.7 before "and."*

343.1   From . . . God,]   T; ⟨From⟩ ↑~ . . . ~,↓ MSp.

343.2   Queen of Saba]   T; queen ~ ~ MSp. *Invariably
               capitalized elsewhere when used as part of a proper
               title.*

343.7   faithful]   T; ⟨fa true⟩ ~ MSp.

343.10   Queen Balkis]   T; ⟨th⟩ ~ ~ MSp.

343.12   note]   T; ⟨observe⟩ ↑~↓ MSp.

343.13–14   had . . . and feared]   T; ⟨had heard of the⟩ ↑had heard
               of↓/ ⟨riches, and wisdom and power of Solomon,⟩
               ↑the great power of Solomon↓/ ⟨and⟩ feared MSp. *In
               restoring a phrase similar to the cancelled one, Irving
               neglected to re-write the necessary "and."*

343.15   waste. After]   T; ~, ⟨she⟩ ~ MSp. *Irving neglected
               to revise punctuation.*

343.16   embassy]   T; ⟨E⟩embassy MSp.

343.19   in state]   T; ~ ⟨style⟩ ↑~↓ MSp.

343.23   presents:]   T; ~, MSp. *Emended punctuation eliminates
               run-on construction following introductory statement.*

343.24   dressed]   T; ⟨richly⟩ ~ MSp.

343.27   riches?]   T; ~?, MSp. *Irving's question mark probably
               written over the comma.*

343.27   said he.]   T; ~ ~: MSp. *Concludes a sentence.*

343.29   Saba. Tell]   T; ~ – ~ MSp. *Emendation reflects Irv-
               ing's usual practice; the dash may be a slurred period.*

343.30–31   God; otherwise]   T; ~∧/ ~ MSp. *Context indicates full
               stop, but Irving apparently did not intend a sentence
               break.*

343.34   to repair]   T; ~ ⟨pay a visit to Solomon; which she/
               did at the head of her⟩ ~ MSp.

343.36   some of which]   T; ⟨how th⟩ ~ ~ ~ MSp.

343.39   Sale's]   T; Sales MSp.

343.39   De Herbelot, &c. &c.]   T; D Herbelot∧/ &c∧ &c∧ MSp.

[A VOYAGE UP THE HUDSON RIVER IN 1800]

344.2   [A VOYAGE . . . 1800]]   T; [*omitted*] 1A.

[A JOURNEY TO SACKETT'S HARBOR IN 1814]

346.2   [A JOURNEY . . . 1814]]   T; [*omitted*] 1A.

LIST OF REJECTED VARIANTS

This list provides a historical record of variants in texts which originated after the copy-texts. The numbers before each entry indicate the page and line. Chapter numbers, chapter or section titles, epigraphs, chapter-summaries, texts, quotations, and footnotes are included in the line count. Only running heads and rules added by the printer to separate the running heads from the text are omitted from the count.

The reading to the left of the bracket indicates an accepted reading; its source is indicated by symbol after the bracket. Any reading which follows the semicolon is a rejected one. The swung (wavy) dash ~ represents the same word, words, or characters that appear before the bracket, and is used in recording punctuation variants. The caret ∧ indicates that a mark of punctuation is omitted. Brief explanatory comments, if required, follow in italics. If more explanation is required than can conveniently be inserted in the table, the entry is preceded by an asterisk * and the necessary comments appear following the same page-line reference in the Discussions of Adopted Readings.

A key to identifying symbols used in referring to manuscript and printed texts is given on pages 348–54.

[REVIEW OF A CHRONICLE OF THE CONQUEST OF GRANADA]

4.38–40	But . . . treated.] 1E, 2A; It appeared to me that its true course and character had never been fully illustrated. 1A.
4.41	world at large had been content to receive] 1E, 2A; world had received 1A.
5.3	fabrication.*] 1E, 2A; ~.∧ 1A. *The footnote to which the asterisk refers—5.39–44—is also omitted from 1A.*
5.5–6	contests which have been sanctified] 1E, 2A; conflicts sanctified 1A.
5.17	smoke] 1E, 2A; and ~ 1A.
6.10–14	He . . . recorded.] 1E, 2A; In the libraries of Madrid, and in the private library of the American Consul, Mr. Rich, I had access to various chronicles and other works, both printed and in manuscript, written at the time by eye-witnesses, and in some instances by persons who had actually mingled in the scenes recorded, and gave descriptions of them from different points of view, and with different details. 1A.
6.14	chronicles] 1E, 2A; works 1A.

8.30	rightful] 1E; righful 2A.
12.21	of mountain or valley] 1E; the ~ ~ ~ 2A.
21.21	wind] 1E; winds 2A.

[REVIEW OF ALEXANDER SLIDELL'S *A YEAR IN SPAIN*]

30.13–16	This . . . where] MSm, T; Iɴ this restless and roving age, this age of expeditions to Timbuctoo and the Pole, when the uttermost ends of the earth have been explored, and its most secret places unveiled, it is a matter of surprise that a country comparatively near at home should yet remain to be described. It is a land, too, of adventure and romance, full of historic, and poetic, and legendary association; yet, withal, a kind of terra incognita—a mysterious realm, un-travelled by the crowd, and where 1E.
30.17	Cockney] MSm; sleek 1E.
30.22	the Pyrenees] MSm; Spain 1E.
30.23–24	Spanish robbers . . . knives] MSm; Spanish blunder-busses and Spanish knives, of robbers on the highways, and assassins in the streets 1E.
30.26	the ear of the simple tourist] MSm, T; the tedium of the *table-d'hôte* 1E.
30.29	well laden] MSm; well peopled 1E.
30.29	well filled] MSm; well/ victualled 1E.
30.29	travelling . . . family] MSm; production of Long-Acre 1E.
30.32	mark] MSm; infallibly ~ 1E.
30.32	English travel] MSm; John Bull 1E.
31.21	little money] MSm; a slender purse, containing merely his lieutenant's pay, and no prize-money 1E.
31.22	and made him depend more upon] MSm; upon 1E.
31.23–24	in making . . . libraries.] MSm; rendering him fresh, new, and original, instead of erudite and common-place. 1E.
31.25	the people] MSm; ~ ~ in their *casas de pupilos*, or boarding-houses, 1E.
31.26	of hotels] MSm; of his own apartment at a hotel 1E.
31.31–32	yet . . . prevents] MSm, T; but with a boldness of touch and a liveliness of colouring, that prevent 1E.
31.43	he was] MSm; ~ is 1E.
31.44–32.1	have dismayed and discomfited] MSm, T; dismay and discomfit 1E.
32.2	enjoyed] MSm; enjoys 1E.

32.3	required] MSm; require 1E.
32.5	verity] MSm; fidelity 1E.
32.14	The little touch] MSm; The captain was one of those veteran campaigners, those hap-hazard men of the sword, gay, gallant, and *farouches,* who had been brought up in the school of Napoleon, had survived the expedition to Russia, and made both love and war in every country of Europe. ~ ~ ~ 1E.
32.15	the officer's] MSm, T; his 1E.
35.1–2	We . . . picture] MSm; We must insert the following picture 1E.
35.3	traveller] MSm; reader 1E.
35.4	way] MSm; weigh 1E.
42.3–6	touching . . . . hand.] MSm, T; touching, and, being drawn from fact, shows us the truth to nature of one of Scott's scenes in the 'Antiquary,' where a similar conflict takes place in the mind of the poor fisherman's wife who had lost her son—an exquisite touch, worthy of the great master that struck it off, and, indeed, only to be effected by a master hand. 1E.
42.41	shewed] MSm; showed 1E. *The same pattern of variants occurs at* 43.23 (shews), 46.23 (shews), 47.24 (shew).
43.3	(el asesinato lo mas feo)] MSm; (*lo mas feo*) 1E.
43.3	committed] MSm; done 1E.
43.5	kind of thing] MSm; business 1E.
43.7	like a dog] MSm; a dog 1E.
43.7–8	—Not . . . criticism;] MSm, T; [*omitted*] 1E.
43.9	him discriminating] MSm; the mayoral a critic in the art of murder 1E.
43.10	pursues] MSm; pursued 1E.
43.14	beholds] MSm; beheld 1E.
43.17	Don Quixote] MSm; Cervantes 1E.
43.19	Sorrowful Knight] MSm; pensive hero 1E.
43.28–29	nor . . . extracting] MSm, T; and nothing can be better than 1E.
*45.39	beauty.] Y; ~.* 1E.
46.24	sailor] T; blue-jacket 1E.
*46.31	girl. Frank] MSm; ~: frank 1E.
46.31	amicable] MSm; warm-hearted 1E.
46.35–36	a Madrid beauty] MSm; the ~ ~ 1E. *1E emendation is appropriate but not necessary.*
46.37–39	It . . . creation.] MSm, T; [*omitted*] 1E.
47.18	As our object] MSm, T; ¶The liberty of the Lieutenant

	must certainly have been in continual jeopardy during this long and adventurous land-cruize; and we doubt whether he has not been often captured and carried into port by these Salee rovers. ¶~ ~ ~ 1E.
47.27	Don Quixote and Sancho Panza] MSm; the Knight of the Woful Countenance and the Squire of all Squires 1E.
48.25–26	We . . . oil] MSm, T; [*omitted*] 1E. *The quotation from Y introduced by this sentence is also omitted from 1E.*
49.9	ancient Spanish] MSm; Spanish 1E.
49.10	which was drawn] MSm; and drawn 1E.
49.12	female] MSm; dame or damsel 1E.
49.12	described] MSm; sketched 1E.
55.18–21	We . . . cruize.] MSm, T; We are tempted to make one more extract, which shows the worthy Lieutenant in a situation of more imminent jeopardy than any other page of his log-book. 1E.
55.34	to their hearts' content] MSm, T; *a gusto*—that is, to their heart's content. 1E.
55.35	enter] MSm; approach 1E.
57.12	delicious perils] MSm; perils 1E.
57.14	curiosity.] MSm; ~∧ as did Yorick when he left untold the delicate dénouement of the affair of the corking-pins. 1E.
57.19–37	In casting . . . instructive.] MSm, T; Before conclud-ing, we would again intimate to the reader, that though our extracts have been confined to personal adventures and travelling sketches, yet these volumes are by no means deficient in grave and judicious remark, and valuable information. The author has evidently tasked his erudition to intersperse his work with historical anecdote appertaining to the places visited; and in the latter part of the second volume there is an elaborate dissertation on the general state of Spain, containing much interesting and curious matter, the result of his reading and his observations. The worthy Lieutenant doubtless regards these rec-ondite passages, which have cost him the most pains, as the most important parts of his work, and those most likely to give it weight and value with the world. He may be surprised and disappointed, therefore, should these pages meet his eye, at finding these, his more learned labours, unrecorded; while those lighter sketches and narrations only are cited which he has

probably considered almost too trivial and personal for publication. Nothing, however, is easier and more common than to fill a book of travels with erudite information, the after gleaning and gathering of the closet; while nothing is more difficult and rare than to sketch with truth and vivacity, and at the same time with the air of a gentleman, those familiar scenes of life, and those groups and characters by the way-side, which place a country and its people immediately before our eyes, and make us the companions of the tourist.

We are sure that the extracts we have furnished will show our young American to possess this talent in no ordinary degree; and we think we can give him no better advice than, in any future work he may undertake, to let us have as much as possible of his personal adventures, and of the scenes and characters around him; assuring him, that when he is most egotistical he is most entertaining, and, in fact, most instructive. He belongs to a roving and eventful profession, likely to throw him into all kinds of circumstances and situations, conduct him to every country and clime, and afford an almost unlimited scope for his talent at narration and description. We anticipate, therefore, further and still more copious extracts from our gay and shrewd Lieutenant's log-book. 1E.

57.37–41   We . . . reading it]   MSm, T; May he long continue his cruizes by land and water; may he have as many adventures as Sindbad—and as happy an exit out of them; may he survive to record them all in a book, and we to have the pleasure of reviewing it! 1E.

[ADDRESS AT THE IRVING DINNER, MAY 30, 1832]

59.23   youth,]   MSv; ~– 1A.
59.24   veneration,]   MSv; ~– 1A.
59.25   whom though] MSv; who, ~ 1A, 2A, 3A, 4A, 6A; who ~ 5A.
59.28   life. And]   MSv; ~. –~ 1A.
59.28   poignant, is]   MSv; ~∧ ~, 1A.
59.28   had been]   MSv, 1A, 2A, 3A, 4A, 6A; have ~ 5A.
59.30   Rumours]   MSv; Rumors 1A; Rurmors 3A.
59.30   had reached me]   MSv; ~ ~ ~ [here Mr. I. betrayed much emotion] 1A, 5A, 6A [2A, 4A *spell the name in full; 3A employs parentheses rather than brackets*].

59.31	feelings;] MSv; ~— 1A.
59.33	charge—] MSv; ~; 1A.
59.34–35	reception . . . landing, and] MSv, 1A, 2A, 3A, 4A, 6A; [*omitted*] 5A.
59.36	groundless.] MSv; ~. (Cheers and clapping here interrupted the speaker for a few moments.) 1A, 2A, 3A, 4A, 5A, 6A.
59.37	¶Never] MSv; ∧~ 1A.
59.38	auspices: on every] MSv; ~. On my 1A, 2A, 3A, 4A, 5A, 6A.
60.2	associates] MSv, 1A, 2A, 3A, 4A, 6A; acquaintances 5A.
60.3	lightly] MSv; slightly 1A, 2A, 3A, 4A, 5A, 6A.
60.4–5	beaming] MSv, 1A, 2A, 4A, 5A, 6A; burning 3A.
60.7	indications] MSv, 1A, 2A, 3A, 5A, 6A; indication 4A.
60.8	sizes and descriptions] MSv, T; descriptions 1A, 2A, 3A, 5A, 6A; description 4A.
60.9	horizon] MSv; ~, 1A.
60.9–10	shewed . . . neighborhood] MSv; showed . . . neighbourhood 1A.
60.13	city] MSv; ~, 1A.
60.14	groves and forests.] MSv, T; green forests [alluding, probably, to Brooklyn and Gowannus]. 1A [*2A, 3A, 5A adopt spelling "Gowannas" and place period within bracket but otherwise duplicate 1A; 6A adopts spelling "Gowanus" but otherwise duplicates 1A*]; groves and forests [alluding, probably, to Gowannas]. 4A.
60.15	emotions] MSv; ~, 1A.
60.17	lighting] MSv, 1A, 3A, 5A, 6A; lightening 2A, 4A.
60.17	spires] MSv; the skies 1A, 2A, 3A, 4A, 6A; the ~ 5A.
60.20	on many] MSv; upon ~ 1A, 2A, 3A, 4A, 5A, 6A.
60.21	stranger] MSv; ~, 1A.
60.23	admired—I] MSv; ~—~ 1A.
60.25	own—my] MSv; ~∧~ 1A.
60.25–26	land!'/ [*space*]/ ¶It] MSv, T; ~."/ ¶Mr. Irving was here interrupted by immense applause: when the cheering had subsided, he went on as follows. "It 1A [*2A, 4A duplicate 1A except that single quotation marks are used and "land" capitalized; 3A duplicates 1A except that "land" is capitalized; 5A duplicates 1A except that single quotation marks are used; 6A duplicates 1A except that a colon is used after "follows"*].
60.28	enjoyment] MSv, 3A, 4A; enjoyments 1A, 2A, 5A, 6A.
60.29	climes] MSv, 1A, 3A, 5A, 6A; climates 2A, 4A.
60.31	trembles] MSv; ~, 1A.

60.31	groans;] MSv; frowns— 1A, 2A, 3A, 4A, 5A, 6A.
60.32	these] MSv; ~, 1A.
60.35	Is not this] MSv; Is this not 1A, 2A, 3A, 4A, 5A, 6A. *The same pattern of variants occurs at 60.36, 60.37; at 60.36 only, 4A prints the locution as "Is not this."*
60.37	the son] MSv, 1A, 2A, 3A, 5A, 6A; a son 4A.
60.38	ambitious,] MSv, 4A; ambition— 1A, 2A, 3A, 5A; his ambition— 6A.
60.40	¶I am] MSv; (A burst of applause, when Mr. Irving quickly resumed:)— "I am 1A, 2A, 3A, 4A [*5A duplicates 1A except that brackets are substituted for parentheses and the dashes appear within the end bracket; 6A duplicates 1A except that the quotation mark is omitted*].
60.40	here.] MSv; ~? 1A.
60.41–42	"Our City—may God continue to prosper it."] MSv; *"Our City*—May Goᴅ ~ ~ ~ ~." 1A.

[REVIEW OF HENRY WHEATON'S *HISTORY OF THE NORTHMEN*]

62.8	Homer] 1A; Homor 2A.
63.22	classical] 1A; clasical 2A.
65.36	translated into Icelandic] H, 1A; ~ in ~ 2A.
67.36	bear me] H, 1A; bare me 2A.
74.3–4	a northern Saga,] 1A; "A Northern Saga," 2A. *See Precopy-Text Rejected Variants 74.5–6.*
83.8	palisadoes] 1A; palisades 2A.

MATHEWS *NOT* AT HOME

87.3	personally] MSv; ~, 1A. *Commas are added in 1A after the indicated words in MSv at the following additional points:* 87.9 since, 87.10 tragedian, 87.11 curricle, 87.12 traces, 87.18 mean time, 87.28 curricle, 87.32 character, 87.33 nightfall.
87.7	point,] MSv; ~: 1A.
87.9	lost,] MSv; ~— 1A.
87.18	mean time] MSv; meantime 1A.
87.23	fidgetting] MSv; fidgety 1A.
87.25	occasion;] MSv; ~, 1A.
87.29	Gipsies] MSv; gipsies 1A. *The same variant occurs at 87.31.*
87.36	post-script] MSv; postscript 1A.

NEWTON THE PAINTER

88.3	talented] MSn; ~, 1A.
88.11	music] MSn; musick 1A.
88.12	good] MSn; ~, 1A.
88.13	Shakespeare] MSn; Shakspeare 1A.
88.13	Sterne, Goldsmith] MSn; Goldsmith, Sterne 1A.
88.13	Bible;] MSn; ~, 1A.
88.15	flowers,] MSn; ~∧ 1A.
88.18	¶Leslie] MSn; ∧~ 1A.
88.23	as altogether] MSn; altogether 1A.
88.26	elegant pencil] MSn; pencil 1A.

THE HAUNTED SHIP. A TRUE STORY—AS FAR AS IT GOES

91.5	Guadalquivir] 1E; Guadalquiver 1A, 2A.
91.34	deuce to pay] 1E, 2A; deuse to play 1A.

[LETTER TO THE EDITOR OF THE NEW YORK *AMERICAN*]

94.12	Greenburgh, Jan. 4th, 1837.] 1A; GREENBURG,* Jan. 4, 1837. 2A. *Asterisk in 2A corresponds to one preceding an explanatory note:* "Greenburg, from which the letter bears date, is the name of the township in which the cottage is situated."

[TOAST AT THE BOOKSELLERS' DINNER, MARCH 30, 1837]

99.2	toast] MSm; ~, 1A.
99.4	Poet] MSm; poet 1A.
99.5	observed that,] MSm; ~, ~∧ 1A.
99.8	Britain] MSm; ~, 1A.
99.8	judgement] MSm; judgment 1A.
99.10	manner] MSm, 3A; ~, 1A.
99.11	manifested, . . . occasions,] MSm, 3A; ~∧ . . . ~∧ 1A.
99.12	writers] MSm, 3A; write s 1A. *Blank type.*
99.15	Rogers] MSm; ~, 1A.
99.16	poems] MSm; ~, 1A. *The same variant occurs at* 99.18.
99.21	side of the] MSm; side the 1A, 3A.
99.21	Atlantic, and I hope] MSm; Atlantic (Hear, hear!). I hope 1A; Atlantic [Hear, hear]. I hope 3A.
99.22	again] MSm; ~, 1A.
99.24	ring] MSm; ~, 1A.
99.25	say indeed] MSm; ~, ~, 1A.
99.25	found,] MSm; ~— 1A.

99.25	friend] MSm, 3A; friends 1A.
99.27	of the grave] MSm; the grave 1A, 3A.
99.27–28	(Mr. Rogers . . . health.)] MSm, 1A; [*omitted*] 3A.
99.27	seventy fifth] MSm; ~-~ 1A; [*omitted*] 3A.
99.31	company] MSm, 3A; Company 1A.

[LETTER OF "GEOFFREY CRAYON" TO THE EDITOR OF THE *KNICKERBOCKER MAGAZINE*]

100.4	TO . . . KNICKERBOCKER.] 1A, 3A; [*omitted*] 4A. *See Emendations* 100.2–3.
100.14	gossipping] 1A, 3A; gossiping 4A.
100.39	classic] 1A, 4A; classical 3A.
101.32	changes . . . notice.] 1A, 4A; changes. 3A.
102.4	Herculanean] 1A, 4A; Herculaneum 3A.
102.22	had been] 1A, 4A; has ~ 3A.
102.34	quaint] 1A, 3A; quiet 4A. *Probably a compositor's misreading*.
103.12–13	New Netherlands] 1A, 3A; ~ Nethelands 4A.
103.22	recollections] 1A, 4A; recollection 3A.
103.26–104.6	I thank . . . . pilgrimage] 1A, 3A, 4A; "~ ~ . . . . ~." 2A.
103.26–35	I think . . . . feelings;] 1A; [*omitted*] 2A.
103.35	and I fancy] 1A, 3A, 4A; I fancy 2A. *See Rejected Variants* 209.28–37.
103.37	my youthful enthusiasm] 1A, 3A, 4A; youthful enthusiam 2A.
103.38	and almost to give] 1A, 3A, 4A; and, as it were, give 2A.
103.39	admired] 1A, 3A, 4A; delighted in 2A.
103.40	dangerous] 1A, 3A, 4A; shifting 2A.
103.41	or perfidious rock] 1A, 3A, 4A; and ~ ~ 2A.
103.43–104.1	forward. Once . . . struggles] 1A, 3A; forward, or, if forced aside for once by opposing mountains, struggling 2A.
104.1–2	immediately resumes] 1A, 3A, 4A; resuming 2A.
104.2	straightforward] 1A, 3A, 4A; onward 2A.
104.5	recovers] 1A, 3A, 4A; resumes 2A.

SLEEPY HOLLOW

105.3	Beside] 1A; Besides 2A.
106.43	rugged] 1A; ragged 2A.
107.26	patroon] 1A; man 2A.
107.27	reigned . . . held] 1A; got the better of the native

savages, subdued a great tract of country by dint of trinkets, tobacco, and *aqua vitae,* and established 2A.

107.29	potent] 1A; heroic 2A.
107.29	lorded it over] 1A; in like manner subdued and occupied 2A.
108.30	drouth] 1A; drought 2A.
108.37	on one] 1A; in one 2A.
108.43	as if in imitation of] 1A; vying with 2A.
109.43	gossipping] 1A; gossiping 2A.
110.21–22	Ichabod Crane and the headless horseman,] 1A; "~ ~ ~ ~ Headless Horseman," 2A.
112.33	verandahs] 1A; verandas 2A.
113.9	can escape the general inundation] 1A; may ~ ~ ~ awakening 2A.
113.14	favored] 1A; spell-/bound 2A.

[LETTER OF "HIRAM CRACKENTHORPE" TO THE EDITOR OF THE *KNICKERBOCKER MAGAZINE*]

113.20	TO . . . KNICKERBOCKER.] 1A; [*omitted*] 2A.
113.21	In your last number, I read with great interest an article entitled] 1A; ¶I HAVE read with great interest 2A.
114.2	etarnal] 1A; eternal 2A.
114.7	or two] 1A; or wo 2A. *Misprint.*
114.13	circumstance, Sir, as I said,] 1A; circumstance, I said, 2A.
114.20	doubt, Sir, this] 1A; doubt, this 2A.
114.33–34	Your . . . St. Louis] 1A; [*omitted*] 2A.

NATIONAL NOMENCLATURE

116.36	Indian local] 1A; local Indian 2A.

DESULTORY THOUGHTS ON CRITICISM

119.17	a—In fine] 1A; ~—. ~ ~ 2A.
122.23	trust to] 1A; trust 2A.
122.32	G.C.] 1A; [*omitted*] 2A.

COMMUNIPAW

123.6	unacceptable:] MSn; ~. 1A.
123.13	New York] MSn, 4A; ~-~ MSnp, 1A. *The indicated compounds in MSn are hyphenated in MSnp and 1A*

at the following additional points: 123.28 moss grown, 124.2 broad brimmed, 124.2–3 broad bottomed, 124.3 shoe buckles, 124.4 short gowns, 124.11 weather cocks, 124.12 grown up, 124.14 close locked, 124.16 old fashioned, 124.28 New Amsterdam, 125.10 New Amsterdam (1A: New-/ Amsterdam), 125.11 round crowned, 127.3 New England, 127.6–7 New Amsterdam, 127.9 crow step, 127.18–19 New England, 127.21 all pervading, 127.26 cabbage gardens, 127.27 oyster parks, 127.35 stocking feet, 128.4 New Year, 128.19 weather cock.

123.15   that,]   MSn, 4A; $\sim_\wedge$ 1A.

123.27   meditate]   MSn; $\sim$, 1A. *Commas are added in 1A after the indicated words in MSn at the following additional points*: 123.27 reverence, 124.1 Doubter, 124.11 street, 124.33 band, 124.42 it, 126.11 known, 126.14 river, 126.23 time, 126.25 front, 126.30 plantations, 127.9 houses, 127.10 erecting, 127.34 banks, 127.43 generation, 128.30 ages.

123.29   look upon]   MSn; ⟨$\sim$ $\sim$⟩ ↑regard↓ MSnp; regard 1A.

123.29   much neglected]   MSn, 1A; $\sim$-$\sim$ MSnp.

123.33   bay–]   MSn; $\sim$, ⟨–⟩ MSnp; $\sim$, 1A. *Irving's dash is written clearly.*

123.37   in truth]   MSn, 4A; indeed 1A. *Emended 1A reading probably prompted by "in truth" in the preceding sentence.*

123.38–39   motherly little]   MSn; simple-hearted 1A, 4A.

123.41–42   New Netherlands]   MSn, 4A; $\sim$-$\sim$ 1A. *The indicated compounds in MSn are hyphenated in 1A at the following additional points*: 124.9 dwelling houses, 125.29 States General, 127.42 black letter, 128.4–5 cherry bounce, 128.19–20 gable end, 128.31 sweet smelling.

123.43   Rome]   MSn, 4A; $\sim$, MSnp, 1A. *Commas are added in MSnp and 1A after the indicated words in MSn at the following additional points*: 124.7 was, 124.13 family, 124.14 doors, 124.16 stoop, 124.25 days, 124.33 band, 124.34 together, 124.37 guidance, 124.38 bay, 125.3 house, 125.4 horses, 125.6 place, 125.11 hat, 125.28 other, 125.28 sure, 125.28 up, 125.35 fuel, 125.36 circumstance, 126.1 Doubter, 126.2 Headstrong, 126.4 reliques, 126.7 grandly, 126.8 crimped, 126.10 word, 126.16 species, 126.20 work, 126.27 land, 126.34 market, 126.38 folks, 126.38 sex, 126.40 market, 126.44 days,

127.4 Communipaw, 127.9 gables, 127.11 stores, 127.14 dealings, 127.14 possible, 127.21 pitch, 127.25 maps, 127.34 cabbages, 127.35 feet, 127.36 pots, 127.40 drawers, 127.41 carved, 128.3 house, 128.6 stockings, 128.9 late, 128.14 winds.

124.2	Golden Age] MSn; golden age 1A.
124.7	"intelligent traveller"] MSn; "~ ~," MSnp; '~ ~,' 1A.
124.14	porches;] MSn; ~, 1A.
124.16	"vrouw"] MSn, 4A; '~' 1A.
124.18	old world] MSn; "~ ~" MSnp; '~ ~' 1A.
124.32	Bowery] MSn; Bower⟨y⟩ie MSnp; Bowerie 1A.
124.37	New Netherlands] MSn, 4A; ~-~ MSnp; ~-/ ~ 1A.
125.9	"The . . . Chimnies."] MSn, 4A; '~ . . . ~.' 1A.
125.13	pusillanimous counsellors] MSn; pusallanimous councillors 1A.
125.20	upon] MSn, 1A; ~: MSnp.
125.26	land;] MSn; ~, 1A.
125.27	Still] MSn; ~, MSnp, 1A.
125.29	Lords] MSn; Lord 1A, 4A.
125.37	say that,] MSn; ~, ~⟨,⟩ MSnp; ~, ~ₐ 1A.
125.43	wench] MSn; housewife 1A, 4A.
126.6	manure] MSn; ~, MSnp; compost, 1A, 4A.
126.7	brims] MSn; brim 1A, 4A.
126.9	rivalling] MSn, 4A; rivaling 1A.
126.10	renowned] MSn, 1A; renowed 4A.
126.36	New York: but] MSn; ~-~.⟨:⟩/ but MSnp; ~-~; but 1A.
126.37	negroes;] MSn, 4A; ~: 1A.
127.10	in stead] MSn; instead, 1A.
127.16	"Governor's Head"] MSn; "~ ~," MSnp; '~ ~,' 1A.
127.17	Governor's Foot,"] MSn; '~ ~,' 1A.
127.27	quays,] MSn; ~; MSnp, 1A.
127.32	confusion;] MSn; ~, 1A.
127.33	shew] MSn; show 1A.
127.33	place; the] MSn; ~.⟨;⟩ ⟨t⟩The MSnp; ~. The 1A.
127.40	clothes presses] MSn; ~-~ MSnp; ~-/ ~ 1A.
127.43	Amsterdam] MSn; ~; MSnp; ~, 1A.
128.3	holydays] MSn; holidays 1A.
128.7	deserts,] MSn; ~; MSnp, 1A.
128.9	portentous] MSn, 1A; portentious 4A.
128.11	city;] MSn, ~, 1A.
128.27	it!–Long] MSn; ~!⟨–⟩~ MSnp; ~!ₐ~ 1A.
128.35	Vander Donk.] MSn; Vanderdonk. 1A.

128.36–129.6   P.S. . . . . village!]   MSn; [*omitted*] 4A.
128.36–37   epistle . . . intelligence]   MSn; ~, . . . ~, MSnp; [*1A, 4A wanting*].
128.39   foothold]   MSn; foot-hold MSnp; [*1A, 4A wanting*].
128.40   smooth tongued]   MSn; ~-~ MSnp; [*1A, 4A wanting*].
128.41   work,]   MSn; ~, MSnp; [*1A, 4A wanting*]. *The same pattern of variants occurs after the indicated words in MSn at the following additional points*: 128.41 heiress, 129.1 event, 129.2 lots, 129.4 wedding.
128.42   cabbage garden]   MSn; ~-~ MSnp; [*1A, 4A wanting*].
129.5   whirlwind!–The]   MSn; ~!⟨–⟩~ MSnp; [*1A, 4A wanting*].

CONSPIRACY OF THE COCKED HATS

130.6   strong holds]   1A; strongholds 2A. *1A spelling characteristic of Irving.*

[LETTER ON INTERNATIONAL COPYRIGHT TO THE EDITOR OF THE *KNICKERBOCKER MAGAZINE*]

134.1   enrol]   1A; enroll 2A.
134.33   Your ob. Servt.]   1A; ~ obedient servant 2A.

[ANECDOTE OF ADMIRAL HARVEY]

135.3–23   Old . . . . obligation.]   MSn; '~ . . . . ~.' MSnc, 1A.
135.3   Harvey]   MSn; HARVEY MSnc; HARVEY 1A.
135.3   told me]   MSn; ~ ~, ↑at dinner,↓ MSnc; ~ ~, at dinner, 1A.
135.4   station]   MSn; ~ ↓station, ↑ MSnc; ~, 1A.
135.7   waggons]   MSn; wagons 1A.
135.7   up home]   MSn; up ↑to their↓ homes MSnc; up to their homes 1A.
135.8   clothes]   MSn; ~, MSnc, 1A. *The same pattern of variants occurs following the indicated words in MSn at the following additional points*: 135.16 scores, 135.21 distress, 135.22 Quaker.
135.10   farmhouses]   MSn; farm↑-↓houses MSnc; farm-houses 1A.
135.11   Hicks's]   MSn; HICKS's MSnc; HICKS's; 1A.
135.14   girls,]   MSn; ~; MSnc, 1A.
135.15   tolerated]   MSn; tolerat⟨ed⟩ing MSnc; tolerating 1A.
135.15   frolicks]   MSn; frolics 1A.
135.16   a thundering bill.]   MSn; '~ ~ ~.' MSnc, 1A.

135.17–18   "You . . . distress,"]   MSn; '~ . . . ~," 1A. *The same*
               pattern of variants occurs at 135.18.

135.19   ¶He has]   MSn; ∧The old ad-/ ↑miral declares he↓
               ⟨He⟩ has MSnc; ∧The old Admiral declares he has 1A.

135.19   true he]   MSn; ~, ↑he says, that↓ ~ MSnc; true, he
               says, that he 1A.

THE "EMPIRE OF THE WEST"

135.27   *North American Review,*]   1A; "~ ~ ~," MSv; ⟨"⟩~
               ~ ~,⟨"⟩ MSvc.

135.29   It gives]   1A; ⟨We⟩ ~ ~ MSv.

135.31   indefeasible]   1A; indefeasable MSv.

135.31–32   and places]   1A; ~ ⟨of the/ artful wiley⟩ ~ MSv.

135.34   our claim]   1A; ~ ⟨having/ ever a decisive⟩ ~ MSv.

135.35   old]   1A, N; Old MSv.

136.2   wily]   1A; wiley MSv.

136.3   He will here find]   1A; ⟨He will find⟩/ [*MS text breaks
               off*] MSv.

*136.18   ¶"We]   1A; ∧∧we N.

137.8   The gradual]   1A; Some parts are very high; but the
               gradual N. *Pitcher's report is quoted entensively in N.
               The passage quoted here—137.8–11—forms part of a
               lengthier one enclosed in N within double quotation
               marks.*

137.19   mountains]   1A; mountain MSv. *Irving is referring to
               the Rocky Mountains.*

137.20   Captain's]   MSvc, 1A; Captains MSv.

137.21   singular]   1A; striking MSv; ⟨striking⟩ ↑singular↓ MSvc.
               *Clark's change was to avoid awkwardness created by
               "strikes" earlier in the sentence.*

137.25   individual,]   1A; ~∧ MSv.

137.25–27   to rear . . . Columbia.]   MSv, 1A; He had once more
               reared the American flag in the lost domains of Astoria;
               and, had he been able to maintain the footing he had
               so gallantly effected, he might have regained for his
               country the opulent trade of the Columbia, of which
               our statesmen have negligently suffered us to be dis-
               possessed. N.

137.28   so as]   1A; ⟨and⟩ ~ ~ MSv.

137.30   character,]   MSvc, 1A; ~∧ MSv.

137.31   that fitted him to follow]   1A; ⟨capable of⟩ ↑that fitted
               him to↓ follow⟨ing⟩ MSv.

[ANECDOTE OF THE FRENCH REVOLUTION]

137.35　　　　Revolution]　MSy; revolution 1A. *The same pattern of variants occurs at 138.8.*

137.35　　　　Abbés]　MSy; abbés 1A. *The same pattern of variants occurs at 137.38 (Abbé), 138.1.*

137.37　　　　noblemen]　MSy; ~, MSyc, 1A. *Commas are added in MSyc and 1A following the indicated words in MSy at the following additional points*: 137.35 Revolution, 138.1 arrived, 138.1 time, 138.2 another, 138.5 tittup, 138.7 day, 138.14 one, 138.14 prisoners, 138.16 Here, 138.18 cart, 138.19 time, 138.19 up stairs, 138.20 chair, 138.20 however, 138.21 while.

138.16　　　　friend!—]　MSy; ~! ⟨–⟩ MSyc; ~!ᴧ 1A.

138.19　　　　¶In the]　MSy; ᴧ~ ~ MSyc, 1A.

138.21　　　　vacant,]　MSy; ~⟨,⟩; MSyc; ~; 1A.

138.21　　　　asked—]　MSy; ~: ⟨–⟩ MSyc; ~: 1A.

138.22　　　　Abbé—]　MSy; ~? ⟨–⟩ MSyc; abbé?ᴧ 1A.

138.22　　　　that time]　MSy; ⟨that⟩ ↓this↑ time MSyc; this time, 1A. *Deletion and interlineation are in pencil.*

[THE TAKING OF THE VEIL,
AND THE CHARMING LETORIÉRES]

145.6　　　　figured]　1A; figure[*MS torn*] MSv.

145.13　　　　it . . . verified]　1A; ⟨if the⟩ it was never ⟨veri⟩/ more verified MSv.

145.14　　　　who]　1A; ⟨a⟩ ~ MSv.

145.15　　　　(capa y espada)]　1A; (⟨capa⟩/ ~ ~ ~) MSv. *The indicated false starts immediately re-written occur in MSv at the following additional points*: 145.22 ⟨s⟩—for "scanty," 145.29 ⟨de⟩, 145.33 ⟨coarse⟩, 145.37 ⟨and repe⟩, 146.43 ⟨to ha⟩, 147.2 ⟨became⟩, 147.9 ⟨Prin⟩.

145.20　　　　temper]　1A; ⟨humour⟩ ↑~↓ MSv.

145.25　　　　chamelion order, and]　1A; camelion/ order, ⟨into the⟩ and MSv.

145.28　　　　merriest]　1A; ⟨happiest⟩ ~ MSv.

145.32　　　　minds]　1A; ⟨the⟩ ~ MSv.

145.34　　　　hackney]　1A; Hackney MSv. *Not ordinarily capitalized by Irving.*

145.34　　　　was passing]　1A; ⟨p⟩ ~ ~ MSv.

145.35　　　　asked him]　1A; ⟨offered the use of his carriage⟩ ~ ~ MSv.

145.35　　　　Letoriéres]　1A; Les-/ toriéres MSv. *The same variant in spelling (MSv Lesto-/ riéres) occurs at 147.22.*

145.38	Palace of Justice] 1A; palace ~/ ~ MSv. *See* 146.5.
146.1	jumped down,] 1A; ~ ⟨off his box⟩ ↑⟨fr⟩↓ ~, MSv.
146.1	carriage,] MSv, 1A; ~: ⟨,⟩ MSvc.
146.5	saloon] 1A; ⟨door⟩ ↑~↓ MSv.
146.6	opened] 1A; ⟨and⟩ ~ MSv.
146.11	afterward] 1A; afterward⟨s⟩ MSv.
146.12	recommendation] 1A; reccommendation MSv.
146.15	The] 1A; ~ ⟨he⟩ MSv.
146.20	with such] 1A; ~ ⟨you⟩ ~ MSv.
146.20	wife;] MSvc, 1A; ~, MSv.
146.21	I'm] 1A; Im MSv.
146.22	seek] MSv, 1A; see⟨k⟩ MSvc.
146.22–23	'charming'] 1A; "~" MSv. *Quotation within quotation.*
146.24	*me*] 1A; me MSv.
146.28	man?] 1A; ~. MSv.
146.29	wife:] 1A; ~ – MSv; ~; ⟨–⟩ MSvc.
146.29	guitar,] MSvc, 1A; ~∧ MSv. *The same pattern of variants occurs after the indicated words at the following points*: 146.35 air, 147.6 applause, 147.40 century, 147.40 present, 147.40 Editor, 147.41 Yours.
146.30	looked so handsome,] 1A; ⟨was so⟩/ ~ ~ ~∧ MSv. *Commas are omitted from MSv after the indicated words at the following points*: 146.40 king, 147.21 consequence.
146.32	taylor.] T; taylor∧ MSv; ta⟨y⟩↑i↓lor∧ MSvc; tailor. 1A.
146.36	mantle-piece] MSvc, 1A; mantle piece MSv.
146.37	¶The captivating] MSvc, 1A; ∧~ ~ MSv. *First line of new page in MSv; Irving probably intended a new paragraph.*
146.40	nobility;] 1A; ~, MSv.
146.44	career] 1A; carreer MSv.
147.4	applauded him] 1A; ↑⟨on recognizing him⟩↓ ~ ~ MSv.
147.5	taste] MSv, 1A; ~, MSvc. *The same pattern of variants occurs at 147.31, after "found."*
147.20	One of] 1A; ⟨A message⟩ ~ ~ MSv.
147.23	days'] MSvc, 1A; days MSv.
147.26	cemetery] 1A; cemetry MSv.
147.27	tender.] 1A; ~⟨,⟩. MSv.
147.27	They exchanged] 1A; ~/ ⟨Princess⟩ ~ MSv.
147.29	After] 1A; ⟨Th⟩ ~ MSv.
147.30	Letoriéres.] 1A; Letori⟨è⟩↑é↓res – MSv.
147.35	and that he] 1A; ~/ [*MS torn*] he MSv.
147.39	and characteristic . . . life] 1A; ⟨I shall for the present Mr Editor ↑respectfully↓ take my / leave -⟩ and

characteristic of aristo- ↓⟨G.C.⟩↑/ cratical French life MSv.

147.40   Mr.]   1A; Mr∧ MSv.
147.41   etc.,]   1A; &c∧ MSv; ⟨&c⟩ ↑etc.,↓ MSvc.

LETTER FROM GRANADA

149.43   dependants]   1A; dependents 2A.
150.8   canvass]   1A; canvas 2A.
151.39   infidel]   1A; infidels 2A.

CORRECTION OF A MISSTATEMENT RESPECTING *ASTORIA*

161.26   Canada]   MStc; ~, 1A.
161.28   fur traders]   MStc; ~-~ 1A.
161.32   country,]   MStc; ~∧ 1A.
161.32   asked,]   MSt, MStc; ~∧ 1A.
162.12–13   public pressure and imprudent investments,]   MSt, MStc; public pressure 1A.
162.20   for this]   MStc; for that 1A. *Probably a compositor's misreading.*
162.23   agent]   MStc; ~∧ 1A.
162.33   enterprizes]   MSt, MStc; enterprises 1A.

THE CATSKILL MOUNTAINS

163.3   ¶The Catskill]   MSt; ∧The ~ 2A.
163.5   wolf]   MSt; ~, 2A. *Commas are also added in 2A after the indicated words in MSt at* 163.13 cultivation, 163.23 Vermont, 163.39 region, 164.3 speak, 164.3 however, 164.16 propensity, 164.19 Kammer, 164.27 month, 164.32 storms, 164.34 animals, 165.13 climate, 165.24 frosts, 165.29 vegetation, 166.4 Laws, 166.5 chiefs, 166.5 usual, 166.32 embarked, 167.1 which, 167.1 examined, 167.22 yore, 167.23 weight, 167.26 adventurer, 167.27 spirit.
163.11   toward]   MSt, 2A; towards 5A.
163.21   sierras]   MSt; chains 2A, 5A.
163.25   Nature]   MSt, 5A; nature 2A.
163.29   unburthened]   MSt, 2A; unburdened 5A.
163.30   milldam]   MSt; mill-dam 2A. *Hyphens are added in 2A to the indicated compound words in MSt at the following additional points*: 163.34 all pervading, 163.36 commonplace, 164.32 thunder storms, 164.38 ever changing, 165.9 cloud weaving, 165.24 snow storms,

165.42 wonder land, 166.19 gold hunting, 166.24 eye witness, 167.8 farm house, 167.25 gold hunting.

163.30	It] MSt; This mountain zone 2A, 5A.
163.31	Country] MSt; country 2A. *See* 163.34.
163.34	¶It] MSt; ∧~ 2A.
163.34–35	feature . . . given it a name] MSt; feature, that might have given our country a name, 2A, 5A.
163.38	wilderness] MSt; labyrinth 2A, 5A.
163.40	character;] MSt; ~, 2A.
163.43–164.1	the beautiful . . . subject;] MSt; their being peculiarly subject to those beautiful atmospherical effects 2A, 5A.
164.2	To me at least] MSt; To me 2A, 5A.
164.6–7	steam boats and rail roads] MSt; steamboats and rail-roads 2A.
164.9–10	in those days,] MSt; then; 2A, 5A.
164.10	not gulping] MSt; not, as at present, gulping 2A, 5A.
164.25	mountain, where] MSt; ~. Here 2A, 5A.
164.26	day and night] MSt; Day and Night 2A.
164.26	only one] MSt; only one of them 2A, 5A.
164.31	showers. Sometimes] MSt, 5A; ~—sometimes 2A.
164.33	every thing] MSt, 2A; everything 5A.
164.39	seemed] MSt; appeared 2A, 5A.
164.41–43	*Some . . . Sketch Book] MSt, 2A; [*omitted*] 5A. *See* Emendations 164.41–43. *The asterisk in the text (164.36) to which the footnote corresponds is also omitted from 5A.*
165.10	Atmospherical Phenomena] MSt; atmospherical phenomena 2A.
165.19–20	whiteness, instead . . . send] MSt; whiteness, and send 2A, 5A.
165.23	Even winter] MSt; Winter 2A, 5A.
165.25	has its] MSt; ~ also ~ 2A, 5A.
165.26	splendor to a] MSt; brightness to the 2A, 5A.
165.27	intense] MSt; intensest 2A, 5A.
165.28	radiance. Our spring . . . bursting] MSt; most limpid radiance—and then the joyous outbreak of our spring, bursting 2A; most limpid radiance;—and then the joyous outbreak of our spring, bursting 5A.
165.30	The splendors] MSt; —and the ~ 2A; —And the ~ 5A.
165.30–31	its evening glory] MSt; evening glory 2A, 5A.
165.34	atmosphere;] MSt; ~— 2A.
165.35	decay;] MSt; ~, 2A.
165.37	sky. Surely] MSt; ~—surely 2A; ~!—surely 5A.
165.39	handy work] MSt, 2A; handiwork 5A.

166.3   Adrian]   MSt, 5A; Adriaen 2A. *The same pattern of variants occurs at 167.23.*

166.5–6   for the ceremony]   MSt; on ~ ~ 2A, 5A.

166.7   Kieft]   MSt, 2A; Keift 5A.

166.10   Johannes de]   MSt, 5A; Iohannes De 2A.

166.16   despatched]   MSt; sent 2A, 5A.

166.16   with a few men]   MSt; and a party of men 2A, 5A.

166.18   procured]   MSt; found 2A, 5A.

166.20   in the]   MSt; on the 2A, 5A.

166.29   Holland]   MSt; Rotterdam 2A, 5A.

166.40   rumor]   MSt, 2A; a rumor 5A.

166.40–41   the mountains]   MSt; these ~ 2A, 5A.

166.42   patroon]   MSt; Patroon 2A.

167.6   in the mountains]   MSt; on ~ ~ 2A, 5A.

167.14   potentate]   MSt; Potentate 2A.

167.18   them;]   MSt; ~, 1A.

167.19   guardianship]   MSt; guardian keep 2A, 5A. *Compositor's misreading.*

167.26   revived]   MSt; renewed 2A, 5A. *Compositor's misreading.*

CONVERSATIONS WITH TALMA

168.4   call]   MSh; ~, 1A. *Commas are added in 1A after the indicated words in MSh at the following additional points*: 168.4 morning, 168.8 Paris, 168.9 country, 168.10 place, 168.13 height, 168.15 with, 168.15 times, 168.16 fleshy, 168.17 animated, 168.17 well, 168.18 unreserved, 168.22 he, 168.27 talent, 168.28 priests, 168.28 old, 168.30 observing, 168.35 fact, 168.37 thinks, 168.37 too, 168.40 Hence, 169.2 eyes, 169.8 noblesse, 169.10 antechamber, 169.11 he, 169.13 drums, 169.23 England, 169.26 wounded, 169.27 them, 169.28 bread, 169.30 confinement, 169.32 money, 169.32 however, 169.33 door, 169.34 frankly, 169.36 bill, 169.38 honor, 169.40 conversation, 169.41 stage, 170.13 periods, 170.14 would, 170.14 doubtless, 170.15 he, 170.21 time, 170.28 true, 170.39 play, 171.2 rises, 171.10 true, 171.12 mischief, 171.16 Polyeucte, 171.26 explanations, 171.28 relished, 171.34 parallel, 171.35 Racine, 171.42 Shakespeare, 171.42 which, 171.42 Talma, 172.2 generation, 172.3 them, 172.5 times, 172.10 gait, 172.10 is, 172.10 course, 172.12 refined, 172.12 powder, 172.15 sieges, 172.16 revolution, 172.17 Napoleon, 172.24 spectacles,

172.28 romances, 172.36 yet, 172.42 poetry, 172.43 prose, 173.1 mystery, 173.3 caught, 173.3 degree, 173.4 style, 173.9 crimes, 173.12 variety, 173.18 prose.

168.10   confusion;]   MSh; ~, 1A. *Semicolons after the indicated words in MSh are replaced by commas in 1A at the following additional points*: 168.20 before, 169.36 receipt, 170.10 characters, 170.24 down, 170.40 audience, 171.14 taste, 172.12 manners, 172.18 away, 173.1 poems, 173.3 him, 173.7 melancholy.

168.11   coloured]   MSh; colored 1A.

168.15   grey]   MSh; gray 1A.

168.16   flexible,]   MSh; ~; 1A. *Semicolons are substituted in 1A for commas after the indicated words in MSh at the following additional points*: 170.7 success, 170.31 drama, 170.34 eyes, 171.11 Aristotle, 171.22 Shakespeare, 172.25 critics, 172.38 Germans.

168.22   in the time]   MSh; the time 1A, 3A.

168.25   Ah,]   MSh; ~! 1A.

168.25   Paris. Every]   MSh; ~—every 1A.

168.28   worn out]   MSh; ~-~ 1A. *Hyphens are added in 1A to the indicated compound words in MSh at the following additional points*: 168.39 every day, 169.31 sea port, 169.44–170.1 constantly recurring, 173.18–19 rough written. *See also* Rejected Variants 172.23, 172.29–30.

168.28   nobility,]   MSh; ~ₐ 1A. *Commas after the indicated words in MSh are omitted in 1A at the following additional points*: 169.37 he, 170.7 Français, 171.26 times, 171.40 moment.

169.8   noblesse]   MSh; *noblesse* 1A.

169.10   soldier caps]   T; soldier/ caps MSh; soldiers' caps 1A, 3A.

169.15   afterwards]   MSh; afterward 1A.

169.15   Restaurant]   MSh, 3A; restaurant 1A. *Apparently intended as part of proper name.*

169.25   round]   MSh; around 1A, 3A.

169.27   shewed]   MSh; showed 1A.

169.31   on a boat]   MSh; in ~ ~ 1A, 3A.

169.36   on receipt]   MSh; or ~ 1A, 3A. *Probably a compositor's misreading.*

169.36   be not]   MSh; are not 1A, 3A.

170.3   Shakespeare]   MSh; Shakspeare 1A. *The variant occurs at the following additional points*: 170.8, 171.22, 171.27, 171.36.

170.12	All this, he observed, required] MSh; "~ ~," ~ ~, "requires 1A, 3A.
170.15	practise] MSh; practice 1A.
170.15	it. "And] MSh; it; ∧and 1A. *See* Rejected Variants 170.12.
170.17	cannot] MSh, 3A; can not 1A. *The same pattern of variants occurs at 171.33.*
171.13	apostacy] MSh, 3A; apostasy 1A.
171.14	idols—and] MSh; ~, ~ 1A.
171.17–18	translation.—All] MSh; ~.∧~ 1A.
171.43	encreasing] MSh; increasing 1A.
172.4	regime] MSy, MSh; *régime* 1A.
172.8	Wolga] MSy, MSh; Volga 1A.
172.15	soldiery:] MSh; ~; 1A.
172.21	nation:] MSh; ~— 1A.
172.23	printshops] MSh; print-shops 1A.
172.29	boulevards] MSh; Boulevards 1A.
172.29–30	melodrames] MSy, MSh; melo-dramas 1A. *The same variant occurs at 172.33.*
172.42	vogue;] MSh, 3A; ~: 1A.
172.43	extacy] MSh; ecstasy 1A; ecstacy 3A.
173.5	ensures] MSh; insures 1A.

[MEMOIR OF WASHINGTON ALLSTON]

173.23	with] MSn, 3A; "~ 1A. *Individual double quotation marks without precedent in MSn occur in 1A at the beginnings of paragraphs at the following points*: 174.15, 174.25, 174.41, 175.4, 175.13, 175.17, 175.29, 176.4, 176.23, 176.40, 177.3, 177.27, 177.32, 178.10, 178.15, 178.17.
173.23	Spring] MSn; spring 1A. *The indicated words capitalized in MSn are emended to lower-case in 1A*: 176.14 Queen, 176.16 Temple.
173.24	France;] MSn; ~, 1A. *Semicolons after the indicated words in MSn are replaced by commas in 1A at the following additional points*: 173.28 form, 174.4 advantage, 174.25 environs, 174.27 paintings, 174.27 halls, 174.35 scenes, 174.36 art, 174.36 monuments, 174.39 law, 175.27 teller, 175.30 despair, 177.4 sensation, 177.6 studio, 177.19 exquisite, 177.38 Feast, 178.11 America, 178.12 life.
173.25	twenty two] MSn; ~-~ 1A. *The indicated compound words in MSn are hyphenated in 1A at the following points*: 175.25 cock crowing, 177.37 day dream.

173.25	age;] MSn; ~— 1A.
173.29	eyes,] MSn, 3A; ~_∧ 1A.
173.30	Every thing] MSn; Everything 1A. *The same variant occurs at 178.4 (1A: everything).*
173.31	animated] MSn; ~, 1A. *Commas are added in 1A after the indicated words in MSn at the following additional points*: 174.11 each, 174.15 beautiful, 174.23 quick, 174.30 atmosphere, 174.33 him, 174.41 here, 175.6 it, 175.7 mind, 175.8 fountains, 175.12 life, 175.16 Allston [MSn Alston], 175.17 America, 175.19 afterwards, 175.38 office, 175.39 wished, 176.17 gloom), 176.23 possession, 176.24 Paris, 176.28–29 subjects, 176.40 Leslie, 176.40 me, 176.41 noble, 177.1 blue, 177.7 there, 177.14 Indeed, 177.15 you, 177.24 it, 177.28 works, 177.30 England, 178.11 Cambridge, 178.11–12 Massachusetts, 178.15 refined, 178.18 noblest.
173.32	general] MSn; genial 1A, 3A. *That is, consistent, pervasive.*
173.34	¶A young] MSn; ∧ ~ ~ 1A.
174.6	"Never . . . collection,"] MSn, 3A; '~ . . . ~,' 1A. *Pairs of single quotation marks substituted in 1A for double quotation marks in MSn occur at the following additional points*: 174.7–14 [*but see* Emendations 174.14], 174.41–42 [*but see* Emendations 174.14], 176.41–177.2; *see also* Emendations 177.3.
174.16	colour] MSn; color 1A. *The same variant occurs at 176.42.*
174.17	grandeur: I] MSn; ~. ~ 1A, 3A.
174.26	in life] MSn; of ~ 1A, 3A.
175.16	project] MSn; prospect 1A, 3A. *Compositor's misreading.*
175.31	paintings.∧] MSn; ~.* 1A, 3A. *The footnote to which this asterisk corresponds—"*Anecdotes of Artists." in 1A, "*Anecdotes of Artists." in 3A—is also without precedent in MSn.*
175.34	United States.] MSn, 3A; ~ ~:— 1A.
175.36	a-back] MSn; aback 1A.
175.37	of—to] MSn; ~, ~ 1A.
175.38	'tis] MSn, 1A; 't is 3A.
175.39	occasions] MSn; vexations 1A, 3A. *Compositor's misreading.*
176.10	him:] MSn; ~; 1A.
176.19	empire!—The] MSn; ~!∧~ 1A. *Double dashes between sentences in MSn are omitted from 1A at the fol-*

lowing additional points: 176.20, 176.22.

176.21	fate. But] MSn; ~; but 1A.
176.22	America."] MSn, 3A; ~.ₐ 1A. *The same pattern of variants occurs at 176.39, after "there."*
176.31	Marques] MSn; Marquis 1A.
176.31	directors] MSn; Directors 1A.
176.40	on the sun] MSn; in ~ ~ 1A, 3A.
176.42	over charged] MSn; overcharged 1A.
177.7	production of] MSn; ~ from 1A, 3A.
177.7	one admirable picture] MSn; an ~ ~ 1A, 3A.
177.16	do it. And,] MSn; ~ ~./ andₐ 1A; ~ ~, andₐ 3A.
177.22	back ground] MSn; background 1A.
177.25	doubt, . . . things,] MSn; ~ₐ . . . ~ₐ 1A.
177.26	portraits."*] MSn; ~.ₐ* 1A; ~."ₐ 3A. *See also Rejected Variants 177.42–43.*
177.29	genius. The road] MSn; ~./ ¶"~ ~ 1A.
177.33	affliction] MSn, 1A; afliction 3A.
177.34	to America] MSn, 3A; to to America 1A.
177.42–43	*This picture . . . New York.] MSn, T; *This picture was lately exhibited in the "Washington Gallery" in New York. 1A; [*omitted*] 3A.
178.12	gray] MSn, 3A; grey 1A.
178.13	world,] MSn; ~; 1A.
178.19	friendship.] MSn, 3A; ~." 1A.

[THE CHRONICLE OF PELAYO]

181.17	bans] MSv; banns 4A. *OED lists both spellings as in use from the sixteenth century, though Irving's was probably obsolescent.*
184.1	a delight] MSv; delight 4A.
184.10	orizons] MSv; orisons 4A. *Irving wished the archaic spelling to lend an antique flavor; see "clerkly craft," 184.13.*
184.14	fond] MSv; a fond 4A.
184.38–39	had left] MSv; left 4A.
188.3	on this] MSv; in this 4A.
188.14	over] MSv; on 4A.
188.26	bonds] MSv; bands 4A. *Irving's intention is clear from another "bonds" in a nearby cancelled passage.*
189.26	thoughts] MSv; thought 4A.
190.5	him] MSv; himself 4A.
194.2	these] MSv; them 4A.
195.36	children] MSv; chil-/ren 4A.

195.37	mountains] MSv; mountain 4A.
198.10	reliques] MSv; relics 4A.
198.12	relique] MSv; relic 4A.

CHRONICLE OF THE OMMIADES

202.5   historian:] MSh; ~. MShc; ~; 1A.

202.5   In his] MSh; in His MShc, 1A.

202.6   mighty] MSh; ~, 1A. *Commas are also added in 1A after the indicated words at* 202.23 palaces, 203.13 country, 204.14 gone, 204.14 men, 204.15 valley, 204.31 roared, 205.4 wanderer, 205.33 strangers, 205.44 it, 206.38 forth, 206.40 xeque, 209.1 men, 209.11 general, 209.15 poetess, 209.19 warriors, 209.22 prince, 209.22 hope, 210.4 Murcia, 211.3 known, 211.3 me, 211.17 villages, 211.40 mules, 212.12 hands, 212.15 which, 212.16 believed, 212.17 Temam, 212.44 colleague, 213.6 and, 213.37 went, 213.41 standard, 214.1 enemies, 214.5 square, 214.10 spared, 214.28 fond, 214.35 daylight, 214.42 way, 215.3 alone, 215.5 case, 216.15 Seville, 216.31 splendor, 217.36 thee, 217.43 funeral.

202.8   despair.] MSh; ~! 1A. *The same pattern of variants in punctuation occurs at* 204.19, 205.27, 209.17.

202.11   out] MSh; ~, MShc, 1A, 2A. *Commas are also added in MShc and 1A after the indicated words at* 202.12 Abbas, 202.16 slain, 202.16 seventy, 202.17 distinguished, 202.20 forth, 202.29 remained, 202.34 demeanour, 203.4 disguise, 203.8 disguise, 203.9 steed, 203.9 passed, 203.9 fugitive, 203.10 ancestors, 203.19 vigorous, 203.20 fields, 203.22 traces, 203.25 sleep, 203.35 young, 203.36 power, 203.37 persecutors, 203.41 evenings, 204.9 place, 204.16 place, 204.22 wind, 204.27 lasts, 204.29 steeds, 204.30 stars, 204.30 wastes, 204.32 blood, 204.34 rise, 204.34 well, 204.36 tree, 205.1 well, 205.4 himself, 205.9 steeds, 205.9 spirits, 205.11 place, 205.13 him, 205.17 Abderahman, 205.24 frankness, 205.25 spirit, 205.28 house, 205.30 him, 205.32 Zenetes, 205.37 Spain, 205.42 Africa, 206.3 purpose, 206.13 he, 206.14 God, 206.17 head, 206.24 landing, 206.27 them, 206.28 head, 206.29 benefactors, 206.35 follow, 208.40 days, 209.32 forces, 210.20 succeeded, 210.25 Cordova, 210.41 tenderness, 212.22 king, 212.22 brother, 212.26 mischief, 212.28 time, 212.37 movements, 213.3 Seguenza, 213.7 friends, 213.11 humility, 213.12 retirement, 213.14 troops, 213.15 where, 213.30 amnesty, 213.39 execrated, 214.4 off, 214.15 sway, 214.21 wali, 214.22 governor, 214.33 vigilance, 214.41 cistern, 215.3 Guadalquivir, 215.4 hearing, 215.7 Guadalquivir, 215.15 wicked, 215.20 men, 215.28 to height, 215.39 disguised, 216.9 melancholy, 216.12 fortune, 216.21 government, 216.25 letters, 216.39 length, 216.42 portals, 217.10 life, 217.11 brothers, 217.14 afterwards, 217.19 away, 217.20 God, 217.35 groves.

202.12   Caliphs]   MSh; caliphs 1A. *The indicated words capitalized in MSh are also lower-case in 1A at* 202.13 Prophet, 202.25 East, 204.21 My, 213.37 Caliph, 217.40 King.

202.15   battle:]   MSh; ~; 1A. *The same pattern of variants occurs after the indicated words at* 209.38 conqueror, 215.36 man.

202.17   of the most]   MSh; most MShc, 1A, 2A.

202.21   pursued]   MSh; ↑&↓ ~ MShc; and ~ 1A, 2A.

202.22   proscribed]   MSh; persecuted 1A, 2A.

202.23   their]   MSh; three 1A, 2A.

202.26   historian:]   MSh, 1A; ~. MShc.

202.26   It]   MSh; it MShc, 1A, 2A.

202.27   his]   MSh; His 1A, 2A. *The indicated words in MSh are also capitalized in 1A at* 209.16 we, 209.38 let, 213.40 east, 214.17 east. *See also* Rejected Variants 204.8.

202.34   demeanour]   MSh; demeanor 1A. *The same pattern of variants occurs at* 205.12; *however, see* Rejected Variants 208.38.

203.2   scymetar]   MSh; scimitar 1A, 2A.

203.4–5   "The . . . caliph,"]   MSh, 2A; '~ . . . ~,' 1A. *Pairs of double quotation marks in MSh are also converted in 1A to pairs of single quotation marks at* 202.26–30, 204.21, 205.16, 205.16–21, 205.26, 205.37, 205.37–206.11, 206.13–20, 209.16–17, 209.37, 209.37–40, 213.26, 214.6–7, 217.16.

203.5   "are]   MSh, 2A; '~ 1A. *Double quotation marks in MSh are also converted in 1A to single quotation marks at* 202.8, 204.17, 204.20, 205.2, 205.9, 205.27, 206.13, 206.22, 206.25, 206.31, 206.36, 206.37, 213.26, 213.30, 215.14, 217.16.

203.6   blood—fly]   MSh; ~. ~ MShc; ~; ~ 1A.

203.6   desart, there]   MSh; desart! There MShc; desert! There

1A, 2A. *The same pattern of variants in the spelling of "desart" occurs at 204.22, 204.29, 206.39.*

203.15 Arabs;] MSh; ~, 1A. *The same pattern of variants occurs after the indicated words at 204.40 destruction, 209.44 conditions, 210.37 Spain.*

203.18 palace,] MSh; ~; MShc, 1A. *The same pattern of variants occurs following the indicated words at 204.37 Bedouins, 206.7 misfortunes, 206.9 men, 206.13 length, 206.36 weapon, 206.42 child, 213.5–6 conflicts.*

203.23 plains,] MSh; ~∧ 1A. *The same pattern of variants occurs after the indicated words at 205.19 me, 205.20 that, 205.39 already, 211.5 tears, 211.11 foes, 211.20 army, 211.29 battle, 215.26 dangerous, 217.41 after.*

203.30 Barca] MSh, 2A; Barea 1A; Bar⟨e⟩ca MSn. *The correction in MSn is by Pierre M. Irving, who also wrote "Barca" in the margin.*

203.32 will] MSh; shall MShc, 1A, 2A.

203.33 shew] MSh; show 1A, 2A. *The same pattern of variants occurs at 206.15 shewn.*

203.42 gently spoken] MSh, 2A; ~-~ MShc; ~-/ ~ 1A. *The indicated compounds in MSh are also hyphenated in MShc and 1A at 204.9 resting place, 204.34 sun rise, 205.12 wayworn, 205.12 travel stained, 205.14 well known, 206.22 sea bord (MShc, 1A: sea-board), 209.21 half disciplined, 209.43 grey headed (1A: gray-/ headed), 210.35 palm tree, 210.38 palm trees, 211.20 short lived, 214.2 sea coast, 214.35 daylight, 215.29 cross bows (1A: cross-/bows), 216.40 twenty eight (1A: twenty-/ eight), 216.41 ninety three (1A: ninety-/ three).*

204.8 wali] MSh, 2A; Wali 1A. *The same pattern of variants between MSh and 1A occurs at 204.19, 211.36, 212.13, 214.21.*

204.14 us,] MSh; ~;" MShc; ~; 1A.

204.15 enquired] MSh; inquired 1A, 2A.

204.16 surprize] MSh; surprise 1A. *The same pattern of variants occurs at 211.35 surprized, 212.35 surprized.*

204.21 prince.] MSh, T; Prince: MShc; ~; 1A, 2A.

204.38 thee; where] MSh; thee? Where MShc, 1A, 2A.

205.20 need] MSh, 1A, 2A; ~, MShc.

205.34 merchants] MSh, 1A, 2A; Merchants MShc.

205.36 apart:] MSh; ~, 1A.

205.37 Omeya; we] MSh, 1A; ~. We 2A.

205.41   dependance] MSh, 1A; dependence 2A.
205.44   prosperity,] MSh; ~; 1A. *The same pattern of variants occurs after the indicated words at 209.42 sway, 212.12 prevailed, 214.43-44 deception.*
206.3   ensure] MSh; insure 1A.
206.19   leader,] MSh; ~∧ MShc, 1A.
206.26   replied,] MSh; ~,: MShc; ~: 1A. ·
206.28   harbour] MSh, harbor 1A.
206.36   honours] MSh; honor 1A, 2A.
207.12   Alabdaries] MSn; Alabdarides 2A. *Irving follows Conde.*
208.10   in chains] MSn; with ~ 2A.
208.33   landing] MSn, 2A; landing in Spain MSh, 1A.
208.35   Ancient Caliphs:] MSn; ancient caliphs; MSh, 1A, 2A.
208.38   demeanor] 1A, 2A; demeanour MSh.
209.3   rejoycings] MSh; rejoicings 1A, 2A.
209.13   encreased] MSh; increased 1A.
209.14   scornful] MSh; a ~ 1A, 2A.
209.16   lot;] MSh; ~! 1A, 2A.
209.19   grey] MSh; gray 1A, 2A.
209.25   valour] MSh; valor 1A. *The same pattern of variants occurs at 217.44.*
209.32   afterwards] MSh; afterward MShc, 1A, 2A. *The same pattern of variants occurs at 217.14.*
209.32   and reunited their forces] MSh; rëunited their forces MShc, 1A; reunited their forces 2A.
209.37   Oh] MSh; O 1A, 2A.
209.38   done;] MSh; ~! 1A.
210.2   tranquility] MSh; tranquillity 1A.
210.39   towards] MSh; toward MShc, 1A, 2A. *The same pattern of variants occurs at 212.3, 212.39.*
211.3   not known] MSh; known 1A, 2A.
211.13   partizans] MSh; partisans 1A. *The same pattern of variants occurs at 212.29 partizan.*
211.20   ¶The] MSh; ∧~ 1A, 2A. *The same pattern of variants occurs at 215.34.*
211.21   Abdelmelec] MSh, MSn; Abdelmelee 1A, 2A. *The same pattern of variants occurs at 211.25, 214.9.*
211.25   Lorca] MSh; Lorea 1A, 2A. *Thus Conde; see also 219.19.*
211.39   compelling] MSh; and ~ 1A, 2A.
211.39   cavalgadas] MSh; cavalcadas 1A; cavalcades 2A.
212.18   center] MSh; centre 1A.
212.29   war] MSh; warriors MShc, 1A, 2A.

212.29	*guerilla*] MSh; guerilla 1A.
212.31	wars] MSh; contests MShc, 1A, 2A.
212.32	dependence] MSh, 2A; dependance 1A.
212.33	licence] MSh; license 1A.
213.6	wall,] MSh, 1A; ~; MShc.
213.10	ambition?] MSh, 2A; ~! 1A.
213.17	relative] MSh; relation 1A, 2A.
213.31	further] MSh; farther 1A, 2A. *The same pattern of variants occurs at 214.13.*
214.11	Abderahman] MSh, 2A; Abdarahman 1A.
214.22	entrusted] MSh; intrusted 1A.
214.44	the means] MSh; the aid 1A, 2A. *Irving uses "means" later in the sentence.*
215.3	Guadalquivir] MSh; Guadalquiver 1A. *The same pattern of variants occurs at 215.7.*
215.5	stair case] MSh; stair-case 1A.
215.21	reappeared] MSh, 2A; rëappeared MShc, 1A.
217.37	wings] MSh; wing 1A, 2A.
217.38	practise] MSh, 2A; practice 1A.

CHRONICLE OF FERNAN GONZALEZ, COUNT OF CASTILE

233.22	councils] MSv; counsels 1A. *Irving is emphasizing the count's physical proximity to the king as well as his companionship with him; the 1A emendation alters this meaning.*
238.14	others] MSv; othere 1A.
241.14	seemed] MSv; seem 1A.
242.2	off of] MSv; off 1A.
242.13	revelry] MSv; gayety 1A. *The emendation in 1A was to avoid repetition of "revelry" earlier in the sentence.*
253.32	dark night] MSv; a ~ ~ 1A.
253.36	toiled] MSv; ~ on 1A.
256.13	called] MSv; call 1A.
257.6	hoof] MSv; hoofs 1A. *The emendation in 1A was probably made for consistency with 257.8, but it was unnecessary; "hoof" is clearly Irving's intention here.*
260.15	Arlanza] MSv; Orlanza 1A.
261.14	woods on] MSv; wood in 1A.
263.25	Pan Cervo] MSv; Pan Corvo 1A.
270.10	buckling once more on] MSv; buckling on once more 1A.
270.43	church] MSv; churches 1A. *Irving's locution is somewhat awkward, but his reference seems to be to the church generally.*

CHRONICLE OF FERNANDO THE SAINT

274.16	King Enrique] MSv; king, Enrique, 1A.
276.9	chevaliers] MSv; cavaliers 1A.
281.3	Giron] MSv; de ~ 1A. *See* Emendations 275.32.
282.7	the mighty] MSv; that ~ 1A.
289.40–290.1	suburb . . . was] MSv; suburbs . . . were 1A. *MSv "suburb" is also emended to "suburbs" in 1A at 290.26, 290.31.*
*290.38	flouting] MSv; floating 1A.
293.14	on the feast] MSv; the feast 1A.
293.20	of power] MSv; of the power 1A.
297.28	which has been said] MSv; which, as has been said 1A.
305.23	created] MSv; erected 1A. *Quite possibly a compositor's misreading.*
306.32	this proud infidel] MSv; the infidel 1A. *Emendation to 1A reading probably made to avoid "pride" and "proud" in the same sentence.*
307.35	benefactor] MSv; benefactress 1A. *Irving's usage is not incorrect.*
309.8	other] MSn; of other 1A.
309.34	sank] MSn; sunk 1A.
312.24	Gazules] MSn; Azules 1A. *See* Emendations 286.17.
314.40	And the raft] MSn; The raft 1A.
315.18	fight] MSn; flight 1A.
317.2–3	a great shout] MSv; great shouts 1A.
318.6	were] MSv; was 1A.
320.10	And Don Lorenzo] MSv; Don Lorenzo 1A.
321.6–7	the bold Admiral] MSv; he 1A. *Emendation clearly to avoid use of the epithet in two consecutive sentences.*
321.12	And the] MSv; The 1A.
321.15–16	defence: and of] MSv; defence. Of 1A.
323.5	dints] MSv; dents 1A.
324.11	these] MSv; those 1A.
328.5	hands] MSva; hand 1A.

[HISTORY OF THE CONQUEST OF MEXICO]

340.3	Scarcely had he] 1A; ⟨While he was sleeping an/ Enormous eagle He had scarce⟩ ↑~ ~ ~↓ MSt.
340.4	awakened] 1A; ⟨wa⟩ ~ MSt. *Indicated false starts immediately rewritten or misspellings immediately corrected occur at the following points in MSt: 340.5 ⟨swop stop swope⟩, 340.6 ⟨him⟩, 340.12 ⟨South⟩.*
340.5	hovering] 1A; ⟨stooping⟩ ~ MSt.

340.6	seizing] 1A; siezing MSt.
340.6	talons,] 1A; $\sim_\wedge$/ MSt. *Comma is the first of a pair.*
340.7	trees, until] 1A; ⟨forests,⟩/ $\sim$, ⟨and sailing with him⟩ $\sim$ MSt.
340.8	diminished] 1A; ⟨faded⟩ $\sim$ MSt.
340.10	eagle mounted] 1A; Eagle⟨s⟩ $\sim$ MSt. *For "eagle," see* 340.5.
340.11	alighted at] 1A; $\sim$ ⟨in⟩at MSt.
340.12	cavern.] 1A; $\sim_\wedge$ MSt.

LIST OF PRECOPY-TEXT REJECTED VARIANTS

This list provides a record of variants in texts which antedate the copy-texts and which are not incorporated in the present critical texts.

The numbers before each entry indicate page and line. The reading to the left of the bracket indicates an accepted reading; its source is indicated by symbol after the bracket. Any reading which follows the semicolon is a rejected one. The swung (wavy) dash ~ represents the same word, words, or characters that appear before the bracket, and is used in recording punctuation variants. The caret ∧ indicates that a mark of punctuation is omitted. Brief explanatory comments, if required, follow in italics. If more explanation is required than can conveniently be inserted in the table, the entry is preceded by an asterisk * and the necessary comments appear following the same page-line reference in the Discussions of Adopted Readings.

A key to identifying symbols used in referring to manuscript and printed texts is given on pages 348–54.

[REVIEW OF *A CHRONICLE OF THE CONQUEST OF GRANADA*]

7.26	scimitars] 1E, 2A; cimeters C.
7.26	lances.] 1E, 2A; ~*. C. *The asterisk in C corresponds to one preceding a citation at the bottom of the page. Similar omissions occur at 15.43, 17.11, 20.29, 24.23, 24.32.*
*15.5–8	"This . . . Granada.'"] 1E; This was a large, wealthy, and populous place, within a few leagues of Granada. It was situate on a rocky height, nearly surrounded by a river, and defended by a fortress, to which there was no access but by a steep and cragged ascent. The strength of its situation, and its being imbosomed in the center of the kingdom, had produced the careless security which now invited attack. C.
15.29	¶"He] 2A; ∧∧~ C. *Paragraph breaks without precedent in C occur at the following additional points in 1E and 2A: 16.12, 18.3, 23.38.*
15.34	relief.] 1E, 2A; relief with all the forces he could raise. C.
15.34	The duke] 1E, 2A; ¶~ ~ C. *Paragraph breaks in C are omitted in 1E and 2A at the following additional points: 17.15, 18.14, 19.6, 19.27, 19.32, 22.4, 22.32, 23.18, 25.11, 25.30, 26.32, 27.10, 27.13.*

16.12   They] 1E, 2A; His scouts brought word, that they C.
16.24–25   admiration;] 1E, 2A; ~: C.
17.13   Guadix.] 1E, 2A; ~ in the Alpuxarres. C.
17.15   set his] 1E, 2A; set the machinations of his C.
17.16   internal feuds] 1E, 2A; great internal feuds and divisions C.
17.21   enemy.] 1E, 2A; ~, whenever an opportunity occurred. C.
18.3   brilliant army] 1E, 2A; force C.
18.4–5   comprising . . . chivalry.] 1E, 2A; most of them his adherents, but many the partisans of his father: for both factions, however they might fight among themselves, were ready to unite in any expedition against the Christians. Many of the most illustrious and valiant of the Moorish nobility assembled around his standard, magnificently arrayed, in sumptuous armour and rich embroidery, as though they were going to a festival, or a tilt of reeds, rather than an enterprise of iron war. C.
18.5   His] 1E, 2A; Boabdil's C.
18.8   befal] 1E; befall C.
18.39   descried] 1E, 2A; had ~ C.
19.14   enemy. He] 1E, 2A; ~: he C.
20.4   the mountains.] 1E, 2A; ~ ~ of Algaringo. C.
20.36   cleft] 1E, 2A; cloven C.
22.1   cavalcade] 1E, 2A; splendid ~ C.
22.12   penaches] 1E, 2A; punaches C.
24.24   assaults, and] 1E, 2A; ~, ~ disheartened by the loss of Hamet el Zegri, who was carried wounded from the field. They C.
25.4   While the holy Christian army was] 1E, 2A; "While the holy Christian army," says Fray Antonio Agapida, "was thus C.
25.4   the infidel] 1E, 2A; this ~ C.
25.32   Egypt, who,] 1E, 2A; Egypt; or, as Agapida terms him, in the language of the day, the Soldan of Babylon. The league, which had been made between that potentate and his arch foe, the Grand Turk, Bajazet II., to unite in arms for the salvation of Granada, as has been mentioned in a previous chapter of this chronicle, had come to nought. The infidel princes had again taken up arms against each other, and had relapsed into their ancient hostility. Still the Grand Soldan, C.

25.35–37   sovereigns . . . territory]   1E, 2A; sovereigns, as well as to the pope, and to the King of Naples; remonstrating against the evils done to the Moors of the kingdom of Granada, who were of his faith and kindred: whereas, it was well known, that great numbers of Christians were indulged and protected in full enjoyment of their property, their liberty, and their faith, in his dominions. He insisted, therefore, that this war should cease; that the Moors of Granada should be reinstated in the territory C.

27.20   Feg]   1E, 2A; Fez C. *"Feg" is also employed at the corresponding point in the ARE Conquest of Granada (1850).*

[REVIEW OF HENRY WHEATON'S
HISTORY OF THE NORTHMEN]

63.36   north]   1A; North H. *The same variant occurs at 68.8, 74.14, 77.29, 78.31, 79.17 (northern).*

63.40   it bears]   1A, 2A; The language, which gave expression to the thoughts and feelings connected with this mythology, and this poetry, bears H.

63.42   and rivals]   1A, 2A; and according to the testimony of one of the greatest philologists of the age, rivals H.

64.26   ¶"The]   2A; ∧∧~ H. *Paragraph breaks not present in H but included at the beginning of quotations in 1A and 2A occur at the following additional points: 76.13, 76.37, 77.42, 79.15, 79.30, 80.16; see also Precopy-Text Rejected Variants 71.6, 76.23–24, 82.14.*

64.35   silver.]   1A, 2A; ~.* H. *Asterisk in H corresponds to one preceding a citation at bottom of page. Reference marks in H pertaining to footnotes are omitted from 1A and 2A at the following additional points: 65.13, 65.43, 67.25, 68.2, 69.38, 74.6, 74.43, 75.33, 76.34, 79.3, 82.18, 84.14, 85.29.*

67.32   had foredoomed]   1A, 2A; have foredoom'd H. *Accepted reading better suited to context.*

67.36   boldest]   1A, 2A; lowest H. *See 67.38.*

68.6   wild]   1A, 2A; mild H. *H almost certainly a typographical error.*

68.18   the gigantic remains,]   1A, 2A; ~ organic ~– H. *See Precopy-Text Rejected Variants 68.19.*

68.19   ruins]   1A, 2A; gigantic ruins H.

69.29–30	'Skidbladner,' . . . 'is] 1A; . . . Odin's wonderful ship Skídbladnir, is that described in the prose Edda, where Gangler interrogates one of the Genii respecting the Ship of the Gods, of which he had before told him, and receives the following answer: "Skídbladnir is H.
69.30	one of the best ships] 1A, 2A; the best ship H.
69.30–31	constructed. It] 1A, 2A; ~, but *Naglfar* is the greatest of all the ships of the gods. The former H.
71.6	¶The slave . . . were] 1A, 2A; ʌThe effects of the original Gothic migration and conquest in Scandinavia are here distinctly marked in the features of the slave caste, descended from the aboriginal Finns, and H.
71.9–10	had reddish hair] 1A, 2A; with their reddish hair H.
71.12	barons, were distinguished] 1A, 2A; ~,–who are distinguished from the others H.
71.13	and by noble employments and manners: from these] 1A, 2A; by their noble employments and manners, from whom H.
74.5–6	"they never . . . fire."] 2A; "And they are rightly named Sea-Kings," says the Author of the Ynglinga-Saga, "who never seek shelter under a roof, and never drain their drinking horn at a cottage fire." H.
74.15–16	they committed] 1A, 2A; these Orlandos committed H.
74.17	the rocks and trees] 1A, 2A; inanimate nature–~ ~ ~ ~ H.
76.23–24	bled. ¶"Ivar changed color] 2A; ~. Sigurdr was so wrapt in attention that he cut himself to the bone, with a knife, with which he was paring his nails. Ivar, above all, anxiously enquiring, changed colour H.
76.27	forbad] 1A; forbid H.
77.27	the contrast] 1A; The ~ H.
79.30	said also] 1A, 2A; said H.
79.33	likewise] 1A, 2A; also H.
79.33	Duke] 1A, 2A; duke H. *The same pattern of variants occurs at 84.20, 84.35.*
80.17	fictions] 1A, 2A; ~ and personages H.
81.31	grandira] 1A, 2A; grandera H.
82.14	¶"The ship] 2A; ʌʌThe army was embarked at St Valery; and the ship H.
82.16	the lions] 1A, 2A; the device of ~ ~ H.
83.36	sword; and if] 1A, 2A; sword; if H.
83.36	all be] 1A, 2A; be all H.
83.37	gain the] 1A, 2A; take the H.

AN UNWRITTEN DRAMA OF LORD BYRON

89.1   hero . . . Alfonso]   1A, 2A; hero of the piece is a nobleman (whom I call Alfonzo) J.

89.2   entering upon the career]   1A, 2A; making his debut on
the stage J.

89.3   have become]   1A, 2A; are J.

89.4   impulses]   1A, 2A; dictates J.

89.4   heedless]   1A, 2A; thoughtless J.

89.4–5   consequences.]   1A, 2A; ∼. These consequences are
obvious enough. Such a moral would be a very common place one but with Calderon I should take a new
and different way of enforcing it and a truly dramatic
one it might be made if treated in the genuine spirit
of Goethe. J.

89.6–8   his . . . figure.]   1A, 2A; our Spaniards entrance into
the world a person in a masque or cloak, that prevents
his features or figure from being recognized (for the
titles of the play leave us in doubt as to the express
nature of the disguise) becomes as it were his shadow
– his second self. J. *See also* 89.16–17.

89.8–11   He . . . irksome.]   1A, 2A; This curiosity at first scarcely
noticed, or only considered as idle impertinence, daily
becomes more irksome. J. *In J this sentence is preceded by one which in 2A appears two sentences after
it; see* Precopy-Text Rejected Variants 89.12–15.

89.11–12   The mystery . . . annoyance.]   1A, 2A; [*wanting*] J.

89.12–15   Alfonso . . . espionage.]   2A; ¶This mysterious being
Alfonzo is unable to identify with any of his acquaintance; his real name or country – or place of abode are
a mystery—and he is equally at a loss to form even
a conjecture as to the peculiar observations and interest of the stranger – J.

89.15–17   It . . . self.]   2A; [*wanting*] H. *But see* Precopy-Text
Rejected Variants 89.6–8, *where a partial sentence
in H corresponding to a portion of the present 2A
reading is given.*

89.16   Alfonso's]   2A; [*wanting*] J.

89.17   the most . . . the latter]   1A, 2A; his most private
actions J.

89.18   seem]   1A, 2A; are J.

89.19–20   he feels . . . spirits]   1A, 2A; though invisible he feels
his presence oppress and weigh upon his spirits J.

89.21   sleeping]   1A, 2A; asleep J.

89.21–22   Alfonso . . . in view]   1A, 2A; he is ever with him or before him J.

89.22–23   He . . . solitude]   1A, 2A; he crosses his path, at every turn he intrudes like ⟨a⟩ ↑the↓ demon in Faust in his solitude J.

89.23   or the]   1A, 2A; in ∼ J.

89.24–25   thwarting . . . ambition.]   1A, 2A; thwarts him in all his deep laid schemes of ambition or fame, J. *The J reading is given here from a paragraph in J following the one which corresponds to the present 2A context. See* Precopy-Text Rejected Variants 89.30.

89.25–29   In the . . . dance.]   1A, 2A; he sees him winding through the assembly & the honied words of seduction that he is addressing to his fair partner in the dance die unfinished on his lips. One voice like the voice of his own soul whispers in his ears and silences the music – J.

89.30   The hero of the drama becomes]   1A, 2A;
                Who can he be
                Is it the false
            Embodying of his fantasy – a shape
            His melancholy spirits have engendered
            out of the ⟨atto⟩ atoms of the day?
        No! It is something more than an apparition that haunts him. Like the Schedoni of the Italians* his evil genius counteracts all his projects, thwarts him in all his deep laid schemes of ambition or fame, unwinds through all their intricacies and shapes the webs of his intrigues, developes the hidden motives of his conduct and betrays that those actions which he wishes to make appear the most disinterested are only based in self – ¶The Hero of the Drama is become J. *The asterisk corresponds to a note:* *Vide – Romance by Mrs Radcliff

89.30–31   power . . . life]   1A, 2A; power all that promised to give life its zest in the outset J.

89.32   of pleasure becomes]   1A, 2A; to others is J.

89.32–35   Existence . . . thoughts.]   1A, 2A; Existence becomes a burthen and to put a terrible [end] to his misery & drive him to a state bordering on frenzy he suspects that the guilty objects of his affections has fallen a prey to her tormentor[.] J.

89.36   Alfonso]   1A, 2A; Alonzo J.

89.36   mysterious stranger]   1A, 2A; unknown J.

89.37	in vain endeavour] 2A; endeavour in vain J.
89.38–39	to . . . attacks] 1A, 2A; ⟨in the⟩ into the house of his mistress & attacking J.
89.39	the fury . . . jealousy] 1A, 2A; all the fury which jealous rage inspires J.
89.40	They fight; his] 1A, 2A; His J.
89.41–44	himself . . . horror!] 2A; himself and the sword of Alonzo at the first thrust pierces the breast of his enemy, who in falling utters "are you satisfied!" his mask drops off and discovers – his own image the Spectre of himself – his self – He dies with horror! H.
90.27	school.] 2A; ∼.* 1A. *For the footnote corresponding to the asterisk in 1A see the Textual Commentary, p. 394.*
90.36	*I.E. A person] 2A; *A person 1A.

CORRECTION OF A MISSTATEMENT RESPECTING *ASTORIA*

*161.25–32	The work . . . . known.] MStc, 1A; [*wanting*] MSt.
*162.2–3	the amount . . . exaggerated.] MStc, 1A; he has greatly exaggerated the amount. MSt.
*162.13–14	when, . . . obliged to seek] MStc, 1A; when he knew I was straitened and was seeking MSt.
*162.19–26	The only . . . . investment.] MStc, 1A; [*wanting*] MSt.

[THE CHRONICLE OF PELAYO]

180.8	historians] MSv, 4A; historiographers MSy, 1A.
180.8	in the obscure] MSv, 4A; for an obscure MSy, 1A.
180.9–10	which . . . country] MSv, 4A; immediately succeeding the conquest of their country by the Moslems MSy, 1A.
180.10–11	wild . . . fables] MSv; groundless fables, and rash exaggerations MSy, 1A.
180.11	Many learned men] MSv, 4A; Learned men MSy, 1A.
180.12	passed] MSv, 4A; worn out MSy, 1A.
180.12–13	the weary . . . contradictions] MSv, 4A; vainly endeavoring to connect incongruous events∧ and to account for startling improbabilities, recorded of this period MSy. *1A duplicates MSy except that a comma follows "events" in the printed text.*
180.14	Pedro] MSv, 4A; Padre MSy, 1A.
180.14	confesses] MSv, 4A; declares MSy, 1A.
180.16	any questions] MSv, 4A; any MSy, 1A.
180.16	rising] MSv, 4A; which rise MSy, 1A.
180.19	indecision] MSv, 4A; state of indecision MSy, 1A.
180.20–26	Let us . . . . paths.] MSv, 4A; [*wanting*] MSy, 1A.

180.27–29	We . . . Pelayo] MSv, 4A; During this apocryphal period flourished Pelayo MSy; During this apocryphal period, flourished PELAYO 1A.
180.30	Wallace . . . Scotland] MSv; Wallace MSy, 1A.
180.31	like his] MSv, 4A; in like manner MSy, 1A.
180.31	band] MSv, 4A; bond MSy, 1A.
180.32	indissolubly mingled] MSv, 4A; inextricably interwoven MSy, 1A.
*186.20–23	The Gascons . . . . dared.] MSv, 4A; The Gascons, says an old chronicler, were a people who used smooth words when expedient, but force when they had power, and were ready to lay their hands on every thing they met. MSy, 1A.
186.23	there] MSv, 4A; for there MSy, 1A.
186.24	plume] MSv, 4A; pride MSy, 1A.
186.24	hijo de algo] MSv, 4A; hijo/dalgo MSy; hijodalgo 1A.
186.25–27	Whenever . . . need.] MSv, 4A; [wanting] MSy, 1A.
186.28	self-styled] 4A; needy MSy, 1A.
186.29	was a] MSv, 4A; ~ one MSy, 1A.
186.30	comrades] MSv, 4A; followers MSy, 1A.
186.30	mounted,] MSv, 4A; ~; MSy, 1A.
186.31	armed] MSv, 4A; furnished MSy, 1A.
186.31–32	This band was] MSv, 4A; They were MSy, 1A.
186.32	gone] MSv, 4A; and ~ MSy, 1A.
186.33	pass of the mountains] MSv, 4A; pass MSy; pass, 1A.
186.33–36	sometimes they . . . them.] 4A; They would make sudden inroads into Spain, scour the roads, plunder the country, and were over the mountains and far away before a force could be collected to pursue them‸ MSy. *In 1A a comma is added following "away" and a period following "them."*

LIST OF COMPOUND WORDS
HYPHENATED
AT END OF LINE

This table is divided into two lists. List I includes all compound or possibly compound words that are hyphenated at the end of a line in the copy-texts. In deciding whether to retain the hyphen or to print as one or two words, the editor has based his decision first on the use of each compound word elsewhere in the copy-text; or second, when the word does not appear elsewhere in the copy-text, on Irving's practice in other writings of the period; or finally, if the word does not appear in Irving's other writings of the period, on contemporary usage. Each word is listed in its editorially accepted form after the page-line number of its appearance.

List II presents compounds or possible compounds that are hyphenated at the end of a line in the present edition. They are listed in the form in which they would have appeared in this volume had they been printed in midline.

LIST I

10.4	bloodshed	68.32	water-sprites
11.21	thrice-proved	68.33	throughout
15.36	forthwith	70.17	supernatural
20.11	horseman	70.35	Godheim
22.6	throughout	71.24	rainbow
24.11	back piece	72.15	soothsayers
24.42	throughout	72.36–37	overthrown
30.19–20	portfolios	85.5–6	hard-earned
37.39	fellow-travellers	87.20	horseman
42.15	household	91.35	overhauled
44.11	oil-cloth	92.22	speaking-trumpet
46.2	well turned	97.30	yourself
49.20	close-built	103.21	writing desk
51.31	fire-engine	103.29	ourselves
54.6	nick-named	105.25	homespun
63.33	Iceland	106.44	chestnut
65.1	Al-thing	107.10	tree-tops
65.21	semi-barbarous	107.32	communion-table

109.25	tomb-stones	145.2	archepiscopal
110.22	horseman	146.7	Louis d'or
110.31	brush-wood	151.40	mock-fight
110.43	house-keeping	152.19	horseback
111.14–15	mill-pond	154.16	sometimes
111.16	knee-deep	155.36	white-wash
112.1	white-haired	157.25	thirty seven
115.12	himself	162.35	lifetime
115.27	namesakes	169.10	antechamber
115.34	god-fathers	173.18	melodramatic
116.23	Saw-mill	186.28	self-styled
117.23	second-hand	194.6	countrymen
117.33–34	northwestern	204.34	themselves
121.1–2	all-pervading	210.21	himself
123.22	antiquity-hunting	227.33	horseback
130.11	button-woods	253.44	archpriest
130.13	cross-road	274.44	overbearing
131.12	low-eaved	288.34	overturning
133.17	New-Amsterdam	322.6	cross-bows
138.8	nobleman	322.34	cross-bow
139.6	eighty five	334.6–7	masterpieces
140.34	midnight	344.41	gray-headed
140.39	archepiscopal		

LIST II

7.5–6	something	52.43–44	marketplace
11.2–3	however	54.32–33	waistcoats
23.29–30	themselves	56.33–34	courtyard
28.3–4	sometimes	57.4–5	Sometimes
28.44–29.1	pack-saddle	60.26–27	Whoever
29.29–30	market-place	64.7–8	sometimes
30.19–20	portfolios	68.33–34	*Ström-kerl*
33.14–15	ourselves	69.8–9	sometimes
34.22–23	Frenchman	72.4–5	something
36.1–2	fretwork	72.36–37	overthrown
40.4–5	withdraw	81.8–9	Northmen
40.32–33	undertone	85.5–6	hard-earned
40.35–36	farewell	90.22–23	booksellers
44.3–4	godsend	91.22–23	forecastle
44.5–6	coffee-houses	92.2–3	brother-in-law
44.37–38	something	96.43–44	passports
50.5–6	half-displeased	102.25–26	new-year
51.20–21	throughout	102.36–37	old-fashioned

103.16–17	weather-cock	186.32–33	sometimes
105.19–20	something	200.24–25	overtook
107.8–9	grape-vines	226.15–16	overlooking
107.33–34	weather-cock	229.27–28	without
111.14–15	mill-pond	229.34–35	grandfather
111.19–20	semi-Gothic	236.2–3	themselves
116.25–26	humdrum	238.4–5	likewise
117.6–7	second-hand	239.13–14	themselves
117.33–34	northwestern	254.30–31	archpriest
118.6–7	subdivided	256.35–36	themselves
121.1–2	all-pervading	259.39–40	themselves
124.36–37	Dutchman	267.28–29	himself
125.14–15	soothsayer	274.18–19	undertake
129.14–15	fate-bound	276.31–32	notwithstanding
129.27–28	chimney-pieces	276.40–277.1	notwithstanding
129.31–32	Nassau-street	278.28–29	however
130.9–10	whitewashed	287.19–20	likewise
131.17–18	Nieuw-Nederlands	293.29–30	Arch-imposter
132.30–31	gunpowder	294.18–19	wayfarers
140.33–34	archbishop	297.8–9	however
141.27–28	archbishop	302.30–31	himself
144.9–10	archbishop	315.18–19	themselves
144.44–145.1	Jean-sur-Moselle	316.29–30	himself
145.36–37	coachman	317.36–37	foot-soldiers
146.2–3	gentleman	320.23–24	overturning
149.16–17	himself	320.26–27	themselves
151.34–35	themselves	321.32–33	overwhelm
153.19–20	case-hunter	327.28–29	throughout
154.14–15	semi-Gothic	330.21–22	himself
155.32–33	whitewash	332.19–20	Goodfellow
160.1–2	heartstrings	334.6–7	masterpieces
160.11–12	home-happiness	337.10–11	sunshine
165.17–18	sunshine	341.13–14	downfall
172.29–30	melodrames	341.21–22	himself
174.5–6	without	343.29–30	themselves
176.31–32	moreover	343.30–31	otherwise
183.42–43	offspring	345.13–14	mountain-side
184.9–10	foster-father	345.21–22	undergoing

INDEX

A separate index is supplied for the contents of Volume I.